The Public History Reader

Drawing on theory and practice from five continents, *The Public History Reader* offers clearly written accessible introductions to debates in public history. It places people, such as practitioners, bloggers, archivists, local historians, curators or those working in education, at the heart of history-making and discusses practical examples of artists, collectors, novelists, activists, curators, those paid to write history and those who do it for fun.

Hilda Kean and Paul Martin address the historical imagination through such concepts as 'embodiment' and 'nostalgia' while using practical examples to demonstrate them. The Reader explores public history as an everyday practice rather than simply as an academic discipline. It is embedded in the idea that historical knowledge is discovered and accrued from everyday encounters people have with their environments and points to the continuing dialogue that the present has with the past, exploring why this has burgeoned on a popular level in recent years.

Divided into three parts, Part I looks at who makes history, focusing on the ways in which the past has taken on a heightened popular sense of importance in the present and the ways in which it is used. Accordingly, history, far from being 'fixed' in time, is fluid and is re-made to serve contemporary agendas or needs in the present. Part II addresses the question of materials and approaches to making history. By using material more commonly within the domain of artists, collectors or geographers and archaeologists, public historians have opened up understandings of the past. Part III looks at the way in which presentations of the past change over time and their different forms and emphases. Throughout, the Reader emphasizes the challenges for public historians today.

Using their own expertise in constructing and teaching a Public History MA, Hilda Kean and Paul Martin have suggested themes and indicative extracts that draw on their understanding of what works best with students. *The Public History Reader* is, therefore, a perfect resource for all students of public history and all those interested in understanding the role of the past in our lives today.

Hilda Kean is former dean and director of public history at Ruskin College, Oxford, where she established the first MA in Public History in Britain. Her books include *London Stories: Personal Lives, Public Histories* (2004) and *People and Their Pasts: Public History Today* with Paul Ashton (2009).

Paul Martin was tutor in public history at Ruskin College, Oxford, during 1997 to 2012. He is currently a distance learning tutor with the School of Museum Studies, Leicester University. His books include *Popular Collecting and the Everyday Self* (1999) and *The Trade Union Badge* (2002).

Routledge Readers in History

The Public History Reader

Edited by

Hilda Kean and Paul Martin

Routledge
Taylor & Francis Group

LONDON AND NEW YORK

First published 2013
by Routledge
2 Park Square, Milton Park, Abingdon, Oxon OX14 4RN

Simultaneously published in the USA and Canada
by Routledge
711 Third Avenue, New York, NY 10017

Routledge is an imprint of the Taylor & Francis Group, an informa business

British Library Cataloguing in Publication Data
A catalogue record for this book is available from the British Library

Library of Congress Cataloging in Publication Data
The public history reader / edited by Hilda Kean and Paul Martin.
    pages cm.—(Routledge readers in history)
  Includes bibliographical references and index.
  1. Public history.   2. Public history—Philosophy.   3. Public historians.
  4. Historiography.   I. Kean, Hilda.   II. Martin, Paul, 1959–
  D16.163.P85 2013
  907.2—dc23   2012030797

ISBN: 978-0-415-52040-9 (hbk)
ISBN: 978-0-415-52041-6 (pbk)

Typeset in Perpetua and Bell Gothic
by RefineCatch Limited, Bungay, Suffolk

Printed and bound in Great Britain by
TJ International Ltd, Padstow, Cornwall

To the MA Public History students at Ruskin, 1996–2012,
from whom we have learned so much.
Paul Martin would also like to dedicate this book to Marie and Elise.

Contents

Acknowledgements

The editors would like to thank the library staff at the Bodleian, British Library, Ruskin College Library and Bishopsgate Institute; Brenda Kirsch, Alan Mann, Steve Mills, Denise Pakeman and Daniel Scharf for comments on various drafts; participants at the Public History Discussion Group and at various public history conferences at Ruskin College, the Institute for Historical Research, the University of Technology, Sydney (UTS) and the Bishopsgate Institute, where many of these ideas were discussed. Also thanks to Colin O'Brien for the cover photograph.

The articles listed below have been reproduced with kind permission. While every effort has been made to trace copyright holders, this has not been possible in all cases. Any omissions brought to our attention will be remedied in future editions.

Part I

1   Raphael Samuel, *Theatres of Memory* (London: Verso, 1994), pp15–25.

2   Roy Rosenzweig and David Thelen, *The Presence of the Past: Popular Uses of History in American Life* (New York: Columbia University Press, 1998), pp15–36, 177–207.

3   Iain J. M. Robertson, 'Heritage from below: Class, social protest and resistance', in B. Graham and P. Howard (eds) *The Ashgate Research Companion to Heritage and Identity* (Aldershot, UK: Ashgate, 2008), pp143–158.

4   Graeme Davison, *The Use and Abuse of Australian History* (New South Wales: Allen and Unwin, 2004), pp80–109.

5   James Green, *Taking History to Heart: The Power of the Past in Building Social Movements* (Amherst, MA: University of Massachusetts Press, 2000), pp73–97.

6   Jorma Kalela, *Making History: The Historian and Uses of the Past* (Basingstoke, UK: Palgrave Macmillan, 2011), pp51–63.

7   Matthew J. Taylor and Michael K. Steinberg, 'Forty years of conflict: State, Church and spontaneous representation of massacres and murder in Guatemala', in J. Santino (ed) *Spontaneous Shrines and the Public Memorialization of Death* (Basingstoke, UK: Palgrave Macmillan, 2005), pp305–331.

Part II

8   Sherry Turkle, *Evocative Objects: Things We Think With* (Cambridge, MA: MIT Press, 2007), pp3–10, 307–326.

9   Hilda Kean, *London Stories: Personal Lives, Public Histories* (London: Rivers Oram Press, 2004), pp1–15, 60–81.

10   Paul Martin, *The Trade Union Badge: Material Culture in Action* (Aldershot, UK: Ashgate, 2002), pp97–127.

11   Daniel Cohen, 'The future of preserving the past', *CRM: The Journal of Heritage Stewardship*, vol 2(2) (Washington, DC: National Park Service, 2005), pp6–19.

12   Deborah Dean and Rhiannon Williams, *Critical Cloth*, Exhibition at Nottingham Castle Museum and Art Gallery, 16 April–19 June 2011, Curated by Deborah Dean and catalogue published by University of Derby, pp2–7, 20–27.

13   Paul Ashton and Paula Hamilton, *History at the Crossroads: Australians and the Past* (New South Wales: Halstead Press, 2010), pp121–133.

Part III

14   James A. Flath, *The Cult of Happiness: Nianhua, Art and History in Rural North China* (Vancouver, BC: University of British Columbia Press, 2004), pp4–10, 81–95, 150–153.

15   Cahal McLaughlin, '"Under the same roof": Separate stories of Long Kesh/Maze', in J. Aulich, L. Purbrick and G. Dawson (eds) *Contested Spaces: Sites, Representations and Histories of Conflict* (Basingstoke, UK: Palgrave Macmillan, 2007), pp233–247.

16   Sandra Prosalendis, Jennifer Marot, Crain Soudien and Anwah Nagia in C. Rassool and S. Prosalendis (eds) *Recalling Community in Cape Town: Creating and Curating the District Six Museum* (Cape Town, South Africa: District Six Museum, 2001), ppvii–xii, 74–94.

17   Lawrence Scott (ed), *Golconda: Our Voices, Our Lives* (Trinidad: UTT Press, 2009), ppxi–xiv, 10–12, 27–28, 69–70, 129–131.

18   Michael Belgrave, 'Something borrowed, something new: History and the Waitangi Tribunal', in B. Dalley and J. Phillips (eds) *Going Public: The Changing Face of New Zealand History* (Auckland, New Zealand: Auckland University Press, 2001), pp92–109.

19   Alan Rice, *Creating Memorials, Building Identities: The Politics of Memory in the Black Atlantic* (Liverpool, UK: Liverpool University Press, 2011), pp32–54.

Hilda Kean

INTRODUCTION

THIS *PUBLIC HISTORY READER* has its origins in our long practice of running an MA in Public History, the first in Britain, at Ruskin College, Oxford, and of teaching lively, engaged and intellectually curious students. The reader derives much from the practice and experience of students who have grappled with concepts underpinning different definitions of public history and then used them in their own work. It is a product of the work of historians of many kinds. The extracts include examples from people who are film-makers, artists, novelists or curators or who have taught history, geography or anthropology.

There are various extant works on the nature of public history. Some have been descriptive accounts of particular presentations of the past; others have been more theoretical explorations of public history and we have drawn upon some of them in our teaching. But this book differs in various ways. As we shall explore, although there are various definitions of public history (and different emphases in different countries), we see public history as a process by which the past is constructed into history and a practice which has the capacity for involving people as well as nations and communities in the creation of their own histories. Discussion of process is an integral part of the practice of public history. This Reader is intended to challenge conventional approaches to history and to facilitate new ways of thinking to enable the engagement with one's own history-making.

Process also implies practice. This includes the materials used for creating history as much as who decides what history is. Thus, although many of the extracts are conceptually based, they also include examples of practice involving people who have not necessarily studied history in a formal sense or obtained qualifications in the field. This selection is deliberate: if public history is not a set body of knowledge but a process by which history is constructed, then it is about 'making' history as much as 'thinking about' history. Although the extracts include examples of practice from China, Guatemala, Finland, Trinidad and South Africa, most of the extracts focus on practice in Britain, North America and Australasia. This is both because of our own expertise but also because the analysis of 'public history' has been most developed, albeit in different traditions, in these English-speaking cultures.

This general introduction provides an overview of debates within the broad framework of public history followed by three related sections – Part I: The past in the present: Who is making history?; Part II: Materials and approaches to making history; and Part III: Intangible and tangible presentations of the past. Each section is prefaced by an introduction that sets a context for the ideas and debates raised within the extracts.

Making history – and being incorporated within 'history'

The Hyde Park Barracks in Sydney, Australia, is now a museum that depicts various aspects of Australia's past by showing the different uses of the building over time, including its use as a military prison, home for destitute women and government departments. When visitors enter the shop to buy admission tickets, they are confronted with a glass cabinet containing real rats who live there as their home and nest. As the accompanying sign says, for most of the nineteenth century the human occupants of the barracks shared the building with rats who scurried about dragging away scraps of clothing, food and bedding to make nests. Because the rats did this, thousands of personal and everyday items relating to humans were found: bonnets, aprons, shirts, shoes, stockings.[1] It was this animal process of accumulation – and then a different, human, recognition of its value – that allowed the archaeological service to document ordinary everyday lives at the barracks in the past. This is still a fairly unusual approach to the display of materials in a museum since it not only explains but also highlights the way in which the institution has constructed its displays. It shows the decisions taken to save what some might see as everyday rubbish and how these ephemeral traces of the past came to be there. It demystifies the work of the professional historians paid to produce such a collection.[2]

Coinciding with this recent visit was another example of history-making outside the former barracks in Macquarie Street. Here the local council had hung bright orange banners from the lampposts declaring 'Find your place in history'. These were advertising for History Week, seen as an opportunity for all members of 'our community to learn about and celebrate the people, places and events that make our City what it is today'. There were various events, including exhibitions organized in libraries. Opening the occasion, the Lord Mayor had urged all city residents 'to get involved'. The inference here was that history already existed and that people needed to become part of what had already been constructed by others, albeit in order to 'find their own place'.[3]

In some ways the rat display inside the Hyde Park Barracks and the banners outside might be useful starting points for discussing the nature of public history. In summary, despite different emphases, public historians recognize that the past and history are not synonymous: history, of whatever sort, is created. The 'past can be made knowable only through an active process of construction, which shapes not only the resulting interpretations, but even the evidence and documentation on which the latter have to be based.'[4] All beings have a past but not everyone is either a historian by profession or training, nor is their particular past included within written or filmed or painted 'history'. By making clear that history is constructed, questions are raised about the nature of history: who decides what is history? Who decides what to include or exclude? Rather than starting with an analysis of the importance of *history* in everyday life, various historians have discussed the value of the *past* in people's lives. In the US, Roy Rosenzweig and David Thelen described the way in which people turn to the past 'as a way of grappling with profound questions about how to live';[5] in Australia, Paul Ashton and Paula Hamilton have shown the range of historical practices people undertake, recognizing that 'formal written history' created by traditional historians is 'only one mode of understanding the past'.[6]

Although inevitably there are different interpretations of the meaning of public history at its most basic, practitioners who conceive of the term broadly would probably agree with the definition used for the editorial policy of *The Public Historian*, the journal of the National Council of Public History –namely, that it involves historical research, analysis and presentation 'with some degree of explicit application to the needs of contemporary life'.[7] 'Contemporary life' can mean many things but in this context it does not mean 'history for its own sake', or history written solely for academic purposes. By implication, given that it relates to life (as opposed simply to study) today, it is also accessible. The 'needs of contemporary life' can embrace nations but also individuals, localities, communities and institutions.

Both the examples given above – of rats and banners – might fit within this broad definition: there was an emphasis on accessibility, an opening up of history and its value in everyday life. But there was a difference in approach. Public history, as defined by Leslie Witz in South Africa, considers 'how histories are represented and created in the public domain'[8] so that 'in approaching the "production of history" one is also approaching history as production'.[9] The Hyde Park rat display was arguably the more radical approach since it showed how the history in the various rooms had been created, thus de-mystifying history-making. The advertising in the street for History Week centred on history having its place in contemporary life, not least by banner advertisements. Here, however, people were encouraged to identify with events already set up for them. The history-making was not of their own creation (it was not about the process of accumulation and sorting that the rats had undertaken, for example); instead, people needed to attend events and fit their own pasts into what someone else had defined as history. Aside from thinking that people are generally just consumers of histories, or, as Jordanova has recently described it, simply acting as 'audiences for the discussions of others',[10] it also implies that the 'thing being consumed' – 'history' – is a given. Although Jerome de Groot called his recent book *Consuming History*, he is far from suggesting that consumption is passive. Instead, he has outlined a range of engagement people undertake, including reading, listening, eating, experiencing, watching, playing or even smelling, in the case of the Jorvik Museum in York.[11] People, he suggests, engage with history on a personal, group and family level. His criticism is not of such engagement but of those historians who exhibit 'professional distaste for the various popular forms of history.... What discussion of history in popular culture there is tends to bemoan the debasing of "history".'[12]

Some have seen public history in different ways – for example, as the creation of accessible history to 'the public'. Aside from the assumptions made about different people being described generically as 'public', this approach also has various ramifications for the way in which history itself is seen as a subject. Such an approach implies that a historian, usually seen as professionally trained, is performing an active role and the 'public' a passive one. Here the historian focuses on history as a body of knowledge than needs to be transmitted in accessible ways. The historian then needs to engage 'the public'. This has the effect of enhancing the status of the historian (as separate from 'the public') both as a possessor of knowledge but also as one skilled in transmission. Such an approach does not necessarily question such roles[13] and has been challenged in various ways. Robert Archibald, for example, stresses the need for active involvement rather than passive consumption by tackling the role of public historians:

> Public historians do not own history. History is owned by those whose past is
> described in the narrative because that story, their own version of it resides in their
> memories and establishes their identities. If public involvement is not integral to
> the process of public history the conclusions are meaningless.[14]

Such an approach offers the possibilities of a participatory historical culture in which people generally – and not just historians – have a clear role in making history.[15] The emphasis is on the active process or the 'making'. As Ron Grele elaborated: 'I do not believe that history is ever unmediated'; it always has a social context of some sort.[16] Reflecting on her own practice working with different communities and their pasts, including those of slavery, in the Bristol area of England, Madge Dresser has suggested that 'true public accessibility also involves the cultivation of trusting, organic relationships. . . . This can be a time-consuming process needing imaginative and sensitive approaches.' This should also apply, she argues, to externally funded projects requiring specific outcomes even though 'It is not always assessable by the reductionist tick-box methods so often favored by officialdom.'[17] Here Dresser uses the term 'organic relationships', but often public historians use the earlier term 'shared authority' as coined by Michael Frisch to suggest a willingness to democratize the making of history.[18] However, some have argued that some 20 years on from its first usage, too often this is a 'signal of worthy intentions rather than an actual description of how people negotiate knowledge about the past'.[19] Rather than thinking of history as a given or a clearly defined body of knowledge, by emphasizing the idea of process it can also be seen as a mechanism whereby 'people can reposition themselves in a changing society and reclaim empowerment by embracing different forms of expression of selfhood in a historical context'.[20] Public history, then, as Alan Newell, a former president of the American National Council of Public History, described it is not a 'distinct field of history' – like women's history or economic history, for example; rather, it is 'an attitude or perception about the use and value of history'.[21]

New definitions and old practices: When did public history 'begin' and what are the implications?

Some of the thinking about the ways in which ordinary people – as opposed to elites – make history owes its origins to developments during the 1960s and 1970s in the field of social history. A key work was Edward Thompson's *The Making of the English Working Class* that emphasized the 'agency of working people, the degree to which they contributed by conscious efforts, to the making of history'.[22] It was also a work written while Thompson was teaching adults in evening classes in Yorkshire and, as he remarked in his preface, he learned a great deal with the members of his classes. Similarly, the feminist history classic *Hidden from History: 300 Years of Women's Oppression and the Fight against It* also owed its origins to life outside academia. The author, Sheila Rowbotham, described its origins coming 'very directly from a political movement' and it was written decades before she was appointed to a university post.[23] The development of oral history and the boom in collecting stories of ordinary people also emerged at this time, including the work of Studs Terkel in the US and Alessandro Portelli and Luisa Passerini in Italy.[24] These approaches had the effect of bringing to light the experiences of people whom mainstream history-writing had ignored. It not only helped to create an impetus for change within history teaching in schools and higher education, but also influenced practice with the development of self-organized groups writing their own histories. This was exemplified by organizations such as Centerprise in East London and QueenSpark in Brighton that issued ground-breaking self-authored collections of narratives of people's ordinary lives.[25] In his thoughtful analysis of such initiatives, Stephen Yeo answers 'everyone's' to the question he poses: 'Whose story?', arguing that '"Everyone's" must start with "mine", because our own (humanity, experiences, feelings and so on) are what we all have in common.'[26]

Those who have seen public history as a recent development of the past 30 years, ascribing its origins, for example, to a course on public history run at the University of California in the 1970s by Robert Kelley, have tended to see public history in a more straightforward fashion as 'the employment of historians and historical method outside of academia'.[27]

In some countries, public historians regard themselves as being perceived to be of a lower status than those employed in universities since the role is recognized as a craft rather than a legitimate academic subject.[28] Certainly, the self-declared 'first book length reference work' on public history published in 1982 was called *The Craft of Public History*.[29] In order to help raise the profile of such work and to defend professional interests in various countries, organizations have been established as trade bodies of professional historians.[30] As Bronwyn Dalley, former chief historian at New Zealand's Ministry for Culture and Heritage, has discussed, the formation of the Professional Historians' Association of New Zealand/Aotearoa was, 'in effect, a credential for historians working in the marketplace to distinguish them from enthusiastic amateurs'.[31] A focus within such professional groups is the maintenance of the 'highest standards of scholarship and critical rigour' that serves then to distinguish such historians from other 'purveyors of the past to popular audiences'.[32] This emphasis on separating historians from people or the public with phrases such as 'historians and their publics'[33] is a different approach than that suggested by historians such as Grele or Frisch – who rather than seeking to differentiate 'historians' from 'people' are looking to the interests we share as human beings and to an equally valued status.[34] Some professional historians have found this difficult to deal with as they feel that their professional standing is being undermined. Yet, as James Gardner, former president of the National Council on Public History, has sharply put it: 'We are often our own worst enemy, failing to share what we do. If we want the public to value what we do we need to share the process of history. . . . This means acknowledging that exhibits (real and virtual) are developed and shaped by individual perceptions. . . .'[35]

Historians who have looked more expansively at the origins of public history have opened up debates about who is creating history. Recognizing in their *The Craft of Public History* that the idea of a *professional* historian (of any sort) is relatively modern, David Trask and Robert Pomeroy III argued that public history 'is an ancient approach to the study of past processes . . . in settings elsewhere than in educational institutions'.[36] This view is common to other countries. Discussing Canadian history, Margaret Conrad has explained that for most of the nineteenth century, Canadian historians were amateurs who came to the field out of enthusiasm rather than university training.[37] In Ireland, scholars have dated the 'public history moulded by the nationalist movement and promoted at a popular level' back to Daniel O'Connell in the 1820s.[38] And in Australia, the origins of public history can be traced back at least to Charles Bean, a journalist who played a major role in shaping the national Anzac legend from World War I.[39] Phyllis Leffler and Joseph Brent contrast nineteenth-century practice with that of a century later in the US:

> When, in the 1870s and 1880s, the discipline of history left public life to enter the academy, its practitioners believed they spoke with the objective and unified voice of science. Now, a century later, as many of them leave the academy to reopen the interrupted dialogue with the world of affairs, they speak in a Babel of voices and languages and cannot even agree on the essential elements of the discipline.[40]

This emphasis on the construction of histories long before there were established degrees in history at universities leads to thinking about the way in which nations – and localities and communities – have taken choices to create particular histories in their own interests and the form such constructions take. Given that history as an academic subject did not exist when nations first started commemorating their particular pasts, it is unsurprising that governments initiated historical constructions. Rejecting the role of academic historians as drivers in this initiative, prolific British historian Jeremy Black has discussed the way in which the past has been reworked in different countries.[41] The type of museums, galleries, monuments, cultural foundations and commemorations that a nation creates is important[42] since people, as Stuart Hall has observed, come to know the meaning of a nation 'partly *through* the objects and artefacts which have been made to stand for and symbolize its essential values. Its meaning is constructed *within*, not above or outside presentations.'[43] Thus the creation of professionalized and institutional national histories particularly through museums started to be important at a time of nation formation, particularly in Europe during the late eighteenth and early nineteenth centuries.[44] In an influential work, Carol Duncan argued that 'To control a museum means precisely to control the representation of a community and its highest values and truths. It is also the power to define the relative standing of individuals within that community . . . wherein the state idealized and presented itself to the public.'[45] The choice of nations about what should be remembered in their pasts has been defined by some historians as the invention of tradition,[46] while others have explored the way in which memory on a collective as well as personal level has underpinned representations of the past.[47] Unfortunately, we continue to witness during modern warfare the destruction of institutions deemed to be integral to a particular nation's identity. In discussing the Serbian siege of cities in Croatia and Bosnia-Herzegovina during the 1990s, in which museums, monuments, libraries and archives were blown up, Pulitzer Prize-winning historian Mike Wallace has called this an effort of 'historic cleansing'.[48]

While the nineteenth century might be seen as a particular period in which ideas of nation developed through museums, these trends have continued in the creation of new national institutions designed to project particular senses of both unity and tradition. Thus, in different ways, recent decades have seen a new National Museum of Scotland and the Te Papa Museum in Wellington, the latter being created both to privilege a neglected Maori past and to signify a new way of thinking about New Zealand as two linked communities of Pakeha and Maori.[49] In the newly reunited nation of Germany, attempts to come to grips with the country's Nazi past have aroused much controversy. 'The Memorial to the Murdered Jews in Europe' by Peter Eisenman in Berlin was finally constructed in 2005 after decades of debate about how to remember this part of Germany history. Previously conceived projects such as the 'Topography of Terror' exhibition on the former site of the Gestapo headquarters remained unresolved for many years, while the former Nazi parade ground in Nurnberg (and nearby unfinished Congress Hall, now the site of a Documentation Centre) remains deliberately in a state of partial decay, almost symbolizing the lack of agreement on how to preserve such sites.[50]

Yet, ideas of nation are not simply created through state institutions. Through works of film and art, popular ideas are maintained and developed as well as being challenged. Tessa Morris-Suzuki has suggested myths created by Hollywood movies are 'important not just because they are national myths, but also because they are global myths'. Landscapes of the historical imagination around the world, she says, have been shaped by Hollywood, whether by depictions of ancient Rome or versions of the American Civil War or World War II, or films such as the controversial *Amistad*, depicting a slave rebellion on a ship involved in the Atlantic trade, because the products of Hollywood have a global market. Films produced in Asia or Africa are far 'less likely to mould the historical imaginations' of cinema and TV audiences in the North Atlantic nations.[51] Sally J. Morgan, for example, has analysed the film *Braveheart*, which did much to awaken sentiments of nationalism in Scotland. Yet, as she discusses, the William Wallace created in the film 'is the ancestor of the New World pioneer. This story is the construction of a "myth of beginnings" in as much as it implies the seeds of racial and class injustice which would eventually make the establishment of America, and the other white colonies, necessary as a haven for the honest working man.'[52]

The past is not settled or decided but contested and changed

Artists and writers of fiction have done as much as historians to disrupt and challenge the way in which a nation views its own past and to make connections between the past and present within the nation. Thriller writers as well as literary novelists have worked in this way. Thus, in his book *The Redbreast*, Norwegian novelist Jo Nesbo explores the way in which fascist allegiances during the war still need to be addressed – and creates a symbolic denouement on Liberty Day, when Norwegians celebrate their autonomy from Denmark in 1814.[53] In Australia, novelists such as Kate Grenville (in her popular books such as *The Secret River* and *The Lieutenant*) or Richard Flanagan (in his *Gould's Book of Fishes*) have used fiction to challenge accepted narratives about nineteenth-century Aboriginal/invader relationships and convict experience during a period in which historians attempting to raise the same issues were subject to vilification.[54]

Although museums, monuments and memorials might suggest some sort of authority and permanence through their physical presence, in practice the past is never settled but open to new interpretations and forms of presentation. The famous quote of novelist William Faulkner, 'The past is never dead. It's not even past', can be interpreted in many ways: embracing the role of the past in people's memories and the influence of the past in the present, but also the way it is still contested and disputed. Another slant on this way of thinking is found in the work of cultural theorist Walter Benjamin, whose work of the 1930s is still seen as pertinent today: 'The true method of making things present is to represent them in our space, not to represent ourselves in their space . . . we don't displace our being into theirs; they step into our life.'[55] The emphasis here is upon ensuring that particular events of an earlier time are not forgotten but made relevant in a particular contemporary moment.[56] A practical example of such an approach is the work of Toby Butler, using oral memories collected along the River Thames and reintroduced into their 'geographical habitat' through a downloadable aural package. Voices from the past are heard in the present in a place that transcends time.[57]

The past is regularly contested and disputed, often fiercely. The controversy over the Enola Gay exhibition in the Smithsonian's National Air and Space Museum in Washington has been widely discussed. Controversy centred on how the dropping of the atom bomb on Japan should be remembered and recorded and the weight that should be given to different perspectives, including the role of the airmen; but it was not unique.[58] Indeed, in Australia such debates about the origins of white Australia and the treatment of indigenous people, which were conducted in the media rather than in scholarly articles, became so fierce that they became known as the 'history wars'.[59] In particular, the contents and approach of the first National Museum of Australia in Canberra were disputed: politicians became involved, displays questioning a benign display of Australia's European past were traduced, and the director of the museum lost her job.[60]

In some ways such controversies are unsurprising, being rooted in both events and places that themselves reflect social relations. Geographer Doreen Massey has argued that places are 'always constructed out of articulations of social relations (trading connections, the unequal ties of colonialism, thoughts of home)' that are not only internal to that locality but which link them to other places. Further, 'the past of a place is as open to a multiplicity of readings as is the present. Moreover, the claims and counter-claims about the present character of a place depend in almost all cases on particular, rival, interpretations of its past.' These rival interpretations, she explains, are based on the different socio-geographical position of the groups that promote them.[61] Dolores Hayden has exemplified who has a role in creating such multiplicities: 'Indigenous residents as well as colonizers, ditchdiggers as well as architects, migrant workers as well as mayors, housewives as well as housing inspectors are all active shaping the urban landscape.'[62] Thus, when discussion took place after the end of apartheid in South Africa about how to present Robben Island where Nelson Mandela and other campaigners had been imprisoned, those creating the history recognized the multiple pasts exemplified in the site, and the island became 'transformed into a microcosm for what the government wanted to see taking place nationally'.[63] In addition to the experience of prisoners, there was also that of the prison guards to be considered, and the island itself was home to more than 100 species of birds. In due course, this World Heritage Site and the museum itself embraced the flora, fauna and even the seabed surrounding the island.[64] In looking to the landscape to create different histories in Australia, Peter Read has engaged with different topographies of pre- and post-invasion Aboriginal settlements. Modern road engineering, he argues, ignores the different landscape experienced by indigenous foot-walkers who used water routes to move around. Realizing the value of places and their different pasts, he has criticized public historians working with museums, monuments, oral history and material heritage, saying: 'we sometimes don't work in the interpretation of historical topography as much as we might. Investigation of a farmstead and its surroundings should involve a good knowledge of soils, imported weeds and their effects, contour lines, watercourses and abandoned roads to understand how it functioned as a working farm.'[65] Using interviews, GPS mapping techniques and Google Earth, he recreated a different Aboriginal past that could be visually imposed upon current non-Aboriginal ways of seeing.[66]

Using the landscape to rethink ways of seeing the past through competing viewpoints has been prominent in the work of American archaeologist Mark Leone, who has spent many years excavating a former slave plantation in Annapolis, the capital of Maryland. The place, he argues, is traditionally known as the site of the US Naval Academy and its importance in the American Revolution; however, Leone was interested in presenting an alternative picture of the past. In particular, through finding hidden crystals used to make mojos or 'hands' that were part of African spirit practices and which were probably placed in the grounds to manage the spirits in the house or to protect the inhabitants, Leone realized that 'our Annapolis discoveries were important to people far beyond archaeology and African American folklore'.[67] Public historians in the US National Parks Service, also in Maryland, have analysed the relationship between different pasts in the landscape by discussing the ways in which slave owner John Blackford, in his plantation at Ferry Hill, specifically 'used a psychological control technique . . . for constant, comprehensive surveillance', ensuring that the social hierarchy of the place was reflected in the landscape itself. Buildings and landscaped gardens were created in such a way as to enable surveillance so that 'the planter elite conceptually devalued the labor of the enslaved population, as well as the laborers' personal dignity as human beings'.[68] Others working within the National Parks Service have discussed possible responses to the idea of a national identity that is infused in landscapes of national parks, such as Yellowstone or Yosemite, being concerned that unless the service connects to the diversity of the population it will become an anachronism. Thus, Lucy Lawliss has suggested that the landscape of the parks is not 'a place of boundaries – political, social, or legal – but a place of relationships. Not so much a place as experiences that change people's lives.'[69] The importance of landscape in different ways in the present is evident in the work of many public historians in New Zealand, particularly those in settling landownership of Maori communities under the Waitangi Tribunal established in 1975. The Treaty of Waitangi, agreeing rights and responsibilities, was signed between indigenous peoples and the British Crown in 1849 although landownership was subsequently disputed in different places. Public historians, rather than lawyers, have been employed to interpret these historical documents in modern law courts. Indeed, recently, it has been authoritatively stated that 'The Treaty sector is the single largest employer of New Zealand historians in the country.'[70]

History outside the archive and the classroom

Thinking about history in the landscape of everyday life is very different than the starting points of conventional history and immediately opens up the topic to those not working as professional historians.[71] The late British social historian Raphael Samuel noted that 'unofficial' knowledge and popular memory was a starting point for understanding the past that comes not from the classroom but from 'civic, ritual, street nomenclature and literary or political statuary' – that is, landscape, monuments and places outside books and archives.[72] Historians have recently shown that archive material itself is a result of decisions taken by archivists to collect particular items – and also by responding positively (or negatively) to what they are offered by people.[73] Many archivists have started to question their conventional role. As Richard Cox has argued, with the advance of technology 'Archivists will be more documentary shapers than documentary custodians, more digital forensic experts then documentary describers and more archival activists than passive reference gatekeepers.'[74] Community groups and political campaigns do create their own archives – and historically have done this.[75] Archivist Andrew Flinn sees 'radical public history' possibilities here of not just celebration and reclamation, but also 'of reflection and explanation' so that a 'community archive can represent not only the establishment of a place where the past is documented and passively collected but, crucially, also a space in which the archive can become a significant tool for discovery, education and empowerment'.[76] Again looking to the future, Kate Theimer, in discussing the implications of Web 2.0 applications, has shown that not only is an opportunity for direct interaction with archival materials possible, but that a physical visit to an archive is no longer necessary since materials can be read at home or on the move.[77] This 'access' also has implications for knowledge formation. What may have been a fairly isolated activity of going to an archive and making notes, usually in silence, becomes a potentially explicitly social activity in which materials found or strands of thought can be shared immediately with friends and partners either through looking at the same web page or through sending a link or text.[78]

In contrast to conventional history-making being seen as a solitary archival act conducted by a professional, Samuel argued that 'history is not the prerogative of the historian. . . . It is, rather, a social form of knowledge; the work in a given instance, of a thousand different hands. . . .'[79] He contrasted this definition with conventional ways of seeing 'the historical discipline', which he criticized as encouraging 'inbreeding, introspection, sectarianism. Academic papers are addressed to a relatively narrow circle of fellow-practitioners.'[80] Such thousands of different hands encompassed, he said, 'the rapidly expanding movements in "do-it-yourself" history'.[81] His definition had a wide remit, including local publishing and family history groups. He embraced family history although such grassroots activity had been criticized by some historians as different than the approach of professional historians and not to be taken seriously as history.[82] While some have seen this historical activity as introspective,[83] more radical practitioners have seen the possibilities of exploring family history as ways of revisiting topics of social history.[84] In recent years there have been examples of family history being used to challenge ways of thinking about migration, or about moments in the nation's psyche.[85] Tanya Evans has suggested that in Australia, family historians have a particular role to play in questioning traditional and largely accepted narratives about Australia's early colonial and convict past, a theme which has been explored particularly in relation to Aboriginal family history by Graeme Davison, as included later in this Reader.[86]

Tim Brennan has analysed family history as the antithesis of both autobiography and biography, genres that tend towards documenting great deeds. By way of contrast, the experience of family history is often mundane[87] and is thus valuable in creating different types of history. Although the work of individual family historians continues to be dismissed as generating 'little insight' unless such researchers work collaboratively with professional historians, thus permitting them to be 'counted as members of the "knowledge society"',[88] others have seen the growth of such work positively, as Martin Bashforth notes: 'family historians collectively represent the most significant opportunity to thoroughly democratise the practice of history. The idea of thousands of families conducting three or four generation family history studies, using the products of family history research and being organised amongst themselves represents a revolution waiting to happen.'[89]

To such self-organized historians, one might add the example of collectors, local guides and creators of blogs of historical interest who, if nothing else, are seeking to disseminate interest in the past.[90] This activity is not a twenty-first-century development.[91] Samuel recognized that people, for the most part, do not obtain their ideas of their family, local or national history from reading history books in school. However, others have used the materials favoured by such researchers to create new ways of thinking. Even academic historians do not necessarily say their passion for history came from history in school.[92] As Italian professor of history Luisa Passerini has recently said: 'I had always hated it, at least the type of history we were taught in school. Dates, facts, great events, the greatness of Italy.' But she was engaged by 'the stories that my grandmother told me: fairy tales, her life-story as well as family stories concerning my great-grandparents, great-uncles and aunts, but also summaries of Italian operas. . . .'[93]

Opening up materials for history

If knowledge of the past is not confined to 'book learning', it also suggests that other materials – outside a paper-based archive – can create value and meaning. This, in turn, can open up different subject matter. Dwight Pitcaithley has recently described the way in which he became a public historian of the US National Parks Service. One of his first assignments was analysing the remains of machines for processing bat guano in a cave with a 180-foot vertical drop into which he was obliged to drop. This unusual location for historical materials forced him to 'recognise that historians could find research material almost anywhere'.[94]

In a different vein, in the weeks following 9/11 (the bombing of the Twin Towers in New York in 2001), historians established The September 11 Digital Archive where they specifically collected materials from 'everyday people', including emails, photographs and pager communications – the sorts of materials unlikely to have found their way into a conventional museum.[95] At the same time, St Paul's Chapel adjacent to the site, which was physically unaffected by the blasts and acted as a resting site for rescue workers, also became a *de facto* museum of the event, receiving – and then saving and displaying – messages and artefacts from around the world paying homage to the work of the emergency services. A project similar to that organized for 9/11 was subsequently created around Hurricanes Katrina and Rita, described as the largest free public archive of Katrina and Rita, with over 25,000 items in the collection.[96] This recognition of the importance of new forms of communication and their use for future researchers has also been noted by Stephanie Ho, discussing the role of blogs as public history in Singapore. However, she has noted that when bloggers venture beyond the 'safe arena of memory and nostalgia' and create histories that are 'incompatible with state narratives [i]t remains to be seen whether the state will treat it as "internet chatter" or bring in the long arm of the law'.[97] Even when digital communication is not explicitly circumscribed by the state it does not mean that contributions are necessarily outside normative constructions, given the strengths of popular memory. The BBC launched a 'People's War' website for people to upload memories of World War II in June 2003, and this continued for some three years, receiving some 47,000 written contributions. While Lucy Noakes has noted how websites can provide a 'more informal space where memories "from below" can be more widely shared and disseminated, than in traditional, formally constituted sites such as memorials, museums and textbooks', she nevertheless noted the way in which 'Cultural memory of the Second World War operates hegemonically, incorporating elements of subordinate memory which can be made to "fit" with the dominant and marginalising or silencing more oppositional, challenging narratives of the war.'[98]

Different approaches to sharing authority

In such approaches there has been an openness about creating history. However, public historians do not always work in this way. Certainly, there have been fierce debates about who decides on what should be presented as history. An article based on decades of personal experience and thinking about public history by Frits Pannekoek, at that time director of the Historical Sites Service, Alberta Community Development, in Canada was provocatively entitled 'The rise of a heritage priesthood'. Describing his recent experience of the historical profession, Frits Pannekoek ironically suggested that 'Professionals no longer advise or counsel – they decide. Only professionals can now make important cultural decisions.'[99] However, he contrasted this with what he had tried to do in Alberta where, he declared, 'Professionals are at the beck and call of the community, not misguided social engineers. Individuals and their community determine historical significance – not professional historians or heritage architects, although they do have input.'[100] Here he discusses various projects with nominal community input leading to controversial outcomes, including the Enola Gay exhibition. By way of contrast, Pannekoek gives the example of approaches to a fur trade site in Alberta. First there was a three-day symposium involving Canada's leading fur trade scholars, representatives from the First Nations communities and members of surrounding communities. The meeting took the decision that the site should be interpreted entirely through the eyes of an Aboriginal woman. As Pannekoek reflected: 'The interpretation ended up being strong, focused, and feminist. Most important it was supported by professional[s] and community. Had the same themes been selected and imposed by the academics, there would have been a riot. Instead, there was insight, acceptance, and dialogue.'[101]

Agreement, however, is not always as easy as this project suggests. James Gardner has looked at what is meant by developing 'radical trust'. He has argued that if, for example, curating an exhibition is about 'making meaning of the past' rather than simply selecting and organizing around personal preference, then this opens up epistemological problems. Therefore, it is not accurate to talk about a blurring between different producers of knowledge, but between knowledge and 'opinion'.[102] Describing issues he has had to grapple with at the Museum of American History at the Smithsonian, he gives the example of having to 'deal with individuals who deny that Japanese Americans were wrongly interned during World War II' and maintains: 'We cannot allow such individuals to use us for their own purposes – or our reputations will end up suffering collateral damage.'[103]

Redefining roles and negotiating positions . . .

Some oral history practice circumscribed by funders' criteria of integration and social cohesion may become a group exercise in nostalgia. In such circumstances, facilitators can see their role as simply 'presenting' the stories of those interviewed rather than undertaking more demanding work analysing, discussing and reflecting critically. An example of this might be the oral history project undertaken with women, called pit brow workers, who had worked sorting coal on the surface of coal mines in the north-west of England. This was a badly paid and physically hard job; yet the effect of discussing the former work in a group led the women to emphasize the social value of the work. Seemingly unchallenged by the project leader, the book produced is a collection of nostalgic reminiscences rather than a more critical reflection. This is exemplified by the title *Ah'd Gaa Back Tomorra!*[104] This example is not unique in the field. Emma Waterton and Laurajane Smith have discussed the ways in which many community-oriented projects 'tend to involve things that are done *for* communities, rather than *with* them', concluding that 'groups affixed with the term "community" . . . are often defined, or have their "authenticity" judged against standards set by the heritage that has been preserved "for them" by heritage agencies and their experts'.[105] As Laurajane Smith, Paul Shackel and Gary Campbell have argued in another work, rather than working in an 'assimilationist fashion' there is a need to 'embrace dissonance'.[106] By simply listening to stories and repeating them uncritically, established histories are not necessarily being challenged – and unheard voices can be devalued and reduced to mere reminiscence.

Some have seen their role in more emancipatory fashion as facilitators offering particular skills to people making their own histories. An example was the collaborative book edited by Raphael Samuel, *The Enemy Within*,[107] which reflected on the miners' strike of 1984 to 1985. While it was written as an intervention in political and public debate, it was also a reminder of 'individual experience and imaginative perception'[108] and the way in which the strike was 'assimilated in popular memory ... both in the pit villages themselves and in the country at large'.[109] Such examples of history-making (and history writing) in the public political domain offer a practical example of the connection between lived experience and formal kinds of learning.[110] This topic has been revisited in an imaginative vein both by, amongst others, artist Jeremy Deller in his Artangel-funded project that was a re-enactment of the Battle of Orgreave during the miners' strike[111] and by Simon Popple, an academic and film-maker. He followed up a project examining the controversial role of the BBC during the 1984 to 1985 miners' strike by giving former miners and police officers the opportunity to produce their own responses to the BBC archival sources and to create their own resources. This new creation of knowledge involved former participants responding to BBC archived material and creating their own response, facilitated by Popple's particular technical skills. Significantly, the project was not about a simplistic nostalgia or memory story, but a reflection on the way in which others had constructed the protagonists' own pasts, and their response to it.[112]

... and bridging boundaries

The very existence of such projects implicitly undermines narrow definitions of professionalized and discrete knowledge by juxtaposing this with ideas of knowledge derived from experience. Such projects can facilitate 'a broadly distributed authority for making new sense of the past in the present'.[113] In London, for example, a project between geographers and archaeologists analysing the material culture found in different sites of a similar date and employing the sorts of detailed materials often used by local and family historians, such as street census returns or Post Office directories, created engaging histories that disrupted conventional ways of seeing class in nineteenth-century London.[114] Artist Jane Palm-Gold also initiated an engaging trans-disciplinary project in London originating from the scenes she observed outside her flat in central London, opposite the site of the nineteenth-century Rookery in St Giles. Later, working with archaeologist Sian Anthony, she both brought to light traces of the cellars and underground passages that helped to facilitate egress for criminals of an earlier age as well as using Hogarth's images of the locality superimposed on her own work to create different narratives of the area.[115] This picture of a place crossing time brought the past into the present in different ways: its display in an art gallery (rather than a museum) also helped to create different audiences.

This breaking down of barriers between people with different expertise is well illustrated by the popular practice of metal detection. In England and Wales alone there are over 200 metal-detecting clubs with the members' initial motivation, according to a recent survey, being an 'interest in the past'.[116] The Staffordshire hoard, 'the largest hoard of Anglo-Saxon gold ever found', of 1500 unique items of precious metals and stones from the seventh century was discovered by Terry Herbert, a metal detectorist, who then informed professional archaeologists. In the past, such amateurs have often been derided by professionals; but Roger Bland of the British Museum paid tribute to Terry Herbert's actions in promptly reporting the find and for 'giving every assistance to the investigation of the site'.[117] The hoard was valued at £3.3 million: a sum was raised within a few months by individuals and institutions, including the Art Fund and National Heritage Memorial Fund, in order to keep the hoard in Britain and on public display. The hoard is now jointly owned by Birmingham Museum and Art Gallery and the Potteries Museum and has been on display in the Midlands, where it originated.[118] Similarly, the work of metal detectorists in mapping important English sites of battle, such as the Civil War site at Naseby, has been acknowledged. This is another example of fruitful crossover, where the outcomes are seen as more important than the status of the person who has discovered the artefact. As Nick Merriman, director of the Manchester Museum and former president of the Council for British Archaeology, has recognized, however hard archaeologists try to create discrete meanings, 'non-archaeologists will re-appropriate, re-interpret and re-negotiate meanings to their own personal agendas'.[119]

Alan Rice, for example, who has done much to bring into the public spaces of the twenty-first century Britain's slaving past, including the creation of a public memorial 'Captured Africans' in Lancaster, at one time the fourth largest slave trading port in Britain, worked with others in the Slave Trade Arts Memorial Project (STAMP), including community activists, creative workers, councillors and academics. As discussed later in this Reader, this was not a project in which the 'expert' told the 'people' the facts of a moment of history and corrected any perceived misunderstandings.[120] The project achieved new ways of thinking about the past and of bringing it into the present not by the scholarship of an individual historian but by all those involved in the project 'reaching in to discover the humanity they share'.[121] Rice's role within the project inevitably drew on his scholarship; but this was not separated from his political commitment to facilitate broad understandings of the past, and his belief that there are many pasts that should be remembered.

What is sometimes forgotten is the way in which people's own creations of history can create distinctive and illuminating meanings. A good example of this is a new book, *London Recruits*, a powerful collection of personal testimonies written by white British people who were recruited clandestinely during the late 1960s and 1970s to distribute illegal leaflets in South Africa at a time when the Apartheid regime was strong and opposition was fragmented, underground or imprisoned.[122] It was only some 35 years later that the individuals met each other and realized that they had all been undertaking this illicit activity: the book arose from this meeting. The book is an excellent subjective account of individuals' experience of their own involvement in this campaign; but it is not – nor is it intended to be – an overarching analysis of the politics of South Africa during the 1960s and 1970s. Another recent book also written from inside a political movement is Dave Hann's posthumous *Physical Resistance or A Hundred Years of Fighting Fascism*.[123]Although based on extensive reading, the bulk of the book is centred on oral interviews of anti-fascist campaigners who were willing to talk to the activist author. As the editorial introduction written by his partner employed in a university explores: 'The academic practice of history, which is often based on the assumption that the story has been told and all that is left to do is interpret it, was regarded by Dave as almost irrelevant. . . .'

In such examples, the reader is offered histories that value experience and have emerged directly as a result of political engagement, creating a particular form of historical knowledge, the type of initiative Raphael Samuel was considering when he talked of a 'thousand different hands'. Reflecting critically on his own former practice, Finnish historian Jorma Kalela has analysed his work with the Finnish Paperiliitto trade union in the 1980s, an extract of which is included in this collection. Creating history research circles, he had assumed incorrectly what they would wish to study and analyses his own attitude as 'patronizing. . . . They had to have the right to study *what in their* view was *their own history*, rather than take for granted a ready-made concept of it [original emphases].'[124]

Conclusion

In different countries and cultures, those who work in museums and archives or undertake guided walks or facilitate educational or community projects may not be the only people who undertake such historical activity. Sources of funding for higher education are such that those employed as 'academic' historians may also undertake consultancy work, advise community history projects or present television programmes. And they may well spend time away from paid employment researching family history, searching eBay to add to their collection or writing their blogs. Their leisure activities may include visiting galleries or ruins, or photographing derelict buildings, or campaigning to preserve areas threatened with development. Therefore, many historians would question how valuable it is to construct rigid boundaries around the different aspects of historians' work since, in practice, the boundaries between different aspects of their professional, scholarly or personal lives are likely to be porous. As Paul Preston, professor of contemporary Spanish history at the London School of Economics and Political Science, recently discussed, he could not have written his new book on historical memory in relation to republicans murdered under Franco without the 'great historian of south west Spain' and the 'great expert' of atrocities in Valencia. Neither is employed in Spanish universities. The former runs a petrol station and the latter a little tobacconist shop.[125]

Helpfully, Paul Ashton and Paula Hamilton have suggested that, metaphorically, history in the broadest sense might be thought of as a house with many rooms inhabited by people such as makers of historical films, community historians and museum practitioners, some of whom inhabit more than one room while 'many make occasional visits to other parts of the house'.[126] Certainly, such a house would need to be an extremely large one to cater for the range of current historical activity of which public history, as this collection demonstrates, is a vital part.

In the three introductions to the selected extracts, bold is used to indicate that what the author discussed is represented by an extract in that section.

Notes

1   Sadly, the rats kept in the case are not Norwegian brown rats – the type found on ships who would have been the type to have lived in the barracks. Instead, they are domestic agouti rats since they were seen as friendlier.

2   For further information on the museum, see P. Crook and T. Murray (2006) *An Archaeology of Institutional Refuge: The Material Culture of the Hyde Park Barracks, Sydney, 1848–1886*, Sydney: Historic Houses Trust of New South Wales.

3   See   http://www.sydneymedia.com.au/html/4353-find-your-place-in-history-this-september. asp 31 August 2010, accessed 14 March 2012.

4   G. Eley and K. Nield (2007) *The Future of Class in History: What's Left of the Social?*, Ann Arbor, MI: University of Michigan Press, p67, as quoted in E. Zelenak (2011) 'Modifying Alun Munslow's classification of approaches to history', *Rethinking History*, vol 15(4), December, p531.

5   R. Rosenzweig and D. Thelen (1998) *The Presence of the Past: Popular Uses of History in American Life*, New York, NY: Columbia University Press, p18.

6   P. Ashton and P. Hamilton (2010) *History at the Crossroads: Australians and the Past*, Ultimo, New South Wales: Halstead Press, p17. See also 'Canadians and their Pasts', a five year project (2006–2011) 'designed to explore the importance ordinary Canadians ascribe to the past and history of their family, their country, and other aspects of their life; to inquire into the level of trust they have in various sources of historical information; and to document the way in which they engage with the past in their every day lives' (http://www.canadians andtheirpasts.ca/about.html, accessed 9 May 2012).

7   *The Public Historian* (2001) vol 23(2), p139.

8   L. Witz (2010) *Museums, Histories and the Dilemmas of Change in Post-Apartheid South Africa*, University of Michigan Working Papers in Museum Studies, no 3, Ann Arbor, MI: University of Michigan Museum of Art, p6. See also, C. Rassool, 'Power, knowledge and the politics of public pasts', www.nelsonmandela.org/images/uploads/PAPER – RASSOOL.pdf, accessed 12 May 2012.

9   D. W. Cohen (1994) *The Combing of History*, p23, as quoted in Witz, *Museums*, p6.

10   L. Jordanova as cited in H. Hoock (2010) 'Introduction', *The Public Historian*, vol 32(3), p18.

11   J. de Groot (2009) *Consuming History*, Abingdon, UK: Routledge, p249.

12   de Groot, *Consuming*, p4.

13   The dissemination of ideas can be a democratic impulse, as John Tosh has argued, defining public history as involving 'the free access of the public to the findings of historical scholarship'. J. Tosh (2008) *Why History Matters*, Basingstoke, UK: Palgrave Macmillan, p119. See also http://www.historyandpolicy.org.

14   R. Archibald (1999) *A Place to Remember: Using History to Build Community*, New York, NY: Altamira, pp155–156.

15   R. J. Grele (1981) 'Whose public? Whose history? What is the goal of a public historian?', *The Public Historian*, vol 3(1), pp44–46.

16   R. J. Grele (2000) 'Clio on the Road to Damascus: A national survey of history as activity and experience', *The Public Historian*, vol 72(1), p3.

17   M. Dresser (2010) 'Politics, populism, and professionalism: Reflections on the role of the academic historian in the production of public history', *The Public Historian*, vol 32(3), pp62–63. See also M. Dresser (2007) 'Set in stone? Statues and slavery in London', *History Workshop Journal*, vol 64, pp162–199.

18   M. Frisch (ed) (1990) *A Shared Authority: Essays on the Craft and Meaning of Oral and Public History*, Albany, NY: State University of New York Press.

19   P. Ashton and P. Hamilton (2009) 'Connecting with History: Australians and their pasts', in P. Ashton and H. Kean (eds) *People and Their Pasts: Public History Today*, Basingstoke, UK: Palgrave Macmillan, p37.

20   P. Martin (1999) 'Look, see, hear: A remembrance, with approaches to contemporary public history at Ruskin', in G. Andrews, H. Kean and J. Thompson (eds) *Ruskin College: Contesting Knowledge, Dissenting Politics*, London: Lawrence and Wishart, p148.

21   Alan Newell as quoted in C. A. Christen and L. Mighetto (2004) 'Introduction: Environmental history as public history', *The Public Historian*, vol 26(1), p12.

22   E. P. Thompson (1980 [1963]) 'Preface', in *The Making of the English Working Class*, Harmondsworth, UK: Penguin, p12.

23   S. Rowbotham (1973) *Hidden from History: 300 Years of Women's Oppression and the Fight against It*, London: Pluto Press, pix. While undertaking some of the research, she had been teaching apprentices on day-release programmes in further education colleges.

24   See, for example, S. Terkel (1970) *Hard Times: An Oral History of the Great Depression*, New York, NY: Pantheon Books; L. Passerini (1987) *Fascism in Popular Memory: The Cultural Experience of the Turin Working Class* (trans. R. Lumley and J. Bloomfield), Cambridge: Cambridge University Press; A. Portelli (1981) 'The peculiarities of oral history', *History Workshop Journal*, vol 12(1), pp96–107.

25   QueenSpark, established in 1972, still publishes community writing. Centerprise was founded in 1970, with much of the early publications initiated by writer and teacher Ken Worpole.

26   S. Yeo (1986) 'Whose story? An argument from within current historical practice in Britain', *Journal of Contemporary History*, vol 21(2), p296. See also L. Sitzia (2010) *Telling People's Histories: An Exploration of Community History-Making from 1970–2000*, DPhil thesis, University of Sussex.

27   R. Kelley (1978) 'Public history: Its origins, nature and prospects', *The Public Historian*, vol 1(1), p16. See also A. A. Jones (1999) 'Public history now and then', *The Public Historian*, vol 21(3), pp21–28.

28   T. Hein (2007) 'History for the people: The field of "public history" gains ground in Canada', *University Affairs: Canada's Magazine on Higher Education*, November 2007, www.universityaffairs.ca/issues/2007/november/_print/history_people.htlm.

29   D. F. Trask and R. W. Pomeroy III (eds) (1983) *The Craft of Public History: An Annotated Select Bibliography*, Connecticut: Greenwood Press for NCPH.

30   The National Council on Public History includes amongst its aims 'promoting professionalism among history practitioners' (http://ncph.org/cms/); the Australian Council of Professional Historians' Associations (ACPHA) aims to increase 'potential clients' and employers' awareness of both the skills of professional historians and the appropriate conditions for their employment' (http://www.historians.org.au/) (websites accessed 14 March 2012). See also http://www.phanza.org.nz/ and L. Dick (2009) 'Public history in Canada: An introduction', *The Public Historian*, vol 31(1), pp7–14.

31   B. Dalley (2009) 'Shades of grey: Public history and government in New Zealand', in Ashton and Kean, *People*, p79.

32   J. Liddington (2002) 'What is public history? Publics and their pasts, meanings and practices', *Oral History*, vol 30(1), pp91–92.

33   Liddington, p88.

34   In an editorial 'Across the great divide' to *The Public Historian* (2007) vol 29(1), p9, Randolph Bergstrom explored this difference while suggesting that public historians 'are reaching people and in turn recognizing people's interests and meaning-making in ways that history's other professions have not always been able to do'.

35   J. B. Gardner (2010) 'Trust, risk and public history: A view from the United States', *Public History Review*, vol 17, p54. See also his earlier 'Contested terrain: History, museums, and the public', *The Public Historian*, vol 26(4), 2004, pp11–21.

36   Trask and Pomeroy, *The Craft*, pxi.

37   M. Conrad, *How Historians Complicate Things: A Brief Survey of Canadian Historiography* (www.histori.ca/prodev/article.do;jsessionid=BF9B12E7B61ECE680930E1A98C0EDB04. tomcat1?id=11635&cview=pf). See also Dick, 'Public history'.

38   B. Bradshaw (1989) 'Nationalism and historical scholarship in modern Ireland', *Irish Historical Studies*, vol xxvi(104), p335, as quoted in J. Regan (2010) 'Irish public histories as an historiographical problem', *Irish Historical Studies*, vol xxxvii(146), p266.

39   Kean and Ashton (2009) 'Introduction' to Ashton and Kean, *People*, p11, and P. Stanley (1993) 'Happy Birthday HRS: A decade of the Australian War Memorial's Historical Research Section', *Public History Review*, vol 2, pp54–65.

40   P. K. Leffler and J. Brent (1990) *Public and Academic History: A Philosophy and Paradigm*, Florida: Krieger Publishers, p28.

41   J. Black (2005) *Using History*, London: Hodder Arnold.

42   P. Carrier (2005) *Holocaust Monuments and National Memory Cultures in France and Germany since 1989: The Origins and Political Function of the Vél d'Hiv in Paris and the Holocaust Monument in Berlin*, New York, NY: Berghahn Books; S. Berger (2009) 'The comparative history of national historiographies in Europe', in S. Carvalho and F. Gemenne (eds) *Nations and their Histories*, Basingstoke, UK: Palgrave Macmillan, pp29–45; C Whitehead (2005) *The Public Art Museum in Nineteenth Century Britain*, Aldershot, UK: Ashgate.

43   S. Hall (2005) 'Whose heritage? Un-settling "the heritage", re-imagining the post-nation', in J. Littler and R. Naidoo (eds) *The Politics of Heritage: The Legacies of 'Race'*, Abingdon, UK: Routledge, p25.

44   For work on ideas of nation, see B. Anderson (1991) *Imagined Communities: Reflections on the Origins and Spread of Nationalism*, second edition, London: Verso; E. Gellner (2006) *Nations and Nationalism: New Perspectives on the Past*, second edition, Oxford: Blackwell; T. Nairn (2003) *The Break-Up of Britain: Crisis and Neo-Nationalism*, third edition, Champaign, IL: Common Ground; D. Boswell and J. Evans (eds) (1999) *Representing the Nation: A Reader. Histories, Heritage and Museums*, London: Routledge.

45   C. Duncan (1995) *Civilizing Rituals*, London: Routledge, pp8–9, 22.

46   E. Hobsbawm and T. Ranger (eds) (1983) *The Invention of Tradition*, Cambridge: Cambridge University Press. See also Berger, 'Comparative history', p34.

47   Key works include M. Halbwachs (1992) *On Collective Memory* (ed. and trans. L. Coser), Chicago, IL: University of Chicago Press; K. Hodgkin and S. Radstone (eds) (2003) *Contested Pasts: The Politics of Memory*, London: Routledge; S. Radstone and K. Hodgkin (eds) (2003) *Regimes of Memory*, London: Routledge; D. Walkowitz and L. M. Knauer (eds) (2004) *Memory and the Impact of Political Transformation in Public Space*, Durham NC: Duke

University Press; P. Nora (ed) (1996) *Realms of Memory: Rethinking the French Past*, vol 1 (trans. A. Goldhammer), New York, NY: Columbia University Press.

48   M. Wallace (1996) *Mickey Mouse History and Other Essays on American Memory*, Pennsylvania, PA: Temple University Press, pviii. Other recent examples include the looting of the Iraq museum in Baghdad and the destruction of the Buddhas of Bamiyan by the Taliban in Afghanistan. L. Rothfield (2008) *The Rape of Mesopotamia: Behind the Looting of the Iraq Museum*, Chicago, IL: University of Chicago Press; L. Morgan (ed) (2012) *The Buddhas of Bamiyan*, London: Profile Books.

49   See http://www.tepapa.govt.nz/AboutUs/history/Pages/default.aspx, accessed 8 May 2012; 'Thinking visually: Doing history in museums, An interview with Bronwyn Labrum', in Dalley and Phillips, *Going Public*, pp176–186.

50   B. Ladd (1997) *Ghosts of Berlin: Confronting German History in the Urban Landscape*, Chicago, IL: University of Chicago Press; B. Niven and C. Pavier (2010) *Memorialization in Germany Since 1945*, Basingstoke, UK: Palgrave Macmillan; S. Macdonald (2006) 'Undesirable heritage: Fascist material culture and historical consciousness in Nuremberg', *International Journal of Heritage Studies*, vol 12(1), pp9–28; P. Carrier (2005) *Holocaust Monuments and National Memory Cultures in France and Germany Since 1989*, New York, NY: Berghahn Books; J. E. Young (ed) (1994) *The Art of Memory: Holocaust Memorials in History*, New York, NY: Prestel; J. Schlor (2005) *Memorial to the Murdered Jews of Europe*, London: Prestel. See also A. Halmesvirta (2011) *Public History in the Making: A New Methodological Approach to Study Memory-Building*, CEuS Working Paper no 2011/12, University of Bremen, Jean Monnet Centre for European Studies.

51   T. Morris-Suzuki (2005) *The Past within Us*, London: Verso, p153. See also N. Zemon Davis (2000) *Slaves on Screen: Film and Historical Vision*, Cambridge, MA: Harvard University Press.

52   S. J. Morgan (1999) 'The ghost in the luggage: Wallace and Braveheart: Post-colonial "pioneer" identities', *European Journal of Cultural Studies*, vol 2, p389.

53   They have also, of course, enforced the status quo. See, for example, Mike Wallace on the role of Walt Disney: 'one might fairly say that Walt Disney has taught people more history, in a more memorable way, than they ever learned in school'. Wallace, *Mickey Mouse*, p134.

54   K. Grenville (2006) *The Secret River*, Edinburgh: Canongate Books; K. Grenville (2010) *The Lieutenant*, Edinburgh: Canongate Books; R. Flanagan (2003) *Gould's Book of Fish: A Novel in Twelve Fish*, London: Atlantic Books; J. Nesbo (2007) *The Redbreast* (trans. D. Bartlett), London: Vintage.

55   W. Benjamin (2002) *The Arcades Project* (trans. H. Eiland and K. McLaughlin), Cambridge, MA: Harvard University Press, p206.

56   W. Benjamin (1970) 'Theses on the philosophy of history', in H Arendt (ed) *Illuminations*, London: Cape, pp247–249. See, too, M. Lowy (2005) *Fire Alarm: Reading Walter Benjamin's 'On the concept of history'*, London: Verso.

57   T. Butler (2009) '"Memoryscape": Integrating oral history, memory and landscape on the River Thames', in Ashton and Kean, *People*, pp223–239. See also T. Butler and G. Miller (2005) 'Linked: A landmark in sound, a public walk of art', *Cultural Geographies*, vol 12(1), pp77–88.

58   A huge literature exists on this. For a chronology see http://digital.lib.lehigh.edu/trial/enola/about/. Other works include L. Jordanova (2000) *History in Practice*, London: Arnold, pp156–159; Wallace, *Mickey Mouse*, pp269–318; E. Linenthal and T. Engelhardt (1996) *History Wars: The Enola Gay and Other Battles for the American Past*, New York, NY: Metropolitan Books.

59   S. Macintyre and A. Clark (2004) *The History Wars*, Melbourne: Melbourne University Press.

60   G. Hansen (2004) 'White hot history: The review of the National Museum of Australia', *Public History Review*, vol 11, pp39–50; D. Casey (2003) 'Culture wars: Museums, politics and controversy', *New Museum Developments and the Culture Wars*, Special issue of *Open Museum Journal*, vol 6, pp8–10; Macintyre and Clark, *History Wars*.

61   D. Massey (1995) 'Places and their pasts', *History Workshop Journal*, vol 39, pp182–192.

62   D. Hayden (1995) *The Power of Place: Urban Landscapes as Public History*, Cambridge, MA: MIT Press, p15. See also J. Urry (2002) *The Tourist Gaze: Theory, Culture and Society*, second edition, Thousand Oaks, CA: Sage.

63   G. Corsane (2006) 'Robben Island: Facing the challenges of creating a national museum in a World Heritage Site', in J. Schofield, A. Klausmeier and L. Purbrick (eds) *Re-Mapping the Field: New Approaches in Conflict Archaeology*, Bonn, Germany: Westkreuz-Verlag, p67.

64   Corsane, 'Robben Island', p70.

65   P. Read (2010) 'Reanimating lost landscapes: Bringing visualisation to Aboriginal history', *Public History Review*, vol 17, pp78, 79.

66   M. Jessop (2008) 'Digital visualization as a scholarly activity', *Literary and Linguistic Computing*, vol 23(2), pp281–293, as quoted in Read, 'Reanimating', p83.

67   M. P. Leone (2005) *The Archaeology of Liberty in an American Capital: Excavations in Annapolis*, Berkeley, CA: University of California Press, p203.

68   R. C. Chidester (2009) 'Critical landscape analysis as a tool for public interpretation: Reassessing slavery at a western Maryland plantation', *CRM: The Journal of Heritage Stewardship*, vol 6(1), pp35, 48.

69   'America's best idea: Musing on national parks past, present, and future, inspired by the new film from Ken Burns. A conversation with E. Carr, J. Reynolds, S. Lewis, D. Kohl, L. Lawliss, T. Davis', *Common Ground*, National Parks Service, Fall 2009, pp17–25.

70   Dalley, 'Shades of grey', p80.

71   See, for example, B. Castles (2011) 'Where we come from: The role of place in family memory', *Memory Connection*, vol 1(1), pp46–57.

72   R. Samuel (1994) *Theatres of Memory*, London: Verso, p11.

73   C. Steedman (2001) *Dust*, Manchester, UK: Manchester University Press. J. Sassoon (2003) 'Phantoms of remembrance: Libraries and archives as "the collective memory"', *Public History Review*, vol 10, pp40–60.

74   R. J. Cox (2011) 'Appraisal and the future of archives in the digital era', in J. Hill (ed) *The Future of Archives and Recordkeeping: A Reader*, London: facet publishing, p231.

75   A good example from the early twentieth century is the British suffrage movement. See H. Kean (2005) 'Public history and popular memory: Issues in the commemoration of the British militant suffrage movement', *Women's History Review*, vol 14(3&4), pp581–604. Later examples include the Black Cultural Archives founded in 1981 in Brixton (http://www.bcaheritage.org.uk/), rukus! Black LGBT Archives launched in 2005 (http://rukus.org.uk/archives) and the Aids History Project at the University of California in San Francisco (http://www.library.ucsf.edu/collections/archives/manuscripts/aids/about).

76   A. Flinn (2011) 'Archival activism: Independent and community-led archives: Radical public history and the heritage professions', *InterActions: UCAL Journal of Education and Information Studies*, vol 7(2), p9, http://www.escholarship.org/uc/item/9pt2490x.

77   K. Theimer (2011) 'Interactivity, flexibility and transparency: Social media and Archives 2.0', in Hill, *The Future*, p134.

78   N. Carr (2010) *The Shallows: How the Internet Is Changing the Way We Read, Think and Remember*, London: Atlantic Books, pp81–98.

79   Samuel, *Theatres*, p8.

80   Samuel, *Theatres*, p 3.

81   Draft Manifesto of History Workshop Centre of Social History, June 1983, History Workshop Archive formerly held in Ruskin College, Oxford, in File RS 6/001, now in the Bishopsgate Archive.

82   E. Hobsbawm (1998) 'On history from below', in *On History*, London: Abacus, pp270–271, 284.

83   Liddington, 'What is public history?', p90.

84   See, for example, Louise Raw's use of census returns to revisit the striking match-workers of East London. Raw helps to create individuals with their own networks and families, rather than nameless people who simply followed Annie Besant. In Derby, the People's History Group has created new interest in Alice Wheeldon, falsely accused and imprisoned during World War I for improbably trying to kill Prime Minister Lloyd George on a golf course with a blow dart poisoned with curare. Her descendants in Australia have been involved in revisiting the research and creating interest in gaining a posthumous pardon. See http://ourhistory-hayes.blogspot.co.uk/2012/01/alice-wheeldon-derby-ww1-martryr.html, accessed 15 May 2012.

85   See M. Stewart (2009) 'Expanding the archive: The role of family history in exploring connections within a settler's world', in Ashton and Kean, *People*, pp240–259, and H. Kean and B. Kirsch (2009) 'A nation's moment and a teacher's mark book: Interconnecting personal and public histories', in Ashton and Kean, *People*, pp187–202.

86   T. Evans (2011) 'Secrets and lies: The radical potential of family history,' *History Workshop Journal*, vol 71, p52.

87   T. Brennan (2000) 'History, family, history' in H. Kean, P. Martin and S. J. Morgan (eds) *Seeing History: Public History in Britain Now*, London: Francis Boutle, p48.

88   M. Drake (2005) 'Inside-out or outside-in? The case of family and local history', in R. Finnegan (ed) *Participating in the Knowledge Society*, Basingstoke, UK: Palgrave Macmillan, pp120–121.

89   He does not dismiss the role of museums, archives and academic institutions but argues that they should allow the family history community to generate research, debates and analyses. M. Bashforth (2009) 'Absent fathers, present histories', in Ashton and Kean, *People*, pp218, 222. See his 'Radical Family History' website, http://radfamhist.wordpress.com/.

90   N. Gregson and L. Crewe (2003) 'Gifting and collecting', in *Second-Hand Cultures*, Oxford: Berg, pp173–195; J. Attfield (2000) *Wild Things: The Material Culture of Everyday Life*, Oxford: Berg; D. Miller (2008) *The Comfort of Things*, Cambridge: Polity Press; S. M. Pearce (1994) *On Collecting: An Investigation into Collecting in the European Tradition*, Oxford: Routledge; P. Martin (1999) *Popular Collecting and the Everyday Self: The Reinvention of Museums?*, London: Cassell.

91   See, for examples, the four-volume series *The Collector's Voice*, Aldershot, UK: Ashgate, 2000, edited by Susan Pearce that documented collecting from *Ancient Voices* to *Contemporary Voices*.

92   This does not mean, however, that governments do not think it important to argue what should be taught in schools and institutions funded by the state. See, for example, T. Taylor (2003) 'Try to connect: Moving from bad history to historical literacy in schools', *Australian Cultural History*, issue 22, pp175–190; S. Collini (2011) 'From Robbins to McKinsey', *London Review of Books*, 25 August, pp9–14.

93   L. Passerini (2011) 'A passion for memory', *History Workshop Journal*, vol 72, p241.

94   D. T. Pitcaithley (2009) 'Taking the long way from Euterpe to Clio', in J. M. Banner and J. R. Gillis (eds) *Becoming Historians*, Chicago, IL: University of Chicago Press, p61.

95   D. J. Cohen (2005) 'The future of preserving the past', *CRM: The Journal of Heritage Stewardship*, vol 2(2), pp6–19.

96   This was a joint project organized by the Roy Rosenzweig Center for History and New Media at George Mason University together with the University of New Orleans in partnership with the National Museum of American History, with the aim of people being able to tell their stories in their own words. See http://hurricanearchive.org/, accessed 14 March 2012.

97   S. Ho (2007) 'Blogging as popular history making, blogs as public history: The Singapore case study', *Public History Review*, vol 14, pp64–79. See also P. Mason (2012) *Why It's Kicking off Everywhere: The New Global Revolutions*, London: Verso, on the role of YouTube in making history simultaneously with undertaking action.

98   L. Noakes (2009) 'The BBC "People's War" website', in M. Keren and H. R. Herwig (eds) *War Memory and Popular Culture: Essays on Modes of Remembrance and Commemoration*, North Carolina: McFarland, p138; and L. Noakes (2013) 'War on the web: The BBC "People's War" website and memories of the Second World War in 21st century Britain', in L. Noakes and J. Pattinson (eds) *Keep Calm and Carry On: The Cultural Memory of the Second World War in Britain*, London: Continuum.

99   F. Pannekoek (2005) 'The rise of a heritage priesthood', in M. A. Tomlan (ed) *Preservation of What, for Whom? A Critical Look at Historical Significance*, Ithaca, NY: National Council for Preservation Education, p29.

100   Pannekoek, 'The rise', p35.

101   Pannekoek, 'The rise', p36.

102   Gardner, 'Trust', p54.

103   Gardner, 'Trust', p55.

104   M. Fisher and S. Donnelly (eds) (2004) *Ah'd Gaa Back Tomorra!: Memories of West Cumbrian Screen Lasses*, Cumbria, UK: Whitehaven Miners' Memorial and Living History Project.

105   E. Waterton and L. Smith (2010) 'The recognition and misrecognition of community heritage', *International Journal of Heritage Studies*, vol 16(1–2), pp7, 13. For further elaboration of the idea of an authorized heritage discourse, see L. Smith (2006) *Uses of Heritage*, Abingdon, UK: Routledge.

106   L. Smith, P. A. Shackel and G. Campbell (2011) 'Introduction: Class still matters', *Heritage, Labour and the Working Classes*, Abingdon, UK: Routledge, p13.

107   R. Samuel, B. Bloomfield and G. Boanas (eds) (1986) *Enemy Within: Pit Villages and the Miners' Strike of 1984–5*, London: Routledge and Kegan & Paul.

108   Samuel et al, 'Preface', *Enemy Within*, pxvii.

109   Samuel et al, *Enemy Within*, pix.

110   Stuart Hall as discussed in K. Jones (1998) 'Against conformity', *Changing English*, vol 5(1), pp22–23.

111   See http://www.jeremydeller.org/.

112   M. Bailey and S. Popple (2011) 'The 1984/5 miners' strike: Re-claiming cultural heritage', in Smith, Shackel, Campbell, *Heritage, Labour,* pp19–33.

113   Frisch, *Shared Authority*, pxiii. See http://www.sudburyukrainians.ca/project.html for an interesting account of the way in which Canadian public historian Stacey Zembrzycki worked alongside her grandmother, interviewing members of the Ukrainian community in Sudbury, Ontario (accessed 13 May 2012).

114   A. Owens, N. Jeffries, K. Wehner and R. Featherby (2010) 'Fragments of the modern city: Material culture and the rhythms of everyday life in Victorian London', *Journal of Victorian Culture*, vol 15(2), pp212–225.

115   'London's Underworld Unearthed: The Secret Life of the Rookery', Coningsby Gallery, London, May 2011. She also discussed her work at the Public History Discussion Group at the Bishopsgate Institute in November 2011; see http://janepalmgold.com/.

116   S. Thomas (2012) 'Searching for answers: A survey of metal-detector uses in the UK', *International Journal of Heritage Studies*, vol 18(1), pp53, 58.

117   See http://www.staffordshirehoard.org.uk/about/the-faces-behind-the-find, accessed 12 May 2012. (Thomas notes that while there is hope for cooperation, trust is still an issue on both sides; see Thomas, 'Searching', p56).

118   Currently on permanent display at the Birmingham museum. Artefacts have also been shown at touring exhibitions around the Midlands, including Lichfield Cathedral and Tamworth Castle. See http://www.staffordshirehoard.org.uk/event/see-it-in-birmingham, accessed 12 May 2012.

119   N. Merriman (2004) 'Diversity and dissonance in public archaeology', in N. Merriman (ed) *Public Archaeology*, London: Routledge, p7.

120   A. Rice (2010) *Creating Memorials, Building Identities: The Politics of Memory in the Black Atlantic*, Liverpool, UK: Liverpool University Press, p48.

121   D. Glassberg (2001) *Sense of History: The Place of the Past in American Life*, Amherst, MA: University of Massachusetts Press, p210.

122   K. Keable (ed) (2012) *London Recruits: The Secret War against Apartheid*, Pontypool: Merlin Press.

123   D. Hann (2013) *Physical Resistance or A Hundred Years of Fighting Fascism*, Blue Ridge Summit, PA: Zero Books.

124   J. Kalela (2012) *Making History*, Basingstoke, UK: Palgrave Macmillan, pp55, 63.

125   Paul Preston interviewed on *Start the Week*, BBC Radio 4, Monday, 14 May 2012.

126   Ashton and Hamilton, *History at the Crossroads*, p8.

PART I

The Past in the Present

Who Is Making History?

Paul Martin

IN THIS FIRST SECTION we will look at the ways in which the past has taken on a heightened popular sense of importance in the present and the ways in which it is used. The overarching concept here is that far from being 'fixed' in time, the past is fluid and is re-made to serve contemporary agendas or needs in the present. The past is, then, shown to be not so much 'a foreign country' as novelist L. P. Hartley or historian David Lowenthal had it,[1] but through our own continual and often personalized re-making of it in the present, a burgeoning number of constantly reinvented ones. As Helen Reddington pleaded in *Lost Women of Rock Music*, which was, to a large extent, based on interviews: 'I urge the reader to value the oral contributions to this book and to understand the fluid nature of perceptions of history.'[2]

The past and the present have always enjoyed a symbiotic relationship. The past from the vantage point of the present has firstly been perceived as something to get back to, but bound up in selective construction and mythologizing of a romanticized 'lost past'. Utopian socialists and pre-Raphaelite artists of the nineteenth century saw the ravenous industrialization of their own age as the destroyer of an idealized Medieval pastoralism which only a return to and redistribution of the land could cure. William Morris's 1890 book *News from Nowhere* is perhaps the most famous articulation of this sensibility.[3]

The Victorian fascination with medievalism, however, as historian Charles Dellheim has examined, was on a broad cultural level and was used to serve contemporary agendas.[4]

As medievalist historian Marjorie Chibnall has shown, the imposition of the 'Norman Yoke' (i.e. the idea that with the Norman invasion of England in 1066, a pre-existing 'golden age' of Anglo-Saxon liberty was replaced by autocracy and enforced servitude by the victorious Normans) was a core concern.[5] Secondly, the past has been viewed as something to escape from. Until late in the twentieth century, it was not something which was favourably 'dwelt on' in the aftermath of two World Wars and a depression between them. Rather, minds were set squarely on the future, as was represented through events such as the Festival of Britain,[6] the promotion of a new tomorrow, typically personified by innovations in domestic furnishing and design.[7]

It is, though, since the early 1980s that an increasingly conscious furnishing of the present with the past has taken place. This is reflected nationally, as literary historian Jerome de Groot has exhaustively demonstrated, through the media and television programming,[8] and in everyday life, as Raphael Samuel explores in his extract. Proactive popular collecting of the material past has burgeoned over the period, possibly as an externalized expression of anxiety about sociocultural change.[9] The exponential growth of internet auction sites, primarily eBay, has massively contributed to the circulation of everyday material culture of the past in the present and helps to fuel this practice.[10]

People's identities are very often strongly embedded in object attachment. This has been extensively studied in Britain, for instance, by social anthropologist Daniel Miller.[11] In the US, the hidden extent to which people have attachments to personal objects is explored in the extract by Roy Rosenzweig and David Thelen. Here, the authors, via questionnaires, look at the ways in which ordinary people encounter the past and how it affects their present. Respondents frequently note how their hobbies (such as dance) led them to an engagement with the past that validates or reinforces their sense of identity in the present. These encounters occur through life experience rather than formal academic study and often stand in contrast to the negative memories of formal history classes when at school. As the authors assert: 'Americans . . . make the past part of their everyday routines and turn to it as a way of grappling with profound questions about how to live.'

Such approaches and engagements with the past can be read as public history. They are outside the academy and speak to a personalized, experiential or autodidactic knowledge that informs the individual on history's role in shaping their present. It is public history also because in its recognition it empowers the individual in their sense of its ownership and as contributors to what history is and how it is made.

The past has often been popularly perceived as 'safe' because it has been and gone and is thus held to be fixed, while everyday life seems increasingly precarious. The past, though, is not a safe haven. It is fluid, mutable and always in flux as new generations look to it to serve present concerns. Hence, the past is constantly being constructed anew with this or that aspect privileged, emphasized or played down. This can be seen in areas as diverse as pop music[12] to national identity.[13]

Ordinary people have conventionally been the subjects of study by sociologists and, later, by social historians. Rather than 'owning' their own history, it was mediated through liberal educated gatekeepers to serve their own agendas. In Britain came the History Workshop in the late 1960s. Through pamphlets and, later, the *History Workshop Journal*, it offered a platform for ordinary people to document their experiences and as a channel for presenting 'history from below'.

Whose history, whose voices?

The forces outlined above motivated people to look to the past in the everyday world around them. Family history, local history, collecting, metal detecting and other historical interests were activated by the sociocultural and economic turn. People now became enthusiastic detectives and took the processes of history construction into their own hands. In the temporal space between inward reflection and outward gaze, the past came to harness a heightened resonance for many people on a personal level. In his influential discourse on the processes of history-making, Samuel proposes that history should be regarded as a practice rather than purely a form of academic study – in which case, he asserts, the vast number of practitioners would be revealed. Rosenzweig and Thelen's survey would seem to bear this out. In his extract, Samuel discusses 'unofficial knowledge'. This may comprise that which does not fit the received version of events or which poses questions of authenticity and absolution to the official or grand historical narrative. It may also simply be that such knowledge is not regarded as 'proper history' by the academy. For Samuel, the likes of collectors of everyday social objects and metal detectorists are historical practitioners. In his extract, he points to antecedents of such practices such as Henry Willet, whose many popular collections are now in the Brighton Museum and Art Gallery (in south-east England).

While greatly empathizing with Samuel, **Iain J. M. Robertson's extract** on 'heritage from below' takes to task the prevailing assumptions of the construction of 'heritage'. It has, he argues, been presented, on the one hand, as conservative, nostalgic and selective. Citing Samuel especially, he posits that, on the other hand, heritage is presented as a democratic process when emphasizing the parochial or small scale over the grand narrative that the former approach adopts. However, Robertson says:

> . . . whilst these more optimistic readings carry considerable merit, both fail to be sufficiently broad or deep fully to accommodate the making and maintaining of an inheritance from the past here recognized as heritage from below.

He distinguishes between alternative and counter-hegemony and further explains that:

> . . . one of the key tasks of heritage from below is that this expression of heritage, tangible or (often) intangible, can offer an alternative construction of the past to that of the hegemonic and, thereby, both galvanize and cohere local communities around alternative constructions of identity and narratives of place.

Using various examples, Robertson shows how readings of heritage as resistance to the dominant heritage discourse function and offer a more democratic path to the understanding of the past in the present through it.

As a further but different example, Graeme Davison discusses the changing nature of white Australian family history, as well as the damage that history has inflicted on Aboriginal people. **In his extract, Davison** examines the interest in family history in Australia beyond literal genealogy. As he notes: 'Democratic family history is the story of those who suffered history, as well as those who made it.' Hence, Davison looks at the value of family history within Aboriginal communities. He juxtaposes this with the turn in settler family history from an unproblematic forward march to a more reflective backwards projection. Thus:

> . . . the new family histories are shaped differently from the old. The genealogist traditionally begins with the family founder, its colonial Abraham and moves forward generation by generation. . . . The new family histories, on the other hand, begin in the here and now, with the writer, and describe a journey backwards in time, and often space, to an uncertain destination.

Hence, the past is something being examined both as a problematic and a wound for Aborigine people, which by extension of the questioning this brings forward, has caused some white Australians to re-evaluate the traditional role of family history in the present. In so doing, the extract serves as an example of the past's mutability and its potential for shifting dominant historical narratives into defensive and, ultimately, more equal discourses. The sense of empowerment and ownership of a revealed history hitherto unspoken in, or ignored by, the master narrative for those marginalized voices is arguably history made and, indeed, fought for in public.

American historian **James Green explains his journey in the extract here** as a labour history teacher with trade union and other movement organizations. His story is one in which he traces an experiential history in moving away from a basic transmission model of 'delivering' labour history to his adult student audience, to a democratic engagement with them in which they have an interactive parity. In doing so, Green asserts, it enabled students 'to get their history into their own hands'.

Beginning with his experiences in Britain at the history workshop of 1976 at Ruskin College, Oxford, Green's narrative is an exercise in communicating the process of historical learning as much as an analysis of the subject itself. The clarity of process in history-making is an important aspect of public history in that it comprises the framework of Samuel's idea of history as social knowledge.

In a similar vein, **Jorma Kalela writes here** about communal, collective or shared histories and notes in his extract that 'shared histories remind us that contrary to many academics' understanding, scholarly works are not the ultimate source on which people's conceptions of the past are based'. He analyses his experience in working with the Finnish Paper Workers' Union. Instead of the members writing about trade union history – as had been the intention – they preferred to research family and local history, thus challenging both notions of 'relevant' history but also the role of the professional historian in needing to respond to such developments. Kalela also analyses both public and popular history in relation to other forms in order to make his case for shared and collective histories.

Memorialization

Memorialization is perhaps one way in which to juxtapose two key aspects of the past's use in the present. On the one hand, memorialization as homage and, indeed, role play is reflected in the commemorative cruise aboard the *MS Balmoral* to mark the centenary of the sinking of the *Titanic*. Departing on 8 April 2012, it followed the exact route of the doomed liner, tickets for which sold out two years in advance, with passengers dressing in period costume. Enchantment by and the enduring fascination with the *Titanic* story at a global level lends itself readily to historical commodification (the on-board gift shop did brisk business). This is not to neglect the family history aspect. Descendants of both those who died and survived have a personal connection to it and were on the cruise. What the wreck of the *Titanic* actually *is* appears more problematic (e.g. a cemetery, tourist attraction or treasure trove for salvage entrepreneurs?).

On the other hand, impromptu memorials for the victims of road accidents or violent assault represent part of the everyday street furniture of our towns and cities. To the bereaved, these are an important part of the grieving process. Small objects relating to the individual are often left or used as ornamentation to further embellish and deepen the memorial's significance. Thus, to the bereaved, the comfort value is presumably increased. To the passing observer, these intensely personal tributes may appear bizarre, devoid of their provenance or biographical context. Unlike the equally personal ancestral photos of *Titanic* passengers and crew coveted by their descendants, the tragic stories of road or violent assault victims often fail to radiate beyond the local news media, thus providing no bigger legend in which to incorporate them (beyond, perhaps, a statistical one). They are, however, shards of historical testimony to an individual's presence/absence in the world and now the history of the location.

In an intensive way, memorialization takes on a crucial dimension in the aftermath of war. In Britain or America, for instance, memorialization of the dead from officially sanctioned international conflicts is taken as an obligation. In civil wars, especially those that garner less global media attention, memorialization is far more problematic and, indeed, dangerous. **Matthew J. Taylor and Michael K. Steinberg explore here** the will to remember and the authority's determination to effect silence through intimidation in Guatemala, even 30 years after the end of a 40-year civil war. They explore officially unintentional memorialization, such as warnings about unexploded bombs. They juxtapose the Catholic Church's will to memorialize the victims through small, named wooden crosses and the state's 'official' memorialization of itself as the country's saviour. The very landscape itself is testimony as they state: 'we stayed in villages "wiped off the map" by military actions in the early 1980s that show no signs of past conflict – in fact, the military often built model villages on the ashes of the destroyed community centres'. Read as public history, this is very much about what is missing, hidden or suppressed, as well as the nature of the 'official line' in what is present. Empowerment through reclamation of their own traumatized history of these times, is still in the making for affected Guatemalan people of the so-called 'red zones'. It has through necessity, at present, to be constructed by proxy outside of the country by exiles and interested researchers, such as the extract's authors. Public, then, in its revelation to the world at large, but still a matter of internalized and mute remembrance for those who survived the military government's violence.

Museums and the people

Museums are perhaps the most obvious spaces where the material culture of the past and people engage. Traditionally, though, the public has been expected to simply assimilate the narratives presented on exhibit labels or through audio guides, etc. This top-down form of communication both privileges and renders anonymous the authorial voice. As museum and heritage studies academic Christopher Whitehead notes about early museum development: 'I believe that a consciousness of previous conceptions of class and the use of the museum as a political agent ... should be an integral part of historical study and narrative ....'[14]

Some 20 years ago, an intervention was made at the (now renewed) Ashmolean Museum, Oxford, in which Classicists Mary Beard and John Henderson placed cards and labels within existing exhibits which questioned their uncritical and almost anonymous presentation.[15]

During recent years, the adoption of more progressive audience development research has become increasingly widespread, with institutions encouraging a more activist engagement with exhibitions. This 'constructivist' or, as it is sometimes called, 'hands on–minds on' approach[16] is very much more in line with the public history idea of process as outlined in the general Introduction. Visitors are encouraged to make their own meaning from what they see, rather than assimilate pre-formatted data on labels. In this sense, the visitor is engaged in recasting or moulding new or personalized meanings from their visit.

Such exhibitions provide an honesty in the information, acknowledging gaps in historical understanding and explaining how exhibits came to be here. It also employs rhetorical questioning in order to invite a deeper probing by the viewer and to encourage a sense of their own meaning-making experience, rather than a predetermined authoritative one. Hence, as meaning is being made by the viewer, a contemporary history of how the material culture of the past is viewed in the present is also being made collectively by the audience. This is well demonstrated in the example of the National Gallery catalogue for a significant but under-reported exhibition, *At Home with Constable's Cornfield*, in 1996.

'People's Shows' were a museum phenomenon of the 1990s, originating at Walsall Museum and Art Gallery, as it then was, in the West Midlands, in which ordinary people were invited by museums to display their collections. Exhibitors were allowed a 500-word caption to accompany their display and collectively these collections were exhibited as a 'people's show'. Inevitably, perhaps, museums were angling for the 'wow!' factor in visitors and so the 'zanier' or more exotic or unusual collections were given privileged positions. The aptly named Colin Painter, principal of the Wimbledon School of Art, designed an exhibition which inverted the people's show idea. He advertised within south London for owners of the image of Constable's famous painting *The Cornfield* (the founding painting of the National Gallery in 1826) to get in touch.

The result was the exhibition *At Home with Constable's Cornfield*, which ran from 14 February to 21 April 1996. In it, owners of the image replicated on objects as diverse as tea trays, ceramic lockets and wall paper gave their opinion of what the image meant to them. Unlike people's shows, *Cornfield* privileged the owner in the exhibition, not the object. A small cabinet of the objects owned was dwarfed by the large freestanding textual boards and enlarged photographs of the owners with their objects *in situ*. Here, what was on show were the stories and opinions of the owners.

As such, the exhibition provided insights into how the past is perceived in the present. It speaks especially to issues of intellectual access and the public meaning-making in something traditionally held to be 'high culture'. It expanded the platform for public engagement with and expression of historical interpretation. Overshadowed at the time by the restoration and re-hang of Holbein's *The Ambassadors*, the exhibition deserves remembering for its democratic empowerment of the people's voice.

Blogging, crowd sourcing and internet communities

The internet operates in a number of ways within history. In terms of history as commodity, digital virtualization is fast replacing the material product. *Encyclopaedia Britannica*, for instance, is now a solely online publication,[17] while e-readers such as Amazon's *Kindle* are becoming more ubiquitous. Provision of information to the public is radically widened via the internet. It has also presented new opportunities for the navigation of history, as exemplified by the social enterprise organization We Are What We Do's *History Pin*.[18] In partnership with Google, this is essentially a digital map of the world that incorporates images from old photographs and postcards. It is thus a worldwide resource for comparing how places used to look with how they look now. Additionally, it calls for active engagement by the user in adding their own images to the map in order to enrich it. It is also available to local organizations (museums, schools, etc.) for their own history mapping projects. As such, it merges the pre-existing local history captioned photography books of 'our town then and now' and the 'memory lane' columns of local newspapers that ask readers to send in their photos and memories of local events and places of the past.

Similar initiatives, such as the Museum of London's *Street Museum* developed by the Brothers and Sisters Company, facilitate an instant historical window. Users point their camera at a present-day street scene or use their GPS to locate one near them in London, and an historical view of the same point will appear on their screen, drawn from the museum's archives, literally pulling the past into the present.[19]

Concomitantly, the internet affords the public the means to both author and convey history. Online social networks have led to new definitions of selfhood manifested through the extent of one's engagement with them. The growth of 'virtual museums' 'curated' by the users themselves has expanded during recent years. Those such as Willenhall (in the West Midlands) are designed to connect the international diasporas of these towns and share memories, photographs, and information of town histories.[20] Essentially, these migrate and expand the longer-standing local history study groups. Other local websites, such as those for Brighton (south-east England), are devoted to single themes and time frames.[21]

Such enterprises can be construed as online or distance learning forums. People learn in public and through peer knowledge and research-sharing. Within at least their own specializations, they collectively enable and empower each other as history practitioners. Perhaps increasingly, academic history will become but one historical path of many, rather than the assumed authority on what history is and what it comprises. The exercise of 'choice' in both saving and presentation is reaching industrial proportions.

Crowd sourcing and history: An antecedence

Crowd sourcing is a method by which objectives are achieved through popular outreach and is not, in essence, a new phenomenon. In Britain, 'Mass Observation' was an initiative of three contributors to the *New Statesman* magazine in 1937. The object was to create an 'anthropology of ourselves'.[22] Based on undeclared participant observation (essentially, eavesdropping on and covertly recording conversations in public places) and open-ended questionnaires from willing participants, activists compiled a database of British public opinion. This was exemplified in director Gavin Miller's film *Housewife 49* (2006), starring British comedian and actress Victoria Wood and based on the diaries of Nella Last during the 1940s and 1950s. In one way, this was a continuation of the social explorer approach that began with Henry Mayhew's reportage of the 1840s and continued in the late nineteenth century with Charles Booth's survey of London.[23] The burgeoning of the new documentary film-making in the 1930s led to such films as *Housing Problems* (1935). Funded by the British Commercial Gas Association to promote the virtues of gas in the home, it was used as an opportunity by the film-makers to highlight slum housing. It was revolutionary in its day in encouraging ordinary people to speak to the camera about their housing problems. In such ways, the voices of ordinary people were 'vox-popped' into the wider historical record.

With the rise of feminist history during the 1970s, the voices of many silent individuals and groups came to be articulated (through ignored diaries, family conversation recording, or even in the first person). During the mid 1990s, the video camera recorder (and later camcorder) superseded other 'home movie' cameras (popularly used since the 1930s). Its mass take-up precipitated programmes such as the BBC's *Video Nation*, comprised of regular five-minute documentaries on what the individual had done that day and which was one of the first of a number of similarly embryonic reality television initiatives thereafter. The digital revolution in mobile and latterly smart phone technology means that there is a far better chance of documenting the witnessing or participation in an event than ever before. Hence, everyone is potentially a history-maker. This, of course, brings us back to Robertson's idea of 'heritage from below' discussed earlier. There are opposite implications. On the one hand, such popular technical enablement of documenting and recording peripatetically means, potentially, how the future will view us and what defined us will be more richly sourced. On the other hand, in such an age of the disposable and recyclable, that will only happen if we save everything.

Crowd sourcing now

The practice of 'crowd sourcing' as we have seen above is not new, but the term might be attributed to *Wired* magazine journalist Jeff Howe whose 2009 book *Crowd Sourcing: How the Power of the Crowd Is Driving the Future of Business* discusses a new economic business model:

> With the rise of user-generated media such as blogs, Wikipedia, MySpace, and YouTube, it's clear that traditional distinctions between producers and consumers are becoming blurry. It's no longer fanciful to speak of the marketplace as having a 'collective intelligence' – today that knowledge, passion, creativity, and insight are accessible for all to see. As *Time* explained after choosing the collective "You" as the magazine's 2006 Person of the Year, 'We're looking at an explosion of productivity and innovation, and it's just getting started, as millions of minds that would otherwise have drowned in obscurity get backhauled into the global intellectual economy.'[24]

For historians, the same ethos can be found in some forms of what might be regarded as public history in the conventional sense: the public volunteering to undertake history work on behalf of a national body, such as the US War Papers:

> The collection consists of 45,000 documents consisting of hundreds of thousands of individual pages from the records of what later came to be known as the Department of Defense. Volunteers register to become a Transcription Associate and then can browse to select whichever document they wish to transcribe or search the collection if they have particular interests. In addition to making it financially feasible, letting the public take a hand in such a project has the benefit of bringing history close to the volunteer and turning that volunteer into an evangelist for the importance of history to contemporary life. Also, it gives the historians involved a sense, as the documents are transcribed, for what the public finds the most compelling.[25]

Another example is the British Births, Marriages and Deaths website[26] in which family historians act as transcribers. Although a worthy initiative, public history is potentially more than simply allowing the public access to, or to take part in, the institutional refiling and taking their findings to a wider public. It is about being the agency of history making itself and having ownership of the methodology and outcome of it. As the authors of a Canadian public history initiative, *The Heritage Crowd Project*, put it:

> Historians who crowd source the writing of historical narratives are able to empower members of a given community who may not have the same institutionalized or professional authority conceded to "experts" in the discipline. This mission is distinctly different from that of most academic historians, whose work is centered around the construction of historical narratives based on the analysis of sources, and that of the museum or public historian, which attempts to provide an impartial and objective narrative of the past for public consumption.[27]

At a London conference on the curating of popular music in 2011, it became clear that nearly every speaker was reliant to some extent at least on crowd sourcing[28] – for example, inviting heavy metal music fans to upload their answers to a set questionnaire. The academic or question setter then becomes the mediator and gatekeeper of the accrued answers, which are, of course, then by necessity rendered anonymous so that the contributors become invisible. Thematic blogs and open discussion boards, forums and discussion groups, on the other hand, have the potential for open recognition of joint effort. Often, the themes of interest (music genres, collecting subjects, fashion forums, etc.) of which contributors have and express knowledge are not presented as historical. Contributors often have, express and share historical knowledge on and through them, but they would not think of themselves as historians or what they are doing as the practice of history.[29] They are, however, to all intents and purposes practising history, often revealing information and discovering objects or raising questions that are not known or acknowledged in formal circles.[30] This, it can be argued, is a version of cooperative crowd sourcing, which creates new history of which those involved have ownership, unlike the top-down institutional allowance of the public to take part in the preservation of already existing material.

Conclusion

The past in the present, then, is not merely about repopulating or furnishing our contemporary environment with commercial and authorized reconstructions of the past (like re-enacted jousts at medieval pageants). It is more the way in which individuals and groups of people, as the extracts here show, come to a deeper or wider understanding of themselves in the present through the variety of ways they encounter and engage with the past on an everyday basis. The mutability of the past is also key. People understand and interpret the past for themselves by making their own meaning from it. This points not to a degradation of historical understanding when unmediated by academics, but to the democratic interpretation of the past when the process of arriving at understanding is part of the narrative. This, in turn, affords a more holistic insight into perceptions of the past in the present which can only benefit historians of the future about us. As some extracts show, the past can also be a weapon of resistance even in the face of the most oppressive circumstances where its material expression is forbidden. This speaks to the will to use the past as a means of re-empowerment in the present or the future.

Notes

1   L. P. Hartley (2004) *The Go Between*, London: Penguin Modern Classics, p1; D. Lowenthal (1985) *The Past Is a Foreign Country*, Cambridge: Cambridge University Press.

2   H. Reddington (2012) *The Lost Women of Rock Music: Female Musicians of the Punk Era*, second edition, Sheffield, UK: Equinox Publishing.

3   W. Morris (2009) *News from Nowhere: Or, an Epoch of Rest. Being Some Chapters from a Utopian Romance*, Oxford: Oxford University Press.

4   C. Dellheim (2004) *The Face of the Past: The Preservation of the Medieval Inheritance in Victorian England*, Cambridge: Cambridge University Press.

5   M. Chibnall (1999) *The Debate on the Norman Conquest*, Manchester, UK: Manchester University Press.

6   B. Turner (2011) *Beacon for Change: How the 1951 Festival of Britain Shaped the Modern Age*, London: Aurum Press; H. Atkinson (2012) *The Festival of Britain: A Land and Its People*, London: I. B. Tauris.

7   B. Quinn (2004) *Mid-Century Modern: Interiors, Furniture, Design Details*, London: Conran Octopus Ltd; G. Stevenson (2003) *Palaces for the People: Prefabs in Post-War Britain*, London: Batsford Ltd.

8   J. De Groot (2008) *Consuming History: Historians and Heritage in Contemporary Popular Culture*, Abingdon, UK: Routledge.

9   S. M. Pearce (1995) *On Collecting: An Investigation into Collecting in the European Tradition*, London: Routledge; S. Pearce (1997) *Collecting in Contemporary Practice*, London: Sage; R. Belk (1995) *Collecting in a Consumer Society*, London: Routledge; P. Martin (1999) *Popular Collecting and the Everyday Self: The Reinvention of Museums?*, London: Leicester University Press.

10   K. Hills, M. Petit and N. S. Epley (eds) (2006) *Everyday eBay: Culture, Collecting, and Desire*, Abingdon, UK: Routledge.

11   D. Miller (2009) *The Comfort of Things*, London: Polity Press (reprint); D. Miller (2009) *Stuff*, London: Polity Press.

12   S. Reynolds (2011) *Retromania: Pop Culture's Addiction to Its Own Past*, London: Faber & Faber.

13   B. Anderson (2006) *Imagined Communities: Reflections on the Origin and Spread of Nationalism*, revised edition, London: Verso; T. Edensor (2002) *National Identity, Popular Culture and Everyday Life*, London: Berg.

14   C. Whitehead (2005) *The Public Art Museum in Nineteenth Century Britain: The Development of the National Gallery*, Aldershot, UK: Ashgate, pxviii; G. Black (2005) *The Engaging*

Museum: Developing Museums for Visitor Involvement, Abingdon, UK: Routledge; N. Simon (2010) *The Participatory Museum*, California: Museum Publishers.

15   M. Beard and J. Henderson (1992) 'Please don't touch the ceiling: The culture of appropriation', S. Pearce (ed) *The Appropriation of Culture: New Research in Museum Studies, Vol 4*, London: Athlone Press, pp5–42.

16   E. Hooper-Greenhill (2000) *Museums and the Interpretation of Visual Culture*, London: Routledge; G. E. Hein (1999) 'The constructivist museum', in E. Hooper-Greenhill (ed) *The Educational Role of the Museum*, London: Routledge; E. Hooper-Greenhill (2007) *Museums and Education: Purpose, Pedagogy, Performance*, Abingdon, UK: Routledge; H. S. Hein (2000) *The Museum in Transition: A Philosophical Perspective*, Washington, DC: Smithsonian Books; F. E. S. Kaplan (ed) (1996) *Museums and the Making of Ourselves: The Role of Objects in National Identity*, London: Frances Pinter Publishers; E. H. Gurian (2005) *Civilizing the Museum: The Collected Writings of Elaine Heumann Gurian*, Abingdon, UK: Routledge.

17   D. Gillmor (2012) 'Encyclopedia Britannica in the age of Wikipedia: The end of Britannica printing its encyclopedia is really just a footnote in the great story of online access to knowledge', *The Guardian*, 14 March.

18   See <http://www.historypin.com/> (accessed 14 June 2012).

19   See <http://www.museumoflondon.org.uk/Resources/app/you-are-here-app/home.html.> (accessed 14 June 2012).

20   See <http://www.virtualmuseum.co.uk/> (accessed 14 June 2012).

21   See <http://www.mybrightonandhove.org.uk/> (accessed 14 June 2012).

22   N. Hubble (2010) *Mass Observation and Everyday Life: Culture, History, Theory*, Basingstoke, UK: Palgrave Macmillan.

23   H. Mayhew (2010) *London Labour and the London Poor*, Oxford: Oxford University Press; C. Booth (2009) *Life and Labour of the People of London*, South Carolina: Bibiolife; R. O'Day and D. Englander (1993) *Mr. Charles Booth's Inquiry: Life and Labour of the People in London Reconsidered*, London: Hambledon Continuum; see also <http://booth.lse.ac.uk/static/a/4.html> (accessed 1 July 2012) for Booth's 'poverty maps' that have formed the basis of the BBC 2012 TV series *The Secret History of Our Streets*.

24   J. Alsever (2007) *The Business Origin and Use of Crowd Sourcing*, <http://www.cbsnews.com/8301–505125_162–51052961/what-is-crowdsourcing/>, 7 March 2007 (accessed 29 February 2012).

25   C. Hopkins (2011) *Crowdsourcing the Preservation of U.S. War Papers*, <http://www.readwriteweb.com/archives/crowdsourcing_us_war_papers.php>, 18 March 2011 (accessed 14 June 2012).

26   See <http://www.ukbmd.org.uk/> (accessed 1 June 2012).

27   S. Graham, G. Massie and N. Feuerherm (2011) 'The Heritage Crowd Project: A case study in crowdsourcing public history', in J. Dougherty and K. Nawrotzki (eds) *Writing History In The Digital Age: A Born-Digital, Open-Review Volume*, <http://writinghistory.trincoll.edu/crowdsourcing/heritagecrowd-project-graham-massie-feuerherm/> (accessed 15 June 2012).

28   Collecting and Curating Popular Music Histories Symposium, Foyle Suite, British Library, London, Tuesday, 5 July 2011.

29   P. Martin (2011) 'A "social form of knowledge" in practice: Unofficial compiling of 1960s pop music on CDR', *Public History Review*, vol 18, pp129–150, <http://epress.lib.uts.edu.au/ojs/index.php/phrj.> (accessed 15 June 2012).

30   These are legion on the net and come and go. Two longstanding and well-regarded blogs are 'Purepop', <http://purepop1uk.blogspot.co.uk/>; and 'Proudfoot Sound', <http://purepop1uk.blogspot.co.uk/> (both accessed 9 July 2012).

Chapter 1

Raphael Samuel

THEATRES OF MEMORY

Invisible hands

IF HISTORY WAS THOUGHT OF as an activity rather than a profession, then
the number of its practitioners would be legion. In the present day they might well
include – if one was concerned to map the unofficial sources of knowledge – the writers
of that new and flourishing sub-genre in which scholars themselves have begun to dabble,[1]
the historical whodunit. Reference might be made to Peter Lovesey, the master of the
Victorian detective novel, whose explorations of London by gaslight draw heavily on
nineteenth-century descriptions of low-life deeps;[2] or Ellis Peters who covers page after
page of her Brother Cadfael books with gobbets of Anglo-Norman history – e.g. the 'anarchy'
of Stephen's reign in the recently televised *One Corpse Too Many* – and uses illuminated
manuscripts for her book-jackets.[3]

In any archaeology of the unofficial sources of historical knowledge, the animators of the
Flintstones, the stone-age family who were rehearsing the rudiments of Palaeolithic living for
1960s TV viewers and who have now been given the accolade of a feature film, surely
deserve, at the least, a *proxime accessit*. Stand-up comics, such as Rowan Atkinson, whose
Blackadder series re-animated the legendary moments of British history for a generation of
television addicts, might get as much attention as the holder of a Regius chair. The impresarios
of the open-air museums, and their ever-increasing staff, would be seen to have made a far
more substantial contribution to popular appetite for an engagement with the past than the
most ambitious head of a department. Space might even be found for those electronically
equipped cowboys of archaeological excavation, the metal detectorists, whose finds have
done so much to enlarge the map of Romano-British settlement.[4]

Even as a form of literary production, history is the work of a thousand different hands.
The books, monographs and articles in the learned journals draw on a whole army of ghost-
writers. Quite apart from the indexers, the copy-editors, and the proof-readers – and in the
old days the typist – without whom a book could hardly exist, one might refer to scholars'
wives who, even if they have been through every line of the text, are likely to be recognized
by no more than a single acknowledgement. F. J. Furnivall, the historical philologist and
founder of the Early English Texts Society, who seems to have married or attempted to

marry not once but twice for the sake of an amanuensis, and who enlisted a platoon of lady helpers for his philological enterprises, is one example;[5] James Murray the Saxonist and the first editor of the *Oxford English Dictionary* another.[6]

Clio's invisible hands in the 1920s might include the musicologists employed on the Tudor Church Music Project, transcribing from cathedral part-books, and scouring the minster archives for manuscripts.[7] There may well have been some, too, in the women readers whom George Gissing describes in *New Grub Street*, buried in the darker recesses of the British Museum, employed as copyists on behalf of the scholars and writers.[8] More skilled, but only slightly less anonymous – they are credited neither on the title page nor in the individual entries – were the young history graduates, all of them female and most of them medievalists, who undertook the work of record-searching and making up slips in the early years of the *Victoria County History* – 'wonderfully plain girls' as they were jocularly referred to by J. H. Round, the cantankerous old Tory who set them to work on their tasks.[9] By the same token, a discussion of nineteenth-century medievalism, if it were to do justice to its anonymous hands, would need to refer not only to the propaganda of Ruskin and Pugin and the church restoration work of Morris and Co., but also to the sewing women, briefly discussed by Roszicka Parker in *The Subversive Stitch*, who produced altar cloths, tapestries and embroideries for the newly ritualized church interior.[10]

If attention was focused, as it should be, on the infrastructure of research, and all those whose labours have gone into the making of archives and sources, then reference might be made to the palaeographers who give names to the anonymous and dates to the undated; the archive staff who calendar solicitors' accumulations and index leases and wills; the cataloguers who make library deposits accessible to the reading public; the conservation officers who perform miracles of invisible repair.

Librarians, though sometimes treated as the Poor Bloody Infantry of the profession, have some claim, historically speaking, to being thought of as among its strategists. They often double in the function of bibliographers, signposting hitherto untravelled terrain. They serve as honest brokers when arranging for the transfer of a collection into public hands. Often, too, they have acted as principals where matters of local history are at stake. The 'Record and Survey' movement of the 1890s and 1900s, to which we owe a great mass of old photographs and the topographical record of now vanished townscapes, is a case in point.[11] City and borough librarians seem to have been instrumental in putting the movement on the map; their libraries were the repositories of the collections; very much later, in the 1960s and 1970s, they played a leading role in bringing them, through exhibition and publication, into the public sphere. The post-war renaissance in local history was similarly beholden to the county record offices. If there is reason to be anxious for the future of historical scholarship, the run-down in library services, the break-up of local history collections, the disappearance of the post of local history or borough librarian and the impending reorganization of the county record offices are at least as much a threat to research as cuts in postgraduate funding.

Bibliographers might also be classed among Clio's invisible hands. Partly because of the revolution in information technology, partly because of the multiplication of subject specialisms, recent years have seen an explosion in the number and reach of bibliographies, while under the influence of the antiques boom there has been an extraordinary proliferation in collectors' handbooks and guides. Whereas thirty years ago bibliography lagged behind research, bringing up the rear with occasional worthy tomes, such as those produced by the Royal Historical Society of writings on British history, today's bibliographers are typically pro-active, bringing the resources of learning to bear on subjects and specialities which researchers have not yet begun to tackle: Martin Hoyle's volumes on garden history are a case in point.[12]

A more generous definition of the historical profession might also include that great army of collectors who, whether in the field of material culture or that of the written word, have so often anticipated the directions which scholarship was later to take. In the seventeenth century one might instance George Thomason, the London stationer who, starting in 1641 and continuing to 1662, contrived to collect some 23,000 Civil War tracts, broadsheets and books, snapping them up as they came off the printing press and then binding them up into 1,983 volumes, the ultimate authority for all twentieth-century commentaries on the Levellers and the Diggers;[13] Samuel Pepys, whose collection of black-letter ballads and broadsides, deposited at Magdalene College, Cambridge, seems to have been one of the original inspirations for Lord Macaulay's version of 'history from below';[14] and that group of royalist antiquarians, such as Thomas Hearne and Edward Rymer, who produced the collectanea on which generations of medievalists were to draw.[15]

The discovery of printed ephemera and its incorporation into library holdings and museum display – a phenomenon of the 1960s – has sensibly enlarged the notion of the historical, turning the spotlight of inquiry on to subjects which would have fallen beneath the dignity of the subject in the past. Who could be interested in a *laundry* list?, the eminent Edwardian historian Sir Paul Vinogradov allegedly exclaimed, giving to the term something of the scorn which Lady Bracknell visited on the idea of someone being spawned in a *handbag*. If such condescension is rarer today, it is partly because feminism and gay history have put body politics on the agenda of higher research, and also because, under the influence of the antiques boom of the 1960s, the notion of the collectable has now been extended to the humblest artefact of everyday life.

Collectors are routinely accused of being obsessive, human magpies or carrion indiscriminately swooping down on everything which falls within their chosen field. Yet, like the Tradescants, whose natural history curiosities were the original nucleus of the Ashmolean Museum, Oxford,[16] their madcap enthusiasms often turn out to be prophetic. Scavenging among what others are busily engaged in throwing out or consigning to the incinerator, they have been the true architects of our libraries, galleries and museums, and, if only at second or third remove, the Svengalis of historical research.

Henry Willett, whose collection of chimneypiece ornaments, or Staffordshire figures, is the pride of Brighton Museum, was a popular educator, as well as a self-made museologist. He collected biological specimens and chalk fossils with the same enthusiasm as he did industrial art. He seems to have been quite conscious of the sociological significance of his collection of porcelain figures, and when he put them on show to the public for the first time, in 1879, offered them as a kind of people's history: 'On the mantelpieces of English cottage homes may be found representations which its inmates or their forefathers admired, revered and trusted in; an evidence of real worship perhaps more accurate than external religious observances and of a truer faith than their lip confessions; a kind of unconscious survival of *lares* and *penates* of the ancients.' Still more ambitiously, and presciently, he made his collection, as he told those who visited it, 'to illustrate the principle, or rather in development of the notion, that the History of a Country may be traced in its homely Pottery.'[17]

John Johnson, whose collection of printed ephemera – a million separate items – has a place of honour in the Bodleian Library (by symptomatic irony, Bodleian throw-outs in the 1930s were one of his principal sources), also seems to have known exactly what he was about. A trained Egyptologist, he would have known how the obscurest hieroglyphic could be translated into substantive historical fact. His collection, assembled over a period of forty years, is an *omnium gatherum* illustrating every phase in the history of the printed word, and the commercial use of graphics. The classification of items, when it was handed over to the Bodleian in 1968, prefigures some of the main new lines of research in subsequent years – thanatology, for instance, in such category heads as 'death' and 'funerary', while in other cases such as body politics, it is only now that it is beginning to be used in its own right.[18]

Aesthetes rather than historians are responsible for constituting our notions of 'period'. Thus the term 'Regency', a profitable one for the writers of historical romance, and for the manufacturers of reproduction furniture, seems to have been a neologism of 1920s interior decorators, and it is only now, with the renewed interest in Holland House Whiggery, that professional historians are beginning to show some interest in taking it up. A camp taste for Victoriana was an aristocratic sport – and a metropolitan fashion – fully two decades before the social historians got 'Victorian people' and 'Victorian values' in their sights.[19] Kenneth Clark gave precocious expression to it in *The Gothic Revival* (1928); Cecil Beaton and the Bright Young Things of the 1920s experimented with it at their fancy dress parties; John Betjeman, pioneering time travel on neglected or forgotten branch lines, gave a taste of it to readers of the *Daily Herald*;[20] while at *Late Joys*, translating a well-worn literary conceit into a species of camp performance art, Leonard Sachs in 1937 began staging Old Time Victorian Music Hall.[21] More recently, the 1960s Art Deco revival, and the brisk trade in Clarice Cliff tea-sets, has been not the least of the subliminal influences in buttressing the argument of those revisionist historians who stress the modernity of inter-war Britain rather than its *ancien régime* conservatism.

Antiquarian and archaeological illustrators, such as those who adorned the guide-books of the later eighteenth century, were the avatars of Victorian medievalism, making the bare ruined choirs of the monastic remains as familiar a spectacle as the gentleman's seat. Thomas Pennant, anticipating the discovery of geology and the invention of pre-history, had his text illustrated with megalithic drawings.[22] Later, the Antiquarian illustrators were among the most effective popularizers of the romantic medievalism of Sir Walter Scott. They monopolized attention in such influential works as Gough's *Sepulchral Monuments of Great Britain* (1786–1799) as also in Stothard's *Monumental Effigies*.[23] The ecclesiologists of the Camden Society, launching their propaganda for a return to the church furnishings of the high Middle Ages, made extensive use of them. The county histories of the early and middle years of the nineteenth century also bear their mark, while transactions of the Record Societies were by the 1850s and 1860s making a feature of their engravings of fonts, naves, and effigies.

Popular illustrators also played a large part in the mid-Victorian turn to the Elizabethan, and the creation of an alternative, more Protestant (and more nationalist), 'Merrie England' to the medieval one of Cobbett, Carlyle and Pugin.[24] W. P. Frith's 'A Coming of Age in the Olden Times' – a crowded canvas showing an Elizabethan squire surrounded by gaggles of his frolicsome tenantry, from which the Art Union, in 1852, extracted the plate 'An English Merry Making in the Olden Time' – was one of the most popular of Victorian prints.[25] 'Archaeological' revivals of Shakespeare, such as those of Charles Kean,[26] and John Gilbert's wood engravings (831 of them) for Boydel's *Shakespeare*, 'one of the most memorable English illustrated works', established a distinctly Victorian idea of the Elizabethan age which has proved remarkably tenacious.[27] Most pertinent of all in creating an appetite for the Elizabethan were the multi-volume works of the architect John Nash, a pupil of Pugin. His *Historic Mansions*, published between 1840 and 1844, and his *Baronial Halls of England* elevated the stately home to a pinnacle of romantic esteem while at the same time making the Elizabethan the morning star of the indigenous.[28]

Another memory-bank which would repay attention in any attempt to draw up a genealogy, or archaeology, of the unofficial sources of historical knowledge would be music. The first histories, in medieval Europe as in ancient Greece, were the ballads, which, starting with Ulysses, made gods and heroes of ordinary mortals. They also served as war memorials, in the case of the Battle of Roncevaux, as also perhaps that of Maldon, giving an epic quality to what in the original event may have been a comparatively minor skirmish. Ballads served as mnemonics in recitations of genealogy and (to follow John Aubrey's account) the learning of dynastic history. They could also be – if radical readings of the Robin Hood legend are accepted – repositories for what Professor Tawney once called 'the doctrineless communism of the open field village'.

From a historiographic point of view, one of the more remarkable instances of the power of the ballad, in consciousness-raising and creating a historical narrative, would be that of the Jacobites, who earned their place in history and romance quite largely on the strength of Lady Nairne's songs. Written and composed in the 1820s – the high point in pan-European Romanticism, and the moment of the Highland tartan's coming-of-age – the songs turned Culloden into a modern Thermopylae and made Charles Edward Stuart into a romantic fugitive ('Over the Sea to Skye' was written by Sir Harold Boulton in 1908). At the present time, music seems even more potent as a period signifier. 'The White Cliffs of Dover' has firmly established itself as a kind of alternative national anthem in any account of Britain during the Second World War, and it is perhaps indicative of this that in the recent controversies over the celebrations of the fiftieth anniversary of D-Day it was neither the Queen nor the Prime Minister who spoke for the soldierly dead, but Dame Vera Lynn. For the cult followers of *Casablanca*, a gravelly-throated rendition of 'As Time Goes By' evokes bitter-sweet memories of the anti-fascist resistance. 'Goodbye Dolly Gray' is famously a kind of signature tune for the Boer War; already well-established, it seems, in 1931, when Noel Coward adapted it for the English family saga of *Cavalcade*. In France it seems that *Le Temps des Cerises* played a similar part for those who wanted to honour the martyrs of the Paris Commune.

Music has also played some part in creating the resurrectionary enthusiasms of our time. The playing of early Baroque music, and the use of original instruments, pioneered by a small group of musical archaeologists in the 1950s, was already able to support an alternative concert circuit in the 1960s; today such performances can command a full house at the Royal Albert Hall. The restoration of old film scores – starting with the mega-musical experience of Abel Gance's exhumed *Napoleon* – is another widely imitated example, while in rock music revivals are so thoroughly mixed up with the production of new music that it is often impossible to know where an old track ends and a new one begins.

Any account of history as a social form of knowledge would need to admit, and rejoice in, the motley character of its following. In the Middle Ages, R. W. Southern writes in his account of the twelfth-century historical revival, it embraced all those who were caught up in the process of collecting and arranging charters, transcribing documents, studying monastic buildings and inscriptions, assembling ancient texts, writing estate history, compiling saints' lives and chronicles. For each surviving work there may well have been many hundreds of constituent fragments.

Clio's under-labourers would also need to include those who worked as visual memory-keepers, in the pictorial representation of the past. One might instance those anonymous ladies – according to some commentators, Anglo-Saxon, and attached to St Augustine's, Canterbury, rather than to a French monastery, or William the Conqueror's court – who sewed the Bayeux tapestry, that incomparable pictorial narrative; or the ecclesiastical painters who turned sacred history into stained-glass windows and frescoes; or the heraldic engravers who inscribed the family coat of arms on seals, banners and fortified keeps. At the crossing-point between the sacred and the secular, pride of place would go to the masons, carvers and goldsmiths who made lifelike statues in churches – a kind of medieval Madame Tussaud's is how they are described by one commentator – and who reproduced, in the *misericordia*, scenes from provincial life. Reference should be made, also, to the members of the artisan guilds, involved in the production and performance of the miracle plays, the moralities and those folk dramas and carnivalesque floats which in the later Middle Ages turned civic ritual into street theatre and an early form of the Elizabethan stage.

Memory-keeping in the Middle Ages, to follow Marc Bloch's admirable pages on it in *Feudal Society*, or the more extended and complex account given of it in M. T. Clanchy's work on the transition from orality to written record, was a public activity in which almost everyone might find themselves involved, if only as witnesses or – in the case of the sermon *exemplum* – silent listeners. This was above all the case in matters of custom and the law where, even after the advent of written documents, a quite special credence was given to the testimony of the elders. In another sphere, there were the members of the parish guilds and fraternities who kept up the *libri memoriales* and prayers for the departed; those who dramatized Bible stories on liturgical feast-days; and that vast number who gave credence to the miracle stories by prostrating themselves before saints' and martyrs' relics.

In the nineteenth century, when history emerged as a great public art, and when its leading practitioners enjoyed the status of men of letters – if not on a par with the poets, then certainly the superior of the novelists – attention might be focused on those new literary forms which shaped the character of historical work and the direction of historical inquiry. Sir Walter Scott, with his anti-heroic heroes, his scenes from everyday life, and his play with vernacular speech would appear as one of the great architects of historical realism, while at the other end of the scale attention might be drawn to that literary underworld where the penny-a-liner, writing drum-and-trumpet histories for one of the boys' monthlies; the poor schoolmaster writing heroic biography for Sunday School prize-books; and the literary lady trying to carve out a corner in the history of philanthropy or the diffusion of useful knowledge lived out a precarious existence.

No less pertinent for nineteenth-century historical awareness would be that small army of popular educators who by means of public lectures and exhibitions, or printed primers and guides, turned nineteenth-century Britain into a showcase of natural history – 'fossilizing' when they went on holiday to the seaside, 'archaeologizing' or 'geologizing' when they visited historic sites, collecting samples of flora and fauna when they went on country walks, and setting up museums of natural history in the home. A genealogy here would range from the pedigree obsessed country squire to the self-educated stonemason or wool-sorter, who week by week took up the 'Notes and Queries' columns of the newspaper and periodical press, either on account of their literary and biographical discoveries, or because they helped to establish a foundation for local research.[29] Numismatists, such as the great Roach Smith of London, a City tradesman who contrived to establish a Roman museum and to publish a small library of Romano-British studies on the strength of workmen's scavengings, might be seen retrospectively as archivists for the future;[30] so might those working-man botanical societies and Saturday afternoon naturalists whose excitements included the discovery of prehistoric remains.

Today history is no longer regarded as a branch of literature, if only because historians themselves harbour quite other ambitions, connecting their work with 'theory' or quantifying their findings in the manner of science. There is no longer, as there was in the nineteenth century, a historical school of painting. Memory-keeping is a function increasingly assigned to the electronic media, while a new awareness of the artifice of representation casts a cloud of suspicion over the documentation of the past. Despite this, history as a mass activity – or at any rate as a pastime – has possibly never had more followers than it does today, when the spectacle of the past excites the kind of attention which earlier epochs attached to the new. Conservation, whatever the doubts about the notion of 'heritage', is one of the major aesthetic and social movements of our time. Family history societies fill the record offices with their searchers. We live in an expanding historical culture, in which the work of inquiry and retrieval is being progressively extended into all kinds of spheres that would have been thought unworthy of notice in the past, the whole new orders of documentation are coming into play.

In any more pluralist notion of the historical profession, or one which paid due respect to those under-labourers without whom historical enterprises would founder, some small space ought to be given [. . .] to the picture researchers – a new breed of Cliographers who owe their existence to the photo-litho revolution of the 1960s, so far as popular historical publication is concerned, or those coffee-table books and Sunday colour supplements which have been the principal medium for the reproduction of 'period' photography. Then there are the television technicians who have the job of synchronizing sight and sound for television docudrama, the writers of screenplays who adapt the literary classics, the film archivists who splice in and select old footage; the independent companies bidding for *Timewatch* slots. In another sphere where do-it-yourself projects have transformed the map of knowledge, family history is a whole industry unto itself, with a bizarre databank at one end of the spectrum – IGI (the International Genealogical Index), the Mormon funded archive of dead souls which is a first port of call for those in search of lost ancestors.

One of the more remarkable additions to the ranks of Britain's memory-keepers – or notable recent augmentation of them – would be the multiplication of do-it-yourself curators and mini-museums. Business houses, goaded into an action by an enthusiast on the staff (quite often, it seems, the principal), have incorporated these into the machineries of self-presentation, putting up display cases in the reception area. The conversion of the home into a kind of miniature historical shrine is even more common, with old photographs – blown up and framed – doing duty for the family portraits and Victorian stuffed squirrels serving as make-believe family heirlooms. Then reference would need to be made to the legions of bargain-hunters who through the medium of the flea market and the car-boot sale have created whole new classes of collectables, or made archives of the future out of the ephemera of the everyday. Walsall Museum discovered dozens of them in 1991, when it staged its first 'People Show', inviting the town's collectors to take up the museum's exhibition space. 'Memorabilia' here appeared in pluralist guise, starting with the veteran jazz musician and his collection of vintage drums and ending up the bedroom culture of the adolescent boy or girl with their collection of football scarves, fanzines or Madonnas.

Graphics

A historiography that was alert to memory's shadows – those sleeping images which spring to life unbidden, and serve as ghostly sentinels of our thought – might give at least as much attention to pictures as to manuscripts or print. The visual provides us with our stock figures, our subliminal points of reference, our unspoken point of address. When we think of eighteenth-century politics we see Hogarth's Wilkes. The bubonic plague brings skeletons out to dance. The Crimean War is Florence Nightingale with her lamp. The retreat from Moscow is Napoleon on a horse looking downwards. The Viking is a man wading ashore from a long-boat; dressed in a horned helmet, and grasping a broad-sword in his right hand: he is off to sack a village.[31] Likewise in a well-worn iconographic tradition, the picture that comes to mind of the ancient Britons may well be that of a caveman wielding a club – long-haired, bare-chested, and protected from the cold by nothing but a primitive sarong. The earliest visual portraits of ancient Britons, Stuart Piggott tells us in *Ruins in a Landscape*, date from about 1575, when a Dutchman, Lucas de Heere, in a description of Britain, made a drawing of a couple of wild-looking naked men, tattooed or woad-painted, carrying long shields, spears and a sword.[32]

The iconography of war would be particularly rewarding to study from the point of view of the visual sources of historical consciousness. Wall panels commemorating famous victories, such as those to be found in the Valley of the Kings, and vase paintings celebrating legendary heroes are among the earliest historical records, while war memorials are among the most ancient of the public arts. The Bayeux tapestry (Napoleon's rediscovery) is probably most people's idea of the Norman Conquest, and we are no less indebted to monumental effigies and ecclesiastical statuary for our idea of the crusades (the nineteenth-century rediscovery of the Knights Templar seems to be responsible for the visual cliché which has the crusader wearing a surplice over his armour).[33]

The nineteenth-century romanticization of war – a subject which awaits its historian – owed a great deal to historical illustration, and to the taste for military antiquities which it was one of Sir Walter Scott's achievements to have made into a pan-European enthusiasm. The knight in chainmail, mounted on a horse, and with his pennant pointing upwards to the sky, was a heroic figure in public statuary (Richard Coeur de Lion outside the Houses of Parliament,[34] Westminster, and the Black Prince in the City Square, Leeds, are well-known examples). Engraved pictures of naval encounters were another nineteenth-century favourite, as for example in the pubs, where marine subjects such as Horace Harral's illustrations to Southey's *Life of Nelson* competed for attention with hunting and racecourse prints.[35] In the pleasure gardens, such as Belle Vue, Manchester, there were also 'living history' firework displays – a kind of Hollywood epic before its time, in which with the aid of the pyrotechnicist's art, the Siege of Gibraltar was symbolically lifted and the Battle of Trafalgar refought.[36]

In the Middle Ages spectacle had been quite fundamental to the dissemination of sacred history. Here the street theatre of the Corpus Christi procession, with its banners, tabernacles and crosses,[37] and the open-air perambulating stages where the miracle and morality plays were performed, dramatically re-enacted the Passion.[38] Legendary history was disseminated in a similar fashion. The Gog-Magog procession in London, celebrating the giants who were supposedly the city's founding fathers, is a well-known example.[39] Then there were those annual turn-outs and open-air demonstrations of the artisan trades, such as the Bishop Blaize procession of the wool-combers, or the St Crispin's Day celebrations of the shoemakers, which seem to have had their origin in a civic ritual. Robin Hood, though he has his origin in medieval ballad, was given a whole new life through the late medieval and early modern development of civic pageantry and ritual; Maid Marian – a great figure at Foresters' and Hospital Sunday demonstrations in the nineteenth century – seems to have been the brainchild of some sixteenth-century parish organizers of May games, who believed the Robin Hood story might show to better advantage if it was played as a drama of young love.[40] In a more carnivalesque vein reference should be made to those folk devils of the popular imagination, in the first place the Pope, later Guy Fawkes, annually consigned to a ceremonial bonfire.[41]

How often has the visual been the original prompt for an historical inquiry? A famous if possibly apocryphal example is that of Edward Gibbon who, according to his own retrospective account, was moved to embark on his *Decline and Fall of the Roman Empire* by the spectacle of the ruins at the Colosseum.[42] A more recent example would be Philippe Ariès whose inquiry into the history of childhood seems to have been sparked off by a portrait of Louis XIII, painted when he was still a child of seven, but in which he is depicted as a grown-up.[43] It seems to have been the spectacle of Père Lachaise, and those November migrations which brought flocks of pilgrims to the cemeteries, 'in the cities as well as the country' which set him off on the thanatological inquiries which eventually produced *The Hour of Our Death*.[44] Ruth Richardson, whose *Death, Dissection and the Destitute* has given a bizarre twist to debates about the New Poor Law, traces her life's interest in the subject to some 'frightening' woodcuts of the Black Death which she saw in a book as a little girl of three, a year or so before she learnt to read. (The book was Johannes Nohl's *The Black Death*, translated from the German, and it has as the frontispiece a skeleton riding on a chariot.[45])

More indirectly, it might be instructive to inquire into the part played by the topographical illustrators in treating, or ministering to, preservationist instincts and historicist tastes. Chorography, the Elizabethan name for the mapping and description of place, was one of the earliest forms of local history.[46] The maps themselves, pictorial in character and very often bordered with county heraldry and sketches of local scenery and seats, were intensely graphic. The 'many cuts' which adorned Dugdale's *The Antiquities of Warwickshire* (1656) – the greatest of the early county histories – marked in some sort topographical illustration's coming of age;[47] henceforth it formed part of the normal repertoire of antiquarian research. Maurice Barley's bibliography of topographical prints shows etchings, mezzotints, copper and steel engravings, photos and lantern slides as well as artists' impressions of buildings and views.[48] When, in the late seventeenth century, Edward Lhuyd (1660–1709) began his topographical researches in Wales – or West Britain as it was then often called – 'he made large collections of drawings of megaliths', and much the same was true of the tragic J. T. Blight's illustrations of Borlase's *Antiquities of Cornwall*.[49]

One of the leading subjects of the topographical illustrators has been that of environments at risk, and one of their recurring inspirations – already a nostalgic subtext in the Elizabethan 'discovery' of England – has been that of creating a graphic archive of disappearing worlds. This was the inspiration of the *Recording Britain* project launched in the dire days of 1940 – the 'pictorial Domesday' for which Sir Kenneth Clark mobilized a galaxy of talents to preserve, in watercolour and gouache, tokens of the civilization which an enemy invasion might be expected to destroy.[50] It was also the urgent impulse behind Sir Thomas Dugdale's frantic journeyings on the eve of Civil War, the one-man crusade of an obsessive antiquarian 'to make notes of those ecclesiastical memorials which might be destroyed in the political storm he saw approaching'.[51] Topographical illustration in the eighteenth century, though less driven by an emergency sense of change, was, if anything, even more seized by the symptoms of decay. 'Drawing ruins' was one of the passions of the eighteenth-century antiquary,[52] as it was of William Stukeley before he converted to an obsession with Druids, and it was also quite central to those picturesque travellers whose late-eighteenth-century writings were in some sort heralds of the Gothic turn in architecture and design.[53]

If one wanted to look for a single figure who would represent the 'new wave' social history of the 1960s, or the turn to those user-friendly, interactive and informal displays which were such a feature of that decade's 'new museology', David Gentleman, the wood engraver and illustrator, would be as strong a candidate as any. He is the man who put living-history pictures on British postage stamps, among them a series on Ironbridge and some of the monuments of industrial archaeology.[54] His Eleanor Cross mural at Charing Cross underground station – a tapestry of medieval labour, with spare, skeletal figures simplified in the manner of an Arts-and-Crafts frieze – is a successful essay in the kind of modernist pastiche which the conservation movement was to make the quintessence of refurbishment.[55] His illustrations to *Ask the Fellows Who Cut the Hay* (1966) or, later, *David Gentleman's Britain* (1982) are very much in line with those of Edward Bawden, Eric Ravilious and John Piper before him – pen and ink with flat washes of watercolour, but without neo-romantic hints of apocalypse or darkling intimations of gloom.[56] His woodcuts to the 1964 Oxford edition of *The Shepherd's Calendar* are also quite strikingly up-beat, indeed positively fecund when it came to August harvest-sheaves, September apple-picking and even the labours of beamless and pale November.[57]

Pedagogically, pictures have usually been the child's first introduction to the idea of the past, from the many woodcuts which decorated the early horn-books to the large-format historical illustrations in today's children's pictorials. In the days of mnemonics, pictures were frequently used as visual aids – as, for example, in those history cards of the kings and queens of England 'showing . . . a remarkable family likeness . . . from William I to William IV'[58] which were a great standby of the Victorian governess; or the board game of 'Sovereigns' in which genealogical information was the counter.[59] Later, with the advent of 'learning by doing' – a phenomenon of the 1920s in go-ahead and progressive junior schools – modelling a Tudor house, drawing an Elizabethan ruff, or mapping the three-field system were fiercely and successfully championed as a modernist and progressive alternative to rote-learning.

Graphics were, of course, quite central to the chap-books, those 'penny histories' which took as their subject legendary heroes, and which owed their street credibility to the juxtaposition of vivid engraving and crude black-letter text.[60] It was the 'horrid and awful-looking woodcuts at the head' which drew the young Samuel Bamford, a workhouse master's son and an apprentice hand-loom weaver, to the legendary histories on sale at a Manchester printer-stationer-bookseller of the 1780s:

> Every farthing I could scrape together, was now spent in purchasing 'Histories of Jack the Giant Killer,' 'Saint George and the Dragon,' 'Tom Hickathrift,' 'Jack and the Bean Stalk,' 'History of the Seven Champions,' tale of 'Fair Rosamond,' 'History of Friar Bacon,' 'Account of the Lancashire Witches,' 'The Witches of the Woodlands,' and such like romances; whilst my metrical collections embraced but few pieces besides 'Robin Hood's Songs,' and 'The Ballad of Chevy-Chase.' Of all these tales and ballads I was soon master, and they formed the subjects of many a long study to me, and of many a wonder-creating story for my acquaintance both at the workhouse and elsewhere. For my part I implicitly believed them all, and when told by my father or others that they were 'trash' and 'nonsense,' and 'could not be true,' I, innocently enough, contrasted their probability with that of other wondrous things which I had read in books that 'it were a sin to disbelieve.' So I continued reading, and doubting nothing which I read until many years after, when a more extended acquaintance with men and books, taught me how better to discriminate betwixt reason and unreason – truth and falsehood.[61]

The nineteenth century was a great age of historical illustration. It was through the medium of the visual that nineteenth-century versions of medievalism imposed themselves, and that the Gothic side of Scott was amplified. While written history moved in a definitely Whig direction, and in the schools parliamentary sympathies in the Civil War were almost unresisted, in the visual a high Tory romanticism prevailed, represented by a whole series of doomed and tragic monarchs, from Lady Jane Grey to Bonnie Prince Charlie. Cheap printing encouraged an astonishing proliferation of educational toys – such as the paper ship game where a very young Eleanor Farjeon waged war, on the nursery table.

One major nineteenth-century addition to the repertoire of visual aids was the Bayeux tapestry. Almost unknown during the first eight hundred years of its existence, and disappearing entirely from view at the end of the fifteenth century, it was discovered by Napoleon in the course of his preparations for the invasion of England, and exhibited for the first time outside Bayeux in 1803, when the preparations for the invasion of England were at their height.

The exhibition was a great success, with Napoleon himself spending some time studying the Tapestry. The parallel between the comet which was seen in France and southern England in November 1803 and the comet shown in the embroidery adjacent to the scene of Harold's coronation was not lost on the audience. A description of the phenomenon was included in the first edition of the handbook which was prepared for the exhibition: 'Dover, December 6, 1803. Last night about five o'clock we observed a superb comet which rose in the south-west and moved towards the north: it had a tail about thirty yards long. The whole countryside was lighted for many miles all around, and after it disappeared, one smelled a strong odour of sulphur.' There was also a story, without foundation, circulated by later English writers, that Napoleon was so struck by the coincidence of the comet that, interpreting it as a bad omen, he abandoned his plans for an invasion of England! The modern propaganda value of the Tapestry was realized for the first time with its Paris exhibition.[62]

It was the enthusiasm of British Gothicists which led to the tapestry's second migration and its return, in the form of imitation and print, to the country where it had originally been embroidered, and whose history it purported to tell. Charles Stothard, whose *Monumental Effigies*, published between 1822 and 1829, were (Mark Girouard tells us) a kind of visual equivalent to the Waverley novels in stirring medievalist sympathies, took up the cause of the tapestry. In 1816, on assignment from the Society of Antiquaries of London, he set about producing a full-size, full-colour reproduction of the tapestry, an undertaking which took two years to complete. 'By closely studying the needle-holes and thread traces Stothard was able to "restore" much of the damaged area and produce drawings of what he considered to be the tapestry's original appearance.'[63]

Historical illustration is, on the face of it, one of the most conservative of art forms. The same stock figures seem to appear in an astonishing variety of contexts, as though there were some puppet-master pulling the strings. Often it seems that archetypal images are involved, even when a picture is ostensibly drawn or painted from life – one could refer to the *pietà* grouping of Daniel Maclise's enormously popular *Death of Nelson*, as of its predecessor and the original of a long line of military martyrologies, Benjamin West's *Death of Wolfe*; the killing fields, in the outstretched hand of G. W. Pabst's *All Quiet on the Western Front*, or Matthew Brady's well-known photographs of the carnage at Gettysburg, in the American Civil War.

Perhaps the most remarkable example of iconographic longevity is that of the woodcuts to *Foxe's Book of Martyrs*, those 'realistic engravings of the horrible tortures inflicted on the faithful Protestant' – as they appeared to a young Spitalfields apprentice of the 1860s[64] – which held their own, almost unchanged, for some three hundred years. John Day, the original illustrator, was an ardent Protestant who had himself been a Marian prisoner, and his woodcuts were re-cut and re-copied, with remarkably little modification, right down to the last popular edition in 1875. They were, writes Hodnett, in his history of book illustration, 'the earliest examples of graphic journalism in England'. The martyrs were pictured being scourged, burned, hanged and stretched on the rack. The horror of the scene was enhanced by the grim but matter-of-fact bearing of the executioners.[65]

Historical illustrations today, in popular educational publishing, such as Kingfisher, Usborne and Dorling Kindersley – the 1990s successors to the 'Ladybird' books – are, in their own way, equally conservative, alternating between extravaganzas of the kind which drew the young Samuel Bamford to the chap-books – e.g. 'How to Draw Ghosts, Vampires and Haunted Houses' – with a 'realistic battlegame' of *Fighting Ships*, in which Viking boats alternate with four-masted Spanish galleons; and a 'time-travelling' series which moves from 'Knights and Castles' to 'Famous Inventors and Explorers'.

The heroic biography which was offered to 1950s and 1960s readers of *The Eagle* – Charlemagne, Alfred the Great and Joan of Arc among them – would not have looked out of place in the self-help manuals and Sunday School prize books of the nineteenth century;[66] while the comic strip serials in the girls' magazines – often with a period setting – loyally continue in the idiom of the Evangelically inspired 'waif' novels. Ringing the changes on court biography and royal romances, the girls' comics have worked a rich vein in little-girl-lost or orphanhood stories, set sometimes in Victorian England, sometimes in Regency times, and typically involving both aristocratic patronage and profiles of people in need. Thus, for instance, 'Sophie Sixpence' (*Mandy*, 3 March 1984) tells the story of a twelve-year-old, rescued from a life of poverty, the workhouse and begging by wealthy Sir John Fielding, who bought her from an unscrupulous couple for sixpence – hence her name. When Sir John goes away on business the wicked step-parents try to snatch her back, rather in the manner of the Artful Dodger in *Oliver Twist*. 'Angel' (*Mandy for Girls*, 26 January 1985) has a Victorian miss, the only child of a wealthy banker, who, stricken by an illness for which there is no known cure, devotes what she thinks are her last days by setting up as a good Samaritan in the London slums. *Nikki for Girls* (27 April 1985) has a bonneted villainess scheming to starve a Victorian orphan to death on behalf of a wicked guardian; while in *Judy and Tracy* (5 July 1986) Hetty Dean, a flower seller in Victorian London, is magically translated into a Moldanian princess.

Closer inspection of any of those images, however, makes them seem a good deal less timeless. The queens who look out from the 'Ladybird' books seem to have been drawn from Julie Andrews or Anna Neagle – fresh-faced or statuesque according to the role in which they are cast. Likewise in the *Royal Story Book of English History* – a popular reader published in 1883 – all of the pictures, whatever the period to which they ostensibly refer, look like those to be found in Victorian moral tales. Except for the inscription 'Lord Have Mercy on Us', the 'Street in London during the Plague', with its tottering, dilapidated tenements, is pure Gustave Doré (after his *London, A Pilgrimage*, 1872). The young King Alfred absent-mindedly burning the cakes, though ostensibly a boy, is a dead ringer for Sir John Tenniel's (and Lewis Carroll's) Alice. Geoffrey Chaucer, the poet, and Edward III, his sovereign, are both pictured as Pre-Raphaelite Merlin-like figures, with long beards reaching down almost to the ground. Forty years earlier, in the illustrations with which Charles Knight used to swell the sales of the *Penny Magazine*, the philosophers and poets, so far from being hirsute, have barely a whisker or a superfluous tuft of hair between them.

It is the genius of television, and especially perhaps television directed at children, that it can reinvent historical characters in such a way as to make them speak in the authentic accent of the here-and-now. Indeed it was under the aegis of that long-running favourite, *Dr Who*, that the idea of back-to-the-future and time travelling – a leitmotif of post modernism – was born. In the 1970s, children's serials celebrated the feats of Richard the Lionheart and the Crusades (*The Talisman*), brought Anglo-Saxon England to life in *Hereward the Wake*, and featured medieval swordplay and chivalrous knights-in-armour in *Ivanhoe*. More recently, through the medium of its eco-friendly and popular *Robin of Sherwood*, children's television has created a kind of New Age outlaw hero, one who was on friendly terms with a Celtic wizard, and a dab hand at conducting Druidic ceremonies. A still more striking case is the recent cult serial *Sharpe*. Set in the period of the Peninsular War, and with some haunting songs of the period to suggest that this really happened, Sean Bean, the male lead, is a cross between a swashbuckling Errol Flynn-type hero, putting cowardly and treacherous enemies to flight, and a more sensitive Lawrentian figure: he falls in love with a Spanish guerrilla who proves her emancipation by knifing someone in every episode; and he cuddles his baby daughter with all the rapture of an Islington-trained 'new man'.

The art of memory as Frances Yates describes it, following a trajectory which leads from ancient Greece to Renaissance Italy and Shakespeare's England, had a very strong graphic side.[67] Beginning as a rhetorical device, it came to be practised, in the Middle Ages, as a kind of visual analogue to thought. It was associated both with the production and storage of images, and with the location of memory places – as, say, burial grounds and shrines.[68] Memory of words becomes memory refracted through the iconography of things, and finally, when it is caught up in occult philosophy, astral figures.[69]

Medieval scribes, with their delight in such mnemonic devices as the visual alphabet, had a genius for discovering the pictorial equivalent of verbal utterance. Words, in the illuminated manuscripts, double in the character of things; while the flora and fauna of the marginalia and the animal heads and facetious figures offset the mysteries of religion or the formalities of the charters by being rooted in the humours of everyday life.[70] Knights announced themselves through heraldry, 'an alternative language of signs, which was peculiar to the knightly order, and distinguished their names'.[71] The merchant class of later medieval London followed suit, 'choosing the same predatory creatures for their emblems as had traditionally appealed to noble families as symbols of power', though the London fishmongers (Sylvia Thrupp tells us) preferred to draw on Christian iconography.[72] Stained-glass windows told the story of the Bible in the form of pictorial narrative and represented saints' lives in gilded tabernacles where the incidents of their sufferings, and their miracles, were rehearsed. Frescoes and friezes depicted scenes of combat and made effigies of the knightly dead.[73]

It is then fitting that Matthew Paris, whose *Chronica Majora*, compiled between 1230 and 1251, is one of the finest medieval histories, should have combined the role of historiographer with that of artist. His text is richly illustrated with relevant scenes, sketched in many cases (it seems) by himself, and he also devised a system of pictorial reference signs, both as an ornament and as a kind of allegorical index. 'We find in one place a fish, in another a stag's head . . . elsewhere . . . two halves of an animal's body.'[74] 'He had such skill in the working of gold and silver and other metal', a fellow monk wrote in 1400, 'and in painting pictures, that it is thought that there has been none to equal him since in the Latin world.'[75]

Antiquarians, with their eye for eccentric and quirky shapes, their love of curiosities and their often very strong aesthetic preference for the archaic, have been much more alert to the visual than historians.[76] Taking then original inspiration, quite often, from exotic objects or the evidence of ruins and relics; using bronze and pottery inscriptions rather than the written or printed word as primary sources; and calling on burial goods or coin hoards to reconstitute the track of ancient settlement, antiquarians have often been concerned to exhibit and display, as well as to write about, the object of their inquiries, while illustration, if only for the purposes of exegesis, has often been a necessity of their published work.[77] In nineteenth-century publication, title pages would often make a feature of Gothic typefaces and archaic words, while decorative borders and end-pieces would simulate some of the effects of the medieval illuminated manuscript.[78]

Architectural history, heraldry and ecclesiology, the leading preoccupations of the county archaeological and record societies, also put a premium on illustration, while the illustrated lecture, using 'dioramic views' of monastic ruins or magic-lantern slides of old English churches, was a firm favourite, it seems, with that large public interested in ecclesiastical antiquities.[79] In the case of popular publishing, such as that of William Hone, Robert Chambers and the egregious S. C. Hall, it was the very basis of their appeal to the reading public.[80] Hone's three-decker *Every-Day Book* was illustrated with 436 engravings, drawn quite often, it seems, by the antiquaries themselves.[81] Charles Roach Smith, the City-of-London chemist who assembled a whole museum of Roman remains, contributed his own etchings in the publication and popularization of his work, improving on the original so that the Roman inscriptions have every letter in place, the mosaic pavements every tessera.[82] His fellow-antiquary Thomas Wright illustrated his wanderings and finds with quantities of engravings and vignettes, drawn (it seems) by his own hand. He enjoyed 'rude forms', and was something of a hurnorist[83] (one of his drawings shows the barrow diggers, sheltering under an umbrella from the storm);[84] but like Roach Smith he seems to have been unable to prevent himself from improving on the original when making his on-the-spot sketches. Wright's triple-decker *History of Ireland* was illustrated with engravings by the President of the Watercolour Society – 'Death of Brian Boru', 'Richard Earl of Pembroke Taking Leave of his Brother', 'Henry II Presenting the Pope's Bull'.[85] His very influential *History of Domestic Manners and Sentiments in England during the Middle Ages* drew on scenes in illuminated medieval manuscripts to illustrate his account of houses, furniture, dress, food and recreations.[86]

Historical illustration was the cutting edge of the introduction of social history into the elementary schools – a phenomenon of the 1920s. The Board of Education, in its *Suggestions* for 1918, argued that children needed 'the picturesque element'.[87] Material culture – in the form of houses, food, dress and means of locomotion – was easier for children to understand than more abstract political and constitutional questions; material artefacts were also – as progressive teachers showed – ideal candidates for 'handwork' (e.g. modelling and drawing), for 'playway' forms of education, and for what was called, after Froebel and Dewey, 'learning by doing'. A model of Stonehenge, 'period' rooms and history friezes were, it seems, among the most popular exercises in junior classes at the time; and the books which catered to them, such as the 'Piers Plowman' histories, were richly illustrated with historical engravings and prints.[88]

By contrast the Historical Association, which established itself in the same period as the gazetteer of masters and mistresses in the senior schools, offered unrelieved acres of print, both in its much-thumbed pamphlets and in its quarterly journal. The university presses – a growing presence in these years – were no less severe, though when Oxford University Press published the Orwins' *Open Fields* it was illustrated by one of the archaeological excitements of the 1920s – aerial photographs.[89]

In an increasingly image-conscious society, and one in which children are visually literate from a very early age, the learned journals stand out as one of the very few forms of publication on which historical illustration has yet to leave its mark. Except for art historians, pictures do not count as a source, nor is there any call for seminars and lectures to be turned into slide-shows. For some, such as those who condemn the open-air museums and theme parks, the visual seems to be disqualified because of its association with the popular. Easy on the eye but undemanding, it is also thought of as being in some sort morally dubious – a kind of pedagogic equivalent to the fling.

'History from below' – the 'new-wave' scholarship which dedicated itself to rescuing England's secret people from the 'enormous condescension' of posterity – stopped short of any engagement with graphics. Caught up in the cultural revolution of the 1960s it nevertheless remained wedded to quite traditional forms of writing, teaching and research. E. P. Thompson's *The Making of the English Working Class* (1963) has not a single print to leaven the 800 pages of a narrative which covers some of the most brilliant years of English political caricature. Nor has Peter Laslett's *The World We Have Lost* (1965), the book which offered a more domestic version of people's history. 'New-wave' social history did take photographs on board, but it was for their reality content rather than their pictorial value or interest – in short, because they were thought of as being of a piece with documentary truth.

It seems possible that history's new-found interest in 'representation', and its belated recognition of the deconstructive turn in contemporary thought, will allow for, and even force, a more central engagement with graphics. It is possible that politics will be studied as a species of performance art, religion as a liturgical drama. Photographs, if in the spirit of postmodernism they are dissevered from any notion of the real, might be studied for the theatricality of social appearances, rather than as likenesses of everyday life.

Whatever historians choose to do, graphics are likely to come more and more insistently on to the agenda of reflection and research. For one thing, there is the fact that more and more information is coming to us in the form of visual display, from cashpoint machines to CD Rom. Then there are the ways in which historical illustration and historical reconstitution are becoming, with the aid of information retrieval and advanced technology, inconceivably more sophisticated than they were in the past. With the aid of laser-beam cutting it is possible to produce, in the built environment, brilliant copies for which there is no original; while animatronics have advanced to the point that it is possible to make a flesh-and-blood figure of a tenth-century Viking skull. Archaeologists, using dendrochronology, allow us to sup, metaphorically speaking, with the Beaker people, while in another sphere the new biogenics – it is believed – can bring long-extinct species back to life.[90]

Finally, and perhaps as a result of the collapse of ideas of national destiny, there is the growing importance of 'memory places' in ideas of the historical past. Landscape, and in particular those vast tracts of it which now come under the administration of the National Trust, is now called upon to do the memory work which in earlier times might have been performed by territorial belonging. The historicization of the built environment is an even more striking case in point, ministering to an appetite for roots at the same time as it often involves dishousing the indigenous population. Old houses, formerly left to decay, are now prized as living links to the past, a kind of visual equivalent to what used to be known as 'a stake in the country'. Even when houses are brand new, they cultivate a lived-in look, as epitomized by the universality of those neo-vernacular styles in which local materials, 'mature trees' and well-established shrubs give a mellow look to starter homes. Conversely, as Rachel Whiteread showed in her 1993 installation, the deserted mid-Victorian house, cut adrift from its moorings, shuttered, blind and empty – a house you could go round but not enter – is perhaps the most disturbing monument to the urban diaspora.

Notes

1   John Bossy, *Giordano Bruno and the Embassy Affair*, London, 1991. Long ago, in a typically compressed but resonant passage, R. G. Collingwood, the historian and philosopher, pointed to the affinities between research and the detective fiction of the day. R. G. Collingwood, *The Idea of History*, Oxford, 1946.

2   The description of 1870s Pedestrianism in *The Detective Wore Silk Drawers*, London, 1971, one of the most successful of Lovesey's novels, might have come from the pen of James Greenwood or J. Ewing Ritchie.

3   The title pages of the Brother Cadfael series say that a portion of the royalties will be devoted to rebuilding Shrewsbury Abbey. An account of the origins of the series runs as follows: 'In 1977, Peters, a lifelong fan of the history of her small corner of the world, began thinking about an historical incident involving the translation of the bones of St Winifred to the abbey in Shrewsbury. What if someone were to use this as an opportunity to hide another body. Who would do such a thing and why? Who would be able to detect such a crime? And so Brother Cadfael was born, a medieval renaissance man who can give Mr Holmes a run for his money in a contest of the clearest and cleverest eyes. Soldier, sailor, crusader and lover, come to the cloistered life late, and of his own volition, the native Welshman forms a small company of monks going to Wales to secure Winifred's relics'. Lesley Henderson, ed., *Twentieth Century Crime and Mystery Writers*, 3rd edn., London 1991, p849.

4   Patrick Wright, 'The Man with a Metal Detector', *A Journey through Ruins: The Last Days of London*, London, 1991, pp139–51.

5   'Missy', as F. calls the girl, 'is his amanuensis and transcribes; takes long walks too with him and others, of ten and twenty miles a day', A. J. Munby wrote of Eleanor Dalziel, the pretty young lady's maid whom Furnivall married in 1862. Derek Hudson, *Munby: Man of Two Worlds*, London, 1972, pp123–24. Twenty years later Furnivall abandoned his wife in favour of his twenty-one-year-old secretary and co-worker, Teena Rochfort-Smith. The story of their tragic romance is told in William Benzie, *Dr. F. J. Furnivall: Victorian Scholar–Adventurer*; Norman, Okla., 1983, pp29–31.

6   Elizabeth Murray, *Caught in a Web of Words: James Murray and the Oxford English Dictionary*, New Haven 1977.

7   Claire Harman, *Sylvia Townsend Warner: A Biography*, London, 1991, pp38–43.

8   George Gissing, *New Grub Street*, London 1891, Chapter 7.

9   Victoria County History Archives, correspondence of J. H. Round with H. A. Doubleday, 1900–1901. R. P. Pugh, 'The Victoria County History, its Origin and Progress', in *Victoria County History*, General Introduction, 1970, pp4–5; W. R. Powell, 'J. Horace Round', in *Essex Archaeology and History*, vol. 12, 1980, p30.

10   Roszicka Parker, *The Subversive Stitch*, London, 1984.

11   For the 'Record and Survey' movement, see Part V of this book.

12   Martin Hoyles, *Gardening Books from 1560 to 1960*, vol. 1, London, 1994. A second volume, covering political themes in gardening literature, is promised for 1995.

13   G. K. Fortescue, ed., *Catalogue of the Thomason Collection*, 2 vols., London, 1908. The Thomason tracts seem to have been little used before the upsurge of interest in the Levellers – and the discovery of the Diggers – at the end of the nineteenth century. G. P. Gooch, *The History of English Democratic Ideas in the Seventeenth Century*, Cambridge, 1889, was a pioneering work in this field. In the 1850s, when David Masson made some use of them for his splendid life of Milton, Thomason's collection was known in the British Museum as 'the King's Tracts'. David Masson, *Life of Milton*, London, 1859, vol. 1, p456.

14   *Catalogue of the Pepys Library at Magdalene College, Cambridge*, vol. III, Cambridge, 1980; *The Pepys Ballads*, ed. W. G. Day, Cambridge, 1987.

15   David C. Douglas, *English Scholars*, London, 1939, is an affecting account of them.

16   Mea Allan, *The Tradescants, Their Flowers, Gardens and Museum, 1570–1667*, London, 1964.

17   Henry Willett, *Introductory Catalogue of the Collection of Pottery and Porcelain in the Brighton Museum lent by Henry Willett*, Brighton, 1879, p3. Willett, a lifelong supporter of Liberal 'not to say Radical' causes, was a friend of Richard Cobden, whose books and papers he donated to Brighton reference library in 1873. An ardent friend of popular education, he conducted public readings at Brighton's open-air forum, The Level. His earliest collecting passion was geology, and the first of a series of privately printed catalogues was one in 1871 on cretaceous fossils (the volume was dedicated to his friend John Ruskin). A precocious ecologist, his next collecting venture was in the field of natural history – he even found dinosaurs and the bones of an iguanodon at Cuckfield, Sussex. Willett's ceramic collection, designed to provide illustrations of popular British history, included masses of militaria (one of Willett's more unlikely enthusiasms) and such up-to-the-minute specimens as the coloured plaster sculptures made by Randolph Caldecott, the well-known *Punch* illustrator, for the Tichborne case. Stella Beddoe, 'Henry Willett (1823–1905): Brighton's Major Benefactor', Brighton Museum, October 1933.

18   *The John Johnson Collection: Catalogue of an Exhibition*, ed. Michael L. Turner, Oxford, 1971. Tom Laqueur, 'The John Johnson Collection in Oxford', *History Workshop Journal*, 4, Autumn, 1977; Louis James, *Print and the People, 1819–1951*, London, 1976, draws heavily on the collection.

19   On early 1930s Victoriana, Robert Graves and Alan Hodge, *The Long Week-End: A Social History of Great Britain, 1918–1939*, London, 1950; on Victoriana and the Bright Young Things, Christopher Sykes, *Evelyn Waugh, A Biography*, Harmondsworth, 1977.

20   Bevis Hillier, *Young Betjeman*, London, 1989.

21   Archie Harradine, 'The Story of the Players' Theatre' in *Late Joys*, London, 1943. Originally the brain-child of Peter Ridgeway and Regency in inspiration, an attempt to recapture the flavour of the 1830s supper rooms, the Players' Theatre evolved into a pastiche of late Victorian music hall performance.

22   Glyn Daniel, *A Hundred and Fifty Years of British Archeology*, London, 1975, pp30–31; John Michel, *Megalithonuania: Artists, Antiquarians and Archaeologists at the Old Stone Monuments*, London, 1983.

23   Charles Alfred Stothard, *The Monumental Effigies of Great Britain*, London, 1811–33. Thomas Stothard, Charles Alfred's father, was a leading painter of medieval subjects and was instrumental in making the Bayeux tapestry known in this country.

24   For an excellent brief discussion of the Victorian turn to the Elizabethan, Alun Howkins, 'The Discovery of Rural England', in Robert Colls and Philip Dodd, eds., *Englishness, Politics and Culture, 1880–1920*, London, 1986, pp70–71; Georgina Boyes, *The Imagined Village: Culture, Ideology and the English Folk Revival*, Manchester, 1993, pp34–35, 39, 70–71, for later stages in the Elizabethan revival. For its influence on architecture, Mark Girouard, *The Victorian Country House*, Oxford, 1971, pp33–35, 55, 65. For typography, Cyril Baxter, 'Andrew Tuer and the Leadenhall Press', *Print in Britain*, XI/8, December 1963, pp31–32; on the reinvention of old English types, Talbot Baines Reed, *A History of Old English Letter Foundries*, London, 1952, p249. The St Bride's Institute has some examples of 'Ye Olde Englishe Fayre' events, staged for charitable purposes in the 1880s, and making a feature of his English fonts. The Holbein Society's facsimile reprints (the first was published in 1876) also helped to propagate the charms of Tudor type.

25   Hilary Guise, *Great Victorian Engravings, A Collector's Guide*, London, 1980, p8.

26   For 'archaeological' revivals of Shakespeare in the 1840s and 1850s, Michael Booth, *Victorian Spectacular Theatre, 1850–1910*, London, 1982, pp34–35, 47–59; J. W. Cole, *The Life and Theatrical Times of Charles Kean*, London, 1859.

27   For Gilbert, Forest Reid, *Illustrators of the 1860s*, New York, 1975, pp20–23; Edward Hodnett, *Five Centuries of English Book Illustration*, Aldershot, 1988, pp123–25; John Jackson, *A Treatise on Wood Engraving*, London, 1861, p561.

28   Michael Twyman, *Lithographers, 1800–1850*, Oxford, 1970, pp213–17.

29   W. J. Thorns, 'Gossip of an Old Bookworm', *Nineteenth Century*, 1881, for autobiographical notes by the founder of *Notes and Queries* (he was also the man who coined the term 'folk-lore').

30   Charles Roach Smith, *Catalogue of the Museum of London Antiquities*, London, 1854; *Illustrations of Roman London*, London, 1859; *Collectanea Antigua*, 7 vols., 1848–80. Smith's *Retrospections* combine memoirs of his forays and friendships with notes on Roman fragments. Brian Hobley, 'Charles Roach Smith (1807–90): Pioneering Archaeologist', in *The London Archaeologist*, vol. XIII, no. 22, 1975, pp328–33. There is brief reference to Roach Smith in Philippa Levine's *The Amateur and the Professional*.

31   See Victor Ambrus's brilliant illustrations to R. J. Unstead, *The Story of Britain: Before the Norman Conquest*, London, 1971.

32   Stuart Piggott, *Ruins in a Landscape: Essays in Antiquarianism*, Edinburgh, 1976, pp66–67. Piggott suggests that the drawings were closely related to contemporary drawings of Native Americans. John White, who accompanied Sir Walter Raleigh on his 1585 Virginia expedition, not only drew Native Americans, but a series of ancient Britons, Picts and 'Neighbours unto the Picts', whose characteristics were profoundly influenced by the New World peoples he had seen and drawn. Ibid., p67.

33   On the nineteenth-century rediscovery of the Knights Templar, James Stevens Curl, *The Art and Architecture of Freemasonry*, London, 1992.

34   Benedict Read, *Victorian Sculpture*, London, 1983, pp13, 59, 31–34. For a contemporary review of Maruchetts's 'Richard Coeur de Lion', *The Times*, 15 January 1862.

35   John Jackson, *A Treatise on Wood Engraving*, London, 1861, p583.

36   Marshall's 'Grand Historical Peristrephic Panorama' in Spring Gardens, Lambeth, was an early form of this particular spectacle, using moving pictures and a light show to re-enact the different stages of the Battle of Trafalgar, and following this up with a series of views of the Battle of Waterloo, Horace Wellbeloved, *London Lions for Country Cousins. . . . A Display of Metropolitan Improvements*, London, 1826, pp57–58. For a magnificent history of the dioramas, cosmoramas and pyrotechnic spectacles on offer in early Victorian times, R. D. Altick, *The Shows of London,* Cambridge, MA, 1978.

37   Miri Rubin, *Corpus Christi: The Eucharist in Late Medieval Culture*, Cambridge 1991.

38   Glynne Wickham, *Early English Stages*, vol. 1, London, 1959, is a superb account – the subsequent two volumes of the work take the story of the processional stage to the Bankside theatre of Shakespeare's London and beyond. See also Richard Southern, *The Seven Ages of Theatre*, London, 1962.

39   Frederick W. Fairholt, *Gog and Magog, The Giants in Guildhall, Their Real and Legendary History*, London, 1859.

40   R. B. Dobson and J. Taylor, *Rymes of Robin Hood: an Introduction to the English Outlaw*, London, 1976, pp39–42, 147, 209, 223–36.

41   O. W. Furley, 'The Pope-Burning Processions of the late 17th Century', *History*, 45, 1959, pp16–23. See Roger Tilley, *Playing Cards*, London, 1967, pp103–5, for 'No Popery' playing cards in 1678–81.

42   *The Autobiography of Edward Gibbon*.

43   Philippe Ariès, *Centuries of Childhood*, London, 1962, pp52–53, 66ff.

44   Philippe Ariès, *The Hour of Our Death*, Harmondsworth, 1981.

45   Ruth Richardson, in conversation with the writer, April 1994.

46   As Helgerson points out, whereas Elizabethan 'histories' were a story of kings and their line of descent, the chorographers offered an England of counties, towns, villages and even wards. Richard Helgerson, *Forms of Nationhood: the Elizabethan Writing of England*, Chicago, 1992, pp132–33.

47   *Life and Times of Anthony Wood*, vol. I, p209, quoted in T. D. Kendrick, *British Antiquity*, London, 1950, p167.

48   M. W. Barley, *A Guide to British Topographical Collections*, British Council for Archaeology, London, 1974.

49   Stuart Piggott, *William Stukeley, an Eighteenth Century Antiquarian*, Oxford, 1950, p8; Frank V. Emery, *Edward Lhuyd FRS, 1660–1709*, Cardiff, 1971, for a fuller account.

50   David Mellor, Gill Saunders and Patrick Wright, *Recording Britain, A Pictorial Domesday of Pre-War Britain*, Victoria and Albert Museum, 1990.

51   David C. Douglas, *English Scholars*, London, 1939, pp36–37.

52   J. L. Nevinson, 'Antiquarian', *Museums Journal*, vol. 59, no. 2, May 1959, p34.

53   Michael Twyman, *Printing, 1770–1970*, London 1970, p88; *Lithography, 1800–1850*, Oxford, 1970, pp29–32,169–74.

54   See 'Resurrectionism' in this volume for this episode.

55   David Gentleman, *A Cross for Queen Eleanor*, London, 1979, is his interesting justification, by reference to medieval sources, of the Charing Cross mural.

56   David Gentleman, *A Special Relationship*, London, 1987, for this illustrator's quite fierce radicalism.

57   John Clare, *The Shepherd's Calendar*, ed. Eric Robinson and Geoffrey Summerfield, with wood engravings by David Gentleman, Oxford, 1964.

58   Lady Peck, *A Little Learning*, p22; Eleanor Farjeon, *A Nursery in the Nineties*, Oxford, 1960, p263, for autobiographical reference to being taught by these cards. Thomas Arnold, in his scheme for historical study, had favoured for young children 'a series of lessons as pictures or "prints" of scenes from universal history portraying remarkable events in striking fashion. Their main object is to give vivid centres of association around which to group the stories'; Thomas Arnold, 'Rugby School – Use of the "Classics"', in *Miscellaneous Works*, London, 1845. Dean Stanley, in his *Life of Dr Arnold* (Chapter 3, p100) tells us that 'In examining children in the lower forms he would sometimes take them on his knee and go through picture-books of the Bible or English history, covering the text of the narrative with his hand, and making them explain to him the subject of the several prints.'

59   Jigsaw puzzles made a feature of chronological tables of English history; Linda Hannas, *The English Jigsaw Puzzle, 1760–1890*, London, 1972, plates 6, 17, 25; pp23–24, 28–32. The book has an inventory of historical jigsaws on pp93–97; an introduction which links them to the 1740s rise of children's publishing; and some fascinating pages on the way the writer tracked her quarry.

60   See Margaret Spufford, *Small Books and Pleasant Histories: Popular Fiction and Its Readership in Seventeenth Century England*, Cambridge, 1981, for a fine history. John Ashton, *Chapbooks of the Eighteenth Century*, has recently been reprinted facsimile by that excellent second-hand bookshop, Skoob's of Sicilian Avenue.

61   Samuel Bamford, *Early Days*, London, 1849, pp90–91.

62   Shirley Ann Brown, *The Bayeux Tapestry, History and Bibliography*, Woodbridge 1988, pp11–12. Cf. also David M. Wilson, *The Bayeux Tapestry*, London, 1985.

63   Mark Girouard, *The Return to Camelot, Chivalry and the English Gentleman*, London, 1981.

64   Thomas Okey, *A Basketful of Memories*, London, 1930, pp17–18. 'Granny had a lot of books very old and worn. One was *Foxe's Book of Martyrs* with all the esses printed like effs and many pictures of poor men and women being tortured'; *Shop Boy*, p24. The grandmother in question kept a small grocer's shop in Morriston, near Swansea.

65   Edward Hodnett, *Five Centuries of English Book Illustration*, Aldershot, 1988, p31. In an extensive literature, reference might be made to J. F. Mozely, *John Foxe and His Book*, London, 1940; William Haller, *Foxe's Book of Martyrs and the Elect Nation*, London, 1963. E. R. Norman, *Anti-Catholicism in Victorian England*, London, 1968, p13, points out that the 1875 edition of Foxe included a print depicting the St Bartholomew's Day Massacre which took place after the original edition. Warren J. Wooden, 'John Foxe's Book of Martyrs and the Child Reaclei' in *Children's Books of the English Renaissance*, Kentucky, 1986, pp73–87. I am grateful to Carolyn Steedman for this reference.

66   Frank Hampson, the creator of *The Eagle's* Dan Dare, brought his career to a climax with a strip cartoon life of Jesus Christ in his autobiography *Before I Die Again*, London, 1992. Chad Varah, who went on to be the founder of the Samaritans, has little to say about his authorial role in the *Eagle* back-cover histories. In a more satiric vein, and enjoying a cult following in the Fourth and Fifth forms, is *Asterix* which, brilliantly translated from the French and with a heady mix of the topical, the antiquarian and a theatre of the absurd, has made Roman Gaul – and a tiny unoccupied part of it – a kind of paradigm for the emancipatory movements of today. (The footnotes at the back keep Asterix within the ambit of education; R. Goscinny and A. Uderzo, *French with Asterix: The Complete Guide*, London, 1993, recycles it for schools.)

67   Frances A. Yates, *The Art of Memory*, Harmondsworth 1978, pp124–27, 129–30.

68   Ibid., pp74–76.

69   Ibid., pp210–12, 217–18, 225–26.

70   M. T. Clanchy, *From Memory to Written Record, England 1066–1507*, first edn., London, 1979, p229.

71   Ibid., p230.

72   Sylvia Thrupp, *The Merchant Class of Medieval London*, Michigan, 1962, pp252–53.

73   George Henderson, *Early Medieval*, Harmondsworth, 1977, pp155–57.

74   Richard Vaughan, *Matthew Paris*, Cambridge, 1958, p211.

75   George Henderson, *Gothic*, Harmondsworth, 1978, p22.

76   'The idea of archaeology as fundamentally connected with artistic values was widely held', writes Philippa Levine in her interesting account of some of its nineteenth-century practitioners. 'Birch rounded off his descriptions by asserting that the value of archaeology was that it "aids in the formation and cultivation of public taste" . . . John Marsden on his appointment to England's first Chair of archaeology at Cambridge, talked of "the close connection between the antiquaries and the poet".' Philippa Levine, *The Amateur and the Professional*, p90.

77   Glyn Daniel, *A Hundred and Fifty Years of Archaeology*, London, 1950, p31.

78   Anastatic printing, a facsimile process invented in the 1840s, was widely used in antiquarian publication, as for example in illustrations of Old English churches. Geoffrey Wakeman, *Victorian Book Illustration*, Newton Abbot, 1973, pp51–55.

79   Archives of St John the Baptist Church, Bridgwater, cuttings book of the Rev. C. Bazell, 1888–90, has the Town Hall crowded for a series of such lectures. I am grateful to Rev. C. Pidoux for exhuming this and other records from the parish chest.

80   Hall's *Book of British Ballads*, London, 1842, contained upwards of four hundred wood engravings 'and was the first work of any consequence that presented a combination of the best artists of the time'. John Jackson, *A Treatise on Wood Engraving*, London, 1861, p564. Hall, a very successful literary impresario, is said to have been the original of *Martin Chuzzlewit's* Mr Pecksniff.

81   William Hone, *The Every-Day Book and Table Book: or Everlasting Calendar of Popular Amusements*, 3 vols, London, 1839.

82   Charles Roach Smith, *Catalogue of the Museum of London Antiquities*, London 1854; *Illustrations of Roman London*, London, 1859; *Collectanea Antiqua: Etchings and Notices of Ancient Remains, Illustrative of the Habits, Customs and History of Past Ages*, 7 vols, London, 1848–80.

83   Wright was an admirer and friend of George Cruikshank. One of his many compilations was *A History of Caricature and Grotesque in Literature and Art*, London, 1875. For an interesting but too brief profile of Wright, Richard M. Dorson, *The British Folklorists, A History*, London, 1968, pp61–66.

84   Thomas Wright, *Wanderings of an Antiquary*, London, 1856, pp186–87.

85   Thomas Wright, *The History of Ireland from the Earliest Period of the Irish Annals to the Present Time*, London, 1854, 3 vols.

86   Thomas Wright, *A History of Domestic Manners and Sentiments in England during the Middle Ages*, London, 1862.

87   R. D. Bramwell, *Elementary School Work, 1900–1925*, Durham, 1961, quoting the Board of Education's *Suggestions for the Considerations of Teachers*, London, 1918.

88   'The Exeter Exhibition of Handwork Illustrative of History', *History*, 7, 1923–24; L. Logie, *Self-Expression in a Junior School*, London, 1928, pp57–59.

89   C. S. and C. S. Orwin, *The Open Fields*, Oxford, 1938.

90   Michael Crichton, *Jurassic Park*, London, 1991.

Chapter 2

Roy Rosenzweig and David Thelen

THE PRESENCE OF THE PAST

Popular Uses of History in American Life

Patterns of popular historymaking

IN APRIL 1994, A YOUNG INTERVIEWER from Indiana University's Center for Survey Research called a 45-year-old man in Memphis, Tennessee. For the next thirty minutes the Memphis man, who owns a consulting company, eagerly described his encounters with the past. In the previous twelve months, he had seen "a lot of TV shows on history," read historical books, and visited at least one history museum. But he did more than passively absorb what others said about the past. One night, while he and his children were watching a TV program about black cowboys, "we got a picture of my great uncle who was a cowboy and, of course, I broke that out and showed it to them." As his children looked at the photograph, he told them what he had learned at family reunions from his mother, grandmother, and great-grandmother about their notable relative.

This man feels passionate about family history; he named "family genealogy" as one of his hobbies. He said he corresponds with a "European American" who has the same last name and wants to work with him on a joint family genealogy. And he makes sure his children get acquainted with his family's "rich history." He took them to a neighboring city so that they could see the headquarters of a major civil rights organization founded by his grandfather and housed in a building bearing his grandfather's name. They also visited another town in Tennessee, where "I can show them buildings that their grandfather had constructed." "In this society many blacks don't know their genealogy," he explained. "Therefore, so many of our kids don't grow up with a sense of self. . . . By knowing my genealogy I have known my family, and that has always made me want to leave something like they have left." He told the interviewer he was organizing his family reunion for the coming year.

In addition to family history, this man from Memphis wanted to learn more about African history. He cited the civil rights movement, in which he participated, as a historical event that affected him greatly and taught him, to "treat everybody, regardless of race, creed, or color, equally." When he talked of his "love for history," he did not speak indiscriminately. Gathering with his family or celebrating a holiday made him feel connected to the past, but only certain museums – those devoted to civil rights or the Vietnam War – moved him. And studying history in school did not leave him feeling especially engaged with the past.

This man, an enthusiastic popular historymaker, was far from unique among the 808 randomly selected Americans and the additional 645 African Americans, American Indians, and Mexican Americans who talked with us about the past. A 36-year-old Georgia truck driver had not been to a history museum, read a history book, or done research on his family's history during the previous year. He said that studying history in school, visiting historic sites, reading about history, and watching films about the past meant little to him. But he does have a coin collection that he adds to as he drops in on coin shops along his trucking routes. As a third grader, he found an 1879 silver dollar and "gave it to my daddy." After his father's death, "the coin was given back to me," and he started his own collection. His favorite coins, he said, include buffalo nickels and flying eagle and Indian head pennies, which he may associate with his mother's Cherokee ancestry. This family-based sense of history probably explains why he told our interviewer that he feels strongly connected to the past when getting together with his family or celebrating holidays.

Our respondents found myriad ways to investigate and forge links with their familial or individual pasts. A 33-year-old psychologist from New Jersey frequently adds to a collection of cups and saucers that started when her grandmother tried to assemble a usable set of china in the rubble of Germany after World War II. "I like things with a tradition, a history," the psychologist said. "I like being able to know where my things come from. My husband and I talk about this all the time – we are the carriers of history in my family. We come from now relatively small families, and we carry the history along. Someone has to be the carrier of the history in every family."

Even more frequently, the people we interviewed carried family history along in diaries, family trees, photo albums, and especially in personal memories, which they shared at family reunions, over the dinner table and around the Christmas tree. A 67-year-old West Virginia man, who grew up in an orphanage, explained the importance of his photo "portfolio full of the kids," which he often looks at. A 20-year-old Oklahoman noted that his family has just been updating "the book that's been passed down from generation to generation" and includes "all our relatives from the 1850s." Embracing new technology, the family has begun to "video my great-great-grandpa" telling his favorite stories, particularly one of a dramatic battle between Indians and settlers. Such attempts to preserve familial history sometimes reflect deeply felt obligations. Investigating his family history, a 30-year-old Long Island truck driver explained, is "a promise I made to my brother before he died; it's always on my mind."

Most Americans pursue the histories of their families; many also explore histories that extend beyond their families. A 73-year-old storekeeper from a small town in central Texas reported that she avidly reads anything she finds on Texas history. She is knowledgeable about local buildings, and says, "I like to pass this down to the younger generation." Another Texas woman in her seventies loves to read "pioneer stories about the settling of the West, the opening up of the Dakota territory, and the Yukon" as well as biographies of Winston Churchill and of Eleanor Roosevelt, whom she admires as a "forerunner . . . who pushed for women's equality."

Hobbyists ardently track the past beyond their family circles. A 20-year-old social work student from a medium-sized city in Oklahoma spends two hours a day working with an African dance group. Dance gives her a "better sense of where I come from." In high school, she complained, "they didn't teach anything" about African American or African culture. Her dancing and her study of the "history behind it" not only give her a sense of "something that was done by my ancestors" but also "can contribute to the African American community." Her interests in African and African American history go beyond dance, inflecting her reading (shortly before talking with us, she'd finished Chinua Achebe's *Things Fall Apart*) and her travel (she said she was planning a trip to Africa and had journeyed to Atlanta to visit Martin Luther King Jr.'s home).

A young mother from Kentucky feels a passionate commitment to the past that has led her in a very different direction. Like the Oklahoma student, she criticized the history she had been taught in high school but said she found deep meaning instead in Civil War reenactments: "I think it's important for people to remember to never forget. . . . We are from the South, and it is important to be proud of our history even if the people from the North think so or not." This Kentucky woman uses the past to think about the present, including current political issues like the display of the Confederate flag. She believes that "our history" is being stolen by the NAACP, which is trying to "take away our right to display our flag," as well as by the Klan and the skinheads who want to appropriate the Confederate flag "as a symbol of hatred." Americans, she said, fought the war over "states' rights" rather than slavery: "Many, many, many" of "our ancestors who fought in the Civil War . . . did not even own slaves." Civil War reenactment "preserv[es] our right to remember our history the way we want to do it . . . instead of the way some of the history books have portrayed it."

Americans, as these sketches show, make the past part of their everyday routines and turn to it as a way of grappling with profound questions about how to live. The people who talked with us did not view the past as distant, abstract, or insignificant. Quite the contrary: through their understanding of the past, this cross section of Americans addressed questions about relationships, identity, immortality, and agency. They also used the past for the business of everyday life – maintaining family and community ties and trying to deal with family health problems. For the young mother from Kentucky, learning about ancestors who fought in the Civil War helped her understand "where I come from." For the man from Memphis, the civil rights movement taught a basic moral lesson about racial equality. For the New Jersey psychologist and her husband, collecting old china perpetuated the memory of their family and themselves to pass down to future generations. For the Oklahoma student, hearing about the past from her mother and grandmother "makes me feel I have a lot of responsibility for what goes on in the world" and "helps me realize the things I need to do in the future."

This chapter provides an overview of what Americans told us about popular historymaking – especially about more formal activities, from watching historical films to investigating family history. The overview illuminates a conclusion that underlies the entire book: people pursue the past actively and make it part of everyday life. The stories of the 1,453 individual Americans we called and the statistical summaries of their responses impress us with the *presence* of the past – its ubiquity and its connection to current-day concerns – rather than its frequently bemoaned absence.

How, when, and why Americans pursue the past: A statistical overview

The pundits who describe Americans as uninterested in history don't seem to be talking about the people we surveyed. Asked whether they had participated in past-related activities during the previous year, more than half said that they had looked at photos with family and friends, taken photos or videos to preserve memories, watched movies or TV programs about the past, attended a reunion, visited a history museum, or read a history book. Between one and two fifths told us that they had joined a historical group, written in a journal or diary, investigated their family's history, or participated in a hobby or worked on a collection related to the past (see Table 1). Almost no one (only 7 of the 808 people interviewed in our national sample) reported that they did *none* of the ten activities we asked about.[1]

Of course, these numbers don't tell the whole story. One of the seven people who answered "no" to all our questions about history-related activities, for example, was an

Table 1 Percentage of Americans surveyed who have done the following in the past 12 months

Looked at photographs with family or friends	91%
Taken photographs or videos to preserve memories	83
Watched any movies or television programs about the past	81
Attended a family reunion or a reunion of some other group of people with whom you have a shared experience	64
Visited any history museums or historic sites	57
Read any books about the past	53
Participated in any hobbies or worked on any collections related to the past	39
Looked into the history of your family or worked on your family tree	36
Written in a journal or diary	29
Participated in a group devoted to studying, preserving, or presenting the past	20

82-year-old widow in Texas who reported that she "never goes out now" except to bowl with other senior citizens on Wednesday afternoons. But she still spent much of her time thinking about the past. "I remember those people that lived around me," she explained to a youthful interviewer. "They were so nice, the people . . . around where I live."

To find out more than the simple frequency of activities, we asked our respondents to use a 10-point scale to describe the intensity of their engagement with the past. Most had no trouble assigning a number between 1 and 10 to describe how "connected to the past" they felt when they celebrated holidays, gathered with their families, studied history in school, read history books, visited history museums and historic sites, and watched historical films and television programs (see Table 2). If we decide that a choice of 8, 9, or 10 indicates a close association with the past, then more than half our respondents felt very strongly connected to the past on holidays, at family gatherings, and in museums.

A 32-year-old physical therapist reported feeling most connected to the past in the three contexts most often given by our respondents. Asked to explain why he felt connected to the past at holiday celebrations, he answered, "Usually when you celebrate holidays, you have your ancestors there – your grandmothers and great-grandmothers. They're bringing a part of their traditions and so forth into the celebration." For him, all family events evoked the past: "Because when you gather with your family, everyone has stories about the way things used to be. It's always story time. We don't gather for that particular purpose,

Table 2 How connected to the past do you feel (1–10 scale)?

	Percent choosing		
	Mean	*8–10*	*1–3*
Gathering with your family	7.9	67.7	6.7
Visiting a history museum or historic site	7.3	56.0	8.6
Celebrating a holiday	7.0	52.7	13.8
Reading a book about the past	6.5	39.5	12.0
Watching a movie or television program about the past	6.0	27.4	14.0
Studying history in school	5.7	27.8	20.8

but we always end up telling stories, and it inevitably ends up being about what life was like when they were kids."

Although respondents described the past as being with them in many settings, they shared the sense that the familial and intimate past, along with intimate uses of other pasts, mattered most. More than two thirds said that they felt very strongly connected to the past when gathering with their families; more than half said the same about visiting museums and historic sites and celebrating holidays – activities they usually did with family members.[2] Only 16 people in the national sample gave gathering with their family the lowest possible "connectedness" score of 1.

Respondents felt most unconnected to the past when they encountered it in books, movies, or classrooms. They felt most connected when they encountered the past with the people who mattered the most to them, and they often pursued the past in ways that drew in family and friends. Five sixths of those surveyed took pictures to preserve memories of their experiences; more than nine tenths looked at photographs with family and friends; more than one third worked on their family trees or investigated the history of their families; almost two thirds attended reunions – three quarters of them family reunions.[3] More than half of the respondents who pursued hobbies or collections related to the past said that family members had initially interested them in that hobby or that the hobby preserved a family tradition. Typically, a 25-year-old student from Massachusetts described refinishing a small chest and dollhouse from her grandmother that she wants "to pass down as an heirloom . . . if I have a daughter someday."

Respondents put great trust in relatives. Asked to rank the trustworthiness of sources for information about the past, respondents gave a mean score of 8.0 to "personal accounts from your grandparents or other relatives" – compared, for example, to a 5.0 for movies and television programs. More than two thirds gave grandparents a rating of 8, 9, or 10; only about one third gave high school teachers such a high ranking (see Table 3). Forty-six people (out of 808 in our national survey) described movies and television as "not at all" trustworthy (by giving them a score of 1); only seven said the same about accounts from grandparents and other relatives. People who talked with us preferred the personal and the firsthand, with one exception: respondents ranked history museums even higher than personal accounts from relatives. But some of the reasoning behind their choices – museums appeared to contain authentic objects from the past, people visited museums with other family members – confirmed the same desire for unmediated experience.

Whatever questions we asked, respondents emphasized the importance they attached to the intimate past and intimate uses of the past. Asked to "name a person, either a historic figure or someone from your personal past, who has particularly affected you," 52 percent

Table 3 Trustworthiness of sources on 10-point scale

| | *Percent choosing* | | |
	Mean	*8–10*	*1–3*
Museums	8.4	79.9	1.3
Personal accounts from grandparents or other relatives	8.0	68.9	2.4
Conversation with someone who was there (witness)	7.8	64.4	2.8
College history professors	7.3	54.3	5.2
High school teachers	6.6	35.5	8.8
Non-fiction books	6.4	32.1	9.1
Movies and television programs	5.0	11.0	22.3

named family members – 29 percent parents, 14 percent grandparents, 9 percent other family members – while 36 percent named public or historical figures. Reminded that the past includes "everything from the very recent past to the very distant past, from your personal and family past to the past of the United States and other nations," respondents were asked, "What event or period in the past has most affected you?" Again, the largest number (nearly two fifths) mentioned a purely personal event like the birth, death, marriage, or divorce of a loved one.

For many respondents the line blurred between "personal" and "national" pasts. Some turned national events into settings for personal stories. For example, more than a tenth reported a public event in which they participated (most often by fighting in a war); more than a quarter chose a public event that had personal significance. Rather than abstractly discussing the significance of World War II or the assassination of John F. Kennedy, they talked about how such an event had figured in their personal development or the setting in which they heard about it. Only one in five chose a public event without also indicating some personal association with that event.

We tried to get at how people thought about the past when we asked which past was most important to them: that of their family, their ethnic or racial group, their community, or the United States. Sixty-six percent named the past of their family. Twenty-two percent named the United States, 8 percent chose their racial or ethnic group, and 4 percent chose their community. Ethnic and racial groups varied in how they responded to this question. But every subgroup of the population – men and women; young and old; rich and poor; white, black, and Indian – listed family history first. To put the statistical findings of our study in a single sentence: Almost every American deeply engages the past, and the past that engages them most deeply is that of their family.

How Americans create their own history

To get a fuller sense of how Americans use the past in their everyday lives, we need to look more closely at the ten past-related activities asked about. On the surface we might distinguish between the four activities that involve interpreting historical information constructed by others (watching films, reading books, visiting museums, looking at photos) and the six that require people to construct, record, or conserve their own version of the past (taking photos, sharing experiences at a reunion, investigating family history, working on hobbies or collections, writing in a journal or diary, taking part in a group interested in the past). But this distinction between "reading" and "writing" the past doesn't always hold. A college student dragged to a family reunion where he half-listens to relatives talk about experiences he views as distant and unimportant is passively consuming history constructed by others. A woman who visits a museum with her children and enthusiastically tells them about connections to their family is actively interpreting and constructing her own historical narrative.

Many respondents told us, for example, about films and books that sparked reminiscences or family discussions. A 39-year-old Alabama woman fondly recalled films on John and Jacqueline Kennedy because "when I see something like that it makes me relate to my childhood, what age I was, what I was doing at that time, what grade I was in, things that I liked to do at that time. I guess it brings back a lot of memories of being in the early sixties." A 46-year-old Arizona woman liked books on the Civil War because her "great-great-great-grandfather was a scoundrel" who was represented by Abraham Lincoln in "the first case he ever lost back in Illinois." A 30-year-old custodian from California remembered reading a biography of Martin Luther King Jr. because his mother had told him about living in the civil rights era "and the things [King] went through when she was growing up." A 27-year-old Rochester glass coater said family reunions linked him to the past because his relatives described the days when his southern sharecropper ancestors picked okra. He noted that the television series *Roots* made him feel equally connected to the past: "There are some things . . . depicted in the movie that my parents and grandparents have gone through – just working in the field most of their life."

If people engage, discuss, use, and interpret the past while watching movies and reading books, they grapple even more directly with the past when they investigate family history or do other things that require (rather than just permit) them to confront memories and artifacts. To borrow a set of categories familiar to professional historians, we can say that millions of Americans regularly document, preserve, research, narrate, discuss, and study the past.

The largest number of respondents talked about documenting the past. Almost one third wrote in diaries or journals. More than four fifths documented historical memories by taking photos or videos, and many shot their photos with a clear archival purpose. "A photograph helps stimulate the memory," said an Albuquerque contractor; it's also something "to show to other people and so that my son can see things that he won't remember and he'll be able to . . . know about us and our lives." Recalling a picture he took of his son wearing a towel "as though it were Batman's cape," the man explained, "he was in this one moment or one stage where Batman means everything to him and I wanted to be able to remember him. . . . It's hard to remember things. . . . If I don't write them down or take pictures, they fly out of my memory."

Many people who keep diaries and journals are attempting to preserve a family record for posterity. A 51-year-old Louisiana nurse said her diary contained "just everyday things – family get-togethers, things that happened at work, the weather . . . the birth of a niece, visiting with a brother from out of town . . . a wedding in the family." "I've done that for ever since I can remember," she explained. "As the years pass, you forget everyday events, but if you write them down you can recall them for yourself and you'll be able to pass this information down to your kids, nieces, and nephews."

Respondents not only discussed this impulse to document the past, they also talked about their efforts to preserve pieces of it. They said they turned photo albums and diaries into treasured artifacts passed from one generation to the next. A 30-year-old South Dakota woman described the "family book" and "family tree" that she was preparing "for my kids." One contained "pictures and paragraphs" of family members going back to the "third generation of grandparents"; the other compiled "stories" about what relatives "were like." Popular preservationists also collect objects that link them or their children to the past. A 42-year-old floral designer from Maryland, raised by her grandparents, explained that she collects kitchen items from the 1940s and 1950s because "it just brings back childhood memories. . . . They were things that my grandmother had too." A retired Missouri woman had recently "dug up some quilts" that belonged to her mother, who "was a very pioneer lady." She told the youthful questioner that she planned to turn them into bedspreads for her "boys" as "a memento from their grandmother."

Collections and hobbies often connect different generations. Many respondents talked about relatives who inspired them – a grandmother who started a South Carolina man on collecting 1930s glassware; another grandmother who started an Illinois woman on collecting old teapots; an uncle who started a Georgia man on collecting trains; a grandfather who started a New York man on collecting coins. A remarkable 39 percent of our respondents worked on a hobby or collection related to the past.

This energetic preservation of the past often requires research. The South Dakota woman who was assembling a "family book" questions relatives about "what they did and when they came over from different countries" and asks them to identify and talk about people in old photos she has gathered. Other respondents, particularly genealogists, told us they spend years searching through courthouses, cemeteries, microfilms, old newspapers, birth and death records, wills, and Civil War pension files. One third of the Americans we interviewed were involved in tracing their family's history – which suggests that more historical research is done on families in this country than on any other subject.

After researching and preserving the past, popular historymakers often create narratives in the form of photo albums, family trees, and family heirlooms. Even more often, they craft oral narratives that they pass on in casual dinner conversations, while watching television, or at reunions, family gatherings, and holiday celebrations. When we asked people why they felt connected to the past at family gatherings, they immediately (and often in great detail) described stories shared on such occasions – narratives of adversity, struggle, and accomplishment or narratives of adventure, nostalgia, and humor. A 47-year-old New Jersey police officer recounted "just reminiscing about the ol' days, talking about fathers and grandfathers and how it was way back when. . . . How you made the most out of very little."

Probably less than 10 percent of our respondents formally studied the past after they left school. One fifth of them belonged to groups related to the past, but fewer than half of these groups study, rather than preserve or present, the past. Evangelical Christians, African Americans, and American Indians, however, showed more interest in formally studying the past. Evangelical Christians said Bible study groups allowed them to examine the past and "the way [it] relates to now," in the words of a 32-year-old Kentucky woman. Several black Americans described informal African American history study groups. A 45-year-old counselor from Cleveland explained that her group "doesn't necessarily have a name" but that it brings together people who "are studying African American history" to find out "the validity of the information we have been given." "For my race of people," she continued, "knowledge" is "the only [thing] that can turn [us] around." One quarter of the Sioux we interviewed (versus one fifth of the overall national sample) participated in groups that study, preserve, or present the past; almost all those groups – the Wounded Knee Pine Ridge Survivors Association, Lakota culture classes, and the Big Foot and Memorial Riders, for example – focus on Indian culture. Through the Grey Eagles Society, a member explained, "elderly tribal members . . . tell about history" and "try to preserve the culture."

Respondents described their activities but didn't necessarily say which of them required the most commitment, energy, and passion. They gave us clues, however, when they talked about a pursuit without any prompting. In our survey, the interviewers took down spontaneous comments. Activities that involved engaging and interpreting historical information constructed by others ("reading the past") provoked relatively few and relatively brief spontaneous comments; activities that required people to construct, record, or conserve their own history ("writing the past") evoked considerably more – almost twice as many – and considerably longer spontaneous responses, even though fewer people took part in those activities. Of the 653 people who reported watching a historical film or television program, only 11 wanted to immediately discuss what they had seen. Although just 290 reported looking into the history of their family, 61 quickly volunteered comments about their historical investigations. Before our interviewer asked about investigating family history, a 71-year-old Philadelphia woman said that she organized annual family reunions, researched the history of her family, and encouraged younger family members to carry the story farther back into the nineteenth century.[4]

Both broad social patterns and particular family histories suggest why some people passionately recover their family histories while others fanatically preserve objects like old kitchen utensils and still others avidly document the past through photos or diaries. Women and men, for example, tend to select different hobbies and collections – quilts and china versus trains and tools. And gifts from grandparents often launch lifelong collections.

But some preferences in historical pursuits – what could be called "historical tastes" – are as difficult to explain as tastes in music, food, and clothes.

Such tastes emerged over and over in our interviews. "I like biographies," noted a Danville, Illinois, woman. An Indiana woman explained her fondness for westerns: "I just like the idea that they had to ride horses and go bareback and they had to hunt for deer and stuff." A 58-year-old Phoenix woman said, "I like tools, wooden spoons, things that can be used day-to-day" as well as "old cookbooks." Other respondents embraced general categories of historical activities. "I always loved to hear my mother tell me stories about the past," said a northern Virginia woman. "I'm a picture nut," reported a 56-year-old Illinois woman who described her particular interest in "family pictures." "My husband loves museums and history," explained a 30-year-old woman from Raleigh, North Carolina. "I like the old cemeteries," noted an Ohio woman, "because I work in a new cemetery and they have so many restrictions. . . . The old cemeteries don't have those restrictions, they have a lot of history in them. The old cemeteries have so many different sizes and types of stones, and you're not going to see that in these new cemeteries." The pursuit of the past is a national preoccupation, it seems, but one with many variations.

Who pursues the past?

Social and demographic variables sometimes predict behavior: in general, wealthy people play golf and working-class people go bowling; women sew and men build shelves. But not always. We spent considerable time with computers and statistical programs looking for variations in patterns of responses based on age, income, education, race, and gender. What we learned can be summarized very simply: participation in historical activities is not for the most part tied to particular social groups or back-grounds.[5]

Black and white Americans, for example, participate in pretty much the same set of historical activities over the course of a year.[6] So do Sioux and Mexican Americans.[7] These broad similarities should not mislead us into thinking that Mexican Americans, American Indians, and African Americans stand in precisely the same relationship to the past as white European Americans. African Americans and American Indians, for example, offered somewhat different answers from white Americans to our questions about connectedness to the past and trust of historical authorities. In general, blacks and Indians seem more likely to distrust mainstream sources of historical authority. African Americans, for instance, trust historical information from schoolteachers and books less than white European Americans do. Moreover, although non-whites center history on their families and pursue pretty much the same set of activities as whites, they take different meanings away from those experiences.

While sociodemographic variables like race, age, and income do not fundamentally explain whether people participate in historical activities, education and gender do have some effect on patterns of participation. For example, people with more education more often read historical books, write in journals and diaries, visit history museums, watch history films, and participate in historical groups.[8] Almost two thirds of the college graduates we interviewed had read a book about the past during the previous year, compared to fewer than one third of the people who had not graduated high school; more than one third of the college graduates had written in a journal or diary, compared to one sixth of the people who hadn't gone beyond high school. Perhaps not surprisingly, education can give people tools that make it easier to participate in historical activities and deal with institutions (like museums) or cultural objects (like books) that assume a certain amount of literacy and historical knowledge.

At the same time, the differences in levels of participation are often relatively small – 35 percent of those with high school education or less participate in hobbies or collections related to the past, compared to 41 percent of those with a college degree. And Americans who don't have college degrees told us that they feel just as connected to the past as those with more education. Demographic variables explain even less about a sense of connectedness to the past than about the level of participation in historical activities.[9]

Our survey offers little support for the claim that an interest in the past or in formal history is the property of "elites." Income, for example, significantly affects participation in only one activity: taking photographs or videos, which requires money to purchase the equipment. And even when education sharply inflects the pursuit of a particular activity, many people with limited education still participate. More than twice as many college graduates as non-high school graduates had read a history book or visited a history museum or historic site in the past year. Yet about one third of those without a high school degree had done both.

The possible associations between gender and historymaking present some of the most exciting themes for speculation and further research. Women reported higher levels of participation in seven of the ten historical activities we asked about; they also told us they felt more connected to the past in two of the six settings we described. More women than men took photos (84 percent of women compared with 82 percent of men), wrote in journals (34 percent compared with 24 percent), attended family reunions (68 percent compared with 59 percent), investigated their family's past (42 percent compared with 29 percent), and participated in groups devoted to studying, preserving, or presenting the past (22 percent compared with 18 percent). More women than men said they felt strongly connected to the past at holiday celebrations (with a mean score of 7.6 for women and 6.3 for men) and family gatherings (a mean score of 8.3 for women and 7.4 for men).[10]

For women, as for men, the intimate and familial past matters most, but for women it is even *more* important. When we asked people which of four different "areas of the past" – that of your family, your racial or ethnic group, the community in which you now live, or the United States – is "most important to you," 73 percent of the women selected family history, compared to 58 percent of the men. When we asked about a person from the past who'd had an important effect on them, two fifths of male and three fifths of female respondents chose a family member.[11] And women preferred activities – investigating the lives of ancestors, writing in journals and diaries, attending reunions – concerned with family history.

In their answers to follow-up questions, too, some women illustrated how they pursued the past to maintain family ties or continuity. Not only did more women than men report keeping journals, they apparently kept them for different reasons. Of the twenty respondents who described a diary or journal as a permanent family record, sixteen were women.[12] Asked what sorts of things she wrote in her journal or diary, a female executive from Cleveland at first diminished the project: "To be honest with you, they were just day-to-day things about interactions with family." But then she added that she thought it gave her a "touch of immortality" to leave a document in which "my children and grandchildren will be able to read what I was thinking on that day."

An 80-year-old widow noted that her work on family history had been sparked by her granddaughter: gathering "all the information before I pass on" is "important so my granddaughter will know what has happened in the family on my side because her mother has also passed away and I'm the only one left on my side." A 63-year-old retired woman from Missouri said that her mother "was working on" a family history when "she passed away last August." After some of the respondent's children and cousins began asking questions about the family, she "took over what [my mother] had been doing." A 58-year-old manufacturer's representative from New York explained that she doesn't "make a study of" family history, but relatives always turn to her for information because "my mother was the record keeper and I have all her books." Family members, our respondents told us, often turn to women, especially older women, for information about the family's past. Of eighteen people who said that requests from other relatives sparked their investigations of family history, fourteen were women – all but two of them more than fifty years old.[13]

Though just as many men as women had hobbies or collections related to the past, women undertook them for quite distinct reasons. Thirty-six respondents described their hobbies or collections as ways to maintain family ties or traditions; thirty of them were women.[14] A Tampa woman reported that her husband collects fishing rods from the early 1900s, while she restores "granny's quilt" from the 1880s. "I want to give it to my daughter one day," she explained. A young mother in Baton Rouge uses her skill at calligraphy to create a "time capsule book" that she will give to her daughter when she turns sixteen.

Both men and women care about the past. Most of the men we interviewed care passionately about family history and feel strongly connected to the past at family gatherings. But the words *past* and *history* (understood as the world of presidents and treaties) may have gendered associations in American society. Men occupy most seats around Civil War roundtables, for example, and three times as many men as women join the History Book Club, which emphasizes military and political history.[15] By contrast, many Americans see the job of maintaining a sense of continuity with the past broadly defined as part of "women's work" within the family. Women often take responsibility for compiling and maintaining family stories and records; they feel comfortable in the more expansive, yet intimate, realm of the past.

But the statistical evidence is not clear cut and some of it can be used to point up other patterns. Men, for example, were more likely than women (by a 40 to 35 percent margin) to select personal instead of public events as the ones most important to them. Men and women felt equally disconnected from the past when they studied history in school. Both men and women were more likely to participate in activities to sustain their families than in more public and formal activities, more likely to attend a family reunion than to read a book about the past, and more likely to investigate the history of their families than to take part in a group devoted to studying or preserving the past. Both men and women felt more connected to the past when they gathered with their families than in any other setting.

When and how Americans engage the past: Formal and informal, unplanned and passionate encounters with the past

Many of the Americans we interviewed "read" accounts of the past – especially in books or films – relatively casually. Although more than four fifths of them had seen a historical film or television program in the past year and more than half had read a history book, few had much to say about them. "I must have read something – right offhand I can't think of what it was," a Minnesota woman remarked. Indeed, only one third of the respondents mentioned specific film titles or TV shows, even when prompted to describe the "kinds of movies or television programs about the past you like."[16] These vague comments contrast sharply with their more detailed commentary on other historical activities. Not surprisingly, perhaps, films and books were two of the three experiences that summoned up the least sense of connection to the past.

The only activity that elicited even less of a sense of connection was the one most widely shared: studying history in school. While respondents spoke of films and books with indifference, they described studying history in vividly negative terms. When we asked some of them "to pick one word or phrase to describe your experiences with history classes in elementary or high school," almost three fifths chose such words as "irrelevant," "incomplete," "dry," or, most commonly, "boring." In the entire study, respondents almost never described encounters with the past as boring – except when they talked about school. "I hated it," a 60-year-old Yonkers, New York, woman said when we asked why she had given studying history her lowest possible score on the connectedness scale.

Obviously, respondents didn't view their most pervasive and formal encounters with the past as the most profound. They often reserved their enthusiasm for unplanned or incidental encounters with the past. Most museum visits, by the evidence of this survey, occur during trips undertaken with some other goal – usually a vacation – in view. "We were on vacation . . . to Sea World and came back through Canton, Ohio, and stopped by the McKinley museum," explained a school custodian from a medium-sized city in Ohio. "I was passing through the town, Carthage, Missouri," recalled a home health aide who lived near Joplin, Missouri. "It was a museum of guns, of Winchester guns and the history of something . . . old guns, stuff from the world war. My husband wanted to go through it; so we did."[17]

Given these often incidental circumstances, it comes as a surprise to learn that visits to museums and historic sites made respondents feel extremely connected to the past. Part of the reason, it seems, is that Americans believe they uncover "real" or "true" history at museums and historic sites. Some sense of the power of encountering a "piece of the true cross"[18] can be glimpsed in the story of a Long Island truck driver who felt more connected to the past when visiting a historic site than when gathering with his family or watching a movie: "I was with a friend – we were stationed in Germany ten or fifteen years ago – and he had a very good knowledge of Roman history. We went out looking for old Roman walls. I figured they were going to be like brick and we wouldn't find them till I fell off them. They were hills! They were thirty feet high, and I suddenly realized they were these old defensive works still standing there after a thousand years." Museums and historic sites also worked a powerful magic because they evoked immediate personal and familial connections. Asked why she had recently visited the Cahokia Indian mounds near East St. Louis, an Indiana woman said, "I wanted my little girl to see something . . . I've seen when I was little."

For this woman and many other respondents, visits to historic sites and museums sparked an associative process of recalling and reminiscing about the past that connected them to their own history. Their visits – far from a passive viewing of a version of the past arranged by a museum professional – became a joint venture of constructing their own histories either mentally or in conversation with their friends and kin. Although respondents said movies and books occasionally stimulated associative reminiscing, they often portrayed museum visits – made in small groups, generally with members of their immediate family – as collective and collaborative.

Looking at old photos also inspired collective reminiscing. When we asked people the reasons or occasions for looking at photographs with family or friends, they described how holidays, family gatherings, birthdays, and funerals led to creating collaborative narratives about the past. "On holidays," reported a young Minneapolis housewife, "you just all get together and start talking about what happened, a specific incident usually, and somebody says 'let me go get the album.'"

Family gatherings and reunions may not start out as deliberate efforts to investigate or examine the past, but they often turn into the equivalent of historical seminars. A 35-year-old female dispatcher from Tennessee described how the past saturates a setting not normally labeled "historical": "You are with family and friends and there is a lot of remembering. . . . The older people get together and talk about the past and they are just remembering things you did when you were a child. . . . There will be a lot of things that you have not talked about in a long time, that you do not necessarily have the time to think about in everyday life. Being with family, somebody will bring up something that leads to something else, and then it starts a conversation about something that happened twenty years ago."

We tried the patience of our interviewees by asking them to explain why family gatherings made them feel so connected to the past, since the answer seemed evident to them. A 44-year-old painter from a dairy-processing town in central Wisconsin explained why he felt more connected to the past in family gatherings than in any other setting: "These are people you have a lot in common with. I'm sure you never get together without bringing up the past; it's something that always pops up. It's your own personal past that you're talking about versus going to a museum, something more impersonal, not connected to you. Any time you gather for a wedding or a funeral – essentially the whole family is present – you bring up deceased relatives or probably happy occasions when we were all children; you remember something fond."

Exploring family history, like visiting a museum, could be casual. "I've discussed it, but I haven't really gone into detail," a Pennsylvania nurse explained somewhat apologetically. An Albuquerque man ascribed his interest in family history to "curiosity" and noted that he hadn't written anything down or looked at a genealogy and that his research consisted of "discussions I have with my family when I'm around them." But after a pause, he explained some deeper motivations: he wanted "to learn who my ancestors were because I feel as though I am a derivative of them and to find out a little more about who I am."

Respondents described how their investigations of history sometimes emerged serendipitously out of family gatherings; at other times they proceeded quite deliberately. Asked why she had looked into her family's past, a Mexican immigrant replied, "We were trying to make a booklet on our history to distribute to all the [150] members of the family" at the annual reunion. "I called some relatives and we decided it was time to make a family tree." Other respondents – particularly those few who described themselves as genealogists – turned investigating family history into a passionate and systematic pursuit. An Indiana factory worker reported that he had used local and national records as well as conversations with his grandparents to trace his family back to Scotland.

Hundreds of thousands of Americans who do not earn their living as history professionals dedicate considerable time, money, and even love to historical pursuits. They volunteer at local historical organizations, lead tours of historic houses, don uniforms for battle reenactments, repair old locomotives for the railway history society, subscribe to *American Heritage* and *American History Illustrated*, maintain the archives for their trade union or church, assemble libraries from the History Book Club, construct family genealogies, restore old houses, devise and play World War II board games, collect early twentieth-century circus memorabilia, and lobby to preserve art deco movie houses. These amateur historians might be considered a third group, distinct from the history professionals who pursue the past for a living and the popular historymakers who made up the bulk of our study.

We encountered many amateur historians. One fifth of those we interviewed reported that they took part in a group that studies, preserves, or presents the past. And two fifths said that they had a hobby or collection related to the past. Many more people watch movies or look at old photos, but hobbyists, collectors, and group members tend to devote considerably more time. (A railroad conductor from an Ohio manufacturing city reported that he spent about a hundred hours per year on his hobby of rebuilding antique farm machinery.) Projecting these results nationally shows that startlingly large numbers of people – 76 million – undertake hobbies and collections related to the past.[19] Even if we decided that only one quarter of the people who said they had worked on a hobby or collection in the previous year were moderately serious about these pursuits, our survey would suggest that 20 million Americans pursue historical hobbies and collections.

Similar projections would put millions of Americans in past-related organizations. To be sure, many respondents defined past-connected groups more broadly than professional historians might: they frequently cited Bible study groups and environmental organizations (since they preserved the past of nature) along with more conventional historical and genealogical societies and hobbyist groups – from the Daughters of the American Revolution to the National Antique Fire Truck Association and the Plymouth Genealogical Society.[20]

These groups include some people – amateur historians – who give much of their free time to historical pursuits. We talked with a retired electrical engineer who had spent six years as a director and three years as president of his local historical society; he also volunteered at a nearby historical museum, working on "some antique horological materials . . . cataloging, repairing, and preparing exhibits." He attributed his original enthusiasm for old timepieces to a pocket watch that his grandfather had given him; then his annoyance at a local watchmaker led him to sign up for an evening course in watch repair. "As is my usual practice," he explained, "I got out lists of books on the subject . . . starting with my interest as a mechanic – that is, my interest in small mechanisms. It increased to an interest in the history of timepieces, both the technology, the philosophy, the social aspects, and so on. And so I became a member of the National Association of Watch and Clock Collectors, and it is through the local chapter that we're doing this work at the museum."

Hobbyists' passions are extraordinarily eclectic. We talked to collectors of old barn paintings, Christian art, needlework, quilts, stamps, coins, Australian money, World War II relics, photos, beer mirrors, tractors, motorcycles, cars, liberty bells, fire equipment, books, trains, china, watches, dolls, clocks, Victorian wreaths, arrowheads, folk art, carpentry tools, old newspaper clippings, early American glass, railroad schedules, bird plates, toby jugs, Indian artifacts, comic cards, old LPs, baseball cards, and Pete Rose items. We also encountered a smaller, but equally diverse, group of people who construct or reconstruct items with historic associations: old tractors and antique cars; needlework and dolls; wooden golf clubs and wooden airplanes; Native American baskets, beadwork, and ceramic sculptures.

These diverse collections and hobbies often inspired great dedication. No other questions (except perhaps those about family gatherings) received such lengthy answers and revealed such close links between historical pursuits and everyday life. A 38-year-old Oklahoma man, who collects motorcycles, could have been speaking for many when he answered our question about "some of the reasons" for his collection by saying: "It is my life." A number of hobbyists and genealogists were so avid in their pursuit of the past that our phone call interrupted them in what seems to be a constant preoccupation. A Florida man, asked about his interest in family history, replied: "Right now in front of me, I'm working on the saga of my great-uncle – he was in Corregidor Island in the Philippines. . . . I've got about 325 pages written about his experiences." When we asked another man about his hobbies and collections, he said: "I'm downstairs polishing antique fire extinguishers for a collection."[21]

Although some hobbyists operate alone, they often create nurturing subcommunities. An Ohio junior high school teacher who collects folk art (and whose husband collects Civil War objects) noted that they meet regularly with other local antique dealers and collectors. "It's a hobby," she observes, "but it's also like a counterculture of people . . . a different breed of people. It's just a very comfortable group of people. You never feel like you don't belong there."

Americans feel at home with the past; day to day, hour to hour, the past is present in their lives. Encountering the past, examining it, interpreting it, living and reliving it, they root themselves in families – biological or constructed – and root their families in the world. Maybe we shouldn't have been surprised that the Americans we called welcomed us so graciously into their lives, shared their memories and their passions, allowed us to be part of their present and their past – allowed us, in a sense, to join the family. Their openness made our survey an arena for cultural conversation, the sort of joint venture they told us they enjoyed. Respondents spent an average of thirty-nine minutes – thirty minutes in the national sample and fifty-one minutes in the minority sample – conversing with people they didn't know.[22] Twenty-one people stayed on the phone for more than two hours; hundreds more took out substantial time to speak with a stranger about their intimate uses of the past.

Everyone a historian

Roy Rosenzweig

History professionals – like most professionals – tend to emphasize the differences between themselves and others. Those who "do" history for a living (whether schoolteachers, university-based historians, museum curators, historic preservationists, documentary filmmakers, staff members at local historical societies, or other public historians) sometimes see non-professionals as ignorant of and uninterested in the past. In his 1989 presidential address to the members of the American Historical Association, the leading bastion of professional historians in the United States, Louis R. Harlan deplored the "present public ignorance of our cultural heritage." "This ignorance and indifference," he argued in a statement that has been echoed by many other history professionals, "has alarming implications for the future of our nation and our historical profession."[1]

The 1,500 people we have quoted in these pages refute the idea that Americans don't care about the past. Two fifths of our respondents, for example, reported that they pursue a hobby or collection related to the past, and they spoke of those pursuits with words like "love" and "passion." An Oklahoma man summarized his reasons for collecting old motor-cycles in one sentence: "It is my life." Two thirds of our respondents described themselves as deeply connected to the past at family gatherings; and the stories they told indicate how the past figures in some of the most intimate corners of their lives. A northern Virginia woman said, "I always loved to hear my mother tell stories about the past," and her comment was typical. Like professional historians, these popular historymakers crafted their own narratives, albeit as dinner-table conversations or family trees rather than scholarly mono-graphs. They preferred constructing their own versions of the past to digesting those prepared by others, and they viewed other sources and narratives with sharply critical eyes. Everyone, as Carl Becker famously observed, is his or her own historian.[2]

Moreover, there is nothing abstract or antiquarian about popular historymaking. In these interviews, the most powerful meanings of the past come out of the dialogue between the past and the present, out of the ways the past can be used to answer pressing current-day questions about relationships, identity, immortality, and agency. Indeed, this was a point that Becker recognized back in 1931 when he wrote his essay about "Everyman His Own Historian" and used the example of popular historical practice to argue that historians need to "adapt our knowledge" to "the necessities" of the present rather than "cultivate a species of dry professional arrogance growing out of the thin soil of antiquarian research." Thus, our interviewees implicitly join Becker in insisting on something that professional historians can too easily forget – "our proper function is not to repeat the past but to make use of it."[3] For our respondents, the past is not only present – it is part of the present.

Such observations about how popular historymakers use the past and what they share with professional historians may contradict the conventional wisdom. Yet they are also commonsensical; anyone who reflects on his or her own experience of family and holiday gatherings – or indeed everyday life – will realize how the presence of the past saturates all of us. Whether surprising or commonplace, these findings have important implications for the practice of history and even for the future of American society. To sort out these findings and their implications would take much closer scrutiny of patterns of popular historymaking than a national telephone survey permits. What follows is one brief effort to describe the significance of what we heard, particularly for history practitioners. Inevitably, this personal statement reflects my own experiences as a scholar and teacher who has worked in a university for the past two decades and has also been involved in trying to present the past in non-academic forums, including museums, films, oral history programs, CD-ROMs, and the World Wide Web.

For historians who want to engage with diverse audiences, this study offers encouraging news and useful advice (as well as some sobering cautions). The interests and passions that our respondents have described suggest bases for forging new connections, alliances, and conversations with those diverse audiences. Of course, many good teachers and history professionals are already aware of these conclusions about popular engagement with the past, about the power of the intimate past, and about the ways audiences actively and critically relate to the past. Our survey strongly supports their most creative approaches to presenting the past and connecting with audiences. This is hardly surprising: the most thoughtful teachers, museum curators, and historical writers listen carefully – if perhaps not always systematically – to what their audiences have to say. The endorsement that this survey provides for their insights and efforts is nevertheless important, since many innovations have recently come under attack from those who seek to reinforce traditional approaches.

Schools have been among the most hotly contested arenas in what have sometimes been called the "history wars."[4] Our respondents had a great deal to say about history in school; they told us that they felt less connected to the past there than in any other setting we asked about. "Boring" was the most common description of history classes. An Alabama man's vivid recollection of high school – "my teacher was 70 years old and she carried a blackjack" – summed up the views of many.

While the history wars have often focused on content – what should be taught in classes or presented in exhibits – our respondents were more interested in talking about the experience and process of engaging the past. They preferred to make their own histories. When they confronted historical accounts constructed by others, they sought to examine them critically and connect them to their own experiences or those of people close to them. At the same time, they pointed out, historical presentations that did not give them credit for their critical abilities – commercialized histories on television or textbook-driven high school classes – failed to engage or influence them.

Given this preference for history as an active and collaborative venture, many respondents found fault with a school-based history organized around the memorization of facts and locked into a prescribed textbook curriculum. Their comments implicitly rejected the recommendations of conservative commentators on history in the schools. For these conservatives, the reason students don't know enough "history" (as defined by standardized tests and textbooks) is the rise of multiculturalism and the decline of a traditional curriculum based on the patriotic story of the American nation – the very curriculum our respondents described as insulting to their ability as critical thinkers. Even if one shared conservatives' desire to cram more facts into students, this survey suggests that the revival of traditional stories and traditional teaching methods conservatives advocate isn't the way to do it.

What respondents told us runs counter to the narrative of declension that says Americans are disengaged from history because cultural radicals have captured the schools (and museums) and are teaching gloomy stories about our nation – stories about McCarthyism rather than America's triumph in the cold war, about Harriet Tubman rather than the Founding Fathers, about destroying Indians rather than taming the West.[5] If only we would get back to the good old facts of American triumph (and the old-fashioned methods of teaching those facts), they maintain, then Americans would be reengaged. The people we interviewed said that they are already quite involved with the past – through formal activities like going to museums as well as informal pursuits like talking with their families. They liked history in museums and didn't like history in schools – not because Harriet Tubman has been added, but because the schools require dry recitation of facts instead of inspiring direct engagement with the "real" stuff of the past and its self-evident relationship to the present.

The fading of the traditional nationalist story has much deeper roots than shifts in school curriculum – one might look at how American misadventures in Vietnam or the racial divisions of the 1960s undercut nationalism, or how the globalization of the economy has made it harder for nation-states to deliver on promises of prosperity for all.[6] Some regard the waning of nationalism as a threat; others see it as an opportunity.[7] Whatever one's position, there is no need to equate history with the nation-state, even though that equation has long been at the heart of professional historical practice.[8] The past, our survey respondents suggest, has many mansions, and in America at least, the past is very much alive, even if traditional textbook narratives of the national past seem to be dying out.

Some teachers are already demonstrating that the narrative of national greatness is not the best way to engage students with the past. Veteran North Carolina high school teacher Alice Garrett tries to help her students develop "personal meanings" of the past through research projects, reenactments, and exposure to firsthand sources. Breaking with "the rigidity of the state's curriculum," she explains, "almost always brings about different power relationships. The teacher becomes a learner; the student becomes a teacher. The parent becomes an expert consultant, and the most energetic individual student in the class emerges as a group organizer."[9]

Garrett is not alone in trying to teach outside the canon. Many other teachers around the country have tried to reshape the formal study of the past by encouraging students to interview members of their families, to explore sites of historical events, or to assume the roles of particular individuals in the past. David Kobrin and his collaborators in the Providence schools transformed the U.S. history curriculum so that students could "grab the power of the historian for themselves rather than rely on the anonymous authors of a textbook." Working from primary documents, teams of students wrote their own histories. Particularly when they could see the connections between the historical issues and their own lives, Kobrin recalls, they worked "past the bell."[10] Creative teachers are tapping into the most resonant patterns in popular historymaking by allowing and encouraging students to revisit, reenact, and get close to the past through encounters with primary documents and living historical sources. "When I teach American history," observes a perceptive high school teacher, "I ask them 'What will your grandchildren ask about you?' History is a living story. It's your story."[11] Such approaches are far from new, of course. In the early twentieth century, "new historians" (like Becker) and supporters of "social studies" advocated historical instruction that closely connected the past and the present and that paid attention "to the present life interests of the pupil."[12]

Teachers who want to connect past and present and to turn students into historians are offering the kinds of classrooms that many respondents told us they wanted. Some public historians (filmmakers, preservationists, museum workers) who speak to largely adult audiences are also aiming to make history less of a top-down enterprise. Implicitly, and sometimes explicitly, our respondents endorsed such attempts to see historymaking as a more democratic activity that allows amateurs and professionals to learn from each other.

One fruitful metaphor for reimagining the relationship between history professionals and popular historymakers is what Michael Frisch has called "shared authority." Frisch urges us to break down hierarchies by redistributing and redefining the meaning of intellectual authority for crafting historical narratives. Scholars and public historians, he argues, "need better to respect, understand, invoke, and involve the very real authority their audiences bring to a museum exhibit, a popular history book, or a public program." The audience's "authority," he notes, may be "grounded in culture and experience rather than academic expertise," but "this authority can become central to an exhibit's capacity to provide a meaningful engagement with history" and to forge a dialogue "about the shape, meaning, and implications of history."[13]

In the 1980s some museums took the notion of shared authority directly into their exhibit halls and created what the Chinatown History Museum in New York called "dialogue-driven" exhibits and museums. Reclaiming the "neglected past" of New York's Chinatown, writes one of the museum's founders, John Kuo Wei Tchen, "must be done in tandem with the people the history is about" so that "personal memory and testimony inform and are informed by historical context and scholarship." The Chinatown History Museum, for example, has found "reunions to be an excellent way to link the felt need for history directly with historical scholarship" – an insight confirmed by our survey. The museum has focused on reunions of Public School 23, since the museum occupies its former quarters. "A dialogue between museum staff, scholars, and P.S. 23ers," Tchen reports, "developed and drove much of the organization's planning during the late 1980s and early 1990s."[14]

Likewise, when the Minnesota History Center in St. Paul opened in 1992, it involved visitors in "active participation with history as a process of inquiry and exploration," according to former assistant director Barbara Franco. Its planning for "A Common Ground: Minnesota Communities" proceeded along "three parallel paths – scholarly discourse about the nature and definition of community, audience research about public perceptions of community, and active involvement of community members in the themes and content of the exhibit." In order to portray an "insider's perspective" on the Winnebago Indians, the curators met frequently with a community advisory board, which helped find artifacts and photos, suggested oral history questions, and shaped the focus of the exhibit. The curators were able to provide "important background information and research skills"; in the process they gained the "trust of the community so that the Winnebago individuals and families were willing to share photographs, precious keepsakes, and personal stories."[15]

Such approaches have influenced curators outside the United States as well. In the late 1980s, organizers of the People's Story Museum in Edinburgh set out to involve local "people in the presentation of their own history." "The term 'People's Story,'" they explained, "was taken literally, as the story was to be told as far as possible in their own words and in this way the museum may be seen to be returning history to those who created it . . . in effect a handing over of some of the power of the Curator to the public." They launched an impressive set of partnerships, particularly with older residents of the community. One project, for instance, brought together "a wide range of community groups, from an Asian girls' sewing club to Adult Training Centres to primary schoolchildren" who created a banner that featured "contemporary people sharing their history with each other, surrounded by the objects, photographs and words which hold most meaning for those individuals who have created this work of art."[16]

Many earlier neighborhood and community history projects also embodied this ethic of shared authority. Such ventures – oral history programs, photo exhibits, walking tours, documentary films, union history classes – often grew out of the social movements of the 1960s and 1970s. Professional historians who were caught up in those movements tried to infuse a more democratic ethos into their historical practice. Frequently with support from the National Endowment for the Humanities (NEH) and its offspring, the state humanities councils, scholars collaborated with amateurs to collect and present stories of people who had been invisible in traditional national histories. Some of these efforts either originated as or became means of creating usable collective pasts for feminists, gays, or union workers.[17]

In the 1980s, funding for these collaborative and non-institutional projects became harder to find; some were derided as "populist" rather than "serious" and "scholarly"; NEH shifted its funding away from them, although a number of state humanities councils continued to provide support. In the 1990s a growing chorus of voices has even argued that the government has no business funding the arts and humanities, that the private sector can do it better. Some conservatives have also made their own "populist" argument, which concludes that public agencies like NEH, the National Endowment for the Arts, and the Corporation for Public Broadcasting concentrate narrowly on topics of interest only to elites. Our respondents didn't agree. They put more trust in historical presentations funded and sponsored by public agencies and non-profit organizations – especially museums, which they regarded as the most trustworthy sources of historical information. (Our survey shows that an interest in history museums cuts across lines of income, education, and race.) Such views offer strong support for continued government funding of museums, documentary films, historic preservation, and other public humanities programs that bring together popular historymakers and history professionals in dialogues about the past.

Why not increase collaboration between professional historians and popular historymakers? Why not set up public humanities programs that bring together Civil War reenactors and Civil War historians? Why not make use of the World Wide Web, which has emerged as a popular venue for amateur historians, to create virtual meeting grounds for professionals and nonprofessionals?[18] Why not connect professional archivists with popular historymakers who document the past through photos and diaries? Why not tap into the intimate ways that people use the past? By assembling wills and treasured objects passed between generations, museum exhibits might illuminate the ways people use the past to address matters of immortality. The personal connections people draw to public historical events – like the Kennedy assassination or World War II – would make excellent subjects for exhibits, class projects, public humanities programs, or documentary films.

All this is easier said than done. Our survey emphasizes not only the commonalities between professionals and popular historymakers but also the differences. The curator for the Winnebago exhibit noted the difficulty of becoming both a trusted insider and a dispassionate outside expert: "There were two sets of ethics operating in this exhibit development process – people ethics and historian ethics."[19] Some history professionals will feel ill-equipped to deal with the intimate issues that popular history-making can easily unearth. After workshops at the People's Story Museum repeatedly evoked painful memories from older participants, staff members decided they needed a family therapist to teach them more about confronting wrenching memories.

There are other differences as well. Professional historians, by training, have often been more suspicious of oral sources than of written documents.[20] And we professionals have also been deeply invested in stories about the nation-state, institutions, and social groups – unlike the people we surveyed, who especially valued the past as a way of answering questions about identity, immortality, and responsibility. Our respondents talked at great length about the past as a source for moral guidance, but morality is not a category that has lately figured in our professional discourse, where relativist notions prevail. Consider the profound engagement with the past that we heard about from evangelical Christians. What does a largely secular group like historians have to say to them? Is there a basis of conversation across such fundamentally different notions about the past?

These differences should not be exaggerated; professional historians have talked about love, tragedy, and morality, just as the historymakers in our survey at times talked about the rise of the nation-state or the experience of social groups. Not surprisingly, history practitioners have found that biography, oral history, and microhistory – which intermingle the everyday and the intimate with larger social and political events – can bridge the gap between professional concerns and popular interests. Still, our professional training often teaches us to shun rather than embrace the moral and personal questions that seemed so important to respondents.[21]

Sometimes historians are also unprepared to deal with the political issues raised by efforts to share authority. Listening to the "community" does not necessarily solve the problem of deciding who speaks for it. The creation of a community advisory board can be a highly political process. And giving a platform to people not usually heard can provoke counter-reactions from those who have traditionally had more power in shaping historical accounts.[22] In 1997, for instance, the Smithsonian Institution's National Museum of American History planned an exhibit based on notions of shared authority, which was called "Between a Rock and a Hard Place: A Dialogue on American Sweatshops, 1820–Present." In a gesture of respect for those whose story was being told, the exhibit organizers planned a section on the notorious El Monte, California, sweatshop to be told in the "participants' voice." Apparel manufacturers were also invited to contribute their perspective to the exhibit, but they refused: the exhibit, they said, gave too much attention to sweatshops and included the views of trade unionists. "Sharing a platform with the union and giving them undue recognition and credibility is something I do not want to get involved with," announced Joe Rodriquez, executive director of the Garment Contractors Association.[23] Can authority be shared with people who are interested in victory rather than conversation?

Popular historymakers are also likely to raise unfamiliar and uncomfortable questions of their own. "I have found it more difficult to write about Chinese New Yorker history with and for fellow community members than for fellow academics," writes Tchen.[24] Linda Shopes captures some of the tensions that can result from a dialogue between professionals and non-professionals in a perceptive commentary on the Baltimore Neighborhood Heritage Project of the late 1970s. She analyzes the many strains and misunderstandings between professional historians and community residents over what was important in the community's history, how to collect and interpret residents' stories, and finally how to report the results. On the one hand, in their collection of stories local residents lacked "the historical background and analytical framework to pursue certain subjects in sufficient depth." On the other hand, the professional historians "failed to appreciate the tapes' value. They used the oral testimony simply as a source of specific information, illustrative quotations, or interesting anecdotes that fit their own analytical framework. They were unable to penetrate beneath the surface of the informants' words."

Shopes concludes that "the deepest impediment to sustained collaboration between the project and the community" was the professionals' "primary affiliation . . . with a nationally organized profession" and their lack of "social commitment to a specific locale."[25] My own experiences in the 1970s with filmmaker Richard Broadman confirms Shopes's point. When we began working on an oral history film about the impact of urban renewal on his Mission Hill neighborhood in Boston, Richard's neighbors were not eager to participate; he was a "newcomer" who had only lived there for five years. Only after another seven years of work on the film and of joint participation in community projects did local residents come to see it as "their" film as well as ours and told their stories for the camera.[26]

The differences are not simply ones of community affiliation. As Shopes recognizes, non-professionals have their own blinders, their own resistance to new approaches. Baltimore residents, for example, wanted histories to avoid anything "even mildly critical of the neighborhood" and to favor a "booster spirit" that made the scholars uncomfortable. Our survey respondents often used the past in complex and subtle ways, but their approach was sometimes in tension with my historical training and preferences. For example, I found their emphasis on the firsthand, the experiential, the intimate, and the familial to be confining as well as illuminating. At times respondents seemed primarily concerned with their own and their family's pasts; the stories of others were often ignored. This privatized version of the past, I worried, can reinforce rather than break down barriers between people, resist rather than promote change. Many respondents were struggling to reach beyond the firsthand, to think themselves into wider histories, and to scrutinize sources of the past that originated outside their immediate circles. Still, I sometimes found their views of the past (as well as they can be judged from these interviews) as narrow and parochial as those of the most traditional professional historians.

Even when popular historymakers avoided overt parochialism, they still tended to draw the circles of their historical interests narrowly. In interviews with white Americans, "we" most often centered on the family rather than other social groups – whether class, region, or ethnicity. The understanding of the past that white Americans get from their families is an enormously potent resource for living in the present, a way of coming to terms with personal identity and of gaining personal autonomy. But white Americans, it seems to me, less often use the past to reach beyond their families and recognize their connections to wider groups of neighbors and fellow citizens. Just as Americans seem to be bowling alone, as political scientist Robert Putnam argues in his commentary on the decline of civic society, they also seem to be writing their histories alone – or at least in small familial groups.[27] Many white Americans understand and use the past in ways that make them suspicious of outsiders.

Black Americans and Sioux Indians drew the circle of "we" more broadly and saw themselves as sharing a past with other African Americans or American Indians.[28] A distinctive view of the past enables both of these groups to maintain a collective identity in the present. Their understandings of the past help them live in an oppressive society. Black Americans, for example, are sustained by a progressive, enabling historical vision rooted in the story of emancipation and civil rights. And for Native Americans, an understanding of their cultural survival in a hostile world is a source of strength for both individuals and the community. Yet even here, the connections drawn – at least in these interviews – often stopped at the boundaries of their own group. Multiculturalist visions of easy border crossings and rich mixings need to confront the suspicion with which these borders are sometimes guarded.

Nevertheless, when people do let down their guard, the common patterns of historymaking that we observed can allow individuals to identify and empathize with others. Moreover, the past can provide a safe, because distant, arena in which people can imagine alternative identities and explore different points of view. We need to marry experience with imagination and enable people to connect with "imagined communities" beyond the ones that they have learned in family circles.[29]

Reading the survey interviews, I also worried that popular historymakers who emphasize the experiential and the firsthand may sometimes underestimate larger structures of power and authority. Families can nurture their members, but many individuals need to earn their livings in exploitative workplaces. And family breakups are often the result of economic crises rather than the failures of individuals. Historical narratives that start (and sometimes end) with the personal cannot readily take account of categories like capitalism and the state – categories, I would argue, that are useful to more than just history professionals.

A history grounded in the immediate and the experiential also runs the risk of neglecting important stories that are temporally or geographically distant. And valuing the experiential can obscure the degree to which reports of "experience" are mediated by existing structures of language and power.[30] As Shopes observes, "Popular ideologies of independence, individual achievement, and respect for the 'self-made man'" shaped the memories reported by participants in the Baltimore project, just as popular ideology, language, and culture (for example, respondents' frequent invocations of "the family") surely stamped the interviews that we conducted.[31]

At stake here, at least potentially, is not simply whether one's sense of the past is rich in context, comparison, and complexity – whether, for example, one sees similarities between one's own experience and the experiences of others or recognizes how employers and politicians might have affected the course of family history. Such understandings of the past have a potential bearing on action in the present. Is it possible to build movements for social change without imagining a set of past and present connections to groups of people who aren't kin and ancestors? Is it possible to work for change without a vision of other alternatives that the past can provide? Is it possible to work for change without an understanding of the structures of power that support the status quo?

By providing context and comparison and offering structural explanations, history professionals can turn the differences between themselves and popular historymakers into assets rather than barriers. History professionals can help to enrich popular uses of the past by introducing people to different voices and experiences. They can help to counter false nostalgia about earlier eras. They can make people aware of possibilities for transforming the status quo. Recognizing how the civil rights movement broke the fetters of a stable and racist social order or how the CIO challenged entrenched notions of management "rights" can inspire people to work for social change in the present. We need a historical practice that is somehow simultaneously more local and intimate and more global and cosmopolitan, more shaped by popular concerns and more enriched by insights based on systematic and detailed study of the past. And, as our interviewees would insist, that historical practice needs to link the past and the present in an active and continuing conversation.[32]

My concerns about the presence of a privatized and parochial past in some of these interviews grow out of a belief that the past should be a vehicle for social justice. Obviously my perspective is not shared by all history professionals or, indeed, by most of the popular historymakers with whom we spoke. The past for many of them (particularly white Americans) is more a source of personal identity and empowerment than group identity and empowerment. Indeed, the prevalence of narratives of declension and defeat among white Americans suggests their understandings of the past may sometimes be disempowering. Their emphasis on stories of declining discipline and rising crime and their celebration of the family as a bulwark in a changing world could much more easily support traditionalist and conservative programs than movements for social change.

Yet this is not a nation of acquisitive and atomized individualists, as some libertarians would want us to believe. Our respondents cared deeply about morality, forging close relationships to others, and leaving legacies for the future. These values and priorities are an important foundation for mobilizing people for a better society – or really for people mobilizing themselves.

Of course, definitions of the "good society" vary widely, and historians play only a small role in bringing about larger social changes. Our respondents told us of beginning with the personal and the intimate, and historians too must begin with their immediate worlds – the places where they teach and talk about the past. The most significant news of this study is that we have interested, active, and thoughtful audiences for what we want to talk about. The deeper challenge is finding out how we can talk to – and especially with – those audiences. History professionals need to work harder at listening to and respecting the many ways popular historymakers traverse the terrain of the past that is so present for all of us.

[. . .]

Notes

Patterns of popular historiography

1   As with all the numbers in this (and any other) survey, methodological cautions are in order. Some respondents may have "telescoped" their responses in a way that made one year into a longer unit; others may have interpreted activities related to the past very broadly; still others may have given us responses they thought we wanted.

2 As noted, we are here arbitrarily – but not without justification – using 8 points on a 10-point scale as a description of feeling "very strongly" connected to the past.

3 After family reunions, the next largest categories were friends (11 percent) and school (7 percent).

4 Spontaneous comments on "reading" the past: look at photos – 8; movies/TV – 11; museums – 35; books – 21; average – 18.75.

  Spontaneous comments on "writing" the past: take photos – 26; reunions – 35; hobby – 31; family history – 61; journal – 24; group – 24; average – 33.5.

  The count for reunions is complicated because interviewers routinely asked respondents for the type of reunion they attended. Our estimate is that about 35 of the 196 comments were offered spontaneously rather than as the result of direct questions.

5 The statistical technique known as "regression" offers one way to gauge which social and demographic factors predict particular behaviors. (A regression is a statistical technique for estimating the effects of one or more variables on another variable. For example, you might use a regression to measure how much fertilizer affects the height of corn when you control for sunlight and rainfall.) In effect, regression equations permit us to ask whether knowing someone's age, income, education level, race, and gender would allow us to predict if they were likely to visit a museum, write in a diary, or watch a history film.

  Even when added together, the five social and demographic characteristics (age, income, education, race, and gender) we used explain only a small part of the variations in the ways that individuals answered the activities questions. For eight of the ten activities, these characteristics explain less than 6 percent of what statisticians call "the variance." (The variance measures the variability from one person to the next in their propensity to do these activities. If these social and demographic characteristics perfectly predicted whether or not someone did a particular activity, they would explain 100 percent of the variance.) For example, only 2.3 percent (a tiny amount) of the variance in the degree to which people have investigated the history of their family is explained by demographic variables. Virtually none (less than .1 percent) of the variance in whether people have a hobby or collection related to the past can be attributed to those same variables. Even in the two cases – visiting museums and taking photos – where demography matters more, the variance is still modest: just 7.5 percent and 14 percent.

  It is possible, of course, that a different set of questions might have yielded more differences, e.g., if we had asked about different kinds of hobbies, if we had mapped frequency, or if we had separated museums from historic sites.

6 When you control for education, income, age, and gender, taking photos is the only statistically significant difference in black and white patterns among the ten activities we asked about. (If you combine numbers from the special African American sample with the blacks in the national sample, blacks also appear to be statistically less likely to participate in hobbies and collections related to the past.) Blacks and whites are, for instance, equally likely to investigate the history of their families or visit museums and historic sites. Adding race to our regression equations thus only slightly enhances our ability to predict whether or not an individual will participate in most activities related to the past.

7 It is more difficult to compare activity patterns for Native Americans and whites and for Mexican Americans and whites because the samples are not strictly comparable. Still, based on what we can see after controlling for other variables (especially education), the differences among these groups are either negligible or relatively easy to explain. For example, although 16 percent of Mexican Americans (as opposed to 29 percent of white Americans) report writing in journals or diaries, these differences largely disappear if you compare people of the same educational level. Even when race or ethnicity does make a difference, it is still a relatively modest difference. For example, social background (including race) never explains more than 13 percent of the variance when the Sioux and white responses are combined, and only on two activities (visiting museums and sites and taking photographs) does it even explain as much as 7 percent.

8 These five differences hold up when we control for other variables like income, gender, and age. Thus, based purely on cross-tabulations, education also correlates with looking at and taking photos, attending reunions, and watching movies about the past. But these differences disappear when we use regressions to control for other variables. On the other hand, the modest difference in levels of participation in hobbies and collections emerges as statistically significant in the regression equations.

9 Only the relationship between education and a feeling of connectedness in visiting history museums is statistically significant. Race, income, age, education, and gender together explain only 1.7 percent – an almost trivial amount – of the variance in the answers that people gave to our questions about connectedness. On only two of the questions (family gatherings and holiday

celebrations) does social background explain more than 1.6 percent of the variance in answers to the connectedness question, and in those cases it still explains only 7.1 percent and 5.7 percent.

10   The differences for attending reunions, working on family history, and writing in a diary are statistically significant based on a chi-square significance test. The regressions . . . which control for income, education, and age, confirm the significance of these three differences in levels of participation in activities. The regressions, in fact, suggest two additional differences are also statistically significant (e.g., taking photos and participating in history-related groups). Another way of comparing differences is to use logistic regressions. By that method, which holds other demographic variables constant, women were 50 percent more likely than men to have investigated the history of their family (the probability of a man doing this was .28 and for a woman .42), 55 percent more likely to have written in a journal or diary (men: .22 and women: .34), and 17 percent more likely to have attended a reunion (men: .59 and women: .69).

11   For men: 86 family; 64 non-family but also non-public figures (friends, etc.); 99 public figures. For women: 166 family; 34 other non-public figures; 74 public figures.

12   These categorizations are necessarily subjective; to control for this, they (and similar counts) were done independently by one of the authors (Rosenzweig) and our research assistant (Andy Draheim) with similar results. Men were more likely than women to offer reasons for keeping diaries or journals like tracking work procedures, exercise schedules, and skill progress.

13   The average age of the 14 women was 55.

14   Women also tended to collect domestic objects, and favored hobbies in which they made rather than just collected objects.

15   Jane Clarke, market research director, History Book Club, letter to David Wilson, 3 May 1994, in possession of authors.

16   Sixteen of the 44 people asked this follow-up question offered a specific title. Another 5 people mentioned titles without a follow-up question. Hence, only 61 of 653 people who said that they watched a film or television program about the past gave us a specific title.

17   To be sure, many people also make quite deliberate trips – even pilgrimages – to specific sites and museums in order to honor a particular history, to instill patriotism in their children, to understand current problems, or to retreat from the present by visiting the past. Below is a breakdown of the reasons given for visits to museums and historic sites: travel – 50; proximity – 11; visiting relative/ friend – 11; taking child – 10; leisure – 9; personal connection/interest – 7; school trip – 7; research – 5; ethnic connection – 4; activism/museum work – 3; work-related – 2; local history interest – 2; understand the present – 2; escape the present – 1; saw movie – 1; other – 9.

18   Brook Hindle argues that "modern man is separated more firmly from the realities of his own world than was man in earlier periods of history." Thus, "man's need to touch the past has increased rather than decreased." "How Much Is a Piece of the True Cross Worth?" in Ian M. G. Quimby, ed., *Material Culture and the Study of American Life* (New York: Norton, 1978), p5. See also Greg Dening, *Mr. Bligh's Bad Language: Passion, Power and Theatre on the Bounty* (New York: Cambridge University Press, 1996), pp339–40.

19   The rough estimate is based on 192 million people over 18 multiplied by 39.6 percent.

20   Below is a breakdown of the types of groups devoted to studying, preserving, or presenting the past in which interviewees participated during the previous year: school-related – 26; church/ religious – 22; local history/local preservation – 17; ethnic or racial – 12; hobbyist/collector – 12; environmental – 11; genealogical – 9; family/friends – 12; work-related – 6; civic/community – 6; art museum – 5; veterans – 4; re-enactor – 3; therapy – 3; fraternal – 2; tourism – 2.

21   This interview was done in pretesting; unless otherwise noted, all quotes come from the main study.

22   The average times were probably longer, according to John Kennedy of the Center for Survey Research, because it is more difficult to keep an accurate time count during long interviews (because of starting and stopping).

Everyone a historian

1   Louis R. Harlan, "The Future of the American Historical Association," *American Historical Review* 95 (Feb. 1990), p3.

2   Carl Becker, "Everyman His Own Historian," *American Historical Review* 37 (Jan. 1936), pp233–55.

3   Ibid., pp252–53. Gerald Figal notes that Japanese "self-histories" (a written form of personal histories that have become popular in Japan since the early 1970s) share this tendency to relate past and present, "shifting easily from a chronology of the past to a commentary on the past and its ramifications

for the present and future." "How to *jibunshi:* Making and Marketing Self-histories of Shōwa Among the Masses in Postwar Japan," *Journal of Asian Studies* 55 (November 1996), pp902–33.

4   See, for example, Mike Wallace, *Mickey Mouse History and Other Essays on American Memory* (Philadelphia: Temple University Press, 1996); Edward T. Linenthal and Tom Engelhardt, *History Wars: The Enola Gay and Other Battles for the American Past* (New York: Henry Holt, 1996).

5   For example, in her *Wall Street Journal* op-ed piece of October 20, 1994, which launched the assault on the national history standards, Lynne Cheney complained that Harriet Tubman was "mentioned six times," whereas Paul Revere, Robert E. Lee, and Thomas Edison received nary a reference. Similarly, columnist John Leo slammed the standards for asking students to learn about such allegedly trivial figures as Mercy Otis Warren ("a minor poet and playwright" included only "so the founders of the nation won't seem so distressingly male") and Ebenezer MacIntosh, a shoemaker and leader of the Stamp Act demonstrations ("a brawling street lout of the 1760s" mentioned merely because he was "anti-elitist"). National Center for History in the Schools, *National Standards for United States History: Exploring the American Experience* (Los Angeles, 1994); Wiener, "History Lesson," pp9–11; Hugh Dellios, "Battle over History May Itself Prove Historic," *Chicago Tribune*, 30 October 1994, Perspective Section, p1; John Leo, "The Hijacking of American History," *U.S. News & World Report* 117 (Nov. 14, 1994), p36. For a recent comprehensive discussion of the controversy, see Nash, Crabtree, and Dunn, *History on Trial*.

6   For some perceptive comments on the decline of nationalism, see Gary Gerstle, "Blood and Belonging," *Tikkun* 9 (Nov. 1994), p68ff, and Kaye, *The Powers of the Past*, pp40–119.

7   For recent defenses of liberal nationalism, see, for example, Michael Lind, *The Next American Nation: The New Nationalism and the Fourth American Revolution* (New York: Free Press, 1995); David A. Hollinger, "National Solidarity at the End of the Twentieth Century: Reflections on the United States and Liberal Nationalism," *Journal of American History* 84 (Sept. 1997), pp559–69. The case for postnationalism and transnationalism is made in such works as Arjun Appadurai, "Sovereignty without Territoriality," in Patricia Yaeger, ed., *The Geography of Identity* (Ann Arbor: University of Michigan Press, 1996) and Saskia Sassen, *The Global City: New York, London, Tokyo* (Princeton: Princeton University Press, 1991).

8   See Duara, *Rescuing History from the Nation*.

9   Alice Garrett, "Teaching High School History Inside and Outside the Historical Canon," in Lloyd Kramer et al., eds, *Learning History in America: Schools, Cultures and Politics* (Minneapolis: University of Minnesota Press, 1994), p75.

10 David Kobrin, Ed Abbott, John Ellinwood, and David Horton, "Learning History by Doing," *Educational Leadership* (Apr. 1993), pp39, 40; Kobrin, "It's My Country, Too: A Proposal for a Student Historian's History of the United States," *Teachers College Record* 94 (Winter 1992), p334. See also David Kobrin, *Beyond the Textbook: Teaching History Using Documents and Primary Sources* (Portsmouth, NH: Heinemann, 1996).

11 *New York Times*, 5 Apr. 1995.

12 National Education Association 1916 report on *The Social Studies in Secondary Education*, as quoted in Hazel Whitman Herzberg, "The Teaching of History" in Michael Kammen, ed., *The Past before Us: Contemporary Historical Writing in the United States* (Ithaca: Cornell University Press, 1980), p476.

13 Frisch, *A Shared Authority*, ppxx, xxii.

14 John Kuo Wei Tchen, "Creating a Dialogic Museum: The Chinatown History Museum Experiment," in Ivan Karp, Christine Mullen Kreamer, and Steven D. Lavine, eds., *Museums and Communities: The Politics of Public Culture* (Washington, DC: Smithsonian Institution Press, 1992), pp286, 301; Tchen, "Back to the Basics: Who Is Researching and Interpreting for Whom?" *Journal of American History* 81 (Dec. 1994), p1007.

15 Barbara Franco, "Doing History in Public: Balancing Historical Fact with Public Meaning," *AHA Perspectives* (May/June 1995), pp5–8.

16 Sandra Marwick, "Learning from Each Other: Museums and Older Members of the Community – the People's Story," in Eileen Hooper-Greenhill, ed., *Museum, Media, Message* (New York: Routledge, 1995), pp140–50. For a Canadian project, see Laurence Grant, "'Her Stories': Working with a Community Advisory Board on a Women's History Exhibition at a Canadian Municipal Museum," *Gender & History* 6 (3) (Nov. 1994), pp410–418.

17 For an overview of some of these projects, see Roy Rosenzweig, "'People's History' in den Vereinigten Staaten," in Hans Heer and Volker Ullrich, eds., *Geschichte entdecken [History Discovered]* (Rowohlt, 1985), pp46–57. See also, for example, Jeremy Brecher, "A Report on Doing History from Below: The Brass Workers History Project"; Duggan, "History's Gay Ghetto"; Sonya Michel, "Feminism, Film, and Public History"; Jeffrey C. Stewart and Faith Davis Ruffins, "A Faithful Witness: Afro-American Public History in Historical Perspective, 1828–1984"; James R. Green,

"Engaging in People's History: The Massachusetts History Workshop," all in Benson, Brier, and Rosenzweig, eds., *Presenting the Past*, pp267–359; and Arthur A. Hansen, "Oral History and the Japanese American Evacuation," *Journal of American History* 82 (Sept. 1995), pp625–639.

18   Michael O'Malley and Roy Rosenzweig, "Brave New World or Blind Alley? American History on the World Wide Web," *Journal of American History* 84 (June 1997), pp132–155.

19   Franco, "Doing History in Public," p8.

20   See Paul Thompson, *The Voice of the Past: Oral History*, 2nd edition (Oxford: Oxford University Press, 1988), pp22–71.

21   Microhistorians set the everyday stories of particular individuals against larger "historical" events. For one promising example, see Dening, *Mr. Bligh's Bad Language*. Professional scholarship, of course, does reflect fundamental moral judgments, even while eschewing explicit discussions of moral conduct or character. On the relationship of historical narrative and moral judgments, see, for example, Hayden White, "The Value of Narrativity in the Representation of Reality," in W. J. T. Mitchell, ed., *On Narrative* (Chicago: University of Chicago Press, 1980), pp1–23; William Cronon, "A Place for Stories: Nature, History, and Narrative," *Journal of American History* 78 (Mar. 1992), pp1347–1376. But on the ways that "the tradition of scholarly detachment," and professional training in general, lead historians to avoid "the emotional places of history" and "the feelings of pride, anger, and loss that accompanies reflecting on the personal past," see David Glassberg, "A Sense of History," *Public Historian* 19 (Spring 1997), p70.

22   For a series of perceptive essays focused on the ways that power shapes history, see Wallace, *Mickey Mouse History*.

23   Megan Rosenfeld, "Clothing Industry Rips into Planned Sweatshop Exhibit," *Washington Post*, 12 Sept. 1997, pC1; Irwin Molotosky, "Furor Builds Over Sweatshop Exhibition," *New York Times*, 30 Sept. 1997, p20; Kristin Young, "Debate over Smithsonian Exhibit Heats Up," *Apparel News*, 29 Aug. 1997, p8.

24   Quoted in Franco, "Doing History in Public," p7.

25   Linda Shopes, "Oral History and Community Involvement: The Baltimore Neighborhood Heritage Project," in Benson, Brier, and Rosenzweig, eds., *Presenting the Past*, pp249–263.

26   *Mission Hill and the Miracle of Boston* (Boston: Cine Research, 1979).

27   Robert D. Putnam, "Bowling Alone: America's Declining Social Capital," *Journal of Democracy* 6 (Jan. 1995), pp65–78. Putnam's work raises a host of complex questions that go well beyond this discussion. For some perceptive critiques, see, for example, Michael Schudson, "What If Civic Life Didn't Die?" and Theda Skocpol, "Unravelling from Above," both in *American Prospect* 25 (Mar./Apr. 1996), pp17–25.

28   I draw this phrase from David Hollinger, "How Wide the Circle of We? American Intellectuals and the Problem of Ethnos Since World War II," *American Historical Review* 98 (Apr. 1993), pp317–337. Hollinger is concerned with the narrowing from a universalist species-centered discourse to an ethnos-centered discourse, and my own focus is on a further narrowing of the "we" to the family.

29   I borrow this phrase from Anderson, *Imagined Communities*. My thanks to Nancy Grey Osterud and Ken Cmiel for suggestions that shaped ideas in this paragraph and some other sections of these afterthoughts.

30   Joan W. Scott provides a well-known critique of the category of "experience" in "Experience," *Critical Inquiry* 17 (Summer 1995), pp773–97. For a perceptive effort to examine more empirically how experience might be mediated by language and culture, see Regina Kunzel, "Pulp Fictions and Problem Girls: Reading and Rewriting Single Pregnancy in the Postwar United States," *American Historical Review* 100 (Dec. 1995), pp1465–87.

31   Shopes, "Oral History," p252. Shopes also notes that "people's sense of their own history is private, personal, and grounded in the family and therefore not congenial to institutional frameworks."

32   Harvey Kaye offers some thoughtful comments on the ways that "the powers of the past" can break "the tyranny of the present" in Chapter 5 of *The Powers of the Past*.

Chapter 3

Iain J. M. Robertson

HERITAGE FROM BELOW

Class, Social Protest and Resistance

> The struggle of people against power is the struggle of memory against forgetting.
>
> (Kundera, 1996, p5)

THIS CHAPTER EXPLORES THE IDEA and possibilities of the notion of heritage from below. Drawing on the widely accepted view that heritage is a social and cultural construct firmly embedded in the power relationships that structure society, this perspective relies on the recognition of the possibility of the expression of alternative forms of heritage that 'work' from below and within, conceived for, from and by local communities with minimal professional help from without. Such heritages, it is also suggested, interact more readily with identity at a local rather than national scale. Examples of these are comparatively rare. Nevertheless, it is argued here that the recently constructed memorial cairns on the island of Lewis, off the northwest coast of Scotland, are one such example. And yet, this chapter will show that, even at these very localized levels, such can be the ineffectual nature of heritage as a medium of communication that heritage from below may be incapable either of wholly circumventing the boundaries created by identity-making and maintaining, or of avoiding the dissonance written into any heritage landscape.

There are two strong sets of views centring on the heritage discourse, the one considerably more pessimistic than the other. One set of views, typified by the work of Hewison (1987), Lowenthal (1985) and Wright (1985), sees heritage as an essentially conservative and nostalgic project. It encompasses a romanticized and idealized view of the past which, in Britain at least, is deployed to reinforce old certainties at times of significant change. Tropes of identity which utilize a sense of inheritance from the past are, according to this view, predominantly rural and evoke a 'lost golden age'. The countervailing view is considerably more optimistic and, drawing predominantly on binary oppositions such as amateur/professional; insider/outsider; history/heritage, recognizes a more democratic form of heritage. Here, heritage is seen to emphasize the 'little platoons' rather than 'great society' (Samuel, 1994, p158). The 'spirit of local places' gains prominence in this construction, as do urban places. And it is not memorialization that is celebrated but 'memorialism' (Dicks, 2000) – attempts by local communities to make and maintain their own heritage. Nevertheless, this present chapter is predicated on the belief that, whilst these more optimistic readings carry considerable merit, both fail to be sufficiently broad or deep fully to accommodate the making and maintaining of an inheritance from the past here recognized as heritage from below.

The view taken is that heritage from below is most often found in, or drawing on, expressions of resistance or memory of resistance amongst the dominated. The chapter will draw on case studies from Australia and England, although the central focus will be on the recent memorialization of acts of social protest in the Highlands of Scotland. Triangulating between in-depth interviews with members of the organizing committee, and theoretically informed work on heritage dissonance, memory and identity, it is argued that, although these memorials are manifestly expressions of heritage from below, the assertion of local identity via heritage and through social memory is even more complex and at odds to other dominant registers of identity than recent re-workings suggest.

Heritage and local identity: An under-explored relationship made meaningful via heritage from below?

The heritage discourse is centred around a number of critical (in both meanings of the word) dualisms: between those who take a pessimistic view of the turn to heritage in the last quarter of the twentieth century and those who take a more optimistic view; between the professional practitioners of the heritage industry and the professional academics; between the past deployed in the service of identity-making and maintaining at a national level and at other spatial scales. Whatever the scale, whether it is a single monument or 'framing stretches of scenery', landscapes, through their seeming ability to exemplify 'moral order and aesthetic harmony', come to figure and 'picture the nation' and thereby 'achieve the status of national icons' (Daniels, 1993, p5). It is, as Short (1991) has shown, only a short step from icon to 'national landscape ideology' in which the supposed values, meanings, beliefs and character of 'the nation' are enshrined in these iconic 'scapes'. Fully imbricated into and playing a constitutive role in this ideology is a sense of inheritance from the past in the form of national heritage (Edensor, 2002, p41).

The key to understanding this link between national identity and ideology as made manifest in iconic national landscapes lies, Osborne believes, in the fact that nations occupy both 'material and psychic terrains . . . often rendered in terms of symbolically charged . . . space'. Drawing on Halbwachs's conceptualization of 'landmarks', Osborne argues that these, through the conflation of history and geography, 'serve to punctuate time, focus space and figure the landscape, converting it into a psychic terrain' (see Halbwachs, 1992; Osborne, 1996, pp24–25) that is at the core of identity at all spatial scales, but particularly the national.

This seeming power of national identities as they relate to heritage is challenged both by other spatial and non-spatial manifestations of belonging and expressions of this relationship. Indeed, according to Graham, Ashworth and Tunbridge, nationalism appears to exist 'largely to structure such heterogeneity into . . . synecdoches of sameness'. Moreover, and most importantly for the current chapter, the role of heritage in identity-making and maintaining 'ensures that it also becomes the focus of resistance at many scales and in many places' (Graham, Ashworth and Tunbridge, 2000, pp84 and 93). Notwithstanding this assertion, consideration of the relationship of heritage to spatial registers of identity other than the national has been somewhat uneven. Indicative of this is the fact that, whilst there is a considerable body of literature investigating this relationship at the supra-national scale, discussion of the manifestation of heritage at the local scale has been, on occasion, somewhat superficial. Graham, Ashworth and Tunbridge (2000), for instance, devote comparatively little space to exploring the relationship between heritage and local identity, notwithstanding the fact that, as Samuel (1994) demonstrates, it is with the local register that the relationship between heritage and identity-making and maintaining is the more meaningful.

Nevertheless, some key interventions have been made. Working on the politics and practice of representation underpinning the commemoration of the war dead in France after World War I, Sherman postulates a sharp distinction between national and local discourses of collective memory. He argues that, whilst 'larger structures . . . and ideological formulations like the national-local dichotomy . . . mediate both the experience and the representation of memory', local artefacts of commemoration enjoy 'considerable autonomy' (Sherman, 1994, pp186–87) from these wider structures, processes and ideologies. Indeed, heritage as an expression of local autonomy is a belief explicitly underpinning the notion of local distinctiveness as formulated by the group Common Ground (in England) and implicitly underlying the notion of heritage from below.

Critical to the main thrust of this chapter is the existence of a fundamental dichotomy within the ways in which heritage can be understood. For Howard, this dichotomy can be captured in the phrase 'conspiracy theory' (2003, p36), although this only implicitly includes the more optimistic readings of the implications of the UK's turn to heritage in the 1970s. More balanced is Smith's attempt to capture this dichotomy through 'the authorized heritage discourse' (AHD), which she contrasts with 'subaltern and dissenting heritage discourses' (2006, pp29–42). Consisting largely of professionals speaking to professionals and within national and international institutions and codes of practice, the AHD lays claim to cultural capital via elite notions of 'inheritance' and 'value'. This is, therefore, according to Smith, a 'professional discourse' (2006, p4) which speaks to and assists in naturalizing dominant practices of identity and belonging. Smith contrasts this with 'a range of popular discourses and practices' which challenge the hegemonic. In particular, she identifies 'subaltern discourses of community participation' (2006, p35) to which this chapter will add alternative expressions of identity-making and maintaining at the local scale.

Much of the basis of these more optimistic perspectives can be found in the work of Raphael Samuel, whose position begins from a condemnation of academic history, albeit without taking into account many of the debates around postmodern historical constructions. For Samuel (1994), academic history is predicated on the belief that knowledge 'filters downwards' (1994, p4) in a strict hierarchy of practitioner acceptability. This he vividly contrasts with what he terms 'unofficial knowledge' – a vast panoply of 'other' forms of history that receive at best grudging acknowledgement from the practitioners of 'real history'. These forms range from the oral tradition through 'children's theatricals' to the 'set-piece historical debate' and reveal history to be a 'social form of knowledge' grounded in an 'ensemble of activities and practices' (1994, pp5–11), out of which, alongside and indivisible from events in the past, emerges a sense of the past in the present.

For Samuel, close consideration should be given to 'the perceptions of the past which find expression in the discriminations of everyday life' (1994, p17). From this he derives his more optimistic reading of the rise of heritage, itself consequent upon the historicist turn (identified by Samuel as 'retrofitting' and 'retrochic') in the UK of the 1970s onwards. One consequence was a significant broadening of what had hitherto been understood as heritage. Moreover, Samuel believes that the past encapsulated by this broadened heritage is culturally more pluralist and radically different from previously hegemonic versions. Thus 'it is the little platoons . . . which command attention' (1994, p158) in the late-twentieth-century version of the national past: urban, feminine and domestic. But most critically, and the point of departure for the idea of heritage from below here delineated, Samuel views the heritage currently enacted as an 'inconceivably more democratic' version of Englishness than any previously enacted and which the 'heritage baiters allow' (Samuel, 1994, pp160–63 and 259–71).

The phrase 'heritage from below' is a deliberate echo of the history from below impulse that was a product of the refashioning and revitalizing of social history in the 1960s. Clearly generating an echo also in Samuel's optimistic conceptualizing of heritage and in the Public History movement of which Samuel was a pioneer, the intention was to challenge elitist conceptions of who history is about, who should 'do history' and who history is for. The intention was to uncover the lives and thoughts of common people and to rescue them from the 'enormous condescension of posterity' (Hobsbawm, 1998, p285). Encompassing a number of forms foregrounded by this movement, not least oral histories and popular memory, heritage from below draws in part on this project, in part also on Gramsci's notion of 'counter hegemony' and on 'unofficial knowledge'.

Gramsci's notion of ideological hegemony has had a significant impact on intellectual thought generally and across the humanities and social sciences more specifically. Unfortunately, the impact on heritage studies has been limited and often negative. Ashworth, for instance, argues that this approach is of limited worth because 'places rarely . . . convey a simple master narrative of the imposition of a single coherent dominant ideology for the establishment of legitimacy by a hegemonic authority or social group' (1998, p113). This negative impact is a matter of some regret as the thesis has much to offer studies of manifestations of social phenomena from below and in opposition to class domination. Equally regretfully, space does not here permit a full discussion of this thesis, thus the following brief outline is offered by way of contextualization for the idea of heritage from below.

The notion of hegemony is closely tied to the cultural means by which one group achieves and maintains dominance over others. Critically, from the perspective of trying to understand the 'work' heritage does, hegemony allows entry into the important ways in which 'culture itself' shapes 'social ideals and social relations' (Billinge, 1984, p34). Gramsci characterized hegemony as the capacity of 'dominant' or 'leading' groups to generate consent among 'the great masses' due to the prestige (or authority or persuasion) and structural position of the dominant groups (Gramsci, 1971, p12). According to Williams, hegemony, as expressed by Gramsci, refers to 'a complex interlocking of political, social and cultural forces' that is also always dynamic, contested and modified (Williams, 1977, pp108–12). It is, perhaps, always in a state of becoming. Apparent in 'the whole substance of lived identities and relationships', hegemony is, therefore, 'a . . . body of practices and expectations' from which the 'lived social process [is] practically organized by specific and dominant meanings and values' (Rudé, 1980; Williams, 1977, pp108–10). For Thompson (1978), such dominance can only be sustained by the constant exercise of skill, theatre and concession. Hegemonic control cannot impose an all-embracing domination upon the ruled and there are always possibilities (latent or realized) for the expression of oppositional cultures.

For the ideas here outlined, this last is critical. In discussing opposition to the hegemony of a dominant culture, we may distinguish between alternative and counter-hegemony. The former is associated with the rise to power of a new class but is only visible in an unrealized state. Once established, it becomes a new hegemonic culture. Counter-hegemony is any opposition to dominant hegemony. It need not be underpinned by an articulated class consciousness and can take both informal and organized forms. Thus food riot or land seizure (see below) can be recognized as counter-hegemonic forms (see Withers, 1988). Furthermore, if 'landmarks' or *lieux de mémoire* can be written into the landscape in support of national landscape ideologies, national identity and the meanings and values of the dominant within society, then counter-hegemonic landmarks can equally be written into the landscape in support and expression of local identity. As heritage from below, such landmarks can celebrate, perpetuate and make material oppositional meanings and practices.

Something of the possibilities in this concept can be discerned in the preface by Studs Terkel to Brecher's *History From Below*: 'Ours, the richest country in the world, is the poorest in memory' (Stonesoup, n.d.). In exactly the same way that history from below sought to prioritize the story of the defeated and non-privileged, the idea of heritage from below recognizes the possibilities of heritages other than those of the dominant in society. One such possibility, and one of the key tasks of heritage from below, is that this expression of heritage, tangible or (often) intangible, can offer an alternative construction of the past to that of the hegemonic and, thereby, both galvanize and cohere local communities around alternative constructions of identity and narratives of place. This, then, provides the opportunity (seldom taken) to celebrate and memorialize *from within* the lives and thoughts of those otherwise hidden from history. Furthermore, recognition of manifestations of this concept takes us further away from the hegemonizing impulse of history than even Samuel would allow. Out of this, heritage from below can be recognized as both an opportunity for the expression of other heritages and identities, and a possibility for the assertion of a structure of feeling that runs counter to the hegemonic.

Much of this derives from the widely recognized assertion (see, for instance, Ashworth, 1994, and Johnson, 1999) that the past, as heritage and a form of cultural capital, assists in the making and maintaining of elite narratives of place and identity. Heritage from below, therefore, draws also on the realization that this inevitably leaves a gap for the possibility of alternative and conflicting expressions of place and identity. Particularly evident in the multi-layered power of landscapes as memory places, heritage from below is grounded in common experience and popular memory and, it will be argued, is self-evidently a product of the local structures of feeling surrounding the creation of the memorial cairns on the Hebridean island of Lewis.

Heritage from below in place and landscape? Common Ground and the Local Heritage Initiative

In the UK, but regretfully actually English-centric, something of the nature of heritage from below is apparent in the campaigning group Common Ground and the Heritage Lottery Fund's funding stream 'Local Heritage Initiative' (LHI). Indeed, the two are explicitly linked through Common Ground's notion of 'Local Distinctiveness'.

Common Ground intervenes to facilitate and stimulate local projects of place-making and maintenance. Working with a philosophy borrowing recognizably from the pheno-menology of Heidegger and Ingold amongst others, the group seeks to work with a con-ceptualizing of the relationship between people, place and identity which it terms 'Local Distinctiveness' (see Clifford and King, 1993). This it sees as 'a starting point for action to improve the quality of . . . everyday places' (Common Ground, n.d.) based on a symbiotic and time-deep relationship between human and natural histories made manifest in the landscape and through everyday artefacts.

Mirroring debates within heritage, both around authenticity and the need for a 'lost golden age' (inescapably rural), Common Ground seeks to be a catalyst of processes of heterogeneity. This it does with 'provocations, examples and questions' but not models or a lead role in local community actions as this would 'deny the basic philosophy that we are expressing'. 'Locality needs to be defined from the inside, with a cultural and natural base, less abstraction, more detail' (Clifford and King, 1993, pp7–18). Notwithstanding these aspirations, professionals from outside often take a central role in Common Ground's interventions. The *New Milestones* project may well be 'a powerful exposition of cultural intimacy with the land' but the most significant claim made about the project is that it required equal input from the artist and local people (Morland, 1988).[1] On one level this reveals an interesting interactive process being played out, on another it reveals that even projects that aspire to 'particularity', 'patina' and 'authenticity' and to enabling the voice from within to be heard, cannot do this without the intervention of professional practitioners from outwith the community.

Common Ground's basic philosophy of 'Local Distinctiveness', in combination with a UK government drive to encourage citizens to take action 'to care for their local environment' (Local Heritage Initiative, 2006, p9), became central to a local heritage funding programme of the late 1990s – the LHI. 'Local Distinctiveness' was one of the four key aims of the LHI as it sought to 'create a holistic programme that could add a new dimension to the understanding and appreciation of heritage at a local level' (Local Heritage Initiative, 2006, p8). This programme would seem to be designed to encourage and foster expressions of heritage from below. Indeed, the founding principles of the LHI encapsulate the belief that 'local people' through 'participatory heritage management . . . are well qualified to identify the heritage of their local area and determine what is of value to them' (Local Heritage Initiative, 2006, p7). Nevertheless the LHI foresaw a role for professionals within that process and established a network of expert advisers and project support workers. There was also a Grant Assessment Panel and a number of centrally commissioned reports and assessments of value (Local Heritage Initiative, 2006, pp10–12). In short, this resembles all the paraphernalia of the AHD. As Dicks (2000) has shown, such local/professional dualisms appear inevitably to involve the generation of tensions and conflicts and, indeed, dissonance from within the project that works to the detriment of local conceptualization of, and participation in, the scheme.

Attempts to delineate and identify expressions of heritage from below are not, therefore, unproblematic. This chapter, however, has not as yet engaged with the processes where such expressions might be most readily located – expressions of resistance or memory of resistance amongst the dominated. Two case studies will be offered here. The first captures in brief the work of Roy Jones and questions of contested urban heritage. The second, more detailed, case study focuses on processes of memorialization in the Scottish Highlands in the 1990s. It is here suggested that these two case studies demonstrate far less problematically the working out of the ideal of heritage from below in the landscape and as an expression of local identity. It must be admitted, nevertheless, that even at this most localized of levels, identity is always contested, heritage is always problematic and dissonance is always present.

The Old Swan Brewery conflict – Perth, Western Australia

This conflict (see Jones, 1997, pp132–55) was about the site and the brewery, and it began with the designation of the brewery complex as official heritage. As with many other landscapes, the history of the 'scape is a contested and polysemic one, only exacerbated by the fact that one aspect of this contestation lies between Aboriginal and white peoples. For the former, this was a sacred site associated with teaching and ceremony; whilst for the latter this was a site of significant industrial heritage. Contestation over whose past was going to be represented centred on the demolition or preservation of the redundant brewery complex. Attempts by the Western Australian state government to reach a compromise only heightened the dispute, resulting in direct action by some Aboriginal groups supported by the construction workers union and Christian groups. Notwithstanding this, the site was eventually placed on the State Register of Historic Places (Jones, 1997, pp140–41). According to Jones (1997, p152), the cause of the protracted nature of the dispute (it had lasted six years and was still ongoing whilst he was writing) was the fact that this was not 'a simple Aboriginal–developer confrontation' but was multi-layered and multi-vocal. For instance, support both against and for the demolition of the complex was evident amongst the white middle class and Aboriginal opinion.

On one level, Jones's summation of this dispute – of the symbolic significance of an Aboriginal victory in 'the establishment heartland of the inner city' – closely accords to the idea of heritage from below as here expressed. However, as Jones argued, the fate of the brewery actually lay 'in white hands' and a more pessimistic reading would recognize this as a 'developers versus NIMBYs battle, with Aboriginals . . . as the pawns of both sides'. Clearly, and despite the fact that the brewery's demolition would be 'a significant and symbolic victory for Aboriginal rights' (Jones, 1997, p154), evidence of non-dissonant expressions of heritage from below must be sought elsewhere.

The Lewis Memorial cairns to the 'land heroes'

From the early eighteenth century, the Scottish Highlands and Islands experienced a significant and prolonged period of social and cultural change that had huge repercussions for ordinary highlanders. These changes took the form of the replacement of small-scale subsistence agriculture with large-scale sheep farming. It also involved the transformation of part feudal, part tribal social relations into purely capitalist relations. Finally, in the period from about 1820 to 1850, it involved the forced migration and emigration of the bulk of the population in the process that has become known as the Highland Clearances. Highland communities did not accept change wholly passively, although a spirit of resistance took some time to emerge from the highlanders' deferential *mentalité*. Nevertheless, by the 1880s a strong protest ideology had emerged and generated extensive and extended episodes of class conflict that have become known as the Highland Land Wars. These declined in the first decade of the twentieth century, only to revive again in the period following the end of World War I.

Both the Clearances and the Land Wars have been memorialized in recent years; firstly in Tiree and Skye and then in Lewis. Here the memorial form is traditional and vernacular. The majority of the Lewis memorials, however, are public-art representational. All memorials, of whatever form, look inward to the crofting community and attempt to create emblematic landscapes of resistance. The particular significance of the Lewis representational monuments comes from the fact that although they were the vision of a professional artist, these were not overly mediated from outwith but were created for, by and from within the local community. What here transgresses the disjuncture created by the deployment of a professional artist is the fact that in this instance the artist concerned had family connections that link him back to the island and directly to the Clearances. As one of the key members expressed it, whilst at first his colleagues on the local committee were opposed to 'some modern artist [being] parachuted in' from outside, the close connections of the artist to the island somewhat allayed these fears.[2]

The Lewis project was for four monuments. According to Angus Macleod, the key figure behind the scheme, inspiration came after he was invited to Tiree to the opening of a memorial there, and by his awareness of memorial cairns on Skye:

> I said to one or two of my friends: 'we are a shamed people, we're forgetting our history. Other people are looking after their history and shouldn't we not?' There are at least four episodes here in Lewis which are well worth commemorating. So everyone was agreed and up and formed a committee and sailed off from then.[3]

This was *Cuimhneanchain nan Gaisgeach*, a committee and group with the aim of commemorating (literally) 'our land heroes'. The individual events chosen to be commemorated[4] were: the riots at Bernera and Aignish; the Pairc Deer Raid; and the meeting between Lord Leverhulme and the crofters from Back, Coll and Gress, consequent upon the land raids in the area in the 1920s. All these events were of great significance in the campaign for land on Lewis (see Buchanan, 1996) and attracted considerable publicity in the (UK) national press and public interest. For Macleod, therefore, these events virtually chose themselves.

The nature of the way in which *Cuimhneanchain nan Gaisgeach* was constituted is of particular interest here. Angus Macleod importantly believed that as the memorials were to be 'about our history', then they had to be 'from and by and for the locality'.[5] To ensure this, the committee had a different chairman (they were always men) in place for each of the different projects. Furthermore, the chairman was always from the part of the island in which (and for which) the particular monument was to be erected. There is a history of place-specific conflict on the island and this policy was an attempt to circumvent this. According to one of the permanent members of the committee, Macleod based this policy on personal experience. When talking about a public meeting to consider the design and location of the cairn for the Coll and Gress land raiders, 'he says [to me] "there is no point someone outwith the area going down there"', as he (Macleod) had been told at a meeting shortly after the end of World War II that he had no right to advise them as he did not come from the area.[6] What underlay this disjuncture, then, was a sense of (very) local identity. For Roddie Murray, Balallan, the first monument to be completed, 'was fine because Balallan was Angus's own home patch and . . . John M. Macleod was also on the committee from there'.[7]

In addition to replacing the chairman, each committee could co-opt local people and a series of public meetings could be arranged to ensure full consultation. In this way, with the emphasis and weight given to opinion from within and from the non-professional, the process of monument-making here described emerges as a manifestation of heritage from below. Key to this is the fact that these are monuments to illegality. They are monuments created by those for whose future protesters were fighting in the Land Wars of the 1880s and 1920s. Events of these periods, class and cultural conflicts, were ideologically driven and expressive of counter-hegemony. And whilst there is no doubt that the cairns were not explicitly constructed as sites of resistance, they do celebrate a culture of resistance and of counter-hegemony. Moreover, those ideas that underlay protest and counter-hegemonic social formations remain evident in the contemporary crofting community. In celebrating and commemorating illegality and in creating landmarks to the memory of an alternative culture, *Cuimhneanchain nan Gaisgeach* was making heritage from below. These memorials are attempts to fix and record authentically what has transpired and offer that past to future generations of insiders. They are, in short, attempts to create distinct landscapes of belonging that are themselves expressive of an alternative hegemony.

Heritage and landscapes of belonging are, however, never unproblematic. As already noted, the original intention was to build four monuments. Ultimately, however, five monuments were built, although only three of these were built by *Cuimhneanchain nan Gaisgeach*. The others were built by independent groups formed specifically to build just the monument in their locality. In one instance, moreover, there is a *Cuimhneanchain nan Gaisgeach* monument and an independent monument, differently located but celebrating the same key event. This was the meeting between Lord Leverhulme and the crofters from Back, Coll and Gress, to which *Cuimhneanchain nan Gaisgeach* intended to build a monument at Back. The land disturbances celebrated by this memorial involved people from at least three separate townships but were coordinated as (virtually) one event. Notwithstanding this, members of the individual townships felt that these events should have been memorialized individually. In addition, people from Upper Coll felt disenfranchised by their lack of representation on *Cuimhneanchain nan Gaisgeach* and further alienated by the public art form of the proposed monument. Their response was to erect an alternative traditional and vernacular monument in Upper Coll.

At Bernera, also, there was tension over both the perceived inappropriate nature of the memorial to be built and *Cuimhneanchain nan Gaisgeach's* role in any memorialization. People from Bernera had been observing *Cuimhneanchain nan Gaisgeach's* proposal for at least two years and had become increasingly uncomfortable with the committee's (to them) ever-more elaborate plans. The result was that the memorial was rejected at a series of public meetings. A Bernera-based group was formed; they raised funds within the area and erected a traditional cairn and dedication plaque.[8]

As with Angus Macleod's concerns over chairing a public meeting in a district to which he did not belong, for Roddy Murray the root cause of this is to be found in Bernera's 'own very territorial reasons'. For members of the group charged with creating their own memorial, attempts by Angus Macleod and other members of the *Cuimhneanchain nan Gaisgeach* committee to persuade them to change their minds only pushed the locality in the opposite direction. As Noreen McIver says, 'it became quite political'.[9]

Tension involving the Bernera and Back/Upper Coll cairns is a manifestation of attempts to maintain a distinctive and very local identity for which the 'other' comprises juxtaposed local communities on Lewis. In both cases, moreover, the failure to accord with the *Cuimhneanchain nan Gaisgeach* project, an explicit attempt to take the mnemonic beyond the purely local, meant that the two cairns became, perhaps unintentionally and unconsciously, inward looking; *for* Bernera and Upper Coll separately and only. It is with no little sense of irony, then, that it should be noted that such actions may well identify the Bernera and Upper Coll cairns as purer expressions of heritage from below than those created by *Cuimhneanchain nan Gaisgeach*. They were wholly local, without any professional design or other help, and were wholly funded by the areas to which they belong. In contrast, the fact that the *Cuimhneanchain nan Gaisgeach* project was part-funded by the Gulbenkian Foundation, and that it was awarded – and the organization accepted – a Civic Trust award for design, must raise some doubt over the autonomous nature of the project.

At the same time, the conflicts around the vernacular cairns demonstrate the dissonance and tensions that emerge when monuments are deployed as mnemonics. The Bernera riot had significance outwith both Bernera and Lewis and for the land protest movement as a whole. An outward-looking public-art memorial would have been representational of this. But by creating an inward-looking monument, the cairn sets up a dissonance between the event and its memorialization, and celebrates only the local district and its identity. This serves, moreover, as a reminder that dissonance and contestation are intrinsic to any attempt to write heritage into the landscape in the form of memorialization. Both heritage and identity are susceptible to contestation from within as much as they are from without. It would seem that the contestations around memorial-making on the island of Lewis arise from traditional local rivalries and from a fear that the strong voices on *Cuimhneanchain nan Gaisgeach* were attempting to disinherit areas from which they did not originate. Undoubtedly these memorials mediate the landscape and comprise a sense of identity at a very local scale. Nevertheless, this attempt to build heritage as commemoration has proved incapable of being able to transgress the boundaries created by these self-same identities.

Conclusion

Unquestionably, the examples utilized in this chapter serve to reinforce the widely held conviction that because heritage is multi-perceived, multi-sold and multi-consumed, then dissonance is intrinsic to heritage landscapes even in this very localized context. Furthermore, heritage from below as here expressed replicates something of the polysemic nature of the heritage discourse. One aspect of the concept is purely academic and is essentially about the recognition of a category of heritage hitherto not given full worth in the academic literature. At the same time, however, the term is expressive of the recognition of the possibility and opportunity of the deployment of the past in service of a present that runs counter to that of the hegemonic and which, operating at the local level, is constitutive of constructions of identity that are at odds with the dominant.

Drawing on the widely accepted argument that heritage is a social and cultural product, it is here argued that heritage from below, as an expression of local identity, is evident in expressions of resistance to dominant discourses such as the conflict surrounding the Old Swan Brewery. The deployment of what we might recognize as a sense of heritage from below is evident also in the campaigns undertaken by Common Ground and in its conceptualization of 'Local Distinctiveness'. This, in turn, was of fundamental influence on the Local Heritage Initiative that of itself may be said to have been an attempt to harness heritage from below to a community regeneration initiative. But perhaps where the concept is here most readily seen 'at work' is with the memorial cairns to land disturbances on the island of Lewis. And yet, even here, at this most localized scale, a sense of a radical inheritance from the past has proved incapable of transgressing the boundaries inherent in identity-making and maintaining. Any attempt, it would seem, to utilize a sense of the past in identity-making and maintaining generates disinheritance, if not dissonance, conflict and contestation.

Notes

1   http://www.commonground.org.uk/sculpture/s-essay.html, accessed 12 February 2007.
2   Interview with Roddie Murray, Lewis, 7 April 1998.
3   Interview with Angus Macleod, Lewis, 6 April 1998.
4   This continues to be an ongoing process. The decision has recently been made to build a fifth monument at Uig.
5   Interview with Angus Macleod, Lewis, 6 April 1998.
6   Interview with Roddie Murray, Lewis, 7 April 1998.
7   Ibid.
8   Interview with Noreen McIver, Bernera, 4 February 2005.
9   Interview with Roddie Murray, Lewis, 7 April 1998; interview with Noreen McIver, Bernera, 4 February 2005.

References

Ashworth, G. J. (1994), 'From History to Heritage – From Heritage to History: In Search of Concepts and Models', in G. J. Ashworth and P. J. Larkham (eds), *Building a New Heritage: Tourism, Culture and Identity* (London: Routledge), pp13–30.

Ashworth, G. J. (1998), 'Heritage, Identity and Interpreting a European Sense of Place', in D. Uzzell and R. Ballantyne (eds), *Contemporary Issues in Heritage and Environmental Interpretation* (London: The Stationery Office), pp112–32.

Ashworth, G. J. and Larkham, P. J. (1994) (eds), *Building a New Heritage: Tourism, Culture and Identity* (London: Routledge).

Baker, A. R. H. and Gregory, D. (eds) (1984), *Explorations in Historical Geography* (Cambridge: Cambridge University Press).

Billinge, M. D. (1984), 'Hegemony, Class and Power in Later Georgian and Victorian England: Towards a Cultural Geography', in A. R. H. Baker and D. Gregory (eds), *Explorations in Historical Geography* (Cambridge: Cambridge University Press), pp28–67.

Buchanan, J. (1996), *The Lewis Land Struggle* (Stornoway: Acair).

Clifford, S. (1994), 'New Milestones: Sculpture, Community and the Land', <http://www.commonground.org.uk/sculpture/s-essay.html>.

Clifford, S. and King, A. (1993), *Local Distinctiveness: Place, Particularity and Identity* (London: Common Ground).

Common Ground (no date), 'Common Ground', <http://www.commonground.org.uk/>, accessed 12 February 2007.

Daniels, S. (1993), *Fields Of Vision: Landscape Imagery and National Identity in England and the United States* (Cambridge: Polity Press).

Dicks, B. (2000), *Heritage, Place and Community* (Cardiff: University of Wales Press).

Edensor, T. (2002), *National Identity, Popular Culture and Everyday Life* (Oxford: Berg).

Gillis, J.R. (ed.) (1994), *Commemorations: The Politics of National Identity* (New Jersey: Princeton University Press).

Graham, B., Ashworth G. J. and Tunbridge, J. E. (2000), *A Geography of Heritage: Power, Culture and Economy* (London: Arnold).

Gramsci, A. (1971), *Selections from the Prison Notebooks* (New York: International Publishers).

Halbwachs, M. (1992), *On Collective Memory* (Chicago: University of Chicago Press).

Hewison, R. (1987), *The Heritage Industry* (London: Methuen).

Hobsbawm, E. (1998), *On History* (London: Abacus).

Howard, P. (2003), *Heritage: Management, Interpretation, Identity* (London: Continuum).

Johnson, N. C. (1999), 'Framing the Past: Time, Space and the Politics of Heritage Tourism in Ireland', *Political Geography* 18:2, pp187–207.

Jones, R. (1997), 'Sacred Sites or Profane Buildings? Reflections on the Old Swan Brewery Conflict in Perth, Western Australia', in R. Jones and B. Shaw (eds), *Contested Urban Heritage* (Aldershot: Ashgate), pp132–55.

Jones, R. and Shaw, B. (eds) (1997), *Contested Urban Heritage* (Aldershot: Ashgate).

Kundera, M. (1996), *The Book of Laughter and Forgetting* (London: Faber and Faber).

Local Heritage Initiative (2006), *Lessons Learnt: A Review of the Local Heritage Initiative* (London: The Countryside Agency).

Lowenthal, D. (1985), *The Past Is A Foreign Country* (Cambridge: Cambridge University Press).

Morland, J. (1988), *New Milestones: Sculpture, Community and the Land* (London: Common Ground).

Osborne, B. S. (1996), 'Figuring Space, Marking Time: Contested Identities in Canada', *International Journal of Heritage Studies* 2:1/2, pp24–27.

Rudé, G. (1980), *Ideology and Popular Protest* (London: Lawrence & Wishart).

Samuel, R. (1994), *Theatres of Memory* (London: Verso).

Sherman, D. J. (1994), 'Art, Commerce and the Production of Memory in France After World War One', in J. R. Gillis (ed.), *Commemorations: The Politics of National Identity* (New Jersey: Princeton University Press), pp186–214.

Short, J. R. (1991), *Imagined Countries* (London: Routledge).

Smith, L. (2006), *Uses of Heritage* (London: Routledge).

Stonesoup Cooperative (no date), 'History from Below', <http://www.stonesoup.coop/historybelow/historybelow.htm>, accessed 12 February 2007.

Thompson, E. P. (1978), 'Eighteenth Century English Society: Class Struggle without Class', *Social History* 3:3, pp133–65.

Uzzell, D. and Ballantyne, R. (eds) (1998), *Contemporary Issues in Heritage and Environmental Interpretation* (London: The Stationery Office).

Williams, R. (1977), *Marxism and Literature* (Oxford: Oxford University Press).

Withers, C.W.J. (1988), *Gaelic Scotland: The Transformation of a Culture Region* (London: Routledge).

Wright, P. (1985), *On Living in An Old Country* (London: Verso).

Chapter 4

Graeme Davison

THE USE AND ABUSE
OF AUSTRALIAN HISTORY

ONE OF THE MOST STRIKING SIGNS of our times has been the widespread revival of ancestor worship. Everywhere it seems – in libraries, archives, churches and graveyards – we encounter the ever-growing legions of genealogists and family historians. Since the mid 1970s genealogy and family history have been one of the most vigorous cultural industries in Australia and, unlike many of the other boom enterprises of the past few years, it shows no sign of collapsing. Australian genealogical societies have experienced almost a tenfold increase in membership over that period, far outstripping the growth of other historical societies. According to Nick Vine Hall, Australia, next to America, continues to have the highest per capita population of genealogists in the western world. It is, seemingly, in modern, recently founded, 'non-traditional' societies that the search for ancestors is most vigorously pursued.[1]

How should we account for the family history boom? One clue to its popularity may be found in the social background and motivation of the genealogists themselves. In 1988 Winnie van den Bossche asked almost 1500 Victorian genealogists to fill out a questionnaire about their personal background, their reasons for taking up family history and their thoughts about the family history boom.[2] (The questionnaire may be compared with a smaller survey among genealogists in New South Wales carried out by Noeline Kyle a year or two earlier.) The identikit genealogist who emerges from these surveys is a forty- to fifty-year-old woman of middle- to upper middle-class background. She is more likely than her peers to have had a secondary or tertiary education. She was probably born in Australia of British or Irish parentage and is more likely to be a mainline Protestant than a Catholic by religion. Genealogy, one may speculate, is more likely to appeal to women, who are the customary nurturers and keepers of family tradition; to the middle-aged who are old enough to appreciate its attractions and to sense its fragility; to the well-to-do who have the education, leisure and means to pursue their hobby; and to the old Protestant Australia which, arguably, has been most threatened by the changes of the postwar era.

Part of family history's appeal is simply as an engrossing hobby. In 1932, in the first issue of the *Australian Genealogist*, one of the fathers of the movement made the point rather picturesquely. 'Collecting stamps, seals, badges and such like hobbies are not to be compared with collecting ancestors,' he remarked. 'Even that bizarre hobby of collecting cactus plants is not to be compared with it.'³ Part of the charm of genealogy lies in the thrill of the chase, the challenge of finding the missing pieces of the puzzle, and the pride of being able to display the trophies of the hunt to an admiring group of fellow enthusiasts. Family historians often invite their readers to share the excitement of discovery, punctuating their narratives with triumphant exclamations. 'I had struck oil!' shouts one exultant researcher at the end of her quest. 'I was hooked on genealogy,' exclaims another addict.⁴

But family history is more than a hobby; it answers a widely felt need to reaffirm the importance of family relationships in a society where mobility, divorce and intergenerational conflict tend to dissolve them. In the United States there have been three major waves of interest in family history – one, in the 1870s, in the immediate aftermath of the Civil War; a second in the 1930s, the decade that also saw the birth of the Australian genealogical movement, and the third, paralleling our own family history boom, in the 1970s and 1980s.⁵ These were times of social disruption when family links were threatened by war, depression or rising divorce rates. By lengthening the sense of generational memory, and by recalling family members to a stronger sense of their inheritance, the family historian seeks to shore up the links of kinship. 'The study of genealogy,' *The Genealogist* reminded its readers in 1978, 'tends to draw families together. . . . In an age when national policies sometimes cause cruel disruption of families, genealogy is one of the counteracting forces that contribute to family reunion and family solidarity.'⁶

The sense of threat and cultural disorientation is a strong theme among the respondents to Winnie van den Bossche's questionnaire. 'I have heard the suggestion that there is a lack of stability in the modern world,' writes a retired insurance officer:

> One no longer trusts one's employer/club/municipality to show the same loyalty to one's self [sic] as say great-grandfather showed to and expected from his employer/regiment etc. Knowledge of one's forebears perhaps helps to fill this gap.

'In a rapidly changing world, individuals have difficulty in maintaining an identity; where they belong in a scheme of things,' confesses another family historian. 'As old truths crumble, the family is seen as a believable reservoir of stable values.' Because it is unalterable, the past is seen as consolingly secure. It is 'something solid in a shifting world', says one genealogist. 'The past is fixed,' declares another who questions 'the prevailing myth that truth and value are relative.'

The dissolving world from which family historians flee is reflected inversely in their family narratives. It is not a world without pain and conflict – since the 1970s family historians have shown a remarkable willingness to drag the old skeletons of illegitimacy, divorce and drunkenness from the family cupboard – but one that continues to provide a touchstone for the moral health of our own generation. It holds up the ancestors to admiration, if not for their virtue, at least for their fortitude. 'I have a deep respect for my ancestors,' declares one genealogist. 'Not only were the men tough, but more so the women. I'd like to see some of the feminists do the same chores under the same conditions as our great-grandmothers.' Some family historians see themselves as defenders of a (British) pioneer heritage against the diluting influence of multiculturalism. 'The more "MULTICULTURAL" we become, the more risk of losing that pioneering identity,' remarks a male accountant. Feminism, multiculturalism, the new reproductive technologies, marital breakdown, inter-generational conflict – these are the perils against which the traditional family historian seeks to shore up the spiritual defences of family life.

Genealogy may be the last refuge of scientific history. There is something reassuringly 'objective' about the task of compiling a family tree. Its lists of dates and names, of births, deaths and marriages arranged in chronological sequence convey an air of exactitude, completeness and inevitability. (Never mind that it suppresses as much as it recovers: a genealogy, after all, charts only one route, the male line, into the ancestral past.) The genealogists themselves are often formidable historical technicians, experts in the 'how' of history. Their domain, however, is essentially a private or tribal one that connects only tenuously with the concerns of national or international history. 'It is my firm opinion that a family tree, whether it boasts of kings or serfs, of bishops or highwaymen, is of little interest to any but the families who have sprung from it,' confesses one genealogist.[7] From the vantage point of the professional historian, the average family history may appear not only trivial but almost inscrutable. It seems plotless, disconnected, unselective. Only if we assume the subjective vantage point of the descendant rather than the universalistic viewpoint of the intellectual, only if we give as much weight to the idea of heredity as liberals customarily give to the influence of environment will we begin to understand its continuing appeal. It speaks, not to our sense of historical significance, but to our need for personal identity. 'I now have an identity, knowing exactly who I am and where I come from,' declares one triumphant genealogist at the end of her quest.

Often, it seems, the decision to begin a family history project is crystallised at those moments of birth, marriage and death when we become acutely conscious of the slender cords binding one generation to another. In the preface to his book *A People called Pointon*, Bruce Pointon recalls that he decided to begin work on his family history 'just a few hours' after the death of his father, Horace. Heather Ronald concluded her book *Wool before the Wind* with the merger of the family wool-broking firm into the Elders conglomerate. Peter Bottomley concludes his history of the Morgan clan, entitled *Just an Ordinary Family*, with the death of its matriarch and the sale of the old family home and effects at Castlemaine. Margaret Beasey first thought of writing the history of her family, the Fleays, after reading an old letter left in her father's safe when he died in 1933. 'Ancestral records are important to me,' she writes. 'I have no children – this book is my contribution to the scheme of the Fleay family.'[8] It is often those who stand at the end of a family line, without children or spouses of their own, who most dutifully tend the memory of its past.

If awareness of the family's past is often stimulated by these moments of discontinuity, it is through the act of reunion that the family's enduring value is most strongly affirmed. 'People still need an extended family and [family history] is a legitimate way of reaching out to them,' writes one family historian. Doing the family tree is often the prelude or postlude to a family reunion; it is the device by which its often far-flung members are made known to each other and summoned back to the home turf. Family reunions are the present-day counterpart of the 'back-to' celebrations that were such a popular feature of rural life in the 1920s and 1930s. Then it was the old country town that the mobile city folk revisited. Now, as the ties of extended kin grow feebler, it is to the old family home that we reverently make pilgrimage.

A striking feature of modern family reunions is their traditional, and often explicitly religious, character. The family customarily gathers at the pioneer homestead or in the old home town, close to the original point of settlement. Often, it is the clergymen of the family who lead the proceedings which usually include a service of thanksgiving even when its members come from a variety of faiths, or none at all.[9] It is as though, by returning to the roots of the family, we seek to recover the certainties of a bygone, perhaps mythological, age of faith.

In recent years, however, family history has subtly changed its character. Thirty years ago, genealogy was still a rather select and selective pursuit, closely linked to the study of heraldry and to the search for a noble or gentle pedigree. In the early 1960s the main genealogical societies had only recently emerged from a period of 'dormancy'.[10] Many of their members were descendents of 'old pioneer' families, monarchists, pillars of the church, especially the Church of England, and of other ancient institutions. Their belief in the 'heredity principle' was at once mystical and scientific. In the person of the monarch they found a supreme example of the 'enduring principle of tribal and family stability'. The pages of their journals were filled with the pedigrees and armorial bearings of European nobility or self-styled Australian gentry.

At a time when eugenic ideas were still current, genealogy also had its scientific uses. Calculating the level of intermarriage in a country town might enable a physician to assess the risks of interbreeding.[11] Checking out a prospective partner's pedigree for possible hereditary disease might be a wise precaution before matrimony. 'The study of genealogy can be a useful preparation for a happy and successful marriage, and the planting of a healthy and fruitful Family Tree,' declared *The Genealogist* in 1977.[12]

In recent years, however, the movement has assumed a more popular and democratic character. In 1967 the editor of the *Victorian Genealogist*, the Pacific historian Neil Gunson, was still obliged to combat the suspicion that genealogists were 'snobs'. 'Nothing,' he replied, 'could be further from the truth. A pride in one's family, no matter how humble, an interest in people, in the human story of man and his way of life, his happiness and his sorrow, does not add up to snobbishness.'[13] By the mid 1970s the Australian Institute of Genealogical Studies opened its arms to all-comers. 'We are not like a trade union, where people are massed together for the purpose of improving their wages, working conditions or social status,' *The Genealogist* explained.

> Nor are we like a cricket or football club, where membership largely depends on specific skills or abilities, for anybody without any skills at all is welcome to join us. Nor are we an elite society where the high and mighty assemble to preen themselves on their importance and superiority, for even the lowliest of commoners has a genealogy and a family history of equal interest to all.[14]

By broadening its constituency, family history has also come to take a broader view of its subject. No longer is it sufficient simply to trace a genealogy – the skeleton of a family history – or to identify the notables in the family line. When even 'the lowliest of commoners' take their place in the story, the story itself broadens out to include those larger forces of social change that shaped their lives. Democratic family history is the story of those who suffered history, as well as of those who made it:

> Our forebears [writes one family historian] were not plaster saints; they were loving, feeling, caring human beings with as many vices and virtues as the rest of us; they lived life to the full and enjoyed their successes and suffered their failures.[15]

Modern family historians look to their ancestors less as moral exemplars than as fellow sufferers. They give little weight to the influence of heredity in their own family fortunes. The bond they seek with their ancestors is an essentially sympathetic one, based more upon fellow feeling than the mystique of blood or ancestral piety. A gentle strain of feminism may be detected in these newer family histories. Instead of tracing the male line of her husband's family, the genealogist may sometimes choose to follow the distaff of her own. For a generation of women who often missed out on tertiary education, genealogy offers direct entry to an alternative world of scholarship, one insulated from the competitive pressures of academia with its examinations, ranking systems and relentless theorising; a democratic community in which everyone is an expert, if only upon her own family.

Patriarchal history

The private hobby of family history stands in contrast, not only to the public values of academic history, but to those elitist forms of genealogy that we may call patriarchal history. The attempt of William Charles Wentworth to create a hereditary Australian aristocracy may have been doomed to political failure, but the great pastoral families have remained the greatest reservoir of hereditary sentiment in Australian society. Land and lineage – the main axes of their identity – are the themes, not only of their own dynastic histories, but of broader accounts of national history into which they merge.[16] The transformation of this tradition in the late twentieth century offers another vantage point on the significance of family history.

The history of Australian family history begins a little later than its American counterpart, but follows a similar trajectory. During the last quarter of the nineteenth century many colonial landowners, and some merchants and politicians, sought to discover or, if necessary, to invent gentle pedigrees and to patent heraldic arms. 'An interest in genealogy,' writes Paul de Serville, 'was a declaration of love and loyalty for the home country' and its popularity – shared, so he says, 'by colonists of every class and background' – 'was indicative of a desire to maintain one's links and roots, to preserve one's identity of background and inheritance, as much cultural as familial.'[17] The Victorian elite, whose origins were often far from illustrious and whose wealth was but newly gained, also led the rush to be ranked. *Burke's Colonial Gentry* (1891) – the most pretentious and the most controversial register of the best Australian families – was dominated by rich Victorians, including some heroes of the land boom whose fortunes had already dissipated before the book was published.

Ideas of blood and heredity – of 'the crimson thread of kinship' – were an integral component of nineteenth century British and Australian patriotism. Ideas of the British people as a great family, headed by the monarch; of the colonies as brothers and sisters; and of their political institutions as a priceless 'heritage' were but an enlargement of those transoceanic, yet intimate, ties which most colonists had recognised in their own family histories and which were regularly reinforced by the processes of migration.[18] Images of blood, kin and race were strong in the patriotic rhetoric of the early Commonwealth. 'These daughters of the Imperial mother will share in the greater conclave of the nation and make manifest in counsel the blood-tie and common racial instinct already proved on the South African battlefields,' declared the *Sydney Morning Herald* as it greeted the federation.[19] The imperial family, as these words imply, was both an inclusive and an exclusive concept; while strengthening brotherly and sisterly ties between fellow Britons, it placed 'lesser breeds', such as Chinese, Aborigines and even Irish, outside the family circle. A multicultural, pluralist Australia may be anxious to forget the extent to which earlier generations of Australians grounded their sense of national identity in notions of blood and breeding.

Pride of lineage is only one of the threads that links genealogy to national history for nationality is itself a genealogical concept, something that is thought to be handed down from generation to generation or, for the newcomer, conferred by a kind of adoption. National identity in a new country is constituted by descent from the first arrival. The 'three significant questions' to be asked by the Australian family historian were: 'WHEN did they come? WHENCE did they come? and WHY did they come?'[20] Descent, for practical genealogical purposes, meant descent through the male line. 'The simplest way is to begin with your father's pioneer forbear,' an experienced genealogist advised the novice. 'Give a brief account of his background overseas and go on to the *when* and *why* he came. Tell of his achievements, his marriage and his family then follow his line, generation by generation, to the present day.'

Genealogy was thus one of the main intellectual props for the pioneer legend, that account of national becoming that conferred the highest honour upon the first-comers. The Women's Pioneer Society of Australasia, for example, was founded in 1928 among female descendants of generally male pioneers. In the 1920s and 1930s members of the Society of Australian Genealogists joined members of the Royal Australian Historical Society in compiling a comprehensive list of the first European arrivals in New South Wales but it was not until 1969, the eve of the Cook Bicentenary, that the Fellowship of First Fleeters was founded.[21]

The Depression years of the 1930s, a period when domestic life and Australia's familial link with the 'Mother Country' were also experiencing new strains, witnessed a renewed interest in genealogy and family history. In the preface to his *Pioneer Families of Australia*, published to commemorate the sesquicentenary of New South Wales in 1938, P. C. Mowle emphasised the value of giving 'a permanent record' to the country's patriarchs and in demonstrating 'the close bonds of kinship which exist between the families in Australia and those of the Mother Country'.[22] In 1934 Victoria also marked its centenary with monuments, ceremonies and historical publications exalting the state's founders and pioneers, and celebrating the imperial connection.

The local genealogist, Alexander Henderson, whose *Pioneer Families of Victoria and the Riverina* was published to mark the centenary, viewed the state's history as the essence of innumerable genealogies. 'We have some measure of responsibility to make our own record worthy of all that is best in that which has been bequeathed to us,' he wrote. 'It is ungracious to forget how great is the amount standing to the credit account of the pioneers of this country in respect of human uplift and high example in treading new paths.'[23] Recording all that was best, totting up the credit account – these are phrases suggestive of a certain wilful blindness to the worst, or debit, side of the moral ledger of pioneering. In Henderson's pages the patriarchal mythology of the state's first families – with their romantic notions of blood, land and gentility – is held up to the admiration of a more democratic age. Like their British aristocratic models, Debrett and Burke, colonial genealogists emphasised the link between lineage and land. Instead of Norfolk of Arundel we have Murray of Borongarook and Wool Wool. Where the record permits, they rooted the history of the Australian pioneer family in a British or Irish prehistory, sometimes illustrating it with a photograph of the ancestral home and a sketchy summary of the British pedigree.

The legitimacy of the Australian pioneer family, however, resided less in the antiquity of its family tree than in the moral fibre and landed wealth of its founding generations. Early arrival in the colonies, preferably but not necessarily as a free settler, contributed to the prestige of the line. P. C. Mowle, for example, included only the most ancient white Australian families, those whose forebears had arrived before 1838. Henderson's pastoral pioneers, on the other hand, rest their claims primarily on the qualities of 'perseverence' and 'enterprise' which they displayed in possessing this 'land of promise'.[24] The imagery of the Old Testament, so familiar to this generation of Calvinistic Scots, provided the moral bedrock for a patriarchal interpretation of their family history.

What this history suppressed or skirted was the conflict between the claims of the pioneers and those of the original tenants of the soil, the Aborigines. Only the scholarship of the last decade has revealed how close to the surface of the land-takers' consciousness was the guilty knowledge of their trespass.[25] But in the family chronicles their descendants supplied to Henderson, the Aborigines – repeatedly characterised as 'troublesome' and 'treacherous' – become merely obstacles to be overcome by the intrepid pioneer.

It took another generation before the pastoral families produced genuine historians of their own, and then it was from the female line of dutiful, but not uncritical, daughters that they mainly came. Judith Wright's *The Generations of Men* (1959), Mary Durack's *Kings in Grass Castles* (1959), Margaret Kiddle's *Men of Yesterday* (1961) and Elyne Mitchell's stories of the Snowy Country are among the first and finest of a remarkable postwar legacy of pastoral sagas written by the daughters of the great pastoral families. It is regrettable that recent feminist historians have so far given little critical attention to these grandmothers of Australian women's history for their careers offer subtle insights into the limits of intellectual independence among the daughters of the squattocracy.

Writing the family history was often a duty imposed by pastoral patriarchs upon their talented daughters, but the women's manner of discharging it did not always accord with parental expectations. 'My father had always wanted me some day to write of the family's pioneering efforts,' Mary Durack recalled in the preface to her story of her forebears, a pioneering family from the Kimberleys. 'He had a keen feeling for history,' she observed, and his journals, kept over sixty years, were an invaluable resource. Yet, she writes, 'only his death, that was so great a loss to me, left me free to write as I have done'.[26] Only as the pioneering age drew to its close, we may hypothesise, were its heirs freed to view their forebears with the pity and irony of the historian. By the time they wrote, the dutiful daughters had often left the land to their brothers or uncles and their writings breathe a wistfulness for a life near enough to remember, too distant ever to be regained.

Judith Wright was barely fourteen years old when her grandmother, Charlotte May Wright, matriarch of the pioneering family, died in 1929. She therefore stood in a less immediate relationship to the 'generations of men' chronicled in her book of that name, published in 1959. Hers is an affectionate, semi-fictionalised account of her grandparents' lives as pastoral pioneers in northern New South Wales and Queensland. It reproduces, yet subtly transforms, the standard themes of pioneer history – pride in land and lineage, the legitimating battle with the elements, the fertile heritage of sons, vines and flocks. But it is a story told largely from a woman's viewpoint, and shaped more by Wright's sense of the cyclical rhythms of the seasons and generations than the straight lines of material progress. Survival and continuity, rather than conquest and progress, are its leading themes. It begins at Dalwood, her family's property in the Hunter Valley, a place that already, at the beginning of her grandmother's life, had assumed 'the quality of legend'. 'There was about their story something of the atmosphere of the Book of Genesis,' Wright reflects. The life of her grandparents, Albert and May, and their search for new pastures in New England and Queensland assumes the shape of an Australian Exodus. And their story concludes, in the mood of Ecclesiastes, with May Wright's musings on the eternal cycles of life and death:

> By the end of the year [1929] she will have gone to her grave on the hill-slope near Wongwibinda – the grave she chose, as though even in death she must overlook what is being done on her beloved property. As for her world – perhaps by then it will have fallen and smashed with the prices on the world's stock exchanges, perhaps it is already vanishing from round her on the quickening tide of change. But at least she is secure; whatever changes, she and her century are unalterable now.[27]

Twenty years later Judith Wright returned to her family history, amplifying and revising it in ways that reveal, not only her changing commitments, but the increasingly problematical character of patriarchal family history. *The Generations of Men* was a hymn to human continuity and growth; *The Cry for the Dead*, published in 1981, is a lament for the victims, black and white, of the European invasion. In the first rendering of her family's story, Wright dealt briefly but sympathetically with the fate of the Aborigines. 'The whites knew that from the tribesman's point of view they were trespassing on country where they had no rights,' she observed. Into the mind of her grandfather, Albert Wright, she inserted some of those awkward 'questions of conscience' that she had evidently begun to ask herself.[28]

But it is only in the second account that these questions are faced head-on. By the time she came to write it, the author was a prominent advocate of both Aboriginal land rights and environmental conservation. The tone of *The Cry for the Dead* is less personal and lyrical than its predecessor. It is as though Wright felt a need to distance herself from her subject, to ground her grim conclusions in verifiable fact. The union of land and lineage that she celebrated in her own forebears' history is now relocated to the Aborigines they dispossessed. Instead of the reassuring images of growth and continuity that bathe the Epilogue of *The Generations of Men* in a kind of autumnal glow, Wright concludes her second book on a tragic note. By 1980 the last speakers of the local Aboriginal tongue have disappeared from the plains of central Queensland, the native forests have been cleared, the grasslands stripped raw by overgrazing and gouged by open-cut mining. 'None of the descendants of Albert and May Wright now own land on the plain or beyond it; and perhaps none of the descendants of the Wadja, if any remain, have seen the country that once was theirs,' she mournfully concludes.[29]

It would be hard to imagine a more striking evocation of the historical disjunction that Wright's generation of pioneer families experienced in the 1970s and 1980s. Her appreciation of the change – crystallised, as it was, by her commitments to the causes of Aboriginal land rights and environmental conservation – may have been more acute than some of her contemporaries. (Mary Durack, always a more resolute upholder of traditional values, continued to write within the broad paradigm of patriarchal family history throughout the 1970s.[30]) It was no more than symptomatic, however, of an entire complex of changes that were simultaneously reinforcing the longing for roots and loosening the soil in which they were planted.

Not the least of these changes was a growing inclination to question the patriarchal order that had first cast the dutiful daughters of the homestead in the role of family historians. In the eyes of their fathers and brothers, we may imagine, family history was women's work; although, as Wright and Durack were to prove, it was not without its intellectual rewards. Only in the next generation, however, did the limitations of the role become fully apparent. Jill Ker Conway's *The Road from Coorain* (1989) is at once an apotheosis and a negation of patriarchal history. In its lyrical evocation of the landscape of western New South Wales and the affecting story of her father's heroic struggle against war neurosis and the droughts of the early 1940s, it stands – along with Wright's *Generations of Men* and Patrick White's *Tree of Man* – in the mainstream of pioneer history.

The crucial difference of *The Road from Coorain* is in the denouement of the story and the stance of the writer. Unlike the traditional story of pioneer life, in which shared trials build family solidarity, Conway's is a story of tragic family dissolution. Her father drowns mysteriously in a dam; her distraught mother returns to Sydney and seeks refuge in pills and alcohol; the children are dispersed to boarding schools. At university Conway eventually becomes a historian and begins a thesis on the colonial wool industry; but she chafes against the insularity and intellectual narrowness of her male colleagues. 'The place I was most at home was the bush,' she recalled. But she knew that 'as much as I loved it I would become a hermitlike female eccentric if I settled into that isolation alone'. In the end, she decides to abandon Australia and pursue higher studies in the United States. The only pang of parting, she implies, was saying goodbye to the family homestead, Coorain. As the plane waits on the tarmac, her mind flies back to the dusty cemetery where her father was buried:

> Where, I wondered, would my bones come to rest? It pained me to think of them not fertilizing Australian soil. Then I comforted myself with the notion that wherever on the earth was my final resting place, my body would return to the restless red dust of the western plains. I could see how it would blow about and get in people's eyes, and I was content with that.[31]

In this passage the link between land and lineage, which was the foundation of patriarchal history, has been stretched almost to breaking point. The cycle of generations has been arrested. The family no longer dwell on the land they fought so hard to keep. And the writer is about to leave her family and her native soil forever. All that remains, it seems, is the haunting after-image of nostalgia.

The reconstruction of family history

It would be easy, but too simple, to dismiss the family history boom as mere atavism, a clod thrown backwards by the chariots of time. Like fundamentalist religion, or voodoo economics, it looks like an essentially regressive symptom of postmodernity. It seeks a sense of continuity in a world of discontinuity, of concord in a world of conflict, of intimacy in a world of impersonality. But it is also something more, for family history has the potential to disturb as well as to console. Not all family histories, as we have seen, are consoling, at least in the sense that they are about happy families. Moreover, it is not necessary to love or respect one's ancestors in order to want to know their story. As the efforts of adoptees to find their natural parentage illustrate, people will endure a good deal of frustration and disillusionment to reclaim their past.

The radical possibilities of family history are well illustrated by the significant role it now performs in the political and spiritual life of those whose ancestral claims were most rudely denied by patriarchal history, the Aborigines. Among urbanised Aborigines, as well as those still living in traditional settings, lineage remains the bedrock of social life. The ancestral claims of the First Fleeters and white pioneers pale into insignificance beside those of the thousand or more generations of Aborigines who preceded them. Australians of European descent have increasingly come to acknowledge the spiritual affinity, if not the legal claim, of Aborigines to their ancestral lands and to look to Aborigines as models of ecological consciousness. When Mary Durack claims that West Australians have 'long since developed an almost Aboriginal sense of identification with their environment', she both acknowledges, and seeks to qualify, the Aborigines' special claim to the soil.[32]

For many twentieth century Aborigines, the ancestral past has also been a hidden past. Separated from their mothers at birth and raised in foster homes or institutions, they know little at first hand of their ancestry, language or traditions. Robert Murray, raised on the Cowra Mission in southern New South Wales, compares his own faint memories of family and Aboriginal tradition with the more continuous oral traditions of Aborigines in the Northern Territory: The Territorians know their family stories 'because there they're retold over and over again to their children's children. . . . Most of our knowledge [he says] comes from books, or from the screen, or from what people tell us. Not from our own people.'[33] Such people must now learn the same techniques of documentary research and oral history as other family historians to pick up the trail of their family past.[34] In her Foreword to *Lookin for Your Mob: A Guide to Tracing Aboriginal Family Trees*, Iris Clayton, a Wiradjuri family historian, reflects on the role of genealogy in the development of Aboriginal identity:

> As Aboriginal people become more aware of their lost lands, heritage and culture, they are increasingly feeling the need for their lost family genealogy. We want our identity returned. This is a need that is growing stronger every year. Our young people need their true identity returned to them with names and stories of their ancestors. This will in turn give them back their self-esteem

along with a purpose in life. Pride in their ancestors and culture will replace oppression, thus interest in Aboriginal culture will grow and hopefully our future generations will have a rich and living heritage to look back on.[35]

There is both irony and justice in the fact that, at a time when many Australians of European parentage look longingly to Aboriginal society as a source of spiritual inspiration, Aborigines should be borrowing the sources and techniques of European history to repair their own shattered sense of identity.

Sally Morgan's bestselling autobiography, *My Place*, describes the search of a young Aboriginal woman to recover her family history. Morgan had grown up unaware of her Aboriginal parentage and had to overcome the resistance of her relatives, long accustomed to the secrecy and shame of miscegenation, before she was able to trace her family tree. Her search led her back, not only to her Aboriginal grandmother, but to the scion of the well-known pastoral family, the Drake-Brockmans, whose child her grandmother had borne. In recovering her family history, Morgan thus illuminates a dark underside of pioneer history, but it is a revelation made without rancour. Far more important, in Morgan's own scale of values, is the release that her discoveries bring from the obscurity of her own origins. 'Can't you just leave the past buried, it won't hurt anyone then?' her mother pleads. 'Mum,' she replies, 'it's already hurt people. It's hurt you and me and Nan, all of us . . . I have a right to know my own history.'[36] It is this redemptive quality of family history, its capacity to release the guilt and pain of the past, which inspires other writers, too, to bring family history to the centre of their concerns.[37]

The last decade has also seen the emergence of a new kind of family history among European Australians. As the children of the rebellious 1960s and 1970s enter middle age, they often manifest an urgent need to rediscover the families they once sought to escape. Germaine Greer's *Daddy, We Hardly Knew You* (1989), Arnold Zable's *Jewels and Ashes* (1991) and Drusilla Modjeska's *Poppy* (1990) each describes a return to the home turf, the disinterring of a painful past and a quest to make peace with the ancestors. These searches are at once an extension and a radical rejection of the old family history. For the old family historians, establishing a lineage was a pursuit that reinforced a sense of certainty amidst doubt, of continuity amidst change. The new family history, on the other hand, is born of a sense of discontinuity, of broken lineages, fractured time and geographical distance. While the old family history records achievements, the new commemorates suffering. While the old celebrates family life, the new – often informed by feminism and Laingian psychoanalysis – radically deconstructs it. The search itself is therefore a more difficult and open-ended undertaking, one in which it is the journey rather than the arrival that matters.[38]

These new family histories are shaped differently from the old. The genealogist traditionally begins with the family founder, its colonial Abraham, and moves forward, generation by generation, tribe by tribe, to trace his large and fruitful issue. By its very shape, the story creates a sense of pattern or purpose that enables the descendants to identify their place in a larger patriarchal scheme. The new family histories, on the other hand, begin in the here and now, with the writer, and describe a journey backwards in time, and often through space, towards an uncertain destination. Family history, to use Modjeska's metaphor, becomes the slow unravelling of a thread, a teasing out as well as a tracing back.

A preoccupation of the new family history, no less than of the old, is the idea of inheritance. 'There is no bucking the genes,' declares Greer, an enthusiastic, if selective, hereditarian. In tracing her father's past, she recognises mysterious affinities of physique and temperament between father and daughter – a strong jaw, a weak stomach, claustrophobia, even, she once fancies, a secret love of aliases.[39] Pondering her mother's breakdown, Drusilla Modjeska raises the resident ghost of genealogy – the fear of hereditary madness:

> When I was in my early thirties, I was afraid, for a long time that, like Lily, I'd have Poppy's breakdown, as if such things are part of our inheritance. The fear that we will follow the patterns laid down by our mothers seems deeply embedded in the female psyche.

But it is a fear she quickly dispels as 'irrational', as she subtly delineates the circumstances that brought her mother low. The inheritance that matters for Modjeska is not biological, but generational. For the feminists of the 1970s, the recognition of what is taken from, or owed to, their parentage is also a revaluation of the freedom they had sought to win. 'While my generation had been noisy in taking our freedoms, I wonder what it signifies in a world in which loneliness is endemic, sexual freedom too easy and too dangerous, and intellectual freedom institutionally hobbled, or fashion-bound,' she reflects.[40]

Like other family historians they follow the standard procedures of genealogical research – the devilling through birth and death registers, the pilgrimages to graveyards and other sites of remembrance, the interrogation of family elders. But there comes a point in each of these narratives when the documents peter out, the gravestones are mute and the elders fall silent. Then the historian has nothing but imagination to sustain a search that still cannot be abandoned. As his train crosses the border into the Soviet Union, Arnold Zable tears up his father's terse outline of the family past and throws it out the window in a gesture symbolic of his own transition from 'outsider' to 'insider'. 'Use your imagination,' Drusilla Modjeska's mother replies, when she cannot, or will not, fill the gaps in the factual record. Even for Greer, the most indefatigable genealogist of the three, fact quickly gives way to conjecture, and conjecture to fiction.

Always implicit, and sometimes quite explicit, in their stance is a critique of the epistemological claims of orthodox history. 'I used to think that truth was single and error legion, but I know now that none of us grasps more than a little splinter of the truth,' writes Greer. For the feminist writers the truth of imagination may be truer, as well as more healing, than the truth of fact. Family history is part of that mysterious domain of women's knowledge that feminists have now set out to reclaim and assert in refutation of the false claims of masculine knowledge. In a series of dialogues with her mother, her lawyer-father and her ex-lover, Modjeska ponders the shifting boundaries between the momentous and the ordinary, between 'evidence' and 'feelings', between 'what can be said and what cannot.'[41]

In a similar dialogue with her brother, Greer insists that her father's account of his own life, as a 'good family man', was 'typical of the lie of *history*', whereas her own more truthful account was 'a classic example of *her*story, punctuating the ideology'.[42]

For each of the writers the return to the past is born of a sense of discontinuity more painful and profound than most family historians own up to. The gulf that divides them from their forebears is in part self-made – a legacy of the struggle for liberation that was the common thread of intellectual life in the 1960s and 1970s. More than thirty years later, Greer still rehearses the conflicts and bears the scars of her rebellion against the strictures of her parents' generation. As the limits of their liberation become evident, and as their own sense of mortality grows stronger, the claims of the parental past reassert themselves. 'We could imagine other ways of living,' Modjeska writes of her feminist contemporaries, 'but we didn't take account of our own histories . . . .'.[43]

Zable also hints at these strains. 'The arguments between us had been, at times, quite ferocious,' he remarks in passing of his relationship with his father, although the issues that were at stake are left unspoken.[44] Modjeska, on the other hand, deals with them head-on, trying imaginatively to reconstruct how their differences looked from her mother's angle as well as her own.

Their youthful desire to escape the family past, like their mature desire to rediscover it, is a frontal attack on that code of silence by which their parents' generation had kept their own painful family pasts at bay. War, racial persecution, sexual infidelity, childhood abandonment, mental breakdown – these were the ghosts that often haunted them, but in deflecting or denying their children's questions the parents of the complacent and conformist 1940s and 1950s had only postponed the day of reckoning.

That moment comes, for Drusilla Modjeska, with the death of her mother. 'My mother had died,' she writes, 'and it was true what I'd said, I did not know her . . . I knew that by not knowing her, I could not know myself.'[45] It was not that she was ignorant of the details of her mother's life for, as her book makes plain, she had been engaged for some time in an effort to reconstruct it. What she did not know, and what she urgently needed to understand, was the truth of those painful ruptures in a family history that had set out to be 'ordinary' – her parents' gradual estrangement, her father's infidelity, her mother's breakdown, her own banishment to boarding school, the anomalous liaison between her mother and a Catholic priest. She finds that the ruptures were, in a sense, implicit in the very pursuit of ordinariness, that her mother's breakdown, for example, came from an accumulation of small, silent injuries rather than the catastrophic onset of one big one.

It is death, too, that releases Germaine Greer from the compact of silence that had surrounded her father's past. 'Now that Daddy's need to have us not know is at an end, my need to know can be satisfied.' She had grown up knowing almost nothing about his parentage or early life. 'He never referred to any kin, neither father nor mother nor sisters nor brothers nor aunts nor uncles, not even in a chance anecdote. He was a man without a past.'[46] From her earliest years, his daughter had carried the hurtful memory of his departure as a RAAF officer during the war and his return as an emaciated and grey-faced invalid. Between father and daughter there had developed an emotional reserve that ripened in her teenage years into outright hostility. To make her peace, if possible, she must try to find that unknown father who preceded, and perhaps coexisted with, the father of painful memory.

Slowly, along faint trails and up dead-ends, Greer unpicks the tangled skein of misadventures and deceptions that made Robert Hamilton King, son of a Tasmanian servant girl, first into the adoptee and Launceston draper's assistant Eric Greeney, and then into the dapper Melbourne advertising salesman, Reginald Greer. The child in her, she admits, had embarked on her search in the hope of discovering a 'hero', a 'prince'. But the man she finds – a liar, a bounder, perhaps a shirker as well – is product not just of his own troubled upbringing and the stresses of wartime service as an intelligence officer in besieged Malta, but, as the author herself finally admits, of her own 'censorious, scrutinising nature'. To understand all, for Greer, is not finally to forgive all.[47]

In all three of these new family histories, the traumas of war-torn Europe cast a long shadow over modern Australia, in none more so than Arnold Zable's *Jewels and Ashes*. Meir Zbludowski, father of Arnold Zable, is the sole survivor of his family, one of only a handful of the once great Polish–Jewish community of Bialystok to escape the Holocaust. In faraway Melbourne, the old man hoards the few scraps of paper that document the family past, but he always deflects his son's questions. '"There are not enough hours in the day for what I want to do," he has told me many times. "Why waste them in recalling things that have long since gone?"' His obstinate refusal to raise the stones of memory only reinforces the son's determination to retrace the family's past. For the second generation, the distance that separates their parents' experience from their own is at once a barrier and an invitation:

> We were born in the wake of Annihilation. We were children of dreams and shadows, yet raised in the vast spaces of the New World. We roamed the streets of our migrant neighbourhoods freely. We lived on coastlines and played under open horizons. Our world was far removed from the sinister events that had engulfed our elders. Yet there had always been undercurrents that could sweep us back to the echoes of childhood, to the sudden torrents of rage and sorrow that could, at any time, disturb the surface calm: 'You cannot imagine what it was like,' our elders insisted. 'You were not there.' Their messages were always ambiguous, tinged with menace, double-edged: 'You cannot understand, yet you must. You should not delve too deeply, yet you should. But even if you do, my child, you will never understand. You were not there.'[48]

In the effort imaginatively to 'be there', Zable returns to the ancestral town of Bialystok. Guided by a map drawn by his parents, he visits the neighbourhood where his grandfather Bishke, the newspaper seller, had rushed through the streets. He returns to the desolate village of Bielsk, once home to his mother's folk, the Liebermans, where he finds a tiny remnant of the Jewish community. He journeys to Pruzhany, a townlet on the edge of the Bialowieza forests, to which, in September 1941, the Gestapo ordered 12,000 of Bialystok's Jews, where his aunt Sheindl met her lover, the resistance leader Yanek Lerner. And he stands near the vacant lot, once known as Prager's Garden, where, on the evening of 5 February 1943, his grandparents, among 900 others, were shot in reprisal for an attack on a German officer.

Zable's journey can never enable him to understand the experiences of the Annihilation as those who were there do; but it is enough to make a bridge of understanding to those who survive. It is only when he returns to Australia and speaks to his father that the barrier of silence is broken down. Only if the past is first remembered can its victims begin to forget.

Conclusion

Our grandparents' generation had a rich vocabulary for describing the relations between past and present. They spoke of 'our heritage', of 'the legacy of the past', of ideas and values, as well as other 'proud possessions', being 'bequeathed' from generation to generation. Such ways of speaking came naturally to a society in which the obligations of children to parents, and notions of blood and heredity, were well and widely understood. When the servicemen of the Great War returned to meet the orphaned children of their dead comrades, it was natural not only that they should think of assuming a responsibility for their welfare, but that the organisation they founded to do it should be called Legacy.

Such ways of speaking are no longer natural to us. Over the past twenty-five years, some of these words have acquired an antique ring and some, like 'heritage' for example, have abruptly changed their meaning. These changes are emblematic of a more pervasive shift in the ways we think of the relations between past and present, and of the mutual relations between the generations. The complex settling of accounts with the past, which is the theme of the new family histories, thus mirrors the preoccupations of national history. Feminism, environmentalism, Aboriginality – each in its way constructs a narrative of loss and guilt, and makes a claim for restitution. Pre-eminent among these claims is that of the Stolen Generations for apology and restitution. These claims raise matters that have to be remembered before they can be forgiven, though perhaps never quite forgotten. It's not that the past, to which we once considered ourselves debtors, can belatedly be handed a bill and somehow made to pay for its unacknowledged debts to the future. In that sense, at least, the past is dead and, if debts have to be paid, then it is only the present and the future that can pay them.[49] But that the past – at least the European past – has exhausted its credit, and that we no longer have to consider ourselves beholden to it, seems to be an unstated assumption of much contemporary culture.

The new family histories supply a telling commentary on that assumption and a partial corrective to it. They not only remind us that there are things we cannot change, but also that even the self that wishes to change them is a product of the past. Perhaps only a nation with a fading legacy of Judaeo-Christian belief, for example, would be susceptible to a claim for atonement and restitution. Just as our ancestors looked to genealogy as the model of nationhood so, perhaps, in these more complex renderings of family history, Australians may find a clue to a new sense of national becoming.

Notes

1   Nick Vine Hall, 'Establishing an Identity', *Society of Australian Genealogists 1932–1982: Golden Jubilee History*, Sydney, 1982, pp82–93; and compare his 'Genealogy and the Writing of History' in Geoffrey Burkhardt and Peter Procter, *Bridging the Generations: Fourth Australasian Congress on Genealogy and Heraldry*, Canberra, 1986, pp391–99; for recent statistics showing a levelling-off of growth, see *Descent: Official Organ of the Society of Australian Genealogists*, vol. 22, no. 3, September 1992, p101.

2   Winsome A. N. van den Bossche, *Amateur Historical Inquiry in the Tracing of Ancestry: Establishing a Profile of a Genealogist, A Victorian Survey*, M.Ed. Thesis, University of Melbourne, 1988. The questionnaire was circulated through the two main Victorian genealogical societies and the genealogical research centre at the State Library of Victoria and is possibly biased towards the more stable element in a floating population of enthusiasts; also compare Noeline Kyle, 'Our Women Ancestors: Illuminating Women on the Family Tree' in Burkhardt and Procter, *Bridging the Generations*, pp217–25.

3   Herbert Rumsey, 'The Collection of Family History', *Australian Genealogist*, vol. 1, Part 1, January 1933, p2.

4   June Elliott, *They Came from Somerset: The Story of Stephen and Emma Harris and their Descendents*, privately printed, Adelaide n.d., pp4–10.

5   R. M. Taylor, 'Summoning the Wandering Tribes: Genealogy and Family Reunions in American History', *Journal of Social History*, vol. 16, no. 2, 1982, pp21–38.

6   'Kaleidoscope', *Genealogist*, vol. 2, no. 6, June 1978, p156.

7   A. Ollier, 'Personal Experiences in Genealogical Research', *Victorian Genealogist*, December 1963, p66.

8   M. Fleay Beasy, *'Belonging': A Research into the Fleay Family through Six Centuries by a Descendant of the Family*, privately printed, Burleigh Heads, 1979, pix.

9   In his article 'Organizing a Family Reunion', *Genealogist*, vol. 3, March 1981, pp143–54, F. J. Robinson gives instructions on how to organise a thanksgiving service 'general' enough to accommodate 'widely varying branches of the Christian faith'.

10   Editorials in *Descent*, vol. 1, Part 1, 1960 and *Victorian Genealogist*, September 1961, p21.

11   W. H. Bossence, 'Genealogy at Kyabram', *Victorian Genealogist*, April 1965, pp97–98.

12   *Genealogist*, vol. 2, no. 3, September 1977, p92; and compare Phil Brotchie, 'Genealogy and Genetics', Ibid., vol. 3, March 1981, pp156–58.

13   *Victorian Genealogist*, April 1967, p147.

14   *Genealogist*, vol. 2, no. 3, September 1977.

15   June Elliott, *They Came from Somerset: The Story of Stephen and Emma Harris and their Descendants*, privately printed, Adelaide n.d., p4.

16   John Hirst, 'The Pioneer Tradition' in John Carroll (ed.), *Intruders in the Bush*, OUP, Melbourne, 1982, pp14–37; and also see his 'Egalitarianism' in S. Goldberg and F. B. Smith (eds), *Australian Cultural History*, CUP, Melbourne, 1988, pp58–77.

17   Paul de Serville, *Pounds and Pedigrees: The Upper Class in Victoria 1850–80*, OUP, Melbourne, 1991, pp191–92.

18   Douglas Cole, 'The Crimson Thread of Kinship', *Historical Studies*, vol. 14, no. 56, April 1971, pp511–25.

19   Gavin Souter, *Lion and Kangaroo: Australia: 1901–1919. The Rise of a Nation*, Fontana Edition, Sydney, 1978, p48.

20   'Compiling a Family History', *Victorian Genealogist*, vol. 2, Part 3, 1965, p85.

21   Women's Pioneer Society of Australia, *Annual Reports, 1958–60*; V. M. E. Goodlin, 'The Hon. T. D. Mutch and his Work', *Descent*, vol. 1, no. 1, 1960, pp5–11; K. S. Inglis, '1788 to 1988', *Overland*, no. 106, March 1987, pp11–13.

22   *Pioneer Families of Australia*, Sydney, 1948, 4th edition, n.p.

23   Alexander Henderson, *Henderson's Australian Families*, vol. 1, A. Henderson, Melbourne, 1941.

24   Henderson, p121 (entry on Yuille family).

25   Tom Griffiths, *Hunters and Collectors*, ch. 5.

26   *Kings in Grass Castles*, Constable, London, 1959, pxiii–xiv.

27   *The Generations of Men*, OUP, Melbourne, 1959, p222.

28   Ibid., pp14, 32.

29   *The Cry for the Dead*, OUP, Melbourne, 1981, pp. 279–80; and compare her *Born of the Conquerors*, Aboriginal Studies Press, Canberra, 1991.

30   See, for example, her *Sons in the Saddle*, Constable, London, 1983, *To Be Heirs Forever*, Constable, London, 1976, and the preface to Ingrid Drysdale and Mary Durack, *The End of the Dreaming*, Rigby, Adelaide, 1974.

31   Jill Ker Conway, *The Road from Coorain: An Australian Memoir*, Mandarin, London, 1989, p238.

32   Mary Durack, *To Be Heirs Forever*, Constable, London, 1976, p19.

33   Robert Murray as quoted in Peter Read (ed.), *Down There on the Cowra Mission: An Oral History of Erambie Aboriginal Reserve, Cowra, New South Wales*, Pergamon, Sydney, 1984, p15; and compare Read, *The Stolen Generations: The Removal of Aboriginal Children in New South Wales, 1883–1969*, New South Wales Ministry of Aboriginal Affairs Occasional Paper no. 1, n.d.

34   See, for example, the description of the part played by Family History and Genealogy Workshops in community development projects in South Australia in Jane Jacobs, 'Women Talking Up Big: Aboriginal Women as Cultural Custodians, A South Australian Example' in Peggy Brock (ed.), *Women, Rites and Sites: Aboriginal Women's Cultural Knowledge*, Allen & Unwin, Sydney, 1989, pp91–93. In 1992 one of the most famous Aborigines, Evonne Goolagong-Cawley, returned to Australia after 17 years' residence in the United States and has since been continuously occupied in researching her family's past. See Greg Roberts, 'Evonne's Greatest Return', *Good Weekend*, 16 January 1993, pp8–11.

35   Diane Smith and Boronia Halstead, *Lookin for Your Mob: A Guide to Tracing Aboriginal Family Trees*, Aboriginal Studies Press, Canberra, 1990, pix.

36   *My Place*, Fremantle Arts Press, Fremantle, 1987, p152.

37   Compare with the perceptive discussion in Bain Attwood, 'Portrait of the Aboriginal as an Artist: Sally Morgan and the Construction of Aboriginality', *Australian Historical Studies*, vol. 25, no. 99, October 1992, pp302–18.

38   Germaine Greer, *Daddy, We Hardly Knew You*, Penguin, London, 1989; Drusilla Modjeska, *Poppy*, Penguin, Ringwood, Victoria, 1990; Arnold Zable, *Jewels and Ashes*, Scribe, Newnham, Victoria, 1991.

39   Greer, p271.

40   Modjeska, pp77, 90.

41   See Greer, p9, and Modjeska, especially chs 4 and 5.

42   Greer, p303.

43   Modjeska, p260.

44   Zable, p63.

45   Modjeska, p5.

46   Greer, p6.

47   Greer, pp6, 311.

48   Zable, pp7, 163.

49   See the exchange between Robert Manne, Stuart Macintyre, Janet McCalman and Graeme Davison in 'The Inaugural Melbourne Debate: That Australia's Historians Should Wear Black Armbands', *Melbourne Historical Journal*, vol. 26, 1998, pp1–16.

Chapter 5

James Green

TAKING HISTORY TO HEART

The Power of the Past in Building Social Movements

T HE YEAR I SPENT IN BRITAIN discovering the History Workshop also started me thinking about teaching movement history and sharing it with workers in a college setting like the one I had seen in Ruskin. In 1975 and 1976 I had a chance to lecture in American labor history at the Centre for the Study of Social History at Warwick University in Coventry, Britain's bombed-out motor city. The Centre had first been directed by E. P. Thompson, who invited David Montgomery to be the first American lecturer in 1969. That was when students occupied the administration building and discovered documents exposing the influence of car industry executives in university affairs. By the time I arrived in Warwick, Thompson had left the Centre, and the sit-in of 1969 was folklore. The new director, Royden Harrison, was an avuncular socialist of the old school who created a relaxed atmosphere in an old farmhouse filled with zealous social historians. I taught labor history to a seminar of master's degree students. Some of them were local working-class people who had joined radical groups and worked in the industrial Midlands, where unions had gained enormous shop-floor power in the postwar years.

One of the Warwick students introduced me to a teacher in the venerable Workers Education Association, which provided instruction in union halls. As a result, I was invited to teach a session on U.S. unions for the shop stewards at the big Massey-Ferguson farm equipment plant near Coventry. My first experience in workers ed was challenging because it was not easy to explain to militant British shop stewards why U.S. union leaders seemed so conservative, and often so far removed from their members. An evening in a well-appointed workingmen's club topped off my first attempt at labor education; it introduced me to middle-aged union men far more interested in what I had to say about labor history than any of my university students had ever been.

Being inspired

Curious about this world where workers met intellectuals, I attended the marvelous History Workshop of 1976 at Ruskin College – a conference devoted entirely to the history of workers education. I learned about worker students and their interaction with radical teachers, and was encouraged to read about Charles Beard, the American progressive historian who founded Ruskin College at Oxford in 1899, and about Mary Ritter Beard, the pioneering historian who taught courses for the Women's Trade Union League. I read about R. H. Tawney, perhaps the most influential socialist intellectual in twentieth-century Britain, who "found himself" through workers education and then became its enthusiastic prophet while writing history inspired by that movement. I also read about A. J. Muste, the radical pacifist whose critical teaching at Brookwood Labor College angered the AFL hierarchy in the 1920s; about Claude Williams, the messianic radical who formed Commonwealth College in Arkansas; and about Myles Horton, who created the Highlander Folk School in Tennessee, which served as a training ground for the new CIO unions in the Depression years and later for the civil rights movement.[1]

Workers education offered a way of learning to teach movement history to workers and a way of engaging with them in movement building. Myles Horton reflected on how educators made this connection in the 1930s. "We had a movement at one time in the CIO," he recalled. "We worked together. There was a social movement that was not just unions organizing for wages and better working conditions and security. It was people organizing to do things in their community, taking political action, learning about the world. . . . Education was part of that; it was a kind of spark that kept those things ignited."[2]

We lacked a vibrant workers education movement like the one I observed in Britain and we missed flash points of worker-student unity that appeared in France during May of '68 and in Italy during the "autunno caldo" of 1969. But in the past, American intellectuals had successfully engaged workers in the process of building radical and progressive movements.

A rocky road

My own engagement with movement politics led me down a road traveled by many New Left radicals, a road we hoped would lead to a revived, radicalized labor movement. This was a kind of toll road, manned by gatekeepers from powerful organizations with conservative leaders. It was a rocky road to run, one strewn with anti-intellectual boulders strategically placed by the founder of the American Federation of Labor, Samuel Gompers, during his war to protect the union members from the radical intellectuals, even though many of these dreamers were workers themselves. Gompers's hostility to the "fool friends of labor" was written into history by Selig Perlman, who told the story as one of a continuous struggle of "organic labor" against the "dominance of intellectuals." During the 1930s, when the left reemerged in the movement, a political challenge would again be posed in "the classic terms of the intellectual problem."[3] This defense of pure-and-simple unionism by the "practical men" prepared the ground for the purge of the left during the Cold War years when workers with radical or progressive ideas were forced out of the movement. At the high tide of popular anti-intellectualism in 1954, the progressive historian Merle Curti explained that some intellectuals had become disillusioned with trade unions, while those who "stuck with the movement either ceased being intellectuals," in a critical sense, or learned to accept and respect the movement's "tough fabric of custom."[4] When the popular anti-intellectualism of the fifties receded, it remained strong in the House of Labor.

The hostility of AFL–CIO leadership to radicals seemed to be shared to some degree by many rank-and-file members who harbored their suspicion of outsiders, like former student radicals. We were constantly reminded of one notorious incident: hard-hatted construction workers beating up on long haired, antiwar demonstrators in New York City.[5]

Nonetheless, in the late 1970s possibilities opened up for former student radicals to participate in workplace and community struggles and to engage working people in educational activities. Perhaps an early enthusiasm for participatory democracy helped prepare former New Leftists for popular education work. In any case, it was not surprising to learn in 1988 that far more of our veterans of '68 engaged in "social and trade union work" than their European cohorts.[6]

When I began to engage workers and their unions in Boston, I hit a wall of suspicion. It was one thing to write labor movement history with a sharply critical view of union bureaucrats and frozen ideas, as I did for *Radical America's* leftist audience; it was quite another matter writing radical history for the actually existing movement. When my first two books on labor history began to reach this audience, some trade unionists reacted negatively. These books would have been ignored by union leaders if I had remained an academic historian. But I was also a movement activist in regular contact with their members, including some determined insurgents. Therefore, my interpretation of labor history attracted some very tough readers who did not like what they saw. They would put me to the test: Would I persist and earn some credibility as a labor intellectual despite their opposition?

Persistence depended on finding allies. My natural allies came from the ranks of younger activists in Boston who shared my political background and values – a cadre of brilliant labor and community organizers (some of them former student radicals, and many others from less privileged backgrounds). They often posed questions about the past derived from their own political practice, and they supported my work as a historian. Allies also came from unexpected places, like the last Catholic labor school in the United States, an institution created after World War II to counter leftist influence in the labor movement. The two Jesuits who ran the church's Labor Guild were intellectuals and students of history (and were quietly independent of the AFL–CIO chiefs); they sold my books to students in their evening labor school and asked me to lecture there.

Most gratifying was the support offered by some Boston trade unionists whose fighting instincts had been aroused by employers' assaults. They were frustrated by a skittish union officialdom. Far from being anti-intellectual, these union loyalists hungered for discussions about history and values, and for serious debates about the issues (though many took the conservative side on the issues we raised). Far from being complacent, they worried passionately about the fate of organized labor and wanted to look back to the past – to find out what had once made their movement strong.

I relied on their support to create a space within our state university for an independent labor education program where union activists could be recognized as thinkers as well as activists, where they could reflect on learned experience, positive and negative, and where they could study movement history warts and all. In this free space we could learn from each other.

Breaking out

Inspired by comrades in the British workers education and History Workshop movements, I returned from England in 1976 determined to break out of my isolation as an assistant professor of history in an elite university by working on the farm workers boycotts and helping our librarians organize a union affiliated with Nine to Five, the women office workers organization. And as previously noted, my work with *Radical America* involved reporting on contemporary rank-and-file struggles and taking up Eric Foner's challenge to write a survey of twentieth-century workers history that would bring the insights of the new social and labor history to a wider audience.[7] I also accepted a promising invitation to lecture on local labor history at the Boston Public Library. In Massachusetts, where all politics is local, it seemed that Boston's labor history provided a promising subject for an initial experiment in doing public history.

The lectures resulted in a book written for a public audience, and addressed questions about trade union conservatism and labor radicalism.[8] The public lectures and the book led to the first opportunities to do worker education at the Boston Community School founded by radical entrepreneur extraordinaire, Michael Ansara, and at the Catholic Labor Guild run by the last two Jesuit "labor priests" in America.

Finding a free space to teach

These opportunities all arose in the last year of my "terminal contract" as an assistant professor of history at Brandeis, and in the depths of the academic "job crisis." Planning to stay in Boston where I had become deeply engaged in movement politics and public history, I considered leaving the academy. But then, more mysterious forces created a temporary teaching job in UMass-Boston's experimental adult education college. My new colleagues wanted someone to teach and write history and remain engaged in community and labor struggles! The college faculty and library staff were fighting for a union contract and there were lots of sixties radicals involved in this campaign and a variety of social causes in Boston's boiling cauldron of movement politics. The action, it seemed, never ended at my new school in the old Boston Gas Building. This experimental college wasn't well appointed or well respected by other academics, but for me it was just the place for doing movement history in public.

In 1966 the University of Massachusetts opened a campus in Boston despite strong opposition from various educational and financial elites. The College of Public and Community Service (CPCS) opened in 1973 as a result of a demand for public higher education to fulfill its urban mission. UMass Boston's Chancellor Frank Broderick, a biographer of W. E. B. Du Bois, thought the faculty's zeal to "provide disadvantaged students with the best in higher education" had tended to isolate the new campus from "large parts of the urban community."[9] Creating CPCS was part of an effort to open the university to a wider range of city dwellers.

The college grew from a few hundred students to nearly one thousand in the early 1980s. The adult students came mainly from the ranks of human and legal service workers, community agency staff and organizers, then later police officers, advocates for the elderly, and union activists. The student body has consisted of over 60 percent females and about 30 percent people of color, a high percentage for a New England college. The college emphasized equity in access and educational opportunity, stressed community service and activism for its faculty, and attempted to blend career education and liberal education – to provide a new kind of access to the university for working-class adults in front-line human service and neighborhood agencies. The faculty offered these workers opportunities to gain new competence in their fields and to become more reflective practitioners and more effective advocates for change.[10]

The curriculum was designed to evaluate student competence in career areas like human services, paralegal work, community planning, and in intellectual areas like political economy, history and culture, the self and society. I joined an interdisciplinary general education faculty organized to infuse liberal education and critical thinking into career-oriented studies. We did not emphasize acquiring knowledge for its own sake, the goal of traditional liberal arts education.[11] We hoped our students would also gain the competence to think critically and "to employ knowledge effectively."[12]

The college's philosophy drew upon Dewey's progressive ideas about the value of experiential learning and the need for egalitarian educational opportunities in a democratic society. CPCS encouraged faculty to evaluate experiential learning and to certify the competence students had gained through performing various social and occupational roles. No credit was given for experience, however.[13] Students were asked to work through a process of assessment and reflection and then demonstrate that their experience met criteria for competence the faculty had developed in various areas – ranging from professional skills like assessing client needs to intellectual skills like legal reasoning. So, instead of the exclusively course-based, graded college curriculum that many of our students had found oppressive in high school and in other college settings, the college developed an alternative curriculum for adults, emphasizing learning as an ongoing process that began before and continued after particular academic courses. Instead of competing for grades, students aimed to meet the same criteria and standards in a kind of contract learning situation; when they came up short, they continued to work with faculty to achieve competence.[14]

All of this put us at odds with those traditionalists in the faculty and the administration who wanted UMass-Boston to be a "Harvard for the poor." In a time when "excellence" was measured only by competitive success, we insisted on certifying competence measured by a person's ability to perform public and community service effectively without sacrificing a critical and an ethical view of one's work. In an era when the experimental programs in higher education began to dissolve, the college provided alternative education for poor and working people, people who would not otherwise have become college students.

The college attracted a faculty and staff of activist-educators who also wrote about the ethics and delivery of human service work, about women's studies, about the politics of community control and the tactics of community organizers, about shelter poverty, about the use of popular music in protest movements, about racism in Boston's schools. It included radicals with diverse political backgrounds, professors like Paul Rosenkrantz, our *consigliere*, a social psychologist who had been a Communist Party activist in the maritime union and in the South. Besides these faculty trained in traditional graduate programs, the College hired practitioners to teach a variety of courses, including Kip Tiernan, the founder of Rosie's Place, the first shelter for roofless women in Boston; Frank Manning, a socialist with a 1930s union background, who became the state's leading advocate for the elderly; Nelson Merced, the first Puerto Rican to serve in the Massachusetts legislature; and Gus Newport, the former mayor of Berkeley. One semester I saw the name "Moses" next to an algebra course. Someone said it was Bob Moses's course. "Do you mean the Bob Moses of the civil rights movement?" I asked incredulously. Indeed, the Robert Moses who had played a now legendary role in the Mississippi freedom struggle had come to teach math at our school.

The college provided support for bridging the gap between citizenship and scholarship created by academic professionalism. It also gave me a chance to overcome the "complacent disconnectedness" of academic teaching and writing described by another radical historian, Mike Merrill, in a fascinating report on his first venture into workers education at about the same time. The union workers he taught were intent on learning the "how" as well as the "what" – a trying experience, he found, for an intellectual not trained to make the connections between knowledge and action that these students wanted. Mike's "sobering experience" of teaching in union halls made him even more doubtful that this kind of teaching and learning could take place in schools, unless, he speculated, "the schools could be made working-class institutions," unless the professors also became organizers, and unless scholarship itself could "be made into a popular activity" like the British History Workshop.[15]

Before I could settle in at the college, there was a battle to fight with older faculty who opposed hiring another sixties radical, but thanks to Ann Withorn, my *Radical America* comrade, and to support from outside my department, I won a tenure-track position on the faculty. I could continue experimenting with how to do workers education and how to present movement history to movement people.

At first, I taught a course on how social movements shaped U.S. history using Howard Zinn's *People's History of the United States*, published in 1980, and asked Howard to take time out of his battles with Boston University czar John Silber in order to talk to our students. But I also wanted to teach about the history of work. Rather than begin by teaching labor history, which seemed too narrow a focus for the wide range of students who enrolled in my courses, I borrowed a leaf from Herb Gutman's book and taught about work and work relations over a broad sweep of history, from the decline of feudalism and the rise of industry, emphasizing the cultural as well as the class struggle over the terms of employment and the measures of work. Students read Maurice Dobb on the breakup of feudalism, E. E Thompson on exploitation, and E. J. Hobsbawm on machine breaking, Eugene Genovese on slavery, Nancy Cott on "the bonds of womanhood," Tom Dublin on the Lowell factory system and its "mill girls," Paul Paler and Alan Dawley on the shoemakers' resistance to the industrial revolution, W. E. B. Du Bois on Reconstruction, Eric Foner on the meaning of freedom for emancipated slaves, and Herb Gutman on immigrants and the shock of industrialization. Using David Montgomery's superb essays on workers' control struggles together with Harry Braverman's revealing book on the degradation of labor in the twentieth century, students learned how concerted activity and trade union militancy arose out of the capitalist drive to control all aspects of work as well as the behaviors of the people who performed it.

One year a seminar of extraordinary students met this extraordinary literature and created a peak experience for me as a seminar leader. The Thursday night gang, which always continued the seminar at Richard's Pub, included Jim O'Halloran, a garrulous man and head of the printer's chapel at the *Boston Herald* who would decide to do a thesis on Dorothy Day and the Catholic worker movement; Mike Bonislawski, a machinist at the GE River Works in Lynn who went on to do Ph.D. work in labor history on the anti-Communist movement that split his local union; Jeff Crosby, another machinist in the same plant, who headed the slate that brought the left back to office in the same Lynn local; Elizabeth Connor, a dedicated socialist who had helped "colonize" Baltimore's Sparrows Point steel plant; Michael McDevitt, an officer of the AMTRAK workers union who became a union-side lawyer; Wally Soper, a troublemaker with a sense of humor who became a union organizer and activist for Jobs with Justice; Janice Fine, a brilliant community organizer, who went on to MIT – of all places – to write a doctoral thesis on new union organizing strategies; and Tim Costello, a Teamster militant and writing partner of radical historian Jeremy Brecher – "Cosmic" Tim, who seemed to have trucked everywhere and read everything. What a group of students, and what a privilege it was to be in the same seminar room with them for a whole year as we traveled down the exciting roads charted by the best social historians.

Since the college's curriculum was highly flexible and not entirely course based, other exciting opportunities arose. Drawing upon the experience of the trade union students at the Ruskin History Workshop, I offered a "doing history" activity for those who wanted to gain competence in researching and writing the history of their own communities, workplaces, and social straggles. Engaging in these learning activities convinced me that the working people in our college needed and wanted to "get their history into their own hands," to use the words of Brazilian educator Paulo Freire.[16]

The British History Workshop approach sought to engage "the imaginations of trade unionists in adult education by getting them to explore their own occupations." Our adult students often found the study of their own occupations a good place to start because it provided more entry points related to their own experiences. Through these specific entry points, they could gain a greater feeling of mastery over a historical problem and learn to think more confidently about addressing broader questions in labor and social history.[17] When our students focused on specific topics, like an industry, a union, a community, or a strike, they could act like historians in their own right and begin to demystify historical scholarship.

Worker-students at our college produced histories of their own occupations, like the impact of Taylorism on postal workers, and wrote fascinating reflections on their own work as organizers of Mississippi pulp wood workers, Maine paper workers, and Miami building-trades workers. From these starting points, they began to study how social movements emerged from workplaces and communities to challenge the forces of capital and the state that now seemed so triumphant. It was easy for our working-class students, who had been pummeled by these forces, to adopt a pessimistic view of the past that "the more things change, the more they remain the same." It was a revelation for them to discover the rich vein of oppositional history uncovered by the new social and labor historians.[18]

Opening the university to union workers

At the same time, other movement historians were reaching out to unionized workers. Herbert Gutman, Steve Brier, Susan Porter Benson, Alice Kessler-Harris, Mike Merrill, Dorothy Sue Cobble, and David Bensman all shared my desire to create spaces in universities, places where we could teach movement history to workers. We also shared an interest in reviving labor education as a medium through which intellectuals could participate in movement building.

During the 1970s and 1980s we tried to connect with a labor movement facing the terrible onslaught described in the previous chapter, and as movement educators and activists, we tried, as Myles Horton reflected, to "anticipate a social movement." You try to "do things in advance that prepare for a larger movement," he explained many years later. "If you've guessed right," he wrote in his autobiography, "then you'll be on the inside of a movement helping with the mobilization and strategies, instead of on the outside jumping on the bandwagon and never being an important part of it." Horton and people at Highlander guessed right about the civil rights movement in the 1950s, and, as a result, their school was built into the movement as it gathered momentum.[19]

In my third year at CPCS, a new dean arrived. Murray Frank came from the college in New York established for union members by District Council 37 of the American Federation of State, County and Municipal Employees. Murray encouraged my efforts to create a labor studies degree program. One student, Darleen Gondola Bonislawski, bolstered my hope that union workers wanted and needed such a program. Darleen was one of the most remarkable of many working-class women who found their way to the college. Raised in a North Cambridge housing project, she worked in the cafeteria in the Harvard Business School, where she inherited union leadership from her feisty mother and nourished her class resentments as she served lunches to the future kings of the Fortune 500. Darleen showed a passionate interest in my labor history course and in our popular history book about Boston's workers, and in 1980 she became the first student to major in our new Labor Studies Program, which drew upon the curriculum already created to train paralegal workers.

The college's curriculum offered several advantages to working-class adult learners. It created possibilities for students to negotiate with evaluators over prior learning and therefore reduced the students' deference to the arbitrary authority some professors exercised in a graded curriculum. It provided valuable flexibility for working students by freeing them from the demand that all credits be earned in the classroom. It encouraged students to present prior learning for evaluation toward their degree requirements and provided an introductory self-assessment course that increased the self-confidence of many students enormously. Our self-assessment workshop helped students to explore their work lives and cultural backgrounds. They were encouraged to make presentations on various workplace and union problems based on earlier learning experiences.

This workshop also raised questions about cultural awareness among diverse groups of workers separated by race and gender, skill and trade, and so forth. The evaluation work and life experience for credit presented some philosophical and pedagogical problems, such as the difficulty of testing academic knowledge in a succinct competency statement based on specific criteria. Since the rest of the curriculum was also divided into specific statements of learning outcomes, we risked cutting students off from the open-ended inquiry into the arts and humanities often denied working-class people. Besides, experiential education created the danger that learning would remained grounded in "prior learning" and fail to move students to "new learning." Genuine education comes about through experience, but as Dewey pointed out, not all experiences are "genuinely or equally educative."[20] Indeed, some experiences may lead to miseducation and inhibit the possibility of having richer learning experience in the future. One of the most difficult challenges for educators who value experience lies in helping students examine the information they have received and the opinions they have formed about "others" and to open the way for new learning about other peoples' experience.

In confronting this challenge the college created some of the best learning experiences we offered. In the initial "assessment" workshop, students from different unions and industries and cultural backgrounds could learn about each other's experience, begin to understand and respect differences, and explore common ground. It even provided an opportunity for improving cultural awareness among workers who were separated in many other respects.

Like the graduates of the AFL–CIO–Antioch bachelor's degree program, our labor studies students usually rated interaction with the other unionists as the most valuable aspect of their educational experience.[21] Excited by the wealth of experience students brought to the college, we attempted to emulate the movement approach to adult education pioneered by Myles Horton at Highlander, where, he recalled, "we took people who were already doing something in their own community, in their unions. They would talk about their problems and how they dealt with them and exchange ideas. It was peer learning; they would learn from each other. Then we'd learn from history and other things, but . . . it wasn't subject oriented; it was problem oriented."[22]

During the past eighteen years ninety-four trade unionists earned their bachelor of arts degrees in labor studies from the University of Massachusetts-Boston because they were willing and able to balance the demands of life, work, and learning, and because they were willing and able to take advantage of the alternative curriculum our college offered students – a curriculum that offered workers meaningful access to higher education.[23] Despite serious cutbacks at the university and despite the decline of labor studies in other state universities, our little program survived and expanded as a result of modest support from the college and critical support from local unions.[24]

Our success in attracting trade union members and helping them complete a labor studies degree required more than offering an alternative, adult-oriented curriculum; it also depended upon offering tuition assistance. Throughout the sixties and seventies the University of Massachusetts at Boston offered low-cost education for working-class people, but with the fiscal crisis of the eighties and cuts in legislative support, tuition and fees were raised to cover costs, thus excluding many of those whom the campus was supposed to serve. Fortunately, the tuition-waiver program offered to many government employees kept the door opened. Our college extended waivers to other groups of workers. Each semester for the past dozen years, ten to fifteen union members belonging to six union locals have received tuition credits – usually the equivalent of 50 to 80 percent of overall costs – generated by their own unions through an agreement with our college. In return for tuition assistance to their union members, officers and staff of several local unions provide instruction and internship opportunities to the program. At first, many of our students were officers, staffers, and radical activists who had dropped out of college and wanted to complete their degrees, but then, because of the tuition support, more rank-and-file members started to enroll, especially from public-sector unions.

Finding friends, encountering enemies

Although individual trade unionists found their way to our program, it was a difficult challenge to convince local trade union leaders that their members could benefit from the kind of college education we offered. Outside of a few public sector union leaders, these officials were not college educated and they simply did not conceive of the university as a place to send their members for education. Many of them encouraged people in the ranks to participate in non-credit labor extension courses to learn the nuts and bolts of bargaining and grievance handling. But they thought college education was for managerial and professional people. If workers went to college, it meant they would leave the ranks to "better themselves." Worse, they might return to the local with their educational credentials and with new ideas about challenging the incumbent leaders. It seemed pointless, therefore, to request official AFL–CIO backing for our program. The answer was a foregone conclusion.

In any case, the program was intended to be independent of union influence, a free space in which union members could engage in critical education, and if they chose, hone criticisms of their own leaders and organizations. As a result, my own standing with the AFL–CIO became more and more problematic during the early years when the program was taking shape. I teamed up with an obstreperous group of union insurgents who held lively conferences in our college on "Putting the Movement Back in the Labor Movement." Some of these militants had been elected to offices in local unions and all of them had been active in struggles to defend unions against hostile employees. The activists who emerged in Boston-area unions during the eighties were extraordinary people. Experienced, tactically talented, and deeply committed, they were determined to reform and rebuild the labor movement. I chose to support their efforts, even though this meant antagonizing powerful union officials.

In 1981 I wrote for the *Globe* on the illegal air traffic controllers' strike in that year. "Where's Labor's Solidarity?" – later reprinted in the dissident magazine *Labor Notes* – asked why other unions did not support the PATCO strikers and provided answers from labor history that explained why the right to strike was lost. The editorial also argued that unjust laws had to be defied in order for the movement to meet the crisis.[25] This initial effort to make labor history public criticized labor law and the unions' capitulation to it and was not well received by AFL–CIO officials.

Following the busting of the air traffic controllers' strike, labor relations in Massachusetts became far more contentious. And by the mid-1980s even old-fashioned business unions felt the tremors of insurgency as younger activists called for change.[26] Struggles against plant closings and concession demands generated surprising militancy among unions, even in Boston, where extreme moderation had reigned since the traumatic defeat of the police strike in 1919.

In the early eighties radical reformers took over the locals of several service-sector unions with largely female and minority membership, locals once ruled by corrupt officials. Two young working-class guys from South Boston were elected to head the union of support staff at Boston City Hospital with the help of some feisty radicals and disfranchised workers of color. Another socialist, Celia Wcislo, who worked in the same hospital, teamed up with hospital organizer Nancy Mills to win election to the largest service workers local in the state,

Local 285, of the Service Employees International Union. They immediately helped recruit their members to our program through an agreement with the college to provide pro bono instructors in return for reduced tuition for their members. Furthermore, Local 285 offered us a solid base of support in a large union with progressive leaders who were willing to encourage their members to study in our education program.

The most exciting and controversial figure on the Boston labor scene was Domenic Bozzotto, an Italian American bartender who had been active in the civil rights movement before becoming the president of the Hotel and Restaurant Workers Union Local 26. He took control away from the front-of-the-house bartenders and waitresses and fought for the back-of-the-house workers, mostly immigrants and people of color. The local quickly plunged into a series of mass mobilizations of its multinational membership, which made us feel like the IWW had risen from the dead. Domenic exuded charisma. He made people believe in the power of rank-and-file workers, and he could mobilize them to win real victories. He also could be a devilish prankster who, it was alleged, threatened to let loose rats in Boston hotels to win wage hikes for the maids toiling at the back of the house. A tactical genius, he willingly allied with radicals of all stripes, confident that he could outsmart and outmaneuver them all.

When I first asked Bozzotto if I could recruit his local's members to our labor education program, he seemed friendly, showing none of the discomfort many union guys felt with academics. I participated in the local's "never surrender" campaigns and shared a cell with some of its members when a bunch of us went to jail after being arrested for sitting in at the bus station during the Greyhound strike. Soon afterward, I asked Bozzotto if he wanted to co-teach a course on organizing. He seemed doubtful at first but then agreed to do so in return for tuition credits for his members. Our association provided further evidence that my work as a labor educator was a threat to the AFL–CIO leadership, because Bozzotto was leading groups of insurgent union activists who criticized that leadership for failing to meet the crisis of the 1980s and for refusing to mobilize their own troops to do the solidarity work unions needed.

The insurgents formed the Massachusetts Labor Support Project, which quickly became an instant mobilization agency – "dial-a-mob" is what activist Rand Wilson called it. A few younger activists from old-line unions like the Ironworkers and the Sign Painters took the risk of getting involved with this left-led coalition movement, attracted by the need to do solidarity work for striking workers at TWA, Greyhound, Hormel, Eastern Airlines, and International Paper at Jay, Maine. Rand Wilson then became the director of a Boston chapter of Jobs with Justice, formed by a coalition of unions determined to seek community allies in an effort to recreate the social unionism of the 1930s. Steve Early, an organizer for the Communications Workers and an experienced labor journalist, played an important role as a strategist and as a critic of AFL–CIO officials who remained committed to the old forms of business unionism created in the years of prosperity when corporations and trade unions could bargain in relative peace. These leaders did not like being told that business unionism no longer met the needs of a labor movement in crisis and they didn't like seeing me quoted to that effect in the *Boston Sunday Globe Magazine*.[27]

What made the situation tricky for these officials was that other labor leaders, including some from established unions, had become increasingly militant in their effort to fight back against management attacks. During the Greyhound strike the stolid building trades, now led by a firebrand named Tommy Evers, filled Copley Square nine thousand strong and battled mounted police to shut down the bus station on the day before Thanksgiving, the busiest travel day of the year.

Evers was a very strong-willed leader raised in Charlestown, a tough Boston neighborhood where he was apprenticed as an Ironworker. In 1972 his local had been sued to force the entry of black workers into the apprenticeship program. As a local union leader during and after "the busing," Evers defended his local. When he became state leader of the building trades he tried to revive a movement lulled to sleep by its monopoly over government work. He even supported others who wanted to fight, including militant interracial unions of hotel workers and school bus drivers. After a life-threatening heart attack, he also reached out to the left and considered hiring radicals to organize non-union construction workers of color.

Evers also participated when the Labor Support Project organized a militant May Day demonstration against Harvard University's investment in Shell Oil. The United Mine Workers' ambitious Shell boycott attracted a lot of union support for the event, causing concern at the AFL–CIO headquarters, which opposed their activities. A smaller group of labor activists also participated in a tally and occupation of a Boston coin shop selling the South African Kruger-Land, when I was made a stunning speech, much to the chagrin of other AFL–CIO officials. As we walked the picket line, I talked to him about enrolling our Labor Studies Program (which he did for a term) and about the idea of organizing a big commemorative event on the next May Day, the centennial of the great eight-hour general strike led by the building trades in 1886. This commemorative event [. . .] created serious problems for the president of the state AFL–CIO, Arthur Osborn, who was deeply suspicious of my work as an educator and historian.

For example, he objected to an op-ed piece for the *Boston Globe* I wrote in 1986 about a surprising strike that erupted at the General Electric River Works in Lynn. That March nine thousand workers walked out to protest the suspension of a shop steward and the company's sabotage of the grievance procedure.[28] I wanted to help the strike leader, Local 201's business agent Ron Malloy, who was a student in our Labor Studies Program. He had just led a progressive slate to victory over the entrenched anti-Communist leadership that had ruled the union since the days in the fifties when the International Union of Electrical Workers (IUE) displaced the left-wing United Electrical Workers (UE). The IUE's anti-Communist leaders fought four bitter battles to keep the original CIO union from regaining power in Local 201.[29] My editorial for the *Globe* infuriated the old-guard powers in the IUE district office because I suggested that its war against the UE had reduced union strength at G.E. The influential IUE district chief had complained bitterly that I had branded his organization "a company union." His suspicions grew when I presented a slide show history lecture to the shop stewards at Local 201 that included a frank discussion of the war between the UE and the IUE, and then invited David Montgomery, a UE veteran, to the union hall in Lynn to speak about that "living history."

About this time, state AFL–CIO leader Arthur Osborn gave a speech to the administrators of public colleges and the two dozen trade unionists whom he had placed as trustees on their boards. He advocated for labor studies, but not the "negative" kind of labor history that pointed up the alleged shortcomings of unions and their elected leaders. Marty Blatt of the History Workshop heard the speech and was sure Osborn was targeting our kind of movement history.

Breaking the ice

But in 1988 more encouraging signs appeared. The desperate strike that year by International Paper workers in the small company town of Jay, Maine, generated inspiring community support and regional backing. The strikers made an attempt through the town meeting to limit IP's use of strikebreakers, a major problem for unions and labor law in the eighties; this reminded me of Herb Gutman's work on how nineteenth-century communities responded to "the invasion of the village green" by industrialists – the theme of a Labor Day editorial I wrote on how the past resurfaced in contemporary strikes.[30] During a support demonstration for the Jay workers I met a paper worker on a picket line who had read the editorial.[31] He asked me to come up and speak at the regular Wednesday night meetings held in the high school gym where, one night, so many people had crowded in to hear Jesse Jackson speak that they had to applaud – as they did long and hard – with their hands raised above their heads.

Jesse Jackson's 1988 presidential campaign generated palpable support from white workers, the so-called "Bubba" vote the Democrats had lost to the GOP in the Reagan years. I wrote an editorial about Jackson's campaign arguing that a new populism had emerged that could make a class-conscious appeal while still emphasizing racism, the Achilles' heel of earlier populist movements. Although most unions backed native son Governor Michael Dukakis, key union activists worked for Jackson, and several won seats as his delegates to the Democratic convention. The *Globe* editorial on Jackson's "class act" elicited some positive responses from mainstream union guys who recognized Jesse's powerful appeal to their members – a sign that movement politics, inspired by the civil rights movement, had begun to penetrate a few corners of the House of Labor.[32]

That summer employers launched a major attack on the backbone of organized labor in the Commonwealth – the unionized building trades. The non-union contractors organized a well-financed referendum campaign to strike down the state's prevailing wage law that helped ensure that publicly financed jobs would be done by union labor. Once again, a struggle erupted over a life-or-death matter for unions because the building trades unions depended largely on public work. These unions had been committed to conservative business practices and had excluded women and minorities, though for a variety of reasons the percentage of females and workers of color in their apprenticeships had grown in the mid-eighties. Led by new progressive state leaders, the building trades mobilized their entire constituency for the first time in a hundred years; they linked up with other unions and social movements through an overall AFL–CIO effort headed by Arthur Osborn, who proved an effective leader and coalition builder.

As vice president of our faculty staff union at UMass-Boston, I noticed how isolated we were as members of the National Education Association. Though we had elected progressive presidents to head the Massachusetts Teachers Association, we remained an island of professionals in a turbulent sea of drowning blue-collar unions. I wrote about the campaign for a teachers' union newspaper that reached over sixty thousand public school teachers throughout the state.[33] Trade union officials appreciated the gesture because our teachers association was politically potent though often at odds with the AFL–CIO and its affiliate, the rival American Federation of Teachers. In 1988 my association stood with the rest of the labor movement.

The unions began the campaign to save the prevailing wage law way behind in the public opinion polls, but the mobilization, using new movement-building tactics, turned the tide. The anti-union measure went down to defeat by a good margin.[34] Jubilant over the victory and the favorable public attention labor received, Arthur Osborn reached out, thanked me, and when I asked, he agreed to speak in public at a forum we organized for the Labor Studies Program on how the movement won this one. The continuing crisis of the movement created a context in which we could cooperate and learn from each other.

Forging a link

The coalition-building that began in 1988 made it easier for us to gain union support for our program. By now dozens of graduates were working in local unions and offering us their support. It took a few years to demonstrate that while many of our students did hope that a college degree would allow them to move to another place in their work lives, they did not want to leave the labor movement.

Two-thirds of all who graduated before 1990 had remained in the labor movement, often in leadership positions. Some needed and wanted the diploma to advance their careers in labor-related vocations, but most seemed drawn to higher education for reasons of personal growth and political commitment – to empower themselves as advocates and leaders for the movement. The program recreated the link "between worker and education and progressive social action" forged by the clothing workers unions and later by the radical teachers at Brookwood Labor College and Highlander Folk School.[35] Our college was a transition house for radicals who had plunged into the unions in the seventies and now needed some time to pause and reflect after being active in their unions during the bitter battles of the 1980s; they needed the free space to think and reflect and to meet people outside their locals and job sites.[36] Many of these students remained active as insurgents criticizing undemocratic and ineffective leaders in their unions, while others had taken on leadership roles in the locals and were pushing to create change at a higher level. Other students were rank-and-file members and local officials who remained union loyalists. Our program welcomed both groups. Despite our critics' belief that we were simply training union radicals, we decided our efforts must remain unbiased and open to all, a requirement of public education. Though most of us who taught had been critics of the union establishment, we did not want to make the program itself part of a "counter-movement" of the left against incumbent labor officials.[37] This was the role assumed by the radical labor schools of the 1930s whose founders rejected public universities as a base for worker education and made their independent schools into oppositional institutions. We chose a different path and attempted to create a space for critical worker education within a university, though this intention did not protect us from the criticism that we were engaged in ideological indoctrination.

By the end of the 1980s, however, even some of our former critics began to acknowledge that we had opened up meaningful access to the state university to union workers who were, in the words of one national union president, largely "ignored and underserved."[38] Our students and graduates were our ambassadors and even our missionaries to union organizations whose leaders remained suspicious, if not hostile, to our efforts.

By the end of the 1980s our students and graduates included the presidents of two large public employees' unions, the business representative for Boston city workers, the president of the State Building Trades Council and of the large electrical workers local in Boston, as well as the vice president of the utility workers and the head of the big industrial union at General Electric in Lynn. They brought an end to the days when our program could be marginalized and red baited. Their experience also showed that our students graduated and continued their work in the labor movement.

The program even began to win some favorable attention from the State AFL–CIO after a talented iron worker named Bobby Haynes became secretary treasurer. Educated at UMass-Boston, he was not especially threatened by intellectuelle. He accidentally defended the AFL–CIO against its radical critics, but he also believed the labor movement had to change and made no secret of his discontent with national union officials. Haynes thought unions needed allies in the universities, in the communities, and in other institutions. As a leader of the 1988 fight to save the prevailing wage law, he concluded that the labor movement could no longer go it alone. Bobby was committed to building, up labor education within the University of Massachusetts, even if it meant taking on some of those who criticized our program. In fact, he drafted a state law placing a union representative on the boards of public institutions of higher learning. When he became a trustee of the university labor educators gained an important ally.

From the beginning the program attracted more women as students than was usually the case in traditional union training efforts. Our early ties to public employee unions with female officials helped start us on the road to leadership development for women activists. Our progress accelerated when Cheryl Gooding volunteered to assist me in developing the program while she worked as the representative of our new faculty staff union. When she became associate director she put her experience to good use. She had graduated from our college while working at Greater Boston Legal Services, where she organized a union of paralegals. Cheryl expanded the agreements we had made with union locals so that students would receive reduced tuition. As a result, we recruited an even larger number of women and more workers of color.

Some students entered the program through the Women's Institute for Leadership Development (WILD), which Cheryl helped to organize with other labor educators. WILD organizers even managed to win the tentative support of the State Federation of Labor for their efforts to train women union members for leadership roles. Women workers responded warmly to the WILD summer institutes, just as they had in the early 1900s to the Women's Trade Union League school in Chicago, attended by Fannia Cohn who later led the effective education programs of the International Ladies Garment Workers Union designed to give workers "the mental and moral equipment" they needed "to serve the labor movement" and "be useful to their class."[39] The account of WILD's effort at coalition building and leadership training written by Cheryl and her successor, Patricia Reeve, is a good example of how the new labor education movement of the 1980s reached union members with new approaches and challenged old barriers to participation.[40] As a result of these efforts, our Labor Studies Program became more diverse, so that by 1992, 60 percent of the students were women and 24 percent workers of color. But beyond inclusion, beyond providing leadership training for women, we needed to offer new learning about issues of diversity, the hardest issues to address in a movement dominated by white males who often held traditional ideas about race, gender, and sexual preference.

In Boston, which remained one of the nation's most segregated cities in terms of housing and labor markets, a critical workers education program needed to examine the hardest issue of all: racism. Our program was fortunate enough to be assisted in this effort by Bill Fletcher who taught as a field instructor. He had been raised in New York by parents who belonged to unions. His father had refused to turn against unionism even though his local was "mobbed up." Fletcher brought his family traditions to Harvard where he joined other students in fighting for a black studies program headed by the socialist Ewart Guinier, a program the university was undermining. He took a job as a welder in the General Dynamics shipyard where several socialists and union reformers were active, and then in 1980 became an organizer for the Boston Jobs Coalition, where he worked on the front lines of the tense fight for affirmative-action hiring in the predominantly white, male construction industry. Bill remained active in these struggles even after he joined a remarkable group of paralegals at Greater Boston Legal Services whose union, District 65, had begun to organize other service workers. He became an organizer for the child care and human service local of District 65 at the time it merged with the United Auto Workers.

I worked with Bill Fletcher in various movement activities, including Mel King's 1983 mayoral campaign, and when I edited a collection of *Radical America* labor history articles that same year, he read my introduction and said he wanted to talk about the commonalities in our approaches to problems of race and class in movement building. Our conversations convinced me that our union students needed to learn from Bill. He agreed to teach courses on black workers history and workplace discrimination.

We shared a passion for doing movement history and cooked up a plan to present it in multicultural format. Through Bill's contacts, we reached Bernadette Devlin McAliskey in

Northern Ireland and invited her to a forum we called "Green and Black" held in March of 1986. The idea was to show the connections and parallels between the black freedom movement and the Irish Catholic civil rights movement. Bernadette enthralled a packed house at our college, describing the influence of our civil rights movement on the new Irish republican movement.[41] The event put movement history on all the evening news programs in Boston and gave Bill what he called "the credibility" to visit the republican groups in Northern Ireland.

The college offered an unusual setting for labor education because it included so many neighborhood activists and students of color who staffed community-based agencies. It seemed like a promising place to open some lines of communication between that world and the largely white world of organized labor. When Pat Reeve became associate director of the Labor Studies Program, she shared my interest in using history to raise questions about exclusion and discrimination. Pat's ambitious course, "Getting a Seat at the Table," used some of the revealing new labor history on race and gender identities to push beyond a discussion of discrimination to a debate about inclusion and power sharing. Using difficult interpretive literature, she encouraged "students to grapple with the past as a means of addressing moral questions in the present."[42] Instead of presenting historical studies based in a scholarly community as received information, she used critical debates about race and gender as stimuli for discussion within a classroom based community of inquiry, where students learned to question their own culture and experience, and confront the problems they faced in a labor movement that lacked a demonstrated commitment to power sharing within its ranks.[43]

New opportunities for teaching movement history

Things were changing in labor education across the country. The old guard that served the house of labor in the Cold War years had given way to a new generation of labor educators influenced by the social movements of the sixties and by the popular education movement's effort to democratize adult learning. One important example of this shift came in 1987 at the prestigious Harvard Trade Union Program, established in 1942 during the heyday of industrial relations as a field. The TUP had survived as a ten-week executive training session for top local and national leaders while being housed in the Harvard Business School. Even after the program left the "B School," it was protected by the labor law scholar Derek Bok when he was president of Harvard and by the influential labor economist John Dunlop, who had been U.S. secretary of labor.

One of our own students, Celia Wcislo, attended the program and suggested that I visit the director and offer to teach labor history for the program. She thought there was plenty of room for improvement. One visit with the director foreclosed that possibility. He told me how much he disliked the new labor history and its harsh treatment of union officials. A year later he retired and was replaced by Linda Kaboolian, an activist in the AFT from Michigan, who asked me to teach the core course in labor history, not to celebrate the institutional survival of unions, but rather to problematize the institutional history and focus students' attention on strategic decisions made – and unmade – in the past. Encouraged by this invitation, I decided not to ask students to borrow knowledge from a history bank where I worked as a teller, but to follow Freire's suggestion that education dialogue begin with problem posing.[44]

Each year for the next decade I taught an often diverse group of trade unionists who came to Harvard from all over the United States and from other nations. At first, I wondered if my radical labor history book and my critical approach to teaching movement history would offend some of the union officials in the class. I adopted a participatory approach in which each student presented a class report on some historical problem, often a case study of some controversial issue. By democratizing the course, and opening up to all voices and opinions, my own voice became one of many, and by no means the only one, drawing critical lessons from the past. The class became a safe place to study current labor problems in historical context. It became a learning community where each student could share a discovery about the past and address a question about a critical choice that once had faced the labor movement.

The new labor history excited many of these trade union students, because it allowed them to discover a hidden past, one in which radicals played a far greater role than they expected; it also allowed them to see a labor movement that often opposed the triumph of "free market" economics, conservative politics, and competitive capitalist values. Indeed, much of that history counters the pessimism that informs contemporary scholarship.[45] These students were eager to learn because they worried deeply about the fate of their unions, which, some Harvard professors told them, were on the verge of extinction unless they changed and abandoned their old adversarial ways. Overwhelmed by data and analysis of labor's current plight, they found in stories about labor's past what one woman student called "a beautiful contrast." Another trade union student summarized the feeling of others when he wrote: "This class has rejuvenated our energy to continue our efforts to regain the power the American labor movement possessed in the past."

Teaching history at the Harvard Trade Union Program created new opportunities for applying a problem-posing approach to the past in union based educational settings. My favorite students at Harvard were the brilliant miners who left the coal fields to join the talented national staff assembled by Richard Trumka, the young reformer elected to lead the United Mine Workers in 1981. I met Trumka when he came to Harvard for a showing of John Sayles's film *Matewan*, which we introduced to an audience of trade unionists and students. He liked my approach to UMWA history and asked me to come down to Beckley, West Virginia, for two days to teach labor history to one hundred organizers. I agreed in a heartbeat, and proposed using the participatory approach to worker education developed by Les Leopold and Mike Merrill at the Labor Institute in New York. I prepared a packet for the session which included a historical chronology that placed UMW history in a national context listing important events and development. I asked them to compare this time line with statistical information represented in graphs that included variables related to the expansion and decline of the union's membership. After my slide lectures focusing on how and why the mine workers' movement grew, the organizers broke up into groups to discuss the historical information I gave them and to address the questions I posed.[46]

The sessions were lively and well received. Trumka wanted a reprise. He invited me to do a similar presentation focusing on the hard work of union organizing for the UMWA International Executive Board in Washington, which was about to invest in a new outreach program. The invitation represented a rare chance to teach labor history to union leaders with pressing concerns about rebuilding their movement.

When I arrived in the dusty old UMWA offices in Washington, Trumka introduced me to Jesse Jackson, who was there to offer the board his support for the union's bitter strike against Pittston Coal Group in Virginia. Hearing the coal miners from all over North America testify their loyalty to Jackson's progressive vision was a memorable experience. I immediately volunteered to work with UMW staff on the Pittston strike, an experience that deepened my relationship with Rich Trumka and some of the gifted, committed staff. With his support, I was able to act as co-chair of the Boston area Pittston strike support committee and build new working relationships with a range of trade union officials, including the president of the State Federation of Labor. In his visits to Boston during the Pittston strike, Trumka did a world of good for my efforts to win union support for the kind of labor education we offered. When he agreed to address our tenth anniversary event in 1990, he had become a new hope for thousands of rank-and-file activists inspired by his honest assessment of the crisis facing unions and his earnest call for a social movement unionism to replace the old ways. Trumka's speech at our dinner in the local electricians' hall charged up our audience of students, graduates, and supporters, emphasizing what we could learn from labor's ordeal and from the black workers' movement in South Africa. His appearance and endorsement of our efforts marked a turning point in our struggle to win union support for our version of workers' education and its role in creating the new labor movement Trumka advocated with power and eloquence.

Besides this political boost, Trumka's support offered crucial opportunities to test the belief we shared about the importance of historical consciousness in the movement building process. Indeed, in subsequent years I have heard numerous union leaders of all kinds call for "more labor history." They want more of it in the public schools where students are being trained to be obedient workers without any sense of their rights, but also for their own members who no longer come from union families and who lack any sense of the struggle that helps them understand why workers need an aggressive labor movement. At a time when the AFL–CIO and some of its affiliates are mobilizing their members for ambitious organizing drives, their leaders fear the case for unionism will not be made in a very compelling way. It is not history in an academic sense they want to convey to their members; it is a sense of the past that helps young people feel like actors in an old morality play, like inheritors of a tradition. Sometimes when they ask me to do history for the members, what they really seem to want is a kind of sermon on values and traditions to revive their passive congregations.

During the 1990s, as the winds of change blew through the house of labor, radical teachers reached a wider audience when they called for critical education that empowered rank-and-file members. Addressing the University and College Labor Education Association in 1990, John Russo of Youngstown State University called upon us to replace the old servicing model of worker training with an organizing model designed to encourage meaningful participation by union members. "Rather than taking advantage of membership knowledge and skills in instructional activities," he said, too many labor educators held on to the traditional delivery methods dependent on the teacher as trainer and expert, because those in charge felt "threatened politically" when the members examined past practices and explored alternative strategies. Speaking in the George Meany Center, the AFL–CIO's official school for workers in Maryland, Russo challenged labor educators to shed their fears and run the risk of upsetting our patrons in union offices. Besides pushing the membership to develop their own strategies, he called upon labor educators to tackle the most controversial issue of all: the lack of union democracy in many unions that functioned much like one-party states. These efforts might be seen as disloyal, he said, but they were necessary if unions expected to revive themselves by mobilizing their members. Like local union members, labor educators should adopt an organizing model of unionism to replace the old servicing model.[47]

For the past decade I have taken a problem-posing approach to teaching labor history to union members, an approach that asks them to think together about what went wrong in the past and what in that past still offers them hope. The dialogue that ensues usually leads to free discussions about what is still wrong in the present. Many students have been willing to make sharp criticisms of the movement in rendering historical judgments, even about controversial issues like anti-Communist purges and the AFL–CIO's Cold War foreign policy. They have also used historical cases to analyze sensitive matters and controversies often too explosive to discuss in their current manifestations, especially patterns and practices of racism and sexism within unions.

Evaluations returned by over four hundred students in the Harvard Trade Union Program who took the history course over the last decade repeatedly emphasized the importance of learning from the movement's "mistakes" including, above all, the mistake of exclusion. These reports, said one trade union student, were critical, "in that we could look back and determine what we considered mistakes," and they were "creative in that we could use history as a way of thinking about new strategies."

My role as a history teacher is to share some of what I have learned from other historians to serve as an intermediary between my scholarly community and the learning community I am trying to create with worker students.[48] This task does not depend much upon delivering prepared lectures drawing on the bank of historical knowledge. Instead, I have been drawn more and more to history telling, to narrating the movement stories I believe are most pregnant with meaning. My job is to provide a kind of master narrative of movement history and then ask the students to share in the story telling, to report on certain chapters in labor's untold story. I must push the learning process beyond narrative reporting by selecting meaningful stories and posing difficult questions about their meanings. But even when worker-students choose not to address my often loaded questions, they convey wisdom in the very ways they tell the story, especially when they connect their report to their own histories and those of their fellow workers. As I have matured as a teacher and storyteller, I have become convinced of what Alan Dawley says when he argues that we understand "narrative, whether as history or myth, as memory or prophecy" as a "pre-condition for historical agency." Whether the goal is redemption or revolution, Dawley argues, "the sense of connection to the past provides identity and momentum, while the belief in an altered future gives hope and purpose." Such narratives can encourage "people of all ranks to engage in strategic thinking" about their past and their future.[49]

My efforts as a teacher of history have paralleled those of a whole new generation of labor educators, some of them veterans of sixties' social movements and some of them products of union struggles. At this point, it is difficult to evaluate the impact of the educational opportunities we have offered union members and movement activists over the past decade or so. Maybe someday historians will look back and say, as Myles Horton did when he looked back on popular education in the 1930s, that what we learned from each other sparked the efforts of union people to survive the crisis of our time and build a stronger movement for the next time.

Notes

1   On Charles Beard's role in founding Ruskin College, see Richard Hofstadter, *The Progressive Historians: Turner, Beard, Parrington* (New York: Alfred A. Knopf, 1968), pp174–77. On Mary Ritter Beard, see Bonnie G. Smith, "Seeing Mary Beard," *Feminist Studies* 10 (Fall 1984), pp399–416, and on the course she taught to women workers, see Nancy Schrom Dye, "Creating a Feminist Alliance: Sisterhood and Class Conflict in the New York Women's Trade Union League, 1903–14," in Milton Cantor and Bruce Laurie, eds., *Class, Sex and the Woman Worker* (Westport, Conn.: Greenwood Press, 1977), p232. For more on Mary Beard, whose "dream" it was "to develop young women to help in the awakening of their class," see Nancy Cott, ed., *A Woman Making History: Mary Ritter Beard through Her Letters* (New Haven: Yale University Press, 1991). On R. H. Tawney the "greatest figure" in British workers education, see Ross Terrill, *R. H. Tawney and His Times: Socialism As Fellowship* (Cambridge: Harvard University Press, 1973), pp36–47. On A. J. Muste at Brookwood, see Nat Hentoff, *Peace Agitator: The Story of A. J. Muste* (New York: Macmillan, 1963), pp56–72; and on Horton, see Myles Horton with Judith Kohl and Herbert Kohl, *The Long Haul: An Autobiography* (New York: Doubleday, 1990). On Highlander, see Frank Adams, *Unearthing Seeds of Fire: The Idea of Highlander* (Charlotte: John F. Blair, 1975), and John M. Glenn, *Highlander: No Ordinary School, 1932–1962* (Lexington: University of Kentucky Press, 1988). Information on these two schools as well as the story of Commonwealth College in Arkansas can be found in Richard J. Altenbaugh,

    Education for Struggle: The American Labor Colleges of the 1920s and 1930s (Philadelphia: Temple University Press, 1990).

2   Myles Horton, interview with Mary Frederickson, "The Spark That Ignites," *Southern Exposure*, 4, 1–2 (1976), p154.

3   See Leon Fink, "'Intellectuals' versus 'Workers': Academic Requirements and the Creation of Labor History," *American Historical Review* 96, 2 (1991), p410.

4   Merle Curti, "Intellectuals and Other People," *American Historical Review* 60, 1 (October 1954), pp272, 275, 280.

5   For a historical treatment of these tensions, and how they were exacerbated, see Joshua Freeman, "Hardhats: Construction Workers, Manliness and the 1970 Pro-War Demonstrations," *Journal of Social History* 26, 4 (1993), pp725–44.

6   *1968: A Student Generation in Revolt – An International Oral History*, Ronald Fraser, ed. (New York: Pantheon, 1988), p367. Fraser's interviews showed that roughly twice as many sixty-eighters in the United States engaged in labor and social work twenty years later than their cohorts in Europe.

7   See James Green, "Introduction," and "Holding the Line: Miners' Militancy and the 1978 Strike," as well as John Lippert, "Shop Floor Politics at Fleetwood," in *Workers' Struggles, Past and Present: A "Radical America" Reader*, James Green, ed. (Philadelphia: Temple University Press, 1983).

8   James R. Green and Hugh Carter Donahue, *Boston's Workers, A Labor History* (Boston: Boston Public Library, 1979).

9   Richard M. Freeland, *Academia's Golden Age: Universities in Massachusetts, 1945–1970* (New York: Oxford University Press, 1993), p333.

10 John Strange, "The Experience of the College of Public and Community Service," *Liberal Education* 63, 2 (1977): pp25–30.

11 Herrick Chapman, "Emancipating the Liberal Arts: The Integration of Liberal and Career Education," unpublished paper by the first CPCS dean of academic affairs, 1975. Copy in author's possession.

12 Russell Edgerton, quoted in Thomas Ewens, "Analyzing the Impact of Competence-Based Approaches on Liberal Education," in *On Competence: An Analysis of a Reform Movement in Higher Education* (Syracuse: Syracuse University Press, 1978), p174.

13 For the use of competency-based education in various settings, see *On Competence: An Analysis of a Reform Movement in Higher Education*, Gerald Grant, ed. (Syracuse, 1978).

14 The curriculum used by the Labor Studies Program at the University of Massachusetts-Boston is described in Ann Withorn and Loretta Cedrone, "Assessing Ourselves: The Experience of the College of Public and Community Service," in *Defining and Measuring Competence*, Paul S. Pottinger et al., eds. (San Francisco: Jossey Bass, 1979), pp65–84.

15 Michael Merrill, "Selling Socialism Door to Door," *Radical History Review* 18 (Fall 1978), pp113–15.

16 Freire, quoted in *We Make the Road by Walking: Conversations on Education and Social Change with Myles Horton and Paulo Freire*, Brenda Bell, John Gaventa, and John Peters, eds. (Philadelphia: Temple University Press, 1990), p218. Also see Paulo Freire, *Education for Critical Consciousness* (New York: The Seabury Press, 1973), p16.

17 Ronald Filippelli, "The Uses of History in the Education of Workers," *Labor Studies Journal* 5 (Spring 1980), pp3–7. Also see Ralph Samuel, "History Workshop Methods," *History Workshop Journal* 9 (Spring 1980), pp162–65; James Green, "Worker Education and Labor History," *History Workshop journal* 14 (Autumn 1982), pp168–70.

18 Herbert G. Gutman, "Historical Consciousness in Contemporary America," in *Power and Culture: Essays on the American Working Class*, Ira Berlin, ed. (New York, 1987), pp400–401.

19 Horton, quoted in Maurice Isserman, "Experiences in Democracy," *The Nation* (12 November 1990), pp569–70.

20 John Dewey, *Education and Experience* (New York: Collier, 1963), p25.

21 Judith L. Catlett and Higdon Roberts Jr., "Looking Back: Meany Center Students Evaluate the College Degree Program," *Labor Studies Journal* 15 (Fall 1990), p10.

22 Horton, quoted in Frederickson interview, "The Spark that Ignites," p153.

23 James Green, "Universities Should Assist Labor Unions in Empowering a New Generation of Workers," *Chronicle of Higher Education* (27 June 1990), pB2. For an earlier discussion of an attempt at Wayne State University to make a labor studies degree program accessible to working adults, see Hal Stack and Oscar Paskal, "The University and Weekend College: Beyond Access," in *Building New Alliances: Labor Unions and Higher Education in New Directions for Experiential Learning*, Hal Stack and Carol M. Hutton, eds. (San Francisco: Jossey Bass, 1980), pp17–28.

24 For a history of the University of Massachusetts-Boston Labor Studies Program, see "Celebrating Ten Years of Workers Education, 1979–89," a pamphlet available from Labor Studies Program, CPCS,

University of Massachusetts-Boston, Boston, MA 02125. Quote from Michael D. Parsons, "Labor Studies in Decline," *Labor Studies Journal* 15 (Spring 1990), pp66–81.

25   James Green, "Where's Labor's Solidarity?" *Boston Globe* (5 October 1981), later reprinted in *Labor Notes* (23 November 1981), p14. A classic and influential statement is by Karl Klare, "The Judicial Deradicalization of the Wagner Act and the Origins of Modern Legal Consciousness," in *Marxism and the Law*, Piers Beirne and Richard Quinney, eds. (New York: John Wiley and Sons, 1981), pp138–68. Karl offered me significant aid in shaping the PATCO editorial.

26   Green and Donahue, *Boston's Workers*, chapter 7.

27   Danny Williams, "The Crisis in Organized Labor," *Boston Sunday Globe Magazine* (6 September 1981), pp25–26.

28   James Green, "Local 201 Shows Labor the Comeback Trail," *Boston Globe* (11 March 1986), p48.

29   James Green, "Not by Bread Alone," *Socialist Review* 90 (1986), pp111–16.

30   Herbert Gutman, "Industrial Invasion of the Village Green," *Trans-Action* 3 (1966), pp19–24, and "The Workers' Search for Power: Labor in the Gilded Age," in *Power and Culture*, pp70–92.

31   James Green, "Labor Day: The Past Resurfaces," *Boston Globe* (6 September 1987).

32   James Green, "For Jackson, Populism Is a Class Act," *Boston Globe* (3 April 1988).

33   James Green, "Save the Prevailing Wage Law," *MTA Today* (30 August 1988), pp3, 26.

34   Mark Erlich, *Labor at the Ballot Box: The Massachusetts Prevailing Wage Campaign of 1988* (Philadelphia: Temple University Press, 1990).

35   Quote from Susan Stone Wong, "From Soul to Strawberries: The International Ladies Garment Workers Union and Workers Education, 1914–50," in Joyce L. Kornbluh and Mary Frederickson, eds., *Sisterhood and Solidarity: Workers Education and Women, 1914–1984* (Philadelphia: Temple University Press, 1984), p54.

36   For a discussion of educational programs, like Highlander Folk School and other resources for social change, which served as "movement half-way houses" for the southern black freedom struggle, see Aldon D. Morris, *The Origins of the Civil Rights Movement: Black Communities Organizing for Change* (New York: The Free Press, 1984), pp139–73. For a discussion of the free spaces needed for radical movement building, see Sara M. Evans and Harry C. Boyte, "Schools for Action: Radical Uses of Social Space," *Democracy* 2, 4 (Fall 1982), pp55–65.

37   Clyde W. Harrow, "Counter Movement Within the Labor Movement: Workers' Education and the American Federation of Labor, 1900–1937," *The Social Science Journal* 27, 4 (1990), pp395–417.

38   Labor/Higher Education Council, "Building Labor Campus Alliances," Proceedings of the National Meeting, 1989; John Joyce, "Address on Labor and Higher Education," to American Council on Education, San Francisco (12 December 1987), pp3, 5–7.

39   See Robin Miller Jacoby, "The Women's Trade Union League Training School for Women Organizers, 1916–26," in Joyce L. Kornbluh and Mary Frederickson, eds., *Sisterhood and Solidarity: Workers Education and Women, 1914–1984* (Philadelphia: Temple University Press, 1984), pp5–42. Cohn, quoted in Susan Stone Wong, "From Soul to Strawberries: The International Ladies Garment Workers; Union and Workers Education, 1914–50," in Ibid., p46.

40   Cheryl Gooding and Pat Reeve, "Coalition Building for Community-Based Labor Education," *Policy Studies Journal* 18, 2 (Winter 1989–90): pp452–60. Besides bringing the women's movement into the labor movement in an effective way, WILD took on a life of its own, taking on the challenge of multicultural education for union women.

41   Both speeches were published in "Ireland Today," a special issue of *forward motion* 7, 2 (March–April 1988), quote from Nell on p32.

42   Patricia Reeve, "'If This Were Steel, I'd Know What to Do with It' – Making Historians' Discourse on Race and Gender Meaningful to Union Members," paper presented at the Organization of American Historians Meetings, Washington, D.C. (30 March 1995).

43   Peter Sexias, "The Community of Inquiry As a Basis for Knowledge and Learning: The Case of History," *American Educational Research Journal* 30, 2 (Summer 1993), p307.

44   Paulo Freire, *Pedagogy of the Oppressed* (New York: Seabury Press, 1970), pp66–67.

45   See Leon Fink, "The New Labor History and the Powers of Historical Pessimism," *Journal of American History* 75, 1 (June 1988), pp115–36.

46   See James Green, "Why Did the Labor Movement Grow? Two Labor History Workshops Presented to the United Mine Workers of America," unpublished curriculum available from author, presented in Beckley, W. V. (1988), and Washington, D.C. (1989), and "A Problem-Posing Approach to Teaching Labor History," paper presented to the University and College Labor Education Association, George Meany Center, Washington, D.C. (1990).

47   John Russo, "The Crisis in the Serving Model and Alternative Labor Education Approaches," address delivered at the University and College Labor Education Association Meeting, George Meany Center, Silver Springs, Md. (1990), pp5–7.

48   For an instructive discussion of how public school history teachers can bridge the gap between "the scholarly community that produces knowledge and the classroom community that produces learning," see Sexias, "The Community of Inquiry As a Basis for Knowledge and Learning," pp305–24.

49   Alan Dawley, "Keeping Time in Twentieth-Century America," unpublished paper presented to the Organization of American Historians, Atlanta (April 1994), pp3–4.

Chapter 6

Jorma Kalela

MAKING HISTORY

The Historian and Uses of the Past

THE RATIONALE OF HISTORICAL RESEARCH IS, from the historian's perspective, to call the audience's attention to one's selection and arrangement of particular past matters in order to demonstrate their present relevance. From the vantage point of history-in-society the same rationale can be given another formulation: historians meet the demand for knowledge concerning the past. This perspective has, however, been underrated by the profession.

'Whose history has been written and whose has not?' This question illustrates the position from which I criticized the profession's establishment in the 1970s. The response was that such an approach is not justified since the historian must be neutral in relation to the different groups in society: rather than showing preferences, one has to abstain from taking a stand. More pertinent to the present chapter was that the premise of my approach was regarded as inappropriate too. Historical enquiry should not be thought of in terms of its 'relevance'; its starting point was not in the present but in the past.

This was the dominant pattern of thought, but it did not mean that all historians took literally the logic of 'history for its own sake'. Many admitted the importance of looking after 'the nation's memory', for instance, and some were even of the opinion that professionals are there to dispose of myths, to correct misinformed interpretations and to meet the demand for knowledge.[1] These kinds of tasks were from my point of view halfway measures: the rationale for historical enquiry was thought of in terms of the profession as a whole, hardly ever in terms of the individual historian's work.

My dissatisfaction remains the same forty years on: prospective historians are left to their own devices as regards their relation to society. Choice of the audience, for instance, cannot be avoided, but to discuss the ensuing issues has been taboo. The purpose of the present chapter is to demonstrate the various ways in which approaching the audience poses questions which have hitherto not been discussed. The most crucial failure from the individual historian's angle is that the role of the audience in the research process has hardly been tackled at all. Yet, the rationale for the historian's work is centred upon those interested in his or her subject.

Different people have different pasts in any society, which means that when historians choose a topic to be studied they also select their audience. In other words, the relevance of the knowledge produced does not depend only on the matters dealt with but also on the people addressed. Or: the message that the historian's study will eventually convey is not important for everyone. Furthermore, advances during the research process are also connected to the audience, since it is the historian's increasing comprehension of why the eventual findings will be significant to those addressed that carries the research work forward – even if historians do not articulate the logic of their work in these terms. Besides, the audience is continuously present in the investigation.

Initially, it is the people to be addressed that the historian has in mind when thinking about the significance of the research – albeit not the audience, as such, but indirectly, by way of evaluating the meanings conveyed by the planned study. Similarly, it is the audience that historians think about when considering which particular aspects of the past should constitute the subject to be studied, and which point of view is best adapted to highlight the relevance of the matters embedded in the topic to be explored. Historians start their work by trying to decide what in particular they want to study and finish the planning stage of the project when they know which matters should be investigated and why these particular matters are significant. By then they will have made up their mind as to what is the study's the central idea and what they want to say by means of their research – that is, to whom it is addressed.[2] This virtual dialogue with the chosen audience continues in the two following phases of the research process.

While the people studied are historians' main 'companions' during consultation of the primary sources – their main task is now to ensure that these people will be given a fair hearing – the people addressed are present at the second stage too. At the same time that historians test their central idea, they collect information with the help of which they can make sense of the beliefs, motives and actions of the people studied in their final account – an essential aspect of making sure their account is fair. This also introduces the third stage that is dominated by those addressed: it is with reference to the audience that historians select the material to be included in the final account and decide how it should be presented. The text must fulfil two tasks: convince the audience that these findings have a sound basis and be readily understood. The idea of this stage is encapsulated, as the American historian J. H. Hexter puts it, on how much knowledge the people addressed already possess and their patterns of thinking.[3]

Thus, the historian's virtual dialogue with the audience lasts from the beginning of the research process to its end. At the same time, the people studied are also present in the investigation, but the dialogue with them (virtual, too, of course) is of a different kind and the stakes are higher. The issue one is now negotiating is about the deeds of the other party, performed in the past culture, and it is necessary to reach an agreement (in the sense of a fair description) to get the permit for conveying one's message. Mary Fulbrook has aptly characterized *the simultaneity of the two dialogues*. 'The historian is the creative intermediary between selected elements of the past and selected audiences in the present; and we would hardly be likely to have any interest in history if this were not so.'[4] The historian's message is based on a particular point of view but he or she must (virtually) make sure that the people studied do not veto it.

That the historian selects his or her audience has been tragically covered up: it is an issue disregarded by the profession even though every historian is confronted with it. True, there has been discussion of the distinction between professional and lay audiences, but that has been conducted in terms of the historian's style, not as a dimension of defining the subject. As regards the research questions asked, a universal single audience remains an undisclosed premise. This is to deceive oneself, and the more frank historian will admit that his or her readers constitute often only a particular group. The varying consequences that selection of the audience has for elaborating the subject to be researched [are] discussed [earlier]. In this chapter I deal with the general implications of choosing the people to be addressed.

Selecting the people to be addressed from the large number of conceivable audiences should actually be thought of as a task on a par with two other exercises performed during the planning stage: defining the subject and delineating the message. And, as with the other two, specifying the audience is not self-evident: all three elements depend on and influence each other. Thinking about the ways in which they interrelate is the substance of the series of steps that eventually leads to formulating the central idea of the research project.

It is the narrow understanding of the professional's rationale that explains the logic leading to the premise of a single universal audience. Regarding the accurate description of the past as the dominating idea of scholarly history is, as such, a task that has no necessary connection to any specific audience other than fellow scholars in the same field. Making sense of the past is very different since it calls for analysing the need of and responding to the demand for historical knowledge. The crucial issue is then about whose view it is that is in need of correction. However, this question has been surpassed by epistemological soundness; accurate description has been thought of as the guiding idea of research instead of being treated as the result of historical enquiry. The same limited ('ivory tower') rationale is evident also in the critique of the prevailing interpretations: it is their status epistemologically that matters, not the stances and policies they sustain.

The conventional inward-looking pattern of thinking also explains why choice of the audience has been covered up; it reveals the blind spot in the rationale of scholarly history. The present relevance of past matters to those potentially interested in them has not been part of mainstream thinking whereas attaining a clear view on why the study is needed is what the professional historian gains from focusing on the people addressed. The following pages seek to demonstrate that, hitherto, in specialist eyes, the audience has actually had no role in the making of history. Instead of thinking about the people addressed as creators of their own histories, professionals have simply regarded them as consumers of academic studies.

Developing a viable concept of the historian in society has been, in retrospective analysis, a task with which I have been preoccupied since 1979, when I was appointed historian of Paperiliitto, the wealthy trade union of the paper and pulp industry. The commission was no coincidence since I had pointed out in my works the virtual total neglect of labour history, a special characteristic of Finland at that time. The key experience of the seven years as an official in Paperiliitto was to grasp the built-in elitism of my profession: we considered all other genres of history-making as subordinate to that of our own discipline. It was not the only lesson that I learnt, the hard way, about the scholar's premises during the 1980s.

It was with the questions raised by our professional arrogance as the vantage point that I reflected during the 1980s and 1990s on the vortex humanities were drawn into. Without actually knowing it at the time, I was an active agent of the paradigmatic change in the discipline of history. The way I designed my commission in Paperiliitto made me one of the proponents of the 'new histories' in Scandinavia, as will be evident from the next pages. Experiences from working in the trade union movement also determined my response to the linguistic turn as its consequences began to unfold. Rather than being upset by postmodernist positions I discussed our basic tenets in the light of the unfolding disruption within the discipline in dozens of publications.[5]

The risk of patronage

I started my work as the historian of Paperiliitto in 1979 by declaring in the union's newspaper that it was neither scholarly questions nor those of the union leadership that should be answered: a professional historian had been employed to investigate what was significant for the members. It is to the great credit of the governing body of the union that this prerequisite to approach history 'from below' was unanimously accepted. The method to be employed was the study circle, the traditional form of self-education for the Scandinavian working-class movement. The new element was that the groups did not study ready-made materials but produced the substance of the work themselves by creating their own histories. Like their Swedish counterparts, these peer groups came to be called research circles.[6]

The idea of research circles worked in practice; at the end of 1986 there were forty groups at thirty-three of the union's sixty-two local branches: over 200 workers engaged actively with history in different parts of the country. The plan was, in other words, a success and it inspired similar initiatives in other unions. My final study, published by Paperiliitto in 1986, was based on the experiences of the workers involved and conveyed my interpretation of the current challenges facing trade unions. It is a treatise that describes the transformation of Finnish society since the 1960s – from the local perspective. However, what is important is that these results were achieved quite differently from how I had initially envisioned it.

Instead of submitting their queries to me, as I had originally suggested, so that I would approach them as a professional historian approaches his own questions, local activists were encouraged to initiate research themselves. Swedish colleagues in workers' adult education had convinced me that the necessary motivation could only be secured by giving the peer groups full freedom to choose their own subjects. As a result, rather than their becoming *de facto* research assistants of mine, the research circles conducted their work independently. What they created were histories in their own right. The Swedish advice caused me to develop a novel concept of history that I managed to persuade the workers to accept.[7]

It took roughly one year's campaigning at the various branches all around Finland to prove to the workers that history did not mean narratives of past ruling groups, and that they too had a role in history-writing. Local activists had to be convinced that the substance of 'history' was not predetermined and that what had taken place in their factory and their neighbourhood was history too. Once they had accepted the idea that they had the same right to define the substance of history as a professional historian, the circles proliferated. This agitation was the hard way in which I discovered that the traditional academic concept of history that I had taken for granted was, by its nature, patronizing. What the workers had been taught at school, in turn, made me reflect on my own lecturing at the university and led to awareness of another problematic nineteenth-century legacy. Given the multitude of pasts, there are also many histories, and one must therefore reserve 'history' in the singular for theoretical and philosophical contexts.

A further lesson about how history is conceived was taught by what aspects of the past turned out to be important for the workers in the paper and pulp industry. Half of the more than 200 people engaged in the project, both social democrats and communists, were primarily interested, to my great surprise, in the transformation of their locality. Most of these towns or villages had originally emerged around a small factory on a stretch of rapids. For one-third of the circles the important theme was changes in their work: this was the time when production was being computerized. The really unexpected matter was that only one-fifth wanted to study the history of the union or labour movement policies – despite the fact that practically all those involved were activists, in addition to being a member of the branch of their union, in at least one of the other local working-class organizations.[8]

The way Paperiliitto activists defined 'their own history' bears in two ways on history-writing, and the first of these is connected to the role of history in the traditional working-class movement. My surprise at their choices revealed that I had in fact shared the socialist version of 'history from above' or 'the history of great men'. In the 1986 book published by the union I coined the term 'the Imperialism of the enlightened worker' to indicate a tendency common to all heirs of the Second International from the late nineteenth and early twentieth centuries. It was not only communists who regarded themselves as the vanguard of the workers' movement but social democrats too – albeit expressing their views in a different way. This is a theme to which I will return in connection with public histories.

The other perspective on history-writing opened by the Paperiliitto activists can be summarized as a piece of advice: beware of patronage. It was apparent that it was the workers' own situation that might engage them with the past, not the history of their union or of some other formal institution. That the risk of patronage is a permanent one has also been demonstrated by, for example, Roy Rosenzweig and David Thelen in their project on the popular uses of history in American life in the 1990s. When people had the opportunity to approach the past on their own terms, that is, 'not as a classroom progress from election to election', they 'grounded historical inquiry in the present circumstances, perceptions, and needs'.[9]

The fundamental message was that the substance of 'history' must not be taken for granted. Scholarly historians should really explore how, and why, the past becomes history. In a more practical perspective, I learned that the professionals must always beware imposing his or her views upon the readership. To make this warning explicitly is called for by the often unintentional nature of patronizing attitudes. The paradoxical difficulty is familiar to any non-authoritarian teacher: to strengthen the student's own motivation while conveying the skills you master.

That the work of the research circles was separate from mine did not, however, preclude cooperation – rather the reverse. Taking the members' ideas seriously led in the long run (it took three years of full-time work!) to a situation where I could communicate with them freely and without misunderstandings (that they were people of roughly my own age and spoke Finnish as their native language was no distinct advantage). At the same time the trust put in me made it increasingly difficult to distance myself from their views. The dilemma has aptly been characterized by Roy Rosenzweig: it really is not easy to be simultaneously 'a trusted insider and a dispassionate outside expert'.[10]

My role in the Paperiliitto history project was that of a supervisor. In addition to taking part in the circles' discussions about their projects, I set up a system of three-day or four-day intensive courses for the circle leaders. Actually, I worked much in the same way that I had done at the university – but free from academic formalities. What ensued in practice, besides guiding the research, was that I had countless diverse conversations in a variety of contexts from the angle of my own research work – the key means by which I acquired the information needed for it.[11] I also took on a new way of thinking about the role of professional historians in society. Rather than just transmitting knowledge, our main contribution is to encourage and support non-professional people engaged with history – and to be available when needed.

Supervised research done by people without academic training proved to be possible but, on the other hand, also raised several issues and problems calling for novel thinking – resulting eventually in the present book. The fundamental lesson was that sensible historians do not think about their audience as mere consumers of 'specialists' findings, but as people who create their own histories – most often, without our participation. What I learned is a good example of the usefulness of reflecting on aspects of the historian's work that conventionally are taken for granted, not to speak of problematizing them in the training of historians.

Not just readers

Whose sense of the past do I intend to influence and why? Along which lines should I proceed? These questions dominate the sensible historian's work when planning a research undertaking. He or she recognizes that history is a mode of making more sense of the world and one's place within it. The grounds for this being a premise for my profession were strengthened while working for Paperiliitto. The new element that entered my thinking during those seven years was a keen awareness of the authoritarian tendency embedded in our work: the risk of slipping into patronizing attitudes is far greater than historians believe.

Avoiding arrogance and condescension calls for taking seriously the views of the people addressed, but this is something historians have to learn the hard way. They are not trained to tackle either the make-up of the audience, or the significance of the topic at hand for the people they are addressing. Hardly any attention has been paid to the particular way the audience, chosen by the historian, approaches prevailing knowledge. Historians are trained to think about the historical interpretations they intend to criticize in scholarly terms, and only imprecisely, if at all, in relation to those outside the academic world.

There was an element of 'from below' in my initial idea of writing the history of Paperiliitto, but it was only gradually that I learned to take into consideration the audience's particular way of thinking. Insight into the role engagement with history plays in people's lives was not only provoked by my experiences at Paperiliitto, however; the key factor was learning a new aspect of the social process of history-making. Today I am able to define this clearly: the everyday casual habit of calling attention to the past was transformed into the purposeful creation of histories. In the early 1980s I learned that there were, in practically all developed industrial countries, a large number of projects where 'ordinary people' were producing various kinds of histories. Professionals were involved in some initiatives, like the best-known one, the British History Workshop movement, but by no means in all of them.[12]

When it gradually became apparent that the kind of historical practice I was initiating in Finland was actually part of an international phenomenon, I considered the deliberate non-academic history-making on a par with the 'new histories'. Their historical significance lay, it seemed, in their function as indicators, and as essential parts, of a wider change in western culture. The world that had been created and was still thought about in terms of the great nineteenth-century ideologies – liberalism, conservatism and socialism – was breaking up: the 'modern' social orders were crumbling. It was actually only later, in the latter half of the 1980s, that I began to think systematically about the new history-connected activities as a challenge to scholarly history. Still later, only through Raphael Samuel's *Theatres of Memory* (published in 1994), did I realize that this was the resurgence of an old phenomenon: the novelty was in its proportions.

Thanks to the intensive Scandinavian cooperation, it was easy to get acquainted with the Swedish counterparts to the Paperiliitto history project. Here, the patrons of the activities were the powerful national organizations for workers' adult education and for the preservation of local arts and crafts. Many initiatives were inspired by the writer Sven Lindqvist's internationally acclaimed book *Gräv där du star* (*Dig Where You Stand*), the point of which was that, in any job, the specialist was the person who actually did the work. For me, a more inspiring writer, in fact, was the architect Gunnar Sillén, whose ideas were intriguing from the professional historian's angle.[13]

The starting point for the purposeful non-academic history-making was, according to Sillén, that many aspects of industrialization and the past conditions of workers were unknown. Or, as Raphael Samuel put it: in industrial archaeology and the retrieval of oral memory one could see that it was a sense of cultural loss that animated the growth of popular enthusiasm for study of the past. The spur for research was not, as many academics think, the ethos of continuity and unity of national culture but rather its unexplored diversity.[14]

It is worth emphasizing once again that creating histories is a multi-faceted practice and that scholarly enquiry is only one genre of making history. As to research done by those without university training, it is reasonable to highlight two matters. On the one hand, the basic demands on any historian are not alien to present-day common sense: what is required is taking seriously the thinking of past people and being fair to them, as well as learning to construct an account based on sound reasoning. On the other hand, acquiring the necessary skills takes time without a trainer. This line of thinking actually leads to [a] vision of history-making. The idea is that of a participatory historical culture: one of collaborative practices where specialists ensure the soundness of the knowledge produced, and where diverse genres of histories are encouraged to flourish.

The expansion of purposeful non-academic history-making at the end of the twentieth century is a laborious subject to be researched because the nature of these activities makes acquiring the information needed difficult. The basic rationale of most projects is intimately connected to their regional, local or familial context and there is seldom any ambition to reach beyond these confines. Connected to this feature is apparently some distinct sense of belonging, an interesting but poorly researched phenomenon. Today, at the beginning of the twenty-first century, these kinds of initiatives seem to be so common that they do not attract special attention. Those who participate come from all walks of life; they are no longer only workers or previously marginalized groups. Scholars from many different fields are also involved.[15]

Even if deliberate extra-mural history-making remains a poorly investigated theme, there has emerged academic interest in popular concepts of history all over the world during the 1990s and 2000s. A pioneering status is enjoyed by the project directed by Roy Rosenzweig and David Thelen on the popular uses of history in American life. Further studies, at least in Australia, Canada and Finland, followed.[16] One of the interesting findings in the American project was the ubiquitous nature of active history-making. Out of 1,453 Americans interviewed about their relationship to the past, 'more than one third had investigated the history of their family in the previous year; two fifths had worked on a hobby or collection related to the past'.[17]

An important finding by Rosenzweig and Thelen is that people are keen to insist that others have no right to foist on them alien opinions of what is important in the past.[18] The issue at hand is, of course, that patronage that does not observe national borders. In Britain, Samuel criticized leftist writers for confusing the commodification of heritage with genuine popular interest in the past. As regards academic historians, there is a strong tendency to dismiss occupations like family history and the collecting of old photographs. These kinds of activities, as John Tosh puts it, are 'largely independent of the cultural *dirigisme* of the major heritage institutions'.[19]

Changes in history-in-society at the turn of the twenty-first century have shed new light on the traditional issue of what should be considered the principal aspects of history, something on which there seems never to have been agreement among historians. The political nature of this question was revealed, and emphasized, by the disruption within the discipline at the end of the twentieth century: the profession could no longer turn a blind eye to societal distinctions and the relative positions of different types of historical research. And, as this book argues, upholding history-making should be accepted as the historians' duty. The audience addressed, however, are not just readers of academic studies, but creators of their own histories, too.

The present pasts of the audience

Giving some thought to the history taught in schools is a rewarding exercise for anyone interested in the uses of the past: one learns that it is a far from straightforward task to decide which topics are important enough to be given attention. That there are alternatives to the history taught in school was something that encouraged quite a few Paperiliitto activists to join the research circles; the curriculum of their (or my) grandchildren today is also of a very different kind to what we were taught all those years ago. This reference to changes in educational policies acts by way of an introduction to the questions confronting historians about to select their audience.

Lists of bestselling books provide another kind of clue to what aspects of history people are interested in, but the sales also provoke reflection (this is covered in the next section). Yale historian Jay Winter, for instance, dealing with studies on the First World War, found that the books that are read most widely are not the ones that took years of research effort, but rather those that allowed families to see the way in which the war affected every British and French household, leaving traces and wounds palpable to this day.[20] The point here is that the historians' findings cannot be separated from other influences, that the reception of historians' works is also determined by readers' previous knowledge.

The example above prompts comment, too, on the mode of presenting the past. It is probably in the overlap between the information that historians present and what is contained in family narratives that the widely disseminated stories of the First World War have their origins. There are certainly other kinds of process too that affect the reception of the historian's work, even if our knowledge of them is limited. What seems certain is that it is not only the way the findings are presented that counts, readers also interpret what they are told in their own way.

The way the historian's results are received is also influenced by the audience's sense of the past. There are many different concepts of history even among professionals, not to speak of the lay readers. However, the variety of ways in which history is understood and the past is used are too great to be summarized in this [chapter].[21] What seems certain is that there are a host of factors that impact upon a work's reception, making it unpredictable, but this does not preclude trying to anticipate the nature of the response. It is, thus, the meaningfulness of the historian's interpretation that is now key: the more intriguing the connection of the subject to the interests of the intended audience, the more eagerly the work will be received. As to how the research project is taken forward, this is the same for both professional and lay audiences.

Ideally, historians start creating the parameters of the subject to be studied knowing what in the past is significant for the people they intend to address, and why. Even if their knowledge of the audience's sense of history is only partial, sensible historians seek to develop the subject starting from the meanings attached by those addressed to the historical interpretations being criticized. Later on, the work is directed by the historian's increasing comprehension of the significance of the research findings for the audience. Normally, the role of the people addressed in this dialogue is passive, but there is nothing really to prevent organizing an actual exchange of views.

As to the historian's role in the dialogue with the prospective audience, the key thing to remember is that 'history is an argument without end'. It is also crucial to bear in mind that there are no 'proper' points of view: in Paperiliitto, for instance, I kept learning of new approaches to the changes that had taken place in the local communities. The point is that history works as 'the citizen's resource', as John Tosh puts it, when historians remember that their job is not to convey absolute statements but well-founded and carefully weighed conclusions liable to be modified.[22] The idea is to open new perspectives on the world of those one is addressing and to invite them to consider whether their existing concepts and values continue to hold true.

The historian looking for an attentive and thoughtful audience to be addressed has been provided with a practical guide on the subject by Roy Rosenzweig and David Thelen in their book *The Presence of the Past*. This summarizes their findings from a large project on the popular uses of the past in American life, and demonstrates their complexity. With an eye to providing some pointers to historians pondering their own relation to the people addressed, the American history professors stress that readers are more attentive when the historian has ensured that those addressed feel they are being invited to approach the past *on their own terms*. In other words, for historians to beware that imposing their opinions on readers is not enough; they must also take the audience's concerns seriously.

The historian must also avoid being misled by scholarly hegemony and remain open to the unexpected. The dichotomy between 'personal' and 'national' is an example of the kind of carefulness needed when treating with consideration the thoughts of the people studied. Separation of the public past from the private does not always make sense; public events are often remembered and perceived as personal ones. A grandmother's story of an event and a meticulous academic study of the same event are very different kinds of histories, and yet, for an individual user of history, they may have the same function.[23]

While developing the subject of the study, the sensible historian also pays attention to the nature of everyday histories as sources for *history-making*, something mentioned above in the context of oral histories. A person's reminiscences do not only tell us which fragments of the past he or she considers relevant in the present, but also reveal the processes by which they are turned into history. The wealth of possible references becomes apparent when one realizes that every historian is surrounded by an infinite number of histories, each with its own purpose. It is worth the historian giving these serious consideration when elaborating their chosen topic.

When historians reflect on the deliberate production of histories by non-professionals, something now quite common in western countries, they would be wise to take on board Raphael Samuel's point: 'The past that inspires genealogists, local historians and collectors is not random' but connected to what for them is important. For many of the local trade union activists whom I trained, the engagement with history resulted from their political views. They were worried about the future of the working-class movement and wanted to restore its traditions. The means to that end was to explore their personal life experiences and to establish connections between these and those of the earlier generations.

It is also good to keep in mind that the sense of the significance of the past and the relevance of history varies depending on the people addressed and the subject studied, a point illustrated by Hilda Kean's description of British 'researchers of family, locality and place'.[24] Some engaged with history are looking 'in a vague way for a wider family', others for an 'educational hobby' and some 'for filling in gaps in family stories'. But there are also those who seek 'the fantasy of connection with someone in the past'. When developing the chosen topic into a subject it is worth the historian's while to reflect on this variety of concerns among the potential audience. As crucial as acknowledging the multitude of different interests is looking at their present impact; it is current concerns, the relevance of the past in the present that is the starting point of all history-making.

People and their Pasts, a collection of essays edited by Paul Ashton and Hilda Kean, makes two important points, the first of which is encapsulated in the plurality of pasts in its title. The second significant aspect of the book is to introduce an issue that hardly appears at all when research conducted is based on conventional premises: how does the past become history, by which processes are histories created?[25] The conclusion of Ashton and Kean, the crucial role of defining history, is illuminated by my change in strategy when engaging the members of Paperiliitto with the writing of their union's history. They had to have the right to study *what in their view* was *their own history*, rather than take for granted a ready-made concept of it.

History provides people not only with a way of learning about 'the external world they inhabit' but is simultaneously for them, as Raphael Samuel emphasizes, a mode of shaping an 'understanding of themselves'. For him, what becomes the content of history is 'directly related to who researched and wrote history'. If history 'is an arena for the projection of ideal selves, it can also be a means of undoing and questioning them, offering more disturbing accounts of who we are and where we come from than simple identification would suggest'.[26] The rationale of engagement with history in case of the local trade union activists whom I trained to be their own historians was similar to that of Raphael Samuel – with the difference that they were not, and had no ambition of becoming, professional historians.

Public histories

'The problem of the working class movement here and now', as I formulated it in the union's newspaper on 14 November 1979, was the starting point for my work at Paperiliitto. Which elements in societal development had made it 'increasingly difficult for the movement to adhere to its original nature as the working people's collective instrument' for improving the conditions in which they lived and worked? Why had the movement failed to help the workers in 'getting a grip on the society and their place in it'? The 'imperialism of the enlightened worker' encapsulated, seven years on, my answer to this. Both social-democrats and communists patronized their supporters by way of sticking to standards of the early socialist movement instead of having the prevailing social conditions as the foundation of their policies.

During my seven years with the union I came to the conclusion that one of the many functions of history is as an instrument of power. 'History is on our side' was the conviction and emblem of the traditional working-class movement. This belief entailed, for both social democrats and communists, the duty to root out social evils; although to be sure, they interpreted the real interests of the working people in their different ways. The method, however, was the same: the parties were there to turn into policies the grievances and demands their members had articulated – since the parties understood the connection between the workers' conditions and the course of history. This was the core of the 'imperialism of the enlightened worker'.

The first step towards recognizing the propensity of the workers' parties to order about their members was to realize the patronizing nature of the traditional historical enquiry that I had come to accept without question. As the work of the research circles and my discussions with those active in them progressed, my perspective widened to cover the 'modern' social orders. 'We have the knowledge' as the prevailing idea among decision-makers and 'from above' as the dominating characteristic of western politics in general gained strength over time. At the twenty-fifth History Workshop in Oxford in 1991, I personally laid the hitherto labour movement to rest in a paper titled 'History-writing, power and the end of the traditional left'. In 2009 my study titled 'Denial of politics as government policy', that highlighted the currently increasing meaninglessness of the idea of responsible use of power, was published in the English volume of the *Parliament of Finland Centennial* series of studies.[27]

Opposition to social, cultural and political predestination was from my perspective, as a contemporary, the crucial dimension in the disruption within the historical discipline at the end of the twentieth century. I came to share the view, common to 'new histories', that history should be thought of as a resource with open-ended applications instead of serving as a course indicator. In his *Identity and Violence* (2006), the Nobel laureate in economics Amartya Sen argues along the same lines regarding moral philosophy. He highlights the current contradiction in which, on the one hand, 'we are becoming increasingly divided along lines of religion and culture', whereas, on the other, the many other ways 'people see themselves, from class and profession to morals and politics' are ignored.[28]

Sen's point denotes the ontological insecurity characteristic of western societies at the turn of the twenty-first century. People are groping around uncertainly in the circumstances in which they find themselves today: what entities actually exist and what is my relation to them? They have created this dilemma themselves in the sense that people now insist on making their own choices. The type of society in which life was culturally predestined has lost its justification; the idea that one's social position dictated one's way of life and thinking has been refuted. True, the possible choices are limited and the liberty experienced is all too often just the creation of skilful marketeers. Still, people refuse to give up their hard-won rights; they want to retain control over their lives.[29]

With the benefit of hindsight, one can argue that it was the ontological insecurity described above that the research circles and myself were confronted with in Paperiliitto during the early 1980s. In the beginning, the project was instigated by the received idea that it is the function of history to tell 'who we are' and 'how we came to be what we are'. Gradually, we had to accept that being able to complete such a task was illusory and that identity poses a real challenge to anyone who is sensitive to the circumstances in which he or she lives. This has been aptly described by Peter Mandler: the collective identities that people once inherited and had to live with, whether they liked it or not, have broken down: 'community', religion, social hierarchy and class, ideology, 'nation'.[30]

Paul Gilroy's recent work on the aftermath of the British Empire is also a good example of the problems an historian has to deal with today. It is, in his opinion, not only the racial hierarchy that must be rejected but also 'the very idea of dividing humankind into homogenous and easily distinguishable biological and cultural groups'. In a similar way 'a healthy distance, even estrangement' is needed from the 'politically over-integrated nation-state'. This is where the sensible historian keeps in mind Stuart Hall's remark, that far from being 'eternally fixed in some essentialised past' identities result from the interaction of history, culture and power.[31] Raphael Samuel referred to the same point in different terms: history is an arena where identities can be both constructed and deconstructed.

The sensible historian also takes note of the most powerful characteristic of public histories – their ubiquitous nature. One meets references to the past anywhere and anytime. In Finland, for instance, scholars have produced excellent studies of descriptions conveying interpretations of history: images of an ancient Golden Age (Derek Fewster), paintings (Tuula Karjalainen) or photographs (Maunu Häyrynen).[32] These are just some examples where interpreting the past has been intentional, but the same effect is also imparted by artefacts which were not designed as contemporary representations of past phenomena. It is also worth remembering that politicians are not always consciously interpreting the past when they refer to it as a reason for a particular decision.

The challenge posed by identity to historians is to bear in mind that it is extremely difficult to separate giving people knowledge that enables them to construct an identity and suggesting one. Defining one's distinctive identity is today an individual affair, in the sense that people are 'freer to tailor it after their own fashion' than before. This is why it is so important, for example, to think carefully about the context in which one uses concepts like middle class, working class and so on. And all the time one must also keep in mind that it is not the historian's responsibility but that of the people addressed to clarify in their own mind who they are and what they want to become.[33]

In historical circles, debates around public histories have been of a different kind. One, actually a continuous debate, is about the competition, if not rivalry, between academic and popular historians. The popularizers aim, in academic eyes, 'at producing compelling and dramatic narratives that will hold the interest of non-professional readers'.[34] Their narratives, according to another common argument, serve 'no higher intellectual purpose' than 'to describe and entertain'. In the opinion, for example, of Exeter historian

Richard Overy, it is popular history, not academic history, that is 'really disengaged from the real world'.[35]

The target of Overy's criticism is the mode in which many of the best-selling works have been written, and one of the academic's arguments is that the popularizer's accomplishments come easily, but at a cost. What is lost is 'an analysis of cultural, religious, or economic developments'. The opposing side, in turn, complains that too many academics 'do not wish to make the effort to relate their little picture to the context provided by the ever-present big picture'.[36] The perspective in this discussion is that of the professional producers of historical knowledge, and, as a result, its field is rather narrow. A wider perspective, that of popular understanding of the past, is embedded in another academic debate.

Criticism of people's ignorance of and indifference to history became common in western countries towards the end of the twentieth century. In rebuttal, it was claimed that the problem was in the substance of historical studies, which was rejected as dull and irrelevant.[37] This debate about the historical awareness of 'ordinary people' has also taken place among professional historians; the views of the people addressed are anybody's guess. Absent is an analysis of the particular patterns of thought among the people addressed and the reasons for them. Why do people, for example, make connections between the various aspects of the past in the way they do?

Why the media and politicians make political use of the past is relatively obvious. What is not so obvious is why popular histories flourish. Why do so many people regard professional histories as insufficient? Why do people find it necessary to create their own history themselves? It is to these questions that I next turn.

Popular histories

Thinking about the ways in which the people addressed deal with one's topic calls for an analysis of everyday history, the multitude of diverse histories prevalent in any society. The practically useful concept here is the social process of history-making, since it both visualizes the context of the historian's work and points to the interplay between public, popular and scholarly histories, their rivalry in 'the terrain of truth'[38] and their competing influences on people's sense of the past. It is positioning one's topic among these different kinds of histories from which sensible historians take their cue for developing the subject of their research. True, public and popular histories are only analytical categories, each of which includes widely divergent types of histories, but they are, at the same time, useful precisely because they encapsulate such varying accounts of the past.

Introductory textbooks on historiography do not devote many pages to everyday history, nor to the various uses accounts of the past are put to.[39] Nor do they discuss the problems confronting the historian as a referee in this field – in fact, the traditionally dominant pattern of thinking discourages assuming such a role. 'The task of history is to understand the past, and if the past is to be understood it must be given full respect in its own right . . . [which] involves, above all, deliberate abandonment of the present.'[40] A great many historians (the majority?) have disobeyed this tenet, however, as has been demonstrated in the section dealing with the specialist's personal contribution, but this has not resulted in a systematic discussion of the professional's role in everyday history.

Thanks to the conspicuous presence of public histories, historians are well aware of these accounts of the past even if they normally disregard them in their writing. The decision to overlook them arises, to some degree, from the undisguised partisanship peculiar to many of these interpretations, but there is also a strong tendency to regard them as unworthy of consideration. In contrast to public histories, historians pay far less attention to accounts that fall into the second analytical category, that of popular histories.[41] These presentations of the past encompass many genres, too. They include, for example, reminiscences of their youth by the elderly or tales and stories of past events learned in the neighbourhood or at one's place of work. They are histories one gets stuck into.[42]

My own sense of the past provides an unmistakable example of the way popular histories are passed on. In the early 1980s I was already an established historian, and it was only to be expected that my aunt should rely upon me as a specialist to assess the manuscript of the biography she had written of her father, a notable Finnish politician in the 1920s and 1930s. To my great surprise, I was confronted with a reconstruction of my own views on Finnish politics during the interwar period twenty years earlier, when I was a young student. As a schoolboy I had not been particularly interested either in politics or history, and my own recollection was that I had tried to avoid listening to my father and his sister talking about my grandfather – yet clearly I had been influenced by their discussions.

It is important to note that popular histories are by and large not meant to be presentations of history, as such; probably much less so than public histories. Notwithstanding this, the interpretations embedded in these accounts influence people's conception of history at least as effectively as those of public histories. A good example in this respect is provided by Jonathan Steele's article in the *Guardian* of 15 April 2005 with the intriguing subtitle 'It was Mikhail Gorbachev, and not Pope John Paul II, who brought down communism.'

The *Guardian*'s correspondent was irritated by the image of the late Pope's dealings with communism conveyed in the obituaries of him. According to Steele, 'the notion that anti-communism was always a consistent part of his motivation is off the mark'. What was ignored in the obituaries was that 'the way Poles saw Communism in the 1970s is not the way they see it now. The Polish Catholic Church was in regular dialogue with the communist authorities, and both worked subtly together at times to resist Soviet influence.' The accounts Steele discusses are public histories dealing with the late Pope; but his article demonstrates that these accounts share an important feature with popular histories. They too are normative by nature, and as a consequence easily become stereotyped. Still, popular histories are probably more effective in conveying customs and traditions, patterns of social behaviour. As Anthony Smith has remarked, 'it is to their ethnic symbols, values, myths and memories so many populations turn for inspiration and guidance.'[43]

As historical sources, both public and popular histories are problematic if our criterion is one of sound knowledge. Their significance for the historian lies in the meanings they attach to the past. They portray social agreements as to what features of the past are considered, by the people who share these accounts, to be indispensable in the present. These aspects of the past support a normative order, common to the people in question, in accordance with which the individual is expected to think and act in the present. But the same norms also govern the perspective on the past. They tell us what to remember and how, as well as what to forget, exclude, render unthinkable or regard as insignificant. In this sense, public and popular histories are political by their very nature.

The meanings attached to the past by public and popular histories are valuable for the historian from two angles. First, in attempting to avoid being unintentionally directed by current circumstances, an understanding of prevalent ideas on the 'right' or 'proper' way of thinking about the past is crucial. Secondly, when one is trying to uncover the functions performed by the interpretations to be re-evaluated, non-scholarly accounts of the past serve as important cues. They help in understanding the meanings currently attached to the topic chosen to be studied.

Attention has been paid to the cultural significance of public and popular histories, but not adequately. There are a host of treatises on the (public) uses of history[44] and on popular accounts of the past,[45] but not on the most significant characteristic of these presentations: the way in which they constantly modify each other while shaping people's sense of the past. This neglect of the interaction between public and popular histories is actually surprising, since it was one of the main points taken up by the well-known Popular Memory Group, active at the turn of the 1980s at the Centre for Contemporary Cultural Studies at the University of Birmingham (UK).[46] Yet, it is the very interaction of public, popular and scholarly histories that defines the position of the historian's topic in the social process of history-making.

There are today, as will soon become evident, an almost innumerable amount of studies on memory (by scholars other than historians) but, comparatively few dealing with popular conceptions of history. The small number of such works actually points to the continuing presence in professional thinking of the idea of 'real' history as an academic preserve.[47] The low academic opinion of everyday history is also demonstrated by ignorance of the variety of lay views on the nature of history; the same controversies that have divided professional historians abound outside academia but in different guise, for instance.

Scholarly histories

Analysing the particular aspects of the past that the intended audience feels are relevant to their current concerns is one of the professional historian's tasks when planning his or her research project. However, a paramount aspect of upholding history-making as a basic social practice must be borne in mind: starting from the histories those addressed have created or cherish does not mean taking them at face value. On the contrary, is it not an essential part of the trained historian's job to try to prevent people from using prejudiced, simplistic or outdated interpretations of the past? Is it not their role to demonstrate and correct weaknesses in prevalent histories? And to provide the people addressed with the knowledge and new interpretations they need?

Discovering that it is possible to produce one's own history often creates an enthusiasm that can be self-defeating: the resulting work can strengthen one's prejudices instead of improving the ability to make informed assessments of interpretations dealing with what one is interested in. This was something I had to emphasize repeatedly in the early 1980s to those involved in the various initiatives. While encouraging efforts to create new, sound interpretations that replace one-sided or otherwise questionable ones, I had to underline that the first step is to put aside one's own prejudices. Taking up a marginalized or forgotten theme was just the starting point and finding new as well as previously undervalued sources only one of the means to the goal. Sound reasoning was the thread running through the intensive courses the research circles of Paperiliitto were given.[48]

The often justified professional concern about the pitfalls in producing popular accounts of the past must not prevent us from acknowledging their potential usefulness. I share Ruth Finnegan's doubt as to 'whether there really is some marked divide between the processes of knowledge creation outside as against inside the universities'.[49] Only arrogance and privilege denies those who do not have academic training the status of 'real' historians: it is argument not authority that counts. This is a theme to which I will return. Here I discuss other aspects that have arisen on the relationship between professionals and lay historians.

One issue is about the historian's relationship to the people he or she is addressing in an age when the internet is on its way to becoming (or has already become?) the key media. How should one go 'about imagining your audience if it is worldwide and online and probably searching for something you wouldn't expect'? It is perfectly reasonable that this issue should be explored thoroughly, but it is, however, beyond the competence of someone who was already about to retire when the internet became an everyday medium.

The same is true of the other considerable effects of electronic communication on historical research.[50]

In any case, it seems probable that the printed word has already been replaced by radio and television as the most influential channel for communicating history. On the other hand, historians such as Simon Schama and David Starkey are still today only a tiny minority; the overwhelming majority of us have to confine ourselves to the world of print. This was the situation to an even greater degree thirty years ago and that is why the research circles in Paperiliitto greatly surprised their academic supervisor.

By far the most popular way for the circles to convey their findings was to put on an exhibition of commented old photographs, which was then visited by hundreds (in some cases even thousands) of people, even in relatively small locations. This medium turned out to be so effective that a special course on displays in general had to be organized for the groups with a specialist from Swedish Travelling Exhibitions. The circles also conveyed their research results in plays, processions, video and music programmes, recitations, as well as one long-playing record. True, there also emerged several books and dozens of articles, but an academic used to thinking in terms of written texts was confronted with unexpected questions about ways of disseminating an historian's findings.

Communication skills have, however, acquired a kind of status in the university training of historians since the 1990s, especially in the United States. The curriculum gives emphasis to the use of non-traditional evidence and formats in the recreation and presentation of history. Conventional methods have been expanded by using not only photographs, oral histories and museum exhibitions, but also television documentaries, multimedia, websites and by reworking traditional historical knowledge into modern, computer-based formats. In this sense, public history (in the singular) refers to a distinctive way of acquiring and disseminating historical knowledge.[51]

In addition to the exhibitions and other forms of presentation used by the circles, an incentive to rethink the professional historian's relationship with his or her audience also emerged in the 1980s from a public debate I had with Gunnar Sillén, one of the authorities for the Swedish research circles. Criticism of professional historians was an integral part of his credo: 'don't regard history as a problem, make it alive instead!' My defence of the specialist referred, in addition to the need to overcome common prejudices, to the role of historical enquiry as critic of a distinct type of using power: there was an obvious need for knowledge about social entities as opposed to dividing society or any other social whole into ever narrower sectors.

In another perspective, the debate with Sillén acted as a stimulus to consider, once again, the relation of historical research to various artistic forms.[52] As regards the present chapter, Sillén prepared the ground for assuming the message of the linguistic turn. In his words, the historian should present his or her findings 'as situations one could re-experience', that is, in ways which made it possible to understand and share the feelings of the people studied. Maybe this was the secret of the remarkable popularity of the circles' exhibitions.

Thinking about the historian's connection with the people addressed also caused me to ponder the question 'what is history for?' from a novel angle. After the historian has, in R. G. Collingwood's words, 're-enacted' a piece of past thinking he or she should present it to the readers in a way that makes, in Sillén's terms, 're-experiencing' possible. This suggestion accords with Markku Hyrkkänen's understanding of 'reflecting' in the Collingwoodian sense: history can give a human being the incentive to 'start thinking about one's own thinking'. What comes out of this is close to Raphael Samuel's view of the relationship between history and historian quoted above.[53] In any case, every historian has reason not only to define their view on the responsibilities of the historian's role as a cultural critic but also to elaborate their personal relation to history.

An additional useful idea, stimulated by Sillén, is connected to the difference between empathy and sympathy. The former means, according to the *Concise Oxford English Dictionary*, 'the ability to understand and share the feelings of another', while sympathy means 'feelings of pity and sorrow for someone else's misfortune'. It is empathy that describes the historian's relation to the people studied, while sympathy, or rather concern and even solidarity, refers to one's relation to the people addressed.[54] This distinction serves as an introduction to Ranke's early nineteenth century maxim *wie es eigentlich gewesen*.

Later generations have failed to notice that there are two elements contained in Ranke's maxim. The one that has attracted historians' attention the most refers to empathy as the required attitude, and has been expressed in our days by, for example, the American historian Gertrude Himmelfarb. Instead of providing lessons the idea of the historian's work is to make 'a strenuous effort to enter into the minds and experiences of people in the past, to try to understand them as they understood themselves, to rely upon contemporary evidence as much as possible, to intrude his own views and assumptions as little as possible'.[55] This refers to empathy, or fairness, as the historian's fundamental duty. The element that has been largely ignored is the logical premise of Ranke's maxim.

Ranke's '*eigentlich*' ('actually') should really be understood as 'contrary to what is claimed or believed', and is the necessary, albeit inexplicit aspect of Ranke's maxim. This refers to the historian's task of producing alternatives to existing interpretations, whether the aim is to improve upon or critique existing histories or to present completely new ones. The historian may have many motives for presenting an alternative interpretation. To condemn these kinds of motives, as the 'objectivists' used to do, is arbitrary.

The two aspects of Ranke's maxim refer to the historian's basic predicament, often expressed in the previous pages: responding to contemporary concerns without compromising fairness towards the people one is writing about. Peter Mandler provides an example of resolving the dilemma in reviewing the 1859 bestseller of the Scottish author and reformer Samuel Smiles, *Self-Help*. According to him, the book provides one with many relevant ideas about developing 'the self – its powers, range, creativity and diversity' for the present day. However, up to its reissue in 2002 the book's title had been enough to label its author a 'Thatcherist of the crudest . . . sort', and since no one has come up with 'anything coherent to say about the positive inspiration provided by *Self-Help* the Thatcherite mud still sticks'.[56]

Demonstrating that something is contrary to what is claimed or believed to have been true means that the idea of persuading the audience is always embedded in the historian's work. 'The chief product (the historian) has to sell', as Stefan Collini puts it, 'is the trained skepticism that says "it wasn't like that"'. Pauli Kettunen, in his turn, underlines that the works historians publish 'open or close, broaden or restrict the perspectives of human agency'.[57] The crucial point here, albeit referring to a neighbouring field, has been aptly made by Ricca Edmondson (teaching at the University of Galway) in her *The Rhetoric of Sociology*[58]:

> . . . in place of objectivity sociologists in fact proceed as follows: they try to tell the truth in a manner which complements and is complemented by, the knowledge and dispositions which their (selected) audience already has. Consciously or otherwise, writers try to gauge the personal and political commitments of the audience they wish to address, or are forced to address, and they adapt the personal and political tenor of their own communication so as to complete or correct their readers' views. Strictly speaking, truthfulness is a product of the joint communicative efforts of both.

As a genre, scholarly histories are on a par with public and popular histories when looking at the different sources of influence on people's views and knowledge about the past. The three categories (all are plural terms) simply represent an analytical division to help historians assess the practical context of their work, everyday history. *Shared histories,* however, open up a different perspective on the social process of history-making.

Shared histories are not analytical tools like public, popular and scholarly histories; they are not coarse categories the historian needs for managing the prevailing knowledge, when organizing the context where his or her study will be conducted. Rather, shared histories are on a par with individual scholarly studies in the sense that they convey substantial interpretations to be evaluated – with the crucial difference that there is no specific author. They are jointly produced collective views of the past, conglomerates of various public, popular and scholarly histories.[59] Analysing the nature of shared histories in the next two sections means studying the elements and mechanisms involved when the people addressed develop their own views on history.

Shared histories

During recent decades there has been marked progress in the historical profession if the criterion is the upholding of history-making as a basic social practice. This is not only due to transformation in historical research, and primarily the emergence of new themes and actors, but also to changed views on gathering knowledge of the past. There seems to be a greater awareness that history is not only taught in a classroom, but learned in a multitude of places, and in a variety of ways.

An increasing number of academics have begun to wonder whether history is something to be approached along the lines suggested by Raphael Samuel. For him history is 'a social form of knowledge', the work, in any given instance, of a 'thousand different hands'. If this is true, he claims, professional studies in history should be discussed in a context created by 'the ensemble of activities and practices in which ideas of history are embedded or a dialectic of past-present relations is rehearsed'.[60] In this book I refer to this 'ensemble' as the social process of history-making.

Nevertheless, shared histories have attracted only a small amount of research. True, a great number of scholars have been interested in the ways in which social groups create their images of the world, but the studies produced concentrate on the various aspects of the agreed upon versions of the past. The shared histories themselves have escaped analysis. As a result, the following discussion of the elements and mechanisms involved when the users of the past create their collective histories are based on studies dealing only with the various aspects of the ensuing whole. This notwithstanding, many scholars have suggested that some shared history is probably a necessity for any community. Michael Howard, for example, writes that 'all societies have *some* view of the past; one that shapes and is shaped by their collective consciousness, that both reflects and reinforces the value-systems which guide their actions and judgements'.[61]

Shared histories then, are the means through which the various groups and communities get to grips with the present and the groundwork for them is done outside university rooms and libraries. It is from the diverse public, scholarly, and especially popular histories and their interaction that these collective forms of knowledge about the past emerge. Often the key role is played by various stories and other forms of folklore, usually passed on by word of mouth. Characteristic of these histories is that they tend to be stereotypical in nature; through constant repetition they become fixed and widely held. Being composite in form, shared histories describe the particular identity of, and often constitute, a community, be it a family, neighbourhood, workplace, institution or nation. They are mutually constructed accounts of the past and, as such, akin to Benedict Anderson's famous imagined communities.[62]

As noted, scholarly accounts of the past contribute to shared histories too. Still, it is important to remember that only a tiny fraction of existing interpretations of the past can be traced back to the work of professional historians. Thus, shared histories remind us that, contrary to many academics' understanding, scholarly works are not the ultimate source on which people's conceptions of the past are based. Professional contributions are not even necessary for shared histories, as the researcher of folkloristics Anne Heimo has demonstrated in her study of a southern Finland municipality.[63] One must not confuse history with the results of historical research.

It is reasonable to depict shared histories as constructions on three levels. First, there is individual remembrance, secondly, public memories and thirdly, frameworks for organizing the ensuing accounts as wholes. During the last three decades a vast number of studies examining these elements has appeared, but hardly anything on the interaction between all three. This disconnection reflects perhaps the most unfortunate effect of the present division of current research on culture and society. There are an almost infinite number of academic 'disciplines', 'traditions', 'orientations' and so on, in addition to the many formal organizations such as 'departments', 'schools' and 'institutes', each guarding jealously its own territory or preserve.

For shared histories as composites, oral history is the most fruitful scholarly orientation even if its emphasis is on the level of individual remembrance. The narratives studied are autobiographical, often organized by the individual lifespan, and these memories reveal, as was indicated above, ways in which individuals reconstruct their past, create histories. A similar perspective on the methods of history-making is opened by works like Thelen and Rosenzweig's *The Presence of the Past* with its focus on the divergent popular uses of history.[64] What all this points to is that providing a *site for personal recollections* is the first necessary prerequisite for shared histories. It is the possibility of making sense of one's own experiences with the help of these collective accounts on the past that makes them shared ones.

The idea of reminiscences or life stories is to make sense of one's past, or rather, as American historian Michael Frisch underlines, to attach personal experiences to their social context. His Italian colleague Alessandro Portelli, in turn, has demonstrated, from the historian's angle, that the significance of the 'errors, inventions, and myths' which characterize these accounts is that they 'lead us through and beyond facts to their meanings'. On the other hand, it is important to keep in mind what specialists in oral history Paula Hamilton and Linda Shopes point out: neither scholars nor people remembering necessarily reflect on 'the process by which the articulation of memories takes place or how they become public'.[65] In highlighting the process through which remembrance is expressed, Hamilton and Shopes prepare the ground for my next point: *unrestricted availability* is the second precondition of shared histories.

The emphasis on the unrestricted availability of shared histories reminds us that remembrance does not take place in a vacuum. On the contrary, individual reminiscences are sustained by *public memories,* for example various memorials, monuments, places and rituals or, in other words, by heritage. This support to individual remembrance (actually history-making) by public memories is the function of *the second level* of shared histories. The question is now of collective remembrance that is the focus of a distinct field of research, often called memory studies that has boomed since the 1990s.[66] This 'memory scholarship' has a very different historiographie trajectory from oral history, and removing the disconnection between the two is what is suggested by the collection edited by Hamilton and Shopes, *Oral History and Public Memories*.[67]

The third level of shared histories, frameworks which organize these accounts as composites, is the least discussed aspect of the topic. True, there are plenty of studies dealing with the different concepts of history, but their function in arranging individual remembrance and public memories has not been systematically analysed. In shared histories the role of these frames is, first of all, to give an impression of the *underlying continuities in history*. An interesting approach in this respect is suggested by Joseph Mali in his *Mythistory*. Another fruitful starting point is provided by the 'schematic narrative templates' (for example, the mode in which the official Soviet narrative of the Molotov–Ribbentrop Pact was presented) suggested by James V. Wertsch.[68]

The most frequently used framework for shared histories is provided by the idea of nation. Not only is the nation frequently taken for granted by historians, it is also often presented as a predetermined condition of anything else in history. The tendency is so strong that historians studying popular views of history (for example, Rosenzweig and Thelen as well as Ashton and Kean) have called into question 'the concept of a common story and national character'.[69] These criticisms of unreflectingness lead to two remarks and with them to the current significance of shared histories.

The liquid social fabric

My first comment on the misuse of the concept of 'the nation' is similar to the point made by Amartya Sen in his *Identity and Violence*. The historian's challenge is the strong tendency, even in this globalized world of ours, to divide people along national lines, and to ignore the ways in which people see themselves. What this means is that historians face the task of demonstrating that nations, communities and ethnic groups change over time and, therefore, should not be taken for granted. Historians must not forget that part of their job is to scrutinize the historical perspective, for example, of political visions and statements and, where necessary, to show that they are anachronistic.[70]

My second comment on the misuse of the nation refers to situations in which the different shared histories are subordinated to a single national narrative – for example, by discussing 'the English' or 'the Finns'. Together, my two comments introduce the key challenge of twenty-first-century politics: customary concepts describing people's associations with each other cannot any more be taken for granted. Not only have nineteenth-century notions of social/class structure become obsolete, but much more recent concepts may also have lost their validity. Culturally different parts of the social fabric, highlighted by the 'new histories' at the end of the twentieth century, can hardly any longer be regarded as fixed.

Shared histories help us in characterizing this dilemma. It is reasonable to assume that those living in circumstances similar enough to want to use the past as a means of coming to terms with the present feel affinity with each other. On the other hand, it is equally obvious that people belong to, and are active in, at one and the same time, several overlapping communities. From the political (or the historian's) angle, these alliances are intriguing not only because the multitude of them exist simultaneously but also because they are characterized by the concurrence of polyphony and unity.

As composites, shared histories allow people to exert control over their present circumstances, but in a counter-intuitive way, similar to that argued by the German sociologist Norbert Elias: individuals are larger than groups because individuals contain within themselves so many different identities. David Thelen agrees and continues:

> An individual could be a woman, lawyer, Republican, Chicagoan, lesbian, Irish-American. Each piece of her identity carries with it materials and traditions that the individual, alone or with others, could turn into a collective past with constantly evolving individual variations. And yet to describe any one of these

groups is also to fall far short of describing any individual who contains so many potential identities and locations between identities with which to describe where he or she has been.[71]

The point, from the perspective of politics and history, seems be that no shared history is a uniform, consistent interpretation of the past, but rather an amalgam of different and often contradictory views. Even so, it is good to remember Elias's point above. Examining shared histories in their capacity as challenging and special forms of knowledge is the scholar's headache: the people studied (and scholars in their private life) do not have any trouble in coping with them in their everyday life.

It seems, to paraphrase the Palestinian-American literary theorist Edward Said, obvious that shared histories are 'as protean, unstable and undifferentiated as anything in the actual world'. Nevertheless, past experiences are arranged with their help, and shared histories also assist in negotiating the present and navigating the future. The problem seems to be our tendency as historians to think almost only in terms of stable identities; to understand 'individuality as a process of becoming and therefore fluid' is unfamiliar to us.[72] With regard to the multitude of oral history and memory studies, however, I would like to take the risk of suggesting that it is the 'fluidity of the self' as their context which gives shared histories the guiding role they have. From this perspective it is unfortunate that scholars have pulled apart the mutually constructed composites of views on the past rather than analysed the ways in which the connections between the different levels within them have been arranged. Nor, because of the lack of studies that focus on shared histories themselves, have the contradictions been examined that result from the heterogenuity of the communities which have produced them.

The trouble with shared histories is simply the lack of research on them. My own work in Paperiliitto opens one perspective. Having directed the union activists while they were doing research in what in their view was their own past, I could have presented their various shared histories – had I known of the concept. Yet, during the first half of the 1980s, 'world view', for instance, was still regarded as a sufficient concept. Shared histories only seem to have attained the key position they hold today with the changes in the structure of western societies during the last two or three decades. I will return to the implications of this situation at the [end of the] book.

I now turn to negotiation as a mode of reaching an interpretation of the past since this method highlights the nature of historical knowledge. The meanings the historian discovers in shared histories emerge through an interactive process, as the researcher of folkloristics Elina Makkonen has demonstrated in her study of popular and oral history projects in three eastern Finland locations. She shows, first, that parties arguing over, for example, a past event or deciding on its meaning move in a hermeneutical spiral, with the result that the explanation arrived at is not reducible to any of the original viewpoints. Her second point is that the resulting interpretation is not a final one, but the starting point for new discussions and interpretations.[73] In other words, Pieter Gevl's 'an argument without end' seems to characterize shared histories, too.

As regards the historian's own work, shared histories remind him or her, firstly, of the necessity of critical detachment from their own position in the social process of history-making. Historians must not forget that they too have been brought up with several shared histories. In other words, David Carr's point that a human being has 'a connection to the historical past, as an ordinary person, prior and independently of adopting the historical cognitive-interest' has to be taken seriously. Secondly, historians must remember that an awareness of this is crucial so as to keep one's own views separate from those of the people studied – thus, analysing one's own thoughts is necessary in order that one produces sustainable knowledge. Such scrutiny is *sine qua non* for carrying out the historian's fundamental duty, doing justice to the people studied.

A further prerequisite for producing sustainable knowledge is that the historian keeps in mind that the audience is always present when he or she conducts the (virtual) dialogue with the people studied and negotiates with them over the meaning of their thinking and actions. Even if the people addressed are, as often is the case, close to his or her own position in terms of locality, ethnicity, political allegiance and so on, their views must not be excluded from critical evaluation. On the contrary, the specialist's obligation is to subject all meanings attached to the past to analysis, and this applies especially to those histories upheld, often even cherished, by people near him or her.

Shared histories emerge from the various comments on and interpretations of the past instigated by the current concerns of those under consideration.[74] The prime function of these mutually constructed accounts is to contribute to the people's daily activities and thinking, not to knowledge in general, and it is from this everyday function that they acquire their significance. Still less are shared histories there to enhance the discipline of history – even if studying them might lead to this. Professional historians have to be content with their duty to replace prejudices and strive to contribute to the sustainability of new interpretations and knowledge.

From the perspective of upholding history-making as a basic social practice, shared histories are useful in the sense that they serve as bridges between the historical understanding of trained historians and the laity. As to supporting the efforts of non-professionals in creating histories, I share the conclusion drawn by Rosenzweig and Thelen. For them, 'the most significant news' of their project was that 'we have interested, active, and thoughtful audiences for what we want to talk about. The deeper challenge is finding out how we can talk to – and especially with – those audiences.'[75] Such an intercourse, involving shared histories as objects of mutual study, entails reassessing the profession's conventions and commencing research work from the perspective of the anticipated significance of the research findings.

Creating such a participatory culture would help to put an end to the scholar's monopoly on history-writing, and to release the study of the past from the one-sided grip of the professionals. At the same time, the move would entail an epistemological issue that has been taken up by Michael Frisch, albeit in connection with oral history, in his 1990 book, *A Shared Authority*. The implications of the close link between authorship and interpretative authority are a [common] thread. Here, Frisch's questions serve as a useful introduction to the politics of history, the historian's relation to the struggle between various interpretations of the past:

> Who, really, is the author of an oral history, whether this be a single interview or an edited book-length narrative? Is it the historian posing questions and editing the results, or the 'subject', whose words are the heart of the consequent texts? What is the relation between interviewer and subject in the generating of such histories – who is responsible for them and where is interpretive authority located?[76]

Notes

1   For more on this, see John Tosh, *Why History Matters*, pp106–10, Basingstoke, Palgrave, 2008.
2   It is worth repeating that 'to whom' is general by nature; it is still relevant, for example, in cases where the audience is made up only of the two people marking an undergraduate's work.
3   J. H. Hexter, 'The Rhetoric of History', *History and Theory*, Vol. 18 (1967), pp1–13.
4   Mary Fulbrook, *Historical Theory*, p162, London & NY, Routledge, 2002.

5   See especially the collection of my essays at the turn of 1990s, *Aika, historia ja yieisö: Kirjoituksia historiantutkimuksen Iähtökohdista* (Turun yliopisto: Poliittinen historia, julkaisuja, C: 44, 1993). For the metaphor of vortex see Gareth Stedman Jones: 'Faith in history', *History Workshop Journal* 30 (1990).

6   For more on this, see Jorma Kalela, 'Paperiliitto history project', *Adult Education in Finland*, Vol. 1–2 (1987), pp33–37. The most comprehensive presentation of the project and its background is Jorma Kalela, *Näkökulmia tulevaisuuteen. Paperiliiton historia 1944–1986* (Helsinki: Paperiliitto 1986), pp11–47.

7   A comprehensive presentation of the revision of my plan is Jorma Kalela, *Näkökulmia tulevaisuuteen*, pp11–15. For an English presentation, see Jorma Kalela, *Paperiliitto History Project*.

8   See Kalela, *Näkökulmia tulevaisuuteen*, pp8–37, for the research circles, and pp37–47 for some of the first steps made towards the concepts outlined in this book.

9   Quoted from David Thelen, 'A Participatory Historical Culture', in Roy Rosenzweig and David Thelen (eds), *The Presence of the Past*, New York, Columbia University Press, p192.

10   Roy Rosenzweig, 'Everyone A Historian' in Rosenzweig and Thelen (eds), *The Presence of the Past*, p184.

11   Unfortunately, I never found time to reflect systematically on my 'participant observation'.

12   See, e.g., Raphael Samuel (ed.), 'History Workshop: A Collectanea 1967–91', *History Workshop*, Vol. 25 (1991), and Jorma Kalela, 'Politics of History and History of Politics: Some Conceptual Suggestions as to Political Aspects of History', in Johanna Valenius (ed.), *Ajankohta: Poliittisen historian vuosikirja 2004* (Turku: Poliittinen historia Helsingin ja Turun yliopistot, 2004).

13   Sven Lindqvist: *Gräv där su står: Hur man utforskar ett jobb* (Stockholm: Bonniers, 1979); Gunnar Sillén, *Stiga vi mot ljuset Om dokumentation av industri-och arbetarminnen* (Stockholm: Raben and Sjögren, 1977).

14   Sillén, *Stiga vi mot ljuset*, passim and Raphael Samuel, 'Editorial introduction' in Samuel (ed.), 'History Workshop'.

15   Since the 1990s I have met a great number of colleagues in Finland, Sweden, Norway and the UK involved in these kinds of projects, but no studies of their proliferation. On the other hand, the relationship between place and belonging as an issue has been discussed by several scholars. See, e.g., Paula Hamilton and Linda Shopes (eds.), *Oral History and Public Memories* (Philadelphia: Temple University Press, 2008), passim.

16   'Quelle histoire pour quel avenir? Whose History for Whose Future?', Sixth Biennial Conference on the Teaching, Learning and Communicating of History, Quebec, Canada, 24–26 October 2008. Information from Pilvi Torsti who took part in the conference.

17   Thelen, 'A Participatory Historical Culture', p190; Roy Rosenzweig and David Thelen: 'Introduction: Scenes from a Survey', in Rosenzweig and Thelen (eds), *The Presence of the Past*, pp12–13.

18   Rosenzweig and Thelen, 'Introduction: Scenes from a Survey', pp12–13.

19   Tosh, *Why History Matters*, pp10–11.

20   The starting point for what follows is Jay Winter's review of several works dealing with the First World War: 'P vs C. The still burning anger when the French talk of the First World War' (*Times Literary Supplement*, 16 June 2006). The comment on the bestselling books was made, according to him, by Antoine Prost.

21   In addition to Jeremy Black, *Using History*, London, Hodder Arnold 2005; Margaret MacMillan, *The Uses and Abuses of History*, London, Profile Brooks, 2009; and Tosh, *Why History Matters*; see also Peter Aronson, *Historiebruk – att använda det förflutna* (Lund: Studentlitteratur, 2004).

22   Tosh, *Why History Matters*, especially pp120–43.

23   Thelen, *A Participatory Historical Culture*, pp195–202.

24   Hilda Kean, *London Stories: Personal Lives, Public Histories,* London, Sydney and Chicago, Rivers Oram Press, 2004, pp12–15. See also Paul Ashton and Paula Hamilton, 'At Home with the Past: Background and Initial Findings from the National Survey' (Australians and the Past, Special issue of *Australian Cultural History*, 22 (2003), pp5–30).

25   Paul Ashton and Hilda Kean, 'Introduction' to Ibid., *People and their Pasts*, pp1–20.

26   The quotations from Hilda Kean, '"Public history" and Raphael Samuel, 'A forgotten radical pedagogy?', *Public History Review*, Vol. 11 (2004), pp52–53.

27   The 1991 paper in Oxford has not been published; the 2009 article appeared in S. Tiitinen et al. (eds.), *Challenges for Finland and Democracy: Parliament of Finland Centennial 12* (Helsinki: Edita 2009).

28   The quotations on Sen's *Identity and Violence: The Illusion of Destiny* are from the back cover of the Penguin Books edition, 2007.

29   This state of affairs began to come into sight towards the end of my assignment in Paperiliitto and analysing its political consequences has been a central theme in my research since. See, e.g.,

ch. 5 in Kalela, *Näkökulmia tulevaisuuteen* and Jorma Kalela, 'Kansalaiset, poliittinen järjestelmä Ja yhteiskuntamoraali', *Tiedepolitiikka*, Vol. 2 (1990), pp5–16.

30   Mandler, *History and National Life*, pp147–48.

31   For Gilroy, *After Empire: Melancholia or Convivial Culture* (London: Routledge, 2005), see Bhikhu Parekh's review in the *Times Literary Supplement*, 9 September 2005; Hall, according to Tosh, *Why History Matters*, p15.

32   Derek Fewster, *Visions of Past Glory: Nationalism and the Construction of Early Finnish History* (Helsinki: Finnish Literature Society, 2006), Tuula Karjalainen, *Kantakuvat – yhteinen muistimme* (Helsinki: Maahenki, 2009), Maunu Häyrynen, *Kuvitettu maa: Suomen kansallisen maisemakuvaston rakentuminen* (Helsinki: Suomalaisen Kirjallisuuden Seura, 2009).

33   Quotation Mandler, *History and National Life*, p147. Connected to the problem of identity is discussion of the histories of various minorities from the angle 'who owns history'; this multifaceted issue is, however, beyond the scope of this book. About its various dimensions, see, for e.g., Grele, 'Reflections on the practice of oral history', pp19–21.

34   Eric Amesen, 'The Recent Historiography of British Abolitionism: Academic Scholarship, Popular History and the Broader Reading Public' *Historically Speaking*, July/August, 2006, pp22–24.

35   Richard Overy, 'The historical present', *Times Higher Education Supplement*, 29 April 2010.

36   The latter quotation from Bruce L. Berger, 'Narrative and Popular History', *Historically Speaking*, May/June 2006, p42.

37   See, e.g., Gerda Lerner, 'The Necessity of History and Professional Historian', *Journal of American History*, Vol. 69, No 1 (1982), quoted in and discussed by Pertti Haapala, 'Sosiaalihistorian lupaus', in Pekka Ahtiainen et al. (eds.), *Historia nyt: Näkemyksiä suomalaisesta historiantutkimuksesta* (Helsinki: WSOY, 1990), pp82–83.

38   The expression has been used by Katharine Hodgkin and Susannah Radstone in 'Introduction. Contested pasts', to Hodgkin and Radstone (eds.), *Memory, History, Nation: Contested Memories, Studies in Memory and Narrative* (New Brunswick: Transaction Publishers, 2006).

39   The commonplace nature of history was the theme of a book titled (in translation) *Everyday History*, which succeeded, at the beginning of the 2000s, in drawing attention to this aspect of history in Finland. See Jorma Kalela and Ilari Lindroos (eds.), *Jokapäiväinen historia* (Helsinki); Tietolipas 177, Suomalaisen Kirjallisuuden Seura, 2001, and Google entry: *Jokapäiväinen historia*.

40   G. R. Elton, *The Practice of History* (London: Fontana Press, 1989 [1967]), p66.

41   In the article referred to in note 11 in this chapter, I used the misleading term 'social memories' to refer to this analytical category.

42   For more on popular histories (albeit not using this term) see, e.g., R. Samuel and P. Thompson (eds.), *The Myths We Live By* (London and New York: Routledge, 1990).

43   For more on this perspective (and for the quotation) see, e.g., Joseph Mali, *Mythistory: The Making of a Modern Historiography* (Chicago and London: University of Chicago Press, 2003); quotation at pp4–6.

44   Examples of recent works include Black, *Using History*, and Peter Aronsson, *Historiebruk: Att använda det förflutna*. An older, more or less standard treatise is M. I. Finley, *The Use and Abuse of History: From the Myths of the Greeks to Lévi-Strauss, The Past Alive and the Present Illumined* (London: Chatto and Windus, 1972; reprint London: Penguin Books, 1990).

45   Recent works are the two volumes edited by Katharine Hodgkin and Susannah Radstone: Hodgkin and Radstone, *Memory, History, Nation*, and Radstone and Hodgkin (eds.), *Regimes of Memory: Studies in Memory and Narrative* (New Brunswick: Transaction Publishers, 2006). These books also display the wide interdisciplinary interest in 'memory' with various attributes (e.g. 'collective memory') since the 1970s.

46   Popular Memory Group, 'Popular Memory: Theory, Politics, Method', in R. Johnson, G. McLennan, B. Schwartz and D. Sutton (eds.), *Making Histories: Studies in History-writing and Politics* (London: Hutchinson, 1982), pp205–52. The terms used by the Group were 'public representations' and 'private memory'. Comments on this article abound in the literature on the study of memory; see, e.g., Hodgkin and Radstone, *Memory, History, Nation* and Radstone and Hodgkin, *Regimes of Memory*. I have myself referred constantly to the Group's work since 1984 (see my 'Minnesforskning, oral history och historierörelsen', *Sociologisk Forskning*, Vols 3–4 (1984), pp47–67).

47   In his article on the subject, 'The historical present', referred to in note 35 in this chapter, Richard Overy writes of the popular 'misperception that popular history and popular history writers are doing in some sense *real* history' (my italics).

48   In the yearly conference for the historians of the labour movement in Linz 1981, I underlined that it was not for nothing that the historical profession had developed their methodological

tools: *Internationale Tagung der Historiker der Arbeiterbewegung, 17: Linzer Konferenz 1981* (Vienna: Europaverlag, 1983), pp581–82. See also Kalela, *Minnesforskning, oral history och historierörelsen*.

49   Ruth Finnegan, 'Should We Notice Researchers Outside the University?', *British Academy Review*, 10, 2007, p60.

50   The quotation is from an anonymous review (in January 2011) of the draft for this book requested by Palgrave Macmillan.

51   For sources, see Chapter 5, note 9, which reads: 'My main source for this discussion has been the internet. In addition to the home pages of several universities offering training in public history, there are those of The National Council on Public History, The Public Historian and The Public History Research Centre (all in the United States) as well as Public History Review in Australia.'

52   The articles of Sillén and myself appeared in *Meddelande från Arbetarrörelsens arkiv och bibliotek*, Vol. 23, Nos. 2 and 3 (1982). For the relationship between history and art, see Ian Mortimer, 'The Art of History', *Historically Speaking* (June 2010).

53   Markku Hyrkkänen, 'All History is, More or Less, Intellectual History: R. G. Collingwood's 'Contribution to the Theory and Methodology of Intellectual History', *Intellectual History Review*, Vol. 19, No. 2 (2009); quotations at p263. See also Thelen, 'A participatory historical culture', p191. About Collingwood himself, see his *The Idea of History* (London: Oxford University Press, 1961 [1946]), Part V, § 4, 'History as Re-enactment of Past Experiences'.

54   See also Peter Mandler, *History and National Life*, London, Profile Books, 2002, pp146–47. I was reminded about the importance of the distinction between empathy and sympathy by Sofie Strandén when giving an expert opinion on her PhD thesis to Åbo Akademi University in July 2010.

55   Himmerlfarb, according to Tosh, *Historians on History*, pp290–91.

56   The review was published by the *London Review of Books*, 19 February 2004.

57   In his review of Raphael Samuel, *Theatres of Memory, Volume 1* in *The Times Literary Supplement*, 10 March 1995; Pauli Kettunen, *Globalisaatio ja kansallinen me: Kansallisen katseen historiallinen kritiikki* (Tampere: Vastapaino, 2008), p24.

58   London: Macmillan Press, 1984; quotation at p157.

59   Questioning conventional thinking about authorship in historical writing is the focus of *A Shared Authority. Essays on the Craft and Meaning of Oral and Public History*, by Michael Frisch (State University of New York Press; Albany 1990, xx–xxiii), but he doesn't use the concept of shared histories, the use and role of which is the theme of the next two subchapters. Still, see below the end of the last section in this chapter, 'The liquid social fabric'.

60   Raphael Samuel, *Theatres of Memory Volume 1: Past and Present in Contemporary Culture*, London and New York, Verso, 1994.

61   In *The Lessons of History* (London: Oxford University Press, 1989), quoted in Tosh, *Historians on History*, p180.

62   According to Anderson nations are 'imagined communities' which do not merely invent but actually consist in myths of historical unity and continuity: *Imagined Communities: Reflections on the Origin and Spread of Nationalism* (London: Verso, 1983), p19.

63   Anne Heimo, *Kapina Sammatissa. Vuoden 1918 paikalliset tulkinnat osana historian yhteiskunnallisen rakentamisen prosessia* (Helsinki: Suomalaisen Kirjallisuuden Seura, 2010); with an English summary: *Rebellion in Sammatti: Local Interpretations of the 1918 Finnish Civil War as Part of the Social Process of History Making*.

64   The fruitfulness of Rosenzweig and Thelen's work is not essentially weakened by their survey method, that is, a method in which the interviewees' world (in this case their past) has been virtually defined by the scholars in advance.

65   Frisch, *A Shared Authority*, ppxv–xx; Alessandro Portelli, *The Battle of Valle Giulia: Oral History and the Art of Dialogue* (Madison, The University of Wisconsin Press, 1997), p12; Hamilton and Shopes (eds.), *Oral History and Public Memories* (Philadelphia; Temple University Press, 2008), px.

66   A standard presentation of this field of study is the two-part collection edited by Katharine Hodgkin and Susannah Radstone, *Memory, History, Nation* and *Regimes of Memory*. According to David Berliner, '"The Abuses of Memory": Reflections on the Memory Boom in Anthropology' (*Anthropological Quarterly*, Vol. 78, No. 1 [Winter 2005]), the reference of memory has been lost because of the inflation of (scholarly) attributes to memory.

67   The quotation at pxi.

68   Mali, *Mythistory;* James V. Wertsch, *Voices of Collective Remembering* (Cambridge: Cambridge University Press, 2002).

69   Quotation from Ashton and Kean, *People and Their Pasts*, p5.

70   Tosh, *Why History Matters*, pp99–139. The Dutch philosopher of history Chris Lorenz, in turn, underlines that the rise of the 'new histories' testifies to 'the declining significance of the nation

state as the "natural" framework of academic history'. Chris Lorenz, 'Unstuck in Time. On the sudden presence of the past', in K. Tilmans, F. van Vree and J. Winter (eds.), *Performing the Past, Memory, History, and Identity in Modern Europe* (Amsterdam: Amsterdan University Press, 2010), pp81–86.

71   Thelen, 'A Participatory Historical Culture', pp199–200.

72   Marina Warner, 'In the Time of Not Yet: Marina Warner on the imaginary of Edward Said', *London Review of Books*, 16 December 2010.

73   Elina Makkonen, *Muistitiedon etnografiaa tuottamassa* (Joensuu; Joensuun yliopiston humanistisia julkaisuja, Vol. 58 [2009]), passim; with an English summary: *Producing an ethnography of oral history*.

74   The historian would be wise to take seriously what for scholars in folkloristics is commonplace: 'Memory need not be dramatic or well told to be a key narrative: the tale can just as well deal with a moment of joy or it can be scant and fumbling in its methods when narrating a trauma.' Annikki Kaivola-Bregenhöj, 'History bursts into story: women's tales of war', *Folklore Fellows' Network*, No. 37 (December 2009), p13.

75   Rosenzweig, 'Everyone a Historian', quotation at p189; Thelen, 'A Participatory Historical Culture', p190.

76   Frisch, *A Shared Authority*, pxx.

Chapter 7

Matthew J. Taylor and Michael K. Steinberg

FORTY YEARS OF CONFLICT

State, Church and Spontaneous Representation of Massacres and Murder in Guatemala

Images of Guatemala

> Guatemala, 1962–present: Two hundred thousand murdered and disappeared Guatemalans, one hundred and fifty thousand Guatemalans seek refuge outside of their patria (homeland), one and a half million internally displaced Guatemalans escape violence, countless orphans and widows, indelible scars of horror deeply ingrained in the minds of victims and perpetrators alike, and counting. . . .
> (CEH 1999)

NO DOUBT, GUATEMALA'S HIDDEN WAR exacted an onerous toll on both indigenous and Ladino (non-indigenous) minds and hearts.[1] The publication of the United Nations sponsored *Guatemala: Memoria del Silencio* (CEH 1999) and the Guatemalan Office of the Archbishops *Guatemala: Nunca Más* (REMHI 1998) reveal to the outside world, in horrific detail, the acts and impacts of almost 40 years of violence. These grisly tomes documenting death and destruction in Guatemala's towns and countryside permit in the words of a witness:

> *Que la historia que pasamos*
> *quede en las escuelas,*
> *para que no se olvide,*
> *para que nuestros hijos la conozcan.*

> (So that the history we experienced
> stays in schools,
> so that it is not forgotten.
> so that our children know what happened.)
> (CEH 1999, vol. 5, p9)

The printed page provides a permanent place for the victims of Guatemala's genocide.[2] Most Guatemalans, however, cannot read or write. How then, do these Guatemalans externalize their memory?

Mention of Guatemala conjures up many exotic images. These images include past and present Maya cultures; majestic Maya temples surrounded by tropical forest, smoking volcanoes, military dictators behind dark sunglasses, and grave human rights violations.[3] Guatemala's natural and culture diversity at first attracts researchers and travelers. Yet these tourists and academic voyeurs often, upon delving deeper into Guatemala's realities, feel compelled to reveal the other side of this small nation's beauty. This contradictory facet of Guatemala is reflected in writings about Guatemala. Recent titles include: George Lovell's *A Beauty that Hurts: Life and Death in Guatemala*, Richard Adams' *Crucifixion by Power*, Jim Handy's *Gift of the Devil: A History of Guatemala*, *Shattered Hope* by Piero Gleijeses, Robert Carmack's *Harvest of Violence: Maya Indians and the Guatemalan Crisis*, Jean-Marie Simons *Guatemala: Eternal Spring, Eternal Tyranny*, and Jennifer Schirmer's *The Guatemalan Military Project: A Violence Called Democracy*. These titles suggest the conflicting relationship these scholars have with their field locations. Guatemalan landscapes exude beauty, but hidden within that beauty lies pain and a history of extreme inequalities and continued repression. When we read the landscape more closely, the beauty appears tarnished or obliterated, just like many Guatemalan families and villages during the "problematic time." We explore these contradictions by presenting images of contrasting landmarks, memorials, and other landscape features associated with the Guatemalan civil war that ended in 1996 with an internationally brokered peace accord between guerrilla groups and the state.

How to read Guatemalan landscapes

We examined Guatemala's landscape for the presence of memorials and less intentional landmarks related to the recently concluded armed conflict. We did this while journeying through mountainous rural areas in the Department of Huehuetenango and Ixil country in the Department of Quiché. We also slogged through tropical lowlands of Ixcán area in the extreme north of Quiché and Huehuetenango. We spoke to locals about how they remember thousands of massacre victims. Upon entering a town or village, for example, we often approached officials in municipal buildings that surround the central plaza of most Guatemalan communities. Enquiries to local police officers and other municipal employees about the existence of memorials (or other ways in which the dead are remembered) that commemorate "the conflict" were received with incredulous stares. Officials often denied the existence of any monuments even if their office sat a mere 50 meters from the Catholic cathedral containing hundreds of crosses that record the name and date of each massacred or disappeared person. We often had to ask long and hard before being pointed to any monuments that commemorate victims because locals still fear talking about the past.

We focused on these rural areas of Guatemala because at the height of conflict in the early 1980s this region bore the brunt of insurgency and counter-insurgency campaigns and thus earned the "red" label from government security forces. Red zones consisted of enemy territories, where "no distinction was made between *guerilleros* (anti-state insurgency forces) and their peasant supporters. Both were to be attacked and obliterated" (Schirmer 1998, p42).[4] These areas received military "attention" during the civil war because, for a short time at least, they were strongholds for the rebel forces, especially the Guerrilla Army of the Poor (EGP) (Ball et al. 1999; Falla 1992; Lovell 1990; Manz 1988; Montejo 1992; Moreno 1998; Payeras 1998; Stoll 1993). We also crossed Lake Atitlán to Santiago Atitlán to investigate how this town remembers the recent violence and the murder of a U.S. priest. The search for monuments also led to Guatemala City. Intense violence wracked the city in the early 1980s and formed the point from which generals and government officials planned counter-insurgency campaigns and subsequent peace negotiations (Payeras 1987).

We became intrigued by what we saw and, just as importantly, what we did not see regarding public memory and commemoration of the civil war. Driving through the poorly maintained back roads and living with residents of former conflict zones, we found it hard to believe that this area formed the focus of state orchestrated murder, massacre, disappearances, and refuge (Green 1999; Zur 1998). Jean-Marie Simon (1987, p16) warns that "many of those who now travel there will be hard pressed to imagine the enormity of its tragedy." An uninformed traveler, tourist, or aid worker not versed in Guatemala's recent violent history and not specifically looking for landmarks might easily continue unaware of clandestine graves and thousands of wooden crosses, one for each victim, nailed to the walls of village churches. In Ixcán, for instance, we stayed in villages "wiped off the map" by military actions in the early 1980s that show no signs of past conflict – in fact, the military often built model villages on the ashes of destroyed community centers (CEIDEC 1990; Nelson 1999). It is in these very villages, as González (1998, pp13–14) bluntly relates:

> . . . in every corner of Yichkan [Ixcán], every turn of the roads of Yichkan, every corner of the bleeding fatherland, every spot was a silent witness to massacres and tortures. The land, the face of the earth, was splattered with the blood of her children. The rivers became the veins of the community in which the blood of the people flowed . . . it was like cutting down a great forest . . . more than four hundred villages were wiped off the face of the earth.

In fact, little evidence of any type of conflict remained after a few months. Simon (1987, p8) poignantly recalls: "scorched earth was overgrown with corn six months later; refugee camps where helicopters dumped grieving widows and children were renamed and reconstructed over razed huts; and model villages were built on top of these camps, often over the ashes of the dead."[5] It is on this landscape that rural survivors must remember. Often, their remembering is an inconspicuous everyday act; simply by living in a humble house that sits on the foundations of a former house, people are remembering. The site of the massacre becomes the monument. These are, intangibly yet palpably, memories of the mind, memories that leave no obvious permanent mark on the visible landscape.

State versus spontaneous memories and memorials

Although few in number, landmarks in post-conflict Guatemala point to a continuing struggle as to how two opposing sides – the state and victims of the state–represent the years of *problemas*. The paucity of overtly public landmarks in many villages and towns severely affected by the war illustrates how residents continue to negotiate and struggle with the aftermath and realities of postwar life and indicates little closure for victims and survivors of violence. Alternatively the absence of monuments may reflect how people choose to internalize their experiences and use their own bodies as sites of resistance and as a way to continue the daily struggle of survival. Internalizing grief may be the only strategy for survival in a country where, in the words of Linda Green (1999), "fear is a way of life." Many rural folk do not see the new government as a significant departure from previous regimes. In fact, under the Portillo government (2000–2004) the tenuous strings of peace are stretched to a maximum as politically motivated murders, land conflicts, and mob lynching continue.[6] Although some Guatemalans feel slightly more inclined to reveal their political leanings and feelings surrounding the war, many remain guarded for fear of future reprisals.

How can villagers build monuments to the dead when many members of civil patrols (government created militias called *Patrulleros de Autodefensa Civil* – PAC), who often participated in military-sanctioned violence directed at other villagers accused of supporting guerrillas, continue to live among relatives of the victims?[7] Thus, many survivors of the war receive little or no closure because they must constantly interact with those who abducted, tortured, or killed their loved ones. Given that both perpetrators and victims continue to live side-by-side, and that communal graves are only now being excavated to provide some sort of closure for relatives (e.g., Prensa Libre 2001b), the momentum to construct public memorials is delayed or muted. Eduardo Galeano attributes such apprehension to the fact that:

> Guatemala sufre de una historia official mutilada . . . como que si recordar fuera peligrosa, porque recordar es repetir el pasado como una pesadilla [Guatemala suffers from an official history that is mutilated . . . as though it is dangerous to remember, because to remember is to repeat the past like a nightmare).
>
> (cited in Wilson 1998)

Certainly, much written work documents the last 40 years of "unrest" in Guatemala – this in itself is a memory. Detailed accounts of death and destruction (Ball, Kobrack, and Spirer 1999; CEH 1999; REHMI 1998) and personal testimonies (e.g., Diocesis del Quiché 1994; González 1998; Menchú 1984; Montejo 1987 and 1992) rapidly multiply in the "safer to speak" climate of the late 1990s and early years of the twenty-first century.[8] Despite the proliferation of printed memories, the words remain unknown to Guatemala's illiterate population. Moreover, only a small portion of the literate population can access the "published memories" that appear to satisfy an international and academic demand for accountability.[9] For example, the exhaustive details found in *Guatemala: Memoria del Silencio* (CEH 1999) cover 12 volumes and cost over U.S. $100. The text and figures now also reside on compact disk, making the information even less accessible to most Guatemalans. The REMHI (1998) publication totals four volumes and sells for U.S. $70, and a summary of the four volumes sells for about U.S. $40.

The memory of those most affected by the war – those who will never access the documents produced by national and international truth commissions, which present a very official, impersonal memory – lies in the hands of the church and the state.

The Catholic Church

Most landmarks commemorating the victims of Guatemala's turmoil fall under the auspices of the Catholic Church. Small crosses inside Catholic Churches bearing the names and dates of murder or disappearance form the only tangible memorial in many villages and towns impacted by the violence. The Catholic Church consistently plays the role of unofficial "moral conscience" because its members and clergy were (and continue to be) persecuted during the conflict. The military targeted members of the Catholic clergy who embraced Liberation Theology, labeling them as dissenters and guerrilla collaborators – these men and women did not last long in the Guatemalan countryside (Diocesis del Quiché 1994; Falla 1992 and 1993). Harassment and assassinations of Catholic Church members continues even after the signing of the peace treaty in 1996. Most infamously, Bishop Juan Gerardi, chair of the Catholic Church's Recovery of Historical Memory project (REMHI), was murdered two days after presenting REMHI's findings to the public on April 26, 1998. More recently, on May 8, 2001, another member of the Church, Sister Barbara Ford, was murdered, in part (according to some of our sources in Guatemala) for assisting in the development of the REMHI project. The REMHI project recorded over 6,500 testimonials that detailed over 55,000 human rights violations, including 25,000 deaths. Strangely, although no large public monument in Guatemala City honors the hundreds of thousands of deaths and disappearances, a large monument, uncovered on April 26, 2000, at a ceremony commemorating the second anniversary of his assassination, commemorates Bishop Gerardi (Nunca Más 2000). Does this monument to Gerardi vicariously represent the victims of 440 village massacres with the words "*Guatemala Nunca Más*" (Guatemala Never Again) replacing the names of the dead?

The Church, through landmarks and memorials to the dead and disappeared, reminds parishioners and the military of human suffering caused by military actions. The large mural painted on the wall of the Catholic Church grounds in Cantabal, Ixcán, and the placement of hundreds of individual crosses inside the Catholic Churches in Nebaj, San Juan Cotzal, and Santiago Atitlán attempt to formalize the past and educate new generations about past atrocities.[10] The Catholic Church in Chajul contains a powerful mural that depicts dead community members and a woman bent in mourning over the prostrate bodies. The mural is entitled "In memory of our martyrs" (Diocesis del Quiché 1994, p200).

The Catholic Church in Santiago Atitlán also contains a memorial to Father Stanley Rother, an American priest who was killed on church grounds on July 28, 1981 and whose remains are interred there. As one arrives by boat to Santiago Atitlán visitors see no obvious, open memorials to the town's troubled past, or of the public outcry that military occupation and repression sparked – again memories remain deep in the folds of the Church. In Santiago Atitlán no overt landmarks in tourist areas indicate the confrontation between the townsfolk and the military that left 19 people dead and which eventually led to popular resistance and the forced abandonment of the town by the military in 1990 – the first successful ousting of the military in Guatemala (Carlsen 1997). If tourists do trek up to the town center, up the steep streets laden with arts and crafts, and make their way into the dimly lit church, they finally reach the memorials. But, is the significance of the tiny brass crosses on a side wall lost on people who come to experience Guatemala's indigenous cultures and natural beauty? Tourists do not make the journey to Santiago to relive a violent past. The crosses on the church wall maybe then, if we think of their intent, serve their purpose – they commemorate the dead for friends and family who frequent the church.

The Catholic Church provides refuge for public commemoration and protest against the actions of the military. The construction of monuments inside churches or on church grounds is the first step toward construction of more public monuments. Foote, Tóth, and Arvay (2000) observed a similar scenario in Hungary, where monuments banned by the communist regimes first appeared in churchyards and cemeteries before the fall of communism.

Not all monuments in Guatemala commemorate civilian victims of the civil war. The military also suffered losses. We now turn to examine how the military represent their soldiers who died on the line of duty.

State sponsored monuments

The military

When interpreting the conflict, the Guatemalan military plays the role of state "savior," without whom a leftist takeover was imminent. The military's portrayal of the war is vastly different than that of the Catholic Church. Their landmarks and memorials often stress sacrifice, unity, national service, and power. In contrast to monuments created by the Catholic Church, military and government landmarks figure prominently in public spaces and take on official tones in both form and content.

After announcing our arrival to Ixcán by thundering across the metal sheets of the bridge spanning the turbulent waters of the Chixoy River, we hit the brakes of the pickup truck to ease over speed bumps, which, at the same time, allows the soldier in an elevated guard post to give us the once over. Next, signs on the massive block wall of the military base at Playa Grande (near Cantabal) flood our vision. The signs invite locals and travelers to visit the military museum inside the walls – the only regional military museum in the country. Paradoxically, or maybe intentionally, this museum sits in the heart of the zone that experienced the most intense conflict in the 1980s and 1990s.

The displays in the museum reinforce the portrayal of sacrifice and salvation of the people from insurgents by the military. For example, a display describes the role of the air force in the counter-insurgency campaign as the *guardian del Ixcán* (guardian of Ixcán). Museum displays include photographs of captured weapons, captured rebels, and battle-ground scenes – features that emphasize military victory and power. Other displays include tributes to military losses such as photographs, examples of field accommodations, and lists of officers killed in the Ixcán, all which emphasize sacrifice to the state. The military depiction of the guerrillas is far from objective. Every verbal and written mention of the guerrillas or insurgents presented to visitors to the museum is prefaced by the word "delinquents."[11] An inspection of the visitor's logbook reveals that most visitors to the museum are local. Locals, who once feared the military, can now openly visit the site of their own torture, pain, and imprisonment.[12]

The Guatemalan armed forces in the Ixcán also constructed roadside memorials in honor of their casualties. Two of the monuments sit on the side of the *Transveral del Norte* (the Northern Transversal route), a road network constructed in the late 1960s and early 1970s by the state to gain access to oil deposits, large tracts of land, and nascent guerrilla camps (Kading 1999; Le Bot 1995). One of the roads cuts east to west though the *Franja Transversal del Norte* (Northern Transversal Strip), parts of which are known as "the land of the generals" because members of the military elite appropriated large tracts of land for cattle ranches and for the promise of oil wealth.

One roadside monument sits at the entrance to the village of San Lucas in the Ixcán. Guatemalan troops occupied this village and created a temporary outpost here for further forays into the rainforests of the Ixcán. Although the monument is slightly defaced, soldiers from the base in Playa Grande saw fit to give the monument a bright yellow coat of paint early in 2001. This new coat of paint represents the new self-proclaimed relationship of the Guatemalan military with Ixcán residents, a relationship in which the military "defends and protects the communities to maintain a peaceful atmosphere in which integral development can occur" (Girón 2000, p3). Yellow is the color associated with the large road building machines that the military now uses; yellow, then, renders a positive air of prosperity and development. Previously, all monuments and machinery bore military olive green paint. With time, though, the yellow coat chips and fades to reveal true military origins – drab olive green.

The monument serves several purposes. In the rainy season, before construction of a shelter, locals sat on the dry concrete base while they wait for transport to nearby Cantabal, or, now that a bridge crosses the formidable Ixcán River, to Barillas in Huehuetenango. The monument lists the names of army engineers killed by guerrillas while they built the road. In this sense, the monument serves its intended purpose – to commemorate the road builders killed by "delinquent" guerrillas. This monument also served its (un) intended purpose by triggering the memory of an Ixcán resident who told me of his experiences as a PAC member, his relationships with military commanders in Playa Grande, and the orders from above that he and other PAC members received to search and destroy suspected guerrilla sympathizers.

The other bright yellow roadside monument is in the form of a castle found on the Army Corps of Engineers emblem. The bright yellow castle also commemorates the death of army road builders. It was barely noticeable until the recent painting campaign brought attention to the diminutive structure by clearing away encroaching secondary growth and by carving a stairway through the red lateritic rainforest soils from the road to the monument itself.

The government

On December 26, 1996, PAN (National Party for Advancement) and URNG (Guatemalan National Revolutionary Unit) signed an internationally negotiated peace agreement that ended almost 40 years of internal conflict. The government erected several monuments that commemorate the peace treaty and victims of the conflict. These monuments always include a dove and the following phrase: "firm and lasting peace." Although these structures represent significant events in Guatemala's history, they are not significant structures themselves. The diminutive nature of the peace monuments is clearly illustrated by the eternal flame and plaque set in the ground in Guatemala City's national plaza. This monument – one-meter high in glory – fades into insignificance against the backdrop of the National Palace, which is still guarded by troops in combat fatigues carrying automatic weapons.

When we visited the peace memorial in mid-2001, the "eternal" flame did not burn, orange peels and trash cluttered the glass case, which sits atop a small stone block. To top off this poor appearance, graffiti adorned the glass casing. When ignited, "the flame is the size of a Bunsen burner" (Smith 2001). Given the length of the civil war (36 years), and associated human suffering, we must question why the state constructed such a small monument. All the same, it is surprising that the state *did* acquiesce to build a monument in Guatemala's most public space. Perhaps answers to our questioning and doubts surface upon examination of the vague and noncommittal words inscribed on the side of the monument, "*A los heroes anónimos de la paz*" (to the anonymous heroes of the peace).

Another diminutive monument to war and peace competes with food vendors and video games in Nebaj, Quiché, the southernmost town in hard-hit Ixil country. Curiously, the barbed wire bounded memorial stands in a hidden corner of the town square. The unstable appearance of the white dove instills little sense of celebration, or even solemn remembrance. Instead, the monument resembles military-controlled model villages during the 1980s, some of which the military encircled with barbed wire to maintain direct control of residents' movements (CEIDEC 1990; Falla 1992). The paint-spattered plaque below the white dove repeats vague nationalistic apologies for the war. The text informs us that this monument honors:

> . . . our brothers who perished in the armed conflict, hoping that this event will never occur again. The people of Nebaj and the municipality offer this monument as a symbol of the new democratic cohabitation and culture of firm and lasting peace.

In Nebaj the real homage to rural Guatemalans resides a mere 20 meters away inside the nearby Catholic Church in the form of hundreds of wooden crosses, which bear the details of each victim of terror. The crosses come from the people and are personal in regard to their message or content (i.e., someone important to me died). The official memorials, in contrast, are vague and platitudinous, and ignored. On the other hand, the military memorials tout their position, power, and achievements, and arc imposed on the landscape.

The lack of investment in public monuments speaks of the current political and cultural climate in Guatemala and how the military and social elite struggle to acknowledge their role in the violence of the past. Despite wide publication and recognition of Guatemala's atrocious human rights record, many upper- and middle-class Guatemalans retort that academics and international agencies side with the Indians and the left. Further, because the elite were physically, as much as geographically, removed from the worst violence in the countryside, they refuse to recognize the magnitude of massacres in rural Guatemala. For example, the minister of defense in 2001, Eduardo Arévalo Lacs, when referring to rapes and land seizures by ex-PAC members in Quiché in July 2001, simply stated that "*ex patrulleros civiles ya no hay, porque fueron disueltos hace años*" (there are no longer any ex-civil patrollers because they were dissolved years ago). In this statement he absolves the military of all responsibility in this case (Prensa Libre 2001c).

The static nature of Guatemala's power structure and class relations means that the state will probably not fund more meaningful monuments representing the violence and victims of almost four decades of war. The act of remembering will remain in the hands of the church and communities that fund their own projects. The highly centralized Guatemalan state and life in the capital city bear little relation to the countryside, so in some respect, rural folk (about 60 percent of the population) increasingly follow their own plans for transforming spaces into places of mourning.

Spontaneous monuments

Some rural communities in Guatemala, in the face of institutional neglect, construct their own monuments to victims and conduct yearly memorial services on the anniversary dates of village massacres (Noack 2001). For example, a large monument commemorates the massacre in Cuarto Pueblo, Ixcán. This twenty-foot high, blue and white concrete structure bears brass plaques listing about 470 residents of Cuarto Pueblo, Xalbal, Zunil, Los Angeles, and Ixtahuacan Chiquito murdered in military massacres in March and April, 1982.[13] A small plaque on the front of the memorial commemorates Father Guillermo Woods, a Maryknoll missionary involved in the early stages of Ixcán colonization in the late 1960s and early 1970s (Morrissey 1978). Father Woods died when the plane he piloted from Guatemala City to Ixcán mysteriously crashed. Many Guatemalans believe the military "downed" the plane (Falla 1992). Candle wax stains the concrete steps around the monument, testament to the active – and ritualistic – use of this site.

González (1998) depicts another spontaneous site and relays plans to build a memorial in the shape of a pyramid in Nueva Esparanza, Huehuetenango.[14] And, in Dos Erres, Petén, where 180 members of the community were massacred and thrown into a well in 1982, the community plans to construct a monument at the site of the well and in the center of the village (Rosales 2000). Residents of Nimlaha'kok in Alta Verapaz and Río Negro outside Rabinal remember massacres and victims by inscribing their names in monuments (Wilson 1997).

A statue of an indigenous woman breaking an M-16 rifle over her head is perhaps the most public and overt memorial in Guatemala. The three meter-high base and statue stand in the busy town square of Chimaltenango, a majority Indigenous town 80 kilometers west of Guatemala City. This memorial occupies a prominent place in the central plaza, which still forms an integral part of social life in many Latin American towns and cities (Low 2000). The plaque tells us about the:

> . . . thousands and thousands of martyrs who fought for peace with social justice
> of the Maya Kaqchikel people and non-indigenous people who were: kidnapped,

disappeared, tortured, massacred, and murdered by the repressive forces of the last thirty-six years [my translation of a section of the inscription from the statue's base].

Residents of Chimaltenango meet, eat, polish shoes, chat, read, gossip, flirt, and simply stroll around the plaza. Erected in January 1997, a mere few weeks after the beginning of "official" peace in Guatemala, the statue makes a bold statement in a time of tender peace. We must note, however, the restrained and vague language used in the memorial. Placing the blame for the violence on "repressive forces" perhaps allows the statue to stand – no specifics about "responsible" forces surface in the text. Even if locals from the capital decide to "finger" the government and openly blame the masterminds and perpetrators of massacres, they remain immune to justice because the June 1994 accord that established the UN-administered Clarification Commission (CEH 1999) stipulates that the information produced "will not individualize responsibility, nor have any legal implications" (Wilson 1997).

Unintended markers of the past

Unplanned markers of past strife riddle Guatemala's countryside. These features provide subtle but important insights into Guatemala's post-conflict environment, and, although unplanned, provide residents with it permanent memory of past events. Driving east from Huehuetenango to Cobin by a back road that hugs the foothills of the rugged Cuchumatán Mountains, we encountered the official road sign that announces the entry into the Ixil Triangle, Quiché. The sign – a leftover from "those times of the guerrillas" – is riddled with bullet holes. It is a constant reminder of Guatemala's worst massacres and remains standing despite the complete inundation of rural Guatemala with new signs advertising banks, money transfer services, fuel stations, development projects, and motels. What is the intent of leaving such a sign in Ixil country?

Another public sign of the past, sadly common in many postwar countries warns residents of unexploded munitions. These posters dot the sides of wooden houses in both Ixcán and Ixil country. Adding further insult to injury, farmers who were denied access to their fields during the height of the conflict so that the military could better control them, now cannot farm those same mine-strewn fields and forests.

These signs contrast with the stunning physical and cultural landscape of the Ixil area, which includes mountainscapes, picturesque wheat and maize fields, and seemingly idyllic villages. Travelers and tourists admire the remote beauty of Nebaj and surrounding villages, bur without cues to the violent past, visitors often succumb to the scenery and the beautiful geometric designs unique to the cloth weavings of the area. Visitors seldom realize that they stand in the middle of former "red" zones of death and destruction. The clues to the past lie deep in the recesses of the Catholic Church in the form of thousands of individually carved crosses bearing the name, age, and date of death of each victim. Other clues lie in the military base a few kilometers outside Nebaj (here no signs invite visitors to inspect the military interpretation of recent events), and an abandoned landing strip (formerly known as "Camp New Life") used in the past to launch bombing missions on isolated Ixil villages and suspected guerrilla camps.

Other public landmarks of the conflict include military outposts at certain strategic geographic locations, such as bridges crossing the Chixoy and Xaclbal rivers in the Ixcán. Over the months of living in Ixcán and traversing its muddy roads with residents, we noted that each time we passed a military checkpoint (current or past) the locals we accompanied broke into stories related to that point in the road. Soldiers carrying automatic weapons still occupy some outposts. We were not allowed to photograph any of the outposts or the soldiers. Again, one wonders about the purpose or message of soldiers guarding river crossings in a "peaceful" country? Because these military installations continue to stand ground in Ixcán and Ixil country, centers of past guerrilla and military activity, the message does not lie too deep beneath the surface. Their presence reminds locals of past and present power relations (e.g., Flores 2003). Military displays of power are especially relevant in the Ixcán, where, according to the soldier who led our tour of the military museum, two local villages continue to reject all government regulations and military control of the region. These villages are made up of residents from former Communities of Population in Resistance (CPR), and returning refugees who fled to Mexico in the 1980s.[15] These villages now enjoy protection because of the presence of international accompaniers and United Nations officials, headquartered in Cantabal, who monitor the postwar activities of the military and verify social reforms promised in the 1996 peace treaty.[16]

Apart from the scars that remain on the minds and bodies of thousands of rural residents in highland towns, the military also left less obvious markers of their years of occupation. In many towns, such as Santa Ana Huista, Huehuetenango, motorists pass guard towers (albeit in ruins) at the entrance to towns where all travelers were stopped, questioned, and checked. These checkpoints stand firm in the memory of residents, who recount hardships endured when revision points functioned.

In the heart of Guatemala City, the military academy (Escuela Politécnica) also conveys a message of continued military power and presence to pedestrians and motorist transiting one of the capital's busiest boulevards. This imposing building, paradoxically located adjacent to the trendy nightclub and restaurant-infested "Zona Viva," resembles a medieval castle and remains a dominant feature in the City, another reminder of the past to the thousands of buses and cars that pass every day. Memories pop into the minds of motorists when traffic slows to permit passage of armored Jeep Cherokees and Mercedes sedans emerging from the recesses of this formidable building. The armed soldiers who patrol the *La Politécnicas* walls send an intimidating image to pedestrians and motorists. The continued presence of armed, ready-for-combat military personnel in the heart of the capital city indicates Guatemala's incomplete transition to a civilian-controlled democracy.

Certainly, military checkpoints and soldiers patrolling in public spaces appear less commonplace today than in the 1980s and early 1990s. Automatic-weapon toting soldiers riding in the back of unmarked pick-up trucks, however, remain fixtures in Guatemala. Today, like the past, the military forms an integral part of the Guatemalan life. This comes as no surprise. Eduardo Galeano, a celebrated Latin American author who writes extensively about the permanent links between politics and the military in Guatemala, writes:

> The president of Guatemala does not wear a prison uniform, but he is a prisoner. The military, his gaolers, have given him permission to enter the National Palace. He has given them a promise of impunity for their killings and has assured them that he will not commit agrarian reform or any other sin.
>
> (Galeano 1967)

Given the recent history and influence of the military in most facets of Guatemalan daily life we cannot expect a radical transition from the past.

In contrast to the imposing presence of the Escuela Politécnica, Jean Marie Simon (1988, p95) points to small plaques and crosses remembering the dead (non-military) scattered throughout Guatemala City. Simon provides examples of these more personal memoirs imprinted in city curbs and traffic islands. These spontaneous shrines constructed by families of assassinated students and politicians do not receive any form of public funding or sanction.

Back out in the countryside evangelical churches make up another powerful feature of the postwar landscape. Guatemala boasts the highest percentage of Protestant members for any Latin American country (although recent conversion rates appear slower with the ending of the war) (Green 1993; Stoll 1993). Although various factors explain the massive conversion to Protestantism, one common theory involves Efraín Ríos Montt, the general who governed Guatemala at the height of military-led massacres in the early 1980s. Ríos Montt, a member and vocal proponent of the "new" religion, claimed that Guatemalans represented the new Israelites. He aimed to create the first Evangelical, anticommunist state in Central America. Many Indian villagers joined Evangelical churches in part to prove allegiance to the state and to avoid persecution by the military (Green 1993; Le Bot 1995). Today Evangelical churches of various sects squeeze into even the smallest hamlets in the Guatemalan countryside. Their loud "broadcast style" of preaching and singing besieges the homes of both Catholics and Evangelicals. Stoll (1993, p5) states that, "the Catholic Church, driven underground after the army killed three Spanish priests and hundreds of local leaders, reported that parishioners were turning Protestant to save their lives." Catholicism was considered tantamount to communism and guerrilla insurgency because of its involvement with liberation theology, church supported cooperatives, and literacy programs, especially in the conflict zones (Green 1993).

Unlike their Catholic counterparts, Evangelical churches do not contain memorials to war victims simply because evangelists avoided some of the direct military persecution (Green 1993). Thus, places where evangelicals worship now symbolize the breakdown of the close-knit corporate, Catholic community that characterized many Maya villages before the war. This developed not only because villages split along denominational lines, but also because the civil patrols and the conflict in general allowed some individuals to violently seek retribution for past personal rivalries and vendettas (Green 1993; Falla 1992; Stoll 1993).

A final, unintended, trigger for memories lies in dead and rotting trees along RN9 (National Road 9) as one approaches the town San Mateo Ixtatán from the south. When we traveled through the foggy, cold, and remote reaches of the 3000 meter high Cuchumatán Mountain ranges, we wondered aloud why so many trees where left to rot in an area where wood is the most important source of fuel. We speculated that perhaps the trees succumbed to disease. Later, we discovered that the military forced local people to cut trees on either side of the road (30–40 meters) to guard against rebel ambushes (Castañeda Salguero 1998; Manz 1988).[17] Today, residents of the area refuse to collect or remove the rotting wood. Residents of the area told Castañeda Salguero "to leave the trees as they lie is like leaving the skeleton of somebody we did not kill. For that reason we do not collect the wood. And they will be there until they turn to dust" (my translation from the original Spanish, p109). Therefore, locals participate now in a subtle form of protest – they leave the tree trunks in place as testament to past atrocities.

Discussing unsettled landscapes in post-conflict regions

Landmarks and memorials in a landscape, overt or discreet, play a powerful role in telling us about a people's values, history, struggles, and successes. Traditionally, landscape studies in the discipline of geography focused on material features expressive of folk, indigenous, and ethnic cultures, such as vernacular architecture, religious icons, settlements forms, and agricultural landforms (Domosh 1989; Hobbs 1995; Jordan 1982, 1985; Kniffen 1990; Mathewson 1984; Sauer 1925). More recently, socially and politically oriented landscape studies have started to examine the messages communicated in buildings, landmarks, and memorials (Atkinson and Cosgrove 1998; Cosgrove 1984; Gillis 1994; Lowenthal 1985; Till 1999, 2003). Most, if not all of these studies focus on landscapes in developed nations and within the context of contestation, but not open insurgency or full-scale warfare. The postcolonial world beyond the North Atlantic realms of relatively tame symbolic and actual political terrains offers rich, if horrific, material for interpretation and analysis. For example, post-revolutionary landscapes, including Cambodia, Sierra Leone, Afghanistan, and Guatemala have received little, if any, attention from geographers. A partial exception is the work of Foote, Tóth, and Arvay (2000) in Hungary. Foote and his colleagues analyze the change in political monuments and historical shrines in Hungary after the fall of the Communist government in 1989.

Perhaps the absence of post-conflict landscape analyses is not surprising given the paucity of monuments in areas of recent conflict. Many post-conflict regions still grapple with new regimes and power relations remain unsteady, thus no one side can claim public space in which to construct obvious landmarks. In other words, states and their citizens do not agree on what or how events should be remembered, thereby delaying construction of memorials or other landmarks (Till 1999). Moreover, many people, just like those in Guatemala, inhibit the desire to build spontaneous shrines for fear of reprisal. Also, post-conflict landscapes present problems of access to outsiders asking questions about past violence (see Santino 2001). Indeed, many of the villages we visited in Guatemala witnessed brutal massacres, making some residents tentative to talk about past violence and how they plan to commemorate past events (Montejo 1987; REMHI 1998). In short, the absence of overt public landmarks and memorials makes the interpretation of post-conflict landscapes more challenging.

However subtle or limited in scale and number, examination of landmarks that do exist in post-conflict landscapes can provide important indicators of past and present political and social relationships. The presence, placement, and prominence of landmarks in post-conflict landscapes can tell the observer about who "won," or, if there are no clear victors, the continuing struggle for power. In the case of Guatemala, although the state successfully destroyed the armed opposition (and anyone remotely associated with it), the government of Alvaro Arzu signed a United Nations' monitored peace agreement in 1996 that mandated a reduction in numbers of armed personnel and the state military budget (Jonas 2000).[18] The state "Victory" remains tainted among much of the Guatemalan citizenry because of the egregious human rights violations (especially against rural residents). Many Guatemalans, especially in rural areas, see the conflict solely as a ploy by the elite to protect economic and social interests. This ploy eliminated those individuals and groups who questioned the power structure within Guatemalan society (Diocesis de Quiché 1994; Kading 1999; Le Bot 1995). Power within Guatemala's post-conflict landscape – as reflected and captured in the landmarks – continues to settle along the dualities of rural and urban, rich and poor, Catholic and Protestant, and military and civilian.

In Guatemala power and social relations continue in a fashion similar to the years prior to the civil war. Ladino elites control politics, land, and capital. Unlike the power shift that Foote, Tóth, and Arvay (2000) document in postcommunist Hungary, Guatemala did not experience a major power shift. Therefore, the construction of new monuments and historical shrines that reflect the ideology of a new regime remains limited. Individuals in Guatemala who desire to construct memorials that contrast with the policies of the military and social elites often do so at great personal risk. In other parts of the world (e.g., Hungary) the radical change from one form of government to another distinct form allows the new government and the people it represents to decide which events and martyrs they wish to memorialize (Foote et al. 2000).

Conclusion

Geographer Steven Hoelscher (1998) writes, "what we see on the landscape . . . stems from the social, economic, and political ideologies of their creators and from their creative exigencies" (p390). In the case of Guatemala, the "creators" of the landscape continue to struggle and compete with one another regarding what is presented to the public. These presentations (both subtle and obvious landmarks and memorials) by groups of citizens, the Catholic Church, and the military/government offer radically different memories of the recently concluded civil war. The Catholic Church commemorates victims. The Guatemalan military emphasizes victory and power.

Sadly, for the people of Guatemala, a long-standing military desire to control the text of the landscape ensures continued tension and violence (e.g., Flores 2003). The military no longer drops bombs on indigenous villages in Ixil country, but military forces and their allies continue to target individuals who seek to portray opposing landmarks and memories of the war (e.g., Nash 2002). The military (i.e., the state) eliminates anyone trying to create a different, victim-oriented post-conflict landscape. For example, Sister Barbara Ford was murdered for her role in the REMHI project. In a separate incident, ex-PAC members raped women, burned several houses, and forced villagers off their plots of land in a Quiché village (Prensa Libre 2001a). The violence in Quiché was attributed to a long-running land dispute between returned refugees and members of the PAC who occupied the land in the absence of the refugees.

Monuments in contemporary Guatemalan landscapes reflect the torturous and tentative path to political and social reform. Competing markers in the landscape send contradictory messages to the Guatemalan public and the world. Memorials and landscape features commemorating victims slowly spread from books to inside churches, to exterior walls of churches and beyond. What will be the next step? Will monuments that provide details of massacres and murders find their way from isolated villages to Guatemala's most public places for all to see? Will the government and church openly sanctify spontaneous monuments and permit memories unfettered by fear? Or, will powerful segments within Guatemalan society continue to control the past?

Notes

1   "The thousands of dead, disappeared, tortured, and displaced, and the hundreds of Mayan communities wiped off the map during the armed conflict all left indelible scars on the minds and hearts of Guatemalans. The impacts of the violence differ according to ethnicity, social class, economic status, gender, age, place of residence, political, and religious affiliation of individuals and social groups. Fear, fright, sadness, depression, sleeping disorders, lack of trust . . . are some of the symptoms frequently shown by people interviewed by CEH" (CEH 1999, Vol. 4, pp14–15).

2   The 12 volumes of CEH also reside on compact discs and on a searchable Web site hosted by the American Association for the Advancement of Science: <http://shr.aaas.org/guatemala/ceh/>.

3   Many Mayan activists within and outside of Guatemala adopted the term "Maya," however, based on discussions with Guatemala's indigenous folk (i.e., nonacademic or activist) in the rural areas of Guatemala, We elect to use the term "indigenous" and "Indian" because most rural indigenous people self-identify using the terms "natural" or "indigena." They use the term "Maya" when referring to "*nuestros antepasados*" (our ancestors). We use the term "indigenous" nor because we negate the relationship between the splendor of the classical Maya culture with their descendents, but because we prefer to use terms that the people themselves employ (some academics claim that the Guatemalan elite refuse to recognize the term "Maya" in their effort to continually belittle the indigenous segment of the population; see Arias 1997; Secaira 2000).

4   David Stoll (1993) reports that many rural Guatemalans existed in a limbo between two armies. Guatemalans we interviewed expressed similar feeling about their lives "between two fires." We

must note, however, that many North American and Guatemalan scholars contest David Stoll's research in Quiché and his reports about how indigenous people coped with the war (e.g., Arias 2003; Hale 1997; Stoll 2003).

5   Nelson (1999, p10) also notes how Guatemalans "live among the eloquent ruins left by the war: model villages built on the charred remains of burned houses, clandestine cemeteries, holding cells for the disappeared built into houses, and military and civil patrol institutions throughout the countryside."

6   Lack of trust in the Portillo regime for many Guatemalans lies in the simple fact that Ríos Montt heads up Guatemala's Congress – Montt was President of Guatemala for 18 months in 1982 and 1983 and, some claim, the mastermind of the worst military massacres and maneuvers in Guatemala.

7   See Prensa Libre 2001a, for an example of strained relationships between ex-PAC members and residents of one community.

8   Although foreign nationals can speak with near impunity, Guatemalan social science researchers, academics, and human rights activists work under renewed death threats and intimidations from "unknown" quarters (Nash 2002).

9   We cannot deny, however, the importance of empirical documentation of massacre victims. Indeed, the type of documentation represented by Falla's *Massacres in the Jungle* (1992) and the CEH and REMHI publications where details surrounding death and destruction surface, in Richard Wilson's words, form "the first act of both remembering and rupturing the silence around violations. Faithfully recording the names of the victims is an attempt to tell the 'public secrets' of a community in order to initiate a break with the official regime of denial. The first statement on the past by Guatemalan society must be a credible and a defensible account of what exactly happened when and to whom, without which other discussions (such as what agents were thinking at the time) cannot begin" (1997, p833).

10   The government carved Cantabal out of the rainforest in 1985 to serve as the administrative center for the newly created *municipio* of Ixán. Cantabal formed part of the "Playa Grande" development pole that consisted of at least 100 villages under army control (CEIDEC 1990). The structure of the villages and towns facilitated military control of rural residents by concentrating residents in geographic areas easily observed by the army in an effort to eradicate the "sea" (rural formers) from which the "fish" (guerrillas) drew sustenance.

11   Visitors to the museum cannot browse the artifacts at their leisure. A civil affairs officer interprets displays for visitors.

12   See the testimonies about imprisonment, torture, and mass graves inside the military base at Playa Grande in Falla (1992, pp192–97).

13   Guatemala's national flag is blue and white.

14   "On this day . . . we will be beginning construction of a great monument to the memory of all the men and women, victims of these thirty-six years of violence. As we raise the monument, we will be embedding into it various objects that we have saved as mementos of our dead: crosses with names, personal objects, or other things that remind us of their existence. I will place at the top of this pyramid . . . the 'deer-eye' seed that I have been wearing around my neck ever since that old lady who gave me her blessing in the darkness placed it in my hand" (González 1998, p157, when referring to reconstruction of lives in Nueva Esparanza, Yichkan [Ixcán]).

15   The Communities of Populations in Resistance resisted military rule during the 1980s and 1990s and eked out a livelihood in the forests of the Ixcán, the Petén, and the mountains of northern Quiché (Falla 1993). They only emerged from hiding after promises from the Guatemalan government to recognize these communities as civilian populations (Primavera del Ixcán 1999; REHMI 1998).

16   Much controversy surrounds the MINUGUA (United Nations Verification Mission in Guatemala) presence in Guatemala. Because MINUGUA protects human rights in Guatemala, many people believe that criminals call in MINUGUA when their rights are in jeopardy. For example, in highland villages around Totonicapán, villagers often deal with their own criminals by cutting off water or electricity rights to offenders of community norms. However, these criminals now call in MINUGUA to illustrate how their rights are in danger. This leads many to believe that MINUGUA is overstepping its bounds and call for its withdrawal. Despite controversy about its presence, Guatemalans voted to keep MINUGUA in country for another four years after their stay expired in 2001.

17   Castañeda Salguero (1998) relates that in "August 1982 the Guatemalan Army gathered the people from various villages of San Mateo Ixtatán to help them cut the trees on either side of the road. In San Mateo Ixtatán, 30 to 40 meters either side of the road were cleared for a distance of 18 kilometers (this includes the road from Santa Eulalia to San Mateo and the road to the east to Yolcultae). This represents about 126 hectares of cleared forest and about 113,400 trees. The rotten trunks still lie on the side of the road as evidence, and none of the locals use them" (p108).

18   Hale (1997) draws on the work of Falla (1992), Stoll (1993), and McCreery (1994) to show how the counterinsurgency campaign of the Guatemalan military mimicked strategies developed during the Vietnam War – security, control, and development. However, Hale goes on to state, that the main difference between Vietnam and Guatemala is that "the Guatemalan army carried the euphemistically defined objective of the first phase, 'eliminate enemy infrastructure' (read noncombatant population) to its beastly logical extreme" (p818).

Bibliography

Adams, Richard, 1970. *Crucifixion by Power: Essays on Guatemalan National Social Structure, 1944–1960*. Austin: University of Texas Press.

Arias, A. 1997. Comments on Hale's Consciousness. Violence, and the Politics of Memory in Guatemala. *Current Anthropology* 38 (5), pp824–26.

Arias, A. 2003. Response to David Stoll. *Lasa Forum* 33 (4), pp22–23.

Atkinson, D. and D. Cosgrove. 1998. Urban Rhetoric and Embodied Identities: City. Nation, and Empire at the Vittorio Emanuele II Monument in Rome, 1870–1945. *Annals of the Association of American Geographers* 88 (1), pp28–49

Ball, P., P. Kobrack. and H. F. Spirer 1999. *State Violence in Guatemala, 1960–1996; A Quantitative Reflection*. New York: American Association for the Advancement of Science.

Blake. K. S. and J. S. Smith. 2000. Pueblo Mission Churches as Symbols of Permanence and Identity. *The Geographical Review* 90 (3), pp359–80.

Carlson, R. 1997. *The War for the Heart and Soul of a Highland Maya Town*, Austin: University of Texas Press.

Castañeda Salguero, C. 1998. *Lucha por la Tierra, Retornados y Medio Ambiente en Huehuetenango*. Guatemala City: FLACSO.

Casaús Arzú, M.E. 1998. *La Metamorfosis del Racismo en Guatemala*. Guatemala City: Editorial Cholsamaj.

CEH (Commission for Historical Clarification). 1999. *Guatemala, Memory of Silence/Tz'inil Na' Tab'al*, Report of the Commission for Historical Clarification. Guatemala City: United Nations.

CEIDEC (Centre de Estudios Integrados de Desarrollo Comunal), 1990. *Guatemala; Polos de Desarrollo. El Caso de la Desestructuración de las Comunidades Indigenas*. Mexico, D.F.: Editorial Praxis, p257.

Cosgrove, D. E. 1984. *Social Formations and Symbolic Landscape*. London: Croom Helm.

Craig, L. 1978. *The Federal Presence; Architecture, Politics, and Symbols in the United States Government Buildings*. Cambridge, MA: MIT Press.

Diocesis del Quiché,1994. *El Quiché: El Pueblo y su Iglesia, 1960–1980*. Santa Cruz del Quiché Guatemala.

Domosh, M. 1989. A Method for Interpreting Landscape: A Case Study of the New York World Building. *Area* 21, pp347–55.

Falla, R. 1992. *Masacres de la Selva: Ixcán, Guatemala (1975–1982)*. Universidad de San Carlos, Guatemala: Editorial Universitaria, p253.

Falla, R. 1993. *Historia de un Gran Amor*. Guatemala.

Flores, O.2003. Ixcán, un pueblo Olvidado, *Siglo Veintiuno*, February 9.

Foote, K. E. *Shadowed Ground: America's Landscapes of Violence and Tragedy*. Austin: University of Texas Press.

Foote, Kenneth E., A. Tóth, and A. Arvay. 2000. Hungary after 1989: Inscribing a New Past on Place. *Geographical Review* 90 (3), pp301–34.

Galeano, E. 1967, *Guatemala: Pais Occupado*. Mexico City: Editoria Nuestra Tiempo.

Gillis, J. R. ed. 1994. *Commemorations: The Politics of National Identity*. Princeton, NJ: Princeton University Press.

Girón, F. R. R. 2000. Coronel de Infantería y Comandante de Zona Militar No. 22, Playa Grande, Ixcán. In *Mensaje de la Comandancia*. Ixcán: Puerta abierta al desarollo. Magazine published by the division of Civil Affairs, Zona Militar 22, Playa Grande, Ixcán, Quiché, Guatemala.

Gleijeses, Piero. 1998. *Shattered Hope: The Guatemalan Revolution and the United States, 1944–1954*. Princeton, NJ: Princeton University Press.

González, G. P. 1998. *Return of the Maya*. Yax Te' Foundation, Rancho Palos Verdes: California.

Green, L. 1993. Shifting affiliations: Mayan widows and Evangélicos in Guatemala. In *Rethinking Protestantism in Latin America*. ed. Virginia Garrard-Burnett and David Stoll, Philadelphia: Temple University Press.

Green, L. 1999. *Fear as a Way of Life: Mayan Widows in Rural Guatemala*. New York: Columbia University Press.

Hale, C. R. 1997. Consciousness, Violence, and the Politics of Memory in Guatemala. *Current Anthropology* 38 (5), pp817–38.

Handy, J. 1994. *Revolution in the Countryside: Rural Conflict and Agrarian Reform in Guatemala, 1944–1954*. Chapel Hill, NC: The University of North Carolina Press.

Hobbs, J. J. 1995. *Mount Sinai*. Austin; University of Texas Press.

Hoelscher, S. D. 1998. Tourism, Ethnic Memory and the Other-Directed Place. *Ecumene* 5(4), pp369–98.

Jonas. S. 2000. *Of Centaurs and Doves, Guatemala's Peace Process*. Boulder, CO: Westview Press.

Jordan, T. G. 1982. *Texas Graveyards: A Cultural Legacy*. Austin: University of Texas Press.

Jordan, T. G. 1985. *American Log Buildings: An Old World Heritage*. Chapel Hill, NC: University of North Carolina Press.

Kading, T. W. 1999. The Guatemalan Military and the Economics of La Violencia. *Canadian Journal of Latin American and Caribbean Studies* 24 (47), pp57–91.

Kniffen, F. B. 1990. Cultural Diffusion and Landscape: Selections from Fred. B. Kniffen. *Geoscience and Man* 27, pp1–77.

Le Bot, Y. 1995. *La Guerra en Tierras Mayas: Comunidad, Violencia y Modernidad en Guatemala (1970–1992)*. México: Fondo de Cultura Económica.

Lewis, P. 1983. Learning from Looking: Geographic and Other Writing about the American Cultural Landscape. *American Quarterly* 35, pp242–61.

Lovell, W. G. 1990. Maya Survival in Ixil Country, Guatemala, *Cultural Survival Quarterly* 14 (4), pp10–12.

Lovell. W. G. 1995. *A Beauty That Hurts: Life and Death in Guatemala*. Toronto: Between the Lines.

Low, Setha M. 2000. *On the Plaza: The Politics of Public Space and Culture*. Austin: University of Texas Press.

Lowenthal, D. 1985. *The Past is a Foreign Country*. Cambridge, UK: Cambridge University Press.

Manz, B. 1988, *Refugees of a Hidden War: The Aftermath of Counterinsurgency in Guatemala*. Albany, NY: State University of New York Press.

Mathewson, K. M. 1984. *Irrigation Horticulture in Highland Guatemala: The Tablon System of Panajachel*. Boulder, CO.: Westview Press.

Montejo, V. 1987. *Testimony: Death of a Guatemalan Village*. Translated by Victor Perera. Willimantic, CN: Curbstone Press.

Montejo, V. 1992. *Brevisima Relacion de la Continua Destruccion del Mayab' (Guatemala)*. Providence, Rhode Island: Guatemala Scholars Network.

Moreno, G. S. 1998. *Guatemala: Contreinsurgencia o Contra el Pueblo?* Colección Gnarus, Spain.

Morrissey, J. A. 1978. *A Missionary Directed Resettlement Project among the Highland Maya of Western Guatemala*. Ph.D. dissertation. Stanford University.

Nash, June. 2002. AAA delegate to Guatemala urges security for anthropologists. *Anthropology News, Newsletter of the American Anthropological Association* 43 (9), pp22–23.

Nelson, D. M. 1999. *A Finger in the Wound: Body Politics in Quincentennial Guatemala.* Berkeley, CA: University of California Press.

Noack, C. 2001. Conmemoración de una massacre. *Debate* 10 (abril 2001), pp14–15.

Nunea Más, 2000, Conmemoran segundo aniversario del asesinato de Monseñor Juan Gerardi. *Nunca Más: Asociación Familiares de Detenidos-Desaparecidos de Guatemala (FAMDEGUA)* 42, pp10–14.

Payeras, M. 1996. *Asedio a la Utopia: Ensayos Pollicos 1989–1994.* Guatemala: Luna y Sol.

Payeras, M. 1998. *Los Dias de la Selva.* Guatemala City: Editorial Piedra Santa.

Prensa Libre, 2001a. *Chajul: Tierra de Nadie en Confrontación.* July 2, Guatemala City, Guatemala, pp1–3.

Prensa Libre, 2001b. *Contra Genocidio.* June 15, Guatemala City, Guatemala, p6.

Prensa Libre, 2001c. *Las PAC Siguen Activas.* June 30, Guatemala City, Guatemala, p8.

Primavera del Ixcán, 1999. *El Derecho Indigena de la Comunidad Primavera del Ixcán, Region Multiétnica de Ixcán.* Comunidad Primavera del Ixcán y Santa Maria Tzejá, Quiché Guatemala.

REMHI (Recuperación de la Memoria Historica). 1998. *Nunca Mas.* Volume 1: Impactos de la Violencia. Oficina de Derechos Humanos del Arzobispado de Guatemala (ODHAG). Guatemala City, Guatemala.

Resales, E. 2000. Erigirán monumentos a victimas de massacre. *Siglo Veintiuno* 4 (December), p12.

Santino, Jack. 2001. *Signs of War and Peace: Social Conflict and the Use of Public Symbols in Northern Ireland.* New York: Palgrave.

Sauer, C. O. 1925. Morphology of Landscape. *University of California Publications in Geography* 2, pp19–54.

Schirmer, J. 1998. *The Guatemalan Military Project: A Violence Called Democracy.* Philadelphia: University of Pennsylvania Press.

Secaira, E. 2000. *La Conservacíon de la Naturaleza, El Pueblo y Movimiento Maya, y la Espiritualidad en Guatemala: Implicaciones para Conservacionistas.* Guatemala.

Simon, J. M. 1988. *Guatemala: Eternal Spring Eternal Tyranny.* New York: W.W Norton and Co.

Smith, P. 2001. Memory Without History: Who Owns Guatemala's Past? *The Washington Quarterly* 24 (2), pp59–72.

Stoll, D. 1993. *Between Two Armies in the Ixil Towns of Guatemala.* New York: Columbia University Press.

Stoll, D. 2003. On the LASA President. *Lasa Forum* 33 (4), pp20–22.

Till, K. E. 2003. Places of Memory. In *Companion to Political Geography*, ed. John Agnew, Kathyrne Mitchell, and Gearóid O'Tuathail. New York: Blackwell.

Till, K. E. 1999. Staging the Past: Landscape Designs, Cultural Identity, and Erinnerungspolitika at Berlins Neue Wache. *Ecumene* 6 (3), pp251–83.

Wilson, R. 1997. Comments on Hale's Consciousness, Violence, and the Politics of Memory in Guatemala. *Current Anthropology* 38 (5), pp832–35.

Wilson R. 1998. *Verdades Violentas: las Politicas de Recordar el Pasado en Guatemala, in Guatemala 1983–1997 Hacia Dónde Va la Transición?* FLACSO, Guatemala, Debate 38.

Zur, J. 1998. *Violent Memories: Mayan War Widows in Guatemala.* Boulder, CO: Westview Press.

PART II

Materials and Approaches to Making History

Hilda Kean

PART I FOCUSED ON THE RANGE of people and institutions making history. This section looks at the materials for this construction (and Part III considers the form of such construction). As we considered in the general introduction, academic historians conventionally go to an archive of printed or written material as the initial step in research. The phrase Joanna Sassoon uses to describe the relationship between history and archival practice is straightforward, but relevant – namely, these are 'active relationships'.[1] Carolyn Steedman has expanded upon this relationship to suggest that the role of the historian in engaging with such material is in some ways more important than the materials themselves. The role of the archive is, she says, to 'do with longing and appropriation. It is to do with wanting things that are put together, collected, collated, named in lists and indices; a place where a whole world, a social order, may be *imagined* [my emphasis] by the recurrence of a name in a register, through a scrap of paper, or some other little piece of flotsam.'[2] This approach, however, has still been seen as contentious by some historians.[3]

Archives and public history

Archives themselves are socially constructed. Dorothy Sheridan, the former archivist of the Mass Observation Archive in Sussex, has argued that any archive involves a 'complex triangular relationship between three agents': those who provide the resources for the archive to exist, those whose stories are held within the archive and those who use it. Each agent, she continues, has a political and social influence and a differing level of both cultural and economic power.[4] Not everything is collected: archivists (whoever they might be) choose what to collect and what to ignore. Certainly some have seen possibilities for 'radical public history' in the creation of community archives as 'a space in which the archive can become a significant tool for discovery, education and empowerment'.[5]

Unlike some innovative practice today that advocates a community approach with a strong sense of common ownership and shared identity between the users and archival activists, particularly in online archives,[6] before the growth of social history in the latter part of the twentieth century much history writing was based on archives held by state institutions. This inevitably included parliamentary papers and those enterprises over which the state had direct influence. Thus, the National Archives in Kew, for example, included reports from spies and informers on industrial unrest, women's suffrage and Irish independence at the end of World War I. These often included dramatic statements such as 'a revolution is to be expected within the next two months'.[7] The archive does not contain trade union or women's suffrage or Sinn Fein records for the same period – since this was not the remit of the official archive. In this example we gain an interesting insight into the state of mind of state officials at the time but inevitably little information on the perspective of radicals. While many historians would now seek to find alternative and additional records by looking at printed records, this can be a rather narrow approach to a subject. It also means that if other materials are ignored very different conclusions can be reached.[8] Martin Pugh, for example, has written on women's campaign for the vote and used the National Archives and parliamentary papers as the main source for his research, concluding that the arguments for the vote for women were won by the turn of the nineteenth/twentieth century. This is seen as highly controversial since the militant movement led by women in the Pankhurst family did not come into existence until the early years of the twentieth century. Thus, their consciously created public spectacles including visually interesting demonstrations or innovative public relations events or hunger striking for political status are then written out of the achievement of the vote for women.[9] Other historians have looked at materials created by activists, such as banners designed by suffrage artists or badges and memorabilia, to show the importance of the movement to women themselves. Therefore, by deciding to focus on such material, other than printed official records, different assessments have been reached about the importance of different aspects of the women's suffrage movement.[10]

Thinking differently about material beyond archives

As public historians are interested in an expansive way in which the past is broadly understood and processed, their starting point is often outside a conventional archive. Dwight Pitchaithley's encounter with bat guano, discussed in the general introduction, is but one, albeit extreme, example.

But looking anew at physical landscape for materials is not unique.[11] Alexander Trapeznik has turned to the neglected waterfront in Dunedin, New Zealand, to look at industrial and mercantile heritage – rather than, as he puts it, 'churches, grand and great houses, and public buildings'.[12] Roy Moxham took further this quest for unusual materials with which to create different histories. Working as a conservator in a university archive he had spent much time poring over maps of India and looking at the hedge that had been erected by the British in the 1860s, extending some 2300 miles and guarded by some 12,000 men. Local people who were obliged to pass through this in the course of selling salt were required to pay a tax. Amongst other things, hostility to the tax had led to civil opposition, including the famous salt march of Gandhi who had declared: 'It is the only condiment of the poor. . . . The tax constitutes therefore the most inhuman poll tax that ingenuity of man can devise.'[13] Moxham assumed that portions of the hedge remained and decided to trace the length of it. However, much to his surprise he found that the vestiges of the hedge had been almost completely obliterated: the hedge remained only in memory or on maps.[14] The absence of the hedge, he realized, showed the disgust with which the tax had been regarded. Thus, the lack of material helped to create deeper understandings about the relationship between British rule and the independence campaign in India. A recent parallel might be found in the symbolic removal of almost all traces of the

Berlin Wall which, if it had remained *in situ*, would probably now be the pre-eminent Cold War monument.[15]

Others have looked at particular neglected materials for history to create new meanings. Andrew Hassam has analysed Indian jute in Australian museum collections that has been, he argues, falsely disregarded. Although Australian wool has been seen as a major topic of history, the sacks in which such wool was transported have not. He argues that this lowly artefact is a new way of looking at the trading networks of the nineteenth-century global economy and that the sacks 'substantiate the lived experience of those who worked with them'.[16]Although the material was in museums it had not been seen as a worthy topic of history in its own right.

While historians can rarely have the 'breakthrough moments' captured in the popular imagination by scientists apparently 'discovering' new things, this can happen. Ann Dingsdale, for example, came across a surviving printed copy of the first petition in Britain for votes of women in 1866 in Girton College Archive in Cambridge by chance. In order to bring these forgotten individuals to light in new ways she first used census and street directories to identify a third (600) of these women. To celebrate the 'lost' two thirds (900) she embroidered their names and created fabric portraits, using traditional 'women's craft', and is now constructing life stories of every signatory using the census and family history materials available on the internet.[17]

Through the focus on individual objects – as opposed to entire collections – different insights can be created, A good example of this approach was the BBC radio series 'The history of the world in 100 objects' in which the British Museum director Neil McGregor picked specific objects through which to re-tell a narrative spanning thousands of years. The re-contextualization of particular objects has also resulted in people seeing apparently known works in a new light. Thus, the exhibition curated by John Mack, again at the British Museum, juxtaposed material from different cultures and times to create new insights.[18] More recently, Turner prize-winning potter Grayson Perry in an exhibition entitled 'The Tomb of the Unknown Craftsman' was commissioned to create new works inspired by individual pieces in the museum with which they were displayed. As the modern artist /craft worker commented at the time: 'This is a memorial to all the anonymous craftsmen that over the centuries have fashioned the manmade wonders of the world. . . . The craftsman's anonymity I find especially resonant in an age of the celebrity artist.'[19]

Material in homes and non-history making places

However, material for creating history also exists in people's own homes. The work of anthropologist Daniel Miller or museum specialists such as Susan Pearce have done much research to show the way in which people value items in their possession.[20] **Sherry Turkle**, a MIT professor and clinical psychologist specializing in people's relationships with technology, is interested in the role of objects **as indicated by the extract here**. She draws on the idea of bricolage developed by Claude Lévi-Strauss, used to describe the construction of a work from a diverse range of materials that are available. Turkle starts from her own experience: 'I grew up hoping that objects would connect me to the world', and used material to explore how this helped her make sense of her own fractured family background. Turkle also applies this understanding more broadly to show how people generally can use objects to make sense of our pasts and ourselves in similar ways. She notes how thinking about objects outside of pure utility or aesthetic indulgences puts us on less familiar or certain ground, describing them as 'companions to our emotional lives or as provocations to thought'. Through such objects we carry our sense of selfhood and of our pasts. This is particularly well illustrated by the '*Casser Maison*' ritual in French-speaking Canada of passing on – before death – particular objects to descendants within families.[21]

Some historians frown upon this subjectivity as outside historical practice – and Turkle is not a historian; but, increasingly, historians, influenced by the pioneering work of Maurice Halbwachs on collective memory, are recognizing the value of emotion. Halbwachs had argued that social groups, including families, had the capacity to remember formed through regular contact among group members.[22] He stated, for example, that emotions and memory were intimately connected to the family holding such sentiments within the family in and across time and generations.[23] Historians have started to use ideas of emotion both to explore their own relationship to material and to make wider connections with groups of people.[24] As Mark Leone has reflected: 'I begin with feelings. My purpose is to make a guide for other historical archaeologists that shows how to start work. That is with your feelings, I suggest.'[25] Turkle uses relationships with materials as navigational tools to create different insights and understandings of the past but also of *ourselves* as interpreters of it.

Daniel Miller, as noted in Part I, has also explored the way in which material objects are 'an integral and inseparable aspect of all relationships' and that 'household material culture may express an order which in each case seems equivalent to what one might term a social cosmology'.[26] How people relate to material that they have acquired in their own lives or inherited from ancestors helps them to create an understanding of their own lives. Such material is both personal but contributes to wide meaning within the population at large. During the 1980s, Chicago sociologists Mihaly Csikszentmihalyi and Eugene Ruchberg-Halton undertook a now famous study of the way in which people related to furniture they owned. They realized that furniture was invested with particular patterns of meanings, especially concerning stability and continuity within the family. Older people, for example, mentioned chairs as invoking memories. They would remember the person who had previously sat in the chair. Thus, the chair helped to evoke memory.[27] While furniture is usually bought and can be expensive and thus has a particular status, it acquires different meaning for those who are fortunate enough to know the person, particularly a relative, who made the chair or other items of furniture. In such examples people do not only summon up the memory of who used the chair, but who made it. The furniture kept alive the name of a dead known relative or a name heard in family stories.[28] Thus, the very nature of material culture acquires different meaning: in the example above it can convey and give status to manual skills often seen to be less valuable than intellectual skills. Although an object is 'dead', writers have seen the way in which it can also embody lived experience. Susan Stewart, for example, has discussed the way in which collected souvenirs represent 'not the lived experience of its maker but the "secondhand" experience of its possessor/owner'.[29] The memories associated with the object are thus retrieved. As Paul Martin discusses in the introduction to Part III, this idea of embodiment or experience is very different from thinking of history solely as information garnered from documents.

Objects outside museums

Some have suggested that within a museum the object itself becomes irrelevant and serves primarily to act as a memory trigger;[30] for others its materiality is integral to its importance.[31] Items deposited in museums are usually dissociated in their presentation – through display cards and so on – from the emotion previously attached to them by the donor.[32] By contrast, items that remain within a home tend to continue to act as conveyors of particular narratives or emotions. As David Craig has shown in his Scottish- and Canadian-based oral history of descendants of Scottish people thrown off their land in the Highland Clearances, objects became an integral part of the narratives told and passed down the generations. He came across a family hastily evicted only able to carry with them what was immediately portable. Even the youngest had to carry the remains of their meagre goods, in this instance a sieve. When he was in Ontario, for example, he came across a mid nineteenth-century memoir of a seven-year-old boy arriving at the family's new place through heavy snow-drifts carrying the tea-kettle, the teapot and a blanket.[33] Here the transporting of the objects, although they had disappeared over time, had acted as a conduit for the transmission of narratives of forced emigration handed down for over 100 years. Equally evocative is the suitcase now used for keeping Christmas decorations by Graeme Whyte. To accompany the publication of London Recruits, the book discussed in the introduction describing the clandestine distribution of ANC leaflets in South Africa, Whyte made a short YouTube film in which he displayed the ostensibly ordinary looking suitcase – divested of Christmas ephemera – to show the hidden bottom for hiding leaflets. The very ordinariness of the suitcase's appearance – and of Whyte's film shot in his home – help to emphasize the drama of the event he is describing.[34]

Less dramatically, Pat Furley has analysed the sewing machine she inherited from her mother, who worked as an outworker making blouses and shirts. Such a machine might be found in social history museums creating narrative on working-class women's home life in twentieth-century Britain. Furley was able to create different meanings: she interviewed the mechanic who serviced the machine; preserved the tiny pieces of thread mixed with oil found in the recesses of the object, exploring the smell they invoked; photographed her brother wearing a shirt his mother had made decades previously. By such approaches she was able to develop different understandings than those created by a museum curator, however imaginative, by focusing on an individual woman's life as an individual and the relationships, including emotional relationships, emanating from the object.[35] When museums have chosen to focus on an ordinary individual person or family these have usually been very popular exhibitions. Examples include the Workers' Museum in Denmark, the Lower East Side Tenement in New York or the exhibition in the South Tyrol Museum in Bolzano on Otzi, a Neolithic man whose remains were found still frozen in 1991.[36]

Collecting and ordinary lives

What people collect, accumulate and fail to discard in their own homes has itself become a process of study, as indicated in the extract here from London Stories. The book starts with exploring the dilemmas faced by a historian – as much as by a daughter – in clearing her mother's flat and the recognition that the lives represented by stuff accumulated over centuries would disappear. The first part of the book discusses some of the found material to be analysed, including a certificate exempting a daughter from vaccination against smallpox, a photograph of a son posting a letter, a turned candlestick, and a memory of desert islands of fluttering palms created on a kitchen windowsill from carrot tops in a saucer of water. But most of the book and the second extract included here is not about the material as such but the process by which meaning was made. This includes the author's wandering through the landscape of England, looking at gravestones, finding a former brickfield, walking the streets of ancestors of some 200 years before, talking to those she met on her travels, and speculating on what she had really found and how to use it to make connections between the past and the present.

Such interrogation of ordinary lives inevitably focuses on ephemeral and small items. Thus, Paul Martin has analysed in the extract below trade union badges that were small and originally inexpensive items and miniaturized the pre-existing iconography of banners (and emblems and posters).[37] While minutes of trade unions can give evidence of numbers of members or votes for policies, they cannot convey in the same way as a badge the value by which trade union membership was regarded. A badge, like emblems before it such as the palm to signify, in medieval times, a pilgrimage to Jerusalem, is a personal item worn on clothing. Thus, it is a personal object meant to convey allegiance in public space outside the home. Like religious symbols these showed the strength of feeling of the owner. More recently, Martin argues, they can be read as symbolizing an alternative attempt to instil meaning into a flagging union movement or 'an almost evangelical revival of self-confidence'. In analysing badges, particularly of the late twentieth century, Martin has also indicated the ways in which gender and race are seen through the lens of badges. Thus, he argues that the iconography used – for example, of a woman breaking chains of oppression proclaiming 'proud and defiant we stand' on a badge issued by Women against Pit Closures – indicates the assertive nature of the campaign.

So far we have discussed people owning objects, but people also collect them. Although public institutions have consciously chosen to collect particular items – for example, art galleries have focused on particular painters or dates, often building on collections donated to them[38] – more recently public historians have decided to collect material that would conventionally be disregarded. Thus, in the days after the bombing of the Twin Towers in New York in 2001 (9/11), public historians realized that much of the mood and experience of that moment was being transmitted through email and ephemeral online material.[39] As **Daniel Cohen**, then director of research projects at the Center for History and New Media at George Mason University, **discusses here**, collecting media no longer means radio broadcasts of a few national broadcasters, as had been the case during World War II. This unusual collection was one of the first to recognize the historical value of digital material and the way in which it needed to be quickly gathered. A website (rather than a museum archive) was established to save personal stories. By autumn 2003 it numbered some 150,000 items and was duly acquired by the Library of Congress, becoming one of the prestigious library's first major digital acquisitions. Not only was the material new, but so too were the methods of collection and, in turn, the nature of the collection. As Cohen notes here, digital collections tend to be 'less organized and more capricious' in their coverage as well as 'larger and more diverse'.[40] In a similar vein, Stefan Dickers, the library and archives manager at the Bishopsgate Institute in London, realized that the posters and flyers produced by the Stop the War Coalition that had helped to mobilize what was claimed to be the largest political demonstration that Britain had ever seen, on 15 February 2003, in opposition to the invasion of Iraq, were important but likely to be discarded in due course. Accordingly, Stefan approached the Stop the War Coalition to take material and to archive it on an on-going basis. He similarly made overtures to the British Humanist Association and Unite against Fascism, and rescued 1960s counter-culture material found discarded under a tarpaulin in the street a few miles away.[41]

Artists, materials and histories

Increasingly, artists have also created works in galleries and museums that have drawn attention to the power of collecting and its relationship to the everyday. Thus, Chinese artist Song Dong has created a work both personally and more broadly significant called 'Waste Not'. It consists of over 10,000 household items collected by his mother Zhao Xiangyuan over some five decades. The collection/artwork includes broken kitchen utensils, paper bags, bits of soap, old umbrellas and used toothbrushes, saved with the original intention of using them at some point. Some would interpret this specifically in a Chinese context of austerity and lack of consumer goods during most of the twentieth century, as publicity for the exhibition in London's Barbican Centre suggested. However, the exhibition has had wider cultural resonance since people in different countries have identified with the habits of collecting, drawing on their own familial and social experience of hardship.[42] Thus, a personal experience of collecting can be transformed, when displayed, into a broader public and social experience.

Many artists have played with the relationship between the ordinary and process, thus creating different perceptions of time and the past. As Derby-based textile artist **Rhiannon**

Williams discusses here, over a period of three years she cut up all seven volumes of Marcel Proust's key work on time and memory, *A la recherche du temps perdu,* and sewed 3000 pages of print into patchwork, taking, she says, considerably longer to hand sew than it took the novelist to create his narrative. In so doing, within this venture she is highlighting the process of construction as much as the end result itself. The emphasis is upon domestic skills of needlecraft, but has become a public artwork in the making (and repairing of it). Her work with lottery tickets has been echoed by Lubiana Hamid in her installation piece *Naming the Money,* exploring the complexity of the legacies of the slave trade. On the back of colourful cut-out figures are accounting pages in which:

> The ledgers' double-entry pages and the neat grid of the invoice gave purposeful shape to the story they told.... Containing only what could fit within the clean lines of their columns and rows, they reduced an enormous system of traffic in human commodities to a concise chronicle of quantitative 'facts' ... erasing from view the politics that underlay the neat account keeping.[43]

By displaying such work, public institutions have imitated the 'ordinary person' who hoards or collects. Susan Pearce's research in the 1990s found that over half the adults she surveyed defined themselves as collectors. People in the present are imitating, albeit not consciously, the practices of wealthy collectors in the past who created cabinets of curiosities or amassed private collections that became the core of public galleries and museums.[44]

Constraints and opportunities of material

Academic historians, particularly those in universities seeking to obtain funding to undertake research, usually must prove that they are aware that particular materials do exist, whether archival material or people willing to be interviewed, and so on. This, however, is a different approach than those historians working on family and locality who have long appreciated that although there may not be very much material at all on a particular ancestor or a personally significant place, one needs to work with it nonetheless. As a result, there can be interesting histories created from previously unconsidered materials. This might include coal-hole covers, trade union buildings, a candle factory or a guide to a particular graveyard.[45] Recently, creative historians have explored the value of dealing with the paucity of traces from the past. Martin Bashforth, for example, has stated that an imaginary archive box for his grandfather would need to be very small comprising just three photos, three campaign medals, a bronze plaque and a certificate of his death in warfare. As he realizes: 'Such a small collection is unremarkable for a working-class man of his time', but then develops this by exploring what is more remarkable: 'how these things were hidden'. It is this absence of material – and familial disclosure – that helps him to develop an illuminating argument about absence, including absent fathers.[46] This willingness to explore scraps to obtain meaning is also well illustrated by the work of Tim Brennan on the small pocket diary of his great grandfather, which he analyses as a conveyor of a past self, a time planner, and a mechanism of foretelling that helps the diarist to manage his life.[47]

The problem of using 'what's there' and 'who decides' is particularly resonant for public historians employed as consultants or as archivists for particular corporations, as **Paul Ashton and Paula Hamilton,** who are joint directors of the Australian Centre for Public History at UTS in Sydney, **explore in the extract below.** They suggest that invariably such historians are employed by historical, institutional, or public buildings to undertake heritage conservation reports as a result of legislative requirements rather than because of 'a passion for the past'.

These clearly affect the type of work such historians are able to produce. Tensions have also arisen in the Australian context, they argue, because of demarcation disputes between 'professional' and 'academic' historians. They describe the ways in which 'authority' is accrued not through quality of writing or research, but through qualifications and professional accreditation. While recognizing the impact of the market place on historians' livelihoods, they also suggest that these debates are too academic-centred and are a diminution of the optimism and enthusiasm that characterized public history practice in the 1980s.

Notes

1   Sassoon, 'Phantoms', p41. See also Flinn 'Archival Activism'.
2   Steedman, *Dust*, p81. See M. O'Neill (2011) 'Restoring the "Mam": Archives, Access and Research into Women's Pasts in Wales', *Public History Review*, vol 18, pp47–64.
3   A good example of the hostility to such approaches is A. Marwick (2001) *The New Nature of History*, Basingstoke: Palgrave, p155ff.
4   D. Sheridan (2012) 'Possession: Tensions in the creation, care and use of archives, with reference to Mass Observation', in G. Dawson (ed) *Memory, Narrative and Histories: Critical Debates, New Trajectories*, Brighton: Centre for Research in Memory, Narrative and Histories, University of Brighton, p42.
5   Flinn, 'Archival Activism', p9. He strikes a cautionary note in discussing the assumptions of official recognition and support for independent community archives since support assumes that they deliver a strong sense of belonging or of identity and that such feelings are socially productive: 'the evidence base for both claims remains for the most part extremely slim'. A. Flinn and M. Steven (2009) '"It is noh mistri, we mekin histri." Telling our own story: Independent and community archives in the UK, challenging and subverting the mainstream', in J. A. Bastian and B. Alexander (eds) *Community Archives the Shaping of Memory*, London: facet publishing, p19.
6   Flinn, 'Archives and their communities: Collecting histories, challenging heritage', in *Memory, Narrative*, ed Dawson, p33.
7   H. Kean (1990) *Challenging the State?*, Brighton: Falmer Press, pp10–16.
8   R. Samuel (1976) 'Local history and oral history', *History Workshop Journal*, vol 1, pp191–208; Samuel, *Theatres*, p161.
9   M. Pugh (2000) *The March of Women: A Revisionist Analysis of the Campaign for Women's Suffrage, 1866–1914*, Oxford: Oxford University Press, p3; see by way of contrast J. Purvis and S. Stanley Holton (2000) *Votes for Women*, Abingdon: Routledge.
10 Amongst others, see L. Tickner (1987) *The Spectacle of Women: Imagery of the Suffrage Campaign 1907–14*, London: Chatto and Windus; Kean 'Public history and popular memory'; H. Swain (2002) 'The Pankhursts – politics and passion', *THES*, vol 25, January 2002, http://www.timeshighereducation.co.uk/story.asp?storyCode=166784&sectioncode=26.
11 Pitcaithley, 'Taking the long way', p61.
12 A. Trapeznik (2011) 'On the waterfront: The historic waterfront precinct, Dunedin, New Zealand', *Public History Review*, vol 18, p65.
13 R. Moxham (2001) *The Great Hedge of India*, London: Constable, pp3,182–236.
14 After three years he eventually found a narrow strip of grassy land near Chakanagar. Moxham, *Hedge*, pp212–23.
15 Thanks to Daniel Scharf for this insight.
16 A. Hassam (2011) 'Indian jute in Australian collections: Forgetting and recollecting transnational networks', *Public History Review*, vol 28, pp108–28. There have been several popular histories focusing on one item as a way of covering many years of history. Some of the most famous include M. Kurlansky (1998) *Cod: A Biography of the Fish that Changed the World*, London: Penguin, and A. Pavord (2001) *Tulip: The Story of the Flower that Has Made Men Mad*, London: Bloomsbury.
17 A. Dingsdale (1995) *Generous and Lofty Sympathies: The Kensington Society, the 1866 Suffrage Petition and the Development of Mid Victorian Feminism*, PhD thesis, University of Greenwich, and correspondence with author.

18   J. Mack (2003) *Museum of the Mind: Art and Memory in World Cultures,* London: British Museum Press. An exception to the norm is the longstanding arrangement for juxtaposing materials from different cultures and times at the Pitt Rivers Museum, Oxford. A. A. Shelton (2011) 'Museums and anthropologies: Practice and narratives', in S. Macdonald (ed) *A Companion to Museum Studies,* Chichester: Wiley–Blackwell, pp64–80.

19   See http://www.britishmuseum.org/whats_on/exhibitions/grayson_perry/introduction.aspx Exhibitions ran 2011–12, accessed 8 May 2012.

20   S. Turkle (2007) *Evocative Objects: Things We Think With,* Cambridge, MA: MIT Press; S. Pearce (ed) (1994) *Interpreting Objects and Collections,* Abingdon: Routledge.

21   J.-S. Marcoux (2001) 'The *Casser Maison* ritual: Constructing the self by emptying the home', *Journal of Material Culture,* vol 6(2), pp213–235.

22   M. Halbwachs (1992) *On Collective Memory* (ed., trans. and intro. L. A. Coser) Chicago: University of Chicago Press, pp54–68. See also A. Landsberg (2004) *Prosthetic Memory: The Transformation of American Remembrance in the Age of Mass Culture,* New York: Columbia University Press.

23   C. Hamilton 'Cultural memory and the emotions: Exploring the connections' in ed Dawson, *Memory,* p65.

24   F. Haug (ed) (1987) *Female Sexualization,* London: Verso; L. Passerini (1996) *Autobiography of a Generation: Italy 1968,* Middletown, CT: Wesleyan University Press; J. Greenway Delight (2008) 'Regret: Discovering Elizabeth Gibson,' *Qualitative Research,* vol 8(3), pp317–24.

25   M. P. Leone (2010) *Critical Historical Archaeology,* Walnut Creek, CA: Left Coast Press, p7.

26   Miller, *Comfort,* pp200, 204.

27   M. Csikszentmihalyi and E. Ruchberg-Hatlon (1981) *The Meaning of Things: Domestic Symbols and the Self,* Cambridge: Cambridge University Press, p59.

28   H. Kean (2000) 'East End stories: The chairs and the photographs', *International Journal of Heritage Studies,* vol 6(2), pp111–27.

29   S. Stewart (1993) *On Longing: Narratives of the Miniature the Gigantic, the Souvenir, the Collection,* Baltimore: Duke University Press, p135.

30   G. Kavanagh (2000) *Dream Spaces: Memory and the Museum,* Leicester: Leicester University Press.

31   See, for example, C. Steedman, 'What a rag rug means', in Steedman, *Dust,* pp112–41; S. Conn (2009) *Do Museums Still Need Objects?,* Pennsylvania: University of Pennsylvania Press.

32   A striking exception is the attitudes displayed in Australian museums towards particular artefacts from Torres Straits islanders. As the National Museum of Australia warns in its collections and online display: 'Visitors should also be aware that the exhibition and website include names and images of deceased people that may cause sadness or distress to Aboriginal and Torres Strait Islander peoples.' See http://www.nma.gov.au.

33   D. Craig (1990) *On the Crofters' Trail: In Search of the Clearance Highlanders,* London: Pimlico, pp138–39.

34   See http://www.youtube.com/watch?v=MRz8gn00gCs, accessed 12 May 2012.
      See also comments made by visitors to Auschwitz about the power of 'ordinary items'. But, as one visitor stated: 'I've heard some comments on the bus trip from Auschwitz II to Auschwitz I from other visitors that what impressed more those visitors were the shoes from kids and the hair. For me, those were not the items that impressed me significantly. What impressed me were the bags with a name painted on it that puts a picture on those who suffered and the fact that when they carried the suitcase they believed that they would make a trip for another horrible place but possibly they would be treated as war prisoners. In those bags and suitcases they carried dishes, polish for the shoes, etc.' Post by José Gomes (Portugal), September 2006, http://www.worldheritagesite.org/sites/auschwitz.html, accessed 16 July 2012 (thanks to Daniel Scharf for this reference).

35   P. Furley (2008) *My Mother's Sewing Machine: An Object of Public History,* MA Public History dissertation, Ruskin College, Oxford, now held in Bishopsgate Institute, London.

36   Within the Workers' Museum are artefacts bequeathed it from a fully furnished flat in Kalkbraederivej in Copenhagen. The elderly woman who left them in 1990 had lived there since 1915 and had made no alterations to the interior. See http://www.arbejdermuseet.dk/; P. Ludvigsen (2009) 'History of the Workers' Museum in Denmark', *International Labor and*

Working-Class History, September, vol 76, pp44–53; Lower East Side Tenement Museum based on excavations of premises in 97 Orchard Street in 1988 found 319 objects, including a ticket stub and confectionary wrapper, but also focused on one family, the Rogarshevskys: R. J. Abram (2007) 'Kitchen conversations: Democracy in action at the Lower East Side Tenement Museum', *The Public Historian*, vol 29(1), pp59–76; the Glasgow tenement owned by Miss Agnes Toward for over 50 years, including a large number of her possessions: S. West (2010) 'Heritage and class', in R. Harrison (ed) *Understanding the Politics of Heritage: Understanding Global Heritage*, Manchester and Milton Keynes: Manchester University Press and The Open University, pp270–303; in Bolzano in the far north of Italy, the South Tyrol Museum of Archaeology has won acclaim for its exhibitions of the corpse of 'Otzi', a Neolithic man whose frozen remains were discovered in 1991 in the Otzial Alps. Forensic analysis has traced how he died, the geographical origins of his tools, and his diet (http://www.iceman.it/en/oetzi-the-iceman, accessed 7 May 2012).

37   See J. Gorman (1986) *Banner Bright*, London: Scorpion Cavendish, revised edition; R. A. Leeson (1971) *United We Stand*, Bath, Somerset: Adams & Dart; A. Ravenhill-Johnson and P. James (2012) *Emblems of Hope: Essays in the Art and Ideology of the Trade Union Emblem (1850–1925)*, London: Anthem; R. Mace (1999) *British Trade Union Posters: An Illustrated History*, Stroud: Sutton Publishers.

38   An emphasis on Italian painters, including Raphael, Titian and Bellini in London's National Gallery, for example, owes much to the estate of Dr Ludwig Mond (http://www.nationalgallery.org.uk/paintings/history/collectors-and-benefactors/ludwig-mond, accessed 20 May 2012).

39   Those involved worked in various institutions but significantly included Roy Rosenzweig, the co-author of *The Presence of the Past*, and projects based both at the Center for History and New Media at George Mason University and the America Social History Project/Center for Media and Learning at the Graduate Center at the City University of New York.

40   See his blog on his on-going work on digital presentation: http://www.dancohen.org, accessed April 2012.

41   As confirmed by email correspondence with Stefan Dickers, May 2012.

42   It has toured worldwide, including London, New York, San Francisco, Vancouver.

43   S. E.Smallwood (2007) *Saltwater Slavery: A Middle Passage from Africa to the American Diaspora*, Cambridge, MA: Harvard University Press, p98, as quoted in Rice, *Creating Memorials*, p207.

44   Pearce, *Interpreting Objects*. See also S. Pearce (1998) 'The construction of heritage: The domestic context and its implications', *International Journal of Heritage Studies*, vol 4(2), pp86–102.

45   See, for example, J. Newman (2009) *Battersea Global Reach: The Story of Price's Candles*, London: History and Social Action Publications; A. D. Harvey (2008) 'Coal hole covers', *Camden Review*, vol 23, pp8–9; B. Hayes (2004) 'Heritage, commemoration and interpretation: Labour and radical movements and the built environment', *North West Labour History*, vol 29, pp48–51; E. Adams (2004) *Grave Matters: A Walk in Kensal Green*, London: Gloucester Court Reminiscence Group.

46   Bashforth, 'Absent fathers', pp204–7.

47   Brennan, 'History', pp40–42.

Chapter 8

Sherry Turkle

EVOCATIVE OBJECTS: THE THINGS THAT MATTER

Things we think with

L IFE, OF COURSE, is not lived in discrete stages, nor are the relationships with objects that accompany its journey. Objects have life roles that are multiple and fluid.

We live our lives in the middle of things. Material culture carries emotions and ideas of startling intensity. Yet only recently have objects begun to receive the attention they deserve.

The acknowledgment of the power of objects has not come easy. Behind the reticence to examine objects as centerpieces of emotional life was perhaps the sense that one was studying materialism, disparaged as excess, or collecting, disparaged as hobbyism, or fetishism, disparaged as perversion. Behind the reticence to examine objects as centerpieces of thought was the value placed, at least within the Western tradition, on formal, propositional ways of knowing. In thinking about science, certainly, abstract reasoning was traditionally recognized as a standard, canonical style; many have taken it to be synonymous with knowledge altogether.

Indeed, so highly valued was canonical abstract thinking, that even when concrete approaches were recognized, they were often relegated to the status of inferior ways of knowing, or as steps on the road to abstract thinking. It is poignant that Claude Lévi-Strauss and the psychologist Jean Piaget, who each in their way contributed to a fundamental revaluation of the concrete in the mid-twentieth century, also undermined the concrete thinking they promoted.[1] Piaget recognized that young children use a style of concrete reasoning that was too efficacious to be simply classified as "wrong." His response was to cast children's "close-to-the-object" approach as a stage in a progression to a formal thinking style.[2] Lévi-Strauss recognized the primitive's bricolage as a science of the concrete that had much in common with the practice of modern-day engineers. He said he preferred to call it "prior" rather than "premature"; yet it was not fully equal.[3]

Beginning in the 1980s, concrete ways of thinking were increasingly recognized in contexts that were not easily dismissed as inferior, even and perhaps especially in the world of science, the very place where the abstract style had been canonized. Scientific laboratories were shown to be places where discoveries are made in a concrete, ad hoc fashion, and only later recast into canonically accepted formalisms; Nobel laureates testified that they related to their scientific materials in a tactile and playful manner.[4] To this testimony from science studies was added the work of feminist scholars who documented the power of concrete, contextual reasoning in a wide range of domains.[5] Indeed, there has been an increasing commitment to the study of the concrete in a range of scholarly communities.[6] To this conversation, [this writing] contributes a detailed examination of particular objects with rich connections to daily life as well as intellectual practice. . . . Choose an object and follow its associations: where does it take you; what do you feel; what are you able to understand?

A jeweled pin, simple, European, clearly of the old country, ties a daughter to her mother and her mixed feelings about their immigrant status. An immersion in the comic books of youth teaches a man how to read the lessons of superheroes in midlife. A lonely graduate student is comforted by her Ford Falcon. The car feels like her "clothing" in the world of the street, a signal of her taste and style. When she becomes a mother, it's time for a trade-in and a BMW station wagon.

Some objects are experienced as part of the self, and for that have a special status: a young child believes her stuffed bunny rabbit can read her mind; a diabetic is at one with his glucometer. Other objects remind us of people we have lost.[7] An artist dies, his collection of Chinese scholars' rocks is left behind. A rock of meditation, "The Honorable Old Man", becomes a presence in the life of his widow, who describes it as she would her artist-husband – "obsession, looking, openness to being surprised and moved, dignity."

Most objects exert their holding power because of the particular moment and circumstance in which they come into the author's life. Some, however, seem intrinsically evocative – for example, those with a quality we might call *uncanny*. Freud said we experience as uncanny those things that are "known of old yet unfamiliar."[8] The uncanny is not what is most frightening and strange. It is what seems close, but "off," distorted enough to be creepy. It marks a complex boundary that both draws us in and repels, as when . . . a museum mummy becomes an author's uncanny "double." Other objects are naturally evocative because they remind us of the blurry childhood line between self and other – think of the stuffed bunny whose owner believes it can read her mind[9] – or because they are associated with times of transition. Transitional times (called "liminal," or threshold, periods by the anthropologist Victor Turner) are rich with creative possibility.[10]

[. . .]

Evocative objects bring philosophy down to earth. When we focus on objects, physicians and philosophers, psychologists and designers, artists and engineers are able to find common ground in everyday experience.

[. . .]

Lévi-Strauss speaks of tinkering; Jean Piaget, of the child as scientist. With different metaphors, each describes a dynamic relationship between things and thinking. We tie a knot and find ourselves in partnership with string in our exploration of space. *Objects are able to catalyze self-creation.* When Igor Kopytoff writes about the "biography of things," he deepens our understanding of how a new car becomes a new skin, of how a change of jewelry can become its own voyage to a new world. *Objects bring together thought and feeling.* In particular, objects of science are objects of passion.

[. . .]

I have also touched on the idea that *we often feel at one with our objects.* The diabetic feels at one with his glucometer, as increasingly we feel at one with the glowing screens of our laptops, our iPods, and our BlackBerries. Theorists as diverse as Jean Baudrillard, Jacques Derrida, Donna Haraway, Karl Marx, and D. W. Winnicott invite us to better understand these object intimacies.

Indeed, in the psychoanalytic tradition, both persons and things are tellingly called "objects" and suggest that we deal with their loss in a similar way. For Freud, when we lose a beloved person or object, we begin a process that, if successful, ends in our finding them again, within us. It is, in fact, how we grow and develop as people. *When objects are lost, subjects are found.* Freud's language is poetic: "the shadow of the object fell upon the ego." The psychodynamic tradition – in its narrative of how we make objects part of ourselves – offers a language for interpreting the intensity of our connections to the world of things, and for discovering the similarities in how we relate to the animate and inanimate. In each case, we confront the other and shape the self.

For me, working with these ideas [. . .] became its own object discipline, my own practice of bricolage. In this sense, *Evocative Objects: Things We Think With* became for me an evocative object. Its elements were new, but the activity of working on it was familiar, as familiar, as carefully handling the objects in the memory closet I knew as a child.

Walt Whitman said: "A child went forth everyday/and the first object he look'd upon, that object he became." With generosity of intellect and spirit, the authors in this collection engage with the objects of their lives. For every object they have spun a world. They show us what they looked upon and what became the things that mattered.

What makes an object evocative?

What makes an object evocative?[1] As I write, *Bodies*, an exhibition of preserved humans from China, is on tour internationally. Its objects, poised between death and new animation, raise questions about the sanctity of what has lived, the nature of art, and the human beings who once were the objects on display. Thinking about the uncanny, about thresholds and boundaries helps us understand these objects with their universal powers of evocation.

And yet, the meaning of even such objects shifts with time, place, and differences among individuals.[2] Some find the preserved bodies the fearsome creatures of night terrors. For others, they seem almost reassuring, an opportunity to contemplate that although death leaves matter inert, a soul may be eternal.

[. . .]

One role of theory here is to defamiliarize [objects]. Theory enables us, for example, to explore how everyday objects become part of our inner life: how we use them to extend the reach of our sympathies by bringing the world within.

As theory defamiliarizes objects, objects familiarize theory. The abstract becomes concrete, closer to lived experience. . . . I highlight the theoretical themes . . . in the hope that theory itself will become an evocative object. That is, I encourage readers to create their own associations, to combine and recombine objects and theories – most generally, to use objects to bring philosophy down to earth.

> It was made of two wheels and an axle, with a pin hanging down from the middle of the axle (not quite hitting the ground), and a string at the end of the pin.
> Mitchel Resnick, "Stars"

Objects of Design and Play

Objects help us make our minds, reaching out to us to form active partnerships. Mitchel Resnick's pull-toy, a wooden car on a string, embodied a paradox: "Since the string is attached to the end of the pin, it seems that the pin should come toward you. At the same time, it seems that the wheels should come toward you. Both can't be true." Resnick had been shown the pull-toy in his high school physics class; he brought the idea of the toy car home with him, but more than this, he brought home the notion of paradox itself. He took apart his own, familiar toys for parts that enabled him to rebuild the pull-toy in his fashion, and even when he had come to understand its mysteries, he continued tinkering: "Even after I 'knew' the answer, I loved tugging on the string and thinking about the paradox." The object took on a life of its own. "No ideas but in things," said the poet William Carlos Williams.[3] And the thing carries the idea.

The anthropologist Claude Lévi-Strauss would say that as Resnick made and remade the pull-toy he was becoming a scientist, more specifically, a *bricoleur*, a practitioner of the science of the concrete. Bricolage is a style of working in which one manipulates a closed set of materials to develop new thoughts.[4] Lévi-Strauss characterizes the primitive scientist as a bricoleur, but modern engineers, too, use this style.[5]

From our earliest years, says the psychologist Jean Piaget, objects help us think about such things as number, space, time, causality, and life.[6] Piaget reminds us that our learning is situated, concrete, and personal. We invent and reinvent it for ourselves. As Resnick plays with pull-toys, he is learning to see himself as capable of inventing an idea, and he is changing in other ways as well. He is learning to be more at home with uncertainty and with his own object attachments.

Object play – for adults as well as children – engages the heart as well as the mind; it is a source of inner vitality. Resnick reminds us of how his mentor, the mathematician and educator Seymour Papert, considered the lessons of his childhood object: gears. An intimate connection with gears brought Papert in touch with ideas from mathematics. As Papert put it: "I fell in love with the gears."[7] Far from being silent companions, objects infuse learning with libido.

[. . .]

[In] Strohecker's "Knot Lab," ten-year-old Jill, a child of a difficult divorce, is preoccupied with tying down the ends of string as she works, using tape, nails, and tacks to keep her knots in place. For Jill, knots are a way to think through her personal situation. Herself at loose ends, Jill is comforted by securing knots in transition. When she builds a knot exhibit that enables passers-by to play with the back-and-forth movement of a True Lovers' Knot, her label for the knot concludes with the phrase "please pull me." Strohecker hears Jill speaking through the knots: "Notice how I am suspended by two knots, one that anchors me and one that holds me. Notice how I am two knots, waiting to be pulled this way and that. I understand being pulled; it is something that I know. Allowing others to pull me is a purpose that I serve."

> My datebook and its events had their own esoteric language. Familiar venues, organizations, and individuals were noted in tiny writing and abbreviations that only I could decipher.
>
> Michelle Hlubinka, "The Datebook"

Objects of Discipline and Desire

Michelle Hlubinka writes about her datebook and her first timepiece – a Mickey Mouse watch that she received on a family vacation when she was four: "Having the watch, I entered a society not just of time-keepers, but time-managers. And I became good at it, perhaps too good at it."

You think you have an organizer, but in time your organizer has you. The organizer is one of many day-today technologies that concretize our modern notion of time. The historian of technology Lewis Mumford examines how the invention of the clock by monks in the Middle Ages transformed social life and subjectivity.[8] Clocks produced time as discrete units, making possible a new way of thinking. Before clocks, there was day and night, morning, mid-day, and evening. Soldiers showed up for battle at dawn. After clocks, there were minutes and seconds. Industrialization needed a clock-produced world of measurable sequences and synchronized action. Capitalism depends on regimenting human time and human bodies.

Our clocks and datebooks do more than keep us on time. Objects function to bring society within the self.

The historian Michel Foucault provides a framework for thinking about how objects such as Hlubinka's watch and datebook serve as foundations of "disciplinary society."[9] In modern times, social control does not require overt repression. Rather, state power can be "object-ified."[10] Every time we fill out a medical questionnaire or take a pill, we are subjects of social discipline. And every time we enter appointments in our datebook, we become the kind of subjects that disciplinary society needs us to be.[11]

When literary theorist Roland Barthes writes that the objects of disciplinary society come to seem natural, what is most important is that what seems natural comes to seem right. We forget that objects have a history. They shape us in particular ways. We forget why or how they came to be. Yet "naturalized" objects are historically specific. Contemporary regimes of power have become capillary in the sense that power is embodied in widely distributed institutions and objects.

From this perspective, Gail Wight's object – the antidepressant medication she calls "Blue Cheer" – produces a patient, just as Hlubinka's datebook produces a time-keeper and time-manager. At the start of Wight's narrative about her pills, she has a sense of herself as an unhappy artist. Soon, psychiatry recasts her identity: she is a broken biological mechanism, but one that medicine can fix. Over time, Wight does not need the presence of a physician to reinforce her medical identity. Over time, the pills alone can do the job.[12]

Eden Medina, like Wight, has her body disciplined. In Medina's case, the social demands are embodied in her shoes. The ballet slippers that haunt Medina communicate the shape of the body to which they want to belong: the ideal dancer's body, conforming to the socially constructed conventions of ballet. Toe shoes put Medina in touch with body practices that teach how the flesh disappoints and how it needs to be disciplined and denied.[13]

> Although it looked like a Braun transistor radio, this object never produced sound. I asked the boy about it and he said: "It can't play music, but I sing when I carry it. One day I'll have a real one."
>
> Julian Beinart, "The Radio"

Objects of History and Exchange

Julian Beinart saw a new object, a mute radio made of wood, and then he could not stop seeing it. His hometown of Durban, South Africa, revealed itself to be rich in technological objects fashioned from the raw materials of an impoverished culture. There were bicycles made from beer cans, cars from bent wire, radios from wood – all technologies of everyday life copied as pure form.

As Beinart found these objects, he saw people and social relationships of which he had been previously unaware. The mute radio and its cousins changed the people who made them and Beinart who discovered them. The mute radio, with no instrumental purpose, was free to serve as commentary on possession and lack, on power and impoverishment.

In a famous passage on commodities, Karl Marx describes how when wood is transformed into a table, it remains an ordinary, sensuous thing. But when the table becomes a commodity in a market system, the object comes alive: it "stands on its head and evolves out of its wooden brain grotesque ideas far more wonderful than if it were to begin dancing of its own free will."[14] Like Marx's commodities, Beinart's wooden radio comes alive as it embodies relationships to power. Yet the wooden radio subverts itself as a commodity and reveals the social relations that commodities are designed to hide.

The social theorist Marcel Mauss, too, describes the animation of objects: gifts retain something of then-givers.[15] As people exchange objects, they assert and confirm their roles in a social system, with all its historical inequalities and contradictions. A gift carries an economic and relational web; the object is animated by the network within it.

From the perspective of the philosopher Jean Baudrillard, the mute radio reveals something profound about the social role of all the radios that can speak. He describes how commodities cultivate desires that support the production and consumption capitalism requires.[16] This process keeps the dominant ideology alive. It becomes invisible and alienates from the real. In such a system, normal radios are taken for granted. But when radios are remade in wood or throw-away tin, the invisible is made visible. In wood, a radio is subversive, a potent actor.

David Mitten finds a Native American axe head that also speaks to him in a subversive way. It subverts his sense of distance between himself and those who came, before him, a theme of the writings of Bruno Latour [. . .]. For Latour, objects speak in a way that destroys any simple stories we might tell about our relations to nature, history, and the inanimate; they destroy any simple sense we might have about progress and our passage through time.[17] Mitten says that when he picked up the axe head, the landscape of his ancestry exploded around him, demanding that it be placed in history, in nature, and in the social lives of the people who had and used it. More than this, Mitten knows that he will part with the axe head only in death, when his daughter will inscribe his life into stories about it.

> A bunny with a soft cotton collar less than half-an-inch wide was named Collar Bunny. . . . He had a small plastic rattle inside his body, and when he sat, the stuffing in his arms made them stick out to the sides.
>
> Tracy Gleason, "Murray: The Stuffed Bunny"

Objects of Transition and Passage

D. W. Winnicott called "transitional" the objects of childhood that the child experiences as both part of the self and of external reality. Collar Bunny (later renamed "Murray") is such an object.

He belongs to Tracy Gleason's younger sister, Shayna. Whatever Shayna imagines herself doing or thinking ("like dressing herself and hopping on one foot and telling a silly joke") can first be "tried on" as bunny thoughts and actions.

Winnicott writes that the transitional object mediates between the child's sense of connection to the body of the mother and a growing recognition that he or she is a separate being. When Shayna starts preschool and its rules insist that Murray cannot accompany her, she is challenged to invent ways of bringing him along. Her solution is to invest Murray with new powers. He develops the ability to read Shayna's mind and intuit her every emotion. In doing so, Murray makes it possible for separation to be not-quite separation. Transitional objects let us take things in stages.

The transitional objects of the nursery – the stuffed animal, the bit of silk from the baby blanket, the favorite pillow – all of these are destined to be abandoned. Yet they leave traces that will mark the rest of life. Specifically, they influence how easily an individual develops a capacity for joy, aesthetic experience, and creative playfulness. Transitional objects, with their joint allegiance to self and other, demonstrate to the child that objects in the external world can be loved. Winnicott believes that during all stages of life we continue to search for objects we can experience as both within and outside of the self.

It is in these terms, as an object in the space between self and surround, that Judith Donath speaks of her much-beloved 1964 Ford Falcon. She inhabits the car like a "skin"; it connects her to her mother, its first owner, and to her children, for whose safety she abandons it. It brings her the joy of an object that traffics, in her words, "between the outside world and the inner self."

[. . .]

Through Donath's sensitivity to the Falcon's cultural biography, she was better able to understand her own. When Donath rides the Falcon as a child in the 1970s, it is a bourgeois suburban object. When it reappears in New York's East Village in the 1980s, the Falcon has been transformed into the neighborhood "cool car." By the 1990s in Cambridge, Massachusetts, the car is exotic and glamorous, congruent with Donath's desire to stand out as a graduate student. "No matter how dully mundane I felt, in the Falcon I was the Driver of that Cool Car."

Winnicott situated his transitional objects in play, which he saw as an intermediate space, a privileged zone in which outer and inner realities can meet.[18] For William J. Mitchell, born in the outback of Australia, the train to Melbourne provided such a space.

The train is the backdrop for a rite of passage, a time of transition that the anthropologist Victor Turner has characterized (for individuals and cultures) as "liminal" or threshold time.[19] For Turner, these times of transition are characterized by the crystallization of new thought and the production of new symbols.

On the Melbourne train, Mitchell is taken from one physical space (his small village in the Australian bush) to another (the cosmopolitan Melbourne), and he is also taken toward a new identity. He writes: "Each warmly lit carriage interior was a synecdoche of urbanity – an encapsulated, displaced fragment of the mysterious life that was lived at the end of the line." Within the liminal space, the self is porous. In train space, Mitchell is open to new associations, sights, and sounds: "And there were wondrous cabinets of curiosities, with friezes of large, sepia photographs over the seats."

In liminal space, Mitchell brings books, words, and objects within his expanding sense of self. It is on the train that he first realized that he can read:

> It was on a train, long before I was reluctantly dragged off to school, that I first realized I could read . . . words in memorable sequence, the beginnings of narrative. . . . As the years went by, and I made myself into an architect and urbanist, I began to understand that objects, narratives, memories, and space are woven into a complex, expanding web – each fragment of which gives meaning to all the others.

[. . .]

Roland Barthes, whose reflections on objects, language, and identity (he writes of "language lined with flesh") also resonate with those of David Mann, writing about the transitions facilitated by the *World Book Encyclopedia* he received as a child.[20]

Far more than a vehicle for the transfer of information, Mann describes the encyclopedia as a means of access to language:

> Its pictures came to life in my mind, parsed into nouns and danced through grammar to the music of verbs. By the time I was four it had taught me to read. Not through my family but through these volumes language became a part of me, the book of the world opened to me and I myself opened to the world as I might otherwise never have done.

Mann and Mitchell make language itself a liminal object, standing outside and within the self, a vehicle for bringing what is outside within.

Mann's description of a self constituted by language is [illuminated by the work of] the psychoanalyst Jacques Lacan. Lacan believes that to talk of "social influences" on the individual neutralizes one of Freud's most important contributions: the recognition that society doesn't "influence" autonomous individuals, but comes to dwell within them with the acquisition of language.[21]

Lacan's theory allows for no real boundary between self and society. People become social with the appropriation of language. You and language become as one. There is no natural man. Lacan's narrative of how language comes to "inhabit" people during the Oedipal phase opens out to larger questions about how we build our psyche by bringing things within. Nowhere is this more in evidence than when we consider what we bring within at a time of loss.

> The logo boasts "Globe Trotter," echoing my grandmother's love of travel. With her newfound liberty after her husband and children had gone, she began to discover the world. . . . But this suitcase is new; she had been saving it for one final trip.
>
> Olivia Dasté, "The Suitcase"

Objects of Mourning and Memory

After her grandmother's death Olivia Dasté packs the old woman's suitcase one last time. A sweater, a handkerchief, a teacup are lovingly arranged in the suitcase. Dasté is afraid to open the suitcase too soon: "[I]t feels dangerous to open it. Memories evolve with you, through you. Objects don't have this fluidity; I fear that the contents of the suitcase might betray my grandmother." But after two years, mourning has done its work. Dasté holds a fragrant red sweater to her face and knows she doesn't have to. Dasté has internalized her grandmother's spirit. "I smile. I am with her in Bordeaux and we have all the time in the world."

In *The Year of Magical Thinking,* Joan Didion describes how material objects may look during the mourning process.[22] After her husband's death, Didion cannot bring herself to throw away his shoes because she is convinced that he may need them. This is the magical thinking that is associated both with religious devotion and the "illness" of mourning. With time, Freud believed, the true object, the lost husband, comes to have a full internal representation.[23] This completes the formal process of mourning; it is only at this point that the shoes can be relinquished. They have served a transitional role.

Susan Pollak, too, begins her narrative of loss with an echo of the tactile – brought back by the way a rolling pin evokes her grandmother's kitchen, the safe place of Pollak's childhood.[24] Pollak's thoughts then go to baking and to the evocative object of Marcel Proust, perhaps the most famous evocative object in all literature. Proust's object is the small cookie called a madeleine. When dipped in tea, the taste of the madeleine brings Proust's character back to his youth, to a country home in Combray, and to his aunt Albertine. Finally, the madeleine opens him to "the vast structure of recollection."[25]

"Never underestimate the power of an evocative object," says Pollak. As a practicing psychotherapist, she is interested in objects for more than evocation. She argues, following Winnicott, that transitional objects can heal. Pollak tells the story of a patient, Mr. B., who was not able to mourn his father until he found the "half-moon" cookies his father had bought for the family when Mr. B. was a child. At that time, money had been tight and his father had only been able to buy day-old cookies. When Pollak's patient went back to his old neighborhood and found the bakery from his childhood, he bought a dozen fresh half-moon cookies. They were unfamiliar, almost displeasing. He had to wait until they were a day old in order to savor them. Only the taste and texture of his childhood could reestablish his lost connection. After finding the cookies he was able to talk to his children about their grandfather. He was able to recall his father's acts of generosity and to think sympathetically about why his father had needed alcohol to endure. The cookie facilitated mourning. Mr. B., a novelist, long blocked in his writing, was able to begin a new novel. For him, as for Proust, memory passed through the body.[26]

Pollak reminds us that Proust himself makes a connection that Winnicott would wholeheartedly endorse. Toward the end of *Remembrance of Things Past*, he says: "Ideas come to us as the successors to griefs, and griefs, at the moment when they change into ideas, lose some part of their power to injure our heart."[27]

> My rocks are un-rock-like. They are plain limestone contradicting itself. The most earthy and banal material transcends itself to become exotic.
>
> Nancy Rosenblum, "Scholars' Rocks"

Objects of Meditation and New Vision

In a narrative in which ideas are successors to grief, Nancy Rosenblum, the widow of a sculptor who collected Chinese scholars' rocks, asks, "How can a rock be a man?"

Scholars' rocks are found in nature, then mounted on meticulously worked bases. The bases transform the rocks into things that are made as well as found, objects that invite reflection on the boundary between nature and culture. Says Rosenblum: "They have the power to provide an effortless, aesthetic experience of mystery. Of infinity in a finite space. Of transformation. Just by looking. Without philosophy."[28]

The rocks displace scale, time, and authorial intent. They are classically liminal objects in Turner's sense: betwixt-and-between categories, the rocks challenge the categories themselves. As Rosenblum puts it, "Gaze at a stone and it disorients."

In traditional rites of passage, participants are separated from all that is familiar. We saw that this makes them vulnerable, open to the objects and experiences of their time of transition. The contemplation of liminal objects can make us similarly vulnerable. In their disorienting qualities, in the way they remind us of the mundane yet take us away from it, scholars' rocks share something of what Freud called the uncanny, those things "known of old" yet strangely unfamiliar.[29]

In his writing on the uncanny, Freud analyzes the etymology of the German words *heimlich* and *unheimlich*, roughly the homelike and familiar and the eerie and strange. The two words seem to be the opposite of each other, suggesting that the eerie is that which is most unfamiliar. But among the meanings of *heimlich* (familiar) is a definition close to its opposite:

it can mean concealed or kept out of sight. Heimlich has a "double." By extension, Freud argues, our most eerie experiences come not from the exotic, but from what is close to home. Uncanny objects take emotional disorientation and turn it into philosophical grist for the mill.

. . . Jeffrey Mifflin, the curator at Boston's Massachusetts General Hospital, uses a 2,600 year-old mummy to ponder ultimate questions: "He had been flesh and blood and bone, and the flesh and bone were still there. His senses had once worked as mine now did. His mind was gone, but neither would I live forever."

Mifflin's mummy frightens him even as it grows in his affections. The man who became the mummy was Padihershef, a stonecutter who lived near Thebes during the Saite Period (XXVI Dynasty) and died in his late forties. His specialty was cutting stone to make tombs. Mifflin begins to identify with Padihershef. When Mifflin opens the mummy's exhibit case and smells the embalming spice and chemicals, he is not overtaken by their pungency, but by the thought that Padihershef's own friends would have smelled something quite similar as they closed his coffin.

Mifflin calculates the generations between himself and the mummy, in his estimate about 130, and he wonders if his "distant progenitors in Britain were mining tin or slicing blocks of peat at the same time that Padihershef was chiseling out tombs in Egypt?" Mifflin thinks about his own uncertainties about religion and the afterlife in relation to Padihershef's probable certainties. Mifflin measures their lives against each other, each seeking to find a place in history and in his generation.

As a curator, Mifflin compares the untidy, chaotic spaces in museum back rooms and the meticulous presentations in the front rooms where all is tidy and ordered. The contrast reveals something too often hidden: we tend to present "front room" knowledge as "true." But its certainties are constructed. We make up a clean story to mask our anxieties about the chaotic state of the little that we know. Chaos compels its opposite: "the orderly presentation of supposed facts" to which Mifflin feels disconnected. He fears that he will always be blocked in his ability to experience certainties by his access to their opposite – his experience in the dirty back rooms. Yet it is the contrast between the front and back rooms that leads Mifflin to a new appreciation of the complexity of knowledge.

In *Purity and Danger*, the anthropologist Mary Douglas examines the evocative power of such contrasts, focusing on how the tension between order and disorder is expressed through our relationship to dirt and pollution.[30] Order is defined in terms of dirt, or that which is not polluting. And dirt is defined in terms of order. Societies create the classification "dirt" to designate objects that don't fit neatly into their ways of ordering of the world.

. . . Evelyn Fox Keller's reflections on her life in science, a narrative about the power of order-disrupting ("dirty") objects to provoke meditation and new vision. Keller takes slime mold as her object, an object full of paradoxes: "In times of plenty, it lives as an individual single-celled organism but, when food supplies are exhausted, it regroups. . . . [It] traffics back and forth both between the one and the many and between sameness and difference."

Turner and Douglas help us see things on the boundary, such as slime mold, as both disruptive and as sources of new ideas. Indeed, for Keller, the "betwixt-and-between" slime mold not only becomes an object-to-think-with for thinking about processes within cells, it becomes a way to think about the politics of science.

In the late 1960s, most biologists argued that slime mold goes from being a unicellular to a multicellular organism, following a signal given by "founder cells." In a 1968 paper, Keller and biologist Lee Segel disagreed. They suggested that changes in the slime mold's state followed from the dynamics of the cell population as a whole. There was no command and control center that took charge of the process. Biologists resisted this suggestion. Keller says: "[D]espite the absence of evidence, [biologists] continued to adhere to the belief that founder cells (or pacemakers) were responsible for aggregation."

Two decades later, while working on a biography of the geneticist Barbara McClintock, Keller again faced the resistance of biologists – this time to a style of doing science. Canonical scientific methods insisted on the researcher's distance from the object of study, but McClintock wanted to be close to her objects, among the corn cells of her research. She imagined herself like a modern-day Alice, brought to their scale in order to feel more a part. Her colleagues in biology were not impressed. Keller began to identify with McClintock. Like her subject, when Keller had looked at cells, she had seen social and decentralized processes. Keller comes to see her career and McClintock's as illustrative of how biology rejects theories that challenge the dogma of single and centralized causal factors.

As Keller wonders why people find causal accounts so compelling, she considers explanations that draw on the Freudian tradition. There, our earliest, profoundly bonded, connections to the world are interrupted by a sudden experience of separation. Keller hypothesizes that "we tend to project onto nature our first and earliest social experiences, ones in which we feel passive and acted upon." Whether or not this particular hypothesis is true, she says, a more general point certainly is: scientists were not open to the "discrepancies between our own predispositions and the range of possibilities inherent in natural phenomena. In short, we risk imposing on nature the very stories we like to hear."[31]

What are the stories we like to hear? Keller suggests that they are often the ones that confirm us in comfortable ways of thinking. But theory can help us to see things anew.

Until now, I have discussed physical objects that engender intimacy. What becomes of this intimacy when people work with digital objects?

Any response needs to be complex, as is apparent in the contrast between two [sections in this extract]. Mitchel Resnick describes his StarLogo program that brings its users to an encounter with ideas about emergent phenomena, much as the concrete objects of Piaget's day put children in touch with ideas about counting and simple categorization. His goal is to have the computer enable a new kind of learning. Yet Susan Yee's testimony about work in a digital archive suggests aspects to life on the screen that may be inherently alienating.

Yee, an architect, begins her relationship with Le Corbusier through the physicality of his drawings. As she works in the Le Corbusier archives in Paris, his original blueprints, sketches, notes, and plans are brought to her in long metal boxes. Le Corbusier's handwritten notes in the margins of his sketches, the traces of his fingerprints, the smudges, the dirt, all of these encourage Yee's identification with the designer. To Yee, the most "miraculous" moment in the physical archive is finding the little colored paper squares that Le Corbusier used to think through his design for the Palace of the Soviets. Yee says that she could imagine Le Corbusier "fiddling" with the design elements, moving them around, considering different shapes and volumes as he worked. The little bits of colored paper connect Yee to his process. Delighted, Yee "fiddles" with them too. The bricolage of the master is re-experienced in the bricolage of the student. As it happened, Yee was visiting the Le Corbusier archive at a dramatic moment, the day it was converted from physical to virtual space. The philosopher Jacques Derrida sees such transitions as "transforming the entire public and private space of humanity."[32] For one thing, while any archive is a selection of material that erases what has been excluded – the digitized archive goes a step further. Its virtuality insures another level of abstraction between its users and what has been selected. It brings to mind Derrida's writing about the word processor where "erasure" is central to his concerns: "Previously, erasures and added words left a sort of scar on the paper or a visible image in the memory. There was a temporal resistance, a thickness in the duration of the erasure. But now everything negative is drowned, deleted; it evaporates immediately, sometimes from one instant to the next."[33]

Derrida's meditation on erasure brings us back to what troubled Yee in the archive. She is aware that, digitized, the Le Corbusier archives will be available to scholars all over the world and be protected from wear and tear. Yet, when the archive is digitized, Yee experiences the loss of her connection to Le Corbusier: "It made the drawings feel anonymous," she says. More important, the digitized archives make Yee feel anonymous. She is grateful for her own position in a generation of architects that knows drawing by hand as well as by computer; her narrative captures an anxiety that digital objects will take us away from the body and its ways of understanding.

Through Yee's essay on the archive, this overview engages the problem of virtuality and its discontents. Yet her cautionary essay must be read in relation to other narratives about computational objects – represented by the promise and enthusiasm of Resnick's writing, as well as that of Howard Gardner, Trevor Pinch, and Annalee Newitz – that suggest how digital objects engage us in new and compelling ways.

Indeed, in Newitz's description of her laptop computer, the flickering screen does not appear cold and abstract, but is integrated into her sense of herself. Her experience of the laptop is reminiscent of how Joseph Cevetello, a diabetic, talks about his glucometer, a device for measuring blood sugar. Cevetello notes how over time his glucometer becomes more than companion: the glucometer "has become me." Moment to moment, its output determines his actions. He lances his finger, readies an insulin injection, and waits "for my meter to tell me what to do." The laptop, like the glucometer, is experienced as co-extensive with the self. Newitz feels so close to her laptop that she cannot tell where it leaves off and she begins. Her self-understanding depends on analyzing the flows and rhythms that pass between herself and the machine. In bed, Newitz remembers not to let the blankets cover the computer's vents so it does not overheat. She is at one with her virtual persona: "I was just a command line full of glowing green letters."

Cevetello and Newitz have achieved couplings so intimate between themselves and their objects that we might characterize them as cyborg.[34] In the cyborg world we move beyond objects as tools or prosthetics. We are one with our artifacts. And in the cyborg world, the natural and the artificial no longer find themselves in opposition. Says the historian of science Donna Haraway: "Any objects or persons can be reasonably thought of in terms of disassembly and reassembly."[35] No object, space, or body is sacred in itself: "Any component can be interfaced with any other if the proper standard, the proper code, can be constructed for processing signals in a common language."[36] Newitz still has to carry her laptop around, but the day is not far off when computation will become part of our bodies, beginning with chips to improve our sight and hearing. Cevetello anticipates the day when his glucometer will be available as an implant; it will provide a digital readout directly sensed by his body.

Once we see life through the cyborg prism, becoming one with a machine is reduced to a technical problem of finding the right operating system to make it (that is, *us*) run smoothly. When we live with implanted chips, we will be on a different footing in our relationships with computers. When we share other people's tissue and genetic material, we will be on a different footing with the bodies of others. Our theories tell us stories about the objects of our lives. As we begin to live with objects that challenge the boundaries between the born and created and between humans and everything else, we will need to tell ourselves different stories.

Notes

Things we think with

1   See Sherry Turkle, *Life on the Screen: Identity in the Age of the Internet* (New York: Simon & Schuster, 1995), pp54–56.

2   See, for example, Jean Piaget and Barbel Inhelder, *The Growth of Logical Thinking from Childhood to Adolescence*, trans. Anne Parsons and Stanley Milgram (New York: Basic Books, 1958).

3   Lévi-Strauss, *The Savage Mind*, 16ff.

4   In science studies, two groundbreaking ethnographies that showed the power of the concrete were Bruno Latour and Steven Woolgar, *Laboratory Life: The Social Construction of Scientific Facts* (Princeton, N.J.: Princeton University Press, 1986 [1979]), and Karin Knorr Cetina, *The Manufacture of Knowledge: An Essay on the Constructivist and Contextual Nature of Science* (Oxford, Pergamon Press 1981). As for Nobel laureates, Richard Feynman wrote extensively about his everyday tinkering in *Surely You're Joking, Mr. Feynman* (New York: W. W. Norton, 1981).

5   One example of feminist scholarship that focuses on a scientist's profound connection with her objects is Evelyn Fox Keller's biography of Barbara McClintock, *A Feeling for the Organism: The Life and Work of Barbara McClintock* (San Francisco: W. H. Freeman, 1983). Other early feminist contributions include Ruth Bleier, ed., *Feminist Approaches to Science* (New York: Pergamon, 1986); Carol Gilligan, *In a Different Voice: Psychological Theory and Women's Development* (Cambridge, Mass.: Harvard University Press, 1982); Sandra Harding and Merrill B. Hintikka, eds., *Discovering Reality: Feminist Perspectives on Epistemology, Metaphysics, Methodology, and Philosophy of Science* (London: Reidel, 1983).

6   To take only a few examples, see Arjun Appadurai, ed., *The Social Life of Things: Commodities in Cultural Perspective* (Cambridge: Cambridge University Press, 1988); Bill Brown, ed., *Things* (Chicago: University of Chicago Press, 2004); Lorraine Daston, ed., *Things that Talk: Object Lessons from Art and Science* (New York: Zone Books, 2004); Mihaly Csikszentmihalyi and Eugene Rochberg-Halton, *The Meaning of Things: Domestic Symbols and the Self* (Cambridge: Cambridge University Press, 1981); Karin Knorr Cetina, *Epistemic Cultures: How the Sciences Make Knowledge* (Cambridge, Mass.: Harvard University Press, 1999); Bruno Latour, *We Have Never Been Modern*, trans. Catherine Porter (Cambridge, Mass.: Harvard University Press, 1993); and Edward Tenner, *When Things Bite Back* (New York: Knopf, 1996).

7   For Freud's description of loss leading to internalization and mental representation, see Sigmund Freud, "Mourning and Melancholia," in *The Standard Edition of the Complete Psychological Works of Sigmund Freud*, ed. and trans. James Strachey et al. (London: Hogarth, 1953–74), vol. XIV, pp239–58. As it is for people and the wishes associated with them, so I believe it is for objects: they become powerful in our psychic lives as we bring them within us, along with their associations, emotional and intellectual.

8   Ibid., "The Uncanny," vol. XVII, pp219–52. In their provocation to discourse, uncanny objects contrast to fetish objects that are stand-ins for thoughts that cannot be expressed; they take the place of what cannot be spoken; "Fetishism," vol. XXI, pp152–57.

9   D. W. Winnicott referred to such objects as transitional. See *Playing and Reality* (New York: Routledge, 1989 [1971]).

10   See Victor Turner, *The Ritual Process: Structure and Anti-Structure* (Chicago: Aldine, 1969).

What makes an object evocative?

1   I thank my research assistant Anita Chan whose work on sources was both meticulous and brimming with good ideas. Ongoing conversations with Kelly Gray enhanced the clarity of this note.

2   As anthropologist Lucy Suchman puts it: "Objects and their positions are inseparable." See "Affiliative Objects," *Organization* 12, no. 3 (2005), pp379–99. On this theme she cites Donna Haraway, *Simians, Cyborgs and Women: The Reinvention of Nature* (New York: Routledge, 1991); Andrew Pickering, *The Mangle of Practice: Time, Agency, and Science* (Chicago: University of Chicago Press, 1997); Marilyn Strathern, *Property, Substance, and Effect: Anthropological Essays on Persons and Things* (London: Athlone Press, 1999), and Karen Barad, "Posthumanist Performativity: Toward an Understanding of How Matter Comes to Matter," *Signs: Journal of Women in Culture and Society* 28, no.3 (2003), pp88–128.

3   William Carlos Williams, *Paterson* (New York: New Directions, 1946), Book I, p7.

4   Claude Lévi-Strauss, *The Savage Mind*, trans. John Weightman and Doreen Weightman (Chicago: University of Chicago Press, 1966), p24.

5   Resnick's experience of the pull-toy as an evocative object is close to what the sociologist Karin Knorr Cetina calls an "epistemic object." Knorr Cetina describes epistemic objects as open, question-generating and complex: "They are processes and projections rather than definitive things. . . . Objects of knowledge . . . are more like open drawers filled with folders extending indefinitely into the depths of a dark closet." From "Sociality with Objects: Social Relations in Postsocial Knowledge Societies," *Theory, Culture, and Society* 14, no. 4 (1997), p12.

6   We form our notions of these things through immersion in our culturally specific object world. And when that culture changes, when it offers new objects, we can come to see the world differently.

This notion of objects and culture change is central to Resnick's work with StarLogo, an effort to provide children with a new world of objects – in this case computational objects – that will enable thinking about emergence. See Mitchel Resnick, *Turtles, Termites, and Traffic Jams: Explorations in Massively Parallel Microworlds* (Cambridge, Mass.: MIT Press, 1994). Seymour Papert makes this point about the power of computer programming as a microworld for learning in *Mindstorms: Children, Computers, and Powerful Ideas* (New York: Basic Books, 1980). While Piaget was a constructivist, stressing how objects are part of children's building their minds, Papert and Resnick consider themselves constructionists, putting the emphasis on children building for themselves the materials that will structure their thinking. For an overview of this activist, "builder's" perspective on objects and intellect, see Idit Harel and Seymour Papert, eds., *Constructionism: Research Reports and Essays, 1985–90, by the MIT Epistemology and Learning Group, the MIT Media Laboratory* (Norwood, N.J.: Ablex, 1991).

7   See Papert, *Mindstorms*, pviii.

8   Lewis Mumford, *Technics and Civilization* (New York: Harcourt, Brace & World, 1963 [1934]).

9   Michel Foucault, *Discipline and Punish: The Birth of the Prison*, trans. Alan Sheridan (New York: Pantheon Books, 1977); *The Birth of the Clinic: An Archeology of Medical Perception*, trans. A. M. Sheridan Smith (New York: Vintage, 1994 [1963]); *Madness and Civilization: A History of Insanity in the Age of Reason*, trans. Richard Howard (New York: Random House, 1965).

10   The literary theorist Roland Barthes describes the objects of disciplinary society as "self-naturalizing." We begin to accept what we have made as what has always been and what must always be. Roland Barthes, *Mythologies*, trans. Annette Lavers (New York: Hill and Wang, 1972 [1957]).

11   Literary theorists Julia Kristeva and Judith Butler approach similar issues from a psychoanalytic perspective, influenced by the work of the psychoanalyst Jacques Lacan who elaborates on language as constitutive of self. Butler stresses that objects, including the body, are never found "in the raw." They are already shaped by language and social discourse and thus ready to shape us. For Julia Kristeva, each individual's psychology reproduces the political relationships of the outer world. So, any change we wish to make in the world first requires a parallel action within. Foucault describes an inner history of objects as it plays out on a social level; Kristeva and Butler bring the story down to the psychodynamics of individuals. See Judith Butler, *Bodies That Matter: On the Discursive Limits of "Sex"* (New York: Routledge, 1993); and Julia Kristeva, *Strangers to Ourselves*, trans. Leon Roudiez (New York: Columbia University Press, 1991).

12   The antidepressants become what sociologist and historian Bruno Latour would call the "foot soldiers" of medical power. The pills confirm individuals in the role of patient. See Bruno Latour, *The Pasteurization of France*, trans. Alan Sheridan and John Law (Cambridge, Mass.: Harvard University Press, 1988).

13   See Butler, *Bodies That Matter*.

14   Karl Marx, *Capital: A Critique of Political Economy*, trans. Ben Fowkes (London: Penguin, 1976 [1867]), vol. I, p163.

15   Marcel Mauss, *The Gift: The Form and Reason for Exchange in Archaic Societies*, trans. W. D. Halls (New York: W. W. Norton, 2000 [1950]), pp11–12.

16   Jean Baudrillard, *For a Critique of the Political Economy of the Sign*, trans. Charles Levin, (St. Louis: Telos Press, 1981).

17   In *We Have Never Been Modern* Bruno Latour describes the subversion of objects as they reveal the cracks in the social constructions that we take as "reality," for example what we call "modernity." We have constructed a notion of modernity that rests on dichotomies between past and present, natural and social, and humans and things, all distinctions that our ancestors, in their world of alchemy, astrology, and phrenology, did not make. Our objects challenge these distinctions. Objects insist on their place in history, on the fact that they are embedded in both nature and culture, and finally, the objects of modern science refuse the distinction between humans and things. On a global level, objects such as "the ozone layer" fuse science, nature, technology, and politics. Technoscientific objects make manifest the social relations of our time. See Bruno Latour, *We Have Never Been Modern*, trans. Catherine Porter (Cambridge, Mass.: Harvard University Press, 1993). See also Bruno Latour and Steven Woolgar, *Laboratory Life: The Social Construction of Scientific Facts* (Princeton, N.J.: Princeton University Press, 1986 [1979]); Bruno Latour, *Science in Action: How to Follow Scientists and Engineers through Society* (Cambridge, Mass.: Harvard University Press, 1987); *The Pasteurization of France*, trans. Alan Sheridan and John Law (Cambridge, Mass.: Harvard University Press, 1988); *Aramis or the Love of Technology*, trans. Catherine Porter (Cambridge, Mass.: Harvard University Press, 1996).

18   For Winnicott, "This area of playing is not inner psychic reality. It is outside the individual but it is not the external world. Into this play area the child gathers objects or phenomena from external

reality and uses these in the service of some sample derived from inner or personal reality." D. W. Winnicott, *Playing and Reality* (London: Routledge, 1989 [1971]), p51.

19   Victor Turner, *The Ritual Process: Structure and Anti-Structure* (Chicago: Aldine, 1969). Turner drew his notion of the liminal from the work of Arnold van Gennep. See *Rites of Passage*, trans. Monika B. Vizedom and Gabrielle L. Caffee (Chicago: University of Chicago Press, 1960 [1909]).

20   Roland Barthes, *The Pleasure of the Text*, trans. Richard Miller (New York: Farrar, Straus and Giroux, 1975), p67.

21   Jacques Lacan, "On the Signification of the Phallus," in *Écrits: A Selection*, trans. Alan Sheridan (New York: W. W. Norton, 1977). For Lacan, the Oedipal period is the time when language and society come to inhabit the child, providing entrée into the "symbolic" order. In Lacan's telling, the Oedipal crisis is resolved through language. The child accepts the father's interdiction to the child's desire for the mother by identifying with the father through an acceptance of his name. (In French there is a pun: the father's *non* and *nom*.) One signifier (the father's name) comes to take the place of another (desire for the mother and desire to be the object of her desire). What is being signified (the primitive, irreducible desire to complete the mother, to be what she is presumed to lack) remains the same. In the course of a lifetime, the individual builds up many chains of signification, always substituting new terms for old and always increasing the distance between the signifier that is most accessible, and all those that are invisible and unconscious, including of course the original signifier. See Lacan, "On a Question Preliminary to any Possible Treatment of Psychosis," in *Écrits*, p200. See also Lacan, "The Function and Field of Speech and Language in Psychoanalysis," in *Écrits*, p68.

22   Joan Didion, *The Year of Magical Thinking* (New York: Knopf, 2005).

23   See Sigmund Freud, "Mourning and Melancholia," *The Standard Edition of the Complete Psychological Works of Sigmund Freud*, trans. and ed. James Strachey et al. (London: Hogarth Press, 1953–74), vol. XIV, pp239–58. Loss and what follows are central to the way psychoanalytic theory tells the story of the evolving self. When Lacan describes the Oedipal moment as the internalization of language and social law, his narrative parallels that of Sigmund Freud. Freud sketched out the process through which loss becomes the motor for objects (here referring to people) to become part of our inner world. Freud considers the moment when a male child gives up the idea that he will displace his father in his mother's affections. The loss requires a radical response. The father, or rather the father's interdiction, is brought inside by creating a mental agency capable of representing it: the superego. (This is the moment that Lacan theorized as the moment of passage to a symbolic order.) Later losses will not result in new psychic structures at the level of the superego. But the basic process has been laid down: a loss, an internalization of an object. Mourning is the painful but necessary process through which this internalization takes place.

24   Psychologists Mihaly Csikszentmihalyi and Eugene Rochberg-Halton investigated people's feelings toward household objects such as the rolling pin, finding that they carry history and meaning. See Mihaly Csikszentmihalyi and Eugene Rochberg-Halton, *The Meaning of Things: Domestic Symbols and the Self* (Cambridge: Cambridge University Press, 1981).

25   Marcel Proust, *Remembrance of Things Past*, trans. C. K. Scott Montcrieff and Terence Kilmartin (New York: Vintage, 1981 [1913]), vol. 1, pp48–51.

26   Mr. B's evokes Henri Bergson as well as Proust. Bergson criticizes any description of memory that divides it into a series of mechanical steps removed from sensation. For Bergson, we must physically prepare ourselves to recall. Remembering is not to re-experience the same thing, but to experience something new and to draw the past into a new realm of possibility. See Henri Bergson, *Matter and Memory*, trans. Nancy M. Paul and W. Scott Palmer (New York: Zone Books, 1990 [1896]), pp133–35.

27   Proust, *Remembrance of Things Past*, vol. 3, p994.

28   The rocks carry ideas and inspire passion. They present thought and feeling as inseparable. In microcosm, the rocks capture what Immanuel Kant called nature's "sublime" and illustrate Gaston Bachelard's thesis that only the infusion of reason with passion can lead to a full comprehension of the world. Immanuel Kant, *The Critique of Judgment*, trans. James C. Meredith (Oxford: Oxford University Press, 1952 [1790]); Gaston Bachelard, *The Poetics of Space: The Classic Look at How We Experience Intimate Places*, trans. Maria Jolas (Boston: Beacon Press, 1994 [1958]).

29   Sigmund Freud, "The Uncanny," *The Standard Edition of the Complete Psychological Works of Sigmund Freud*, trans. and ed. James Strachey et al., vol. XVII, pp219–52.

30   Like other boundary objects, dirt and pollution provoke strong emotions and carry powerful ideas. To make this point, Mary Douglas looks at the taboo foods of Jewish dietary tradition. In Douglas's formulation, every kosher meal embodies the ordered cosmology of Genesis in which heaven was separated from the earth and the sea. In the story of the creation, each of these realms is allotted its

proper kind of animal life. In the heavens, two-legged fowls fly with wings; on the earth, four-legged animals hop or walk; and scaly fish swim with fins. It is acceptable to eat these "pure" creatures who behave in harmony with their realm, but those that cross categories (such as the lobster that lives in the sea but crawls upon its floor) are unacceptable. Every kosher meal carries a theory of unbreachable order. Holiness is order and each thing must have its place. Mary Douglas, *Purity and Danger: An Analysis of the Concepts of Pollution and Taboo* (New York: Routledge, 1966), especially chapter 3, "The Abominations of Leviticus."

31   Evelyn Fox Keller, *Reflections on Gender and Science* (New Haven, Conn.: Yale University Press, 1985), p157.

32   Jacques Derrida, *Archive Fever: A Freudian Impression*, trans. Eric Prenowitz (Chicago: University of Chicago Press, 1996), pp17–18.

33   Jacques Derrida, "The Word Processor," in *Paper Machine*, trans. Rachel Bowlby (Stanford: Stanford University Press, 2005), p24.

34   Donna J. Haraway, "A Cyborg Manifesto," in *Simians, Cyborgs, and Women: The Reinvention of Nature* (New York: Routledge, 1991), p162.

35   Haraway, "A Cyborg Manifesto," in *Simians, Cyborgs, and Women*, p162.

36   Ibid., p163

Chapter 9

Hilda Kean

LONDON STORIES. PERSONAL LIVES, PUBLIC HISTORIES

Collecting material

AT FIRST IT SEEMED EASY. Sitting in her hospital bed with a broken leg, Mum had already made a list of the furniture she wanted with her in the residential home. Other items had already been allocated for local good causes. The washing machine and fridge had been taken away by the National Children's Home to give to a 'deserving' single mother and her children. Jean from the Loughton branch of the Essex Handicraft Association had arrived and together we had lifted the heavy sewing machine complete with its own table into her estate car. Boxes of knitting wool, scraps of material for patchwork and piles of *Cross Stitch Monthly* had already caught Jean's eye and she loaded the boxes into her car with the anticipation of future pleasure. I had taken the heavy Victorian and Edwardian furniture hand-crafted by my paternal grandfather. My mother had wanted none of it. But a dressing table and tallboy, utility furniture made in 1946, the year of her marriage, she took with her. What remained seemed simple for me to organise and to process.

I just needed to make separate piles for the books, or so I thought. The needlework, tapestry, embroidery, patchwork and quilling coffee-table books had already been distributed to the ladies of the Essex Handicraft Association for their bring and buy stalls. In another pile I had put the hundreds of religious books: the Bibles in a series of editions – Moffatt, *New English Bible, Good News Bible*; the William Barclay commentaries; the homilies from Patience Strong. These would go to the Loughton Methodist church for a jumble sale. They would all be going to a useful new home; someone would find a place for them, just as Mum and Dad – Winifred Kean (née Mankelow) and Stanley Kean – had, in their own way.

The remainder of the books were mainly about the history and topography of London: these were old, often rare and invariably in hardback and I would take these. I too would use them, for researching and writing, these books that my father had collected over the years about his home town. As Stan, who was born in London Fields in Hackney, used to say, he was a Cockney, born within the sound of Bow Bells, if the wind was in the right direction. Books that Winifred deemed to be still 'useful' or of sentimental value would be going with her to the Methodist residential home in which she would now live. These included the prizes for good conduct at Sydney Road elementary school in 1920, the Bible presented on her conversion to Methodism, and music scores of *Messiah*, *Elijah*, *Creation*, and *The Crucifixion* that she had sung in the London Choral Society with her husband before I was born.

Sorting through the rest of the books and ephemera should have been a simple task of objective categorisation, a sort of Dewey system for house clearance, but it became more complicated than this. For here I was engaging with collections of things that were now simultaneously anchored in the spaces of a 'past, yet stubbornly present' domain.[1] Here were objects, things, material, which crossed time. I had thought the books were simply books but they were also receptacles of notes and jottings, artefacts that had belonged to people, people I had known, and had been used as part of their daily existence. The books had transformed themselves into testimonials of many lives: of my mother who wrote sermons and the order of services, drawing on her Bibles and religious texts, writing out every word neatly in spiral notebooks; of my father who had died ten years before and whose possessions had never been sorted (I only now realised) by his widow, since the slips of paper, the notes, remained sticking out undisturbed from the piles. But the books and ornaments also went back to at least another, earlier, generation. There was the example of the Walter Scott novel given to my father, as the inscription explained, by his mother Ada. It had been a birthday present in 1914 that neither of them – to judge by the book's good condition – had ever got round to reading. But my father had not thrown the book away; nor did I. As Sally J. Morgan has described, in the account of her own father leaving a selection of photographs to his children before he died, 'The raw place where "history" begins is in the fear of oblivion. Out of that fear we begin to look for immortality and for meaning in narrative. . . . When my father gave me his photographs he was giving me his own narrative of his own life.'[2] What was surrounding (or was it overwhelming?) me in the jumble and mess of this tiny council flat on the London/Essex borders was material from the past from which a history might be made. These were not tides that I had called up in the reading rooms of the Bodleian Library in Oxford or scrutinised, carefully using just a pencil, in the Rare Books room of the British Library. The material here was stuff that I had probably lived with as a child (I could not have been sure amidst the quantities and mess), and which my parents had lived with at least since their marriage. However, many of the things went back beyond the twentieth century into at least the last decades of the 1800s. In her illuminating exploration of the art of writing history Ludmilla Jordanova has suggested that what is 'relevant' material in the creation of history is 'never straightforward'.[3] I was surrounded by artefacts from the past; were they things that would assist me in writing a history of the family within which such items had been held?

I did not just observe books, or scribblings in them. Here too were minutes of meetings: Toc H, Women's Toc H, a typed report of a National Trefoil Guild conference my mother had attended in 1958;[4] accounts of the day care centre she had run; reports of Islington council care meetings, for whom my father had done voluntary work on his retirement; running orders for concert parties given to old people's clubs, churches and day centres; jokes and quizzes with bits of paper marking the questions. In Stan's hand there were notes, bookfuls of them, garnered from systematic and regular attendance at London evening classes over a period of thirty years. No scholar, he always said of himself (he'd left school at 15), but he'd made up for it in other ways. Those who spend their employed hours as clerical workers are not supposed to engage in such activities in their leisure time; conventionally this is left to the middle classes, the students, the lecturers, the professionals. But here were History notes, mainly of London, notebooks listing slides taken throughout mainland Britain of famous buildings, interesting cathedrals, 'sights' rather than 'sites'; and philosophy too: Hobbes and Locke and *Zen and the Art of Motorcycle Maintenance*, set texts from classes at the City Literary Institute. Here were notes on Religion, Comparative Religion, Islam, Judaism, Hinduism, all made by this life-long Protestant Non-Conformist. Although the evening class note-taker was dead, the sermon writer and Women's Fellowship class leader was not.

If I had asked Mum what to do with these things she had not divested onto others, she might have said chuck them out, they are no use now; so I didn't ask and I chose what to keep and to 'use' – in my way, as historians (and probably daughters) always do.

My mother had never known when things might come in 'useful' and so plenty had been hoarded. Used stamps were carefully cut from envelopes and placed for safe-keeping in a jar, to be forwarded, at some unspecified future time, to a charity. Here too were custard-cream biscuits in a royal wedding tin from 1981, given away free, she said, by the milkman; kept untouched on top of the kitchen cupboard for eighteen years. There were drawers full of receipts for Christmas presents to my mother from my father for kitchen goods, which themselves were rarely taken from their boxes. Instructions, too, existed in carefully kept booklets for the unused sandwich maker, unused filter coffee funnel and unused foot spa. Here were never opened gadgets purchased in a heady moment at a 1940s Ideal Home exhibition, an indication of what might have been.[5] They stayed in their boxes – a reminder of the self-denial of daily life. Here were boxes of presents: presents received and putative gifts, often the self same items, a recycling of good intentions. Drawers of Avon talcum powder bought for others; tea towels from a Trefoil Guild penpal in Australia or from the Canadian couple met on a coach tour two decades before or from the church bazaar for missionary work. Over twenty such tea towels were kept, used neither for drying dishes nor display: never to be used by this couple. Their lives had not been 'good enough' to allow the extravagant use of bright tea towels or a choice of talcum powders and soaps for their own use. There would always be a 'best occasion' to wait for, a right time, a better time, which never came. The flat was full of such reminders of a bygone era: the unopened wedding presents – the tablecloths in their crinkly cellophane wrappers, being kept for some future 'best'; the wedding photos in their presentation folders never distributed to the guests. As I moved my 85-year-old mother's effects with her into a residential home, they were still there in her flat.

The ephemera of these lives lived in working-class London were kept and not thrown away. These were the traces of existences lived in some ways set apart from contemporary time, adhering to outdated Liberal politics or Non-Conformist religion, staying in jobs in declining industries. The possessions hoarded reflected a coming together of lives of different generations and times into one place and moment. The existence of a world of hoarded bits and pieces, fragments and shards – I never used to think of them as materials for the writing of history when I lived amongst them as a child – were of a familial world into which I was born but which always seemed to be of a much earlier time. When I was young I never quite understood the fuss about Miss Havisham, the woman abandoned on her wedding day, in Charles Dickens's *Great Expectations*. Living a life in frozen time, the appurtenances of a previous event not removed, seemed a normal part of present life, to me. We did not quite have mouldering wedding cake for decades but uneaten Christmas cake kept in the tin to the following year, slivers of piccalilli residing in a jar in the bottom of a cupboard, paper bags and string in their own kitchen drawer, or in later years washed plastic bags, part of a present, redolent of a past, were all part of a daily routine. Here, as the twentieth century was turning into the twenty-first, was an almost illegible George III penny with the accompanying note of an unspecified child antiquarian explaining its historicity; Victorian hand-carved furniture; tiny and repeated relics of Southend-on-Sea; the World War One blanket used by the Rayleigh guide camp in the 1930s. These traces of earlier times had been gathered in my parents' and grandparents' lifetimes: they were still there.

Although I had started researching my family's history several years before my mother's accident and my role as a house clearer, it was seeing this physical substance of different lives that had given me the impetus to start to write about it. If, however, I had found such material in a public archive I would have been more confident about what to do with it. Discovering ephemera, particularly bits of paper carelessly left in otherwise ordered bundles, tied with ancient string, I would usually be excited. It would suggest that I had 'found something' that no one else had read, or noticed. It would have been obvious that here were materials for the writing of history since they had been preserved in archives, libraries, repositories, museums, created specifically for this purpose. I would have got out my pad of lined file paper and started scribbling. If it had been in a venue maintained by English Heritage or the National Trust I would have kept the glossy leaflet with key dates and facts, probably talked to the staff to get their perspective or, more likely, to provoke an argument about the rationale for the restoration or presentation. It wouldn't have seemed a problem getting material for writing history. But a council flat on an ex-Greater London Council (GLC) estate in Debden is not conventionally the stuff of history. Ordinary homes in the past are not the usual repositories of historical material. The commonplace childhood homes of Beatles Paul McCartney and John Lennon have not been preserved because of any apparent architectural merit but because of who these 'ordinary' children had become. My parents' cultural milieu and influence was surely in a qualitatively different league.

Since at least the 1960s, it has been 'permitted' to write histories of ordinary people's lives. This was how writers such as E. P. Thompson with his ground-breaking *The Making of the English Working Class* made their living and reputations as historians. Such history, however, was usually based on documents in archives, rather than what was found tucked away in a cubby hole, or dumped into plastic black bin bags. What elderly women decide to keep – or discard – is still not usually the substance of academic history although family historians may operate otherwise. However, as Tim Brennan has suggested in his exploration of his great-grandfather's diary, dates of births, marriages and deaths, census returns, memories and heirlooms, are used by the family historian to construct a notion of self and to reject 'conventional cultural institutions as the sole arbiters of legitimacy and value'.[6]

Such items are personal but the experience of keeping things, using them, making connections between the past and the present is one shared by thousands of researchers engaged in writing about the lives of their own families. When I teach classes about writing family history or public history, students always have things that they are happy to bring into the group to share: a wooden spoon owned by Scottish peasants whose cottage Queen Victoria visited; the posthumous medal of a now-dead father who had been a London fire-fighter in the Blitz; a photo of 1950s children eating ice cream from a van on an ordinary day on their estate; a rent book, a ring, a badge.

Historians and their histories

Such ephemera are not usually indicative of lives conducted centre stage in a conventional political or a social historian's idea of important events. In my own family, there are no documents to link my East London ancestors with the 1880s dock strike or to indicate political agitation for weavers' jobs; indeed there are no traces to link them with either conventionally defined significant local or national events. No close male relative died in the trenches of the First World War nor in the Normandy landings in the Second (indeed they conveniently managed to avoid direct participation in both of these wars); no one joined the Labour party (and certainly not the Communist party). These were lives conducted off-centre-stage in the margins, of what has been seen, even by progressive historians, as the sidelines of history. Social historians of the 1970s insisted that the lives of working-class people like my parents, or grandparents and great-grandparents and their parents, covering in my case a traced time of a mere 200 years (a mixture of late breeders and long livers), were hidden from history.[7] History as a set body of knowledge existed but there were omissions;

the lives of working-class men and women were – they said – ignored, often because of historical indifference or because of who wrote history. Minute books of union branches, diaries of working men and women were found and used;[8] interviews were conducted in the 1960s and 1970s with those who had been born as the nineteenth century had turned into the twentieth.[9] Emphasis was placed on the value of the spoken word, its alleged authenticity, its warmth and character, for the history of working-class lives.[10] There was an assumption that working-class people spoke, perhaps more truthfully, more engagingly, than the middle class who preferred to convey their life experiences by the written word.

But less attention was given to the places in which people lived, the things people possessed from the past and valued, items which were personal but reflected broader times. When one elderly man, for example, in Wilmott and Young's famous study, *Family and Kinship in East London*, proffered papers of his family's past this was treated quite casually: '[He] brought out an old paper written in somewhat strange French in the year of the Revolution, which as far as could be made out was a petition from a man who was his ancestor beseeching the Governors of the French Hospital in Hackney to employ his grand-daughter.'[11] In such times histories were written of big – and certain – events: *The Making of the English Working Class*; *Hidden from History: 300 Years of Women's Oppression and the Fight against It*; *The Voice of the Past*.[12] The definite article, 'the', reflected the grand narratives and optimistic overview of working-class activity facilitated by the contemporary politics of those years of radical campaigns. The political world we live in now has changed; so have the concerns of historians. There has been a reaction to the positive broad sweep of class action or socialist-feminist tales. No longer are the Luddite croppers, the obsolete handloom weavers and followers of religious utopian Joanna Southcott being rescued from the enormous condescension of posterity, as E. P. Thompson first described it some forty years ago.[13] The experience of surviving through times of acute social disturbances and of trying to change the world now attracts little interest in, at least, mainstream history. Indeed, the idea of experience itself has often been debunked.

[. . .]

In contrast to admittedly difficult attempts to explore how past experience might be seen in the present, a slippery elision has instead seemed to develop between the knowledge of the impossibility of ever being able to re-create the past 'as it really was' and the idea that the past is of no relevance to the present. Keith Jenkins argues this position in his *Refiguring History*:

> The past contains nothing of intrinsic value, nothing we *have* to be loyal to, no facts we *have* to find, no truths we *have* to respect, no problems we *have* to solve, no projects we *have* to complete (original emphases). . .[14]

Jenkins is, quite rightly, criticising the conventional view of an historian seeking 'truth' and 'objectivity' whilst refusing to acknowledge the role of the historian herself in the making of history. However his approach begs the question, Why bother writing history? And, needless to say, Keith Jenkins doesn't. Although he has written a number of thought-provoking works on the nature of history he does not even attempt in practical ways to create a different sort of writing about previous times. The past, experience, the existence of everyday lives have become utterly irrelevant – at least to writers of this outlook in their professional work.

My history

[. . .] I want to argue that while it is impossible to recreate the past as it really was we can nevertheless create meaning, understanding and, even, interest by drawing on the substance of past lives. The idea of 'materials', however, is also controversial. Writing in very different ways from Keith Jenkins, Richard Evans, who [. . .] acted as an expert defence witness in the libel case brought by David Irving,[15] has declared, 'Argument between historians is limited by what the evidence allows them to say.' Evans treats the reader to a metaphorical comparison of historians acting like figurative painters sitting around a mountain, painting it in different lights or angles. However they paint, they will all be painting the same mountain. 'The possibilities of legitimate disagreement and variation are limited by the evidence in front of their eyes.'[16] Of course, documents should not be deliberately falsified (nor erroneously translated),[17] but Evans's argument assumes that there is a consensus amongst historians about what 'evidence' is. This, I suggest, is not a given. To notice that there may be traces of earlier lives in a cubby hole in a council flat in Debden also requires a recognition that such lives may be constructed by material other than material written by the state, philanthropists, or do-gooders. However, those who use artefacts other than that found in official archives are by no means dominant amongst historians.

Here I use material that exists inside – and outside – archives, in the local streets of the present, in graveyards and cemeteries, souvenirs and trinkets, photos and maps, memories and stories. In doing so I am not trying the impossible task of re-constructing the past 'as it really was', but rather, as cultural commentator and activist Walter Benjamin described, to attempt to bring the past into the present, 'The true method of making things present is to represent them in our space, not to represent ourselves in their space . . . we don't displace our being into theirs; they step into our life.'[18] The traces that I draw on to write the stories here are, in some senses, about my family but they are also part of broader cultural and social histories. When I teach courses on public history or writing family history I am always engaged and fascinated by the ephemera, the traces of former lives that students choose to bring to class: a sailor's embroidered picture from the early nineteenth century, a saying 'all fur coat and no knickers', a photograph which evokes sad memories. Inevitably, the rest of the group can relate to these apparently personal materials because of the social, and shared, nature of the way in which historical and cultural knowledge is created. Those who bring such material to history classes have chosen what to bring; what is written in this book is what I have chosen to write. The materials make it possible, provide the basis, the underpinning, but the written history is that which an historian attempts to create.

My family history – and family historians

This [writing is] about a past characterised by traced and traceable ephemera, an archaeology of lives lived in particular places and spaces, but a history that is being written in twenty-first century London. The 'protagonists' lived amidst the distressed weaving of early nineteenth-century Bethnal Green, the furniture trade in Shoreditch in the late 1800s and early 1900s, the workhouse in Hackney, the lunatic asylum in Surrey, farmlands in Shropshire, the brickfields in Kent, the home for inebriates in Norfolk, the London Electricity Board (LEB) and the Inner London Education Authority (ILEA). Attached to the chairs, bricks, graves, ornaments and photographs are stories; in the state records of the census of birth, marriage and death certificates are narratives of a different sort. By using them in the context of this [writing] of the twenty-first century there will be further narratives, other types of stories. This history, then, is itself a story of the process of creating past lives for present times. These are lives which were ordinary enough, mapped out against the routine of everyday existence: a getting by, a pulling through, of things not being what they might have been, of wanting them to have been better. In these stories there are traces of living on a peculiar sort of margin never in the worst slums but next to them, teetering on the edges of respectability, but, for the most part, remaining the right side of upright. They are lives that can be constructed because of the traces that still remain.

For some, the nineteenth century was a time of imperialist expansion and emigration, of possibilities in other lands or even other towns or suburbs. While others travelled thousands of miles to look for a new life, mostly my paternal family stayed put, not exactly stationary but moving in circles, in a radius of a few miles round and round the streets of East London, particularly Bethnal Green and Hackney. I currently live a 30-minute walk away from where Esther, my grandfather's grandmother, lived. Unknowingly I used to drive down her street every day taking the short cut to Tower Bridge, crossing the river southwards for work. I'm not sure Esther and I would have much in common if we were to meet in some East London form of Aboriginal dreamtime. But we would share a knowledge of the same geographical area; although our lives are very different and separated by nearly 200 years we have in common a place, a place which has changed, but a place which physically still exists. It is against this physical – and metaphorical – space of London and the south of England that I am seeking to create a contemporary map for the lives of these people.

The self and history

What is it that we are doing, those of us who, as John Aubrey the antiquarian put it, go 'grubbing in churchyards',[19] rummaging in the archives or hoarding inherited photographs? Are we looking for a past, searching for an elusive fragment which will help us in detective-like mode to give us an answer about a different time? Or are we trying to use this material to create a particular present and imagine a future? As Raphael Samuel suggested:

> If history is an arena for the projection of ideal selves, it can also be a means of undoing and questioning them, offering more disturbing accounts of who we are and where we come from than simple identifications would suggest.[20]

Certainly the absorption in the activity and the engagement with the bald material of 'family history' surpasses many of the practices of the scholars in the British Library. Unlike the British Library, which rations its books, especially during the summer when scholars really do want to read them, the materials in the Family Records Centre* are readily available: no rationing here – and helpful staff. This is the heart of 'non-academic' research into past families today in England and Wales. As the repository of records of births, deaths and marriages since 1837 and full census returns from 1841 to 1901, the Family Records Centre is an exemplar of autodidacticism. In the Family Records Centre in Finsbury there is not just the activity of reading but simultaneous interpretation: the details of the family or street found in the census need to be picked over, usually at that very moment, to ascertain whether it is indeed the 'correct' one. In contrast to an academic reading intent on garnering as rich sources as possible, which, in the case of social and cultural historians, might mean nice stories, plentiful anecdotes, new sidelines, or, rarely nowadays, grand overviews – the family historian while relishing material is also looking very explicitly for only certain information. The social historian might scrutinise the war memorial in the Hadlow church outside Tonbridge for 1914–19, looking at the numbers of young male dead and considering how many of the families in the small village lost a son, brother or father; the family historian might note the name of only one, either to be pursued as a son of another scion of the family or be discarded as the 'wrong one'.

Some might reject the work of the family historian as a form of regressive train spotting, simply filling in the boxes in the genealogical tree. Certainly some of the material is precise, but family history is a much less 'objective' practice than it first seems. Family historians, like those working in other historical fields are, whether they necessarily realise this or not, privileging the role of the historian as a maker of narrative. Tim Brennan has characterised this approach as one which jettisons modernist views of an unfolding historical process, 'in favour of a more internalised and intersubjective invention of the past'.[21] The historian of family – like the conventional historian – is not recording every detail, every piece of material, but only the ones which fit their purpose. There is indeed the fascination with the illusion of apparently 'discovering' what isn't known, to use this as a source of imagination. Some are looking in a vague way for a wider family, others for an educational hobby, some for filling in the gaps in family stories. Some seek the fantasy of connection with someone in the past in not dissimilar vein to the excitement expressed by Studs Terkel meeting Bertrand Russell and 'shaking the hand of the man who shook the hand of the man who shook the hand of Napoleon',[22] or as an historian of British homosexuality has described in wittier ways, 'I once kissed a man who'd once been kissed by Lord Alfred Douglas . . . a man now in his forties is thus only two pecks away from Oscar Wilde.'[23]

Traces of stories do already exist in census records, birth, marriage and death certificates, ledgers of the lunatic asylum and workhouse minute books. But such fragments are also re-fashioned through their juxtaposition in the present. . . .

[. . .]

My immediate family and their predecessors covered with silence the difficulties, the pain of uncomfortable realities; they did not talk about them. Thus many of the starting points for my own exploration have been based on physical materiality, a material culture which does exist, and which is being pursued by those engaged creatively in museum, anthropological and cultural studies as well as those researching their own families' lives.[24]

[. . .]

The fragments of materials I use are connected to me through a notion of family: the gravestone inscription, 'I waited patiently for the Lord and he inclined unto me and heard my cry'; the strange photograph of a mother's son posting a letter; the certificate exempting his daughter from vaccination against smallpox; fashioned stools and turned candlesticks; the memory of desert islands on the kitchen windowsill, fluttering palms created from carrot tops.

The bits and pieces of personal lives can also be the subject matter of public histories, histories created outside university rooms and libraries that emphasise the engagement with history now:

> Public history can act as an umbrella, under which the historical mind can be brought to bear on areas of research and thought which are often seen as mutually exclusive . . . it relies on a collective and collaborative effort of people working in different fields. This very process, of itself, helps to avoid academic navel gazing.[25]

[. . .]

These pages contain London stories; they are stories of personal lives but in the process of their construction they have also become part of a broader public history.

Graveyards and Bricks in Kent: The Mankelows

Graveyards in the heat

. . . [It] was time to explore nearer London, to seek out traces of ancestors of my mother's father. It was summer and proved to be the hottest day of the year so far. In hindsight the heat of 80+ had not been the ideal weather in which to trek up a steep hill to a Kent church in the vague hope of finding dead Mankelows. Earlier in the day I had already visited two churchyards in Pembury, further south along the Maidstone Road, since this village had featured in the family's eighteenth-century itinerary. In the old church of St Peter, Pembury, there had been the opportunity to photograph the grave of engineer and Liberal MP Sir Morton Peto, the first Non-Conformist to be buried in Anglican ground,[1] and the unusual gravestone image of the New Testament story of Mary and Joseph's flight into Egypt I'd read about previously; but there had been no grave of any Mankelow – however one spelt the maternal surname. I had also been unlucky in the graveyard of the church of the Holy Trinity in nearby East Peckham. Perhaps this walk to a disused church would prove to be another false trail, caused by wandering in places I did not know.

Fortunately, the woman in the supermarket where I'd replenished my bottled water pointed me in the direction of the other, older, church, St Michael in East Peckham, while warning me about the uphill walk. But, she advised, it was worth it: although the church itself was closed (and now run by the Churches Conservation Trust) it was a good visit and she had enjoyed it on the annual open weekend. This church was clearly a local landmark, as the owner of the garden centre subsequently confirmed when I lost my way. He too had researched the history of his family and was happy to point me in the right direction (together with four plants for the pond).

The ascent from the hamlet of a few houses, the former centre of the East Peckham village before it had translocated into the valley floor, was not unpleasant but tiring in the 80s heat, reminiscent of walks in the Apennines rather than rambles in the Home Counties. In the shimmering afternoon heat the view too was almost northern Italian. From the summit of the hill I could see parcels of fields and villages in the distance faded by the sun: Hadlow with the distinctive landmark of the castle folly; Pembury, where I'd started the day; and the newer settlement of East Peckham, with its supermarket, down the hill. Hidden from view by the ancient pines, to the north east, would be my last destination of the day, Yalding, a confluence of the Medway, Beult and Teise rivers.

These villages I had noted had not been selected randomly in my panorama but ones I had known existed because of my – and others' – digging in the records. My mother's paternal family had lived in this part of western Kent, on the borders with Sussex, for over 350 years from the 1650s – and some still lived nearby and had researched the family's long history in the area. William Mackello had been born in Pembury in 1658; his married life took place where his children were raised, further east in Yalding, a settlement recorded in the Domesday book.[2] Subsequent generations had moved via East Peckham and Yalding to Hadlow where in 1795 my great-great-grandfather, also called William, but now with a surname spelt Mankelow, was born.

The summary here of names, places, and years, in just a few sentences does not reflect, of course, the years of collective effort it has taken to unravel the basic genealogy; a result of my own efforts and of others researching the same family and those met when, as John Aubrey the antiquarian put it, I go 'grubbing in churchyards'.[3] Here, those who prefer family history as a day-out-in-the-countryside to being stuck in front of a computer screen, might find words on a stone which chronicle a lifespan. Often the gravestone might describe familial status and, sometimes, the nature of the individual's work or the esteem in which they were held. At most there might be words enough to suggest elements from which a researcher might make a history for the present. The complex of symbols – names, dates, relationships – certainly suggests material for the making of family stories. As Hayden White, an historical philosopher has suggested, we place value on story-telling in the representation of real events, 'out of a desire to have real events display the coherence, integrity, fullness, and closure of an image of life that is . . . imaginary'.[4] And on this hot July day this was what I had been attempting to do: find material for my story.

However, the helpful woman in the supermarket had been wrong: it would have been possible to drive to the lychgate of the churchyard and park – and cars were already there. Within the ancient burial place surrounded by trees, many of which were even older than the graves, there was the sound of an electric lawn mower and a hot, excited, dog. A young man naked to the waist emerged from behind the closed church apologising for his state of undress to this solitary, middle-aged woman swathed in clothing, sensible hat and barrier suncream. The man was not, he was at pains to explain, the regular gardener, but he was, it was clear, someone who knew the nearby land in particular ways. He had local knowledge of the landmarks which he shared with me: the folly at Hadlow owned, he said, by a German who made porn movies; the village of East Peckham which had itself translocated and grown, down in the valley; and the course of the river, which he picked out amidst the trees. The contours of the land, the Weald and the Downs, were a framework for his visualisation of this locality that I, as a Londoner and driver, tended to see through the A21 and A26 roads that skirted the Sussex and Kent borders. From the vantage point of high ground and seeing the villages I had read about through the unofficial gardener's eyes, the land seemed different. The distance between Hadlow, Peckham and Yalding was small if they were seen in relation to the Medway river. The movement of the Mankelows between villages, I could now see, made a different sense. Over generations they had followed the course of the river to new villages, a traversing of the river valley now seemed logical and coherent in a way that merely plotting data from documents had not.[5]

In his recent book on graveyards, Mark Taylor has argued that what one thinks is deeply conditioned by where one thinks – and certainly standing on the top of a hill provided a different perspective to poring over a map.[6] A conventional historian is thought to know about things 'because you have been there', there being an archive.[7] But 'being there' can also mean being here in the present, in actually existing places in the contemporary landscape, where objects created in the past can transcend time and be with us here in the present. Landscapes created centuries ago remain visible today, at least in traces, if we have the eyes to see it.[8] Unlike a so-called objective historian, who seeks to engage in a supposedly unmediated way directly with the archive, family history research also seeks to involve others in an exploration and construction of a past. In contrast to the solitary note-taking observed in the British Library, many visitors to the Family Records Centre are accompanied by a spouse, partner or elderly mother who is prodded to remember family stories, to guess ages or places, to hypothesise about the apparent disappearance of an ancestor from the registers. Others choose to make contact with researchers through the Rootsweb website or regional family history groups, posting questions on internet message boards – and receiving answers.[9] And here in the graveyard of St Michael's in East Peckham this social construction of historical knowledge, as historian Raphael Samuel would describe such a process, involved discussing the landscape and exploring the movement of people with a sweating young man and his hot dog.

The headstones at St Michael's were interesting – I'd guessed that before I'd visited from a book outlining some striking examples.[10] An initial walk through the yet-to-be-mown-grass revealed lovely angels, skulls acting as *memento mori*, an hourglass with shifting sand and a horse bending its head in grief, but not, at least not in this hot wandering, any ancestral graves. A subsequent, cooler, September visit would confirm the absence of Mankelow graves. My family's connection with the place may have been confined to a happier occasion – the wedding in 1794 of John Manktelow, the great-grandson of William Mackello, and father of William Mankelow, before his move to Hadlow. This seemed, then, a landscape through which they had passed rather than one that suggested the permanence of settlement associated with death and family gravestones.

Gravestones in Hadlow

Wandering around in St Mary's church Hadlow, near Tonbridge, some years before, on the first occasion I had gone looking for dead Mankelows in Kent, it had been different. The impetus for that visit had been my mother's recollection that the family of her father, Fred Mankelow, had come from there, although she had never visited the place nor known his parents nor, indeed, any of his family. Before that visit I had never been to this part of Kent. Although, as a child, I'd spent most summer holidays in Kent, or the 'garden of England' as my parents told me, this was usually in Broadstairs. The environs of Tonbridge had never been on our itinerary in those times – our own mapping and travelling through Kent had been very different.

These had been the first of 'my' dead people who I had supposedly 'found', recorded on a gravestone, and I had the emotional illusion that the discovery was itself significant. Although it was not the case that there was new knowledge here as such about the Mankelows, in an analogous way to that described by Victor Seidler holding in his hand the notarial deed outlining what happened to one of his uncles shot by the Nazis in Warsaw, 'The materiality of the document somehow helped me feel the reality of what had happened.'[11] It gave an additional meaning to previous researches. For me, being in this place, Hadlow, was a way of reconfiguring fragments of the past in the present and making more of them than simply words on a microfilmed parish register.[12]

Surrounding the Hadlow church of St Mary's is a closed churchyard. As Hilary Lees has explained, a churchyard, as opposed to a cemetery, has the feeling of antiquity, indeed many stand on prehistoric sites predating the churches they surround.[13] As this headstone was the first gravestone I had 'found' belonging to an ancestor it seemed important to commemorate the discovery in a visual image. I needed to create an additional layer of permanence and record, perhaps to confirm to myself that I had, at last, found 'something tangible'. But on the first occasion it was too dark to photograph the gravestone clearly, so further visits became inevitable.

The stone had first been erected to remember Mary Mankelow, nee Hayward, born in the last year of the eighteenth century, who had died aged 60 in August 1859. *Morbus cordis* the death certificate had declared – Latin for straightforward heart disease. Under her name was recorded that of 73-year-old William, her husband of nearly 40 years, who had survived his wife by a decade. The brick-maker and farmer had, his death certificate declared (in English), passed away due to 'general decay'. The stone itself had also suffered decay in the intervening 140 years and it was difficult to read the inscription clearly. Although the names of her seven surviving adult children were listed,[14] the quote from Psalms 40 was more weathered: 'I waited patiently for the Lord and he inclined unto me and heard my cry.'

The sentiment expressed on the stone was different from the warning I would see on an 1840s stone in Pembury, 'Learn to die'; in contrast a different sort of homily was being offered to visitors here, which may have been deliberate. In a rural churchyard manual of 1851, Kelke had specifically advocated the inclusion of a biblical text so that stones themselves could become an effective medium of conveying religious instruction and improvement.

Texts from the Psalms were particularly recommended for those suffering from a long illness (however, unfortunately, he does not cite this one). He also suggested the motif of assuming the character of a voice from the tomb. Thus, he continued, there could be a permanent lesson with gravestones 'perpetually teaching from generation to generation'.[15] In some ways he was proved to be right, although teaching family historians about facts in their ancestors' past was surely not what he had in mind. For those like Mary Mankelow, who in life was illiterate,[16] there was a particular sort of transformation in death. Her 'voice' became both articulate and literate, and one that still remained in the landscape of her native village nearly one and a half centuries after her death. As Jacques Ranciere has analysed, 'The availability of writing – of the "mute" letter – endows any life, or the life of anybody, with the capacity of taking on meaning, of entering into the universe of meaning.'[17]

At one time the stone would have provided a recording, in the then present, of former lives known to those who had erected the stone; but, as Mark Taylor has suggested, 'a graveyard is where we keep the dead *alive as dead* [original emphasis].'[18] I cannot 'remember' a person, outside the public domain, whom I never knew. But churchyards themselves are embodiments of memory; they are places which make explicit the passing of time. Now it is the grave itself that is 'remembered' and which I photograph, making this new artefact a conduit of meaning.[19] In the materiality of the stone the past connects with the present; it remembers for me someone I do not know. There is no relative either I, or my mother, would have ever known who knew the woman that this stone remembers. However, by its very existence the gravestone suggests that once there was a woman who did indeed exist – and one who should be remembered and commemorated. It also suggests that a story can be told in the present.

The last verse of the chapter of the Psalms used on Mary's gravestone defined the psalmist thus, 'I am poor and needy; yet the Lord thinketh upon me.' However, by local standards, these Mankelows were neither poor nor needy; after all, they had money for the headstone and jobs which would sustain them throughout the year. William Mankelow, Mary's husband, had worked as a brickmaker, and farmer, and from the 1820s developed a carrier business, running a daily service transporting goods – and people – to and from Tonbridge. Their oldest son, also called William, would join his father, in the carrier business, moving, eventually to London and taking a younger brother, Thomas, my great-grandfather with him. Other children had continued working on the land or as a dressmaker or carrying goods. The men, at least, were of sufficient status to be mentioned as those with trades worth recording in the local directories.

Although I was pleased to have found my 'first' ancestral gravestone even I realised that this was neither the most interesting nor important stone in the churchyard. The commemoration of this death was indeed a small moment compared to the bigger event recalled in the far corner of the churchyard in the shade. Here was an obelisk dating from October 1853 commemorating 30 migrant hop pickers – from London – drowned when the horse and cart capsized on a nearby bridge while taking them back to their campsite near Tudeley, known today as the only church in England which possesses a stained-glass work by Marc Chagall. For me this has personal resonances too, for this was the church where James Mancktelow, the grandfather of William and Mary Mankelow, had married Ann Richards from Yalding in 1767. Hop picking was labour intensive and much of the harvest was carried out by women and children from London, or Ireland, who came down for the summer work and some sort of holiday, returning every year to work for the same farmer.[20] Hop pickers were often criticised for excessive drinking or petty theft and there are also stories of their supposed extravagance. As a local woman commented on the hop pickers' penchant for buying flowers to take back home, 'We told them time and time again that chrysanthemums would travel better, last longer, but they loved the brilliance of the dahlias.'[21] Local residents had testified to the inquest that they had complained about the poor state of the bridge for many years and the jury returned the verdict of accidental drowning entirely due to the defective state of the bridge. The dead included 16 members of one family.[22]

This event was bigger and locally more important, as befitted the size of the memorial stone, than the lives I was tracing in the same graveyard. In the normal course of events those who picked hops would have been unlikely to be able to afford to commemorate in stone those relatives who died of natural causes.[23] Rupture and disaster had given these transient hop pickers a permanent place in the Kent landscape. In contrast to a time of movement or even migration for work the hop pickers' memorial is about a specific time and place, a moment which changes the course of the London hop pickers' lives.[24] In contrast to the Mankelow stone, this was not a commemoration enacted by, or for, the families of the dead – in several instances whole families from babies to grandparents had perished and there were none left to remember in this way. Rather it was a way of a community recording an event out of the ordinary in their own locality, creating a mark on the local landscape of an important occasion.[25] This recording of names was not the same as those on the gravestone of the wife of the brickmaker; there was no encouraging verse from the Psalms here. The obelisk was not to a single (nor related) family but – confronting the norm – to 30 individuals buried together in one grave on successive days united in death because of their work, rather than familial bonds.[26]

I do not know whether the event in October 1853 or the subsequent erection of the memorial impinged on the daily lives of the Mankelows. Did they carry on harvesting their hops? Did they make their bricks as usual? Did this bigger event affect their lives in any way?

. . . I cannot make a clear connection between the bigger event and 'my' Mankelows in 1850s Hadlow. In death, however, they share the same place of commemoration within the same village. Together – the hop pickers and the Mankelows – they have made a particular mark on the landscape.

Stones in Yalding

On the same hot July day in which I had seen the layout of the villages of the Medway with the eyes of another, I also visited the graveyard of St Peter and St Paul church in the village of Yalding – a place that had been dismissed by a gazetteer of 1834 as 'a place of little importance', declaring the church to be old 'with a square tower but [which] possesses nothing worthy of notice'.[27] My perception was rather different, for here to the left of the side path of the churchyard was a group of seven stones almost sheltering together near a side wall, and all sharing the same surname of Mankelow. In life these people had shared at least a common name through descent or through marriage.[28] But it was not just the common surname which suggested a closeness. The stones were of brothers and sisters, husbands and wives, cousins as well as those more distantly related. The gravestones' physical location in a distinct group almost suggested an emotional closeness and a particular sort of familial bond for which there are no other fragments or traces. The very material of the stone seemed to suggest an affective, human condition because of the juxtapositions of the graves.

However, it was not only the existence of graves which had linked the Mankelow family of the past with the present landscape. Some years before the research of this sweltering day, when I had returned to the Hadlow church in light good enough for a photograph, I met 'H', a local historian, who was explaining to visitors the history of the thirteenth-century church of St Mary.[29] As a local woman she had known descendants of the Mankelows in the graveyard; she told me about a bomb falling on their pub, a child who was disabled, and directed me to the Mankelows' land. 'H' also knew the name of another descendant of the buried

Mankelows. He too was researching his family history. She said she would contact him and then write to me once she had checked this with him. And this she did.

Bricks

'A' still lived locally, and I realised through our correspondence that we shared great-great grandparents in common, William and Mary Mankelow, who were buried in Hadlow – and, of course, an interest in history. 'A' is a careful researcher and has compiled detailed charts which trace back, as far as he can, the lineage of the Mankelows, emphasising the line which leads directly to him. The more recent family tree is recorded in a chart that has pride of place on his dining-room wall alongside the ancient pipes and objects which he and his wife have found at low tide in the Thames estuary on the north Kent coast. For several years he has collected material on the Mankelows including maps and photos, which he willingly shares. An aspect of his research is a means to an end, of getting back further in time. We meet and talk about our respective explorations; this confirms for me again that this isn't my main rationale. I don't want to go back into the past; I want the Mankelows to come forward into the present.

'A' possesses and values an annotated map inherited from William Mankelow's son, George (his great-grandfather), born in 1827, who had continued to work the land after one of his younger brothers, Thomas (my great-grandfather), had moved away. The framework of the map was the ownership and renting of land, rather than natural topography. It noted the different types of land used for hop gardens, orchards, cottages with gardens, roads, the processes for brick-making – kilns and faggot yard, pond and brickearth, brickyard – as well as a cricket field. Brick-making (like cricket) was a seasonal activity: brick earth dug in autumn was left over winter to be broken down by frosts before being fired in the spring and summer.[30] A source of fuel was needed for firing the bricks: hence the area, outlined on the map, set aside for faggots.[31] Conventionally brick-making was hard work needing unskilled and skilled labour, a trade learnt within a family.[32] Certainly some familial handing-down of skills can be surmised. In the 1700s, when based further south in Pembury, William Mankelow's father had worked as a collier, probably as a charcoal burner.[33] The Kent Weald had been famous for its use of wood in iron making and the first modern blast furnace in the area had been established in Tonbridge in the 1550s, ensuring that by the late sixteenth century the Tonbridge parish was an important focus for ironmaking in the Weald.[34] However, the overuse of timber had led to its lack of availability and, in turn, an increase in the price of charcoal: the owners closed down the works and many relocated to Aberdare and Merthyr Tydfil in Wales.[35] The Mankelows had not gone away. However, in order for them to remain in Kent, they themselves had needed to change their ways of earning a living.[36] Or, as Lampedusa, the author of *The Leopard*, phrased it more elegantly, 'In order for things to stay the same, things will have to change.'[37]

The Mankelows, who had come to Hadlow most recently from Yalding, stayed, working the brickfield, renting the land from some of the 2,400 acres owned by the local worthy Sir William Geary, the former attorney general in Accra on the then Gold Coast.[38] Staying – and not going – was a new feature of the Industrial Revolution. Previously, itinerant brick-makers had traversed the country testing the local clay and then working it until the building, for which the bricks and tiles were needed, was completed.[39] Locally, brick-making skills stretched back to the Tudors with the clay of the Weald maintaining an excellent reputation for producing some of the finest bricks available.[40] Some Kentish bricks were destined for London, the largest single market in the country, but most bricks fashioned around Tonbridge were for local use.[41] In 1836 alone there were over 5,700 brick-makers in England,[42] and Tonbridge itself boasted six.[43] The Mankelows' brick-making venture may have been successful. The brick tax, that had been introduced in 1784 to help pay for the wars with France, was repealed in 1850. This led to a general expansion of the industry,[44] which had been further assisted from the 1830s by the railway boom: a turnpike road over a railway, for example, would require 300,000 bricks.[45]

Hadlow Common where the Mankelow brickfield (and the cricket field) existed, was – and still is – part of rural Kent. As 'H', the Hadlow local historian, had indicated, although the cottages where William and Mary Mankelow and their children had spent their days were gone, the site of their former brickfield – with a local cricket pitch in front – was still here. According to 'A', who possessed not only documents but local knowledge, the present cricket field was a former large clay pit, that had been an integral part of the Mankelow business.[46] When 'A's' great-grandfather George had finished digging clay he had apparently filled it with faggots and seeded it to make the current cricket field. It was slightly lower, 'A' had observed, than the surrounding fields because of the rotting of the faggots over the years causing subsidence.[47] Neither the map of the landholdings nor my viewing of the land would have revealed this: the small changes in the landscape, that an outsider can neither know nor see, would only be observed by one who knew the place, who lived in the same place but in the present. As Raphael Samuel noted in an article published nearly 30 years ago, though still timely and relevant:

> Local history demands a different kind of knowledge than one which is focused on high-level national developments, and gives the researcher a much more immediate sense of the past. He meets it round the corner and down the street . . . [and can] follow its footprints in the fields.[48]

I can, however, at least in some way, interpret maps. The entire rented land as covered on 'A's' document was calculated as 'A r p – 21.0.13'. In those far gone 11-plus days we were taught to know what this meant (and forgot once the exams were over) but at least I know the initials stand for acre, rod and perch. This, I realised, was a bigger area than the 12-acre farm occupied by the Eickes on the Staffordshire/Shropshire borders (and considerably larger than the houses that Esther and William Keen inhabited in Bethnal Green). However, when I look at this document and the large-scale Ordnance Survey map of the same land I see shapes, possible buildings, but I have difficulty imagining people or signs of activity. Others see it differently. One of my MA students sees the Ordnance Survey map in other ways when I try out this writing on them for feedback. As a professional surveyor 'M' is able to calculate the size of the brick kilns, add up the square footage and estimate the numbers of people who could have worked there:

> There are some outbuildings so perhaps you could assume a maximum of 30 employees, not all there at the same time, including the manager. As the area had lots of these works and kilns, this may be an overestimate on numbers.

He apologises for not going back to research this more thoroughly in his office library but he does know, in a way I do not, that 'the various cricket fields are approximately two thirds of an acre and the measurements are in acres, rods and perches . . . a perch is a quarter of a chain . . . about five yards I think'.[49]

'A's' documents also suggested that the Mankelows grew hops. The local directory had stated that not only was Hadlow known for its clay and loam soil, but for its fruit, wheat and hops. Hadlow was seen as a brewery village and unsurprisingly William and Mary's son, George, developed beer-making as a sideline.[50] In its nineteenth-century heyday more than 330 of the 400 rural parishes in Kent boasted hop gardens.[51] But few hop fields remain today. In Yalding where an earlier generation of the Mankelows had lived and died there are still remnants of hop fields; and along the Maidstone Road, linking Pembury and East Peckham villages, tourists can pay for the 'experience' of a hop field with a hop garden country park. In 'A's' modern house on the outskirts of Tonbridge he points to the trees, at the back of the well-maintained garden, that formed the perimeter of the local hop fields of his childhood and on which his house and garden were built.

Brick-making, like hop farming, was part of an earlier Mankelow history. By the late 1800s brick-making had become a large-scale industry: publications such as the *Brick and Pottery Trades Diary*, published in the first years of the twentieth century, became primers of technology, gadgets, calculations and contract management.[52] This was a new age of steam and engines; bricks fashioned on the land were part of an earlier time. In the same way that the Eickes had carried on farming and the Keens weaving, the descendants of 'William and Mary Mankelow had continued the trade into the twentieth century with George's son, also called William, continuing to work as a brickmaker'.[53] George himself had kept the business going through diversification. As a flier in the possession of another Mankelow descendant asserts:

George Mankelow
Manufacturer of
Bricks, Tiles, Drain Pipes and Pottery
Hadlow Common
Tonbridge
Birch and Heath Brooms always on hand
Orders Respectfully Solicited[54]

But, these distant relatives advise me, the solicitation for work was not entirely successful. George, so the story goes, drank away the family's money.

Thomas the carrier: Moving through the landscape

On the gravestone in Hadlow churchyard had been listed some seven children of William and Mary. They included the eldest son, William, running the carrier business, George, of whom 'A' was the direct descendant, and Thomas, my great-grandfather born some 15 years after the first child, in March 1835. However, unlike his brother George, Thomas did not work on the land, but instead moved through it, delivering parcels. The seasonal nature of brick-making and hop farming alike did not provide sufficient income for survival throughout the year. As bricks tended to be used locally and the conveying of bricks was part of the production process, brick-makers often developed a sideline in transport.[55] For some this meant work as coal merchants, but the Mankelows developed a transport business delivering goods. Three of William's sons – William, Thomas and John – ran a daily carrier service for parcels, goods and people to and from Hadlow to Tonbridge.

[. . .]

Different histories of the same family

When I met 'A', a fellow researcher and distant relative, in his Tonbridge home I was slightly taken aback. He was older than me by some years and looked both like a long-dead aunt of mine and a man whose appearance I only knew from a photograph, my grandfather, Frederick Mankelow. I'd brought his photograph with me to display, in a sense, my credentials – to show that I was who I said I was, a descendant of the Mankelows – which would give me some sort of right to research the family, to ask questions of people I had never met, and to accept their kind hospitality. Such 'proof' of probity, of belonging to the same family, seems to carry far more weight with family history researchers than a printed business card outlining academic qualifications. You need to give 'proof' of your actual research, of the different ancestors you have tracked, the certificates you have accessed (and purchased), the census returns you have photocopied. Such ephemera indicates that you are no outsider to this form of historical practice and therefore able to be included within this particular community of researchers. I had a fantasy that 'A' being local, and rather older than me and thus closer to 'the past', could tell me 'what the Mankelows were like'. I found he could, indeed, understand the landscape differently but he could no more pronounce authentically on their inner lives, or on 'what the past was really like', than I could. However, I did relish the anecdote, the personal snippets and note that the Mankelows he knew 'were Tories and drinkers' in contrast to my Liberal and abstemious grandfather, Frederick Mankelow.

I am not sure that 'A' and I are looking for the same things, nor that we are looking for them in the same way. 'A' scrutinises the documents, especially during a wet winter; I prefer the outdoors, the artefacts, the places – history as a day out away from London. Nor are we particularly interested in the same line of the family – at least from the 1830s when our respective great-grandfathers were born – but we continue to exchange material. It is through 'A' that I meet 'B', one of his cousins, who, he recalls, has a quantity of photographs handed to her many years before by an old aunt. Noting that the addresses of the photographers on the back included Chelsea and other London addresses, and remembering my interests in the Mankelow carriers who had moved to that part of London, 'A' suggests a possible connection worth pursuing.

'B', a founder member of her local history society in East Anglia, also has her own interests. She describes herself as having 'a passionate interest in history', and when she replies to my initial letter she explains that we are second cousins once removed, 'It's lovely having a relative one didn't know one had.' She is interested in the census returns for the village in which she now lives, which are difficult to access there and in due course I forward photocopies of the microfilm in the Family Records Centre. She is also hoping that I might be able to help her discover more about a mystery woman from her childhood past: a Lucy Jones who visited her family in Hadlow and arrived by motor cycle from Portsmouth and was either married to (or the daughter of) a ship's engineer. But despite our mutual interest in completing a puzzle of a common past neither of us can join together these places, these names, these stories. Although we appear to have parts of the same jigsaw that does not apparently fit we realise that what we do have in common is a knowledge of London and a love of Benjamin Britten's operas. As a young woman 'B' had queued all night for seats for *Peter Grimes* when it was first performed at Sadler's Wells on 7 June 1945 and we find ourselves talking enthusiastically about recent Britten productions.[56]

I was more optimistic than 'B' about her photos, passed on to her from another relative. Neither she nor 'A' had recognised any of the people or the places. She viewed my hypothesis that these could be part of the Mankelow family who moved to Chelsea to work as carriers extremely sceptically (although she was generously prepared to photocopy me both the images and backs of the cards which displayed the names of the photographers). 'No', she pronounced authoritatively, as we looked through them in turn – 'they don't look like Mankelows.' As 'B' suggests, I do realise intellectually that these unlabelled and unnamed images could, of course, be of anyone; however, I do not want them to be thus. I want them to have a connection, to contribute to meaning, to help explain a move from Kent into London. I speculate on who the people might be, the common aspects of their features, the locations of the photographers. I consult the post office directories for the names of photographers in London to correlate obsessively the dates of the photographers' businesses with Thomas Mankelow's move to Chelsea. I want to make the images fit to 'my' Mankelows, my story. And certainly there were matches between the locations of photographers and the streets in which Thomas lived. I showed the photo that I wanted to be Thomas and his son to my mother and my aunt Lily in the vain hope that they might have seen a similar image when they were children – and had remembered this. But it meant nothing to them; it was just an old-fashioned photo. Notwithstanding the fact that the child in the picture is in a dress, I recalled that both boys and girls wore similar clothes when very young and hoped – without substance – to convince myself that this was indeed my maternal grandfather Thomas, with his baby son, Frederick.[57] But, I cannot make such connections with my photographs, however much I might desire it; the material just is not there. 'B' is right: I cannot achieve such a knowingness any more than she can make connections with a mysterious Miss Jones on a bike.

[. . .]

Notes

Collecting material

*   Now closed down
1   Elizabeth Hallam and Jenny Hockey, *Death, Memory and Material Culture*, Oxford, 2001, p119.
2   Sally J. Morgan, 'My father's photographs: the visual as public history', in Hilda Kean, Paul Martin and Sally J. Morgan (eds.), *Seeing History. Public History in Britain Now*, London, 2000, pp33–34.
3   Ludmilla Jordanova, *History in Practice*, London, 2000, p102.
4   The Trefoil Guild is the organisation of retired girl guides. Toc H was an ecumenical movement founded in the First World War to provide social activities for servicemen; it continues as a social, philanthropic organisation.
5   A contemporary review had described the thousands who thronged the Ideal Home Exhibition: 'many are still looking eagerly for a home, not so much an ideal home, but any sort of home'. Deborah S. Ryan, *The Ideal Home through the 20th century*, 1997, p92.
6   Tim Brennan, 'History, family, history,' in Kean, Martin, Morgan, *Seeing History*, 2000, p48.
7   Classically Sheila Rowbotham, *Hidden from History*, Pluto 1973, and the early issues of *History Workshop Journal*, 1976 ff.
8   See pamphlets issued by Ruskin History Workshop, for example, Bob Gilding, *The Journeyman Coopers of East London*, Oxford, n.d.; Raphael Samuel (ed.), *History Workshop. A Collectanea 1967–1991*,Oxford, 1991; David Englander (ed.), *The Diary of Fred Knee*, Society for Labour History, 1977; John Burnett (ed.) *Useful Toil*, 1971, reissued Harmondsworth, 1984.
9   Notable examples are Paul Thompson, *The Edwardians. The Re-making of British Society*, St Albans, 1977; the work of the London History Workshop as discussed in Samuel, *History Workshop. A Collectanea*, 1991; Raphael Samuel, *East End Underworld. Chapters in the Life of Arthur Harding*, London, 1981.
10 It must be acknowledged that such views have been challenged in the more recent past and Paul Thompson, for example, has re-evaluated his earlier approach.
11 Michael Young and Peter Willmott, *Family and Kinship in East London*, Harmondsworth, revised ed., 1962, p114.
12 E. P.Thompson, *The Making of the English Working Class*, Harmondsworth, 1963; Sheila Rowbotham, *Hidden from History: 300 Years of Women's Oppression and the Fight Against It*, London, 1973; Paul Thompson, *The Voice of the Past: Oral History*, first edition, London, 1978.
13 Thompson, *The Making of the English Working Class*, p12.
14 Keith Jenkins, *Refiguring History. New Thoughts on an Old Discipline*, London, 2003, p29.
15 Described as such by, inter alia, Verso Books, the publisher of Richard Evans's book *Telling Lies about Hitler: The Holocaust, History and the David Irving Trial*, London, 2002.
16 Evans, *Telling Lies about Hitler*, 2002, p257.
17 He rightly accuses Irving of doing this in *Telling Lies about Hitler*.
18 Walter Benjamin (translated by Howard Eiland and Kevin McLaughlin), *The Arcades Project*, Harvard, 2002, p206.

19   As quoted in Hilary Lees, *English Churchyard Memorials*, Stroud, 2000 p11.

20   Raphael Samuel, *Island Stories*, London, 1998, pp222–23.

21   Brennan, 'History, family, history,' in Kean, Martin, Morgan, *Seeing History*, 2000, p49.

22   Joanna Bornat, 'Oral history as a social movement', in Robert Parkes and Alastair Thomson, *Oral History Reader*, London, p191.

23   Hugh David, *On Queer Street: A Social History of British Homosexuality 1895–1995*, London, 1997, pix.

24   Paul Martin, *Popular Collecting and the Everyday Self. The Reinvention of Museums?*, Leicester, 1999; Susan Pearce, *Collecting in Contemporary Practice*, London, 1998.

25   Introduction, Kean, Martin, Morgan, (eds.), *Seeing History*, p13.

Graveyards and Bricks in Kent: The Mankelows

1   Sir Samuel Morton Peto 1809–89. Baptist, Liberal MP for Norwich 1847–54, Finsbury 1859–65, Bristol 1865–68. He was partly responsible for building the Houses of Parliament and for constructing a large part of the south eastern railway between Folkestone and Hythe, *Dictionary of National Biography*. See also Deborah Wiggins, 'The Burial Act of 1880', *Parliamentary History* 15:2, 1996.

2   Arthur Hussey, *Notes on the churches in the counties of Kent, Sussex and Surrey*, London, 1852, p169.

3   As quoted in Lees, *English Churchyard Memorials*, p11.

4   Hayden White, *The Content of the Form: Narrative Discourse and Historical Representation*, Baltimore, 1990, p24.

5   The landscape of the nineteenth century remains at least visible to this day in traces. Walter Benjamin, *The Arcades Project* (translated Howard Eiland and Kevin McLaughlin), London, 2002, p478.

6   Mark Taylor and Dietrich Christian Lammerts, *Grave Matters*, London, 2002, p40.

7   Steedman, *Dust*, p145.

8   Doreen Massey, 'Places and their Pasts', *History Workshop Journal*, 39, 1995, pl83ff.

9   www.rootsweb.com.

10   Lees, *English Churchyard Memorials*.

11   Victor Jeleniewski Seidler, *Shadows of the Shoah. Jewish Identity and Belonging*, Oxford, 2000, pp32–33.

12   Michael P. Steinberg, *Walter Benjamin and the Demands of History*, New York, 1996, p66.

13   Lees, *English Churchyard Memorials*, pp12, 21.

14   Only one child had died in infancy, namely, John, born 12 June 1825, who had died 1 July 1828. Those surviving to adulthood were William, Sarah Ann, George, Henry, Jonathan, Thomas and Eliza Jane. Information from Arthur Mankelow and also Hadlow parish registers, Kent County Council archives, Maidstone.

15   William Hastings Kelke, *The Churchyard Manual Chiefly Intended for Rural Districts*, London, 1851, pp59–60, 63, 103.

16   William Mankelow signed his name; Mary Hayward gave her mark. Marriage record, Hadlow parish, 29 February 1820, in Kent County Council archives, Maidstone.

17   Jacques Ranciere, 'The Archaeomodern Turn', in Steinberg, *Walter Benjamin and the Demands of History*, p29.

18   Taylor and Lammerts, *Grave Matters*, p23.

19   Jetter Sandahl, 'Proper objects among other things', *Nordisk Museologi*, 1995:2, pp97–106, as translated into English on website (visited 26 February 2002): www.umu.se/nordic.museology/ NM952/Sandahl.html. Thanks to Paul Martin for this reference.

20   They were also often the indigent inhabitants of the casual wards of workhouses. Raphael Samuel, 'Comers and Goers', in eds. H. J. Dyos and Michael Wolff, *The Victorian City. Images and Realities*, vol.1, *Past and Present/Numbers of People*, London, 1976, pp138–39; Taylor and Lammerts, *Grave Matters*, p20.

21   Michael J. Winstanley, *Life in Kent at the Turn of the Century*, Folkestone, 1978, pp79, 82, 85.

22   Ann Hughes, *Hop Pickers' Memorial*, Hadlow, n.d.

23   Raphael Samuel, 'Comers and Goers', pp138–39.

24   Ibid.

25   A similar example concerning Pegswood colliery, Northumbria, is discussed in Jack Halliday, 'The Land of Lost Content. The Life and Death of a Mining Village', Certhe dissertation, Ruskin College, Oxford, 1999.

26   Hughes, *Hop Pickers' Memorial*, Hadlow, n.d.

27   T. Collings, *A New and Complete History of the County of Kent*, London, 1834, p134.

28   In the case of Ann Richards through marriage. Most of the inscriptions are difficult to read, however it is clear that one is of Ann, who died 27 November 1830 aged 87(?) years. This would appear to be

the grave of Ann Mancktelow née Richards who was married to James Mancktelow grandson of William Mackello (b. 1658) and grandfather of William Mankelow born in Hadlow in 1795.The dates correspond with the dates of 1743–November 1830 on documents transcribed by Arthur Mankelow.

29   The west tower dates from the thirteenth century, though much restoration took place in the nineteenth century. John Newman, *West Kent and the Weald*, Buildings of England series, Harmondsworth, 1969, pp299–300.

30   Edward Dobson, *A Rudimentary Treatise on the Manufacture of Bricks and Tiles*, London, part 1, 1850, p21.

31   Ronald W. Brunskill, *Brick Building in Britain*, new ed., 1997, p18.

32   Molly Beswick, *Brickmaking in Sussex. A History and Gazetteer*, West Sussex, 1993, p76.

33   William Mankelow/Mackello born 1701 in Pembury. After his marriage to Mary Hills in Pembury he moved to East Malling/Pembury where he died in 1778. Thanks to Arthur Mankelow for this information.

34   By the early eighteenth century there were only three furnaces and one forge in Kent producing ordnance. Michael Zell, *Industry in the Countryside. Wealden Society in the Sixteenth Century*, Cambridge, 1994, pp126–27, 242.

35   Robert Furley, *A History of the Weald of Kent*, vol.2, part 2, Ashford, 1871 p.607; Zell, *Industry in the Countryside*, p132.

36   Faggots of wood had been plentiful in Kent and these had long been used in burning bricks and lime. John Boys, *General View of the Agriculture of the County of Kent*, 2nd ed., London, 1813, p198.

37   Giuseppe di Lampedusa, *The Leopard*, 1958 (English translation, 1960).

38   Entry for Sir William Nevill Montgomery Geary, barrister and inhabitant of Hadlow, Kent. He had contested both Durham and later Gravesend for the Liberals. *Who was Who*, vol.4, 1941–50.

39   Alec Clifton-Taylor, *The Pattern of English Building*, London, 1962, p217.

40   Clifton-Taylor, *The Pattern of English Building*, p229; Kenneth Graven, *Timber and Brick Building in Kent. A Selection from the J. Fremlyn Streatfield Collection*, London, 1971, p22–23.

41   Christopher Powell, *The British Building Industry since 1800*, 2nd ed., London, 1996, p43.

42   Extract from *The Digest and Index of the Report of the Commission of Excise Inquiry*, 1836, as published as appendix to part 2 of Dobson, *A Rudimentary Treatise on the Manufacture of Bricks and Tiles*, 1850, p81.

43   C.W. Chalklin, *Early Victorian Tonbridge*, Maidstone, 1975, p14. Many new houses were built in Tonbridge – not necessarily of high standards. Houses were often constructed directly over sewers and few possessed piped water; the brick-makers also benefited by 'recycling' the waste from the privies and cesspools to make further bricks. M. Barber-Read, 'The public health question in the 19th century. Public health and sanitation in a Kentish market town, Tonbridge 1850–75'. *Southern History*, 4, 1982, pp174–79.

44   Nathaniel Lloyd, *A History of English Brickwork*, London, 1925, p52.

45   Dobson, *Rudimentary Treatise*, part 1; 340,000 bricks were sufficient for paving a mile of road nine feet wide. Boys, *General View of the Agriculture of the County of Kent*, 2nd ed., 1813, p200.

46   The local historian places it slightly to the north.

47   Arthur Mankelow, 'The Mankelow Family History', unpublished account. I am most grateful to Arthur for a copy of his history.

48   Raphael Samuel, 'Local history and oral history', *History Workshop Journal*, 1, 1976, p192.

49   My thanks to Alan Mann for his observations.

50   Alan Everitt, *Landscape and Community in England*, London, 1985, p123; Alan M. Everitt, *Transformation and Tradition: Aspects of the Victorian Countryside*, Norwich, 1985, p24. Hadlow was also known for its fair share of drunkards as court reports indicate in *Tunbridge Wells Standard and Southborough and Tonbridge Journal*; see, for example, August 1869.

51   Everitt, *Transformation and Tradition*, pp24–25.

52   See, for example, *The Brick and Pottery Trades Diary and Year Book*, London, 1910. Lists were given of the trademarks of different firms.

53   From Mankelow, 'The Mankelow Family History', Unpublished account.

54   Thanks to Beryl Hatton for a copy of this flier from her personal archive.

55   Beswick, *Brickmaking in Sussex*, pp40–43.

56   Michael Kennedy, *Britten*, London, 1983, p45.

57   Anna Davin, *Growing Up Poor*, London, 1996.

Chapter 10

Paul Martin

THE TRADE UNION BADGE

An Epoch of Minority Symbolism?
The Pervasion of the Badge and the
Contraction of the Union

Wearing badges is not enough.[1]

[H ERE I] WILL EXPLORE the resurgence in the use of badges over the last two decades in the labour movement, and question if they might articulate a deeper meaning than might at first seem to be the case. Questions of gender, race and particularism are addressed to site the badge in a wider context. The badge has become a familiar appendage of the trade union movement, entrenching itself in many areas. Yet its use as a propaganda tool in the labour movement in Britain was late in coming. This use, although perceivable in earlier decades, has only become predominant since the 1970s.

It is useful to note the spread of the badge, and especially the tin or button badge into wider spheres of popular culture and society, in order to place trade union adaptation of it into context.[2] Primrose Peacock in her book *Buttons for the Collector* gives some indication of the tin badge's early permeation. Buttons in the sense used by Peacock are those normally used for the fastening of garments as opposed to the lapel badge variety, although she does talk briefly about 'pin-backs':

> To a button collector, the term lithograph includes photographs and other methods of printing, and is used to describe a variety of buttons which were first made during the 1880s, but which did not become very fashionable until the early years of George V (1911). During that time there was a fashion craze, first for buttons which portrayed actresses and other personalities and later, when waistcoats became popular with men's sportswear, sets of buttons depicting any pretty girl or sporting activity were worn. Such buttons were popularised by the development of celluloid, but in Britain were considered common by the upper classes. Ladies of breeding would not 'know' a man who wore theatrical buttons, in the same way that my grandmother did not 'know' any woman that dyed her hair.[3]

After the first mass-production of the button badge in 1896 it would have been a simple matter of modification to transform the celluloid waistcoat buttons into lapel badges by altering the fixing on the back, and the 'craze' for such items would seem to have become an established custom: 'The majority of modern "pin-backs" are celluloid or plastic and they range from quaint to vulgar. British people will remember the "I like Ike" campaign after WWII. More recent slogans are not so complimentary.'[4]

In America, the button badge has, since 1896, been used for every conceivable purpose, including protest. In the 1960s it was used in large numbers there, reflecting the disillusionment with the establishment of the time. It was used by the civil rights movement, anti-Vietnam war lobby, nuclear disarmament groups, and as an expression of alternative culture in musical, social and political culture generally. In Britain, the establishment political parties had used the button badge from the later 1900s to a small extent as a publicity tool, by issuing buttons with portraits of the candidates on them. The Communist Party had also used button badges for hunger marches in the inter-war period, as well as for the commemoration of May Day before the Second World War. Although they were issued in Britain in the 1950s and 1960s, it was never on the same scale as in the US, and it was not until the 1970s that the button badge made a real impact on labour culture in Britain.

The material conditions of the 1970s must be sketched out to some extent in order to trace the pattern of the current distribution of the badge. These conditions broadly follow political agendas of the period: first the Heath government of 1970–74, second the Wilson/Callaghan government of 1974–79, and finally the various Conservative administrations beginning in 1979. The badge in these periods becomes a symbolic iconographical expression of the ebb and flow of industrial relations and sociocultural practice, marking beginnings and ends of certain trends, and perhaps in recent years, of an epoch.

The first significant phase, from which the rise of the badge as a conveyer of cause or as an explicit protest weapon in the modern period in Britain is traceable, is that of the Heath government, and especially the 1971 Industrial Relations Act. From the end of the Second World War until this time, union disputes had been largely internalised and concerned observation of demarcation, and spheres of influence, which were largely resolved through the TUC and union amalgamation. Two major national issues, however, were the implementation in the early 1960s of the Beeching cuts in rail services and the widespread pit closures of the late 1960s under Lord Robens. The Beeching cuts were to be commemorated posthumously by the train drivers' union, ASLEF, in the form of [a] badge. . . . The pit closures of the 1960s were hardly contested, the focus of attention being the level of severance pay, and so does not relate to the union badge in its role as a means of protest.

The 1971 Industrial Relations Act marks a major discontinuity in post-war labour history. For the first time since 1945 overtly anti-union legislation had been enacted (*In Place of Strife*, drawn up by Harold Wilson and Barbara Castle in the 1960s was never implemented and so cannot be said to mark a discontinuity). The effect of the 1971 Industrial Relations Act however was to cause a major rupture within the TUC over registration and compliance with it, and caused several large unions (albeit temporarily) to disaffiliate from the TUC. The use of legislation from that time on was to become the norm in industrial relations. The dockers known as 'The Pentonville Five' gave British labour its first post-war martyrs. The notorious builders' strike of 1972 and the Shrewsbury trials reiterated this trend. Balanced against this were the victories of the workers in the Upper Clyde Shipyards (UCS) and the two miners' strikes of 1972 and 1974. These victories, which were contributory towards bringing down the Heath government, were set against a background of continuing amalgamations, the two most notable ones being the engineers (AUEW) in 1970 and the building workers (UCATT) in 1971. The tradition of unity being strength via amalgamation, and the ultimate victories of the two miners' strikes represented to the unions the justness of their cause and the victory of labour over repressive anti-trade union legislation. The UCS dispute in particular highlighted the influence of the shop stewards' movement. This had been growing and consolidating itself since the 1950s and was partly responsible for the resurgence of the badge in the labour movement in the later 1970s, as will be examined later.

The introduction in this period of anti-union legislation and the resistance of the shop stewards *ipso facto* marked both the beginning of iconographical resurgence and discontinuity of design. The demonstration against the Industrial Relations Bill in 1971 saw the biggest procession of trade unionists since the 1926 May Day celebrations, many of the old banners being given their first public airing for years and probably in many cases, their last. It is noted that several of the then more recently established unions had prepared new banners especially for the demonstration, far more simplistic in design than their opulent predecessors,[5] and this implicitly was to become the norm in banner-making in subsequent years. Poplin and silk-screened designs replaced the expensive banner silk and embroidery of the past. Meanwhile, the legislation of the time and the solid shop steward-organised resistance to it saw the first sparse use of the badge as a propaganda weapon in the labour movement.

Button badges such as 'Kill the Bill' and 'Free the Shrewsbury Pickets' were issued in this period, whilst 'Solidarity with the Miners' button badges were issued during both the 1972 and 1974 miners' strikes (and reappeared in 1984). Sparse as the use of the badge was in this period, it was used when the struggles were in progress. Only two commemorative (enamel) badges were issued after the events were successfully concluded. These were the Kent and South Wales area NUM badges for the 1972 miners' strike. None at all were issued for the 1974 miners' strike, compared with the many hundreds that were issued for the 1984/85 miners' strike. This seems to indicate that the burgeoning of the badge in the postwar labour movement occurs only when it is losing or after it has lost, rather than when it is winning a battle. In 1989, only one commemorative enamel badge was made to mark the fifth anniversary of the 1984 miners' strike; in 1994, there were at least six to commemorate the tenth anniversary. That more pits had been closed as a result of the 1992 Heseltine cuts no doubt increased the imperative of commemoration – a faint echo and personal token of a community's existence. Designs from 1985–86 were revamped and struck in different colours to commemorate the repetition of the same process of protest, as with for example, the Lancashire Women Against Pit Closures, who camped outside colliery gates on anti-closure vigils during 1992.[6]

The election of a Labour government in 1974 was seen as the ultimate victory over the 1971 Act. The legislation passed under it was favourable to organised labour, and for the first half of its administration, there was general industrial contentment and an absence of the badge in a campaigning role is noticeable in this period. By 1977, inflation was increasing, unemployment was rising and public sector wages were being eroded, along with cuts in public expenditure, leading ultimately to the 'winter of discontent'. An increasingly directionless and moribund Labour government seemed incapable of solving the problems. It is at this point that the button badge as a campaign weapon and a conveyor of protest came into its own. An early example was the 'Stuff the Jubilee – Fight the Cuts' badge issued by the Socialist Workers Party (SWP) in 1977 on the occasion of the Queen's silver jubilee.

The tin badge enjoyed a renaissance in 1970s Britain, but not only in the political or labour field. It was seized upon by advertising agencies, and used as an effective promotional medium for the sale of everyday items. It was also used by newspapers and magazines in a similar way, and by record companies to promote rock bands and the culture that surrounded them. The button badge was also being used as an introspective proclaimer of esoteric statement. Slogans such as 'keep on trucking', 'just passing through' and tantric designs were commonly reproduced on button badges at this time.

There were also the 'fun' button badges. Statements such as 'I'm Bored', 'Tomorrow We Must Get Organised', etc. were quite prevalent. These were reflective of a kind of office humour, but also proved highly popular with school children usually to the alarm of parents who viewed them with distaste.[7] Enamel and button badges however, had been utilised for children's clubs by cinemas, newspapers, comics, magazines, etc. since the 1920s, many of which are now highly sought after by collectors with a taste for nostalgia.

It was not directly from the labour movement that the phenomenal outbreak of badge wearing occurred at first, but from two outside sources. The increase in racist attacks, the rise of the National Front, and the alienation and disaffection felt by much of youth at this time expressed itself in opposition to a seemingly ineffective Labour government.[8] It was ethnic minorities and working-class youth who were *losing,* and it was they who acted as a catalyst for the explosion in the use of the badge. The Socialist Workers Party (SWP) had organised 'Rock against Racism' (RAR) and 'The Anti-Nazi League' (ANL) movements in 1976 and they took off in a big way, especially with youth who were the specific target. Anti-racist button badges were issued for all sorts of social groups. Many rank-and-file trade unionists wore the badges of Engineers, Miners, Nurses, even TUC 'against the Nazis'.

Coinciding with this was the emergence of the youth cult of 'punk rock' in 1977. Culturally this incorporated largely anti-racist, nihilistic and socialist tendencies and was naively political in its music. It offered a mass youth market for the SWP/ANL/RAR. Racists sought to infiltrate the punk scene early on, encouraged by the naive fashion amongst punks at first, for wearing Swastika armbands as a form of shock tactic to an older generation rather than an assertion of political conviction. Punk's mass expression was overwhelmingly anti-racist. The two big Carnivals Against The Nazis in 1978 and 1979 were RAR/ANL's high point.[9]

In conjunction with the musical badges, which expressed in the main either nihilistic or socialistic slogans and which were produced largely by record companies and petit-entrepreneurs out to exploit the phenomenon, the ANL/RAR badges were sold and worn in vast quantities. The button badge was a popular part of the livery of any punk. The SWP's 'Bookmarx' outlet did a roaring trade in anti-establishment slogan badges. Initially badges were issued in three-inch (75 mm) diameters but these proved unpopular, and were soon reduced to minuscule size, down to a half-inch (12.5 mm), but more usually between one and one-and-one-quarter inches (25–31 mm), in order that the maximum number of them could be worn on one lapel, which was the fashion at the time. The Better Badges firm in London's Portobello Road for instance, issued enormous quantities of such badges.

The implicit informal alliance between left-wing politics and youth culture was symptomatic of Labour's failure to act as a campaigning body. This gave the impression of cutting the ground from under the unions' feet, temporarily usurped by external bodies. The movement represented vigour to youth, an outlet for frustration. They had as little respect for the unions as they did for the government – they were all regarded as part of the establishment. It is from this point that trade unions began to try and recruit more young workers into the movement as a whole. Similar campaigns had been tried in the early 1960s, when youth culture had offered an alternative identity to that of the work place. Notably, campaigns were initiated by the National Union of Boot and Shoe Operatives (NUBSO) and the National Union of Tailors and Garment Workers (NUTGW) at that time. 'Anarchy in the UK' as a youth anthem was not one which trade unions saw as conducive to the next generation of their officials and activists.

With the election of a Tory government under Thatcher in 1979, the SWP placed its emphasis in other areas. ANL and RAR were largely abandoned (although ANL was revived in the late 1980s). Youth culture changed again, and the populist upswing of the late 1970s ebbed away. One of its practices though, the use of the button badge, remained and was used from below to a great extent by groups of workers in dispute, in a way it had not been (prior to 1977) used before in Britain. The innovative idea of making badges for various groups 'against the Nazis' and so making the cause that more close to those who wore them, was perhaps the idea for the issuing of localised dispute badges. To commemorate Thatcher's election in 1979, the *Morning Star* newspaper hurriedly issued a copious number of 'I Didn't Vote Tory' button badges. In origin a bitter political statement, the slogan was quickly appropriated by commercial interests, and was printed on posters, t shirts, mugs, postcards, even teatowels. Whilst illustrating the power and wide distribution of the badge, this example also shows how 'serious' rhetoric is often converted into music-hall satire or self-mockery. The unions, seeing the popularity of the button badge, probably adopted it as a propaganda tool, as a means of regaining their established position as the vocal expression of the working class. This tendency seems to have begun at the bottom and percolated upwards via shop stewards at branch level in disputes. Shop stewards, the means by which rank-and-file dissent had come to be articulated, now used the badge as a means for that articulation. Unions such as the TGWU had recognised and accommodated the stewards' movement, rather than try to distance itself from it; by such means the badge percolated upwards, to be used also as a means of expression of conviction at national as well as local level, from around the end of the 1970s. The steel strike of 1980 was probably the first instance in which the button badge was overtly issued by British trade unions on a large scale.

The button badge as a campaign tool was again invoked in the 1980s, principally through the Campaign for Nuclear Disarmament (CND), but also in other areas, though nowhere as explicitly as in the 1970s. CND's use of the badge was revived when the movement itself revived in the early 1980s. It imitated the RAR/ANL device of issuing badges for various social groups 'against the Nazis', by adopting the same and other social groups 'against the bomb'.

It is important to differentiate between the two types of badge that have become prevalent as a means of protest in the last three decades. From 1977 to 1982, it had been the button badge that had been utilised. From 1982, and especially from 1985, it has been the enamel badge. The earliest use of the enamel badge as a protest or publicity tool in the contemporary period seems to have been one issued by the South Yorkshire Regional Committee of the Iron and Steel Trades Confederation (ISTC), to commemorate the 1980 national steel strike, again a campaign that was lost. But it was 1982 which marks the real beginning of the renaissance in enamel badge manufacturing. This is not an arbitrary date. It was the year of the ASLEF strike, which coincided with the Falklands War. The dispute (over flexible rosters) was lost, and the enamel badge was used by ASLEF to commemorate the loyalty of those who had struck, branch and regional badges being issued in their hundreds, and which were still being issued for several years afterwards. The ASLEF dispute has poignancy perhaps because of its coincidence with the Falkland Islands war. A placard on an English naval dockside seen in a television news broadcast warned: 'Call off the Rail Strike, Or We'll Call an Air Strike'. An industrial dispute at a time when so many people were wrapping themselves in the Union Jack was never likely to curry much favour with the public. The use of the enamel badge rather than the tin one was perhaps also symbolic of the ambivalence towards the union from the public. As such, the dispute needed a more permanent symbol of loyalty than a transient button badge.

The nature of industrial relations under Thatcher had deteriorated rapidly. The onslaught of the Tory government, and the reactionary atmosphere engendered and encouraged amongst employers, meant that strikes were no longer short protest affairs, but had rapidly turned into lockouts, with the replacement of strikers by non-union labour. As days turned into weeks and weeks into months, those in dispute needed a source of income to sustain their struggles. One way of providing this was by the sale of enamel badges. The more ephemeral button badge was unsuited for this purpose, as it was more like a give-away item, or could only be sold for pennies, whereas enamels could be sold for much-needed pounds. As a fund-raiser, the enamel badge has come into its own. Quite apart from the social connotations, this has been enabled by competition amongst manufacturers. Two firms in particular, Adams Badges of London and Badges Plus of Birmingham, both established in the late 1970s, issued a large portion of the enamel dispute badges of the 1980s. A reduction in the cost of production of enamel badges, by these firms at least, made the enamel badge as a fund-raiser and proclaimer of cause an even more lucrative idea.

The 1984–85 miners' strike

The threatened mass closures of mines on supposedly economic grounds all over Britain by the then National Coal Board in 1983, led to a national strike against pit closures in March 1984 which lasted until March 1985. During 1984,[10] enamel badges were issued by striking miners, but with the minimum of wording, usually, just the name of the pit and the date '1984'.[11] This is because they were intended as a means of identification for pickets, picketing away from their home colliery. The button badge was also used to a great extent during the strike, acting as a means of celebrating support from other areas and unions (often more in spirit than in action, as will be discussed later). Photographs of miners festooned with badges, looking like walking exhibitions,[12] bring back to mind General Gordon's suggestion that blue cockades should be worn for mutual recognition. However, the majority of the badges worn were ordinary membership badges of other unions, as well as of county miners' unions that formed the highly federalised NUM. They are perhaps symptomatic of the need for and the belief in outside support, characterised by the extensive swapping of badges between miners and supporters on picket lines and at rallies, galas and demonstrations during the miners' strike. They were none the less badges that had already existed before the strike began of all sorts of unions including overseas ones.

The conclusion of the Miners' strike in 1985 marks the real acceleration of the production of the enamel badge, again after the strike had been lost. Such badges are regarded as war medals and battle honours, especially those issued during the strike, and shortly afterwards. Those issued later on were produced mainly to raise funds for the sacked miners, and were seen largely as precisely that. Some later issues, however, were also produced by NUM branches who did not have the means or funds during or shortly after the strike to issue their own badges at the time. All of these, though, would be bought for fundraising purposes. They were (and still are) seen as different from those issued closer to the dispute itself. Such cathartic and traumatic experiences often require counselling. As both a form of therapy and of commemoration, clubs are formed which act, at least subconsciously, as self-help groups. In 1985, the '5.3.85 Club' was formed. This denoted the date on which a national return to work was made. Only those miners who had stayed out until the end of the strike were admitted, and entitled to wear its badge. This has at least one historical precedent in the 1918 Australian organisation known as 'the Lilywhites', veterans of the 1917 New South Wales strike. . . . Nothing is recorded in that instance, however, to suggest that the women – wives, mothers, etc – equally affected by such a turn of events, had any formal mutual support network, in the way that miners' wives had in the Women Against Pit Closures (WAPC) movement. More work needs to be done in this area, to allow such history to be uncovered, particularly in the field of experience outside the formal organised trade union movement, and with special reference to oral history and testimony.

The 1984–85 miners' strike resulted in a return to work without a negotiated agreement and allowed the wording on the commemorative badges to assert honour and dignity in the struggle without admitting defeat. 'Loyal and Undefeated' and 'Loyal to the Last' were common statements on these badges, as was 'One Year's Unbroken Allegiance to the NUM'. In areas where scabbing was notable, 'Loyalist' and 'Loyal Members' are appended to the badge to distinguish them. The recurring use of the word 'loyal' though is the ultimate testimony of conviction and lack of regret in taking part in the strike.

In the contemporary sense, the invoking of principle and historical struggle, carried as much by folk memory as by documentation on the badge, again seems to be prevalent from the miners' strike onwards. Scargill's (and many others') assertion that the strike was not simply about jobs in the present, but that pit closures meant the loss of hereditary jobs which were the miners' children's by right, perhaps struck a chord with other sections of the labour movement. Certainly the miners' strike was an intensely personal one. This is demonstrated through the wording on some of the button badges issued during the strike. The Wearmouth lodge in Durham, referred to itself both as 'Harry's "F" Troop' and 'The Zulus'. The Whittle lodge in Northumberland named themselves 'The Warriors' and an enamel badge of the Northumbrian pickets refers to 'Murphy's Marauders' thus suggesting the prosecution of the strike (in a union historically, highly federal in nature anyway) on the basis of guerrilla warfare, perhaps in answer to the police armies of occupation of the colliery villages. The enamel commemorative badge of the Hickleton Main branch of the National Union of Mineworkers (NUM) in Yorkshire, declares 'Forget Not the Lessons of Our Past', explicitly suggesting the remembrance of historic sacrifice as a reason for continuation.

The emotional resonance evoked by the miners' strike badges runs deep. In 1986, Dick Hall, a Derbyshire miner, decided to auction off his collection of four hundred miners' strike badges, in order to raise funds for the sacked miners' fund that Christmas. *The Miner*, in October 1986, reported on the decision: 'The collection of well over four hundred badges includes some exceptionally rare first editions, which are virtually impossible to obtain.' Hall himself, states 'Of course it hurts to be parting with them, most were collected in the heat of battle – but I think my feelings have got to come second to the victimised lads.' Hall's friend, Billy Seaton continues:

> It must really pain him to part with the badges; some of them are priceless – about as rare as an honest Tory. For example the collection includes South Derbyshire's 'Time the Avenger'; the 'Kellingly Black' Allegiance badge and much prized 'Hucknall No. 2' and many others which were struck in very limited numbers from a few dozen down to a handful.

Even before the miners' strike, in 1983, a postcard published by the National Graphical Association (NGA) in connection with the Warrington print dispute, pictured a ghostly appearance of the Tolpuddle Martyrs, angrily addressing a TUC General Council sitting on a fence holding its 'bottle' (that is, courage) saying 'we all broke the law when we fought for union rights.' Such invocations though, are not a phenomenon confined to recent decades. It is itself a phenomenon, each succeeding generation invoking the sacrifices of the last as the rightness of their cause. As long ago as 1919, the gold medal awarded by the Women's Trade Union League bore the motto 'Lose Not Those Things That We Have Wrought'.[13] Perhaps this tradition had been lying dormant until the 1980s, awaiting recall. The idea of preserving jobs for the next generation acted as a spark, triggering off an attestation to values. A rebirth of adhesion to traditional trade union principle is expressed in the handbill accompanying a badge of the Shirebrook (Derbyshire) branch of ASLEF in 1985. It pictures a seagull, with the words 'avarice', 'cronyism', '£7.32' and 'principles first'. The accompanying note explains the usage of the wording: 'As a branch Shirebrook supported the stand against DOO [driver-operated-only trains] putting "principles first", but within our midst we had "seagulls" that by "cronyism" and because of "avarice" were prepared to and actually did accept "£7.32" for working DOO trains before an agreement was reached.'

The other side of the coin in badge iconography is the re-emergence of 'new realism' in the 1980s rebranded as 'new unionism' in the 1990s.[14] The evangelical reaffirmation of historical struggle on the badge has been largely (though by no means entirely) in relation to dispute badges and commemoratives, usually in the wake of defeat. The more 'moderate' badges are usually in the nature of membership badges. Given the hostility to trade unionism in Britain during the 1980s and 1990s, it is perhaps a little difficult to believe that in 1975, the Australian government established the Trade Union Training Authority 'to train and develop trade union officials and members in skills required to run a trade union', which also issues its own badge.[15]

Not all redesigning of union emblematics, though, is necessarily symbolic of any compliance with softer approaches to modern industrial conditions. R. A. Leeson tells us that the Patternmakers badgered their executive for (almost) twenty years to have an emblem made.[16] The pace at which events now occur requires more speedily available iconography, almost with a sense of urgency. The changing of such union names as the 'Amalgamated Society of Wire Drawers and Kindred Workers' to the more upbeat 'Wire Workers Union' (WWU), or of the 'Post Office Engineering Union' to the 'National Communications Union' (NCU) in the 1980s (in both instances of which, the clasped hands of unity were retained in the design) is symbolic of the changing nature of industry and commerce. From the 1990s, new names were adopted which did not even incorporate the nature of the industry or profession in which the union organised. In a decade personified by the emphasis of style over content, three public sector unions amalgamated to become 'UNISON', and the Barclays Bank Staff Association became 'UNIFI' (the 'Uni' of union and 'Fi' of finance). These at least arguably adopted a soundbite name which encapsulated a key aspect of trade union rhetoric. The Society of Telecom Executives, however, in a millennial gesture, on 1 January 2000, became simply known as 'Connect'.[17] The badges incorporating the new titles are quickly ordered by unions to help promote the identity of it with the membership, whereas branch banners often take a lot longer to change. Although it has been said that the majority of branch badges are issued by the laity of the union, the NCU and WWU examples came from head office. In the cases of the Greater London Staff Association (GLSA) and the National Association of Teachers in Further and Higher Education (NATFHE), badges were issued in direct response to requests from ordinary members.[18] It is not only the badge that is used for publicising events or commemorations, although it is the most utilised and immediate one. Plates, mugs, postcards, posters, T-shirts and all other traditional and modern means of communication are being used to publicise cause and principle, with the badge at the forefront.

ASLEF continued to issue badges to commemorate branch anniversaries amongst other things, many of which were for eightieth anniversaries. This is because many of the branches concerned did not expect to reach their centenaries before they were closed, perhaps symbolising the issue of badges in advance of defeat rather than in its wake. Many ASLEF badges were issued in the late 1980s for 'dead' stations and branch lines closed under Beeching in the 1960s, though there were none issued at the time. This could be seen as no more than a ploy to cash in on the growing collectors' market, but is perhaps also symbolic of a lament for a ravaged industry, a posthumous symbol of pride in spite of defeat. It could be recognition of where the rot started, belatedly or otherwise, or as a poignant reminder of the results of that wholesale attack on the industry, acting as an implicit warning. With the privatisation of the railways in the 1990s, this seems even more relevant.

The Wapping dispute

If the 1984–85 miners' strike symbolised Thatcher's attitude towards the state's employees, then the Wapping dispute was the imposition of this same credo in the private sector. In 1986, Rupert Murdoch manipulated a situation whereby the print unions working for his Fleet Street titles were coerced into strike action. Having got his employees out of his premises, he then sacked them, and moved his operation to Wapping, employing non-union labour and de-recognising the print unions. The dispute lasted for twelve months. The Wapping dispute also saw a large number of badges issued once the strike had turned into a lockout, and increased in number as the dispute wore on.[19] Mines, rail and print are the three best examples of this phenomenon, but many smaller local disputes have used the enamel badge for fund-raising and proclamation of cause, while the dispute is actually on (see below).

An overt assertion of alternative principle or policy by a branch to its national leadership is expressed through the badges of the London Press Branch of the former Electrical, Electronic Telecommunication and Plumbing Union (EETPU, since amalgamated with the Amalgamated Engineering Union). This branch was loyal to the sacked workers during the Wapping dispute in 1986–87 in contradiction to the national leadership's policies of sweetheart deals and scabbing. It first issued its own branch badge initially in tin, later in enamel. After the Wapping dispute it issued its own long-service badges for 20, 30, 40 and 50 years, awarded in preference to the national long-service badges covering the same periods. The branch badges all picture a clenched fist as opposed to the national ones which all use Walter Crane's Angel of Light and Liberty design, as did the former Electrical Trades Union (ETU), except for their fifty-year badge which also pictures the 'Angel of Light and Liberty'.

Since Wapping

The success of Murdoch's tactics at Wapping signified to the corporate world the legitimacy of disregard for employee rights. Following Wapping, there was an intensification of such tactics throughout British industry. Many smaller disputes, caused by the same tactics as those used by Murdoch, became the norm.[20]

By the late 1990s, nothing had changed. The Liverpool dockers,[21] Magnet Kitchens,[22] Critchley Labels[23] and Project Aerospace[24] are all examples of the employer response of sacking and locking-out workers who made moderate claims for pay increases and union recognition. As a result of this position, trade unions (officially) and sacked workers (unofficially) have adopted different tactics. In the run-up to the general election of 1997, the TUC and its larger affiliates were at pains to stress a new 'user-friendly' image to both members and employers from whom they sought recognition. In imitation of New Labour's 'New Britain' mantra, the 1997 TUC congress adopted as its slogan 'New Unionism'. However, this was a far cry from the militant adoption of the label used by the new unions of unskilled workers in the 1890s, and was partly conditioned by the fear of New Labour's distancing itself from trade unions,[25] and partly by its traditional fear of union militancy. An intensification of its new realist approach of the mid-1980s was characterised by its adoption of the music and culture festival concept as a means of attracting new members and getting its message across to the young disaffected. In this, unions were learning the lessons of the 1970s. Emphasis is placed on the services the union provides (legal aid, cheap car insurance, health care plans, etc.) which are now seen as central to people's lives.[26] In so doing, John Monks, the TUC General Secretary, sought to equate the militant unionism of the 1890s with the new realism of the 1990s by linking their central focus on the unskilled and semiskilled worker.[27]

Conversely, there are those who have fought and lost under such circumstances, not least the miners. They also learned a great deal tactically as a result. Some of these have now grouped together in the spirit of 'worker flexibility' on their own terms. The Magnet Kitchens dispute in Darlington, England, where three hundred workers were sacked for legally voting for a stoppage in pursuit of a wage claim, is a case in point. During the miners' strike, workers from the Darlington factory donated money, goods and support to the miners in Derbyshire, where most of the mines are now closed. The ex-miners then returned the favour:

> 'We brought the long dispute to trade unionism', says Terry Buckeraitis, one of the miners. 'We can't picket lawfully any more, but we can do other things'. Since their defeat in 1985, he and 'about 70' other former members of the National Union of Mineworkers have reinvented themselves, first as a sacked miners support group, then as 'free-range trade unionists'. Where they used to bellow on picket lines, they now 'look for new avenues'.[28]

There is also a much closer working relationship between trade unionists in this situation, environmental activists and other direct action lobby groups. The absence of any meaningful and nationally applied industrial relations apparatus over the last two decades has perhaps sown the seeds from which we are now reaping the harvest. The lapel badge in this scenario becomes another symbol of solidarity and principle, a visual testimony both to the legitimacy of the cause being advocated and the solidarity of others in its support. The wearing of hats and caps bearing multiple examples of badges of unions who (at local level) have assisted is the evidence of this assertion.

Gender

Given the sheer numbers of badges issued over the years, it would not be possible to say to what extent women have been represented in union badges, but they would seem to have been largely hidden. This is not to say that women were more active in trade unions in the early years of the century, but that as many unions had considerable numbers of female members, it would be only logical to assume that some expression of this fact would have been manifested in the badge, but apparently did not to any great extent. The National Federation of Women Workers, Society of Women Welders,[29] National Union of Women Teachers, National Union of Women Civil Servants and the Association of Women Clerks and Secretaries are a few examples of all-women unions that issued badges, the best example of which is perhaps the beautiful medal issued by the Women's Trade Union League, previously mentioned. This was awarded to a Miss Ann Loughlin in 1919, the last of its kind before the WTUL merged with the TUC in 1920. The narrative accompanying a picture of the badge relates:

> Its winner was the daughter of an active trade unionist but she found that she started work in the Leeds clothing industry [and] that the local union branch committee of the union was not at all enthusiastic about enrolling women, although the wages of the girls were sometimes as low as 3s for a week of fifty two and a half hours or more. Joining the union the day she started work at the age of 15, Miss Anne Loughlin was shop steward and propagandist before she was 21. . . .[30]

Another similar example can be found in the special medal minted for the retiring presidents of the National Union of Women Teachers (NUWT). A commemorative history of the NUWT was published in 1928, a copy of which was found by a collector, Andy Redpath. The presidential medal was introduced in 1917–18 shortly after the union was formed by ex-members of the National Union of Teachers (NUT), angry at male teachers' attitude towards women's suffrage and equal pay. The wording in the badge's centre reads: 'Pass On The Sacred Flame' and pictured a female hand passing on a flaming torch (of enlightenment) to another, and was the work of Miss Neal, the NUWT secretary and Miss Phipps, the commemorative book's author.[31]

Other than this example, however, there seems to be little representation of women on mixed-gender union badges. It is also indicative of the indifference with which badges have been met by feminists, those working in visual culture and historians generally, that this has not been noticed sooner. Over the last two decades, books have been written on the use and importance to the women's movement of banners and emblems[32] and even postcards,[33] and yet the badge has still to be recognised as an aspect of women's history, even within the women's suffrage movement when many portrait buttons of the Pankhursts and other suffragists were issued as fund-raisers.

The Women Worker's Union of Ireland issued a badge, the union being formed because of Larkin's interpretation of the word 'person' in the ITGWU rule book, to mean 'man'. The horses entering the Cork docks had to have the ITGWU 'Cork Carriers' badge in their bridle to be allowed through the gates, and therefore the ITGWU once organised men and horses but not women![34] Both ASLEF and the NUR had women's societies which issued badges, but these were supportive auxiliaries, not unions in their own right. One ASLEF member aged 70 in 1997, proudly showed off a souvenir teaspoon, the finial of which was the enamel badge of the ASLEF Women's Society. It was given to his mother on the occasion of his birth by the then new women's society branch in Eastleigh, Hampshire, he being the first baby to be born into the branch. The member remembered his mother's role in the women's society during the 1955 train drivers' strike: 'My mother helped keep the Eastleigh pickets supplied with refreshments.' He, his father and two brothers were all train drivers, and he remembered his mother 'work[ing] hard washing our overalls with the old fashioned copper. No washing machines in those days. Four sets of overalls and always clean for us every Monday.'[35]

A number of unions once issued women's section badges, including the National Union of Lock and Metal Workers, the General, Municipal, Boilermakers and Allied Trades Union (GMB), the National Warehouse & General Workers Union and the AEU (during the Second World War). This last example did not signify it was a women's section badge, rather it was made of chrome as opposed to the usual brass to make the distinction. This last example reveals a hidden element in union badges that disguises women. Some unions incorporated women into the title of the union, and hence the badge if there was a big enough female membership (though the officers seemed always to have been men). These include the National Amalgamated Society of Male and Female Pottery Workers and the Amalgamated Society of Tailors and Tailoresses. In some cases, iconographical concessions were made in the union's imagery, for example, the design of the insignia of the Amalgamated Society of Lace Makers and Auxiliary Workers which shows two clasped hands, one of which is female.[36] The Scottish Textile Workers Union, established in 1907, also issued a badge picturing both a male and a female textile operative. However, even where recognition of women is cited in the title 'male' usually precedes 'female', perhaps indicating the ratio of male to female members, but more probably asserting a male hegemony. Moreover unions such as the Dundee and District Union of Jute and Flax Workers and the General Union of Textile Workers, which both had very large female memberships, make no concession to their female members either in wording or iconography, the only distinction being that those badges intended for female members had pin rather than buttonhole fittings on the reverse. The Felt Hatters and Trimmers Unions were two separate unions, one male, one female, but which shared the same (male) general secretary and premises.[37] They also shared a common badge of membership. Women are not recognised on this badge, other than via the pin fitting (although there is a silver version of this badge in the TUC collection which has a fitting consisting of two metal loops through which a two-pronged pin is slipped, as in a cap badge fitting). This then suggests a hidden female element, masked behind an all-embracing title and the male definition of the iconography. To be fair however, even in rare instances when a union was a predominantly female one, and run by a woman, the badge chosen neither reflected these facts, nor made much of an assertive display. Such was the case of the National Union of Domestic Workers (NUDW). It was formed in 1938, by the TUC itself, as a campaign to organise poorly paid female domestics.[38] In a circular sent to members in July 1938, the question of a badge was mooted by Beatrice Bezzant, the NUDW national organiser:

> Another question on which I would like to have your opinion is that of a badge for members. As you know, most if not all Trade Unions have a Badge for members, and I have received several letters from members of our own Union, asking if and when we are going to have a badge. Would you like a badge? And do you think it would be a good idea to have a small round badge with a dark blue background and the letters N.U.D.W. in gold upon it?

Evidently, the membership were either more or less in agreement, or failed to significantly respond, as the badge eventually issued was as described, but lozenge-shaped rather than round. This perhaps reflected the conservatism of the TUC who spawned the union rather than any particular desire of the union, which by May 1953 was wound up, as domestic service had largely ceased to exist as an industry by this time.[39]

Since the 1980s, it has often been heard from women delegates that the composition of union and TUC hierarchies are overwhelmingly, white, male and middle-aged. Without discussing the number of women members of unions or their proportion on executive committees etc. it is sufficient to say that during the 1990s the recruitment of women into trade unions was one of the main objectives of the labour movement. For this purpose, women's officers were appointed and recruitment material was produced specifically aimed at women. Two kinds of badges are aimed at women made by trade unions nationally, outside of the unisex national membership badge. The first are those that are issued for recruitment campaigns which often sport the female symbol and slogans such as 'a woman's place is in her union' or which utilise assertive graphics and maxims as a form of self-belief.

On the other hand, unions have also offered their female members since the late 1970s what are usually advertised as 'the ladies' brooch', as an enamel, more permanent form of badge. These are usually round in shape and similar in design to a scarf ring. The GMB offer their women members a brooch in the shape of a brass leaf with the union logo on it, both of which are overtly and conventionally femininely decorative.

This seems to be a visual contradiction in emphasis that needs resolving. The assertive and positive nature of women is more clearly expressed in the badges of the 'Women Against Pit Closures' movement, such as the Coventry Colliery branch issue, picturing a woman breaking the chains of oppression, and proclaiming 'proud and defiant we stand'. Such imagery away from the heat and intensity of a single issue such as the miners' strike, is perhaps a little overbearing for everyday wear, but is more representative of women's strengths and portrays women in a more positive and assertive manner. It would be desirable to either replace the 'ladies' brooch' with something more representative of the campaign button variety of badge, or to do away with separatist badges altogether. At the moment it is uncomfortably tempting to ponder that the assertive tin campaign badges might be a means of attracting women into the union, but once in they are considered converted. The implicit docility of the 'ladies' brooch' or neck chain, which is also issued, seems to imply this to be the case. Attitudes are changing in some areas however. The health service nurses union, COHSE (now part of UNISON) abandoned their 'Branch Chairman' badge in 1987, and replaced it with a 'Branch Chairperson' badge. UNISON itself, in recent years has produced a 'Lesbian and Gay Members' sectional badge whilst the Manufacturing, Science and Finance Union (MSF) have also a produced a 'Lesbians and Gays in Management' (LAGIM) badge, whilst grassroots support groups such as the 'Lesbians and Gay Men Support the Miners' produced their own enamel badge during the 1984–85 miners' strike. All of this is some indication of the distance travelled and reminds us that such activity is contextualised by a wider progressive change in social and cultural attitudes in recent years.

Race

Another theme that has received attention in the trade union movement is that of race. Trade unions are now seeking to present themselves as more open towards black workers, which was not the case thirty or forty years ago. Given this emphasis, the question of race in badge iconography is a pertinent subject to examine. The most obvious way in which badge iconography could be improved in this area concerns the still common clasped handshake design. This is pointed out quite interestingly in a song recorded by Ewan MacColl and Peggy Seeger, written by Charlie Mayo, about an unpopular colour bar strike that took place at King's Cross by a minority of ASLEF and NUR members in 1957.[40] The strike had no official support and was soon crushed by local leaders and activists. The claim was that promotion of black members was affecting the overtime of white members. The first verse of the song is as follows:

> My union badge shows two joined hands with a lighted flame in common fight
> but troubles brewing in the sheds for both these working hands are white.[41]

The reference to the hands being white is to make the point of the song, as ASLEF and NUR badges of the time show the hands as either gilt or chrome, not white or indeed black, but it is a salient point. The NUR issued a badge in 1987 for the South African Railway & Harbour Workers Union, with whom they were twinned, in order to raise funds for the latter. This does indeed picture two clasped hands – one white, one black. The old GMB badge pictured two white hands, although there was no deliberate racial connotation in their colouring. Many unions that use the clasped hands device picture it in base metal, or colours other than black and white. If serious attempts are to be made in recruiting non-white workers, then the badge's iconography needs more careful consideration in some cases. If this sounds a flippant point, one has only to look at the biennial conference medals of the American Federation of Labor/Congress of Industrial Organisations (AFL/CIO), the American equivalent of the British TUC, which always picture two clasped hands, one white, the other black. Whether this came about through pressure from union members or whether it was a conscious decision is not known, but it should be borne in mind and seemed to be taken on board by some badges of the late 1980s such as that of the Southwark Trades Council amongst others.

The issue by the Union of Shop Distributive and Allied Workers (USDAW) of an enamel badge to mark the victimisation of two supermarket employees, 'Gary and Ross, sacked for opposing apartheid', shortly before Nelson Mandela's release from Robben Island, evoked the internationalist aspect of racism. The issue by UNISON of a 'Black Members' sectional badge (although the union name is not mentioned on it) and the Public Service, Tax and Commerce Union (PTC) 1996 black members' inaugural conference badge perhaps indicates the importance with which the question of equality and anti-racism is now treated in the trade union movement.

Symbolism

What does this burgeoning of the badge symbolise? It could be argued that the badge, rather than converting people to a cause, serves only to convey recognition of a cause from one member of a minority to another and gives the impression that a cause has been all but won before it has been even fully asserted. Many contemporary badges are issued by branch lay officials and activists. Compared to the small attendances at branch meetings, the badges perhaps overstate support for a cause or campaign. Many union members would perhaps not wear union badges. The badges perhaps are worn by the same activists and give a false sense of awareness of a cause, in the same way that ostensibly 'public' meetings are usually only ever attended by the same activists; this is perhaps implicit in the statement on one badge proclaiming 'Wearing Badges Is Not Enough'. The number of badges seen adorning the lapels of the converted are often quite out of all proportion to the small numbers of workers actively involved in the causes which they espouse. Many others perhaps wear the badge as a kind of trendy fashion accoutrement. In this sense modern badges are quite different from the older union badges that were worn only by the members concerned. They would be worn for years, unlike the majority issued today, which are of a temporary nature in a lot of cases, worn only whilst the cause to which they appertain is in operation, or worn by non-members to signify recognition of principle. The wearing of the badge today though probably most often symbolises a general empathy with the cause that it espouses rather than the active support which it enjoys.

It could be argued that such a burgeoning of badges acts as a smoke screen behind which the contraction of traditional industries such as mining and the railways and therefore the membership of the unions organising within them is going on apace. The miners' badges, for instance, could be said to represent an assertion of unity that was not really there. The reality, it could be argued, was division, and therefore the badges are symbolic of a cleaving together of the strikers themselves in the absence of wider support, especially so where the badge commemorates the unity of two colliery branches. The increased use of legislation during the Thatcher years aimed at breaking the unions cannot be denied. It was the second phase of Tory attack which had begun in 1971 with Heath. It was only interrupted by an undynamic Labour government, which towards its end looked increasingly as though it would have to use modified legislation of a similar nature itself. The difference was that in the early 1970s, there was nothing like the contraction of industry that took place under Thatcher; in the earlier period, industry was kept alive by artificial injections of government cash, a policy continued by Labour. The unions emerged victorious and defeated the legislation, the stewards' movement was strong and the badge was not used to express or commemorate victory. In the 1980s, legislation was implemented with a vengeance, and contraction of industry was intense. Compared with Thatcher, Heath now appears the very image of Tory moderation and the badge has been used extensively. In this sense then, the badge perhaps symbolises the end of an (albeit interrupted) epoch of Tory attack on the position of trade unions. The pronouncements of New Labour, made to placate potentially troublesome unions, have in practice only served to codify and legalise pre-existing customs (for example, the level and applicability of the minimum wage) and seem to offer little improvement.

The burgeoning of the badge has come at a time when unions are losing the battle for jobs and services. The badge then can be seen as a means behind which an ever-contracting industrial landscape is seeking to retire with grace, maintaining dignity whilst retreating, mimicking perhaps, Britain's withdrawal from empire in earlier decades of the twentieth century. Some of the largest unions seem to be collaborating with this theory. John Edmonds, General Secretary of the GMB is on record as saying '"Unity is Strength" is very, very old fashioned.'[42] It is hard to agree with him when the full name of his union is the antiquated 'General, Municipal, Boilermakers & Allied Trades Union'. The union is now known by its abbreviated initials 'GMB'; 'Unity is Strength', a slogan more pertinent now than at any other time since 1926 given the level of casualisation and temporary employment under the guise of 'worker flexibility', has been replaced by 'Working Together'. Gone are the clasped hands of unity, and in come two matchstick people symbolic of harmonious working (between union and management?). This is the trade union equivalent of New Labour's abandoning of the crossed quill and spade for the softer red rose. So does this new (or rather, idealised) realism mark a departure from trade union traditions? The historical precedent of the Mond-Turner talks of 1927[43] would suggest not, but if the labour movement is to turn its back on its past heraldics and traditional symbolism, it does then mark the end of resistance and the admission of defeat and the beginning of acquiescence with policies from above.

But is this the true picture of the contemporary labour movement? There is another side to the question which is equally valid. The labour movement has since the 1980s in branch structure been busy invoking all the imagery and martyrdom of its past, not least of all through the medium of the badge. The bicentenary of the Calton Weavers strike of 1787 was commemorated on the badge of the Glasgow May Day in 1987. The Wapping dispute saw the commemoration of the fiftieth anniversary of the battle of Cable Street linked with the Wapping dispute in 1986, proclaiming 'Fifty Years against Fascism'. This is symbolic of the bolstering of morale in the movement, to commemorate past glories in the absence of them today. Many unions have taken to issuing branch badges, perhaps rediscovering their own regional history and this highlights the nature of 'national' unions as actual 'federations' of branches.

Regionalism

Regionalistic representations of national union badges are not uncommon. Even in earlier years unions such as the ASW and NUR issued special badges for their Irish memberships. The Railway Clerks Association issued a special badge in 1932 for their conference in Dublin, whilst the ASE made a special badge for its delegates to the 1893 TUC conference in Belfast. The British TGWU have also made a number of special badges for their Northern Irish membership, prefixing the name with 'A' for 'Amalgamated', to distinguish it from the Irish TGWU, with whom it sometimes competes, prior to it becoming the Services, Industrial and Professional Trade Union, (SIPTU).[44] Unions such as the ASW, ASRS and ASE are known to have issued medals and badges for their branches set up in South Africa, Canada, Australia and America. An even stronger sense of regional identity can be found in the badge of the Anglesey Workers Union (an organisation comprised predominantly of agricultural workers), first issued in 1918 for the increased number of members that year.[45] The name appears only in Welsh (*Undeb Gweithwyr Môn*) and the establishment date of 1911. The central design is the Anglesey coat of arms and the motto '*Môn Mam Cymru*' – 'Anglesey, Mother of Wales'.[46]

An example of modern regional badges are those issued by UCATT in the 1980s. All bear the 'chain links' of the national design (symbolising strength through unity), but many have regionalistic representations, such as the white rose on the Yorkshire badge, the red dragon on the South Wales badge, the thistle on the Scottish badge and London Bridge on the London badge. Even a scarce badge of the Isle of Man branch of the TGWU (produced originally in the early 1930s) was issued to commemorate the opening of their new offices on the island in 1982, which bears the three legs of Man design. The technical and scientific union ASTMS, not known for its proliferation of badges, did in the late 1980s issue several badges, two of which are for health service branches. This perhaps implies a desire to commemorate the union's separate identity in these areas after the merger with the Technical Administrative and Supervisory Staffs Association (TASS) in January 1988 (now the Manufacturing, Science and Finance Union, MSF). All of this is a far cry from the days when a union would simply issue one national badge. The National Asylum Workers Union for instance, noted in its proposal for a national badge in *The National Asylum Workers Union Magazine* in March, 1914 that:

> . . . it has been suggested to us that if the union does not soon adopt an official badge, the London County Council section of the union will obtain one of their own! This of course would be an undesirable (and we might add unauthorised) proceeding, and it would be a ridiculous state of affairs for different 'circles' of the union to have different kinds of badges. We must have unity on the badges question as on any other.[47]

One can only wonder at what they would make of the iconographic and symbolic representations that now exist! Even the smallest outposts of empire are not without their unions and badges to represent them. The Gibraltar Taxi Drivers Union and the Falkland Islands General Employees Union (which had 450 members out of a total population of 1,759 in 1975) are two examples.

Important anniversaries have been commemorated in the 1980s and 1990s of the establishment of general unions and trades councils, which have been used as tools through which to reinvoke the traditions and principles on which the movement was traditionally based. Another perspective is offered, at least in the health service, by Andrew Redpath, a UNISON activist and trade union badge collector. During 1997, over twenty health-care branches of UNISON, issued their own badges. Redpath suspects that:

> . . . the reason for this is either the need to establish a strong separate identity for the union as a health care union or the fact that since the formation of NHS Trusts and local bargaining, branches have taken on more of the roles that were carried out nationally, and the local branch is now much more important within the union and branches are affirming their strong local identity.
>
> It seems that branches are much more likely to produce their own badges now than in the past, when you had to try to get the union to produce badges nationally. The nurses, midwives and health visitors badge produced by North Tyneside has spread to many other Unison branches and is getting national distribution without it being a national badge.[48]

A distinct lack of leadership from the TUC has possibly also caused unions to assert their own points of view at local level. Thatcher sought to alienate the labour movement from the very people who needed it most, portraying it as something detrimental to their interests. Events such as the Manchester Trade Union Week have been efforts at combating this, the badge playing an important role. Handbills and leaflets [for] the public are seldom read, but the badge invites the curious to question [an issue] further.

The localised badges are not then smoke-screens to hide behind, but are weapons to be brandished as a means of drawing strength through tradition, as reasons for continuing the collective organisation, invoking sacrifices of previous generations as moral obligations and incumbencies to resist attack, rather than a retreat, dignified or otherwise. Such badges are perhaps symptomatic of the resurgence of principle and organised discipline. If this is the case, then far from being the end of an epoch, they mark the beginning of a new one, with evangelical fervour. The badge becomes the material representation of the will to fight back, the re-inculcation of past events on the badge is perhaps to underline the thin dividing line between legality and illegality.

In Australia, which is highly federalised, state-issued badges of national federal unions have always been and still are common, many often making local distinction in both wording and imagery. These may be as simple as the fobs issued by unions such as the Grocers Employees Union, Australian Plumbers and Gasfitters Employees Union or Federated Mining Employees Union of Australia, which have stamped on the reverse: 'Property of union' and the initial of the state.[49] The next step up from this is expressed by the Federated Railway Loco Enginemen's Association of Australasia. Between 1904 and 1920, they issued a generic watch chain fob featuring a map of Australia in the centre picturing a train. On the reverse the state emblem was embossed, as opposed to a simple key letter. Until 1920, each state organisation remained autonomous within the association until registration was granted.[50] The Australian Telegraph & Telephone Construction and Maintenance Union on the other hand, went one step further by making the initials of the issuing state the central design of the badge.[51] Other unions such as Australian Timber Workers Union issued badges of their own design, incorporating the state name into the design.[52] The ultimate expression of this distinction, is the different coloured badges of a generic design, each colour representing a separate state. The Australian Tramway and Motor Omnibus Employees Association, in the 1930s and 1940s at least, had each state branch issuing 'a badge with its own initials and different coloured enamels: NSW light blue; Victoria red; Tasmania green'.[53] The Transport Workers Union of Australia in the 1940s and 1950s, issued a generic badge, to which were attached a specific coloured enamel rectangle, denoting the state. Tasmania had an: 'attachment in the shape of Tasmania'.[54] In the 1980s, the Australian Bank Employees Union issued similar badges: light blue South Australia; dark blue Tasmania; green Queensland and Victoria; red New South Wales; white Western Australia. They also issued key rings in these colours.[55] We can see therefore the progression of an assertion of autonomy or at least a strong local identity within the context of the need for a localised control system of membership.

The immediate aftermath of the 1984–85 miners' strike is probably the point at which the phenomenal resurgence of the badge took place in Britain. The miners for years had been the industrial trade unions' front-line troops. In 1972 and 1974 they had emerged victorious, recompense for 1926. In 1984–85 they were defeated, which to the Tories was recompense for 1972–74. The front-line troops had been beaten in the largest industrial dispute since 1926. The rest of the labour movement held its breath, unable to decide what position to adopt. Ideological and strategical concerns were an all-pervading concern in 1980s British trade unionism. The TUC and GMB as examples on one hand (not to mention the extreme example of the former EETPU) determined that the future laid in a sort of 'business unionism', making the union feel 'comfortable', like executive-class suites on airplanes, turning away from rank-and-file resistance, as occurred after 1926. This was reiterated in the 'new unionism' theme of the TUC's 1997 conference, the first under 'New' Labour. On the other hand, a grassroots determination to win through regardless, seeking aesthetic inspiration in the face of so many defeats has also grown since the 1980s. The revival of the theme of historic sacrifice, via the medium of the badge, helps facilitate this. Here, the badge has its role turned full circle, acting to help inaugurate a new generation into the struggle for justice that it was originally produced to uphold (as in the case of the sacked Liverpool dockers, who contrasted strongly with the suits and mobile phones of many delegates at the 1997 TUC conference), and acting 'as a useful conversation piece in recruitment work'[56] as it originally did.

The trade union badge of the 1980s seemed to symbolise either a desperate attempt to instil meaning into a flagging union movement, increasingly at odds over its aims and objectives, or an almost evangelical revival of self-confidence and self-assurance, and in so doing seemed to mark either the end of one epoch or the beginning of another, depending on the standpoint adopted. The 1990s witnessed the further decline of traditional industries, most vividly symbolised by Heseltine's pit closure programme of 1992 and its aftermath (evocatively dramatised in the film *Brassed Off*), and the election of a business-friendly 'New' Labour government. Indeed, by 1999, Trade Union Printing Services (TUPS) had been formed: 'TUPS Books was founded by redundant miners and shipyard workers who, by producing books which chronicle the social history of the North of England, have provided themselves and others with jobs.'[57] Here, what was so recently the daily working lives of so many has now been remarketed as glossy illustrated books, the covers of which picture shipyards and coal mines at sunset, in the same style as the National Trust or natural history photography, or which could also be seen allegorically as the sun setting on their particular industries. As a means of survival, and an attempt to ensure employment we all become tourists even of our own lives. The examples of spin doctoring and the heritage industry have been learned well here. In the spring of 1999, TUPS published the first issue of a magazine on the life, history and culture of North-East miners and mining, *Bands and Banners*, titled after the most commonly associated image of North-East mining. Thus, the Durham 'big meeting' which by its 110th anniversary in 1993 was virtually dead as a celebration of a living industry, found regeneration as a re-enactment ceremony, and was vigorously remarketed as a tourist attraction instead.

Many veterans from the labour disputes of the 1980s have found as much to protest about under 'New' Labour as they had under the Conservatives. At present, the TUC's new realism/new unionism of the 1980s and 1990s seems to be dominant overall, but in a still changing and ever shifting labour environment, there is everything to play for. As knowledge becomes the new currency, and as the notion of 'the citizen' is increasingly narrowly defined by technological knowledge, material ownership and the will to personal financial investment, the marginalised increase in number. The fallout from this is still to be tested, but if recent critiques are anything to go by[58] the campaigning zeal of the 1980s may have been just a foretaste of bigger things to come. As globalisation and standardisation[59] move on apace with ever expanding international corporate amalgamations (for example, in retailing, supermarkets, e-commerce, etc.), so trade unions have sought to respond. One example takes us back to the 1890s, when the American Knights of Labor organised in Britain. By 1999, the American union, the Association of Flight Attendants, was recruiting members at London's Heathrow Airport, and as such had affiliated to the British TUC.[. . .]

Notes

1   Billy Bragg, singer/songwriter, 1980s.
2   For a general overview of the history, development and uses of the button badge, see F. Setchfield, *The Official Badge Collectors' Guide*, London, Longman, 1986.
3   P. Peacock, *Buttons for the Collector*, Bath, David & Charles, 1972, p80.
4   Ibid., p82.
5   J. Gorman, *Banner Bright*, p48, Scorpion (revised and updated, 3rd edition), 1986.

6   It should be noted however, no badges were issued for the fifteenth anniversary in 1999. Rick Sumner of the Justice For Mineworkers Campaign, through whom most of the NUM badges are now sold for fund-raising purposes, explains that it was not possible to find a British badge manufacturer who would have the badges made in Britain rather than China where labour costs are cheaper and non-union (personal communication, 1999).

7   For example, see M. Merritt, 'Your Verdict on Craze that's big Business', Brighton *Evening Argus*, 17 September 1979, pp2–3.

8   If anything, the situation is worse today. Recent high media profile cases of fatal racial and suspected racial attacks include Stephen Lawrence, Michael Menson, Ricky Reel, and Howard and Jason McGowan.

9   D. Widgery, (1986) *Beating Time: Riot 'n' Race 'n' Rock 'n' Roll*, London, Chatto & Windus.

10   There is a copious literature on the history and course of the 1984–85 miners' strike and its aftermath. The following are a selective but representative selection. National studies: L. Sutcliffe and B. Hill, *Let Them Eat Coal: The Political Use of Social Security during the Miners' Strike*, London, Canary Press, 1985; P. Wilsher, D. Macintyre and M. Jones, *Strike – 358 Days That Shook the Nation: A Battle of Ideologies: Thatcher, Scargill and the Miners*, London, Coronet, 1985; D. Reed and A. Adamson, *Miners' Strike 1984–1985: People Versus the State*, London Larkin Publications 1985, S. Milne, *The Enemy Within: The Secret War against the Miners*, London, Pan, 1994. Local studies: A. Thornett (ed.), *The Miners' Strike in Oxford*, Oxford, Oxford Miners' Strike Support Group, 1985, J. Williams, N. Dickinson and L. Jaddou, *Hanging on by Our Fingernails: The Struggle at Lea Hall Colliery 1984–1987*, Nottingham, Spokesman Books, 1987. Photo-texts: R. Huddle, A. Phillips, M. Simons and J. Sturrock, *Blood, Sweat and Tears: Photographs from the Great Miners' Strike 1984–1985*, London, Artworker Books, 1985; I. Jedrzejczyk, R. Page, B. Prince and I. Young, *Striking Women: Communities and Coal*, London, Pluto Press, 1986; C. Salt and J. Layzell, *Here We Go! Women's Memories of the 1984–85 Miners' Strike*, London, Co-operative Retail Services Ltd, 1985.

11   B. Seaton, *Justice for Mineworkers Badge Collectors Guide*, Nottingham, private publication, 1987.

12   For examples, see, for example, N. Clark, 'Worn with Pride: Union Badges', *Labour Research*, 1987, February, pp19–20.

13   TUC collection, London.

14   Which is the same thing, not to be confused with the militancy of that term as applied to the 1890s.

15   G. Smith, *Emblems of Unity: Badges of Australia's Trade Union Movement*, New South Wales, Littlehill Press, 1992, p239.

16   R. A. Leeson, *United We Stand*, Bath, Adams & Dart, 1971, pp39, 68. Between 1879 and 1889 three concerted efforts were made by branches to have an emblem made, but not until 1897 were they successful.

17   This of course mimics the corporate rebranding of formally identifiable industries such as British Steel as Corus; British Gas as Centrica and for business purposes at least, the Post Office as Consignia. See, e.g. the Midlands commuter free paper *Metro*, 1 January 2001, p15.

18   N. Clark, 'Worn with Pride – Union Badges', *Labour Research*, February 1987, p19–20.

19   See L. Malvern, *The End of the Street*, London, Methuen, 1986, for a full account of the dispute.

20   For example, the long-running lockout and dismissal-based disputes at Keetings and Senior Colemans engineering companies, and Morris Curtains in the 1980s. There were many others.

21   J. Pilger, 'They Never Walk Alone', *Guardian Weekend*, 23 November 1996, pp14–23; S. Miller, 'Reminder Of Old-Fashioned Struggle', *Guardian*, 10 September 1996; S. Milne, 'Uphill Struggle For Forgotten Strikers'; *Guardian*, 1997, reproduced in *Trade Union Badge Collectors' Newsletter*, No. 61, September 1997. See also the television documentary *Dockers: Writing the Wrongs* and the dramatisation of the dispute *Dockers*, both screened on Channel Four, 11 July 1999.

22   Milne, 'Uphill Struggle. . .'; A. Beckett, 'Poles Apart At Magnet', *Guardian G2*, 16 March 1998, pp1–3.

23   Milne 'Uphill Struggle. . .'.

24   Ibid.

25   S. Milne, 'Battered Unions Cut Adrift', *Guardian*, 14 September 1996, p1; S. Milne 'How Unions Found They Were On The Menu', *Guardian Comment*, 14 September 1996, p3. See also 'Blair and the TUC', *Guardian Comment*, 14 September 1996; 'Union Dues', A. Culf, 'BBC Drama Puts Labour In A Spin', *Guardian*, 14 September 1996; *Guardian Weekend* (letters page), 7 December 1996.

26   R. Thomas and T. Hunter, 'Unions Strike Out In New Direction', *Guardian Jobs and Money*, 7 September 1996, pp1–3.

27   M. Halsall, 'Monks Aims at 5m "Union Wannabes"', *Guardian*, 10 September 1996, p8.

28   A. Beckett, 'Poles Apart At Magnet' *Guardian G2*, 16th March 1998, pp1–3. Other expressions of contemporary worker dissatisfaction are expressed humorously and subversively; a Rotherham

gardener, unfairly sacked during the winter for instance, sowed bedding plants in such a way as to spell out the word 'Bollocks' come the spring. *Trade Union Badge Collectors' Newsletter*, No. 70, January, 2000. Elsewhere, 30 staff made redundant at the Ibstock Himley brick plant, near Dudley, on being instructed by management 'to make sure the last batch of bricks were up to scratch before leaving', produced 30,000 bricks with the same expletive impressed in their surface. They were distributed to the company's customers before the prank was realised, *Guardian*, 29 March 2000.

29   See J. Gorman, *Images of Labour*, London, Scorpion, 1985, p33 for illustration and history.

30   *Labour*, August, 1949, p269.

31   See A. Redpath in *Trade Union Badge Collectors' Newsletter*, No. 68, Summer, 1999.

32   L. Tickner, *The Spectacle of Women: Images of the Suffrage Movement 1907–1914*, London, Chatto & Windus, 1987; T. Campbell, *100 Years of Women's Banners* (second edition), Dyfed, Wales, Women for Life on Earth, 1990; D. Atkinson, *The Purple, White and Green: Suffragettes in London 1906–1914*, London, Museum of London, 1992; T. Campbell and M. Wilson, *Each for All and All for Each: A Celebration of Cooperative Banners*, Manchester National Co-operative Education Association, 1994.

33   I. McDonald, *Vindication! A Postcard History of the Women's Movement*, London, Bellew Publishing, 1989.

34   F. Devine, 'Who Dares Wear the Red Hand Badge', *Liberty*, Journal of the Irish Transport and General Workers Union, June 1984.

35   Anon, 'Spooning Up On History With a Selhurst Veteran', *Locomotive Journal*, July 1997, p3.

36   Which is reproduced as the frontispiece of the book on their history. See N. H. Cuthbert, *The Lacemakers Society*, Nottingham, Amalgamated Society of Lace Makers and Auxilliary Workers, 1960.

37   A. Marsh, V. Ryan and J. Smethurst, *Historical Directory of Trade Unions Volume 4*, Aldershot, Scolar Press, 1994, p480. For further reference to women's representation in labour history and women's iconography, see E. Hobsbawm, 'Man and Woman in Socialist Iconography', *History Workshop Journal*, 1978, No. 6, Autumn, pp121–38; S. Alexander, A. Davin and E. Hostettler, 'Labouring Women: a reply to Eric Hobsbawm', *History Workshop Journal*, 1979, No. 8, pp174–82; A. Davin, 'Feminism and Labour History' in R. Samuel (ed.), *People's History and Socialist Theory*, London, Routledge, 1981, pp176–81; L. Tickner, *The Spectacle of Women*. . . .

38   P. Martin, 'The National Union of Domestic Workers', *Trade Union Badge Collectors' Newsletter*, No. 35, 1992, October, p11.

39   Ibid.

40   For a further example of such negative action in the labour movement in this period, see M. Dresser, 'The Colour Bar in Bristol, 1963', in R. Samuel (ed.), *Patriotism: The Making and Unmaking of British National Identity, Volume 1: History and Politics*, London, Routledge, 1989, pp288–316.

41   J. Rose, *One Hundred Years of King's Cross Aslef*, London, King's Cross branch ASLEF, London, 1986, p48.

42   *Morning Star*, 23 June 1987.

43   The Mond-Turner talks were held between Sir Alfred Mond of ICI representing the employers and Ben Turner of the TUC in 1927 in the aftermath of the 1926 General Strike. The purpose was to find a way of avoiding such a situation again by finding more effective machinery for unions and employers to settle differences. The talks came to little especially against the background of vindictive Conservative anti-trade union legislation in 1927 which remained on the statute book until after the Second World War.

44   For further reference to these and other Irish-related trade union badges, see the leaflet issued for the exhibition *In Solidarity*, held at The Ulster Museum, Belfast, from 7 February to 22 April 1984.

45   D. Pretty, *The Rural Revolt That Failed: Farm workers trade unions in Wales 1889–1950*, Cardiff, University of Wales Press, 1989, p105.

46   For the union's full history, see D. Pretty, 'Undeb Gweithwyr Môn: Anglesey Workers Union (Part One)', *Transactions of the Anglesey Antiquarian Society and Field Club*, 1988, pp115–48; D. Pretty, 'Undeb Gweithwyr Môn: Anglesey Workers Union (Part Two)', *Transactions of the Anglesey Antiquarian Society and Field Club*, 1989, pp43–79; D. Pretty, *The Rural Revolt That Failed*.

47   This, though, cannot have been a unanimous view in the labour movement, even at that time, as an 'East Coast District' key chain fob exists of the National Union Of Gas Workers and General Labourers, based in Hull, dating from between 1889–1916 (see K. Sinclair, op cit.).

48   A. Redpath, personal communication, 13 January 1998.

49   Smith, *Emblems of Unity*, pp160, 67, 130.

50   Ibid., pp134–35.

51   Ibid., p75.

52   Ibid., p79.

53   Ibid., p81.
54   Ibid., p240.
55   Ibid., pp45–46.
56   'Trade Union Badges', *Man and Metal*, 1965, November, pp326–27.
57   Trade Union Printing Services publicity sheet, 1999.
58   For example, W. Hutton, *The State We're In*, London: Jonathan Cape, 1995; C. Lasch, *The Revolt of The Elites and the Betrayal of Democracy*, New York: Norton Publishers, 1995.
59   See G. Ritzer, *The McDonaldization of Society* (new millennium edition), London, Sage, 2000. Ritzer shows how the rise of the McDonald's fast food chain has become universally adopted as a model for the global standardisation of industrial and commercial process, practice and employment, etc.

Chapter 11

Daniel Cohen

THE FUTURE OF PRESERVING THE PAST

CONSIDER THE EFFORT EXPENDED TO SAVE a rich and representative historical record of perhaps the two most tragic days in American history in the past century: December 7, 1941, and September 11, 2001. The National Archives preserved military photographs of the chaos at Pearl Harbor on December 7 as well as communications and damage assessments. The Office of Naval Records and Library recorded the names of those who died or were wounded. Meanwhile, other government branches and institutions undertook more wide-ranging preservation activities. The Library of Congress acquired the annotated typescript of the National Broadcasting Corporation's breaking news account. In addition to saving military records, the National Archives catalogued the reactions of government officials in public announcements and private correspondence. The National Park Service administers the USS Arizona Memorial of Pearl Harbor in Hawaii to preserve the underwater remains of the ship, while providing visitors a sense of the day's events and repercussions.

In a mode more active than reactive, others sought to save the character of the Pearl Harbor attack by seeking out the views of average Americans. Pioneering folklorist Alan Lomax, working at the Library of Congress's Archive of American Folk Song, sent out an urgent telegram on December 8 to like-minded colleagues around the country imploring them to record the sentiments of the American people. In the next three days these interviewers, using cutting-edge technologies such as direct-to-disc machines that recorded sound directly onto platters that could be played immediately like normal records, gathered commentary from dozens of people in 15 states – a total of 4 1/2 hours of powerful expression. In subsequent years, historians have mined other national and local archives, letters and diaries, and the memories of Americans and Japanese to create a comprehensive picture of this day of infamy.

Sixty years later, on and after another day of infamy, September 11, 2001, professional and amateur archivists and historians again sought to record the aftermath of a horrific event. Widely varying initiatives began almost immediately, engaging in selective acquisition and broad opportunism, active outreach to historical subjects and passive collecting of artifacts, short-term haphazard gathering and careful long-term preservation. Projects modeled on those of 1941 quickly arose. At Columbia University, the Oral History Research Office and the Institute for Social and Economic Research Policy created the September 11, 2001 Oral History Narrative and Memory Project, which has conducted more than 300 interviews with people affected by the terrorist attacks in New York, New Jersey, and the Boston and Washington, DC, regions, including interviewees who escaped the World Trade Center or lived in its shadow and Afghan and Muslim immigrants.[1] As it had 60 years earlier, the American Folklife Center at the Library of Congress, the descendant of the Archive of American Folk Song, sent out a notice to folklorists across the United States to record the "thoughts and feelings expressed by average citizens." This distributed network of oral historians donated approximately 300 hours of audiotape to the library, collected in 19 states and a military base in Italy.[2] The library's September 11, 2001 Documentary Project also gathered a smaller number of video interviews, written narratives, drawings, and photographs.[3]

Despite the efforts following September 11, which were orders of magnitude larger than those of Lomax and his small band of colleagues, the nature of the historical record had changed in many ways. Media no longer meant the radio broadcasts of a few national networks but now meant hundreds of audio and video broadcasts. Far more expansively, the record of 9/11 was to be found in new media such as websites, email, and other forms of electronic communication and expression, forms that have become an increasingly significant part of America's and the industrialized world's cultural output.

To be sure, in the weeks and months after September 11, museums, libraries, CRM and archives began to address the changing nature and scope of the historical record. In doing so, however, they had to abandon, at least in part, well-established models drawn from oral history and archival science. The explosion of historical sources in a digital age necessitated this evolution in preservation tactics. For example, whereas photographs of the attack at Pearl Harbor number at most a few thousand – the largest collection, at the National Archives and Records Administration, comprises a mere 5 boxes with about 200 images in each box – the photographic record of September 11, 2001, likely numbers in the millions of images. Indeed, with the proliferation of personal cameras since 1941, and especially with the spread of digital cameras in the last decade, 9/11 may be among the most photographed events in history.

Given the enormous size of the photographic record of 9/11, a variety of organizations, not just those in the preservation business, have had little trouble building impressive archives. The United States National Institute of Standards and Technology (NIST), as part of its investigation into why structural elements in the twin towers failed, gathered more than 6,000 images from 185 professional and amateur photographers, from almost every conceivable angle and covering virtually every moment, and in some cases fractions of a second, of the towers' collapse.[4] As seen in the remarkable Here is New York "democracy of photographs" collection of 5,000 images from hundreds of contributors, each photographer literally as well as figuratively had his or her own perspective on the event.[5]

Some preservation institutions recognized the proliferation and importance of new digital media. Looking to supplement their standard accessions of the printed editions of newspapers after September 11, the Library of Congress, in partnership with the Internet Archive, WebArchivist.org, and the Pew Internet and American Life Project, archived 30,000 websites from September 11 to December 1, 2001. This massive collection of digital materials will undoubtedly be of great value to future researchers. But even this impressive undertaking saved less than *one-thousandth* of the roughly 32 million websites in existence in September 2001.[6]

Others took a more active role, soliciting a variety of digital reactions and artifacts through online projects not dissimilar from Alan Lomax's grassroots effort to capture a wide range of perspectives from across the country after the Pearl Harbor attack. The September 11

Digital Archive at the Center for History and New Media at George Mason University, co-produced by the American Social History Project/Center for Media and Learning at the City University of New York Graduate Center, which I co-directed, tried to capture digital sources from everyday people. We used a website, available at http://911digitalarchive.org, digital telephone lines, and less technologically sophisticated methods like note cards that were later scanned, to save personal stories, emails, photographs and works of art, instant messages, pager communications, and other forms of expression and communication from 9/11 and its aftermath. Thus far the archive has collected more than 150,000 items from thousands of individual contributors. In the fall of 2003, the collection was accessioned by the Library of Congress, one of the library's first major digital acquisitions.[7]

Concerns about digital collections

The vast expansion of the historical record into new media between December 7, 1941 and September 11, 2001 presents serious challenges that will have to be surmounted in the coming years if future scholars and the public are to have access to an adequate record of the past. Yet despite the urgency of dealing with this mutating record, many in the cultural heritage community have major reservations about digital collecting, due in part to an understandable aversion to the complicated hardware and software involved, but more importantly because of some very real concerns about the nature of online work. At the same time that the web has enabled an exponential increase in cultural production, some argue that online collecting misses those older, less educated, or less well-to-do subjects who may not have access to the necessary technology.[8] Furthermore, the shift from analog to digital entails a change from well-known and relatively stable forms such as paper to forms for which the preservation path is unclear.

Digital collections are characterized as being shallow and less useful for research than traditional archives, for which provenance and selection criteria are critical. It is unrealistic to expect that the Library of Congress could pre-screen 30,000 websites for quality or relevance to 9/11. The staggering numbers possible in digital collecting renders ineffectual some central tenets and time-honored procedures of archival and library science. Another common problem, encountered by many online collecting projects that actively solicit digital materials, is the opposite of this abundance: the failure to collect much at all because few people hear about or contribute to their websites. An inverse relationship between the quantity of digital artifacts gathered and the general quality of those artifacts may exist.[9]

> Perhaps the most profound benefit of online collecting is an unparalleled opportunity to allow more varied perspectives in the historical record than ever before. Networked information technology can allow ordinary people and marginalized constituencies not only a larger presence in an online archive, but also generally a more important role in the dialogue of history.

Digital collections are indeed more susceptible to problems of quality because they often lack the helpful selection bias of a knowledgeable curator and the pressure to maintain strict criteria for inclusion engendered by limited physical storage space. Web collections formed around the submissions of scattered contributors or thousands of websites and blogs have a very different character from traditional archives. Digital collections tend to be less organized and more capricious in what they cover.

On a more positive note, digital archives can be far larger, more diverse, and more inclusive than traditional archives. Perhaps the most profound benefit of online collecting is an unparalleled opportunity to allow more varied perspectives in the historical record than ever before. Networked information technology can allow ordinary people and marginalized constituencies not only a larger presence in an online archive, but also generally a more important role in the dialogue of history. "The Net is a people's medium: the good, the bad and the ugly," Brewster Kahle, the founder of the Internet Archive, has said. "The interesting, the picayune and the profane. It's all there."[10]

A less obvious but perhaps more important measure of the "quality" of a digital historical collection becomes apparent when the collection is assessed as a whole. Like any collection, there will be a minority of striking contributions among a sea of mundane or seemingly irrelevant entries. Historians who have browsed box after box in a paper archive trying to find key pieces of evidence for their research will know this principle well. The propensity of digital collectors to save virtually everything given the low cost of digital storage and the difficulty of using selection criteria may make these percentages worse. Yet, a few well-written perspectives or telling archival images may form the basis of a new interpretation, or help to buttress an existing but partial understanding of a historical moment. At the same time, the greater size and diversity of online collections allow more opportunities to look for patterns. Why do certain types of stories recur? What does that reveal about popular experience and the ways that experience is transformed into memory?

Because of a digital collection's superior ability to be searched, historians can plumb electronic documents in revealing and novel ways. The speed of analysis can enable quick assessments of historical collections and more substantive investigations. For instance, when historian Michael Kazin used search tools to scan the September 11 Digital Archive for the frequency of words such as "patriotic" and "freedom" he came to some important conclusions about the American reaction to the terrorist attacks. Kazin discovered that fewer Americans than one might imagine saw 9/11 in terms of nationalism or another abstract framework. Instead, most saw the events in personal and local terms, the loss of a friend, the effect on a town or community, the impact on their family or job.[11]

Active solicitation of digital materials

Reaching out to and interacting with historical subjects online, either in real time or asynchronously, is far more economical than traditional oral history. With subjects writing their own narratives, the cost of transcription is avoided. While live individual interviews are often quite thorough and invaluable resources, online initiatives to collect personal histories can capture a far greater number at lower cost and acquire associated digital materials, such as photographs, just as cheaply.

Of course, even if highly successful in the future, online interaction with historical subjects will not mean the end of traditional ways of gathering recent history. As oral historian Linda Shopes observes, newer technological methods will have a hard time competing with many aspects of the oral historian's craft: "the cultivation of rapport and . . . lengthy, in-depth narratives through intense face-to-face contact; the use of subtle paralinguistic cues as an aid to moving the conversation along; the talent of responding to a particular comment, in the moment, with the breakthrough question, the probe that gets underneath a narrator's words."[12] Instead, using the Internet will likely complement these older methods.

Acquiring historical materials and recollections online is more difficult than setting up a rudimentary website because it entails digital tools to receive, process, and store submissions. To adequately capture the past in this way, more technical hurdles must be surmounted to allow for historical documents and artifacts to flow inward rather than merely outward, as they do on the web pages of most museums, archives, and historical sites.

The good news is that online interactivity is becoming easier each year. The same digital technologies that have made the historical record proliferate into new forms give us the best hope to capture that record. Not everyone needs a custom-programmed archival system such as the one constructed for the September 11 Digital Archive. Much of the infrastructure and software required to do simple or even moderately complex online collecting is available and cultural institutions and independent scholars should take advantage of these technologies.

Probably the oldest and still quite useful technology for online collecting is email, the choice of some of the most successful projects. Keith Whittle's Atomic Veterans History Project, devoted to the community of veterans who participated in nuclear testing during the Cold War, has collected and posted more than 600 personal narratives from former soldiers, acquired solely through email. As Whittle discovered, emailers include attachments such as scanned photographs, many of which grace the website alongside the narratives. Email also allows for long-term interactions, follow-up, and detailed exchanges. An online collecting project can get started right away with a simple web design that uses email links to encourage and accept submissions.[13]

Blogs have given millions of Internet users a taste of what it is like not just to read and view the web, but also to post to it. Many ways of maintaining a blog also allow for more than one person to post and for contributors to add images and multimedia files, creating an ever-expanding and multifaceted discussion about topics of interest. The ease with which one can add materials makes blogs an attractive possibility for a basic collecting site. Blogs have built-in search features and the ability to export whatever is collected to other locations.[14]

New forms of instantaneous communication on the Internet will further expand the toolkit for collecting history online. Millions are now using instant messaging (IM) software that permits real-time communication with individuals around the globe. Although they do not have the tonal inflections of a spoken dialogue, these typed conversations have the advantage of being self-documenting, unlike oral history interviews, which require expensive transcriptions. More recent versions of these IM programs also allow rudimentary audio and video chats, which opens up the possibility of a future that is much like the past of traditional oral history. Technical concerns such as installing and configuring appropriate software and hardware for digital collecting should recede, ultimately, into the background.

What will remain in the foreground are the qualitative concerns, especially the question of provenance raised by the solicitation of historical materials from unseen contributors. Given the slippery character of digital materials, how can we ensure that what we receive over the Internet is authentic, or that historical narratives we receive really are from the people they say they are?

Some of these worries are relatively easy to address. Concern about the falsification of digital historical documents and metadata (information about such artifacts) has mostly turned out to be a phantom problem.[15] I am not alone in this assessment. Newspaper websites have found that relatively few people enter fake information. In one study, the *Philadelphia Inquirer* discovered that only 10 to 15 percent of their 300,000 registered users had entered bad email addresses, and some of those were merely by accident or due to technical difficulties. Zip codes and other less problematic bits of personal information are falsified at an even lower rate.[16]

The nonprofit mission of online historical archives should produce even higher rates of honesty. Most people who take the time to submit something to a digital project share a cultural institution's or dedicated researcher's goals and interest in creating an accurate historical record. In addition, some technical methods can help double-check online contributions. Every computer connected to the web has an Internet Protocol (IP) address.

A small bit of programming code can capture this address. If a researcher is skeptical that a contribution has come from a specific person or location, a WHOIS search, which translates an IP address into a semi-readable format that often includes a contributor's Internet service provider and broad area of service, may result in helpful information.[17] Less cloak-and-dagger is a simple email or telephone follow-up with a contributor to thank them for their contribution; this presents an opportunity to ask contributors if they might have any other documents or recollections and whether they might know of other contacts.

The best defense against online fraud comes from traditional skills. Historians have always had to assess the reliability of their sources. Countless notable forgeries exist on paper. As Donald Ritchie has pointed out, written memoirs and traditional oral histories are filled with exaggerations and distortions.[18] Historians will have to continue to look for evidence of internal consistency and weigh them against other sources. In any media, new or old, solid research is the basis of sound scholarship.

Despite the challenges and insecurities surrounding digital collecting, it has become a burgeoning practice. Recently, for example, the British Library, the Victoria and Albert Museum, the Museum of London, and a number of other British museums and archives pooled their resources to display and collect stories of immigration to the United Kingdom in a project called Moving Here. Thus far the project has posted almost 400 stories and artifacts, mainly digitized versions of existing archive records but also new materials acquired via the site, ranging from a documentary video on Caribbean life to the reflections of recent African immigrants. The British Broadcasting Corporation's online project to gather the stories of Britain's World War II veterans and survivors of the London Blitz, entitled WW2 People's War, has been even more successful, with over 1,000 narratives gathered through the BBC's website after only 8 months, including dozens of harrowing accounts of D-Day.[19]

In the United States, the National Park Foundation, the National Park Service, and the Ford Motor Company are using the Internet to collect first-hand narratives of life during wartime for the Rosie the Riveter/World War II Home Front National Historical Park in Richmond, California. So far more than 6,000 former home front workers have contributed stories. *National Geographic's* Remembering Pearl Harbor site has received over 1,000 entries in its memory book. Over 500 people have recorded their personal stories and artifacts of the Civil Rights Movement on a site co-sponsored by the American Association for Retired Persons, the Leadership Conference on Civil Rights, and the Library of Congress. The Alfred P. Sloan Foundation has supported dozens of online collecting projects on science and technology in the belief that the history of these subjects is growing much faster than our ability to gather it through more conventional means.

Although there remains a healthy skepticism in the oral history community about the usefulness and reliability of narratives collected online, several new projects by major oral history centers demonstrate the benefits of online collecting. Even Columbia University, the home of the nation's first oral history program, is encouraging alumni to join in writing Columbia's history by contributing stories online.[20]

Saving existing digital sources

The main challenge for those interested in a more passive form of digital collecting is how to preserve what is collected for the long term. This is a serious challenge faced by actively acquired digital collections as well. Electronic resources are profoundly unstable, far more so than physical objects like books. The foremost American authority on the longevity of various media, NIST, still cannot give a precise timeline for the deterioration of many of the formats we currently rely on to store precious digital resources.

A recent report by NIST researcher Fred R. Byers notes that estimates vary from 20 to 200 years for popular media such as the CD and DVD. Anecdotal evidence shows that the imperfect way most people and institutions store digital media leads to much faster losses. For example, a significant fraction of collections from the 1980s of audio CDs, one of the first digital formats to become widely available to the public, may already be unplayable. The Library of Congress, which holds roughly 150,000 audio CDs in conditions almost certainly far better than those of personal collections, estimates that between 1 and 10 percent of the discs in their collection already contain serious data errors.[21]

Moreover, nondigital materials are often usable following modest deterioration, while digital objects such as CDs frequently become unusable at the first sign of corruption. We have gleaned information from letters and photographs discolored by exposure to decades of sunlight, from hieroglyphs worn away by centuries of wind-blown sand, and from papyri partially eaten by ancient insects. By contrast, a stray static charge or wayward magnetic field can wreak havoc on the media used to store digital sources.

Beyond the possibilities of data corruption, all digital objects also require a special set of eyes, often unique hardware, and an accompanying operating system and application software, to view or read them properly. The absence of these associated technologies can mean the effective loss of digital resources, even if those resources remain fully intact. There have already been several versions of HTML, the underlying language of the web, enough to cause many of the web pages created in the early 1990s to be partially unreadable. The University of Michigan's Margaret Hedstrom, a leading expert on digital archiving, bluntly wrote in a recent report on the state of the art, "No acceptable methods exist today to preserve complex digital objects that contain combinations of text, data, images, audio, and video and that require specific software applications for reuse." In short, historians, archivists, librarians, and museum curators, even those strongly committed to the long-term preservation of recent history, enter uncharted waters when they try to save the past digitally.[22]

Computer scientists and digitally savvy librarians and archivists are working on possible solutions to these challenges, from software like the Massachusetts Institute of Technology Libraries' and Hewlett-Packard's DSpace or the University of Virginia's and Cornell University's Fedora, and through broad initiatives like the Library of Congress's National Digital Information Infrastructure and Preservation Program. But we are still in the very early stages of the creation of these new digital archives, and many prototypes and methods will undoubtedly disappear. Most readers of this article will not become active participants in these complex projects, but they are worth keeping an eye on to understand when possible solutions might become available.[23]

Worrying too much about the long-term fate of digital materials in many ways puts the cart ahead of the horse. The average web page exists for a mere 44 days, after which it can never be reproduced. Instead of worrying about long-term preservation, most of us should focus on acquiring the materials in jeopardy in the first place and on shorter-term preservation horizons, 5 to 10 years, through well-known and effective techniques such as frequent backups stored in multiple locations and transferring files regularly to new storage media, such as from aging floppy discs to DVD-ROMs. If we do not have the artifacts to begin with, we will never be able to transfer them to one of the more permanent digital archives being created by the technologists.[24]

Taking first steps

The importance of moving quickly to save extant digital materials is exceedingly evident in the case of 9/11. People turned to the Internet as a "commons"; it became a place to communicate and comment and share their feelings and perspectives. For example, nearly 20 million Americans used email to rekindle old friendships after 9/11. Thirteen percent of Internet users participated in online discussions after the attacks. People approached the Internet as a place to debate the United States government's response to terrorism (46 percent), to find or give consolation (22 percent), and to explore ways of dealing locally with the attacks and their aftermath (19 percent). Rather than in tangible diaries and letters, there was an outpouring of thoughts and emotions in thousands of blogs on September 11 and the following days, and in millions of emails and instant messages.

"For the first time," wrote one electronic newsletter editor, "the nation and the world could talk with itself, doing what humans do when the innocent suffer: cry, inform, and most important, tell the story together." Just four years later, many of these potent reactions already have been permanently lost in a discarded email or blog account, to willful or unconscious deletion, or on the unrecoverable magnetic surface of a crashed hard drive. Had the Library of Congress and its partners decided months later, instead of within mere hours, to save the web pages from 9/11 and immediately afterwards, many already would have vanished into the digital ether.[25]

Humans have always found ways to express their feelings and their history to each other and to a wide audience. Today this is being done increasingly in digital rather than analog forms, instantaneously to a vast global audience. In an age in which a significant segment of the record of modern life exists in digital form – a segment that will only grow in the years to come – ways will need to be found to capture digital documents, messages, images, audio, and video before they are altered or erased if our descendants are to understand how we lived. A future in which the cultural heritage community does not make extensive use of digital technologies as part of their mission is difficult, if not impossible, to imagine. Much more can, and must, be done if those interested in preserving a robust historical record are to fulfill their mission in the 21st century.[26]

Notes

1   Oral History Research Office, Columbia University, *September 11th 2001 Oral History Narrative and Memory Project*, http://www.columbia.edu/cu/lweb/indiv/oral/sept11.html, accessed May 11, 2005; Mary Marshall Clark, "The September 11, 2001, Oral History Narrative and Memory Project: A First Report," *Journal of American History* 89 (September 2002), pp569–79.

2   American Folklife Center, The Library of Congress, *September 11, 2001 Documentary Project*, http://www.loc.gov/folklife/nineeleven/index.html, accessed May 11, 2005.

3   The Library of Congress, *September 11, 2001 Documentary Project* in the American Memory Collection, http://memory.loc.gov/ammem/collections/911_archive/, accessed May 11, 2005.

4   National Institute of Standards and Technology, "Documentary Information Received by NIST," http://wtc.nist.gov/media/docs_info_received.htm, accessed May 11, 2005.

5   *Here is New York: A Democracy of Photographs*, http://www.hereisnewyork.org.

6   The Library of Congress, *The September 11 Web Archive*, http://www.loc.gov/minerva/collect/sept11/, accessed May 11, 2005; Netcraft, *Netcraft Web Server Survey*, September 2001, http://www.netcraft.com/Survey/index-200109.html, accessed May 11, 2005.

7   The Center for History and New Media at George Mason University and the American Social History Project/Center for Media and Learning at the Graduate Center at the City University of New York, *The September 11 Digital Archive*, http://911digitalarchive.org, accessed May 11, 2005.

8   According to the Netcraft web server survey in February 2005. See http://news.netcraft.com/archives/web_server_survey.html, accessed May 11, 2005, for the latest numbers.

9   On the vast digital corpus of the Clinton White House, see Adrienne M. Woods, "Building the Archives of the Future," *Quarterly* 2, no. 6 (December 2001), http://www.nasm.si.edu/research/arch/temp/marac/the_quarterly/Dec2001.html, accessed May 11, 2005. On the strange potential of future digital archives to contain either enormous numbers of documents or very few, see Roy Rosenzweig, "Scarcity or Abundance? Preserving the Past in a Digital Era" *American Historical Review*

108, no. 3 (June 2003), pp735–62. For more on how to create a successful online collecting project, and how to promote it, see Daniel J. Cohen and Roy Rosenzweig, *Digital History: A Guide to Gathering, Preserving, and Presenting the Past on the Web* (Philadelphia: University of Pennsylvania Press, 2005), chapters 5–6.

10   As quoted in Lee Dembart, "Go Wayback," *International Herald Tribune*, March 4, 2002, http://www.iht.com/articles/2002/03/04/itend04_ed3_.php, accessed May 11, 2005.

11   Michael Kazin, "12/12 and 9/11: Tales of Power and Tales of Experience in Contemporary History," *History News Network*, September 11, 2003, http://hnn.us/articles/1675.html, accessed May 11, 2005.

12   Linda Shopes, "The Internet and Collecting the History of the Present," paper presented at *September 11 as History: Collecting Today for Tomorrow*, Washington, DC, September 10, 2003. For more on this "rapport" and the way rich historical accounts arise during the live interaction of interviewer and interviewee, see Alessandro Portelli, *The Battle of Valle Giulia: Oral History and the Art of Dialogue* (Madison: The University of Wisconsin Press, 1997) and Michael Frisch, *A Shared Authority: Essays on the Craft and Meaning of Oral and Public History* (Albany: State University of New York Press, 1991).

13   Keith Whittle, *Atomic Veterans History Project*, http://www.aracnet.com/~pdxavets/, accessed May 11, 2005.

14   There are two main types of blogging systems: those hosted on one's own server and those hosted on a blog company's server. Certain versions of both types are free, though there are also paid versions that have more features. By far the three most prevalent hosted blogging systems are Blogger, owned by Google, http://www.blogger.com, accessed May 11, 2005, LiveJournal, run by a small team of software developers and staff, http://www.livejournal.com, accessed May 11, 2005, and AOL Journals, owned by TimeWarner, http://hometown.aol.com, accessed May 11, 2005. Although it exists in a commercial version, LiveJournal can also be downloaded for free and installed on your server. LiveJournal and Six Apart's Movable Type, http://www.moveabletype.org, accessed May 11, 2005, are the predominant do-it-yourself blogging systems (Six Apart also runs a commercial hosting service for Movable Type blogs called TypePad, http://www.typepad.com, accessed May 11, 2005).

Many other free and commercial blog sites and programs (including the open source WordPress) exist for those who find the dominant software and hosts too basic, or who demand other features like message encryption or the automatic resizing of images for web display. A full list of software packages can be found at http://en.wikipedia.org/wiki/Weblog# Blogging_systems, accessed May 11, 2005, and hosts for a variety of blog packages can be found at http://directory.google.com/Top/Computers/Internet/On_the_Web/Weblogs/Tools/Hosts/, accessed May 11, 2005. In general, however, the top four systems will be suitable in most cases. Two of the more sophisticated blogging systems are the free *Nucleus CMS*, http://www.nucleuscms.org/, accessed May 11, 2005, and pMachine's *ExpressionEngine*, http://www.pmachine.com/expressionengine/, accessed May 11, 2005.

More information on blogs can be found in National Institute for Technology & Liberal Education, "Market Share," *NITLE Blog Census*, http://www.blogcensus.net/?page=tools, accessed May 11, 2005; Weblogs Compendium, "Blog Tools" and "Blog Hosting," http://www.lights.com/weblogs/tools.html, accessed May 11, 2005, and http://www.lights.com/weblogs/hosting.html, accessed May 11, 2005.

15   My rough estimate is that over the last 4 years less than 10 percent of the nearly 1,000 submissions to the Echo Project, a set of experimental online collecting efforts in the recent history of science, technology, and industry, have been off-topic or suspect. Center for History and New Media, *Echo Project*, http://echo.gmu.edu, accessed May 11, 2005.

16   *San Jose Mercury News*, "Web Newspaper Registration Stirs Debate," Mercurynews.com, June 13, 2004, http://www.mercurynews.com/mld/mercurynews/8915529.htm, accessed June 2, 2005. Online collecting projects that focus on sensitive topics obviously may encounter more resistance to revealing accurate personal information. See R. Coomber, "Using the Internet for Survey Research," *Sociological Research Online*, 2, no. 2 (1997), http://www.socresonline.org.uk/2/2/2.html, accessed May 11, 2005.

17   The American Registry for Internet Numbers has a free IP lookup service at http://www.arin.net/whois/, accessed May 11, 2005. Non-U.S. domains (those with two-letter country codes at the end) can be located through Uwhois.com, http://uwhois.com, accessed May 11, 2005. Domains that end in .aero, .arpa, .biz, .com, .coop, .edu, .info, .int, .museum, .net, and .org can be located through the governing body for the web, the Internet Corporation for Assigned Names and Numbers (ICANN), at http://www.internic.net/whois.html, accessed May 11, 2005. There are several

commercial services that scan worldwide IP addresses, e.g., Network-tools.com, http://network-tools.com/, accessed May 11, 2005, and Network Solutions, http://www.network solutions.com/en_US/whois/index.jhtml, accessed May 11, 2005.

18   Donald A. Ritchie, *Doing Oral History: A Practical Guide* (2nd ed.; Oxford: Oxford University Press, 2003), p32.

19   Moving Here, *Moving Here: 200 Years of Migration to England*, http://www.movinghere.org.uk/, accessed May 11, 2005; BBC, *WW2 People's War*, http://www.bbc.co.uk/dna/ww2/, accessed May 11, 2005.

20   National Park Foundation, "Rosie the Riveter Stories," *Ford Motor Company Sponsored Programs*, http://www.nationalparks.org/proudpartners/partner_ford_rtrs.shtml, accessed May 11, 2005; National Geographic, *Remembering Pearl Harbor*, http://plasma.nationalgeographic.com/pearlharbor/, accessed May 11, 2005; *Voices of Civil Rights*, http://www.voicesofcivilrights.org, accessed May 11, 2005; The Alfred P. Sloan Foundation, "History of Science and Technology," http://sloan.org/programs/scitech_historysci.shtml, accessed May 11, 2005; *C250 Perspectives: Write Columbia's History*, http://c250.columbia.edu/c250_perspectives/write_history/, accessed May 11, 2005; *Vietnam Archive Oral History Project*, http://www.vietnam.ttu.edu/oralhistory/participation/index.htm, accessed May 11, 2005.

21   Fred R. Byers, *Care and Handling of CDs and DVDs: A Guide for Librarians and Archivists* (Washington, DC: Council on Library and Information Resources, 2003), http://www.clir.org/pubs/reports/pub121/sec4.html, accessed May 11, 2005; Peter Svensson, "CDs and DVDs Not So Immortal After All," Associated Press, May 5, 2004, http://www.usatoday.com/tech/news/2004-05-05-disc-rot_x.htm, accessed May 11, 2005; Basil Manns and Chandru J. Shahani, *Longevity of CD Media, Research at the Library of Congress* (Washington, DC: Library of Congress, 2003), http://gort.ucsd.edu/mtdocs/archives/diglet/001522.html, accessed May 11, 2005; Eva Orbanz, Helen P. Harriso, and Henning Schou, eds., *Archiving the Audio-Visual Heritage: A Joint Technical Symposium* (Berlin: Stiftung Deutsche Kinemathek, 1988); Diane Vogt-O'Connor, "Care of Archival Compact Discs," *Conserve O Gram*, 19/19 (Washington, DC: National Park Service, 1996), http://www.cr.nps.gov/museum/publications/conserveogram/19–19.pdf, accessed May 11, 2005.

22   Margaret Hedstrom, "It's About Time: Research Challenges in Digital Archiving and Long-Term Preservation," white paper sponsored by the National Science Foundation and the Library of Congress, August 2003, p8. For more on the challenges libraries and archives currently face with the proliferation of digital artifacts and collections, see Daniel Greenstein, Bill Ivey, Anne R. Kenney, Brian Lavoie, and Abby Smith, *Access in the Future Tense* (Washington, DC: Council on Library and Information Resources, 2004), http://www.clir.org/pubs/reports/pub126/contents.html, accessed May 11, 2005, and *Building a National Strategy for Preservation: Issues in Digital Media Archiving* (Washington, DC: Council on Library and Information Resources and the Library of Congress, 2002), http://www.clir.org/pubs/reports/pub106/contents.html, accessed May 11, 2005.

23   *DSpace*, http://www.dspace.org; fedora, http://www.fedora.info, accessed May 11, 2005; National Digital Information Infrastructure and Preservation Program, http://www.digitalpreservation.gov, accessed May 11, 2005.

24   On the longevity of web pages, see Gail Fineberg, "Capturing the Web," *Library of Congress Information Bulletin* 62, no. 4 (April 2003), http://www.loc.gov/loc/lcib/0304/digital.html, accessed May 11, 2005.

25   Pew Internet and American Life Project, *The Commons of the Tragedy* and *How Americans Used the Internet after the Terror Attack* (Washington, DC: Pew Internet and American Life Project, 2001). Quotation from *The Commons of the Tragedy*. See also Amy Harmon, "The Toll: Real Solace in a Virtual World: Memorials Take Root on the Web," *New York Times*, (September 11, 2002), pG39.

26   For more on the growth of Internet usage, especially as a place for communication, expression, and dialogue, see Deborah Fallows, *The Internet and Daily Life* (Washington, DC: Pew Internet and American Life Project, 2004).

Chapter 12

Deborah Dean and Rhiannon Williams

CRITICAL CLOTH: TO BE CONTINUED ... and THE TIME I'M TAKING: SEWING PROUST

Critical Cloth: To be continued . . .

Deborah Dean

R HIANNON WILLIAMS REFERS to her ongoing project *Critical Cloth* as 'a collection of paper works' and so leads us naturally to thoughts of accumulation and acquisition. This is the stuff of museum practice but also gets to the heart of the ideas she is exploring in each piece of work in the collection, in particular *My Loss is My Loss*.

My Loss is My Loss is the pivotal piece around which the other four works orbit. It is a patchwork cloth, made from lottery tickets; Williams buys £10 worth each week, makes the losing tickets into neat, hexagonal tessellations or patches, and stitches them on to a growing length of patchwork, in a process which she intends to continue for the rest of her life. She began the piece in 2002, playing the same set of ten numbers each week and relinquishing the occasional ticket to claim a prize. The rest are destined to become paper patches, accrued to this great document of loss. Each year the piece grows in length by half a metre, at a cost of £520 and in April 2011 when this publication was made, it measured 4.5 metres.

Williams describes *My Loss is My Loss* as 'an intellectual exercise which critiques late capitalist culture; it faces our ambiguities around appropriate uses for money and is perhaps a distasteful record of how I have spent my money, time and labour; I gamble, I lose, I work with my loss. But rhetorically, I am always giving to "good causes"' (Williams, 2009).

As well as recording financial loss, the piece tells a story of spent hopes and dreams. A new lottery ticket is a moment of fantasy and potential; for however long it sits in a purse, or waits on a mantelpiece unchecked, it represents the possibility of winning a life-changing sum. But it is more likely to be a loser and each patch in *My Loss is My Loss* is a little tale of disappointment or resigned shrug of the shoulders. This is a familiar story, emphasised by the repeated use of the ubiquitous pink and white ticket on one side of the patchwork. But there is a second, more intimate narrative emerging on the reverse, where each patch is reinforced with a scrap of birthday or Christmas card. Received by the artist each year, these snippets provide a glimpse into a private world. Before the mid 19th century all paper was handmade and costly and so it was common for patchwork to be backed with recycled personal documents. Usually, such backing was removed when sewing was complete, but Williams retains it to give extra strength to the fragile layer of ticket paper. In so doing, she also imbues the piece with autographical detail: an annual roll call of special occasions mark the passage of time and underline her life-time commitment to *My Loss is My Loss*.

This layering of narrative is evident in *Money Talks,* begun in 2008 as a companion piece to *My Loss is My Loss. Money Talks* is stitched from used scratch cards and backed with financial reports from daily newspapers. One side records the artist's private 'flutter', her hurried scratching away of the surface in search of the hoped-for winning numbers standing in for the gestural marks of drawing. On the reverse, the drama of the global economic crisis is played out over the weeks and months; from the announcement that 'the boom is over' on the first patch in January 2008, an increasingly alarmed vocabulary emerges with each week's row of careful stitches:

> I find I am stitching my way through an extended financial crisis. Each week,
> I take ten scratch cards, cut and back them with a new and troubled language –
> 'recession', 'slump', 'home repossessions', 'financial gloom', 'bankruptcy',
> 'capitalism in crisis'. . . .
>
> (Williams, 2009)

Over centuries, patchwork has demonstrated its capacity to commemorate major historical events as well as private domesticity; but in *Money Talks*, there is a sense of immediacy, with history unfolding as the artist works.

Other pieces in *Critical Cloth* are more reflective: in *Hoops for My Art to Jump Through,* a single-sided square of patchwork, Williams has sorted through the administrative paperwork that underpins the business of being an artist, cutting segments from it to make patches. The piece recounts the loan of her work to exhibitions, correspondence with galleries, negotiations and contracts.

Reportage – notable for not being a patchwork – is a series of three necklaces, each made from thousands of small discs, cut from the articles and images of three daily newspapers. The flimsy paper circles are threaded chronologically onto filament and densely packed so that together their edges create a rich band of colour, which changes with each new report. The necklaces are snapshots of time; a day's worth of news and events is hidden within the structure of each one. However, the sequence of headlines is faithfully transcribed in the title of the work, creating a disjointed narrative from the remnants of the dissected newsprint.

Both *Hoops for My Art to Jump Through* and *Reportage* are made meticulously and completed to a predetermined format and time frame. They operate as short spin-off stories to the central, non-stop narrative of *My Loss is My Loss*.

Yet within all these works lies a subtler narrative, implied through the process of making but invisible: that is, the time spent by Williams in the creation of each piece, marked stitch by stitch. In *Taking Time: Craft and the Slow Revolution,* Helen Carnac describes how an artist 'thinks through the act of making', opening up a space for themselves and others 'to interact and become immersed in time' (Carnac, 2009). The making of patchwork requires patience and precision: measuring, cutting, folding and stitching, piece by piece, on and on. This slow, contemplative work is the antithesis of our frantic, fast-paced technological age. Williams speaks of reaching a point where her repeated actions create a rhythm that frees her mind to reflect (Williams, 2010).

In her introduction to *Quilts 1700–2010: Hidden Histories, Untold Stories,* and referring to an essay by Joanne Bailey in the same publication, Sue Prichard describes how the making of patchwork in middle-class households of the 18th and 19th centuries (patchwork made for pleasure rather than out of necessity) 'provided a refuge from the day-to-day operation of the household, a momentary pause for quiet reflection and rare seclusion' (Prichard, 2010).

The value of patchwork as a means of occupying time positively was recognised by the 19th century prison reformer Elizabeth Fry. Fry and her supporters distributed fabric and sewing equipment to female prisoners and convicts on transportation ships, believing that needlework offered not only a practical skill and mode of employment but also, as Claire Smith writes, 'an enlightened state of contemplation, whereby the focus required for the act of stitching would have allowed the maker to enter a mental space removed from the everyday' (Smith, 2008). Moreover, patchwork seemed particularly suited to this doctrine:

> The creation of intricate patchwork required a heavy investment of time. With a lack of active employment, the experience of prison life for many in the early nineteenth century was reduced to the soul-destroying slippage of hours into days. Fry was keen to instill in the prisoner the transformative potential of this experience, turning simply 'doing time' into the positive experience of having the time in which to do something, and restoring a sense of control and independence to the inmate.
>
> (Smith, 2008)

Time as a concept, a metaphorical space and a means of structuring content and process, runs throughout *Critical Cloth* and is typified by the most recent work, *The Time I'm Taking*. Three years ago, Williams mapped out her latest task: to systematically dissect all seven volumes of Marcel Proust's *A la recherche du temps perdu* (c. 1908–22; translated both as *In Search of Lost Time* and *Remembrance of Things Past*). She chose an edition that prints the seven volumes in six books and has undertaken to hand-sew the three thousand pages of this monumental work into six sets of patchwork. At the time of writing, the first eighty pages of all six books have been completed.

Her system involves cutting tessellations from each page of the novel and backing them with fine white fabric interfacing. These two layers have a translucent quality and when held to the light, the text from the reverse of the page shows through to the front, one line colliding with another to create a soft slurring of words. This fragmentation and slippage means that it will take the viewer time and patience to decipher the text. Thus they experience something of the time and labour required by Proust to write the novel, and by Williams to deconstruct and remake it into cloth.

The act of taking apart Proust's fiction, only to stitch it together again as a new object, finds an echo in Williams' continuing work on *My Loss is My Loss*. Now over eight years in the making, the earlier sections of the patchwork are beginning to display the impact of time and light on ephemeral materials. Williams finds that she must now conserve and repair at one end of the cloth, whilst adding new patches to the other. The original linear process of making has become circular, like Penelope's shroud which, Homer tells us in *The Odyssey*, she wove by day for her father-in-law Laertes, only to unravel her work each night, in order to re-weave the following day. In this way she hoped to buy herself time until her husband Odysseus returned from the Trojan War, in the meantime warding off the persistent suitors who wished to take his place.

My Loss is My Loss therefore makes demands; it has grown in scale beyond the confines of the domestic space in which Williams works and beyond any notion that it might function as a quilt or cover:

> The physical bulk of the patchwork is now considerable and difficult to sew – I need to move round the piece, supporting, folding and unfolding to reach the different angles of each seam.
>
> (Williams, 2009)

It is at once old and new; it represents its own past, present and future, as well as that of the artist for whom it is, we are reminded, a lifetime commitment.

In February 1992, Canadian artist Germaine Koh made a similar commitment to *Knitwork*, a life-long piece made by unravelling used woollen garments and re-knitting the yarn into a single continuously growing object. By 2002, it was eighty metres long, comprised three hundred reused garments and weighed four hundred pounds; in 2005, when it was presented at Angel Row Gallery, Nottingham, it had increased further in scale, flowing over the gallery floor in an exuberant tide of colour, whilst the artist sat knitting steadily at its source:

> Although the slow accumulation of layers of obsolete goods might recall geological processes, the limits of the piece are actually human; the work will be finished when I cease [to be].
>
> (Koh, undated)

Like *My Loss is My Loss*, *Knitwork* has no function other than to be itself and to measure out the artist's life, in materials that also have their own history.

In *Critical Cloth*, Rhiannon Williams is creating a body of work – a collection – whose quiet intensity is apparent in every slow and measured stitch of its making. Yet the tasks she has set herself are monumental, pushing the work to a scale of endeavour which makes it (to borrow words used by Germaine Koh to describe *Knitwork*) 'both sublime and absurd, both excessive and banal, both rigorous and formless' (Koh, undated).

References

Carnac, Helen (2009), *Taking Time: Craft and the Slow Revolution*, Craftspace.

Koh, Germaine (undated), *Knitwork: Frequently Asked Questions*, information sheet.

Prichard, Sue, ed. (2010), *Quilts 1700–2010: Hidden Histories, Untold Stories*, V&A Publishing.

Smith, Claire (2008), 'Doing Time: Patchwork as a Tool of Social Rehabilitation in British Prisons', *V&A Online Journal*, Issue 1.

Williams, Rhiannon (2009), *Critical Cloth*, statement of practice.

Williams, Rhiannon (2010), in conversation with Deborah Dean.
. . .

The Time I'm Taking: Sewing Proust

Rhiannon Williams

Over the last three years I have begun to cut up systematically all seven volumes of Marcel Proust's prodigious novel *A la recherche du temps perdu* (c. 1908–22) and sew three thousand pages of print into patchwork. It will take considerably longer to hand sew this book than it took Proust to construct its narrative. Our mutual preoccupation, however, is to tease out and quiz the nature of time. Proust's achievement as a Modernist writer was, in the words of Samuel Beckett 'to examine in the first place that double-headed monster of damnation and salvation – Time' (1999, p11). In choosing to re-work Proust's work, to take apart then stitch together his fiction a hundred years after its production, I commit my time and labour to a task of critical practice. Sewing the *Recherche* extends and intensifies, perhaps even sets askew, the Proustian project. If nothing more, *The Time I'm*

Taking compounds a literary figuring of time with the practical, haptic and time-consuming routines of needlework.

Narrative time and stitched time

For Proust, who wrote *In Search of Lost Time* (also translated as *Remembrance of Things Past*) in somewhat irregular fashion over fourteen years leading up to his death in 1922, the making of an expansive, literary universe provided a philosophical vehicle for understanding dimensions of time lost, time passing, time regained through the mechanisms of memory and, ultimately, time outwitted by art. To conjure the subjective knowing of time, lived out by a complex self, constitutes the structural and principal theme of Proust's semi-autobiographical fiction, a *roman-à-clef* 'spanning the whole long arc of seven books' (White, 1999, p141). Narrative space, often besieged by prolonged evocations and metaphors, gives us the renowned 'Proustian sentence' and the narrator's manifestation of life's drama sits voluminous on the written page. Ollendorf declined to publish early volumes in 1913 with a note of sarcasm: 'I don't see why a man should take thirty pages to describe how he turns over in bed before he goes to sleep' (Davies, 2003, pxxviii). Literary critics of the twentieth century, however, are united in celebrating the singular importance of the *Recherche,* acclaimed by Walter Benjamin as 'this great special case of literature' (1992, p197) and later by Roland Barthes, as 'a complete system for reading the world' (Bowie, 2001, p514). Introducing his recent companion to Proust, Richard Bales is quite adamant, 'he is *the* author when it comes to treating the theme of time, time which can be apprehended in unexpected ways, the most spectacular being sudden resurrection of the past' (2001, p1).

Setting out now, at the beginning of the twenty-first century, to reconfigure the *Recherche* with needle and thread, I work the printed page to re-iterate and make dense the actual and conceptual time synthesised in Proust's study. The old labour of writing is doubled-up with the new labour of sewing and my own musing on time continues as I practise. With hexagonal template and a simple over-stitch, the temporal narrative of Proust's 'tapestry' (Benjamin, 2008, p94) is transposed piecemeal, into a paper-cloth-prose object, opened out in a panorama of writing and stitching.

Louise Bourgeois knew how 'doing' by sewing gave 'a structure and rhythm to time and thought' (Harrison, 2008, p37). Stitching was a conscious taking or appropriation with disciplined intent, distinct from 'respite and relaxation' sought in spare time or leisurely sewing (Stalp, 2007, p70). For Bourgeois, the motion, gestures and embedded habits of needlework were a pre-condition, allowing the mind to settle on memories and history and thus make art (Harrison, 2008, p36). My own protracted cutting into and re-assembling of the *Recherche* is akin to this strategy, absorbing time along a trajectory of sporadic, yet attentive handwork. Often working in pockets of negotiated or snatched time, I too settle, at once compelled by the tessellation of patches, and my mind returns to Proust's phraseology. His words come up close just as I fold and prick them: '. . . had I not tormented myself . . .', '. . . The love of Albertine . . .', '. . . his philoprogenitive zeal . . .', '. . . my original suspicions . . .' (1996, pp6–15). By the stitch, all is levelled to simple method and orderliness, not dissimilar from Maxine Bristow's inclination for plain sewing. Bristow sees the stitch in continuum as witness, a temporal measure that builds through 'the habitual return of the same' (Mitchell, 2006, p31). This is especially true of patchwork, given that the architecture of making is regulated entirely through the logic of repetition, governing form, stitch, pattern and praxis. A liking for re-iteration and sheer 'investment of time' (Jones in Prichard, 2010, p7) is enough to bulk out and make the piece. Marking time as so much labour can be its own spectacle by virtue of quantity and extent. This is stitching ad nauseam, but it is also technique as continuum. In all areas of textile practice, persistence of the handmade as 'laboured-over process' continues to be, observes Sarat Maharaj, 'a force that cannot be shrugged off' (Johnson, 2000, p20). I propose that a re-casting of Proust's fiction as patchwork distils narrative time into 'craftsman-time' (Sennett, 2008, p251), and re-positions the written text as subject and object of a prolonged, artisanal, cogitative and essentially material practice. The compatibility of one with the other seems palpable, for, '[i]n an age that values speed, brevity, efficacy, performance, and appearance, Proust "signifies" slowness, length, labor, contemplation, resistance, transcendance' (Gray, 1992, p153).[1]

Intrinsic to Proust's narrative figuration are the vital agents of metaphor and memory. Both are active in moving the parameters of time in a 'powerful vision of impermanence' (White, 1991, p155). Linear time has no dependable chronology in the *Recherche*, challenged as it is by continuities and discontinuities, swings from past to present, setting up an oscillation and a 'then/now rupture' (Watson, 1999, p164). In this context, and in deference to Classical precedence, Proust draws upon a somewhat platitudinous textile metaphor to convey longitude and longevity. The very sweep of time resides in textile analogy. Not only is his entire text conceived as 'the tapestry of lived life' wherein weaving of memory evokes Penelope's web (Benjamin, 1992, p198), but the necessity of long sentences is justified by a likeness to spinning: 'I really have to weave these long silks as I spin them. [. . .] If I shortened my sentences, it would make little pieces of sentences, not sentences' (Davis, 2003, pxxx). In the final volume, *Time Regained*, the narrator sees 'that the nimble shuttles of the years weave links between those of our memories which seem at first most independent of each other' (1996, p194). Human relations, once 'swollen' in importance, are ultimately reduced to a 'thin, narrow, colourless ribbon of an indifferent and despised intimacy' (p358). And in his final assessment, 'the thread of life' is seen to have passed through individual characters, eventually, 'all these different threads had been woven together to form the fabric . . . of the complete whole' (p353). By extension, *The Time I'm Taking* allows Proust's metaphorical cloth to reside in a literal equivalent, a paper cloth stitched in another time, through new agency, to form again the fabric of the complete whole.

Metaphor combines in the *Recherche* with the equally potent work of memory. Indeed, Proust's incentive to write results from the transformative nature of his own childhood memories, taking him on through the 'vast structures of recollection' (Proust, 1996, p54). As profound as any resurrection, history overcomes the protagonist in startling episodes of 'involuntary memory' (coined the 'Proustian rush'). Induced by touch or taste (a starched napkin, lime-blossom tea), spontaneous memory erupts and resides entirely in sensual experience. And it saturates the text. Transposed into patchwork, this text, laden with fictive re-callings and recollections, supports another mnemonic function. This refers to the textile artefact conceived as repository of commemorative or personal narrative and affiliation. With meaning that 'continue[s] to resonate across time' (Jones in Prichard, 1996, p7), cloth kept for posterity, is often enchanted and itself a 'sensory trigger' (Prichard, 1996, p21). A patchwork quilt in vernacular form, for example, can present an intense semiotic surface where fabrics worked with thread vouch for the subjectivity of the maker. In a similar way, *The Time I'm Taking* has the potential to be just such a 'repository', recalling the writer and the sewer, one heroic, the other stoic, both taken up with the lived-out vicissitudes of time submitted to a project of work.

Proust in patches

In one sense (the post-modern sense), cutting into the *Recherche* may be construed as an act of violence, but sewing is its amelioration. Gathering patches is a matter of harvesting the text. And this image suggests reduction, a possible 'fracturing and abbreviation' (Gray, 1992, p155), which appears to render Proust's 'stupendous length' (Bales, 2001, p4) an eroded and lesser entity. Moreover, cutting-up is preceded by an act of scanning (something less than reading), aligning choice words in windows barely two inches across. By necessity, scraps of print are discarded – I have made remnants of Proust, as well as requisitions. But the *raison d'être* of patchwork is to pursue aesthetic integrity founded precisely on this economy of redeployment; to select, cut up, disrupt, collage and quote are intrinsic to its effect. I am most aware of slicing through acclaimed 'architectonic sentences' (Davis, 2006, pxxiii) to arrive at a new semantic order, one of highlights and magnification. Through exhaustive production of hexagonal pictograms, prose melds with honeycomb pattern and generates a suggestive and cryptic surface. The iconic 'madeleine moment', for example, which launches the *Recherche* through the narrator's first encounter with involuntary memory, is rendered thus a partial, if knowable sign:

after

scattered, taste a

enduring, more immater

remain poised a longtime, li

oping, amid the ruins of all

the tiny and almost impalpa

structure of recollection.

recognised the taste of the

coction of lime-blosso

I did not yet

is

In this respect, the new modular whole now emerging from the *Recherche* may depend upon broken text familiar to the 'post-writing' age (Ellison, 2001, p201), but the overall unity of the sewn piece is a gestalt and amplification of its component parts. *The Time I'm Taking* is no 'cheeky collapse' of Proust, examples of which Margaret Gray associates with 'kitschification' and a gimmicky perversion of meaning (1992, pp153 and 156). Laid out page-by-page, stitched patch by patch, the entire complexity, epic proportions and 'gigantism' of the *Recherche* (White, 1999, p99), comes to be marked out and measured in space as well as in time.

    Transposition of the *Recherche* from paperbacks to paper cloth requires some consideration of the organising structure and collation of the novel. How might this inform a scheme for sewing? Proust's own thoughts on the formal arrangement of his *magnum opus* illustrate a wish to avoid any apportioning to volumes or parts. He would have preferred 'the whole of it' to be 'printed in a single volume, with two columns to the page and no paragraph divisions at all' (Benjamin, 2008, p94). By 1913, however, Proust is resigned to convention: 'I am like someone who has a tapestry too large for present-day apartments, and who has been obliged to cut it up' (Proust, 2008, p116). The *Recherche* has a complex publishing history and major revisions and re-orderings take place prior to Proust's death – the last three volumes are published posthumously.[2] C. K. Scott Moncrieff and Terrance Kilmartin's translation into English (1922–30), currently presents seven volumes in six books numbering up to five hundred pages in each (Vintage, 1996). It is this edition that provides both the material and the logic for sewing *The Time I'm Taking* as six sets of patchwork. To date, the first eighty pages of all six books have been stitched in panels measuring 80cm square. I anticipate the lengthier volumes could eventually produce up to eight metres of patched paper.

Taking stock of my own practice, I find patchwork in sympathy with Proust's approach to writing. The notion of working through an accumulation of 'patches' was not alien to Proust, although it facilitated a more organic method than I can adopt. His narrative skills have been likened to those of a 'mosaicist' (Carter, 2001, p39), and others point to the importance of 'montage' allowing the author to 'assemble hitherto disparate fragments into a more coherent sequence by means of a sophisticated "cut and paste" technique' (Schmid, 2001, p60). Moreover, the pragmatic value of patching assisted Proust in the management of his preparatory notes and transcripts. Céleste Albaret (Proust's housekeeper in the last eight years of his life) recounts his incorporation of copious 'additions' or 'paste-ons', small scraps of paper folded and glued to the page, scribbled with endless corrections (Albaret, 2001, p272–77). The idiosyncrasies of such an approach delighted the author who compares himself to a dressmaker combining swatches of cloth, 'I am pasting papers at the top, at the bottom, to the right, to the left' (Davies, 2003, pxxxviii) and, 'pinning here and there an extra page, I should construct my book, I dare not say ambitiously like a cathedral, but quite simply as a dress' (Proust 1996, p432). Proust's object was thus made and written in the manner of 'paning'[3] and its narrative structure is similarly one of patching 'scene, anecdote, impression, image, and crafting it to completion' (Carter 2001, p39).

The cumulative habit of patchwork assures my continued and steady conversion of text to cloth for years to come. Stitching continues and reading continues, for *The Time I'm Taking* is as much an exploration of literary criticism as it is the pursuit of art practice; reading and sewing converge in a mutually engaging and critical exchange. D. H. Lawrence found reading Proust was like 'trying to till a field with knitting needles' (Grey, 1992, p154), but I find at the interface between reading the *Recherche* and sewing the *Recherche* lies an opportunity to synthesize narrative time with stitched time and explore how one dimension augments the other. And no doubt I have elected by my work to be more fully, as Beckett would have it, a Proustian 'creature', 'victim of this predominating condition and circumstance – Time'. For in work, in life and in Proust, '[t]here is no escape from the hours and the days. Neither from tomorrow nor from yesterday' (Beckett, 1999, pp12–13).

Notes

1   Length and memory are two themes often explored by contemporary artists working with the *Recherche*. Most recently, Theodora Varney-Jones presented *Combray* (2005), exploring 'metaphorical skins of time and memory' (Don Soker Contemporary Art. San Francisco), and Véronique Aubouy continues her project, *Proust Lu*. Since 1993, Aubouy has filmed a sequence of readings from Proust – she expects to complete the work in 2050. www.veroniqueaubouy.fr/proust.html.

2   Eight volumes published in 1919 by Gallimard are now in the public domain and can be viewed online at the Internet Archive of the University of Toronto, http://www.archive.org/detals/ductdechezsaOl.

3   'Paning' refers to 'panes' of fabric sewn together for decorative effect. The term predates 'patchwork' which only appears in common use from the mid-18th century (Browne in Prichard, 2010, p24).

References

Albaret, Céleste (2001), *Monsieur Proust*, New York: New York Review of Books.

Bales, Richard, ed. (2001), *The Cambridge Companion to Proust*, Cambridge: Cambridge University Press.

Beckett, Samuel (1999), *Proust and Three Dialogues with Georges Duthuit*, London: John Calder.

Benjamin, Walter (1992), 'The image of Proust' in *Illuminations*, London: Fontana Press.

Benjamin, Walter (2008), *The Work of Art in the Age of Mechanical Reproduction*, London: Penguin Books.

Bowie, Malcolm (2001), 'Barthes on Proust', *The Yale Journal of Criticism*, 14 (2), pp513–18.

Carter, William C. (2002), 'The vast structure of recollection: from life to literature' in Richard Bales (2001), *The Cambridge Companion to Proust*, Cambridge: Cambridge University Press.

Davies, Lydia (2003), 'Translator's introduction' in Marcel Proust, *The Way by Swann's*, London: Penguin Books.

Harrison, Antonia (2008), 'Weaving, unweaving and reweaving: the legacy of Penelope' in *The Fabric of Myth*, Warwickshire: Compton Verney.

Ellison, David R. (2001), 'Proust and prosterity' in Richard Bales, *The Cambridge Companion to Proust*, Cambridge: Cambridge University Press.

Gray, Margaret E. (1992), *Postmodern Proust*, Philadelphia: University of Pennsylvania Press.

Johnson, Pamela (2000), 'Thinking Process' in *Art Textiles 2*, Bury St Edmunds: Bury St Edmunds Art Gallery.

Mitchell, Victoria (2006), 'Clothing the grid: alterations and alternations' in Maxine Bristow, *Sensual Austerity*, Sleaford: The Hub, National Centre for Art and Design.

Prichard, Sue, ed. (2010), *Quilts 1700–2010: Hidden Histories, Untold Stories*, London: V&A Publishing.

Proust, Marcel (2008), 'Swann explained by Proust' in *Days of Reading*, London: Penguin Books.

Proust, Marcel (1996), *In Search of Lost Time Volume Six: Time Regained*, London: Vintage.

Schmid, Marion (2001), 'The birth and development of *A la recherche du temps perdu*' in Richard Bales, *The Cambridge Companion to Proust*, Cambridge: Cambridge University Press.

Sennett, Richard (2008), *The Craftsman*, London: Allen Lane.

Stalp, Marybeth C. (2007), *Quilting: The Fabric of Everyday Life*, Oxford: Berg.

Watson, Janell (1999), *Literature and Material Culture from Balzac to Proust: The Collection and Consumption of Curiosities*, Cambridge: Cambridge University Press.

Chapter 13

Paul Ashton and Paula Hamilton

HISTORY AT THE CROSSROADS: AUSTRALIANS AND THE PAST

The new professionals: Public history

Public history can be broadly defined as a diverse set of practices that communicate and engage with historical meanings in public arenas. But to gain an understanding of public history it is as important to ask what specifically do public historians do?

In some ways, public historians perform much the same activities as academics. Unless extremely privileged, they are invariably involved in administration and workplace politics. Heritage practitioners often find themselves involved in debates over legitimate uses of history in heritage practice or in outright battles with bureaucrats or other professionals; major projects can be as administratively demanding as running a history department. Some public historians also teach, which is a highly public form of historical work.

A comprehensive cultural geography of public history practice is yet to written. But an outline is possible. Various areas of state and also local government are employers but in Australia private enterprise is a much less important employer of historians than in the USA. A few major corporations engage historians on a full-time basis. These positions are primarily located in archives and special historical collections or in property/heritage management. The Australian Post Office is one such employer. Power providers, road and water authorities have employed historians, or at least have units devoted to heritage, though historians are often viewed as being interchangeable with archaeologists by these agencies.

Large private corporations only on occasion employ professional historians – as opposed to retirees or insiders – to undertake one-off projects. However, this tends to be serendipity. Corporations and government departments with property holdings that include heritage buildings – State departments of Health, with extensive holdings of historic institutional public buildings, are a prime example of the latter – also employ historians to undertake heritage conservation reports. This is more than occasionally done as a result of responsibilities under the various state heritage acts or their enabling legislation rather than a passion for the past. State heritage agencies such as the Heritage Council of Victoria and the Heritage Branch of the NSW Department of Planning employ a small number of historians. The federal Department of Environment, Water and Heritage likewise employs historians in its heritage unit.[1] Unlike the North American example, there are almost no firms of historians or corporate historical enterprises in Australia. Most public historians are independent freelancers. The few exceptions include groups such as Crozier, Shute and Associates (based in Brisbane), Rosen and Associates (in Sydney) and Historica, a business which is mainly concerned with presenting 'contemporary, inspirational, and highly authentic cultural productions of "living history" across diverse spatial venues and media formats'. Founded by Stephen Gapps and Brett Kenworthy in 2003, Historica focuses on historical re-enactment and living history as 'powerful mediums for communicating the past in the present'.[2]

While the heritage industry generates a large proportion of work for public historians in Australia, those involved in training public historians have been drawn to more popular forms of history to diversify employment opportunities. Of all mainstream radio and television, only the Australian Broadcasting Commission (ABC) can count historians on its staff. Michelle Rayner, executive producer of the ABC's history shows *Hindsight* and *Verbatim*, is a graduate of the UTS graduate public history program. Budget cuts in recent years, however, clearly indicate that history on ABC radio will not be a growth industry. But this does mean that occasional freelance work may be available.

One freelance historian, Kate Evans, was engaged in research for the *Timeframe* series on ABC television in the late 1990s. Opportunities for historians in TV and radio will ultimately depend upon the internal political economy of individual channels and station, the appeal of individual historians – conservative historian Professor Geoffrey Blainey, who is now a freelance historian, once had his own series during an era of heightened nationalism in the early 1970s – and the whim of management. In 2004, after having investigated various options for historical programs, the ABC launched *Rewind* which was presented by historian Michael Cathcart. This program, however, had mixed responses.[3] The Australian multicultural TV broadcaster SBS screened its historically based 'reality' program *Colony* in 2006. There are also a few public historians who are film makers. Jeannine Baker had her documentary on the flooded town Adaminaby screened on the ABC in 2003.[4]

Local government is a significant employer of historians, but not in the field of heritage, though it has varying levels of input into a sizeable number of local and site specific studies commissioned by developers and others. Nor does it generally recruit historians as permanent staff. There are, however, notable exceptions. After directing the major Sydney City Council Sesquicentenary History Project from 1987, Shirley Fitzgerald was appointed City Historian. This is in part a reflection of Australia's wealthiest municipal authority's admirable perception of itself as a leader in civic cultural life rather than a trend in public history in Australia. Under Fitzgerald's leadership (until her retirement in 2009), and with the involvement of historians such as Chris Keating, Lisa Murray, Hilary Golder and Margo Beasley, the Sydney City Council has developed the largest and most impressive public history enterprise in the country. The council has also embarked on an ambitious on-line Dictionary of Sydney which was awarded a large Australian Research Council (ARC) grant in 2006. In Melbourne, academic and public historian Andrew Brown-May oversaw the creation of the Encyclopaedia of Melbourne which was sponsored, among other organisations, by the City of Melbourne and which was also awarded an ARC grant.[5] Many other local government authorities have commissioned local histories or histories of entire municipalities. The City of Adelaide, for example, commissioned Peter Morton to write *After Light: A History of the City of Adelaide and Its Council, 1878–1928*.[6]

Community history is another site for the practice of public history. Clubs – including ethnic and sporting bodies – professional associations, private schools and charities also commission histories. Anniversaries often provide the impetus for such work. The broad range of fields in commissioned histories is also impressive. Apart from institutional and local history, work is being done in Aboriginal history, oral history, medical history, sporting history, religious history, transport history, environmental history, planning history and urban history.[7] Perhaps the strongest growth area in recent years for public history has been in the field of Native Title where indigenous communities are obliged legally to demonstrate continuous connection to their land in order to succeed in a land claim. The practice and politics of work in Native Title claims is complex and often fraught.[8]

The professionalisation of history

Before World War II, Australia had only six small universities with five professors of history and one associate professor.[9] By the mid-1970s, most professional historians – around 750 – were concentrated roughly equally in universities and colleges of advanced education. As elsewhere, the growth of professional history was associated with the rise of the nation and nationalism. A combination of factors, however, led to a new development in the professionalisation of history. These included urban environmental activism, the emergence of new histories culminating in the new social history, the growth of the heritage industry from the 1970s and developments in cultural tourism. And they facilitated the emergence of a sector of academically trained historians working professionally with a wide range of employers and publics outside universities. This began in the late 1970s in the USA and in the early 1980s in Australia. The field was known initially as Applied and, later, Public History. Public historians work in heritage conservation, commissioned history, museums, the media, education, radio, film, government and other areas. They ask the question: 'What is history for?' and they are concerned with addressing the relationship between audience, practice and social context.[10]

Changes in the tertiary education sector also had an impact on the professional practice of history. Career paths for historians in academia were to diminish after the onset of economic recession in the early 1970s. Australian universities and colleges weren't initially affected to the extent of many of their overseas counterparts. In terms of investment in social capital, the largess of the Whitlam Labor government was to generate a wave of material comfort which washed the humanities in the academy until the late 1970s. But career opportunities for young historians had largely dried up by the early 1980s.

As a result, growing numbers of academically trained practitioners looked outside universities for work which would sustain them in their chosen profession. Thus it is not coincidental that professional historians' associations (PHAs) sprang up from the 1980s: South Australia, 1981; Victoria in 1983 (as part of the History Institute of Victoria; self-determining from 1991); NSW, 1985; Western Australia, 1989; Queensland, 1990; and Tasmania, 1992.[11] The Professional Historians Association of the Northern Territory was established in 2001.

The formation and initial growth of these organisations, however, was generally characterised by debate over their nature and purpose. Questions concerning historical authority lay at the heart of the matter. As Ruth Donovan has observed, the History Institute, Victoria, was 'conceived as a bridge linking institutional historians and others working outside the university'.[12] Modelled in part on the London Institute of Historical Research and co-funded by four Victorian universities, it was promoted by academics such as Geoffrey Searle, and acted as a sort of brokerage between organisations and freelance historians. Its two principal interest were 'to establish and expand a market for the historical training provided by universities [and] . . . to promote the interests of the history sector, to heighten the community's awareness of historical questions, and to develop a sense of the cultural importance of a sense of history'.[13] By the mid 1980s it had a membership of between 350–400 roughly divided equally between academics and university-qualified historians and others with a general interest in history. By and large it did not concern itself with industrial matters. A rift, however, was to emerge within the Institute. Brian Crozier, who was largely responsible for the Institute's initial progress, had a particular view of not just the organisation but of history more broadly. As Greg Denning was to write, Crozier:

> . . . saw before most of us that history was a public thing. It didn't belong to academic history departments. It didn't belong to establishment antiquarians . . . there were historians in museums, galleries, in archives, in newspapers, in schools whose needs were not being met by academic history departments.[14]

Ultimately, a Public History Sub-Committee of the Monash Public History Group was set up in 1990. In the following year, this became the Professional Historians' Association of Victoria. A decade later, facing financial difficulties in a stringent tertiary environment, the History Institute, Victoria closed its doors.[15]

Rumblings in and between groups involved with the new public history were evident at what became known as 'The Adelaide Meeting'. During the Australian Historical Association's 1986 conference in South Australia's capital, a meeting was held between the Association of Professional Historians of South Australia, the Professional Historians Association of NSW, the History Institute, Victoria, the Centre for Western Australian History (set up in 1985) and the Public Historians Association, Canberra. Some groups had adopted membership restrictions, flagging an industrial trajectory. The South Australia association had a minimum requirement of a BA including a history major; the New South Wales association insisted on an honours degree in history for associate or full professional membership, though it did have a nonprofessional category. Having represented the PHA NSW at the meeting, Heather Radi – a Senior Lecturer in Australian History at the University of Sydney – reported what was essentially a demarcation dispute to that association's members. The Centre for Western Australian History, she wrote in *Phanfare*:

> . . . is established within the University of Western Australia and appears to be under the management of academic historians who see themselves as the only ones qualified to write history. It intends charging a management fee for arranging to have a 'history' written which it will 'edit'. Concern was expressed that this policy will disadvantage historians working outside the universities and may lead to exploitation. . . . Both the Centre and the Victorian History Institute are prepared to take a Management Fee for arranging and advising clients commissioning a history.[16]

The situation, however, was more complex. Some academics equated such professional guidance with research degree supervision. University departments could also lend freelancers and their fledgling associations professional recognition and support. Academic qualifications had also been adopted as the primary professional accreditation rather than professional experience, though the latter could secure membership. Later, growing numbers of history departments offering 'applied history' programs also pointed to their need to work in the field and secure work for their masters and doctoral students.

The PHA NSW also experienced teething problems, with some teeth eventually being pulled. Richard White, an academic at the University of Sydney, left the steering group that was setting up the organisation as a mark of protest over what he felt was a far too prescriptive approach to developing objectives and rules. In its early years, PHA NSW members struggled over prioritising their immediate professional needs, a desire for academic approbation, developing networks and generally promoting history. Reflecting on the PHA NSW's origins, Tony Prescott, a past President, remarked that a 'lot of attention was still being focussed on the legitimacy of public history and, in retrospect, it is evident that undue attention was given to attempting to justify this aspect of professional practice to academic colleagues'. For Prescott, the latter was a 'distraction' from their main object: the marketplace.[17]

The New South Wales association was to take a hard line on its role as a professional body. In 1990, it attempted unsuccessfully to have itself listed on the state's Industrial Register.[18] Subsequently, after a series of protracted and difficult negotiations, it amended its constitution in 1993 to remove a non-professional membership category which had been important to the association's initial viability. As a direct result of this action, in that year the PHA NSW lost 60 of its 100 members.[19] Memberships were gradually restored with a significant number coming from the public history programs at the University of Technology, Sydney, and the University of Sydney.[20]

During the 1990s, other PHAs wrestled with questions of membership. States with smaller populations especially needed to buttress their numbers. Thus the Professional Historians and Researchers Association in Western Australia sought to attract members not solely from history but from across the humanities and social sciences. The Queensland History Institute – facilitated by the Brisbane History Group and established in 1990 with the distinguished historian Professor Geoffrey Bolton as its patron – had 'Fellows' as one of three categories of membership to accommodate people without academic qualifications who had contributed significantly to the state's history. In some instances, questions over membership were finally settled after formation of the Australian Council of Professional Historians Associations (ACPHA) in 1996. In December 1999, each of the six member associations of the ACPHA endorsed a National Standard for the Accreditation of Professional Historians. In the following year the Western Australian organisation, for example, 'amended its rules and membership categories accordingly' and became the Professional Historians Association (WA).[21]

The stated aims of the Council are 'to increase potential clients' and employers' awareness of both the skills of professional historians and the appropriate conditions for their employment; to maintain and encourage adherence to professional standards and ethics among historians; to encourage mutual support and co-operation among professional historians; and, to provide a forum for critical discussion of historical scholarship.'[22] Though the Council has been unsuccessful in supplying public forums or generating a dialogue about the nature of historical practice and its role in the culture, its creation underscored public history's arrival as the latest development in the professionalisation of history in Australia.

University history departments were slower to respond to this change though there were varying and various links between these professional bodies and the academy. The first public or applied history courses offered at tertiary level were at the University of Technology, Sydney, NSW, in 1988; Monash University, Victoria, in 1988; Murdoch University, Western Australia, in 1991; the University of Queensland in 1994; and the University of Adelaide, South Australia, from 1996.[23] The University of Canberra and Charles Sturt University, Bathurst, also offered subjects and courses in cultural heritage management. Freelance historians now outnumber the 350 academic historians currently in Australian universities. These programs and professional organisations did not touch all public historians. Geoffrey Blainey has yet to join the Victorian chapel and most 'accredited' public historians do not have graduate qualifications in public history. But the rise of professional associations and courses have meanings for public history which relate to another issue: that, as novelist Doris Lessing declared, academic historians had 'lost the right to interpret the past to the public' for having spoken to themselves for too long.[24]

From the 1970s much academic history tended to become increasingly specialist. Specialisation came at a price to many areas of academic history. Specialist, often esoteric knowledge, independence from lay input and closed, professional discourses contributed ultimately to the disasters that befell many history departments in Australia in the 1980s and beyond. This was initially exacerbated by the absence of a corresponding professional environment outside the academy. History departments had been reproducing themselves in an increasingly inhospitable corporatist and economically rationalistic climate. Unlike most professions, academic historians did not receive the support of powerful, external counterparts – who often accredited programs of study and influenced income streams – to champion their cause in the academy. In some universities the word 'history' slipped out of departmental titles. Academic discourses also saw shifts in nomenclature: historical landscapes, for example, became cultural landscapes. Official responses to the discipline of history indicated its ambivalent status. On the one hand, history was deemed to be worthy as an object of cultural warfare. On the other hand, history's subsumption in name indicated an official recognition of its seditious potential.

Change placed question marks against some old professional certainties. In terms of authority, professional historians have traditionally derived their status from academic qualifications and positions, academic publications and academic referees. Public historians, however, can also derive authority from legislation – such as heritage acts – or from government agencies, whether directly or indirectly. And it can be gained or enhanced by non-academic skills and reputation. Professional associations can confer degrees of authority through processes of accreditation, though there have been instances in Australia where accusations of 'gate keeping' have been made.

Questions of authority – or its recognition – in part underlie continuing tensions between academic and non-academic professional historians. For public and community historians, however, issues of authority can be particularly fraught when working with communities. In a post-colonial era where history has been democratised, professional practitioners can find themselves in negotiation with a range of individuals, groups and organisations over the content and nature of history.

The Koori Centre for Aboriginal Education at the University of Sydney, for example, has developed a set of principles and procedures to conduct research. Two of the principles state that the 'researcher/s shall ensure that through consultation and collaboration the needs and aspirations of the Aboriginal and Torres Strait Islander people, their community/ies, or organisations participating in the project are met'. Further, there is an instance that indigenous people and groups involved in research projects 'shall have a principal role in decision-making within the research project'. This covers consultation mechanisms; the definition of the area of research; project aims; control over benefits to the Aboriginal and/or Torres Strait Islander community; the research process; the research structure; the budget; terms and conditions for employing Aboriginal or Torres Strait Islander/non-Aboriginal participants in the research; evaluation procedures; the ownership of research outputs; and control over publication conditions.[25] These principles do not sit at all well with a traditional professional model. And although lacking any legal weight, they have had a significant ethical and moral impact on the ways in which some historians engage in historical undertakings with indigenous Australians.

While on the one hand public history represents a new development in professional history which has had a mixed reception in the academy – reflected, for example, in its very gradual and still uncomfortable integration into 'mainstream' history conferences – these changes have also contributed to the destabilisation of older definitions of what it is to be a historian. Indeed, the term public history has also been caught up in definitional debates.

Graeme Davison, in the *Oxford Companion to Australian History*, has neatly described public history as the 'practice of history by academically trained historians working for public agencies or as freelancers outside the universities'.[26] While useful this definition is perhaps too neat and excludes a range of both professionals and amateurs who practice history with effect in various public arenas. Davison, indeed, immediately goes on to note that while the North American term 'public history', coined in the mid 1970s,[27] was not adopted until a decade later in Australia, practitioners could be traced back at least to C. E. W. Bean. Bean, however, was not an academically trained historian. He studied law at Oxford University and subsequently became a journalist.

In drawing on the example of Charles Bean, Davison indirectly acknowledges tensions and growing debates over the term 'public history'. We say growing since to date most public historians – whether academic or non-academic – have been largely content to get on with their practice, leaving reflections on the field to a handful of individuals.[28] The only Australian periodical devoted specifically to public history – *Public History Review* – has few contributions that address public history per se.[29] Professional associations generally limit their activities to directly work-related matters and publications such as codes of ethics.

Public history in Australia has been shaped by specific local conditions that vary from state to state, region to region and place to place, and by largely British and American influences including England's people history movement and the less influential applied history model that emerged in the United States.[30] As mentioned earlier, the rise of graduate university programs across the country led by academics with different styles and ideological persuasions has also impacted significantly on public history.

In his *Use and Abuse of Australian History*, Graeme Davison recollects that his engagement with public history evolved out of a hobby and a sense of 'professional obligation' to enthusiasts. 'Only gradually', he notes in the preface to this work, did he realise that 'everyday forms of history-making' were both transforming and challenging the academic discipline of history. Elsewhere, Davison has depicted public history as an expression of a desire to bridge a perceived gap between academic history and the Australian public. Earlier, British academic Raphael Samuel, a founder of the *History Workshop Journal*, who founded a public history program at Ruskin College, Oxford,[31] had put this rather differently when he proposed that:

> . . . history is not the prerogative of the historian, nor even, as postmodernism contends, a historian's 'invention'. It is, rather, a social form of knowledge; the work, in any given instance, of a thousand hands.[32]

The differences in approach are vital in coming to a fuller definition, hard as this might be, of public history. Davison's conceptualisation of public history is academy-centric. Public historians emerge from universities and their practice is a vernacularism of academic history. In this view the public historian's role is to lead the laity by example.

For Samuel, history in the public arena is 'the ensemble of activities and practices in which ideas of history are embedded or a dialectic of past-present relations is rehearsed'. In this sense, public history is an engagement with such activities and practices. These can range from ceremonies and rituals of 'social integration'[33] to public landscapes, monuments and memorials, museums and exhibitions, school texts and classrooms, historical films and novels and family and local 'history-making'. Most of these activities – including history teaching in high schools – do not involve professionally trained historians.

Going back to Davison's definition, we might draw a distinction between public history and public historians. Public historians are generally concerned with a wide range of audiences. They bring historical skills into a variety of contexts. And they are concerned with the social and cultural uses of history. But further definition is difficult. Some public historians are pragmatic, even conservative in their approach to public history. Others view engagement with public history as a vehicle for cultural interventions and social activism. Some see themselves as independent scholars (though some independent scholars such as Humphrey

McQueen do not necessarily see themselves as public historians). Others do not identify as history scholars.

In Australia, as in the USA and Canada, there is significant interest in pursuing a career in public history. And there is a range of possibilities which currently look more promising than traditional alternatives in history. For many future historians, the academy – offering training, pastoral care and some opportunities for employment – will be part of a network of organisations and institutions, such as the professional historical associations, that sustain professional historical practice. The future, however, is uncertain and public history remains marginal, and occasionally disdained, in the academy. Eminent academic historians, such as Ludmilla Jordanova, have argued for the importance of public history, noting that it 'raises exceptionally complex issues upon which all historians must reflect. We cannot dismiss public history', she rightly contends, 'as "mere" popularisation, entertainment or propaganda. We need to develop coherent positions on the relationships between academic history, institutions such as museums, and popular culture'.[34]

Clearly, tensions abound. Even professional historians' associations – which themselves are at a crossroad with memberships peaking and the first generation of professional, non-academic historians moving towards retirement – struggle with the term 'public history'. Few of them use it in their literature. And only a tiny handful of their members have articulated their views on what has become a sub-discipline or field of history. The same can be said, with a few exceptions – including Graeme Davison, Peter Spearritt and Shirley Fitzgerald[35] – of academic historians. The situation is similar in Britain and America. In an insightful article concerning academic definitions of 'historian' and 'audience', Patricia Mooney-Melvin noted with some frustration that:

> Even in studies such as Theodore S. Hamerow's *Reflections on History and Historians*, with its focus on 'what it is like to be a professional historian' as opposed to an examination of the nature of historical scholarship, the definition of historian is treated as a fixed category, unrelated to time and place. The only time and place of importance in the defining process, at least as far as the professional historical community is concerned, is that of the period when the professionalizers' construct of historian emerged and took root. Given the way in which we subject everything else to reinterpretation and contextualization, I find it curious that we are so loath to examine – even at the most superficial level – the appropriateness of this definition in light of other aspects of the profession's past and present experiences.[36]

In Australia, as elsewhere, this question of redefinition remains largely unaddressed.

Ruth Donovan has argued, rightly, that public history organisations have achieved their workaday objectives. Now, she wrote, 'better history is being undertaken beyond the academy than ever before and the trained historians undertaking it are increasingly perceived as professionals'.[37] Such an academy-centric view, however, belies ongoing professional insecurity. Queensland's PHA notes on its website that it is 'akin to other professional associations for persons such as architects, doctors, engineers and planners. It is not an historical society at all'.[38] The situation, too, is more complex. Despite its successes, as Donovan rightly observes, 'the optimism and enthusiasm that characterised and drove the development of public history practice [in Australia] in the 1980s has faded'.[39] Pressures of freelance life, an aging first generation of public historians and the consolidation of professional organisations have been major contributing factors. The relative smallness of these groups, however, has at times been problematic and on occasions some have been accused of gate-keeping.[40] This has been exacerbated by vicissitudes of the market place.

Questions of authority – or its recognition – in part underlie continuing tensions between academic and non-academic professional historians. Today, professional associations confer authority through processes of accreditation which is now nationally prescribed. But in a post-colonial era where history has been democratised, professional practitioners can find themselves in negotiation with a range of individuals, groups and organisations over the content and nature of history. Around twenty years ago, Michael Frisch coined the term a 'shared authority'.[41] While still in vogue, [. . .] [it] is more often than not 'a signal of worthy intentions rather than an actual description of how people negotiate knowledge about the past.'[42]

Finally, we return to Raphael Samuel's call for a 'more generous definition of the historical profession'.[43] For some academic historians, public history paradigms – including heritage conservation – have already become important, for example, in grounding research and attracting increasingly competitive research grants. And the growing importance of university-community engagement in the tertiary education sector should increase public history's appeal. For freelance historians, generosity may have other rewards including broader professional recognition and status.

Notes

1   For details of the politics of history in heritage at the federal level, see Paul Ashton and Jennifer Cornwall, 'Corralling Conflict: The Politics of Australian Federal Heritage Legislation Since the 1970s', in Alexander Trazpeznik (ed), *Conflicted Heritage*, special issue of *Public History Review*, vol 13, pp53–65.

2   See http://www.historica.com.au.aboutus.

3   See Michelle Arrow, '"Want to be a TV Historian When I Grow Up!": On Being a *Rewind* Historian', *Public History Review*, vol 12, 2006, pp80–91.

4   For a review of the documentary see Pauline O'Loughlin, 'Jeannine Baker, Adaminaby', in *Public History Review*, vol 10, 2003, p134.

5   Andrew Brown-May and Shurlee Swain (eds), *The Encyclopedia of Melbourne*, Cambridge University Press, Melbourne, 2005.

6   Wakefield Press, Adelaide, 1996.

7   See, for example, Paul Ashton and Chris Keating, 'Commissioned History' in *The Oxford Companion to Australian History*, op cit, pp139–41.

8   For example, see David Ritter and Frances N.A. Flanagan, 'Stunted Growth: The Historiography of Native Title Litigation in the Decade Since Mabo', in *Public History Review*, vol 10, 2003, pp21–39.

9   Stuart Macintyre and Anna Clark, *The History Wars*, Melbourne University Press, Melbourne, 2003, p25.

10 Paul Ashton, 'The Past in the Present: Public History and the City of Sydney', in Tim Murray (ed), *Exploring the Modern City: Recent Approaches to Urban History and Archaeology*, Historic Houses Trust NSW and La Trobe University, Sydney, 2003, p2.

11 Paul Ashton, 'Duncan Waterson: Public Historian', in Paul Ashton and Bridget Griffen-Foley (eds), *From the Frontier: Essays in Honour of Duncan Waterson*, special issue of *Journal of Australian Studies*, vol 69, and *Australian Cultural History*, vol 20, 2001, p18.

12 Ruth Donovan, 'Australian Public History: Growth of a Profession?' PhD Thesis, University of Western Australia, Nedlands, 2006, pp155–56.

13 Brian Crozier, 'The Historical Community; or Seeing the Whole Elephant', *Newsletter*, History Institute, Victoria, vol 6, no 9, October 1989, p7, quoted in Donovan, op cit, p119.

14 Greg Denning, 'Some Beaches are Never Closed: Foundation and Future Reflections on the History Institute Victoria', *Rostrum*, vol 19, December 2001, p29.

15 University of Melbourne Archives, acc no 10214, historical note.

16 *Phanfare*, no 18, October 1986, p4.

17 Tony Prescott, 'The Professional Historians Association in New South Wales: A Seventeen-Year Overview', *Public History Review*, vol 10, 2003, pp90–91.

18 *Phanfare*, no 61, October 1990, p4.

19 Prescott, op cit, p91.

20   Twenty per cent of the current professional membership have degrees in public history from UTS. See http://phansw.org.au/member_list.html, accessed 1 August 2009.

21   See http://www.phawa.org.au/about%20us.html, accessed 21 July 2009.

22   See www.historians.org.au.

23   Paul Ashton and Paula Hamilton, 'Streetwise: Public History in New South Wales', in *Public History Review*, vols 5/6, 1996–97, pp15–16.

24   Ibid

25   The Koori Centre, 'Principles and Procedures for the Conduct of Research', in Christa Ludlow (ed), *Ethics for Historians*, Professional Historians Association NSW Inc, monograph series, no 1, Sydney, 1995, p35.

26   Graeme Davison, 'Public History', in Graeme Davison, John Hirst and Stuart Macintyre (eds), *The Oxford Companion to Australian History*, Oxford University Press, Melbourne, 1998, p532.

27   Robert Kelley, 'Public History: Its Origins, Nature and Prospects', *The Public Historian*, vol 1, no 1, 1975, p16.

28   See, for example, Graeme Davison, *The Use and Abuse of Australian History*, Allen and Unwin, Sydney, 2000 (reviewed in *Public History Review*, vol 8, pp198–200); John Rickard and Peter Spearritt (eds), *Packaging the Past? Public Histories*, special issue of *Australian Historical Studies*, vol 24, no 96, April 1991; and Paul Ashton and Paula Hamilton, 'Blood Money? Race and Nation in Australian Public History', *Radical History Review*, vol 76, Winter 2000, pp188–207.

29   See http://epress.lib.uts.edu/journals/phrj.

30   On public history in Britain, see Hilda Kean, Paul Martin and Sally J. Morgan (eds), *Seeing History: Public History in Britain Now*, Francis Boutle Publishers, London, 2000, and Paul Ashton and Hilda Kean (eds), *People and their Pasts: Public History Today,* Palgrave MacMillan, Basingstoke, 2009. For the American experience, see James B. Gardner and Peter S. LaPaglia (eds), *Public History: Essays from the Field*, Krieger Publishing Company, Florida, 1999.

31   See Hilda Kean, 'Public History and Raphael Samuel: A Forgotten Radical Pedagogy?', in *Public History Review*, vol 11, 2004, pp51–62.

32   Raphael Samuel, *Theatres of Memory: Volume 1: Past and Present in Contemporary Culture*, Verso, London, 1994, p8.

33   E. J. Hobsbawm and Terrence Ranger, *The Invention of Tradition*, Cambridge University Press, London, 1984, p263.

34   Ludmilla Jordanova, *History in Practice*, Arnold, London, 2000, p171.

35   See Graeme Davison, *The Use and Abuse of Australian History*, op cit, and 'Public History', in *The Oxford Companion to Australian History*, op cit; Peter Spearritt, 'Money, Taste and Industrial Heritage', in Rickard and Spearritt, op cit; Shirley Fitzgerald and Kathryn Evans, 'Reflections on the Commissioning Process: An Interview', in *Public History Review*, vol 2, 1993, pp125–34. Fitzgerald was an academic at the time and became an adjunct Professor at the University of Technology, Sydney from 2005.

36   Patricia Mooney-Melvin, 'Professional Historians and the Challenge of Redefinition', in Gardner and Paglia (eds), *Public History: Essays from the Field*, pp6–7.

37   Ruth Donovan, 'Australian Public History: Growth of a Profession?', PhD thesis, University of Western Australia, 2006, p321.

38   See http://www.qldhistorians.org.au/au/phaq/information.index.shtml, accessed 20 July 2009.
      39 Ibid.

40   Paul Ashton, 'Duncan Waterson: Public Historian', in *From the Frontier: Essays in Honour of Duncan Waterson*, Paul Ashton and Bridget GriffenFoley (eds), special issue of *Journal of Australian Studies*, no 69, 2001, p19. *Meaning of Oral and Public History*, State University of New York Press, Buffalo, 1990.

42   Ashton and Hamilton, 'Connecting with History', op cit, p37.

43   Op cit, p19.

PART III

Intangible and Tangible Presentations of the Past

Paul Martin

I N THIS SECTION WE WILL LOOK at intangible interpretations and understanding of history and their tangible realizations. The intangible is discussed in how the past is experienced, felt or reflected upon and the ways in which history is constructed or engaged with other than through written documents. It also relates to the idea of embodiment. That is to say, something that sensually (visually, aurally, etc.) or physically seems to represent or symbolize a feeling, idea or value held by people. In this way people discover or develop relationships with the past that are formed at least in part through acculturation, of being in the world[1] rather than through study of established documents (but which it might also lead to as well). The tangible is demonstrated through the extracts, in how such emotional engagements either result in representative material constructs, such as museums and memorials, or are triggered by memories of life experience in existing buildings, such as plantations and prisons. In this sense, the practice of public history is about the externalizing or articulating of this historical embodiment through a variety of routes explored in the extracts. The extracts themselves are introduced and discussed using either comparative examples or with each other to contextualize and reflect the ideas and issues in them.

Telling stories

History, from a conventional Western perspective is usually held to be constructed by the search for empirical evidence often in the form of documents or records which 'testify' to a course of events.[2] From an everyday experiential and public history perspective, it is more about, as the extract by James A. Flath notes and echoing Pearce on popular collecting,[3] 'how people make sense of the past and present', especially in an intangible, non-written context. Flath examines *nianhua* (New Year pictures) from rural China and the socio-cultural role they played and how they changed in the twentieth century. He finds their representation and physical production intrinsically bound: '*Nianhua* may be understood through two essential sets of considerations. [. . .] the physical and social production of the visual text, followed by the way the images are put together to form a narrative or evoke a certain impression.'

A Western example of this intangible understanding is expressed by Katalin Lovasz in her essay 'Playing Dress Up: eBay's Vintage Clothing-Land'.[4] She discusses the dichotomy between her objective academic stance as a researcher and her subjective imagination as a collector of that which she is researching – vintage women's dresses and their effect on women's movement in social space during the 1930s to 1950s. She notes that in wearing the vintage dresses and imagining herself into the role of a 1930s American woman, she:

> ... thereby dissolve[s] the conventionally static barriers among researched, imagined and real and make[s] of them something organic, mobile and changeable, something that escapes the constraints of the traditional segregation of the researcher and her subject.[5]

Gendered language notwithstanding,[6] French social theorist Jean Baudrillard asserts in his essay 'The Systems of Collecting' that collecting is discourse orientated towards oneself:

> ... whatever the orientation of a collection, it will always embody the irreducible element of independence from the world. It is because he feels himself alienated or lost within a social discourse whose rules he cannot fathom that the collector is driven to construct an alternative discourse that is for him entirely amenable, in so far as he is the one who dictates its signifiers – the ultimate signified being, in the final analysis, none other than himself.[7]

Lovasz's embodiment of her collection both exemplifies yet transcends Baudrillard's assertion. It is subjective and immersive, but also objective in its recognition as an additional and alternative research process and how it differs from her formal academic training. As she freely acknowledges:

> It is not recommended research practice to seek physical identification with the subject of one's research. I've just never been able to compartmentalize myself. I generally find my research echoed in the bits and pieces of my daily life. . . .[8]

Although not exactly an Aboriginal 'dreamtime'[9] Lovasz seemingly enters a similar form of transcendence of the present, via a material culture medium:

> My body is the transition between the here and now that I inhabit while imagining the past, and the past I imagine. [. . .] By wearing a dress from the 1930s, I become the act of imagining and I embark on a bodily engagement with the reconstruction of the past.[10]

Thus, the tangible and visible in the form of the vintage dress acts as a conduit for an intangible and deeply felt historical connectivity. This then feeds back into and through Lovasz's research, adding an extra dimension of historical perception.

Flath argues that the printed visualization of historical narrative through *nianhua* was significant in rural China while academic history was not. It was the signification that mattered, as it is for Lovasz in her example. This signification, Flath asserts, could therefore be appropriated by elites to impart their own messages and agendas. He notes, for instance, that 'Socialist icons gained legitimacy because they were produced using traditional peasant-oriented techniques. . . .' Hence, an apparent seamlessness with the past is given continuity in the present.

Lovasz experiences a similar seamlessness after opening her packages of vintage clothing and associated material, bought through eBay: 'I proceed to do the same things that women in the past did: I try on my new dresses, flip through the pages of my new-old magazines. I thereby overlap the past habits of these women with my new ones.'[11] In both Flath's and Lovasz's cases, the past is a matter of perception and, importantly, embodiment. For the rural Chinese, *nianhua* were visually recognizable as a print form of narrative that spoke both to the classical tales they told and the age-old practice of physically making and using them, all of which embodied a sense of the past and continuity in their perception. For Lovasz, it is the literal bodily engagement with the dresses through wearing them that affect a similar perception. Hence, an internalized sense of the past is formed which offers a different understanding and engagement than 'encountering it at a physical remove'.[12] Both Flath and Lovasz in their different ways are articulating an intangible or sensed past through familiar with everyday physical mediums.

The physical in the form of a building, for instance, may more intangibly signify very different histories. As Cahal McLaughlin observes in the extract on the Long Kesh/Maze prison/internment camp in Northern Ireland, it was 'for some a site of political struggle and for others a place of punishment for "terrorist" crimes'. McLaughlin describes the process of making a documentary film, *Inside Stories*, about the prison and its inmates and service personnel while being careful to maintain a parity of screen time for all involved. He explains the various receptions the film received in different locations, which highlights the constructivist responses (i.e. audience members creating their own meaning-making from the viewing). McLaughlin asks: 'in what contexts is it possible for individuals and communities emerging from conflict to listen to the accounts of others from whom they have been divided for thirty years, if not for very much longer?'

One example, not of an emergent conflict but still of a contemporarily relevant issue, was an extraordinary meeting held between historians, old British Communist and Fascist veterans of the 1936 Battle of Cable Street in 1991 at the Institute of Historical Studies, London.[13] This is a historically celebrated event in which a vast number of East Londoners gathered to stop the planned march through their area of Sir Oswald Mosley's British Union of Fascists. The sheer numbers and strength of opposition caused the police to advise Mosley to call off the march, which he did. Both this and *Inside Stories* were exercises in what McLaughlin calls 'memory telling' and 'giving space to stories'. In so doing it is perhaps the human context more than the political that is highlighted. On the question of the veracity of physical confrontation or moral persuasion away from fascism, Charlie Goodman, an active anti-fascist in the 1930s, recalled the mass unemployment of the era:

> I remember playing football in Victoria Park (east London) we used to play about
> 30 a side in those days for about four hours at a time. And many of the blokes
> I played with, and I saw them once, on a march wearing black shirts and black
> boots and all that sort of thing, and afterwards I said to them 'What the bloody
> hell are you doing with Mosley?' and they says to me 'Charlie, don't worry we're
> getting half a crown [12.5 pence] and a pair of boots.' So, which you may laugh,
> but it was something. So are you going to beat up a bloke because of that?[14]

They are both, as well, stories about place. Both are legendary. Both Long Kesh/Maze and Cable Street loom large in historical consciousness.[15] Both involve adherents of diametrically opposed political positions and the resultant violence. Both have deep experiential histories and narratives that shape the historicization of those places. This public testimonial history is, on one level, intangible in that it is born of acculturation. But such is the strength and collective sum of testimony that once recorded or published they are rendered the tangible history of those places and events. Certainly no official history based on the events as evidenced by the then home secretary Sir John Simon or police chief Sir Philip Game would measure up against the oral testimony of participants in the Cable Street events. No less than the official Cabinet or parliamentary records or memoirs of home secretary Merlyn Reese would convey the 'meaning' of Long Kesh/Maze beyond the perfunctory and utilitarian.

The time and distance is a lot less in the Northern Irish case and its historicization is still in the making. The construction of a full historical narrative is still a fragile process.[16] As McLaughlin notes: 'the representation of "Troubles" narratives continue to be contested'. As such, his chapter is an exercise in the analysis of a documentary structuring process that enables first-hand experiential accounts to be articulated. It is about the use and occupation of space, both physically in terms of the prison itself and visually on camera. Eschewing conventional editing approaches, McLaughlin gives each participant 30 minutes screen time in one go to tell their story.

This differs from another narrative of the Maze/Long Kesh in the 2008 film *Hunger*, directed and co-written with Enda Walsh by Steve McQueen. The film stars Michael Fassbender as Bobby Sands, the Irish republican prisoner and elected MP for Fermanagh and South Tyrone. It is centred on the 'dirty campaign' of 1976–81 and the subsequent hunger strikes[17] for the recognition of the 'five demands' which included the reinstatement of political prisoner status, free association and the right of prisoners to wear their own clothes, all of which had been withdrawn. McQueen is a British artist and this was his directorial debut; hence, it is as much if not more an artistic statement than a feature film. Its dialogue comprises a segment of a near 20 minute ideological exchange between Fassbender's Sands and a visiting priest, Father Dominic Moran, played by Liam Cunningham. The rest of the film has sound but little dialogue, and conveys its narrative through the physical movement and visual condition of the men's bodies and their movement and confinement within the camp's space. This is prison as a dark vista or spectacle; but unlike McLaughlin's film, it is a narrative on a single if powerful and important moment in the camp's history and from a partial perspective. What they have in common, though, is the use of space and physicality, as McLaughlin notes: 'As the participants negotiated their way around Long Kesh/Maze, through its cells and corridors, control rooms and exercise yards, they were stimulated by the materiality of the site, remembering '"things they had forgotten" and using their bodies to "relive" and retell some of their experiences.' Hence, as noted at the outset, an embodied sense of the past is projected outwards to the world.

Prejudice is also the originator of the events in Cape Town, South Africa. **In their extract** on the District Six Museum in Cape Town, South Africa, **Sandra Prosalendis, Jennifer Marot, Crain Soudien and Anwah Nagia, and Ciraj Rassool** analyse the process of contesting the traumatic loss of their forcibly destroyed community under the Apartheid regime. They describe the way in which former residents and their relatives were brought together in a movement for land restitution, community development and political consciousness through a museum project. They describe the daunting nature of creating a museum dedicated to District Six: 'Our dilemma was that what seemed to make museums distinctive was their concern with material objects and collections, whereas what made District Six distinctive was that is was a story of complete destruction.'

In District Six, 'the tenancy rate was high, many people's bonds were not with houses and possessions but to their histories.' Hence, the recall and memories of the former residents became of central importance. The past can sometimes be recalled through what we might call 'time shock': an instance where long relegated or seemingly forgotten memories are triggered causing a sudden confrontation with them. Historian Roger Griffin, for instance, writes that:

> Time can be experienced by humans in a number of modes, some involving a
> powerful sense that the emptiness often equated with linear or 'clock' time can be

transcended in a distinctive, deeply meaningful higher time. This time can be called 'ecstatic' since it allows the individual to stand 'outside' ordinary time.[18]

This seems to be what happened to Dougie Erasmus, a former District Six resident who had started a Latin American band there in 1949 which became very popular. He was forced to move away in 1978 having until then lived in the same room in which he was born. He then became a taxi driver and apparently put all his memories of District Six behind him. Then in 1995:

> . . . a Museum founder managed to bring him to the museum by hiring his taxi to the museum. Once inside he sat down at the old Church piano and playing Stride style with lots of tremolo, he launched into 'They Can't Take that Away from Me'! To our shock, Dougie died shortly after his visit, but we know that here in the District Six Museum, he had managed to recapture moments of glory that had been taken away from him by the forced removal and his own attempts to forget the past.

The authors assert the on-going relevance of the museum: 'The museum raises all sorts of issues around memory: remembering and forgetting. Who are the people who want to remember District Six and who are those who would prefer to forget?' Tangibly, the museum acquired a range of street signs, perversely enough from one of those responsible for bulldozing the town. These then became their first exhibition, which they called *Streets*. The museum's floor became a grid map of the former District Six which acted as 'a means for ex-residents to reclaim their addresses by writing their names onto the map'.

We need to contextualise the welcome with which memory telling is often embraced with the usually dismissive regard for nostalgia. This helps us to understand the nature of intangibility in the personal engagement with the past.

Nostalgia?

Life experience, memory and the way they are expressed by the individual in the present often seem intangible to the outside observer. They have, though, a real presence for the story teller whose history it is.

Nostalgia's origins lay in its early diagnosis as a pathology or malady from which mercenary soldiers especially were often held to suffer.[19] Contemporary dictionary definitions include '1. a yearning for the return of past circumstances, events, etc.; 2. the evocation of this emotion, as in a book, film, etc.; 3. longing for home or family; homesickness'.[20] All of these definitions we would readily recognize. However, a deeper and contemporary cultural analysis points to a much more fluid and practical use which is applicable to a number of the extracts here. Media artist and writer Svetlana Boym[21] differentiates between 'restorative' and 'reflective' nostalgia:

> Restorative nostalgia is at the core of recent national and religious revivals; it knows two main plots – the return to origins and the conspiracy. Reflective nostalgia does not follow a single plot but explores ways of inhabiting many places at once and imagining different time zones; it loves details not symbols. At best reflective nostalgia can present an ethical and creative challenge. . . . This typology of nostalgia allows us to distinguish between national memory that is based on a single plot of national identity, and social memory, which consists of collective frameworks that mark but do not define the individual memory.[22]

In *Stasiland*[23] journalist and writer Anna Funder explores post-unification East Germany a dozen years after the event through interviews with both victims and former agents of the East German secret police, the *Stasi*. She unsurprisingly found largely sadness, regret and bitterness amongst her victim interviewees' memories of their past because they are centred on lost life chances and betrayal of and by loved ones. Historian Maria Todorova and sociologist Zsuzsa Gille, in *Post-Communist Nostalgia*,[24] though, argue that a wider nostalgia is part of a healing process accommodating the change between the communist and post-communist eras. We can understand both District Six and Golconda (discussed below) in all of these terms. What all these examples speak to is that although politics and socio-economic systems may be different within them, the human condition remains consistent. Memory and its confrontation, the negotiation of the recalled past in the present, is part of how people reconcile themselves with the past and enable themselves to move forward. For Janelle Wilson, the importance of nostalgia lies not so much in the accuracy of recall but in why and how it comes to prominence:

> Placing oneself – in the past, present and projecting into the future – is vital to each of us. The experience and expression of nostalgia need not only be an escape, nor does the past need to be viewed as static. Individuals decide – in the present – how to recall the past and in the process imbue the past with meaning which has evolved over time and which is relevant in the present.[25]

That meaning is then arguably historically valid because it speaks to the future about how people perceive the past in their present. Wilson identifies several uses of nostalgia, including, most obviously, as a form of idealizing or mystifying the past and being age or generationally embedded. Importantly here, though, she also offers that 'Nostalgia is an intra-personal expression of self which subjectively provides one with a sense of continuity' and further that it 'is a form of inter-personal conversational play serving the purpose of bonding'.[26]

As novelist **Lawrence Scott shows in his extract** in conjunction with the University of Trinidad and Tobago, all of the above are demonstrated. He describes the history of a former sugar cane estate, Golconda. Former employees then recall their lives and experiences presented in dialect as well as in other forms, including dance. The formal overview of the plantation's history prefaces the contributions from the former employees whose recollections make up the bulk of the book. Scott observes that 'It became apparent that, with some of the participants not being formally literate, the project would look for its outcomes through oral contributions.'

This extends the idea of Boym's 'reflective nostalgia' into the area of psychogeography.[27] This was originated by Guy Debord, social theorist and founder of the Situationist International,[28] an artistic and crypto-political movement. Psychogeography is founded in the idea of the *derive*.[29] Essentially, this is an abandonment of everyday purpose to a wandering through the city in search of encounter and happenstance. It was proposed as a way for people to reimagine or engage with their built environment that circumvented the intended functional (and capitalist) purposes of the city. This approach now takes in all manner of marginalized spaces, as explored by poets Michael Symmons Roberts and Paul Farley in their book *Edgelands*,[30] which considers gravel pits, business parks and landfill sites amongst other places. Psychogeography can, though, also be restorative in the form of the reimagining of lost sites, buildings and communities by those long since expatriated from them or which have completely disappeared. International studies specialist Benedict Anderson has more expansively analysed this.[31] A more contemporary application of psychogeography is succinctly summarized by post-graduate student Emma Smith:

> The possibilities the concept of psychogeography provides are unlimited. It can provide a framework for literary critiques in terms of identity, and space and

place, journeys of a physical or metaphorical nature and most importantly the development of identity and characteristics in synch with a static or changing environment.[32]

Scott relates about Golanda that:

> Repeatedly, members of the group said they wanted the story of their generation told. They wanted the life in the barracks to be told. They wanted the hardship and injustice of estate life to be remembered. . . . there was also pride in belonging to a way of life which created a closely knit community who worked together. There was an esteem for themselves in belonging to an industry whose processes are captured in the language of the industry as used by the workers as they describe their lives. We were saving language as well as memories. There was nostalgia for a childhood which was remembered both for its hardship and for a fun created out of simple pleasures. . . .

Hence, another characteristic of nostalgia, its bitter-sweetness, comes into play: the attempt to balance, weigh or reconcile the good with the bad. It also demonstrates Smith's assessment of psychogeographical validity.

Like District Six, the Golconda project aroused emotionally conflicting memories, but both examples are predicated on a sense of lost community. Both the cases of District Six and Golconda err on the side of Boym's reflective nostalgia. In District Six's case, restorative nostalgia was not an option because that belonged to the remaining adherents of the Apartheid regime that passed the Group Areas Act that destroyed their community. Both, though, serve as platforms for those affected to navigate and negotiate their pasts and sense of identity in the present – who they have been and who they are now.

History – but not as we know it?

Michael Belgrave's extract discusses the roles and work of public historians employed as 'expert witnesses' to determine the ownership of land claimed by the Maori population under the 1840 Treaty of Waitangi, the meaning of which has always differed between Maori and English interpretations. Tribunals were set up under the 1975 Treaty of Waitangi Act, since when historians have been employed for these tribunals to interpret evidence under an adversarial system and to defend their analyses. Belgrave notes that while historians may be commissioned by the farming or fishing industries, most commissions come from the Tribunal, Crown or claimant. Importantly, he asserts that: 'Maori claimants will continue to see academic history as yet another barrier to the recognition of Maori knowledge and whakapapa [genealogy]-based history.' As Davison notes in relation to aboriginal history in Australia, history is a wound for the indigenous people.

Public history, then, has a duality here. On the one hand, it can be held to connote historians for hire as in an original 1970s American sense of the term. More pertinently, though, indigenous peoples who have a different sense of what the past is and what happened in it are challenging Western historical orthodoxy with their own approaches to the same events. The Western problem with its validity is analysed by Fabri Blacklock, who observes about the on-going 'history wars'[33] in Australia, which concerns the history of British colonization:

> The enduring 'history war' has been largely underpinned by Anglo Australian perspectives and research methodologies whilst the perspectives of Indigenous

people are seldom evident. This is hardly surprising given history has largely been written and interpreted by non-Indigenous historians and unique perspectives of Indigenous historians are still only emerging.[34]

The perceived dismissive Western attitude to orality as non-evidential is also highlighted:

Indigenous histories have largely been written by non-Indigenous historians and this has impacted on how Indigenous history is perceived by the wider community. Many non-Indigenous historians employ traditional historical methods to conduct their research whilst Indigenous methodology like oral history is often dismissed as myth and unreliable evidence. It is important to recognise Indigenous methodology and oral history, as it is based on many thousands of years of the survival of our culture and is an important part of our understanding of our history.[35]

It is interesting that in 2003 'intangible heritage' was formally defined and declared to be protected by the United Nations Educational, Scientific and Cultural Organisation (UNESCO), and this includes Maori cultural practice.[36] Concepts of 'intangible history' have yet to make a convincing inroad to orthodoxy when Maori or Aboriginal historical approaches are regarded as 'myth'. From the visible and publically acknowledged indigenous campaigns for compensation in New Zealand, **Alan Rice in his extract** discusses the invisibility (until recently) of Lancaster's role in the slave trade in Britain.

Rice discusses the historical amnesia, until very recent years, of the presence, outside of the Lancaster Maritime museum, of any acknowledgement that the City of Lancaster in Lancashire, north-west England, was an active participant in the slave trade. Lancaster's maritime importance has long since declined and it has few Afro-Caribbean or African residents today. It therefore lacks the pressure for acknowledgement of a past built on slavery that exists in cities such as Bristol and Liverpool. In this sense, the slave trade was rendered intangible and absent from official narratives about the city's past, which instead emphasized historically civic pride and commercial mercantilist success. It should be noted, however, that even in Bristol, it was as recent as 1999 that the first public material cultural acknowledgement of that city's role in the slave trade was acknowledged. This was via the opening of 'Pero's Bridge' named after a slave of Bristol sugar planter and merchant John Pinney.[37]

Rice uses the case study of 'Sambo'/'Samboo', an African slave arriving in Lancaster in the 1730s, who dies shortly afterwards, it was said, from profound culture shock. Sambo was buried by sailors in common ground (not being baptised), at Sunderland Point, near Lancaster. Rice deftly demonstrates changing attitudes to issues such as slavery, racism and exile by examining visits to, and tokens left on, Sambo's grave. This is juxtaposed with the absence of formal memorialised recognition of Lancaster's slaving past. Instead, Sambo's grave became *de facto* that memorial. As Rice notes: 'Sambo's grave and memorialization show how the actions of ordinary citizens can be just as important to effective historical retrieval.'

Two years ahead of the 2007 bicentenary of the abolition of the Atlantic slave trade in Britain, a sculpture remembering Lancaster's slaving past, 'Captured Africans', was finally unveiled – a partnership between the city council, museums service, county education service, the campaigning group Globalink and University of Central Lancashire:

STAMP (Slave Trade Arts Memorial Project), inaugurated in September 2002, was an ambitious arts education outreach project. It culminated in this permanent memorial to Lancaster's role in the slave trade on the quay side in 2005. The sculpture reflects the decks of the ships that carried the people, with various cargoes in perspex blocks. The front stainless steel column lists many of the ships that sailed from this quay and the number of slaves they picked up in Africa. A mosaic shows the origins and destinations. The statue was unveiled on Columbus Day, October 10th 2005.[38]

The history of Sambo's grave has served as a compass of social and moral attitude over the decades. Rice asserts:

> This public acknowledgement of the dissident memories that Sambo's history ignites outlines a politics which seeks to intervene in the traditional amnesia about its slave past and reinvigorate the narrative, not as sentimentalized panegyric, but rather as radical counter memory.

'Captured Africans', 'Pero's Bridge' and other contemporary memorials like it serve as a statement to the future of how we arrived at them, reflecting, as they do, the greater willingness, in a much more diversified age, to criticize and critique the contributors to the economic and civic flourishing of Britain's port cities. As S. I. Martin notes:

> A square in Plymouth commemorates John Hawkins. A statue of Sir Francis Drake overlooks Plymouth Sound. The story of how these mariners repulsed the Spanish Armada of 1588 is seen as a cornerstone of popular British history, yet few know of Hawkins' voyage to West Africa in 1562, in search of human cargo. His delivery of 300 Africans as slaves to the Spanish Caribbean is generally credited as being the first instance of an Englishman engaging in the transatlantic slave trade. Hawkins' cousin, Francis Drake, would join him on a later slaving voyage to the African coast. Which story is remembered, and why?[39]

Rice believes that: 'Memorials at their most effective speak to their future contexts as much as to the past they commemorate, to a future orientated responsibility, rather than a guilt-charged retrieval of a static past.' There should now, and increasingly, be more parity in what is remembered and why and by whom.

Conclusion

Intangible history as discussed here is very much public history in that it originates in us all and finds expression through collective effort as the extracts demonstrate. Hence, it is a grassroots form of engagement with the past that does not take the academy as its starting point. It has been introduced in two ways here: firstly, in the form of the forgotten or ignored as the sections on District Six, Golconda and Lancaster address, and then the hidden. We have seen, for instance, how the experiential history of Long Kesh/Maze prison evolved by its very rationale for existence behind closed doors. Secondly, through exploring acculturation and embodiment and the re-assessment of nostalgia we can point to other forms of engagement with the past that affect nearly everyone in some way, which academicized history does not. Indigenous people's sense of the past has always had more in common with such approaches than conventional Western historical insistence on documented evidence. The extracts that follow go some way to exploring the ways in which the tangible can be retrieved from or articulated through intangible history.

Notes

1   The Embodiment Organisation online, <http://www.embodiment.org.uk/definition.htm>, accessed 3 July 2012.
2   Oxford Dictionaries online: 'a continuous, typically chronological, record of important or public events or of a particular trend or institution': <http://oxforddictionaries.com/definition/history>, accessed 3 July 2012.
3   S. M. Pearce (1995) *On Collecting: An Investigation into Collecting in the European Tradition*, London: Routledge.
4   K. Lovasz (2006) 'Playing Dress Up: eBay's Vintage Clothing-Land', in K. Hills, M. Petit and N. S. Epley (eds) *Everyday eBay*, London: Routledge, pp283–95.
5   Lovasz, 'Playing', p291.
6   S. M. Pearce (1998) 'Women and Men', in *Collecting in Contemporary Practice*, London, Sage, pp125–51.
7   J. Baudrillard (1994) 'The Systems of Collecting', in trans. R. Cardinal, J. Elsner, R. Cardinal (eds) *The Cultures of Collecting*, London: Reaktion Books, pp7–24.
8   Lovasz, 'Playing', p283.
9   T. Griffith (2001)'Deep Time and Australian History', *History Today*, vol 51(11), November, pp20–25.
10   Lovasz, 'Playing', p292.
11   Lovasz, 'Playing', p283.
12   Lovasz, 'Playing', p287.
13   P. Catterall (ed) (1994) 'The Battle of Cable Street', *Contemporary Record*, vol 8(1), summer, pp105–32.
14   Catterall, 'Battle', p119.
15   T. Kushner and N. Valman (1999) *Remembering Cable Street: Fascism and Anti-fascism in British Society*, Middlesex: Vallentine Mitchell.
16   Henry McDonald (2012) 'US court says IRA member's secret testimony can be handed over to police', *Guardian*, Sunday, 8 July 2012, <http://www.guardian.co.uk/uk/2012/jul/08/us-court-ira-secret-testimony>, accessed 17 July 2012.
17   T. P. Coogan (1980) *On the Blanket: The Inside Story of the IRA Prisoners' Dirty Protest*, Turtle Island Books; Basingstoke: Palgrave Macmillan, 2002; D. Beresford (1987) *Ten Men Dead: Story of the 1981 Irish Hunger Strike*, London: HarperCollins.
18   R. Griffin (1999) 'Party Time: The temporal revolution of the Third Reich', *History Today*, vol 49(4), April, pp43–49.
19   J. Starobinski (1966) 'The idea of nostalgia', *Diogenes*, vol 54, pp81–103.
20   The Free Dictionary online, <http://www.thefreedictionary.com/nostalgia>, accessed 3 July 2012.
21   S. Boym (2001) *The Future of Nostalgia*, New York: Basic Books, pxviii.
22   Ibid.
23   A. Funder (2003) *Stasiland*, London: Granta Books.
24   M. Todorova and Z. Gille (eds) (2010) *Post-Communist Nostalgia*, Oxford: Berghahn Books.
25   J. L. Wilson (2005) *Nostalgia: Sanctuary of Meaning*, Pennsylvania: Bucknell University Press, p7.
26   Wilson, 'Nostalgia', p19.
27   M. Coverley (2010) *Psychogeography*, Harpenden: Pocket Essentials; W. Self and R. Steadman (2007) *Psychogeography*, London: Bloomsbury.
28   S. Ford (2005) *The Situationist International: A User's Guide*, London: Blackdog Publishing.
29   T. McDonough (2010) *The Situationists and the City: A Reader*, London: Verso Books.
30   M. Symmons Roberts and P. Farley (2012) *Edgelands*, London: Vintage.
31   B. Anderson (2006) *Imagined Communities: Reflections on the Origin and Spread of Nationalism*, London, Verso, revised edition.
32   E. Smith (2011) 'Introducing Psychogeography', <http://critical-regionalism.com/2011/03/27/introducing-psychogeography/>, accessed 16 July 2012.
33   S. Macintyre and A. Clark (2004) *The History Wars*, 2nd ed, Melbourne: Melbourne University Press.
34   F. Blacklock (2009) *The History Wars: Acknowledging Indigenous Oral History,* SELF Research International Conference, Refereed Journal, United Arab Emirates University,

UAE, 13–15 January 2009, <http://www.self.ox.ac.uk/documents/Blacklock.pdf>, accessed 4 July 2012, pp1–2.

35   Blacklock, *History Wars*, p2.
36   The UNESCO definition of intangible heritage can be found online at <http://www.unesco.org/services/documentation/archives/multimedia/?id_page = 13&PHP SESSID = 99724b4d60dc8523d54275ad8d077092>, accessed 4 July 2012. See also L. Smith and N. Akagawa (2008) *Intangible Heritage*, Abingdon: Routledge; D. Fairchild Ruggles and H. Silverman (eds) (2009) *Intangible Heritage Embodied*, New York: Springer Books.
37   C. Eickelmann and D. Small (2004) *PERO: The Life of a Slave in Eighteenth-Century Bristol*, Bristol: Redcliffe Press.
38   Waymarking.com online, <http://www.waymarking.com/waymarks/WM3G75_Slavery_Memorial_Lancaster_UK>: 'Captured Africans' slavery memorial, Lancaster website, accessed 5 July 2012.
      An audio-visual Lancaster slavery trail recorded by Year Five School children can be viewed at <http://www.globallink.org.uk/slavery/towntrail.php.>, accessed 4 July 2012.
39   S. I Martin (undated) *Your Local Slave Trade History*, BBC History, <http://www.bbc.co.uk/history/british/abolition/local_trade_history_article_01.shtml>, accessed 2 July 2012.

Chapter 14

James A. Flath

THE CULT OF HAPPINESS

Nianhua, Art and History in Rural North China

Introduction

[. . .]

This [chapter] is about how people made sense of past and present by visualizing the world through block-print representations known as *nianhua* (New Year pictures). *Nianhua* provide unique insight into the cultural and social history of rural China, but we cannot read them without making extensive inquiry into their nature and the role they played in the society in question. As a result, it has been impossible to separate the representation of *nianhua* from their physical and social production in the North China village. What has emerged from study of these prints is not a history of rural society but of how certain forms of understanding of culture and society have been produced in village China through the medium of print.

This [chapter] treats production and representation of *nianhua* as complementary, and argues that the single most important aspect of the village-based print industry was that it engaged in prescriptive mass production – a process by which a uniform object was collectively produced using a defined set of tools and techniques and in deference to collectively defined social values. Moreover, the physical factors of environment, economy, and physical geography, and the intellectual factors of entertainment, religion, custom, history, and artistic conventions also imposed limits on the free appropriation of texts, and directed the way in which texts were read. Only when these factors are delimited may it be possible to consider how perceptions of the social and physical world were put into print, and how print, in turn, configured perceptions of the social and ethical world.

Complete details on the nature of *nianhua* will emerge in the course of this [chapter]. For the moment it will suffice to explain that during the late nineteenth and early twentieth centuries, rural centres in North China, like Shandong's Yangjiabu, Hebei's Wuqiang and Yangliuqing, and Henan's Zhuxianzhen, supported extensive cottage industries devoted to the production of *nianhua*. During the winter months of each year, these towns and villages printed millions of copies in a wide variety of subjects ranging from household icons to theatrical illustrations, historical tales and legends, harbingers of good fortune, calendars, and floral decorations. Local agents and outside traders distributed the products virtually nationwide, and by New Year there was scarcely a home in the land that did not have at least a Stove God print.

Like most popular culture texts, however, interpretation requires resolving a long list of interpretive difficulties. The problems of Chinese popular culture studies, in general, have been stated nowhere more eloquently than in the conference volume *Popular Culture in Late Imperial China*.[1] In the introductory comments to the volume, editor Evelyn Rawski asks historians to consider culture in terms that Clifford Geertz identified as "structures of signification," wherein cultural phenomena contain multiple levels of significance and of understanding. Co-editor David Johnson responds from Antonio Gramsci's position that culture is governed by the communication-based structure of dominance that allows "official culture" to impose its values as beliefs to which people willingly defer. But whatever their individual approach may be, Rawski, Johnson, and other contributors to this volume generally agree that structures are the lens through which we may understand consciousness.

Roger Chartier has been critical of this type of methodology, arguing that it is not consciousness, but "classifications, divisions and groupings . . . [that] serve as the basis for our apprehension of the social world as fundamental categories of the perception and evaluation of reality."[2] Cultural statements are governed by the place (or milieu) in which they were made, the conditions that made them possible, the schemata that lent them order and the principles of regularity that governed them, and the specific forms dictating the separation of "truth" from "fiction."[3] Chartier's critique does not entirely discredit the analytical concepts of signification or communication, but it does insist on a more rigorous appraisal of culture as "a social history of the various interpretations, brought back to their fundamental determinants (which are social, institutional and cultural), and lodged in the specific practices that produce them."[4] If this method of analysis is to be used in the study of *nianhua,* then some caution must be exercised when reading them broadly as expressions of popular culture.

Of course there is little question that *nianhua* currently fit the description of popular culture, but since the category of popular culture is a relatively modern invention, that particular rubric will not be helpful in understanding how *nianhua* functioned in the late nineteenth and early twentieth centuries. Categories of evaluation are a principal concern for me, and this [chapter] is largely devoted to working out which categories were relevant to the makers and users of *nianhua* in their own time and space. But while the categories are many and diverse, the one point that needs to be asserted is that *nianhua* are primarily an expression of print culture.

Print culture, plainly stated, is a means of understanding the world through print. In the physical sense, print culture is the act of producing, disseminating, obtaining, displaying, and reading print. In the social sense, print culture is the abstraction of the world created by the repeated and systematic application of ink to paper, and the penetration and transformation of social relations by print. Take, for example, the practice of worshiping the Stove God through his printed image . . . essentially attention to the Stove God required a ceremony that involved the annual immolation and replacement of his printed image. For the people involved in the cult, this was primarily a ritual designed to gain the favour of the god, but since print was the medium, that ritual should also be understood as a specific practice of reading within a culture defined by print.

The study of *nianhua* as an academic subject began with the Russian sinologist V. M. Alekseev (1881–1951), who (along with Edouard Chavannes, his academic supervisor) began to collect and research *nianhua* for his doctoral thesis in the early twentieth century. Unfortunately the expense and technical difficulty of reproducing the images limited the breadth of his publication on the subject, and, excepting a small volume published in England in 1927, his collected essays were not published until 1966 with the posthumous volume *Kitaiskaia Narodnaia Kartina* (*Chinese Popular Pictures*).[5] Yet even this volume does not specifically focus on *nianhua*, but rather uses *nianhua* to illustrate discussions of related matters, such as theatre or the "Twin Gods of Harmony."

In China there was little academic interest in *nianhua* until after 1949, when folklore became an imperative field of study, and researchers began to reconstruct the history of the art form. Much of the material that is extant owes its survival to folklore research of the 1950s when Wang Shucun, the most prolific researcher on the subject, accumulated a massive collection of prints and began to write the first of his many discourses on the subject. Bo Songnian (Po Sungnien), too, has been working with the genre since that time, and although Wang has developed more specific historical subjects in a variety of compilations, Bo's *Zhongguo nianhua shi* (*History of Chinese nianhua*) stands as the most comprehensive historical overview on the subject in Chinese.

Outside of China, excepting a number of annotated albums, there has been little research on the topic of *nianhua*.[6] Clarence Day's *Chinese Peasant Cults* (1940) used iconic *nianhua* to analyze Chinese popular religion, but although Day made some useful observations, much of his data was actually drawn from Henri Doré's *Researches into Chinese Superstitions* (1914–38), which took a dim view of the subject and provided little specific information on the print industry. David Holm dealt with *nianhua* at some length in his doctoral dissertation, "Art and Ideology during the Yan'an Period" (1979), as did Tanya McIntyre in her dissertation *Chinese New Year Pictures: The Process of Modernization* (1997). McIntyre subsequently published a part of her research in Antonia Finane and Anne McLaren's *Dress, Sex, and Text in Chinese Culture* (1999). John Lust's *Chinese Popular Prints* (1996) appeared as the culmination of a long devotion to *nianhua*, but the work is regrettably inconclusive. Political and resistance themes in twentieth-century *nianhua* have also received attention from both Chang-tai Hung, "Repainting China" (2000), and Ellen Johnston Laing's "Reform, Revolutionary, and Resistance Themes in Chinese Popular Prints, 1900–1940" (2000). Laing has also discussed wartime *nianhua* reforms in *The Winking Owl: Art in the People's Republic of China* (1988). But while there is a limited secondary literature on the subject, there has been no comprehensive effort in any language to treat *nianhua* as primary historical documents that can illuminate a subject other than *nianhua* themselves.

Notwithstanding earlier works, such as Thomas Carter's *The Invention of Printing in China and Its Spread Westward* (1925) and Tsien Tsuen-hsuin's "Paper and Printing" (1985), the study of Chinese print culture in general has only recently begun to emerge as a distinct field of study. There is, of course, extensive discussion of journalism and literature in China, but the idea of a more narrowly defined Chinese print culture only gained explicit attention in 1996, when *Late Imperial China* carried a special issue on Chinese printing and commercial publishing, with introductory remarks by Roger Chartier. Of the widely ranging contributions to that volume, Cynthia Brokaw's discussion of the Ma family publishers bears the most relevance to the present study, owing to her emphasis on the social organization of a local printing industry in Fujian and its regional trading networks in late imperial times.[7]

Robert Hegel has also considered Chartier's argument that the text is inseparable from the material conditions that make it available. In *Reading Illustrated Fiction in Late Imperial China* (1998), Hegel argues that it is most important to be concerned with "*how* literature signified in Ming and Qing China, and only thereafter with *what* it signified."[8] This also reflects my own strategy in dealing with *nianhua* as historical texts, even though the approach is driven as much by necessity as by theoretical consideration because particular readings of the text are simply not available. In all of China's literate tradition, down to the early twentieth century, there are no more than a dozen works that even mention *nianhua*, Gu Lu's *Qing jia lu* (c. 1855) providing one of the more comprehensive accounts with its

80–word introduction to *nianhua* and some 400 words on door gods. This absence of published opinion thus disqualifies any pretension to extract an authorial or otherwise personal meaning from *nianhua*. As a consequence I have retained focus on production and representation.

Reading nianhua

Nianhua may be understood through two essential sets of considerations. As Robert Hegel suggests, these are first the "how" and then the "what" of signification – the physical and social production of the visual text, followed by the way the images are put together to form a narrative or evoke a certain impression. The importance of considering both is illustrated in the following images. The first is an outline block of an ordinary image of the Stove God and God of Wealth. Even without their faces and coloration, one can already see that in its finished form it would be an effective and sensually gratifying image in all its iconographic complexity and overflowing imagery contained by a systematic oppositional structure. With no further information, one might be able to draw some general conclusions about the culture and aesthetics of the society that produced or consumed the image. Assuming the block would be used in a polychrome printing process, it might be safe to guess that the consumers had a taste for colour and basic contrasts. Assuming that the central figure was a god, one might also guess that they placed a high priority on ritual, as represented by the Stove God. Following the same reasoning, one might also draw some basic conclusions about the training and social orientation of the print maker, guessing him to be a typical folk artist schooled in techniques passed down through the generations.[9]

The next outline block is quite different portraying a folk story in which a youth pays a visit to the arbiters of birth and death in order to secure an extension on his foreshortened lifespan. The graphic construction is much different from that of the Stove God just discussed, and although it is just as complex as the Stove God print, it is organized around an entirely different set of principles. The elegant rockery at the base of the print balances the finely written calligraphy in the upper left, angles are justified, perspective is in order, the mulberry on the right balances the chess players on the left, and the image is centred around the staff of the boy, which also functions to frame the text. Once again, the image appears as a comment on its maker and consumer, suggesting a somewhat discriminating interpretation of the world and a sophisticated appreciation of how space could be manipulated within the two-dimensional image.

Seen separately, it would be difficult to draw any connection between the two blocks, since they appear to be done by people of completely different backgrounds and education. This, however, illustrates the perils of disregarding the more concrete factors of production, because on that basic level the two images are fixed to each other in a way that could not have been known by merely studying the impressions. The simple fact is that these two very different images are found on opposite sides of the same printing block, and thus could not be more closely related, having been produced in the same place, at the same time, and probably by the same hands. The printing block brings disparate texts together in a way that is perhaps unusual, but it cautions us against essentializing the image based on appearance, and suggests a range of issues that need to be brought under consideration when analyzing the printed text.

Print, whether graphic or written, plays an integral role in human relations and must be examined in terms of when, where, and how the printed items were produced and displayed, and how these factors in turn formed and confined the interpretative space in which they could be read. Given the diversity of humans and human relations, the meaning of any piece of print must be considered equally diverse, since its interpretation can potentially change with each individual reader. Consequently, the reading of print must be considered a function of the reader's position in that web of human relations. Realistically, we will never be able to account entirely for the full range of meaning in any particular piece of print. But although it is true that print is individually read, it is also socially produced, and the circumstances of reading restrict the range of possible interpretations for a reader in a certain time and in a certain place. Only by taking these configurations under consideration is it possible to interpret and reconstruct the significance of something apparently so simple, and in fact so complex, as a colourful piece of paper innocuously posted in a North China village household.

The demand for and interpretation of *nianhua* depends on the space and time in which they were displayed, and the ethical regime under which they were produced. For many *nianhua*, this space was the home, and the perception of time corresponds to the ritual and agricultural calendar. By the declining years of the Qing dynasty, a representation of space and time began to develop that was more expansively cosmopolitan and more immediately local in the sense that place, event, and period became related concepts important to the reading of the representation.

Since *nianhua* were socially derived, the prints and their interpretation must be considered in the context of social change. Of particular interest are the processes of infrastructural, technological, and political change in the early twentieth century that not only affected the capacity of the village to sustain print production, but also brought print makers into contact with an expanded print environment and new printing and viewing technologies. Village printers attempted to meet and adapt to this challenge, but the changing technology and shifting aesthetic sensibilities eventually undermined (but did not eliminate) the local industry. Technology and infrastructure also contributed to the increasing capacity of centralized agencies to direct and control the production of print actively.

The emergence of a putatively secular state in the twentieth century created the challenge of establishing secular legitimacy in an environment that was deeply attached to ritual. With few political or ideological resources to promote their program, the Republican-era state could do little more than meddle with village print As such resources were consolidated under the People's Republic, however, the state was increasingly able to direct, control, and finally monopolize print production, directing it toward the construction of a metanarrative that was more comprehensive than any witnessed under previous regimes.

[. . .]

Retelling history through the narrative print

In the introduction I argued that history, in its academic sense, was not important to the cultural life of rural China. Historical narrative, on the other hand, and the way it was visualized in print, was far more relevant. Understanding how that past was visualized requires that the process of signification be reviewed in light of the theory of prescription. In that context, the present chapter asks how historical narratives could also be understood not as an infinite body of unique representations, but as a finite body of finely crafted conventions.

Central to this discussion are the conventions of theatre and their expression in the highly popular form of theatrical *nianhua*. A second set of considerations critical to under-standing how these representations were conceived are the artistic principles and motifs drawn from the wider field of graphic representation, including classical landscape and figure painting, and the more popular forms of iconic associations found in nature symbolism. Finally, there are the standards established by formal and popular historical interpretations as they appear independent of theatre, although it should be stated that these distinctions are never entirely clear. But while theatre, art, and history are important to this discussion, it must be understood that these were also distinct forms of representation, so that when their conventions are delivered into the medium of *nianhua,* the message takes on a new level of significance.

If historical representations are so heavy with graphic and narrative formulae, then another question naturally arises regarding whether historical narrative itself was any less formulaic. The evidence presented here suggests that aside from the visual references, historical tales were largely construed as parochial interpretations of Confucian virtue. It would be unjust, however, to claim that all historical tales were so neatly arranged, since there is also a significant body of material that engages in a boisterous re-imagining of the past that clearly fell out of line with the way the past was viewed in more formal schools of thought. The fact that there was room in the *nianhua* industry for such diversity in representation is a reminder that while *nianhua* were highly prescriptive, their makers were never obliged to uphold an orthodoxy that was, in any case, never perfectly understood.

Nianhua *and the pacing-horse lantern theory of history*

The idea that Chinese history is cyclical has been a cliché in the West at least since Tennyson wrote his famous phrase "a cycle of Cathay." But as Dun Lichen demonstrated in his "pacing-horse lantern" theory of history, there is a grain of truth to the matter, if only because people such as Dun believed this to be an accurate description of the Chinese past:

> "Pacing-horse" lanterns are wheels cut out of paper, so that when they are blown on (by the warm air rising from) a candle (fastened below the wheel), the carts and horses (painted on the paper) move round and round without stopping. But when the candle goes out, the whole thing stops. Though this is but a trifling thing, it contains in truth the whole underlying principle of completion and destruction, rise and decay, so that in the thousand ages from antiquity down to to-day, as recorded in the Twenty-four Histories, there is not one which is not like a "pacing horse" lantern.[1]

The important question is not whether history actually functioned in this way, but why Dun Lichen subscribed to this view. Dun's views were likely structured in part by his Confucian education, and by the fact that he was a Manchu watching his dynasty and career fall into ruin. But in concentrating on social and historical background, it is all too easy to overlook that although it was a "trifling thing," Dun Lichen's perspective on history was prompted by a toy lantern spinning mindlessly somewhere in the streets of Beijing.

Nianhua are like the pacing-horse lantern in that they were among the many representations that flourished outside the bounds of recognized categories but still had a profound effect on how people saw history. Whereas Dun Lichen has passed on a precise commentary on his perceptions of the lantern, however, we do not have the benefit of such insights to clarify exactly what historicisms *nianhua* may have provoked. Understanding how *nianhua* signified history therefore requires that historical *nianhua* narratives be treated in the same terms as other examples of the genre. That is to say, narrative *nianhua* need to be studied through their physical production, their classifications, divisions, and groupings, and their social, institutional, and cultural determinants.

When V. M. Alekseev travelled through North China in the early twentieth century, narrative prints were dominating the market, and the researcher was able to acquire hundreds of different theatrical scenes – most representing historical narratives. This available variety supports what has been said about the exuberance of this prescriptively organized industry in the early twentieth century. But it remains to be shown how processes that should naturally have limited variety instead provided the market with seemingly unlimited variations.

As mentioned earlier, the top-producing *nianhua* artists in Yangliuqing could design as many as 170 *nianhua* drafts in a year – an average of one draft every two days. But if the designer increased production in the winter, as was likely the case, then it would not be an unreasonable guess to say that the most efficient designers could have finished a draft in a single day. Despite this rate of production, *nianhua* designers maintained a high standard and often provided their products with extensive detail. As Lothar Ledderose has recently argued in his study of mass production in Chinese art, this union of quality and quantity in other arts, crafts, and even written language, could only have been achieved through the application of modular processes, in which craftsmen and artists did not create each piece independently, but assembled the objects from standardized parts, or modules.[2] Just as with Ledderose's example of thirteenth-century temple painters, *nianhua* artists painted the same patterns time and again in a process that caused Alekseev to comment that *nianhua* were not painted so much as they were written.[3] Unlike temple painters, however, the *nianhua* artist did not rely on duplication through stencils or other forms of direct transfer, but on the close approximation of established forms of dress, settings, postures, and so forth. And like the repertory of the theatrical company, these components could be combined with a convenient plot to produce a vivid representation.

This approach to artistic production can be illustrated through the comparison of a series of separate battle scenes involving mounted horses. A complete survey of Yangliuqing material could easily involve a dozen extant prints in this comparison, but the point can be made with scenes taken from two prints in particular – *Changbanpo* and *Records of Patriotism*.[4] Although the scenes represent distinct historical episodes, it may appear that the artist or artists cut corners by copying the same three horses time and again, changing only the riders and their relative positions. However, a more thorough comparison reveals that while the outlines for some representations are virtually indistinguishable, they are nonetheless unique and have been drawn individually.

But if *nianhua* designers did not object to producing multiple images as near-duplicates, why did they not simply use stencils and save themselves the trouble of redrawing each module as a distinct image? One possible explanation is that the standard form was not used simply to expedite production, but rather was intended to provide the viewer with stock characters drawn from a common pictorial vocabulary that could be assembled into a pattern having narrative appeal. Because the narrative was composed of familiar elements, it was accessible and meaningful to any viewer educated in that cultural form. While the simplicity of the equestrian representations suggests a rather limited stock of types, and therefore a limited potential for narrative development, if we take the human form into consideration, that vocabulary is infinitely expanded. It may be noted that while there are essentially only three distinct horses in this example, each of the six riders are rendered with unique costumes and martial styles. In this sense the *nianhua* designer was working on the same principle as painters of the literati tradition, where true accomplishment was measured in terms of the mastery, but not replication of artistic conventions. *Nianhua* designers knew that the purpose of their product was to tell a tale and that innovation would only obscure the message, while an endless variety of narrative could be produced and appreciated through the employment of the archetypes familiar to the members of that culture.

Theatrical conventions in narrative **nianhua**

There is little question that by the turn of the century, theatre was at the centre of both rural and urban cultural life. Arthur Smith's Shandong survey of the 1890s paints a picture of an extremely vigorous industry circulating at all social levels and including entertainers ranging from amateur artists taking time away from their farms, to elite professionals travelling in processions that led them to the performance halls of the cities and major entertainment centres and to temple fairs and village markets.[5] There is, however, little primary quantitative data on which dramas were being performed in rural China. Smith, for example, confessed that he found the music "excruciating" and so left no account of dramatic content save that they often involved "high-class historical characters, like Chiang Tai-kung etc."[6] Tao Junqi's catalogue of 1,300 *jingju* (Beijing Opera) shows that with some 155 different plays the Three Kingdoms period is by far the best represented historical period on stage, owing to the unrelenting popularity of *Sanguo yanyi* (*Romance of the Three Kingdoms*).[7] This popularity extends also to the *nianhua* genre, from which Boris Riftin has compiled published and unpublished sources to identify no less than 337 extant prints based on the novel.[8] Fifty-eight of the 120 chapters of the novel are represented in *nianhua*, although distribution is by no means even, with most of the prints being devoted to a handful of popular scenes. Of particular interest to the *nianhua* genre are the scenes *Fengyi Pavillion* (Chapter 8), various scenes involving Liu Bei's initial visits to Zhuge Liang's thatched cottage (Chapters 36 and 37), and various scenes set in Changbanpo (Chapter 41). There are also numerous interpretations of "Dragon and Phoenix Stratagem" and "Returning to Jingzhou" (Chapter 54), "Zhao Yun Intercepting A Dou" (Chapter 61), and "Ruse of the Empty City" (Chapter 91).

Although it is tempting to use *nianhua* as an index of the relative popularity of various narrative forms, *nianhua* are not a literal representation of the theatre. Inconsistencies exist because the print excludes the social and aesthetic context, including the religious circumstances of the festivals at which they were often held, not to mention the music of the original event. As Tanaka Issei argues in his discussion of Ming and Qing local drama, while there were discernible patterns in the performance of plays, these patterns were evolutional and changed with the social context.[9] Thus, no single text can give full representation to the complexities of live theatre.

Print did, on the other hand, provide a single "freeze-frame" view of a single play that was taken out of its original context and isolated in the home, thereby forming a distinct mode of viewing the narrative as a graphic text. Print could represent the optimum visual configuration of the drama. The most exciting battles, the most dazzling costumes, and the most grandiose gestures could all be combined into a single climactic moment when, for example, Cao Cao is duped by Zhuge Liang, or Monkey creates havoc in heaven. Print could also bring to life aspects of the art that were not possible on the physical stage by simultaneously involving a single actor in multiple scenes, or by importing more characters into a scene than would be possible on stage. Moreover, where the actual theatre was confined to the stage and to the use of stage props, the print could transcend these limitations by placing the action in a "realistic" setting with "real" horses, architecture, scenery, and so forth, even while populating the setting with heroes dressed in theatrical costume. Print could also ignore the narrative distinctions that separated staged theatre from the printed novel or the storyteller, transposing the best elements of each into the graphic genre.

Finally, theatrical print was relatively free in what it could represent, and so could satisfy the preferences of its clientele without the interference of disapproving county magistrates or other authorities. Arthur Smith observed that it was normally the wish of the magistrate to restrict all theatrical performances, as they were seen to be a public nuisance.[10] Failing this, local magistrates moderated the event by insisting that whenever romantic dramas like

Romance of the Western Chamber were performed, the troupe was also required to perform dramas stressing fidelity, filial piety, chastity, and charity.[11] As Zheng Banqiao wrote on his City God temple tablet: "Theatrical performers, who instruct the people by bringing before them the occurrences of ancient times, representing them in such a lifelike way as to call forth in their audiences magnanimous feelings, joyful emotions, or sorrowful expressions, are benefactors of humanity in no small degree. Only let low vulgar and clandestine affairs and such as relate to the grosser passions be strictly prohibited, then the erection of the theatrical stage will not prove a matter of supererogation."[12]

These guidelines were supported by a program of censorship aimed at curtailing "licentious" dramas and novels, and limiting material such as "Pictures of Wandering in the Marsh" that the Daoguang emperor, for example, felt encouraged readers to "regard violent persons as heroic."[13] As Smith commented in 1899, however, these restrictions had retained little moral force, and given the difficulties that late Qing authorities had in maintaining control over open and public spectacles like theatricals, there was little hope of controlling the production and distribution of broadsheets that merely represented them.

The most important distinction between theatre and its representation in *nianhua* is the fact that while *nianhua* artists were surrounded by theatre, there is little to suggest that their images of the theatrical performances were drawn from life. The image was therefore not a direct representation of any particular event, but rather was designed in respect to established standards of representation.[14] This process may be clarified by comparing some of the surviving illustrations of the *Romance of the Three Kingdoms* classic "Returning to Jingzhou." This tale, incidentally, stands out with "Ruse of the Empty City" and "Changbanpo" as a clear favourite among narrative *nianhua*, with twenty-four extant versions according to Riftin's count. For this reason, "Returning to Jingzhou" serves well for comparative purposes and will help to demonstrate the extent to which conventions were applied in different production sites.

In the version of "Returning to Jingzhou" found in the Ming dynasty novel *Romance of the Three Kingdoms* by Luo Guanzhong, Liu Bei and his wife, Lady Sun, fled the southern State of Wu with Zhao Yun to take refuge in Jingzhou under the protection of Zhuge Liang. With General Zhou Yu of Wu in pursuit, the pair were apprehended by Generals Xu Sheng and Ding Feng, who had been sent to cut off their retreat. Just when all seemed lost, Lady Sun (who was the sister of Sun Quan, King of Wu) soundly rebuked Xu and Ding for showing her such disrespect. Impressed by this display, the captors allowed the group to pass, and after a frenzied chase across the Yangtze River, the company finally broke through to safety in Jingzhou.

The *nianhua* version is able to take liberties with the story, representing the already romanticized literary account as a dramatic but formulaic performance. The first example originates with Yangjiabu's Nangongxing workshop and represents the essentials of the theatre, with richly clad actors but a bare minimum of props and settings, as demonstrated by the substitution of a stage prop for Lady Sun's carriage.[15] A second print from Yangliuqing includes a larger set of actors in similar surroundings, but with the added luxury of a fully equipped carriage for the heroine – something not seen on stage. A third print from Yangliuqing takes the viewer back a step, allowing for a wider perspective on the scene in which all apparent references to theatre are absent.[16]

Despite the variation in setting and arrangement, one singular message shines through in all these theatrical *nianhua,* and that is the basic structure of the plot. No one having the least understanding of the theatre and its conventions could fail to identify the primary characters and, with the aid of props, associate the scene with the famous historical episode and its representation on stage. Lady Sun is immediately identifiable by her carriage, Liu Bei infallibly stands by his woman, and Zhao Yun bristles for a fight while Xu Sheng and Ding Feng stand humbly aside. The scene is therefore given its narrative integrity by deferring to standards of representation set by the theatre. But once that form was adhered to, there was little compunction to draw the remainder of the scene as it appeared to the theatre patron. Although such "realism" remained an option, the *nianhua* designers tended to interpret the scene through forms that extended the narrative beyond the confines of the stage.

One final point may be made in reference to the relationship between illustrated drama and *nianhua*. It is true that *nianhua* frequently depict the same scenes found in illustrated versions of drama scripts taken from novels such as *Romance of the Western Chamber, Yang Family Generals,* and *Romance of the Three Kingdoms*. A comparison of illustrated drama with *nianhua*, however, shows little graphic relation. Robert Hegel demonstrates that illustrations in printed books were generally understated, functioning primarily as visual aids to the written text, rather than aiming to impress the viewer with detail.[17] With *nianhua* this situation is quite the opposite, with the written text acting as a prop for the graphic narrative that is rendered with overwhelming colour and action. If illustrated drama did not have a profound influence on its *nianhua* counterpart, it was because the two types of illustration existed for explicitly different purposes, and told the story in entirely different ways.

Artistic conventions

Few literati in classical China accepted graphic print in any form as a legitimate form of art. Even encyclopaedias that thrived on categorizing the arts did not provide graphic print with its own classification, designating it instead as a subtradition of various crafts. As a further subtradition of print, *nianhua* did not even qualify for this lowly distinction, receiving no mention at all in any of the compendiums of art. With no recognized categorical existence, there could be no context for discussion or standards for appreciating *nianhua* in literate culture.

The basic problem with seeing *nianhua* as art in classical China is the ironclad distinction between the commercial crafts and what Joseph Levenson deemed the "amateur ideal" of the fine arts. This ideal, attributed to Dong Qichang and his followers in the late Ming and early Qing, prompted the cultural elite of Qing China to regard art as the casual expression of the cultivated gentleman, and not something to be bought or sold, much less produced for money.[18] Even Chen Hongshou (1598–1652), whose works of illustration and graphic print are generally regarded as the finest of that genre, never dared take the title of artist. And while ranking himself above the artisans who actually rendered his work into the printed form, Chen insisted on the designation of *zuojia* (fabricator, professional) for himself.[19]

To discuss *nianhua* in terms of artistic conventions is therefore somewhat anachronistic, since it is unlikely that many *nianhua* designers were ever so proud as to regard themselves as artists. Nonetheless, in looking at *nianhua*, one is frequently impressed by some very convincing interpretations of the finer techniques of landscape and figure painting. Much has been made of Qian Huian's tenure in Yangliuqing during the mid-Guangxu period (c. 1891), and the *nianhua* designed by this particular artist are often considered the ultimate achievement in the form. And while countless other *nianhua* designers laboured their whole lives in obscurity, Qian Huian was the only one to have received mention in any pre-modern Chinese publication, despite the fact that he devoted only a few years to this occupation. Qian's recognition by literate culture, if only at its margins, is attributable to the fact that he alone signed his name to his work, and he could be so bold because he used established artistic principles that his literate contemporaries could describe as "lofty, ancient, handsome and free."[20]

Qian Huian's commentator also mentions that after the artist's departure from Yangliuqing, his techniques disappeared and the trade reverted to products that were garishly coloured and so "Vulgar and despicable."[21] This reversion was most directly due to the incapacity of the majority of *nianhua* designers to reproduce Qian's style. But the long-range failure to incorporate the finer elements of "Bird and Flower" painting into *nianhua* should also alert us to the likelihood that Yangliuqing printers had no commercial incentive to perpetuate this style. Given the right demand, Yangliuqing printers might have retained Qian Huian, rather than losing him to the more lucrative Shanghai market. Or they might at least have replaced him with one or more of the many fine artists available to the commercial art industry at that time. That neither of these avenues were pursued was most likely due to the declining interest in fine prints in Beijing. Meanwhile, in the growing provincial market for theatrical prints there was probably minimal demand for his subtle historical narratives and artistic devices.

Although many of Qian's techniques were later abandoned, some print designers did continue to draw on the same stock of decorative motifs that Qian had employed. It is difficult to say with much certainty what Yangliuqing prints looked like before the arrival of Qian Huian, although the evidence does suggest that Qian simply enhanced their existing style and focus. One popular source of illustration must have been *Jieziyuan huazhuan* (*The Mustard Seed Garden Manual of Painting*), on which Qian himself seems to have based some of his figures. Techniques used in such printed volumes as *Shizhuzhai* (*Ten Bamboo Studio*) and even the cheaper *Dianshizhai huabao* (*Dianshizhai Pictorial*) are sometimes also evident in *nianhua*. In general, however, it is less productive to try to trace *nianhua* to their literal origins than it is to place them within the broader range of iconography that pervaded the environment. While the *nianhua* painter may very well have used a painting manual while designing a print, he may just as easily have copied motifs from a commercial painting, illustrated fiction, painted pottery, another *nianhua*, or any of the host of representations that also employed these figurative models. So not only were print designers filling their works with the conventional narrative elements that would make the print comprehensible as a story, they were embroidering the pieces with the artistic conventions that, however vulgar they may have appeared to the artist's eye, still made the print artistically relevant.

Moreover, while the casual viewer might see these motifs as merely decorative attributes scattered at random through the composition, many motifs are used in discriminating patterns to evoke certain themes within the narrative. As in all Chinese decorative arts, the most popular *nianhua* motifs are flowers, especially the plum blossom, lotus, peony, and chrysanthemum; and trees, mainly bamboo, pine, willow, cassia, and palm. The plum blossom is regarded as a harbinger of spring because it is the first blossom to appear at that time. Because it is extremely hardy and continues to flower until the very end of its lengthy life span, it has also come to stand for fortitude, hope, and respect for old age. The lotus (*lian*), which blooms out of the abysmal mud, represents purity and detachment from worldly cares, but also represents fertility due to a play on its name, which may also be read as "continuity" (suggesting a continuous line of descendants). The peony may represent riches and honour, hut also love, affection, and feminine beauty. The chrysanthemum, because it is supposed to last until late into the year (ideally until the ninth day of the ninth month), represents longevity and integrity; and because of Tao Qian's poetic eulogies, it is also associated with that poet's tranquil retirement from public office. Bamboo is upright, strong, and resilient, and yet gentle, graceful, and refined, so it has been claimed by the scholars who paint them as a representative of the best scholarly qualities. Scarcely less popular is the pine, whose longevity and solitude can represent maturity, lasting friendship, and self-discipline. The palm indicates scenes of cultivated retirement, and the cassia, like the carp, suggests literary success. The willow branch is a traditional farewell gift, and like the wild goose, evokes parting and sorrow.

The conspicuous placement of any of these attributes in a narrative *nianhua* should therefore not be taken as a mere accident of aesthetics, because to the perceptive viewer these images could evoke the essential character of the scene and its protagonists. The *Romance of the Three Kingdoms* episode "Series of Stratagems," for example, tells the story of how Wang Yun successfully destroyed the evil alliance of Dong Zhuo and Lu Bu by secretly promising his beloved consort Diao Chan to both despots and so provoking a feud. The scene in two parts shows Diao Chan expressing her willingness to join the plot with Wang Yun on the left, and on the right Dong Zhuo and Lu Bu engage in bloody combat while Diao Chan looks on. In the left-hand scene, the beauty of Diao Chan and the love between master and consort is expressed by the placement of peonies above and below; the right-hand scene is overshadowed by a weeping willow that articulates the pain of Diao Chan's separation from her home and patron.

Even where motif and narrative have no apparent relation, their mutual effect cannot be dismissed. In a simpler depiction of *Romance of the Three Kingdoms* heroes Zhang Fei and Zhou Yu, titled *Thrice Angering Zhou Yu*, the rivals strike theatrical postures on the left, while the right is decorated with a flowering plum, magpies, and a poem, which work together to cheerfully welcome the spring. There are few possible parallels between the two halves of the print, but they are nonetheless inextricably linked by the confines of the paper on which they are printed. One cannot look at Zhang Fei and Zhou Yu without also thinking about the season of birth and regeneration – not a standard narrative equation, but an equation all the same. So while trees, flowers, and other motifs are frequently used to balance and decorate the image, they must also be recognized as symbols that evoke specific sentiments and connotations, and thereby act as elements of the narrative.

In general, the artistic conventions used in *nianhua* give the impression that the historical narrative happened in a fairytale landscape modelled after idyllic southern landscapes, such as Hangzhou's West Lake. It seems instructive that the scenery in depictions of *Legend of White Snake*, which are actually set at West Lake, differ little from those of *Outlaws of the Marsh*, set in the swamps of western Shandong; or that the scenery displayed in depictions of Tao Qian's legendary visit to the Utopian Land of Peach Blossoms is virtually the same as that found in the representations of historical events that happened in less idyllic locations, such as the featureless North China plain. By sharing in the techniques and motifs of his literati colleagues, the *nianhua* designer placed the historical narrative in a cultured space. Regardless of how roughly interpreted or incongruously employed, these are the conventions of artistic practice that made the work meaningful as art.

Historical conventions

The presence in folk art of theatrical and artistic conventions raises some interesting points about the historical nature of the subject. If the graphic representation of historical narratives was produced as a set of conventional but evolutional motifs, can the historical narrative be understood in those same terms? I have thus far insisted that *nianhua* cannot be taken as a literal representation of anything that they may represent, and that the most we can take from *nianhua* is some indication of how subjects were cognitively ordered. So, without claiming that people really believed history to be synonymous with endless variations on the themes of classical romances, *nianhua* may still provide some insight into how history was understood, not as a grand cycle of rise and decay as Dun Lichen would have it, but as a conventionalized historical landscape.

The theatre was thoroughly historical by nature, and as if to prove the point, one of the few theatrical prints to place the action in the context of an actual theatre includes the following inscription: "We (actors) praise good and punish evil by differentiating what is good and what is not; and the deeds of a thousand years are before your eyes. We'll tell tales about the world, sing ballads of ruin, and show where happiness is and where it is not. The history of seventeen dynasties lies before your eyes."[22]

Much as aesthetic and narrative considerations have interceded to provide the "Seventeen Dynasties" (or elsewhere "Twenty-Four Dynasties") with a nonlinear reconciliation, the influence of more orthodox views of the past continue to be apparent in the world of *nianhua* print. In one excellent work on Yangliuqing *nianhua*, Li Zhiqiang and Wang Shucun have carefully organized a broad selection of prints to represent historical tales from each of China's major dynasties from the reign of the Sage Kings through to the Qing dynasty.[23] Their volume does demonstrate that *nianhua* printers had a profoundly developed historical consciousness, but the clear progression through the dynasties is very much the work of the editors and does not suggest how or if the original artisans shared that conception of order.

Fortunately, *nianhua* printers did produce a number of works that combine a selection of historical tales within the same print. Because they are fixed ill their relative positions, the arrangement of the components provides a better perspective on how the artist organized the past as relative themes. What is most evident from these examples is that *nianhua* printers were not bound by linear temporal rules. Two such examples from the Alekseev collection, published by Wang Shucun and Boris Riftin, contain a total of sixteen historical episodes.[24] A fixed order of printing, of course, does not predetermine a fixed order of reading, but assuming that the literate viewer read them in a literary manner – from top to bottom and right to left, then the order proceeds with no regard to chronology. Nor can any but a completely random order of reading produce a chronological sequence. It must, on that evidence, be concluded that the examples were not chosen for their adherence to dynastic succession, but for their moral, didactic, or narrative qualities. A few examples will suffice to give the tone of these narratives:

- Yan Guang (Yan Ziling) of the Eastern Han refuses to take up office when invited by Emperor Guangwu, preferring to spend his days fishing.
- The Han dynasty royal consort Wang Zhaojun is betrothed to a Xiongnu chieftain and goes to live beyond the Great Wall.
- Su Wu (a Han dynasty envoy) is captured by the Xiongnu but refuses to cooperate with them, preferring to herd sheep instead.
- When Zuo Botao dies, his best friend Yang Jiaoai takes the body back to the state of Qi for burial. Zuo Botao appears to Yang in a dream, saying that the spirit of the assassin Jing Ke opposed the burial. Yang cuts his own throat so that he can join Zuo in the afterlife, and together they vanquish Jing Ke.
- During the Warring States period, Yu Boya, a Jin envoy, finds an understanding friend while playing the qin (zither) on Ma'an Mountain.
- During the Three Kingdoms period, Zhao Yun and Zhao Fan, governor of Guiyang, become blood brothers until Zhao Fan offers Zhao Yun his widowed sister-in-law as a bride. Zhao Yun angrily refuses out of respect for filial piety and overthrows Zhao Fan.

The historical narratives originate in a variety of historical classics and vernacular novels, such as *Jingshi longyan* (*Comprehensive Words to Admonish the World*, seventeenth century), *Shi ji* (*Historical Records*, first century BC), *Fengshen yanyi* (*Enfeoffment of the Gods*, sixteenth century), *Lienü zhuan* (*Traditions of Exemplary Women*, first century BC), and *Sanguo yanyi* (*Romance of the Three Kingdoms*, fourteenth century). In most cases, these narratives were made available to the general public through the medium of theatre and various forms of oral performance. Yet the preceding examples are not represented as theatrical, as none of the characters wear appropriate theatrical costume. What is more surprising about this selection is that there are relatively few references to the sword-fighter tales that one might assume to have commanded the greatest popularity. To the contrary, most deal in some way with the virtues of filial piety and fraternity, chivalry, and withdrawal from official duties. These frequent references to virtue support V. M. Alekseev's conviction that although not a single example from his collection of 3,000 *nianhua* depicted Confucius, and in spite of frequently unorthodox interpretations, *nianhua* prints were nonetheless fundamentally Confucian.[25] While they may have failed to appreciate the logic of Confucianism, *nianhua* printers nonetheless incorporated the moral aspects of the teaching into their work. Considering much of the material presented in the remainder of this chapter, this appears as a somewhat selective reading of the material, but in reference to the serialized historical narratives, there would seem to be some truth to the statement.

The unofficial history of nianhua

The point of much of the preceding discussion has been to demonstrate that *nianhua* artists defined their production in deference to the social and cultural themes and standards of their time, including standard histories and historicized Confucian values. This, however, neglects the presence of what might be called "unofficial history *nianhua*" and glosses over those many narratives that do not adhere to artistic, theatrical, and historical conventions. We may know from the literary histories (official or otherwise) that Shen Wansan, for example, was a wealthy subject of the Ming dynasty, but without the input of *nianhua*, how could we have known that "unofficially" Shen was given his fortune by the Dragon Ring?

Equally colourful renditions of history and historical figures can be found in many examples from the *nianhua* genre. One such design from the Yangjiabu Gongyi workshop that is supposed to have originated in the early Qing, but which was reprinted with sufficient frequency to deliver it to the present, portrays the highlights in the early life of the Ming dynasty founder Zhu Yuanzhang. Historically, Zhu was born a commoner, educated in a monastery, and became a bandit chief before embarking on his meteoric rise to power. The Yangjiabu print edition of the story endeavours to cover the whole string of incidents in a single sheet. Zhu Yuanzhang appears three times in different situations: involved with his various confederates, with the mystical forces that bestow the mandate of heaven, and with a bit of money for good measure. There is little in the arrangement of the print that contemporary viewers could consider temporal or spatial order, and the only means of division is to interrupt upper and lower strata by a convoluted line.

A similar structure exists in the print *Bao Gong Takes Office*, also of Gongyi workshop and attributed to Yang Fang (1806–90).[26] Historically, "Judge" Bao Gong (Bao Cheng, 999–1062) was born in Anhui province as a commoner and rose to fame as chief investigative censor in the Song capital of Kaifeng. Bao Gong began his ascent to cult figure status through a series of Yuan and Ming courtroom dramas that portray the Judge as a stern but just official.[27] According to a more unorthodox legend, however, when the imperial court first sent for him to take his position, he refused to leave his unharvested crops. Fortunately the Heavenly Official (Tianguan), seeing that Bao was a worthy man, dispatched a team of immortals to take in the harvest, thus allowing Bao Gong to fill his post without sacrificing his precious grain.

Compared to the sombre and orderly format of the serialized historical tales, these interpretations of the past illustrate that there was still more than one way to tell a tale through the graphic text. The latter examples are unstructured insofar as they do not conform to standard historical accounts, and the graphics do not adhere to the relatively linear representational practices used at some Yangliuqing workshops. The presence of conflicting styles of representation within the same production centre, and even the same workshops, should caution the reader against assuming too much in terms of industry standardization. While the practices and conventions of representation from across the spectrum of Chinese representational and cultural practice had influenced the representational styles of village printers, this effect did not eliminate alternative styles or subjects of representation. The industry was, as I have said, prescriptive, but it was not perfectly prescriptive and so did not narrow the field to a single standard of representation.

Conclusion

There have always been multiple ways in which the past could be read, and through their particular forms of representation, the theatre, finer arts, and literature all offer unique interpretations of history. Each has its own logic, and artists tell their stories using patterns and conventions dictated by the appropriate medium. These conventions also influenced the theme and appearance of *nianhua*, but as graphic print also has its own particular logic, *nianhua* printers too told their stories in a manner unique to the demands of print.

Print took theatre, art, and history beyond the social and intellectual context that had structured them in their original form, and twisted and compacted them to fit the boundaries of its predetermined format of ink on paper. The printed form was thus an abstraction of what it represented, but while it did not tell the story in the same way as theatre, art, or history, the purpose of print was still to give representation to the subject. To be certain there was room for variety, and the original medium never held complete authority over the embellishments in style and narrative that were the stock in trade of the *nianhua* printer. But there was also an impressive deference to order and standards of representation, and in pursuit of that end, printers adopted many of the conventions prescribed by the original medium. In that way, print artists did accept the core vocabularies and the conventions of representation by which the essence of the subject could be understood by anyone having a basic familiarity with those traditions. Print was just one of many forms of representation, but print, in particular, helps to understand how this society mass-produced its classical history, and why Dun Lichen perceived the past in terms of the grand cycle of rise and decay, as if it were a pacing-horse lantern. Such perceptions were guided not by the repeating cycle of past events, but by the repeating cycle of archetypes through which the past was represented through media such as *nianhua*.

Exorcising modernity

It had been a week or two since my visit to the monastery of Donge, and I was in Yanggu to see the Shizi Lou, where Wu Song reputedly became inebriated just prior to his famous tiger-killing episode in the novel *Outlaws of the Marsh*. The building was in good repair, and a large statue of Wu Song and his feline adversary helped to confirm my conviction that good history was synonymous with a good narrative. But passing a row of shops, I was confronted with yet another image, and as it was the "evil fifth month" (or thereabouts), I was interested to see the demon-quelling Zhong Kui affixed to the door of an electronics shop. In place of a severed devil's head, or other horrific sign of his supernatural prowess, this Zhong Kui hoisted high a shiny new television set.

In doing so, the demon queller seemed to demand that we understand not just how such visual texts exorcised the past, but how they continue to exorcise the present. In all practical respects, the age of woodblock *nianhua* should have come to a close in the 1930s when lithography began to overcome the technological and distribution disparities that had preserved xylography as a viable form of media until that time. This demise was postponed by the wartime retrenchment of those disparities, and by the development of political considerations favourable to "peasant art" that kept *nianhua* afloat in various forms through the 1950s when, as Chang-tai Hung has shown, they continued to be produced under the supervision of the state.[1] But when those sympathies were officially retracted in the 1960s, it must have appeared to all involved that the industry had finally run out of borrowed time.

The apparent death of *nianhua*, however, was really only the precondition for its latest reinvention as tradition. In fact, *nianhua* never really "died," and a trickle of print continued to flow out of production villages even after their condemnation in the mid-1960s. In Yangjiabu the woodblock prints cooperative was disbanded in 1970, and some fifty independent production units surfaced briefly before disappearing again until 1974. By 1975 *nianhua* production was on the rise, and by 1984 annual production had reached levels equivalent to the previous high of 11–12 million items in the 1950s and early 1960.[2]

For most people today, *nianhua* are no longer a text of the home, and have instead become fleeting images made available through televisions, magazines, and advertisements, and they are embodied, as they have always been, by festival. Mechanically printed door gods appear intermittently on rural gateways, the God of Wealth has made a fitting comeback in the era of economic reform, and pictures of chubby babies still appear in the shops at New Year. Against all odds, a handful of village printers are still actively producing woodblock *nianhua* – some for the tourist trade, others for their original manifestation as New Year's harbingers of happiness. Most *nianhua* production centres now host government-sponsored research institutes for the study of woodblock prints; Yangjiabu, Gaomi, Wuqiang, and Mianzhu in Sichuan have museums and galleries; and although much of old Yangliuqing has been obliterated by urban development, the Yangliuqing Picture Society continues to operate a showroom in Tianjin.

But while *nianhua* may represent tradition, there will never be a return to the regime of really traditional *nianhua* produced in the traditional way. Only through the exhibition of museum, television, and journalistic print is the productive form and representational content of *nianhua* reunited as a mutually reinforced tradition. *Nianhua* printers are fully aware of their new status in society and are quick to point out that their *nianhua* now have national and international appeal. I was reminded of local product pride when I once over-zealously bargained for a collection of prints: "This is ART!" I was brusquely informed by a Yangjiabu *nianhua* shop-clerk.

The transition of *nianhua* from a part of everyday life to conspicuous tradition arguably began in the May 4th movement when a few visionaries began to drive a not-always-benevolent wedge between folk art and the needs of contemporary society. By separating *nianhua* form and content in the Yan'an era, the CCP achieved a sort of formal traditionalism, invoking the shades of an iconographic history even while denying iconography the dignity of tradition. So under communist direction, *nianhua* ceased to be represented by content, and it became the *practice* of woodblock printing that represented the essence of tradition. Socialist icons gained legitimacy because they were produced using traditional peasant-oriented techniques, and socialist government gained, and continues to gain, legitimacy by supporting the peasant artisan.

In the constant struggle to define modernity in the twentieth century, *nianhua* and other forms of tradition were alternately called upon and attacked amid the advance into that uncertain territory. But then, *nianhua* have always been articles of social articulation, and where they once helped to define the time and space of domestic life, they now help to configure the time and space of modernity, if only by proving an irrevocable separation from the ways of doing things "then" (in the past) and "there" (in the village). In making that distinction, as Nicholas Dirks puts it, "the modern not only invented tradition, it depends upon it. The modern has liberated us from tradition and constantly conceives itself in relation to it."[3]

Zhong Kui, holding a television, printed in colour-offset on a plastic sheet, and hung outside an electronics shop is definitely *not* traditional. But the image is compelling because the obsolete exorcist is permitted relevance to the modern, and modernity is given its relevance to the past – the television is needed in order to understand Zhong Kui as traditional, and Zhong Kui is needed to understand the television as modern. And while an advertisement poster detailing that relationship may seem rather blunt, in its subtler form the media seamlessly blends tradition and modernity. Whether posted in its original form on a wall, projected into the living room through technology, displayed in the marketplace as advertising, hung in the gallery or museum as art, or written as history, *nianhua* and their iconography are still there to help us understand the spaces we inhabit.

This reconstruction of *nianhua* as text has involved them in many contexts – from family altar, to village marketplace, to revolutionary headquarters, and back to family altar in a complex relationship of appropriation that befits their nature as print. The reality of appropriation has also led to the conclusion that a straightforward visual analysis of a printed picture cannot be used to ascertain an expression of interest, social class, education, and the like. In other words, the printed picture can never be judged simply as an index of feeling. I have argued instead that the subject is given historical substance by the structures of propagation and control through which knowledge of the subject is made available. If the circumstances of propagation and control actually produce, or are involved in a conscious discourse of resistance, modernity, or nationalism, then there is a valid context, even a necessity, for relevant discussion. Likewise, we cannot approach village print as a representation of popular culture either having symbolic autonomy from, or dependence on, dominant culture. Essentially, we cannot begin a discussion of the past by presuming to find evidence of an ideal primarily configured by the present, because the past will certainly disappoint us in that respect.

When events are submerged in the processes that create comprehension of them, they often appear confused and not implicitly organized into any particular ideal through which we in the present often view the past. However, appreciating the confusion of the past does not deny the fact that out of all the narrative and visual potentialities that arise in any particular time and place, certain trajectories do emerge as dominant discourses. Regardless of how influential certain interpretations of past or present experience may become, rarely do they limit the field to a single perspective or account. What appear as trajectories in narrative and visuality are constantly subjected to fluctuation and variation, and they are comprehended through the larger body of existing narrative and visuality that conditions all subsequent reading and interpretation. Although this may suggest a contradictory position that history is both chaotic *and* ordered at the same time, the methodology is primarily concerned with understanding how people in rural China, and those who presided over it, attempted to extract order *from* chaos. As David Carr argues, narratives of past and present do not represent reality; they are only the extension and configuration of its primary features.[4]

The visual text as a representation of history needs to be understood primarily through its structuring qualities, and the classifications, divisions, and groupings that make its comprehension possible. As an artistic expression, images are internally structured to form a narrative or evoke a certain impression, while externally the contextual, physical, and social structures of the visual text control its meaning. Structures of both natures control the image and aid comprehension because they demonstrate the limits of free appropriation and possible interpretation, and they bring things together in ways we might not have imagined if visuality and social production were treated separately. Internal graphic structures and external social structures helped people in the past to make sense of what they were looking at, and these reconstructed frameworks help us in the present to appreciate how those same people looked at an image and used it to organize their environment The challenge of writing cultural history through predominantly graphic texts thus begins by defining which structures and principles were most relevant to the society in question, and how those structures and principles were understood and configured through the graphic text. The graphic text does suggest the measures people took to control their world, but most directly the graphic text tells us how people sought to control their sense of it.

Notes

All unattributed translations are the author's own.

Introduction

1   David Johnson, A. Nathan, and E. Rawski, eds., *Popular Culture in Late Imperial China* (Berkeley: University of California Press, 1985).

2   Roger Chartier, ed., *Culture History: Between Practices and Representations,* trans. Lydia Cochrane (Cambridge: Polity Press, 1988), pp4–5. For his other criticisms of this methodology, see his critique of Robert Darnton's *The Great Cat Massacre and Other Incidents in French Culture History* (New York: Vintage, 1984), in "Texts, Symbols, Frenchness," *Journal of Modern History* 57 (1985): pp682–95, and Darnton's response in "The Symbolic Element in History," *Journal of Modern History* 58 (1986): pp218–34.

3   Chartier., *Cultural History*, p10.

4   Ibid., p13.

5   Alekseev wrote that after having been engaged in classical Chinese studies at the Institute of Oriental Languages in St. Petersburg, "a small, luminous picture (a *nianhua*), as if a bomb, fell into our vapid swamp. This bomb was thrown by V. L. Komarov, a botanist who had returned from a Manchurian expedition in 1896. At the Geographic Society he pointed out that nobody in Russia studies Chinese folklore . . . yet no one can ignore its presence. . . .. A fracture of the bomb that ricocheted into my consciousness has had drastic consequences for me because when it was my turn to go to Peking and experience the celebrations of the Chinese New Year, not only did I . . . start to collect and study these pictures, but I also decided to write my dissertation on this topic. . . .. Unfortunately, when I presented my prospectus to the Academy of Sciences, I was immediately informed that it was folly. The Academy refused to finance the publishing of my album due to the lack of funds, and all my plans collapsed. I was forced to look for a new topic for my dissertation." V.M Alekseev, *Kitaiskaia Narodnaia Kartina* (Moscow: Nauka, 1966), pp16–17 (translated from Russian by Vlad Sobol). Although Chavannes never published his collection either, a representative sample can be found in Danielle Eliasberg, *Imagerie populaire chinoise du Nouvel An* (Paris: Arts Asiatiques, 1978). V. L. Komarov's *nianhua* are mainly held in the collection of the Geographic Society in St. Petersburg. A selection of these can be seen in Wang Shucun, *Sulian cang Zhongguo minjian nianhua* (Beijing: Renmin meishu chubanshe, 1989).

6   Regarding annotated albums in Western languages, see Edith Dittrich, *Glück ohne Ende: Neujahrs bilder ans China* (Köln: Eine Ausstellung des Museums für Ostasiatische Kunst der Stadt, 1984); Maria Rudova, *Chinese Popular Prints,* trans. V. Sobolev (Leningrad: Aurora Art Publishers, 1988); Wang Shucun, *Paper Joss: Deity Worship through Folk Prints* (Beijing: New World Press, 1992); Iris Wachs, *Half a Century of Chinese Woodblock Prints: From the Communist Revolution to the Open Door Policy and Beyond* (Israel: Museum of Art Ein Harod, 1999); David Johnson and Po Sung-nien, *Domesticated Deities and Auspicious Emblems: The Iconography of Everyday Life in Village China* (Berkeley: University of California Press, 1993); Ellen Johnston Laing *Art and Aesthetics in Chinese Popular Prints* (Ann Arbor: Center for Chinese Studies, University of Michigan, 2002).

7   See Cynthia Brokaw, "Commercial Publishing in Late Imperial China: The Zou and Ma Family Businesses of Sibao, Fujian," *Late Imperial China* 17, 1 (1996): pp49–92. Other contributors to this special edition of *Late Imperial China* are Roger Chartier, Lucille Chia, Timothy Brook, Kai-wing Chow, and Catherine Bell.

8   Emphasis in original. Robert Hegel, *Reading Illustrated Fiction in Late Imperial China* (Stanford: Stanford University Press, 1998), p3.

9   The masculine is used whenever referring to an anonymous artist because of the high probability, as dictated by social norms, that the artist was in fact a man.

[. . .]

Retelling history through the narrative print

1   Dun Lichen, *Yanjing suishi ji* (Beijing, 1906). This book was translated with an intoduction and commentary by Derk Bodde as Dun Lichen, *Annual Customs and Festivals in Peking as Recorded in the Yen-ching Sui-shi chi by Tun Li-ch'en* (Beijing: Henri Vetch, 1936), p80.

2   Lothar Ledderose, *Ten Thousand Things* (Princeton: Princeton University Press, 2000).

3   V. M. Alekseev, *Kitaiskaia Narodnaia Kartina* (Moscow: Nauka, 1966), p20.

4   For further examples, see Li Zhiqiang and Wang Shucun, *Zhongguo Yangliuqing muban nianhua ji* (Tianjin: Yangliuqing huashe, 1992), pp6, 20.

5   Arthur Smith, *Village Life in China: A Study in Sociology* (New York: Fleming H. Revell, 1899), p65.

6   Ibid., p57.

7   Tao Junqi, *Jingiu jumu chutan* (Beijing: Zhongguo xiju chubanshe, 1963).

8   Boris Riftin, "Sanguo gushi nianhua tulu," parts 1 and 2, *Lishi wenwu* 76, 11 (1999): pp31–49; 77, 12 (1999): pp5–22.

9   Tanaka Issei, "The Social and Historical Context of Ming-Ch'ing Local Drama," in *Popular Culture in Late Imperial China*, ed. David Johnston, A. Nathan, and E. Rawski (Berkeley: University of California Press, 1985), pp143–160.

10   Smith, *Village Life in China*, pp59–60.

11   Robert Ruhlman, "Traditional Heroes in Chinese Popular Fiction," in *The Confucian Persuasion,* ed. Arthur Wright (Stanford: Stanford University Press, 1960), p145.

12   D. B. McCartee, "Translation of the inscription upon a stone tablet . . .," *JNCBRAS* 6 (1869–70): p175.

13   Hsiao Kung-chuan, *Rural China: Imperial Control in the Nineteenth Century* (Seattle: University of Washington Press, 1960), p241. On banning of "Pictures of Wandering in the Marsh" see Wang Liqi, *Yuan Ming Qing sandai jinhui xiaoshuo xiqu shiliao* (Shanghai: Shanghai guji chubanshe, 1981), pp206–7.

14   One exception to this rule is discussed in Chapter 5, Figure 5.2 [of the original work].

15   Wang Shucun, *Jingju banhua* (Beijing: Beijing chubanshe, 1959), p37.

16   Wang Shucun, *Zhongguo meishu quanji: huihua bian* 21 (Beijing: Renmin meishu chubanshe, 1985), p134.

17   Robert Hegel, *Reading Illustrated Fiction in Late Imperial China* (Stanford: Stanford University Press, 1998), p325.

18   Levenson's argument is found in Joseph Levenson, *Confucian China and Its Modern Fate* (Berkeley: University of California Press, 1958) 1: pp15–44.

19   Hegel, *Reading Illustrated Fiction*, p287.

20   Cai Shengwu, *Beijing suishi ji*, cited in Claudia Brown and Ju-hsi Chou, *Transcending Turmoil: Painting at the Close of China's Empire, 1796–1911* (Phoenix: Phoenix Art Museum, 1992), p134.

21   Ibid.

22   Alekseev, *Kitaiskaia Narodnaia Kartina*, p77, Figure 37.

23   Li Zhiqiang and Wang Shucun, *Zhongguo Yangliuqing muban nianhua ji* (Tianjin: Yangliuqing huashe, 1992).

24   Wang Shucun and Boris Riftin, *Sulian cang Zhongguo minjian nianhua* (Beijing: Zhongguo renmin meishu chubanshe, 1989), Figures 148–49.

25   Alekseev does mention one image of Confucius, but adds that he doubted its folkloric nature; *Kitaiskaia Narodnaia Kartina*, pp115, 133. The image he refers to may be that reproduced in Wang and Riftin, *Sulian cang Zhongguo minjian nianhua*, no. 48, from the collection of the Russian Academy of Social Sciences, Moscow.

26   Qu Zhengli, *Yangjiabu nianhua fengzheng zhuanji* (Welfang: Zhongguo renmin zhengzhi xieshang huiyi, 1989), p162.

27   George Hayden, *Crime and Punishment in Medieval Chinese Drama* (Cambridge, MA: Council on East Asian Studies, Harvard University, 1978), p2.

Exorcising modernity

1   Chang-tai Hung, "Repainting China: New year prints (nianhua) and peasant resistance in the early years of the people's republic," *Comparative Studies in Society and History* 42, 4 (200), pp779–810. This period is also discussed at length in my PhD dissertation, "Printing Culture in Rural North China" (University of British Columbia, 2000).

2   Zhang Dianying, *Yangjiabu nianhua* (Beijing: Renmin meishu chubanshe, 1990), pp197–98.

3   Nicholas Dirks, "History as a Sign of the Modern," *Public Culture* 2, 2 (1990), pp27–28.

4   David Carr, *Time, Narrative and History* (Bloomington: Indiana University Press, 1986), p16.

Chapter 15

Cahal McLaughlin

'UNDER THE SAME ROOF'

Separate Stories of Long Kesh/Maze

War of words

THE PRISON THAT ONCE HELD, according to Her Majesty's Chief Inspector of Prisons, James Hennessy, 'the largest concentration of terrorists in Western Europe', has been completely empty since 2002.[1] The 1998 Good Friday Agreement provided for the release of prisoners charged with conflict-related offences and over a period of two years 445 were freed from Long Kesh/Maze, a huge jail complex near Lisburn, ten miles south of Belfast. One of the most significant sites of the conflict that is often referred to as the 'Troubles', it has remained controversial since its closure.[2] There is, for example, still no agreement about its name. The current administrators of the site, the Office of the First Minister and Deputy First Minister, who will oversee its redevelopment, call it the Maze after its official title, HMP Maze, given with the onset of British rule in the north of Ireland in 1972. Many former prisoners, their families and supporters refer to it as Long Kesh, the name of the internment camp established in 1971, which preceded the now more famous H-blocks, erected between 1976 and 1978.

The different names reflect some but not all of the different meanings that the prison holds for those who were held there, who worked there, who visited it or only knew the place through its media representations. These meanings changed over time. Prisoners were subject to different penal regimes at different historical periods: internment, criminalization, and then acceptance of their political status.[3] Republican prison struggles, the blanket and no wash protests, the hunger strikes of 1980 and 1981 dominated the early years of II-blocks, while a remarkable degree of political freedom within the blocks' wings was the key feature of the later years. Republican and Loyalist prisoners[4] occupied separate and separated spaces within Long Kesh/Maze and there were only brief periods when their integration was attempted. Prisoners' collective control of their own space structured the changing, but always oppositional, relationship between prisoners and prison officers. For example, during the Republican prison protests prison officers patrolled the wings throughout extensive lock-up periods, for twenty-four hours a day at times of intense conflict. Then, as their demands for political status, including free association, were won, prisoners' movement along their wings increased and that of prison officers correspondingly decreased, with their access to both wings and cells restricted or prohibited altogether. Put simply, as prisoners gained control over the spaces of the prison, prisoner officers lost it.

While Long Kesh/Maze was shutting down and since its closure, it has remained a relatively secret place, with entry for visitors restricted and controlled. Despite, or perhaps because of this, Long Kesh/Maze has become a site of investigation for artists, photographers and filmmakers. This chapter reflects on the production and reception of *Inside Stories: Memories from the Maze and Long Kesh Prison* (2005), a video documentary that I produced and directed.[5] In 2003, I separately recorded three former occupants: Billy Hutchinson, a former Ulster Volunteer Force commander who became a member of the Progressive Unionist Party; Desi Waterworth, who was still a serving prison officer when he participated in *Inside Stories*; and Gerry Kelly, a leading member of the Irish Republican Army and now Sinn Fein's spokesperson on justice and policing. Negotiations for access to the prison with these former occupants took several years and involved the Northern Ireland Office, the Northern Ireland Prison Officer's Association and republican and loyalist ex-prisoner groups, Coiste na n-Iarchimi and Epic.

Because of the sensitive nature of the prison's disputed iconic status – for some a site of political struggle and for others a place of punishment for 'terrorist crimes' – recorded interviews at the prison site have rarely been permitted, either when the prison was operational or since its closure.[6] I was only able to record Desi Waterworth, Billy Hutchinson and Gerry Kelly at the prison because Desi was still in the prison service and Billy and Gerry were political representatives, elected to the Northern Ireland Assembly and afforded access by the Northern Ireland Office.[7] Ownership of the site has since been passed over to the Office of First Minister and Deputy First Minister, which faces political pressure to prevent the prison being open to ex-prisoners. An example of this kind of political reaction followed a private commemoration inside the prison's hospital block by family and friends of the ten republican prisoners who died on hunger strike in 1981. Under the heading, 'Unionist Anger at Use of Jail for Event', an *Irish News* article of 6 June 2006 quoted Democratic Unionist Party, MP, Nigel Dodds: 'To say that I am furious at the government for permitting the former Maze prison to be used for this republican jamboree would not be an exaggeration.'[8]

Thus, the making of *Inside Stories* took place in a particular kind of 'post'-conflict situation. While there have been, and still are, many attempts to record, remember and memorialize the events which different communities consider significant, fears about the past and its opposing interpretations continue unabated. *Inside Stories*, which presents an analysis of the power of place and how the return to it is a key moment in the process of relating individual and collective histories, counters or even overrides any political imperatives to forget. The editing and viewing of the documentary, however, are very much affected by the demands of a transitional society, moving from a war footing to a culture of peace. This chapter, on the production and reception of one video documentary, raises questions about the conditions in which memories are recorded and then replayed to a wider audience. In what contexts is it possible for individuals and communities emerging from conflict to listen to the accounts of others from whom they have been divided for thirty years, if not for very much longer?

The recordings for *Inside Stories* explore the role of place on the content, structure and performance of memory-telling. As the participants negotiated their way around Long Kesh/Maze, through its cells and corridors, control rooms and exercise yards, they were stimulated by the materiality of the site, remembering 'things they had forgotten', and using their bodies to 'relive' and retell some of their experiences. While I had assistance carrying equipment, only I accompanied each of the participants on the recording of their return to the prison, using a hand-held camera and radio microphone, in order to reduce the intervention of the film-making process, creating an intimacy and trust that I hoped would offer the possibility of personal recollection. I returned on another occasion without any participants to record the visual and sound characteristics of the space.

Giving space to stories

Collaboration between myself and each of the participants, with each retaining equal share with me in their own recorded memories, was essential to the success of the project, since the representation of 'Troubles' narratives continue to be contested. The fragmented peace process has not yet led to the sustained operation of a local assembly and while disagreements about political power-sharing persist, it remains difficult to find common ground to hear each other's stories.[9] Discussions during research, recording and post-production encouraged participants to claim control over the directing and editing. Ultimately, I offered a veto, the right to withdraw the material if they were unhappy with it.[10]

Of course, the organization of material that had been subject to these agreements into a structure and format that was coherent if not meaningful remained my task and my responsibility. My previous professional experience included the directing and producing of television programmes and community videos, both of which entailed linear narratives. The dominance of cinema and television in the construction of documentary stories is such that the conventions of linear, inter-cut, three-act structured narratives seem unproblematic. Early attempts at fitting the material into this structure proved frustrating, but this is not an uncommon experience, and the film editor Walter Murch, describing the transition from recording to editing, writes: 'The director, of course, is the person most familiar with all the things that went on during the shoot, so he is the most burdened with this surplus, beyond the frame information.'[11] Since the edit suite provides the opportunity to retell the story, the editor is to some extent starting afresh. Having arrived at a certain point as researcher, director and camera operator, it can be daunting and difficult to regain the momentum, at a point when new possibilities are wide open and you can begin the journey once more. It is the equivalent of the writer's blank sheet, but in reverse, that is, the page is full of random letters and commas that you are now required to make a story of. Of course, film language exists that encourages you to adopt certain codes for audiences to interpret. These include overall 'types' of documentary that encourage expectations that you can develop, for example, investigative, observational and video-diary. Film language transverses these types and allows the editor to suggest mood and tone. Examples of such grammar include the intercutting of two interviews or images that contradict or challenge one another. The effect of such 'montage' is to suggest a third meaning arising from this clash and it has been refined to become a staple part of editing. Another common example of film grammar is the use of a narrator, where a disembodied voice can set the context and give guidance to the audience on how to read the film. Like this 'voice of god', a non-diagetic soundtrack can be more subtly applied to guide the mood and expectations of the audience. A further example of grammar is the use of visual cutaway over the edited speaking contributor, which can function practically to cover up any jump-cuts in the visuals, and can also be used to offer depth to the immediate storyline or interview as well as offering the audience breathing time to move from one theme to another.[12]

These working practices were at the forefront of my early editing attempts. But whatever strategy I applied, whether to construct a narrative chronologically, thematically, or aesthetically, they proved unconvincing. One belief in the edit suite is that the material often begins to edit itself. Murch elaborates when referring to a particular editing process:

> Whereas the advantage of the KEMs linear system is that I do not have to be speaking to it – there are times when *it* speaks to *me*. The system is constantly presenting information for consideration, and a sort of dialogue takes place.[13]

Once a structure is found, if you 'listen' to the material, pieces will start falling into place and the end product will be greater than the sum of its parts. So the theory goes. In whatever way I tried – either to work with an overall structure or to cut together small sections – the reverse process seemed to occur. The material was being diminished, not enhanced, by the editing. Any integrity that the participants possessed was being undermined by attempts at intercutting them, which took the form of fragmenting their contributions and forcing them together. One of the reasons dated back to the rationale behind the recordings. No clear line of inquiry was established other than the site's influence on the memory-telling. No set of questions were prepared and each participant was encouraged to respond to their rediscovery of the site, with occasional questions posed for clarification only. In this, the methodology corresponds to the oral history tradition of life storytelling, where the significance of developments can be interpreted through episodic moments.[14] Also, although the choice of participants was intended to represent different experiences, this was limited by who was given access by the site owners. The three participants spent different historical periods at the prison, so their stories rarely overlapped and did not inform or directly challenge each other.

The negotiations to arrive at the recordings were jokingly referred to by a colleague as 'a mini peace process'. I now felt like the colonial governor attempting to bang heads together. Attempts at forcing a mainstream linear intercut formula onto this material were inappropriate and I began to look for alternatives. The inspiration came from cinematographer, Humphry Trevelyan, who had used a gallery to exhibit multi-screen 'unedited' work from his documentary on an Iranian coach driver.[15] The opportunity to minimize the editing and to screen separately in a non-theatrical space seemed worth pursuing.

I began to edit the three participants' contributions in turn, each section lasting approximately half an hour. This length was determined by the first edit of Billy and involved removing a minimum of material that was visually awkward, such as messy focus changes. There still remain such moments but these were kept because of the importance of the accompanying synch, that is, the contemporaneous soundtrack. There were also moments in Billy's contribution when I had to fight my professional instincts to cut him early, when he stopped talking and gazed thoughtfully at the horizon. This was slowing the story down, and my urge to keep it moving was proving hard to resist. But this project was not for television and therefore little concern was needed for the income-disposable viewer channel-hopping. I cut the other contributions down to 30 minutes to allow a balance of screen presence and prioritized memories that were triggered by the return to the site. Importantly, it was then that the participants decided which memories remained. I changed one edit minimally and another substantially, in both cases because the participants referred to events that were considered by them to be too difficult to deal with at this fragile stage of the peace process.[16] This management of memory, or at least of making memories public, which has tended to dominate the hesitant attempts at conflict resolution and runs alongside the more wide-ranging demands for a truth and reconciliation process, was one necessary effect of allowing those I filmed editorial and copyright control.

This strategy of editing each piece to the same length with minimal intervention in substantial content and handing over the final say to participants created three coherent but separate narratives and almost immediately offered interpretations of the whole recordings that were lying just under the surface. Segregation, the separation of prisoners according to political allegiance, was a defining feature of the Long Kesh/Maze regime and was regarded by both Republicans and Loyalists as a victory over the prison authorities, since it demonstrated acceptance of the continued existence of their organizations and allowed them increasing amounts of space free from prison officer control. Not only were these spaces contested on a regular basis, often violently, and involved all those who spent time in the prison, but the narratives on the outside were contested through the mass media. The British government referred to the armed movements and their prisoners as 'terrorists' and 'criminals', while they referred to themselves as 'volunteers' and as 'political'. These disputes persist in the public discourse, most recently around plans for the future of the prison site. Although a panel representing most political parties has agreed to preserve a symbolic number of buildings under the umbrella of a Conflict Transformation Zone, there are calls by one victims' group, Families Acting for Innocent Relatives, for the prison to be completely demolished.[17]

Seeing and hearing the other

Just as there were separate memories of these experiences, there were separate narratives. The first edit consisted of three self-contained half-hour stories and involved jump-cutting each contribution (eschewing continuity editing and cutaway coverage of cuts), as well as book-ending each of the sections with visuals from the space with actuality sounds, such as gates opening and wire scraping. The next question was how to screen these and a number of possibilities suggested themselves, resulting in different forms in different situations. During April 2004, the film was shown at Catalyst Arts in Belfast on three screens in three constructed rooms, along with a screen in the foyer for visual shots of the empty prison. In October 2005, it was screened at the Imperial War Museum, London, as part of its War, Memory and Place film season, and in February 2006 at Constitution Hill Gallery, Johannesburg, on both occasions in the form of a linear 100-minute documentary, with the three stories running consecutively. Northern Visions Television, a community channel in Belfast, screened each story on consecutive nights in September 2005. At the Practice as Research in Performance International Conference at the University of Leeds in 2005 and at the London South Bank University Digital Gallery in 2006, it was again shown on three separate screens, but without walls, in Leeds using distance to prevent sound bleeding and in London using directional speakers.[18]

At all venues, the audience response was part of the performance of *Inside Stories*. Responses took different forms, for example, written notes in comment books, informal spoken comments, and organized public debates. The question of editing as an ethical and political practice, including the rights of editorial control, was a recurrent theme. A panel discussion held in Catalyst Arts, organized by the post-conflict initiative, Healing Through Remembering,[19] elicited comments about the effect of resisting conventional mainstream media intercutting techniques.[20] Because *Inside Stories* eschewed this method for continuous thirty-minute accounts from each former occupant of Long Kesh/Maze, the editing of their movement around the prison became visible. The process of constructing the film was transparent as it was viewed, giving its viewers an opportunity to reflect on its making as well as documentary practices more generally. Intercutting has lent itself to the mechanistic analysis of the conflict as a matter of 'two sides', the juxtaposition of opposites driving the story. While Billy's, Desi's and Gerry's narratives were screened separately, they were not placed in direct opposition.

In the discussion that accompanied the showing at London South Bank University Digital Gallery, another three-screen installation, the presentation of each narrative according to its own internal logic as opposed to the usual attempts to impose a storyline was considered again. The importance of allowing 'each one to speak in their own right' and 'to see people talking more openly' was noted in the comment books. And, a report on BBC2's *Culture Show* suggested that this arrangement of screened narratives offers a mode for conflict resolution: 'Perhaps this is the best way forward, telling everyone's story, separately, but under the same roof.'[21]

What kind of space was required for the telling of multiple and conflicting stories was another key issue of debate. Brendan O'Neill of Catalyst Arts explained that one purpose of exhibiting *Inside Stories* was to offer a 'neutral space where memories could be explored and opportunities offered to listen to "other" stories'. Imperial War Museum curator, Toby Haggith, also argued that this was a relatively untampered viewing experience because of the 'time given to each contributor' and 'the insight that each offers in a way rarely seen before and unmediated by other images'.[22] The creation of space and subject position from which it is possible to listen to other narratives is identified as a crucial element in the peace process itself. As Kevin Whelan points out in a 2005 conference report entitled *Storytelling as the Vehicle?*:

> As well as having the right to tell stories, we also have an ethical duty to hear other people's stories. In a post-conflict situation, this becomes a very pressing issue. This . . . may be the most difficult one because in some respects it is what makes possible a shared version of the past, and therefore a possible future.[23]

The notion that a particular kind of film practice and exhibition, an art gallery or a museum, can create a space for such listening because of a generated or inherent neutrality did not go unchallenged. Martin Snodden, a former prisoner who had shared a Long Kesh Loyalist compound with Billy Hutchinson, who is now Director of the Conflict Trauma Research Centre, reminded us at the Catalyst Arts exhibition of the variety of forms that the same story can take: 'I have told my story many times, but not the full story, always a version of it, depending on the context.'[24] The filmed return to an empty jail, the editing suite, the art gallery or museum are, of course, specific kinds of contexts. Mark Snodden points out how telling stories is an act of negotiation between speaking and listening, between speaker and listener at a particular time and place. It is not an absolute truth that characterizes memory-telling, like all forms of communication, it is contingent. For Whelan, this has a positive effect:

> Testimony means that it is always possible to tell it another way. It means that it is also possible to hear it another way. Testimony in that sense always has the possibility of opening a space for dialogue and negotiation with the other.[25]

I did detect an interest, a curiosity if not sympathy, for the 'other' stories that *Inside Stories* presented. A community arts worker, someone from a world quite removed from that of the prison officer, stated that it was this story that was most 'intriguing', and a representative of the Loyalist community suggested it was only seeing (and, therefore, listening) to all three narratives, rather than isolating the one to identify with, that made proper 'sense'. A comment from an Irish émigré in London developed this idea of the exhibition's interlinking nature, referring to the individual and political contexts of memory-telling:

> The juxtapositions and points of connections working across these pieces . . . enhances our awareness of the pragmatic realities that are inseparable from the bigger ideological and political questions.[26]

As a documentary filmmaker, with experience of providing 'packages' for televisual output – linear, intercut and driven by a narrative impulse – this decision to produce material that allows prolonged presence on the screen, with little visual or audio interference, has been a challenge and a discovery. Although the surface of the work appears uncluttered, the performances of the participants are compelling and allow for a rich audience engagement precisely because the structure allows time to contemplate both the content and the architecture of the production.

For an audience from the north of Ireland that lived through the 'Troubles' as I did, there is a consciousness about privileged access to a site that was secret to some and divisive to all as well as in being accorded some insight into the feelings and memories of particular men who survived violence and incarceration. The structure of separate screen time for each participant suggests that efforts to engage with our violent past may benefit from allowing memories of that contested past to be heard and seen in a way that acknowledges audiences' ability to use their own critical faculties and in a sense to become their own editor of the material. This suggests a triangular structure to storytelling – the original participant, the filmmaker and the audience – where the audiences generate the meanings. In a society that has not yet passed the 'post' of 'post-conflict', the act of seeing and hearing 'the other' is a step we recognize as necessary, but that many of us still find difficult to take.

Notes

1   *Report of an Inquiry by HM Chief Inspector of Prisons into the Security Arrangements at HM Prison, Maze* (London: HMSO, 1984) Cmnd.203, p59.

2   L. Purbrick, 'Long Kesh/Maze, Northern Ireland: Public Debate as Historical Interpretation', in *Re-Mapping the Past: New Approaches in Conflict Archaeology*, ed. J. Schofield, A. Klausmeier and L. Purbrick (Berlin: Westrauz-Verlag, 2006), pp72–80.

3   See L. Purbrick, 'The Architecture of Containment', in *The Maze*, by D. Wylie (London: Granta, 2004), pp. 91–110; L. McKeown, *Out of Time: Irish Republican Prisoners Long Kesh 1972–2000* (Belfast: Beyond the Pale, 2001); C. Ryder, *Inside the Maze: the Untold Story of the Northern Ireland Peace Process* (London: Methuen, 2000).

4   Republican prisoners belonged to either the Provisional Irish Republican Army (PIRA), the Official Irish Republican Army (OIRA) or the Irish National Liberation Army (INLA) and Loyalist prisoners were members of the Ulster Volunteer Force (UVF), Ulster Defence Association (UDA), Ulster Freedom Fighters (UFF) or Loyalist Volunteer Force (LVF).

5   Other documentaries that I have directed include *Telling Our Story: the Springhill Massacre*, Victims and Survivors Trust, 1A Rockmore Road, Belfast, BT12 7PD (2000), and *We Never Give Up*, Cape Town: Human Rights Media Centre (2002).

6   *The Hunger Strikes*, Dir. Margot Harkin, BBC Northern Ireland, 27.7.96, is one of these exceptions.

7   I hoped that the successful completion of *Inside Stories*, always intended as a pilot for a larger study – the recording of an archive of interviews at Long Kesh/Maze – would have led to greater access being granted. However, at the time of writing, applications to record interviews at the site have been refused, although recording of the site itself has been permitted. *Inside Stories* has developed into a wider project, the Prisons Memory Archive, initially funded by the Heritage Lottery Fund. To date, 30 former occupants (prisoners, prison officers, visitors, teachers, chaplains, welfare workers) have been recorded inside Armagh Gaol, which was used during the 'Troubles' primarily to imprison women.

8   'Unionist Anger at Use of Jail for Event', *Irish News*, 6 June 2006, p12.

9   Initiatives relating to the telling and listening to 'Troubles' narratives have come from organizations outside government, such as Healing Through Remembering, see www.healingthroughremembering.org.

10   For a fuller account of this process see C. McLaughlin, 'Inside Stories: Memories from the Maze and Long Kesh Prison', *Journal of Media Practice*, 7(4) (2006), pp123–33.

11   W. Murch, *In the Blink of an Eye: a Perspective on Film Editing* (Los Angeles: Silman-James Press, 2001), p24.

12   For a very brief introduction to editing strategies, including montage, see *The Cinema Book,* ed. P. Cook and M. Bernink, 2nd edn (London: British Film Institute, 1999), pp319–20. For a brief discussion on documentary film language and strategies see B. Nichols, 'The Voice of Documentary', in *New Challenges for Documentary*, ed. A. Rosenthal and J. Corner (Manchester: Manchester University Press, 2005), pp17–19.

13   Murch, *In the Blink of an Eye*, p46. The KEM Universal is a film editing system, which like the Moviola and Steenbeck systems, has been superseded by digital editing systems.

14   K. L. Rogers and S. Leydesdorff, *Trauma: Life Stories of Survivors* (New Brunswick: Transaction Publishers, 2004), pp12–13.

15   Exhibited and discussed under the title 'Film in Gallery: the Space Within' at the Practice as Research in Performance conference, Bristol University, 2003, www.bristol.ac.uk/parip/trevelyan.htm.

16   That those who agree to participate in site-specific memory and film projects, such as *Inside Stories*, feel it is necessary to withdraw some material for viewing at a later stage, is confirmed in the Prisons Memory Archive project where 'storage' of footage is required until one participant reaches retirement.

17   See Maze Consultation Panel (2005), *Final Report. 'A New Future for the Maze/Long Kesh'*, http://www.newfuturemazelongkesh.com (1.3.05) and account of their workings in Purbrick, *Long Kesh/Maze*, pp72–80. Under the title 'Maze Must Go' on Families Acting for Innocent Relatives (FAIR) website (http://www.victims.org.uk,) (17.09.06) is the statement: 'We fully intend to bulldoze it no matter what the consequences may be. The Maze will not be set up as a shrine to Republican terrorists.'

18   For the Practice as Research in Performance screenings see http://www.bristol.ac.uk/parip/2005 (17.09.06) and for the Northern Visions Television see http://www.nvtv.co.uk/allschedules (17.09.06).

19   See note 9.

20   http://www.catalystarts.org.uk (17.09.06).

21   The report on future plans for the Maze/Long Kesh, which included the Catalyst Arts installation, was by Shelley Jofre on the *Culture Show*, BBC 2, 12 May 2005.

22   Toby Haggith, 'War, Memory and Place', Imperial War Museum, 25 September 2005. The decision to give over uninterrupted and separate time to the participants was highlighted when the linear version of *Inside Stones* was screened in the gallery space at Constitution Hill, Johannesburg, alongside a photographic exhibition of former prisoners in the Apartheid system. (The parallels and differences in scale and political solutions between South Africa and Ireland were referred to in the comments book here.)

23   K. Whelan, 'Right of Memory', in *Storytelling as the Vehicle?*, ed. Grainne Kelly (Belfast: Healing Through Remembering, 2005), pp19–29.

24   On 20 April 2005; see http://www.catalystarts.org.uk (17.09.06).

25   Whelan, 'Right of Memory', p20.

26   Comment Book, London South Bank University Digital Gallery, Professor Edward Hughes.

Chapter 16

Sandra Prosalendis, Jennifer Marot, Crain Soudien and Anwah Nagia, and Ciraj Rassool

RECALLING COMMUNITY IN CAPE TOWN

Creating and Curating the District Six Museum

Introduction: Recalling community in Cape Town

Ciraj Rassool

THE DISTRICT SIX MUSEUM OPENED its doors in the old church of the Central Methodist Mission at 25A Buitenkant Street on 10 December 1994. The exhibition with which it opened *as a museum* was called *Streets: Retracing District Six*. Described as an 'archaeology of memory', the Museum was the culmination of years of planning, dreaming and imagining on the part of the District Six Museum Foundation. The Foundation was one of a range of organisations, institutions and cultural projects which had emerged between the 1970s and 1990s to preserve the memory of District Six, the area of inner-city Cape Town at the foot of the mountain, which had seen the forced removal of 60,000 people from the heart of the city.

Streets was due to be open for only a couple of weeks. However, since that day in December 1994 when ex-District Sixer and then Minister of Justice Dullah Omar opened the exhibition, the District Six Museum was not able to close its doors. As funds were raised, the Museum grew in complexity, as an institution and in its museum work of collecting, exhibitions and education. While the *Streets* exhibition became the core of its exhibitionary work for more than four years, a number of other exhibitions were curated alongside it, expressing the Museum's desires to tell more complex stories, to work with different mediums, to address specific audiences and even to go beyond the story of District Six. Among these exhibitions were *(Dis)playing the Game*, on the sporting and cultural heritage of Cape Town, *The Last Days of District Six: Photographs by Jan Greshoff*, a display of the architecture of the District before its bulldozing, *Buckingham Palace*, based on the Richard Rive work, and aimed at school learners, and *Tramway Road*, about the forced removals in Sea Point and attempts to build community.

Recalling Community in Cape Town is a book about the history, the cultural work and the ongoing thinking on the part of the District Six Museum. It is a book about the Museum by members of the Museum – by its staff, and its trustees and founders. It is very much an insider's view of the District Six Museum. It recounts the multiple stories that members of the Museum tell about the District and the Museum. It attempts to chart the growth and development of its collections and exhibitions, to explore the political and cultural questions that have shaped it, and to reflect upon the specific contributions it has made to, and challenges it has posed for, museum curatorship and the transformation of heritage in South Africa. This book articulates how the histories, legacies and political challenges of District Six have been reflected in the work of the Museum. It thus follows in the historiographical footsteps of the seminal book, *The Struggle for District Six: Past and Present*, which had been edited by Shamil Jeppie and Crain Soudien for the Hands Off District Six Committee, one of the organisations to which the Museum traces its beginnings.[1]

This book is divided into four parts. Part I, 'Beginnings and trusts', introduces readers to most members of the Trust of the District Six Museum. It records the memories and thinking on the part of trustees about the origins and early history of the Museum. It also reveals very particular relationships of trustees with District Six and the work of the Museum. There are different ways in which the story of the District Six Museum is narrated. There are institutional histories of committees and founders, political histories of civic politics, agitation and mobilisation around the scarred landscape of the District, and cultural histories of District Six memorial projects and social history research. Among the issues that emerge out of these accounts is a productive ambivalence that exists in the Museum about the categories of 'museum' and 'exhibition'.

This uneasiness expresses itself in two ways. When the District Six Museum Foundation was created and the Museum itself formed, the choice of the category of 'museum' did not necessarily express a specific commitment to the institution of the museum. The Foundation certainly wanted a project through which it would be able to contest the past and use history as a means of mobilisation around the traumatic landscape of District Six. Records of the early days of the Museum's existence reveal a debate about what the priorities of the Museum should be and where it should allocate its energies and capacities. While some were concerned about the links between the District Six Museum and other museums in South Africa and beyond, a strong position was articulated that the mission of the Museum was *not* to network with museums, but to mobilise the masses of ex-residents and their descendants into a movement of land restitution, community development and political consciousness.

Nevertheless, it was indeed fortuitous that a District Six *Museum* was created as a cultural institution at the same time as the challenges of museum and heritage transformation in South Africa were being identified, and the frameworks for such processes of transformation created. The Museum emerged as an independent, non-government organisation. As a museum institution, it was unburdened by the baggage of old collections and outdated museum classificatory systems. And as a new community-based independent museum, it did not face any pressure to conform to the state authorities and emerging, centrally directed, national heritage policies or frameworks. These circumstances necessarily, saw the District Six Museum, explicitly and implicitly, engage with processes of museum and heritage transformation in South Africa. As a small, community-based initiative, the Museum never-theless saw itself as being of national significance, as an institution which told a national history of forced removals. And as an independent space of knowledge-creation that was confident about its achievements and ways of working, and which was also attempting to address its shortcomings, the Museum wanted to tell its story nationally, thereby intervening in the field of cultural representation. The publication of this book is another contribution to these objectives.

The ambivalence about being a 'museum' is also expressed in the approaches of trustees, Irwin Combrinck and Peggy Delport. Combrinck has said about the District Six Museum: 'It is not a place where you just come to view artefacts. It's something that you become involved in.'[2] This view is echoed by Delport, who has been the central curator of the Museum's key exhibitions. Delport regularly refers to the processes of inscription, performance, annunciation and theatre that are the life's blood of the Museum's work. It is these, sometimes ephemeral, processes that give the Museum's distinctive curatorial features – the map, the cloth, the street signs, the hanging portraits and the hand-coloured enlarged streetscapes – their meaning.

These are some of the themes that are taken up in Part II of the book, 'The Museum at work'. Here, staff and trustees describe, analyse and reflect upon different aspects of the Museum's work. These accounts include records or everyday encounters, exchanges and visits that take place on the Museum map, the narratives that museum education officers recount to tour groups and a description of youth education programmes co-ordinated by the Museum. Peggy Delport reflects upon the cultural genealogy and the curatorial history and context of the *Streets* exhibition. Crain Soudien and Lalou Meltzer analyse the features of popular claims on District Six's past, which they contrast with official representations. Sandra Prosalendis *et al* reveal significant moments in the Museum's history and discuss how cultural and political challenges facing the Museum were approached at different times between 1995 and 2000. This discussion highlights the close relationship that the development of the Museum has had with the process of land restitution in District Six, and argues that the Museum's commitment to healing, nation-building and capacity-building necessarily expresses itself in the desire for District Six to be redeveloped and resettled.

Part III, 'Museum interjections', charts more recent debates and analytical approaches that have found expression in the District Six Museum, outlines recent research into the collections of the Museum as well as research conducted in preparation for new exhibitions. Whereas *Streets: Retracing District Six* was the core exhibition of the Museum for most of its history, a new exhibition, *Digging Deeper,* was created for the newly restored and renovated Buitenkant Street church building in 2000. A number of the contributions to this section signal the unveiling of *Digging Deeper* the questions that it sought to address and the multifaceted research and curatorial processes that produced it. Crain Soudien defends key myths about the nature of District Six and its history, while Lucien le Grange analyses the District's rich urban quality. In reconstructing the history of Bloemhof and Canterbury flats, Shamil Jeppie analyses attempts by the state to plan and create modern forms of accommodation for the employed working class as well as the ways in which Bloemhoffers built community in the flats.

Three articles signal *Digging Deeper's* concerns and changes in relation to the history of collecting and display in the Museum. Tina Smith and Ciraj Rassool analyse the multifarious lives of photographs in the Museum's collections and exhibitions and identify ways in which more complex approaches to photographic images and genres have begun to be addressed in the new exhibition. Valmont Layne and Ciraj Rassool examine the ways in which the central concerns of the Museum with life history, orality and memory are reflected in the work of three memory rooms created in the new exhibition and the refurbished Museum. Peggy Delport ends off this section with a discussion of the curatorial features of *Digging Deeper*. She draws attention to the spatial character of the Museum, the aesthetic principles and concepts that inform the exhibition, as well as the interpretive eloquence of voices which it wants to unleash. This section also contains a parallel text of the timeline produced for *Digging Deeper*. More than just a chronology of facts, this timeline attempts to reveal the choices the Museum has made in the questions it has posed about District Six's past.

Digging Deeper, as a self-conscious and self-reflexive exhibition, sought to address a restlessness within the Museum that wanted to tell the story of District Six with greater complexity. Whereas *Streets* tended to focus on public spaces and lives constructed in public, *Digging Deeper* sought to examine the private and interior spaces of people's lives. In making *Digging Deeper,* the Museum chose to enquire into its collection and to ask deeper questions about the District, rather than merely to produce more facts. The approach in the new exhibition is to avoid taking a single, safe narrative, and sets out consciously to disrupt and unsettle certain conventions about District Six's past: that the District was a 'coloured' place, that District Six was a 'slum', and even the idea that social life in District Six was without contradiction. In adopting such an approach, the District Six Museum has asserted that it is not a space of innocence. The Memorial Text at the entrance to the Museum reflects the desire to ask difficult questions: 'we seek to work with our memories, our achievements *and our shames,* our moments of glory, courage and love for one another, *and also the hurts we inflicted upon each other'* (emphasis added).

In the work of the District Six Museum, certain features have emerged as core values and approaches that inform its memory work. Informed by the social character and political history of District Six that it has come to understand, the Museum is convinced that one of the most important contributions it can make to the fields of culture and history in South Africa is to articulate a position which questions the validity of race and racial categories. One of the most important aspects of the mission of the District Six Museum is to question race at every turn and to assert a politics of nonracialism and anti-racism in every facet of its work.

Secondly, the Museum is aware that its capacity to continue to be effective depends on how it is nurtured as an independent space of engagement and contestation about history and knowledge of society. The Museum seeks to open up questions of *relations of knowledge* as contained within and generated by all aspects of its work, and about the possibilities and limits of self-representation. In part, this is an attempt at a self-critical and reflexive pedagogy on the part of an institution which has brought together community-connected academics – some of whom see themselves as 'activist intellectuals', but who often bear the restrictive marks of the academy – and former residents, many of whom have been activist intellectuals for decades, with their roots in District Six-based political and cultural organisations. The synergies and contests of such a membership mix lie at the heart of the curatorial methods of the District Six Museum and are expressed in the insider knowledge represented in this book. The questions that the Museum wants to ask extend to developing a questioning approach to academic forms of knowledge appropriation as well as to challenging the assumed neutrality of tourist discourses of diversity. Through such questions and challenges, the Museum places a more complex model of the community museum, as a space of contestation, on the agenda for heritage transformation.

It is out of its 'core business' of memory work conducted in support of the struggle for the restitution of land rights in District Six that the District Six Museum seeks to recall community in District Six. The notion of 'recall' used here and in the title of this book refers both to the Museum's memory work on District Six and its desire to see the community of District Six restored and called back to resettle, redevelop and heal the scarred landscape at the foot of the mountain. From the perspective of the Museum, the recovery and restoration of memory is just as important as, and needs to be a vital component of, the recovery and restoration of land. The District Six Museum once again takes this opportunity to place on the agenda the development of a Memorial Park as part of the reconstruction and redevelopment of District Six. These concerns about memory, memorial and their fundamental relationship with redevelopment and restitution are reflected in the final text contained in Part IV of the book, 'Memory restitution and conscience'. This text is an edited extract from an interview conducted in 1998 with Museum trustee and District Six Beneficiary Trust Chairperson, Anwah Nagia, about the politics of land restitution in District Six.

When this interview was conducted with Anwah Nagia, the state was understood to have been dragging its feet on land restitution, and to not have publicly campaigned for the widespread lodging of land claims as vigorously as campaigns were developed around voter education. As final preparations were being made for this publication, the groundwork was in progress for a landmark ceremony in District Six on Sunday 26 November 2000 to be presided over by President Thabo Mbeki, at which the final stages of the District Six land restitution process would be launched and 4 hectares handed back to claimants. This process would ensure that 17,000 tenant families, described under apartheid law as 'African' or 'coloured', would return to District Six after successful land claims. At the ceremony Thabo Mbeki, Anwah Nagia and Land Affairs Minister Thoko Didiza were billed to speak and special efforts were taken to ensure that trustees of the District Six Museum would be in attendance. In the first public announcement of the event, Anwah Nagia eloquently expressed the views of both the Beneficiary Trust and the District Six Museum:

> History must begin to judge us as victorious over apartheid social engineering and separate development. We are celebrating the return of stolen land from the people who were defenceless, voiceless and disenfranchised in the land of their birth. Let this victory teach us to share and shape a common destiny for a united people.[3]

It seems clear that the 'recalling' of the community of District Six and the resultant restoration of the 'heartbeat back to the city' will be held up no longer. With estimates of between 8,000 and 10,000 people set to move back to the city the process of land restitution had seemingly entered 'the last lap', and was 'moving forward fast'.[4] The memory work of the District Six Museum has hitherto taken place on the basis of the empty traumatic landscape of District Six and the desire for its healing. The redevelopment of the area, the building of houses and the reconstitution of a community of District Six would pose new challenges for the District Six Museum. These are challenges that the Museum awaits to address with enthusiasm.

[. . .]

Punctuations: Periodic impressions of a museum

Sandra Prosalendis, Jennifer Marot, Crain Soudien and Anwah Nagia

In this article, we present snapshots and impressions of the museum at different times: Sandra Prosalendis, Director of the District Six Museum, and Jennifer Marot, the Administrator, present their views of the Museum in November 1995, December 1996 and April 2000 while the September 1998 piece was written by trustees Crain Soudien, Anwah Nagia and the Director, Sandra Prosalendis, to provide the rationale behind the Museum's contribution to the conference entitled 'Local Tradition and Global Destiny' held in Stockholm.

November 1995

> One year later and against all expectations the *Streets* exhibition of the District Six Museum is still resolutely here in Buitenkant Street, recalling for all who pass by the mystique that was District Six.

Yesterday, a milk bottle was delivered to the old front door of the Methodist Church in Buitenkant Street. This bottle dates back to the 1920s, to the People's Dairy, Hanover Street. It has done its round from District Six to London and now back home to the District Six Museum.

Here in the 'Freedom Church', a little space has been created that resurrects the spirit of District Six once again in the centre of Cape Town. In this space, the original street signs hang in ladders, signposting nothing now but memories. The floor is a map of the District Six streets through which people walk, and on which children play, where ex-residents can mark their homes and other significant places. The alcoves contain windows, glimpses of small vignettes of District Six homes. Family photographs line the walls and draw us into the intimacy of personal histories. A series of larger-than-life portraits, among them civic leaders and artists, look down from the gallery at the gathering of people below.

The Museum is more than just a static display. It is a space that enables us to confront the issues of our past. Each day it bears witness to poignant stories hitherto untold that are inspired by this environment of memory and celebration. The District Six Museum has broken with the traditional ideas of museums and collecting. It has created this concept of an interactive public space where it is people's response to District Six that provides the drama and the fabric of the museum.

In establishing the museum and speaking to ex-residents, we are discovering again what we mean by public, by 'community' and by 'the people'. In District Six, where the tenancy rate was high, many people's bonds were not to houses and possessions but to their histories. Identity lay in each person's position within the community, within the street, within themselves and their interaction with others. Individuals who were scattered during the destruction of District Six and other displaced neighbourhoods could survive as 'people' and as 'the public' but not as a 'community'.

The Museum was started without any material collection. What had to be collected was, in fact, this intangible spirit of community. The Museum is attracting people who care and want to understand what was destroyed in the name of 'community development' and what needs to be done in terms of community redevelopment.

People have brought and continue to bring photographs and objects from their lives in District Six: such as Constantine Nell's set of wedding photographs taken in a photographic studio in Tennant Street in 1902, or the green hawker's cart along with the paving stone on which it rested. The opening exhibition was the result of the enthusiasm and dedication of an extraordinary and diverse group of volunteers: ex-residents of District Six, narrators, architects, artists, poets, printers, friends, family members and strangers – spanning four generations at least.

The Museum touches people's lives and hearts

Mr Petersen is 82 and was brought to the Museum by his daughter. Together they walked the map and he marked with his walking stick the block where he was born, Queen Anna's Place. Overcome with emotion, he wept over a model of a building, and kissing the cardboard cutout he whispered, 'What a beautiful place was the National Cinema.' On leaving the Museum, he remarked that today it was as if he had received a hundred pounds!

Twenty-five years ago, a photographer captured a group of children playing under a fig tree in De Korte Street. Two of those children, Moosa and Jenny, lost contact with each other until last year, when they met again and fell in love. Visiting the museum as part of their courtship, they came upon the photograph. Ecstatic with the coincidence and the magic,

Moosa rushed to mark the fig tree on the map, only to discover that someone else had already done so: his cousin, who had been there the week before!

Groups of schoolchildren populate the Museum during the week. Most heart-warming are those groups who come from the townships to which District Six families were moved. Even though these children have no experience of District Six, you can see their eyes light up as they make the links between the old streets and the names of the tenement blocks in which they live. It doesn't matter that the story of District Six is history: this familiarity gives them a feeling of ownership of the centre of the city as they shout out the names of *their* streets.

However, we would be doing a disservice to the notion of community and to District Six if we were to sentimentalise it and to imagine it having been without its dangers and divisions. Community is about struggling with these issues and, because of the bond of shared identity, caring about each other in spite of the differences.

People have always seen District Six in different ways; to many, it was home and community, to others a vibrant cultural experience, and yet others have described it as a 'rathole'. District Six was many things: an extraordinary place that inspired artists to capture its essence. The National Gallery is to host an exhibition that will feature paintings by artists of District Six. The paintings will reflect not only the development of art but the changing image of the area because of the varying external pressures, perceptions and shifting populations during the twentieth century.

The area affected by the Group Areas legislation was determined by the demarcations on a nineteenth-century map of Cape Town that divided the city into six districts. By the mid-twentieth century, the area was covered by municipal wards five, six and seven. The term 'District Six' did, however, survive as an expression of endearment or embarrassment depending on the individual's social aspirations. The 1966 declaration gave it a new political potency in the anti-apartheid struggle. In the post-apartheid period the District, because of its history of cosmopolitanism and tolerance, acquired a new dignity and significance in the quest for reconstruction and reconciliation.

Ultimately, the story of District Six is not just about District Six. It has been used and will continue to be used as a symbol of wider issues of civil justice and a unique instance of 'multicultural' living.

December 1996

> Two years after its opening, the District Six Museum stands in Buitenkant Street in all its shabby splendour. People jostle in and out of the entrance, alongside the makeshift graffiti-style sign; foreign and local tourists to Cape Town brush shoulders with ex-residents, a mixture as heterogeneous as the spirit that the museum celebrates. Inside, to a background of impromptu piano recitals, three exhibitions compete for space. An air of festivity reigns as old friends meet and rediscover their past, and yet there is still a sense of repose and remembrance that lingers in the museum, a legacy of the building's past roles as church, school, community centre and political sanctuary.

District Six was named for the sixth municipal district of Cape Town in 1867. Originally established as a community of freed slaves, merchants, artisans, labourers and immigrants, District Six was a centre with close links to the city and the port. By the beginning of the twentieth century, however, the history of removals and marginalisation had begun. The first to be 'resettled' were Africans, forcibly displaced from the District in 1901. The more prosperous began moving away to the suburbs and the area became the neglected ward of

Cape Town. In 1966, it was declared a white area under the Group Areas Act, and by 1982 the life of a community was over. Sixty thousand people were forcibly removed to a then barren outlying area aptly known as the Cape Flats, their houses razed to the ground by bulldozers.

It was virtually impossible to resist the removals. Once the area had been flattened, only the mosques and the churches remained. The community from the mosques and churches continues to worship in District Six, refusing to sell or deconsecrate their grounds. The last protest was to 'salt' the earth to prevent anyone from building until there was a democratic political dispensation. Fierce and bitter political battles were fought as the state and wealthy business concerns tried to occupy and develop the land. Today, only 35% of this land remains vacant. The concept for a museum grew out of the struggle to fight forced removals, and so the Hands Off District Six Committee, the Ratepayers and Residents Association, the Roman Catholic Church and the Methodist Church formed a board of trustees to found a District Six Museum.

Over a period of six years, these community activists developed ideas through vigorous argument, conflict and community consultation to a point where they and their ideas inspired the Central Methodist Church and an international human rights trust to donate, respectively, the space and a small grant to be used to start a museum. With the acceptance of these donations, it was necessary to develop from an entirely voluntary process, with an inherent impermanence, to a sustainable organisation accountable to the donors and the community. There was a dawning realisation that it is one thing to have a dream and to be filled with moral passion, another to give this a material reality. The solution appeared to be to employ a project director to be responsible for raising more funds and opening the space and ideas to the public at large. An exhibition to announce the formation of a District Six Museum was planned.

It is hard to believe that, at the same time, two and a half years ago, we sat in an empty church feeling anxious and uncertain about the task ahead. Our dilemma was that what seemed to make museums distinctive was their concern with material objects and collections, whereas what made District Six distinctive was that it was a story of complete destruction.

In our casting about, we became aware of a secret collection of street signs and traced them to the cellar of a house in Mowbray. The collector was in fact a foreman, who acting on behalf of apartheid's infamous and ironically named Department of Community Development, had been briefed to 'dump District Six in Table Bay'. He did his job well: the rubble of District Six is the landfill beneath Duncan Dock. However, the street signs did not accompany the rubble. For whatever reason, these he systematically collected and saved.

Negotiations were difficult: He was anxious about meeting us, scared of being prosecuted for 'war crimes'. Some of our members were bitter and resented him, wanting no dealings with everything he stood for. However, the power of this remaining concrete evidence of District Six was stronger than both fear and anger. It took several meetings to negotiate his donation of the signs to the museum, but eventually – with the assistance of a local artist – they were hung in a series of ladders, filling the empty space of the church. They began to work their magic: a step in healing and reconciliation in a divided society. It was interesting that, having acquired a 'collection', we realised that our museum would be more than just a static display. It would be a space that would enable us to confront the issues of our past.

The signs acted as a catalyst for new ideas and, at last, our exhibition had a name: *Streets*. We converted the floor of the museum into a giant map, retracing the original street names and the grid of District Six – a means for ex-residents to reclaim their addresses by writing their names onto the map. The map is a fitting memorial, since, in an attempt to erase District Six from the map of local history, many of the street names, even the grid itself, were changed to make way for the white suburb of Zonnebloem and the development of the Technikon.

During this flurry of enthusiasm, there was the behind-the-scenes slog of fundraising, as well as the co-ordination of requests for material from ex-residents. In the beginning we did not have sufficient funds to mount such a huge exhibition or run a sustainable museum. Every day we continued to act, there was always the risk that financial support would not materialise. And yet, caught up in the power of this phenomenon of creating something from nothing, more than two hundred volunteers offered their time and expertise. Hard work paid off – funds to build the exhibition did materialise, and on 10 December 1994, our two-week exhibition entitled *Streets: Retracing District Six* was opened by Dullah Omar, then Minister of Justice.

The success of the exhibition exceeded our every expectation. At the end of two weeks, we realised that the public had taken ownership of the idea and that we would not be able to close the doors. With a dawning sense of terror and unpreparedness we realised that the Museum had begun and that we were committed to raising R2.5 million to sustain it into the future.

In the next two years, the museum became an interactive space in which it was the people's response to District Six which provided the drama and fabric of the Museum. What we continue to collect is the intangible spirit of community. The path through which each object arrives, and the relationship of the community to the objects that they have entrusted to us, animates the Museum. We attract people who care and want to understand what was destroyed in the name of 'community development' and what needs to be done in the name of community redevelopment.

The Museum raises all sorts of issues around memory: remembering and forgetting. Who are the people who want to remember District Six, and who are those who would prefer to forget? Consider the tale of Dougie Erasmus. In 1949, Dougie Erasmus of Windsor Street started the first Latin American band in Cape Town, the Copacabana Band, which became famous throughout the city. Dougie was eventually forced to move to Mitchells Plain in 1978. Up until that time, he had still been sleeping in the same room in Windsor Street that he had been born in. Falling on hard times, Dougie became a taxi driver and resolutely put his memories of District Six behind him. It was only in June 1995 that a Museum founder managed to bring him to the Museum by hiring his taxi to the Museum. Once inside, he sat down at the old church piano and, playing stride style with lots of tremolo, he launched into 'They Can't Take That Away From Me'! To our shock, Dougie died shortly after his visit, but we know that, here in the District Six Museum, he had managed to recapture moments of glory that had been taken away from him by the forced removal and his own attempts to forget the past.

A banner that was hung from the balcony when the Museum opened stated:

> In this exhibition, we do not wish to recreate District Six as much as to re-possess the history of the area as a place where people lived, loved and struggled. It is an attempt to take back our right to signpost our lives with those things we hold dear . . . the exhibition is also about pointers to our future. We, all of us, need to decide how as individuals and as a people we wish to retrace and re-signpost the lines of our future. Such a process is neither easy nor straightforward. It is not predictable either.

The birth of the Museum has not been easy or straightforward. It was the result of an organic process of interaction between community and organisers, of hard work, enthusiasm and vision. However, none of these perhaps was as instrumental in its success as the inadvertent perfect timing of its opening in the South African political and social landscape. Its success also lies in the tacit understanding of all the players that achievements are collective and not solely the result of any one person's efforts. The absence of individual ownership of the museum means that every participant, donor, visitor, employee or trustee can lay equal claim to owning the museum.

September 1998

> This piece comments on the Museum and its intersection with the process of land restitution, especially through its links with the District Six Beneficiary and Redevelopment Trust.

In order to understand the significance of the Museum in the process of reconstituting the city of Cape Town as a nonracial and open city it is important to locate District Six in South Africa's larger history. It is the site of one of the most publicised experiences of forced removals in the country. While the forced removals of people from District Six cannot be said to be more traumatic than those of other communities in South Africa, it is certainly the best documented. The process of documenting this experience has assisted other affected communities in recalling how they too might fight to win back their dignity and even their land.

District Six is significant also for its urban history. Much of this history has been about impoverished and marginalised people managing to build a sense of community and retain their own humanity in the face of considerable state neglect and oppression. District Six is remembered by many who lived there as a place where they were able to cross religious, class and social boundaries. As a place where they were able to share their everyday experiences and to live not as 'coloured', 'whites', 'Africans' or 'Indians' but as South Africans, District Six occupies a special place in the history of South Africa. It is argued by many that it was destroyed precisely because it offended the racist inclinations of the apartheid government. It was one of a number of places, like South End in Port Elizabeth and Vrededorp and Doornfontein in Johannesburg, that disproved the apartheid ideal. People lived together in relative harmony. The colour of their skins was not the only factor that mattered in their lives. Often much more important was the fact that they all shared a bond of poverty. The memory of District Six, and the sense of community and solidarity it generated, is important for South Africans who have been forced into apartheid townships and into apartheid identities.

The Museum has played an important role in the many struggles around the social, cultural and civic renewal that are taking place in the city. It has provided a forum for the discussion and debate of the future of the city of Cape Town. It has emerged as one of the few sites and structures in the city with the legitimacy to talk to and about the future of all its citizens. It is one of a handful of institutions able to speak about Cape Town and its people in terms that include the entire spectrum of its social makeup. It has also created the space for ordinary people to intervene in the bigger politics of urban renewal and to express their views about the future of the city. It has facilitated several cultural events, mainly in the form of exhibitions, which have drawn heavily on the input of ordinary District Sixers. These events have been path-breaking in so far as ordinary people have been able to describe themselves as they wish to be seen.

While these developments have not been without their difficulties, the museum has, thus far, proved to be an enormously generative space. It has brought to the fore the complex role an institution such as the District Six Museum plays in providing a bridge between the different experiences and knowledge of the everyday world and the more traditional academic approach of the museum. How knowledge is produced in this, through exhibitions, publications and other presentations, is a key area in which the Museum is poised to contribute museologically but also in terms of urban planning.

At the heart of these developments has been a specific conception of history with which the Museum has worked. As part of this historical work, the Museum has sought to draw on the rich urbanity which has characterised the life of District Six. It is this resource that the museum, and indeed the District, offers to the process of reconstruction in the city. The resource is mediated through the museum's exhibition policy, which is fundamentally about finding ways of incorporating the subjects of the stories of District Six – the people themselves – into the exhibition process. In this process, attempts are made to have people participate in the decisions about how they are to be represented. The past is not so much an archive awaiting unveiling, but a tapestry on which individuals and groups are able to inscribe themselves. They announce their positions and interests and take responsibility for their self-portrayal.

An important feature of this process is to show how human – as opposed to natural – our histories are, and how susceptible to shifts in power the storytelling is. In working in this way, the Museum has helped to show how stories and the histories that are constructed around them are seldom free of the personal interest of the storyteller. Difficult as this stance might be, the Museum has sought to use this as a resource and a strength, rather than as a problem.

Conflicts and solutions

Having spoken of history as a social activity, it is clear that museum work cannot, of course, be without its conflicts and contradictions. Memories, and the ways in which memories are transacted, mediated, represented and made use of, are questions which invoke difficult debate. In the process of establishing the Museum, evident from the very beginning were contrasting understandings of what the Museum ought to do, how it ought to deal with the past and how it dealt with the various claimants who spoke on behalf of District Six. On the one hand, there were stake-holders, many of whom were in the Trust which oversaw the establishment of the Museum, who saw it as a place which would serve as a reminder of the oppression experienced by the ordinary men and women who had built the city. There were, on the other hand, pressures to freeze and package the memory of District Six in ways which were distinctly inimical to the struggles that were taking place around District Six. Apologists for the apartheid era, for example, sought to enshrine the District Six Museum as a 'coloured' monument. Interestingly these struggles persist in one form or another.

Much more complex have been occasions when the Museum, either in the person of individual trustees or museum workers, have had to speak publicly or participate in one or other public process on the question of District Six. Born out of the struggle to save District Six, the Museum's broad stance has been to align itself with the dispossessed people of District Six and to offer itself as a vehicle for their participation in decisions about the future of the area. In practice, this stance has not been without difficulties, because situations have arisen where different people claiming to speak on behalf of District Six have sought to appropriate the Museum or to enlist its endorsement. Each of these occasions has been dealt with individually. The overarching approach of the Museum has, however, been that of inclusiveness.

An important issue for the Museum, which illustrates this approach, has been the question of the restitution of the rights of the dispossessed people of the area. The restitution process is based on a commitment by the state to compensate communities who lost their property and their homes as a result of the implementation of the Group Areas Act. It invites affected communities to make application to have their rights restored or made good monetarily or by way of the award of an alternative property in another area.

In this process, which involves the Museum, there have been debates about democracy and legitimacy.

Stakeholders within the community of District Six have been divided over the processes and the structures that have emerged to deal with the state and the local government (the City Council of Cape Town). While the question of history has been subdued within this debate, interestingly, it has been the spirit of inclusiveness which has prevailed. Borrowing from the heritage of District Six and its ability to assimilate into its fold new individuals and communities, the debate has been resolved through the invocation of District Six as an urban space that provided refuge to all and sundry. This achievement has been due, in no small measure, to members of the Museum.

The approach that has been taken has been to work with people's demands. Museum representatives in the process worked from the premise that the victims of forced removals were the first priority. Victims were engaged through a series of community participation projects and forums and venues. They were given 'hearing space' in all of these projects. Attempts were made to appreciate people's personal experiences as the building blocks of the eventual reconstruction. This community has become a coherent group and channelled their thoughts and demands into a central vehicle called the District Six Beneficiary and Redevelopment Trust. This Trust enjoys legitimacy as the negotiating instrument to interact with other bodies, especially Council and Government. In other words, the Council and Government must join the community rather than the other way around.

While the process has been uncomfortable and often acrimonious, it has been resolved in a way that is typically District Six in its character. The process has involved hard talking and repeated attempts to be sensitive to different people's experiences and backgrounds: it has involved listening to each other; appreciating other people's limitations and seeing them as strengths. Holding the process together has been a constant reminder of what there is to lose if the process were to fail.

Pitfalls and possibilities

What the restitution process has highlighted are the possibilities that are offered to public debaters by knowledge-producing institutions like museums. While the Museum recognises the dangers of producing a self-serving history which legitimates graft, greed and the abuse of political power (both individual and corporate), it seeks to argue that it can facilitate, in what it exhibits and how it exhibits, the coming-together of people of different mindsets. Looking at the difficulty, in the District Six example, of returning 45,000 people to the city and including their history in the many histories of South Africa, it is clear that the Museum is a site of profound reconstruction. In this sense, the role of the Museum, and the way in which it has offered its space for people to affirm their own delegitimated identities and to question their own pasts, is an important example to the rest of South Africa.

Rationale

The rationale of the Museum and, by implication, of the different projects in which it finds itself, is to contribute towards healing, nation-building and also capacity-building, but from the bottom up. The process must be in control of the 'victims' who for the first time in their history have a direct say and influence in the return, reconstruction and occupation. The rationale is to keep the process as participatory and transparent as possible, and in so doing build confidence and trust.

Impact

The impact of the Museum has been overwhelmingly positive. People feel a sense of ownership and responsibility towards the city. Unfortunately it has also engendered some impatience. Long delays in the restitution process have allowed mistrust to creep in as people's hopes have been stalled by the complexity of the bureaucratic process.

April 2000

Elevated above the city, on the slopes of District Six, the Museum waits out the last few days of its temporary occupation of the Moravian Chapel. It has been minimalist, a place of light and space and anticipation: the brightly coloured '*strukkies*' strung across the hall as if waiting for a celebration to begin. It has been a year of change, of new audiences, new experiences and a new atmosphere. A busy year which has fully justified the decision and the effort involved in keeping the District Six Museum open during its renovation phase.

The Museum's long-term plan was always to renovate and restore its Buitenkant Street premises in the Methodist Mission. This was an ambitious project, likely to take a long time. Again, the Museum was confronted with the dilemma of closing its doors in the face of public demand and the need to maintain its income from its Museum Shop. Instead, we decided to relocate for the period of the renovation to the Moravian Chapel. This white-painted building has stood for twenty-five years in visible contrast to the flattened landscape, a headstone to the ravages of forced removals.

Moving from the bustle of the Buitenkant Street premises, bordering District Six and the city centre, to the central emptiness of the District set up a whole new dynamic for the Museum. Although the District Six community still played a central role in the life of the Museum, especially with regard to the land claim research process and school curriculum programmes, no longer did ex-residents simply pop in on their way to do their business in town. Here caught between sea and mountain, we were suddenly disconnected from everyday routes and public transport. However, we did become part of a new route, one dependent on motorised transport (and facilitated by our sudden wealth of ample parking on Moravian Hill!). At least seven tourist buses visited us every day on the newly developed tourist route from 'city to township and Flats', a route that the Museum is proud to be part of and to have facilitated. Our return to Buitenkant Street will hopefully develop the interest of both the new and old visitor groups.

Just as the exhibition in the Moravian Chapel echoes the openness and sparseness of the current District Six landscape, the Museum in Buitenkant Street will reflect the busyness, variety and detail of the city centre and the old District Six, a place of community collectives and rich organisational and political life. This exhibition continues the processes integral to the genesis of the Museum and its particular curatorial practice of continuity, inclusivity and spontaneity: working with youth, communities and the disengaged from spheres as diverse as religious groups, street children, prisoners at Correctional Services institutions, unemployed youth, young artists, established artists, professionals and intellectuals, both academic and community.

Together with these community groups, the curatorial team is weaving a complex skein of themes into a bright and textured exhibition that will allow the material (objects, photographs, artworks, stories, music and oral history) collected over the past five years and the works of artists and writers inspired by District Six to find expression. It will question notions of home and belonging and issues of identity, while exposing apartheid, forced removals and the debate around global urban renewal.

The themes that thread through the exhibition will deal with the processes of memory, and we have included three memory rooms in the reconstruction of the Museum. The first is an actual interior that existed in District Six, 'Nomvuyo's Room'; the second is an artistic representation of the poignant memory of a room; and the third is a recording studio where we will collect oral testimony and will be able to operate as a broadcasting studio. The memories of District Six are precious because in reality we have very few authentic artefacts from the District: the hawker's cart, the street signs, the Little Wonder Store doors, some personal mementoes and archaeological fragments. The museum continues to be about abstract issues, about loss, memory and recovery. The physical and metaphorical heart of our new museum will be a facility that will attempt to capture these intangibles.

As we sit looking out the chapel doors over the empty lands towards the sea, we try to imagine what an occupied District will look like. The old street grid of District Six no longer remains; most of the names have gone and exist only in the Museum, but there is the promise that the City, the District Six Beneficiary Trust and the National Land Commission will soon begin the rebuilding of District Six as a residential area. In the meantime, we look forward to our return to Buitenkant Street in order to prepare it as a community centre that will cater to the reestablished District.

Notes

1   Shamil Jeppie and Grain Soudien (eds), *The Struggle for District Six: Past and Present*, Cape Town: Buchu Books. 1990. This book is unfortunately out of print and copies are very difficult to obtain.
2   Cited in David Goodman, 'Cape Town's District Six Rises Again', in *The Ford Foundation Report*, vol 28, no 2, Spring 1997, p17.
3   Henriette Geldenhuys, 'Thousands to move back to District Six', *Cape Times*, 22 November 2000.
4   Henriette Geldenhuys, 'Putting the heartbeat back into the city', *Cape Times*, 24 November 2000; Henriette Geldenhuys, 'Thousands to move back to District Six', *Cape Times*, 22 November 2000.

Chapter 17

Lawrence Scott (editor)

GOLCONDA

Our Voices, Our Lives

Prologue: From Golconda to Golconda

A FEW MILES OUTSIDE the great Indian city of Hyderabad, perched squarely on the Deccan Plateau, stands what remains of a once mighty fortress known as Golconda. Its name, in native Telugu, literally translates "round hill", which is most appropriate as in the year 1143, during the Hindu Kakatiya dynasty, a mud fort on a granite hill became by the 15th century the centre of power and wealth ruled by the Qutb Shahi kings.

In 1689, the Qutb Shahi dynasty and Golconda fell to the Mughal emperor Aurangzeb. The subsequent kings were called Nizams. They went on to become some of the richest kings of the time. For 600 years, Golconda was the storehouse for an endless stream of diamonds extracted from mines around the city. Some of the more famous ones are the Kohinoor diamond and the Hope diamond. This, apparently, was the only known source of diamonds until the discovery of the New World mines.

By 1750 the Mughal Empire in Delhi had all but collapsed. The British first arrived in Golconda in 1779. By 1806 it had become one of the largest cantonments of the East India Company in India. The British had set up three major trading posts in Calcutta, Bombay and Madras. These soon became fortified cities.

The East India army was commanded by famous generals like the Duke of Wellington and Robert Clive. The regiments left for India from the Cape of Good Hope and were then dispatched to East India forts. In 1798, the Madras regiments had 11,000 Europeans and as many Indians. And we know that these regiments moved or were disbanded as and when necessary.

Many thousands of miles away over the *Kala Pani*, the little Spanish colony of Trinidad was experiencing its first real economic growth since the Spanish arrived in 1498. Hundreds of French immigrants, enticed by Roume de St. Laurent's Cédula de Población of 1783, were arriving in the island, attracted by promises of rich land for them and their myriad slave chattels. The rich plains called Annaparima by the native Yao and Shebaio peoples were ideally suited to the growing of sugar cane.

Several names of Cedula grantees in the Naparimas have survived, including Rambert, Bordenarve, Bontour, Sipriani and Godineau. The land that would later become Golconda in

Trinidad was part of sugar plantations developed by one of these French settlers. They occupied the site of an Amerindian village, the artefacts of which have been re-discovered in the area of a small teak forest outside the modern-day village of the same name. Though the records for this period are now lost, the Mallett Survey of 1797 shows that the Naparimas, to which Golconda belonged, boasted eight rum distilleries, twenty-eight cotton mills, twenty-five coffee mills and twenty sugar refineries worked by mules. Thus, the agronomy of the original Golconda grant may not have been in sugar alone, but also under cotton and coffee. Mallett describes the area thus: "Few hills and very fruitful, producing the finest sugar of the colony; has two navigable rivers (the Siparia, now known as the Cipero, and Guaracara Rivers)."

The first emergence of the name 'Golconda' in the annals of Trinidad local history actually pre-dates the arrival of East Indians in the colony by at least six years, as the government Blue Books for 1839 show that George Monkhouse, proprietor of Golconda estate, paid dues of four pounds three shillings on his property. Presumably, this is also the Lt. George Monkhouse who was buried at St. Clement's Anglican Church in 1853. The now obliterated epitaph describes him as being "lately of the East India Regiment."

Though the mists of time have shrouded all details as to his past, we may assume that Lt. Monkhouse christened his Trinidadian holdings in memory of his time in Golconda as part of the East India Regiment. The Trinidad Golconda, like its Indian namesake, also occupies the top of a round hill. Further, there is evidence that the York and Lancaster regiments, which served in Martinique in 1793, left for India in 1800 and were then posted to the West Indies in 1829.

The estate, like its neighbouring Corinth, would have been worked by African slaves before emancipation in 1834 and the end of apprenticeship in 1838. "The Deed of Separation and articles of agreement, Francois and Rose Debonne Cazabon," dated 1837, shows clear mention by name of the "thirty apprenticed labourers who were formerly slaves belonging to the said estate and duly registered in the Registrar of Slaves office of the said island." A similar situation on the neighbouring estates of the Naparimas must have existed. There is further documented evidence of life on these estates in the diary of Friedrich Urich in *The Urich Diary 1830–32*, which gives clear evidence of the conditions and the arrangements of labour on the estates.

Around 1850, the first East Indian indentured labourers began to arrive on the estate, and would indelibly become the dominant fibre in the fabric of life in Golconda for more than a century thereafter. There is evidence in the records of arrival in the National Archives in Port of Spain of indentured workers who were sent to Golconda in the middle of the 19th century and continuing.

Though records specific to Golconda are scarce, the estate and its newly settled immigrant population would not have escaped the scourge of cholera, as it decimated the colony in 1854. In a generic account written in the Port-of-Spain Gazette, it was said that Indians on the Naparima estates "died like flies".

Around 1870, Golconda entered a new era of history as it was annexed to the formidable possessions of the Colonial Sugar Company, owners of Usine Ste. Madeleine, and the largest sugar producers in the empire.

In 1872, the village received its first house of prayer. St. Luke's Anglican Church was constructed as a chapel of ease to St. Clement's, which was consecrated in 1853 by the Rev. Jones Gabbett. The chapel became a focal point for almost all the Scottish and English overseers of the surrounding estates, as a few old tombstones of these persons in the churchyard seem to suggest. The Presbyterian Church's Canadian Mission to the Indians (CMI) constructed the first Golconda Presbyterian Church in 1875, under the auspices of pioneer missionaries, Rev. John Morton and Dr. Kenneth J. Grant.

In 1884, the unvarying thunder of drums smote fearfully upon the white colonial ears in the Naparimas. Since the 1850's when it was first celebrated on Philippine Estate, *Hosay* had been observed by almost every plantation where Indian immigrants were resident. The festival gained a reputation of being a wild and noisy affair which was frowned upon by the petit bourgeois and middle classes of the period. Following a season of unrest on the estates which employed immigrant labour (culminating in a riot at Cedar Hill in 1881 and the death of an Indian during the *Hosay* of that year), the colonial authorities on 30th July 1884 issued an ordinance which would prevent the immigrants and their gaudy *tadjahs* from entering San Fernando. Labourers from Philippine, Golconda, Retrench and Petit Morne estates met in the dead of night at St. Clement's churchyard and planned their triumphant parade in defiance of the Ordinance. On Thursday 30th October 1884, thousands of Indians, armed with lethal hakka sticks, thronged the way to Cipero Cross where they were confronted by twenty armed policemen. Stipendiary Magistrate Arthur Child read the Riot Act to the mob, with little or no effect. When the Indians were almost upon the police, they opened fire. When the smoke cleared, twelve lay dead, and over one hundred were injured. During the fray, the majority of the procession hastily abandoned their *tadjahs* and fled. The dead were placed on carts and buried in a mass grave where the present San Fernando Central Market now stands.

Golconda continued as part of the Colonial Company's empire, and received a new mode of transportation, when in 1900 a sugar-cane railway was laid to the collection scales in Barrackpore and Debe. The railway crossing just outside Golconda was a landmark, and boasted a guard's tower and what was perhaps the last surviving crossing barrier, which was de-commissioned in 1998 when the last leg of the railway was scrapped.

The last years of the 19th century were difficult ones for the sugar industry as low prices on the international market caused an industry-wide recession. The indentured immigrants of Golconda must have felt the sting of the contraction, probably by having their wages or "tasks" reduced. The Indians themselves were to become permanently tied to the Trinidadian soil when immigration ceased in 1917, and the final umbilical cord with Mother India was severed.

Though relatively little is known about the indigenous religious practices of the immigrants, it is at least understood that a *khutiya* or communal worship space, complete with a small *mandir* or shrine, existed in the centre of the barracks behind the Presbyterian Church as early as the 1920's. There is no record of any pronounced Islamic presence in the village at this time.

In the 1930's, 40's and 50's, Golconda Estate was managed as part of the nearby Petit Morne Estate. There are many remnants of these and earlier periods. The overseer's house, where many English and Scots overseers lived through the time of the Usine Ste. Madeleine Sugar Company, still exists. Walls of the water cistern which fed the barracks and the estate can still be seen. Parts of the old pens, stables and work houses remain in the transformed house belonging to Balchan and Farida Rampaul, whose garden is becoming a museum of the remnants of the old estate and cane railway.

The next great event in Golconda's history was the arrival of electricity in 1954 as part of an island-wide electrification programme. In the early 1960's a new Presbyterian church was constructed, replacing the old wooden structure.

In the 1960's the barracks were demolished, and with Caroni Social Welfare Loans, many estate workers built their homes in the Golconda Settlement.

During the 1970's more dramatic changes occurred with the departure of the British presence which had dominated the area for so long and the formation of state-owned Caroni (1975) Limited as the new overlords of the canefields. The years of the 1980's and 1990's saw a gradual decline in the importance of the sugar industry as a generator of income in the village. In 1998 the cane railway was scrapped. The final blow came in 2006 when Caroni (1975) Ltd. was closed for good.

The Golconda Project

The writings which appear in this collection have grown out of a community, oral history project with villagers who were sugarcane workers or related to sugarcane workers from the village of Golconda, just outside San Fernando. We were looking to collect what has been called, 'Public History': "Not history told to you from the top down, something you have to be qualified in, involving using fancy words that only a few people understand, something that you keep secret, which involve academics talking down to the public."[1] We were looking for a history which entails, "Any investigation into the past using any method that people feel is appropriate to help them to make sense of any aspect of the past. It is a meeting between the professional world and members of the public who are interested in investigating the past. It uses public and private collections, archives, memorabilia, oral history, the landscape, memory, photographs, family stories to investigate public and private pasts."[2] We have particularly used some of the latter points in this definition in our research. The project was begun in a series of eight three hour workshops which I conducted at the UTT's Corinth Campus in September–October 2007 and continued through 2008–2009 with interactive meetings in the community as part of The Academy for Arts, Letters, Culture and Public Affairs' Outreach Programme at the UTT.

Corinth borders the village of Golconda, once a sugar estate since the early 19th century and now a thriving village, the birth place of Michel Jean Cazabon and a landmark on the southern landscape. The estates of the Naparimas have formed part of a broader research area: Hidden Cultures (French Creole) with which I have been involved and to which this project is connected.

Apart from myself and the teachers and local southern historians who participated, all the other participants are from the village of Golconda. Some have lived all their lives there and some came to the village through marriage.

My original idea was to conduct a creative writing project with ex-sugarcane workers at a time when the industry was in decline and experiencing its last crop. My aim was to work with people who had lived and worked on the estates near to Usine Sainte Madeleine.

This was the landscape in which I was born and grew up until I was nineteen, and continued to visit. It has been the well-spring of inspiration for my own writing of fiction. It has remained as a landscape which most essentially gives me a sense of place in the world, a sense of identity, as I have come and gone from Trinidad over the years. I wanted to work with people who wanted to tell their story of living and working in the sugar industry in this landscape.

I was born at Petit Morne Estate. My father had been an overseer at the nearby Union Hall Estate. Petit Morne was a promotion to manager for him. Golconda was managed as a part of Petit Morne in the 1940s and 1950s, as part of the Usine Sainte Madeleine Sugar Company, U.S.M. So arranging to recruit people for the project from Golconda was to fulfil one of my first ideas. I could not believe my luck.

Through the support of Deosaran Jagroo, the CEO of Caroni Ltd., I was invited to a meeting of supervisors in the field who were working on the closure of the company at the time. I put my idea to them. There was some scepticism. But at that meeting was Kenneth Benjamin, a member of the Transition Team in Human Resources, from Golconda, and almost immediately, he informed me that he had the right people for the project. He knew people who wanted to tell their story. Benji would organise it. That was Mr Jagroo's prediction, and so said, so done.

In May 2007 we organised a meeting at the Community Centre in Golconda for me to meet those villagers who thought they were interested. The group that met the villagers, myself apart, included Mario Lewis, a cultural-artist colleague from The Academy at the UTT, together with David D. A. Maharaj, a teacher and local historian from St Stephen's College in Princes Town, and two other non-village participants, John Ramsaran and Mungal Chatergoon, both of whom knew the history of the estates well. Radha Benjamin prepared the community centre for the meeting, and Benji introduced the meeting.

John brought his knowledge of the Presbyterian Church on the estates, Mungal brought his local history knowledge and kept from that first day a photographic record of all our meetings, as well as writing poems which evoked some of the themes that we were developing. All of us then who met with the villagers at that first meeting were associated with the life in the sugar and with that particular landscape. Mario was observing and recording with his video camera as someone new to the landscape and the life in the sugar.

Of the seventeen villagers who attended that first meeting, twelve committed themselves to attending the workshops arranged to begin in September of 2007. Dennis Armoogan declined to continue after the first workshop because of other commitments, but allowed us to publish his one detailed, striking piece on estate life. His decision to publish came just before his sudden death on 23rd April 2009.

Attendance was excellent. We were a group ranging from the oldest Mrs Bernadine Sandiford, eighty five years old, to the youngest at forty one.

It became apparent that, with some participants not being formally literate, the project would look for its outcomes through oral contributions which would then be recorded and transcribed, rather than through written pieces. Yet, once we began, there were a number of written pieces offered, a piece on estate life by Moonan Amichan and effectively formed poems by Jhaimany Seeta Seebaran and Moonan Amichan. The teachers and I have contributed written pieces.

After the first introductory meeting, Mario and I visited the village again, to record with Benji's introductory tour, the shape of the village, to see for ourselves how the landscape evolved from sugar estate into settlement and then into village. This was going to be one of the stories which would emerge in our workshops. On that visit, Mario taped some of the villagers as an experiment in recording and we got some memorable pieces which are now published as poems: Radha Benjamin's poignant 'Somebody Walking' and Ralph Chanan's freshly remembered 'Birth and Death'. We ended up filming in Taramatee Rajbally's bar and being refreshed with a complimentary cool drink.

Before beginning the workshops, we arranged an introductory session at The Academy in Barataria which then gave a formal stamp to our project. We wanted commitment. Participants would receive a modest stipend for that commitment. But the real value that we exchanged was the desire to tell our stories as freshly told lived experience. We were looking for those kinds of stories of how life had been as the village evolved, not academic pieces, not second hand experience, though we have included an historical note, Angelo Bissessarsingh's 'Golconda to Golconda', on what so far we have managed to speculate is the early history of the estate, and David D. A. Maharaj's 'Sugar: A Snapshot from 1987' which nods towards the academic.

An 1846 map of Trinidad shows clearly the situation of Golconda, marked more prominently than many of the surrounding estates of the Naparimas. We have speculated that possibly the estate got its name from Lieutenant George Monkhouse, a member of the East India Regiment who once owned the estate in the early part of the 19th century and is buried in the nearby St Clement's church yard cemetery. The name may have been given nostalgically in memory of Golconda in Andhar Pradesh outside Hyderabad. It does seem, from presently available documents, that the estate got its name before Indentureship. Angelo Bissessarsingh, a researcher and local historian, writes the story in 'Golconda to Golconda'.

At one of our last meetings of the project, Soumya Sastry Didon, who comes from Hyderabad and has been living in Trinidad with her husband Luc Didon, the current Director of the Alliance Française in Trinidad, and who was fascinated to learn that there was a Golconda in Trinidad, gave a talk on the history of the ancient fortress. Angelo Bissessarsingh also gave a talk at that meeting on the early history of the village and has woven Soumya's account of Golconda in India into his piece.

Celebratory meals have played a significant part in keeping the various members of this community project together. After the meal on this occasion, cooked by Radha Benjamin and her women helpers, Jhaimany Seeta Seebaran and Lystra Samaoo, we were offered an Indian Golconda dessert, kubbani kamitha, cooked by Soumya Sastry. This was another way in which Golconda had come to Golconda.

In the afternoon a group visited the St Clement's church yard to see the sites of the Monkhouse graves and other significant graves of the 19th century, guided by Angelo Bissessarsingh.

One of the aims in transcribing our oral recordings was to maintain the oral qualities of these pieces. We wanted the collection to be truly 'Our Voices, Our Lives'. Standard spelling has been used for the most part and punctuation has been used for clarity, but not in any way to alter the dialect of the spoken voice, but rather, to enable and maintain the oral qualities through the syntax. The pieces by the teachers, the Rampauls and myself are written pieces. There has been an attempt to standardise Hindi spellings and for this we sought the advice of Professor Brinsley Samaroo who assisted us in compiling the glossary.

At the workshops held at the UTT's Corinth Campus we took a thematic approach. Each week we would take a particular theme. We began with ancestors, then moved on to childhood, school and growing up. We looked at estate life and family life, at religion, traditions and festivals. Of course there was work. An interesting theme which evolved was the importance of the train, and in estate life, the role of the midwife in the community emerged as a vividly remembered figure.

We began each session with reading extracts from novels, stories and poems which reflected the life in the sugar, from novelists like Isaiah Boodoo, Ismith Khan, Vidia Naipaul, Sam Selvon and Jan Shinebourne. We read historical accounts of life in the sugar. We read the poets Edward Braithwaite, Martin Carter, the San Fernando poet, Rajandaye Ramkissoon-Chen and Grace Nichols. The literature was to stimulate our own stories which we then told among ourselves. After this warm up, as it were, for the first hour, we broke into recording groups, two or three people going with one of the teachers to record stories on the day's theme. In this way we collected eight hours of recording over a range of eight themes. In our third hour we would come back from our recordings and share our experiences of telling stories. Once the transcriptions began to be done, our own stories became a stimulus for talk and new recordings.

A highlight of these sessions was when we broke from the classroom sessions and spent our time on a walk-about of the village, creating a map of the main landmarks and remaining artefacts of Golconda as a sugar estate. The overseer's house is still there. There are remnants of the old barracks and the cistern which gave the estate water. The old mule pen and workshops have now been transformed into a home by Balchan and Farida Rampaul. There is the old railway signal box and remnants of the old railway lines. Maps by Moonan Amichan and David Maharaj grew out of our walk-about.

These stories were told with great feeling and commitment, often resulting in tears for the teller and for the listeners. Story-tellers got in touch with stories they did not know they had in themselves. Often these were of parents and the poverty which they experienced. A majority of the group were of the 1940 generation who left school at fourteen to go and work in the fields because of the situation of their parents. There are graphic stories of childhood by Sookier Amichan and Soodeo Freddie Ragoonanan. Life stories, as by Taramatee Rajbally, are detailed and freshly remembered.

Our oldest member, Bernadine Sandiford, who never missed a session and gave generously of her experiences, died on New Year's Day 2008. Sadly, she has not lived to see her stories in print. Her family and friends within the community buried her in the cemetery at St Luke's Anglican Church, a landmark, and one of the oldest buildings in Golconda, with which she was associated throughout her life. She was a great example to the group and her own remarkable story as an African Trinidadian living among East Indians in the barracks as family, nursing her neighbour's child, Jaitoon Mahabir, who was herself a member of the group, was a moving moment in the group's exchanges. This is celebrated in the joint piece 'Mother and Daughter' by Jaitoon Mahabir and Bernadine Sandiford. She passed on this connection to the village to her daughter Wendy Mitchell, whose pieces on school and religion create a generational contrast with the pieces by her mother.

Repeatedly, members of the group said they wanted the story of their generation told. They wanted the life in the barracks to be told. They wanted the hardship and injustice of estate life to be remembered. While hardship was a theme, there was also pride in belonging to a way of life which created a closely knit community who worked together. There was an esteem for themselves in belonging to an industry whose processes are captured in the language of that industry as used by the workers as they describe their lives. We are saving a language as well as memories. There was nostalgia for a childhood which was remembered both for its hardship and for a fun created out of simple pleasures as we see in Sookdeo Freddie Ragoonanan's childhood piece which, in describing a fishing expedition, says, "The old man used to say, just how the stars break, just so the fish go take the line, and until he catch a fish, he aint coming, home you know.'

With the sugar industry pretty well gone, there is some faint hope to revive some part of it, keeping the Usine Ste. Madeleine factory working with the farmers' canes, along with foreign and local companies interested in making paper, sugar, molasses for rum and the new rum straight from the sugarcane juice. But there is no doubt that a landscape and way of life is changing radically. This I think is one of the main values of this community project, to record a swiftly disappearing way of life.

Some of our stories from the younger members of the group are by those who came into Golconda by marriage, and their stories draw a striking contrast between the sugar estate and the very different landscapes of Penal Rock Road in pieces by Lystra Samaroo, and Tableland by Radha Benjamin. Taramatee Rajbally's pieces also reflect a life outside Golconda, at Penal. Kenneth 'Benji' Benjamin's piece 'How growing Up Was' tells the story of a new generation, as a child born in the Golconda Setdement and not in the barracks, a child who benefited from the new secondary education of the 1960s and who went on to continue his education as a trade unionist, rising to top positions in the All Sugarcane Workers Trade Union.

As an intermediary celebration of our work, once we had completed all the transcriptions, we had a series of readings by the younger generation reading the pieces by their elders. A short video film of the project so far, edited by Mario Lewis and myself was shown.

In the end, as well as the oral pieces, many in the group wrote poems, some well formed pieces. The moving evocation of the sugar by Sookier Amichan in 'Sugarcane' was an oral piece transcribed by Naila Arjoon, who at the time realised as she transcribed it that we had a spoken poem on our hands. I think it is only now at the very end that we fully realise what it is we have been reaping here, truly a Golconda of stories as we were taught by Soumya Sastry Didon to use the word as a superlative.

There are also the written pieces by the teachers. David Maharaj's piece on his ancestors, 'The Maharaj Families of Usine Ste Madeleine', is important for its detail of family history. His essay 'Sugar: A Snap Shot from 1987' has contextualised Golconda in the general life of the history of the sugar industry. Marilyn Temull's poems and particularly 'Golconda Voices' express the themes of this project, while Naila Arjoon's 'Sweet Memories of Sugar' laments the passing of the sugar landscape while expressing memories of its beauty in her own growing up. My own piece, 'The Mark of Ramdaou', shows my connections to the world of the sugar. All these pieces form part of this anthology of lived experience in the sugar. There is also John Ramsaran's piece on the Presbyterian Sunday School experience at Golconda, 'Sunday School at Golconda', an important historical marker from his own experience and his knowledge of the stories of the some of the early Presbyterian missionaries. Mungal Chatergoon's poem 'For Mrs Sandiford' is a rewrite of one of Mrs Sandiford's stories in Mungal's representation of the dialect, giving the story a broader resonance by having it shaped as a poem. Each of the teachers did their own transcriptions and became intimately involved in the pieces. Jenny Scott assisted me in some of the transcriptions of my groups, and together she and I carried out some additional editing as the book came closer to publication.

There are many people to thank for their support and this is done formally in the acknowledgements. But above all it is the villagers themselves who have to be thanked for giving so generously of their experiences as is Kenneth Benjamin, "Benji", who introduced us to his village.

It was generally agreed that we wanted to remember Bernardine Sandiford in a very special way as the senior member of the group who gave so plentifully of her unique experiences as an African Trinidadian living among East Indians; acknowledgement of her memory forms part of our dedication. When Dennis Armoogan died on 23rd April, 2009 it seemed fitting that he too should be remembered in our dedication.

We want to thank Ms. Judith Elcock, the Manager of the UTT's Corinth Campus, for her warm welcome and making the facilities at the campus available to us. She took a special interest in our work and was a guest at our celebration of readings when we had completed our transcriptions, and afterwards joined us for lunch in the village at the Benjamin's.

We thank Professor Ken Ramchand for supporting this project as part of The Academy's outreach work, and attending our meetings, including our walk-about day and celebration of readings and other general meetings. Equally, we want to thank Brinsley Samaroo for his contributions on the history of the sugar, and Pandita Idrani Rampersad's spirited video interviews with villagers during our walk-about session, which in turn received spirited responses. Mr Sham Shu Deen, the genealogist, conducted a very important session introducing an exhibition on indentureship, which was originally mounted at the National Archives, and offering ways into tracing genealogies, carrying out spontaneous interviews to illustrate how one might go about getting the first leads into the genealogy search. We thank Kim Johnson, one of my UTT colleagues, who while interviewing Nassalou Ramaya for his music project, interviewed Betty Mahabir Ramaya on her husband's work. Betty, as Betty Mahabir, came from Golconda and we have used part of that interview here, comprising detailed and well told stories connected to many of our themes. Her contribution has enriched the collection. We also thank Kim for access to and use of some of his sugar photo archive.

Let me close by acknowledging the privilege it has been for me to work with all the members of the project, the teachers, the consultants, and to remember Kenneth Benjamin's original desire, that we are passing on our stories to a younger generation to understand the lives of their elders. I also wish to thank again, in particular, the villagers themselves, whose stories are at the heart of this project, for their many warm expressions of cooperation and hospitality throughout the life of the project. Their commitment was genuine and sustained.

[. . .]

Bound to sugar

Moonan Amichan

Different type of people have different type of job. Now take for instance, when I go to work, I do eight hours work. I come home, my wife stay home, prepare all she cooking. That is how we do.

I work three to eleven in the evening. But I do different work from cutting cane. I load cart. I drive trace mule. That is a mule that used to pulling the cart. In those days I wasn't married. But when I starting load cart, drive cart, I get married at that time.

But my wife stayed home. In other words I work and do all the maintenance, and she maintain the family. She had to send the children to school, cook their food, wash clothes, my clothes, children clothes, and prepare all the things. All that I do is the outside work, bringing in the income, and she do all the house work.

All the grocery, pay bills, she do all of that most of the times. She get up sometimes three o'clock in the morning when I was to cut cane and load cart, but when I was to work three to eleven in the evening, she get up same hour most of the time, six o'clock, five o'clock. But she has a habit of getting up and do all her work early and then sit down and relax, because she get that habit from my mother who used to tell she, 'Better to get up before the sun rise, do all your house work.'

In the barrack days the most education the girl get is they learn them sewing, not education, and cooking. Sewing and cooking is the most essential things for a girl in the barrack days.

My father work in the estate, but I never see him work, I hear he work and he tell me he work. I never know him working, because in the barrack days he used to sell.

Usually two person used to sell in the barrack days, my father and a next Muslim fella, they call him Mia. We sell fig, orange, grapefruit. We had donkey cart.

Well, my mother, I see my mother working on the estate. Well, when my mother goes to work and come back, my father take care of everything at home. He take care of the children, cook, wash, change clothes, whatever necessary, because my father resign before my mother. Then my mother started to work in the estate. After seeing its advantage I had was to leave school and stop she from work.

When I was working first I start driving trace mule, I start load cart, when the carter man ent come I work. When he ent come I used to take my sister and drive cart and she used to load. She used to load cart with me. Then they abolish the cart now.

They start driving a Farm-all, they call it Bell trailer. It had a Farm-all in the front pulling the trailer, winching up the load in the back. After that I drive bush cutter, then I start driving fire engine. During the season I cutlass, I break bank, I weed, all these laborious things.

Even when I gone in the factory for employment, the manager himself say they cannot employ people from the cultivation. It was very difficult. They have a system that if they pull people from the cultivation, they wouldn't get nobody to work in the cultivation.

I started to work about fourteen years, when I leave school. Because of the condition of my parents and them.

I remember when the foreman stand up and watching the work, but those days wasn't a bed of roses you know. I remember when I see my mother toting the paragrass down from the centre of the field, to the trace, with all this mud and thing running down in she face, and dirty clothes. Sometimes the foreman wife alone used to get water. When they bring one tin of water for the day, that is that, no more water for them.

I sometimes see my mother take she dress, wipe she hand and eat she roti. It wasn't like now, when you getting a whole gallon of water. Nobody else couldn't get to carry no water, excepting the foreman wife.

And then, you cannot call them by they name, you have to call them *Sadarin*, and calling the foreman *Sadar*, and calling the white man *Sahib*. If they want to say the white man coming, they talk in Hindi, 'Sahib a wailla'. The white man does not know that language, some white man know it and some don't.

Sometime the foreman and they, when you do one task, you now start to work. They tell you go and do a next half task, and tomorrow they will tell you, 'I helping you, today.' That is you done do it as a next half. The next day you go back and do it again, and you start again, so you already have work in hand, pile up. And the foreman take that and give it to the white man, give that to the company.

When my mother and father come home, and I see the condition of them . . . I have a picture of them, sixty years. I see people work, fifty years, sixty years. Sometimes when they sit down to work, take the water from the river, wash they hand.

It have a foreman they call Blacks, if you working there, you could never done work. People working in Golconda, and they leave Golconda and gone Bronte to work, and they come back and meeting people in Golconda who working. He was not a good fella to work with, pressurizing the workers. He was Indian. Most of the people working in Caroni was Indian.

When the younger generation started to work in the company, some of the work started to change. The foreman start to 'fraid the younger generation. They couldn't work them as how they want. Sometimes a foreman measuring, where a rod is ten feet, they pushing the rod, when they push the rod, is fifteen feet they getting. So you have to do it.

Sometimes you working in big cane, you wet down head to foot, in the morning when you come three o'clock, four o'clock in the morning. You do a task, you soak down head to foot with the dew, and whether rain or sun, or thunder, you have to do your task. Sometimes five rod, fifteen, twenty rod in length, so when you multiply that now, is a hundred and something feet. So for the day, you come back one o'clock, two o'clock. How much you making? You can't even make five dollars a day.

Look, sometimes when I used to work and pay loan, to make five dollars, I had to pay five dollars and twenty five cents for loan. Now sometimes you getting two days for the fortnight.

When Panday rake over, then we start to get a little improvement, guarantee work. When Bhadase Maraj was the president general, when you go for more you getting a penny or a cent increase, hardly get a penny, you get a cent increase. And how much you could make with that? When you have to mind three children, you wife, yourself.

I mind my mother, my father, my brother, myself, three children, my wife. How much you could make with that, when you have to pay five dollars and twenty five cents for loan? We get the loan through the sugar welfare, but that was Caroni land, for house. You get the land free but we have to pay back the loan.

[. . .]

Canefield on fire

Jhaimany Seeta Seebaran

> In the middle of the night
> The room get bright.
> 'Nanee, Nanee!'
> 'what's wrong, Sarah?'
> 'Come and see.

The room on fire.' Sarah say, amaze.
'No; Sarah, is canefield in a blaze.'
Sarah cry in shock,
'where I'll get cane to suck?'
Nanee say, 'Girl, go to sleep.'
Sarah get up and peep.
she look and look, admire
The long green leaf on fire.
she wake up in the morning
Hearing the folk.
Realising they come out to work.
[. . .]

People and customs

I didn't have an Indian name. My Christian name was Evelyn, Betty Evelyn Mahabir. I was born 1930 at Golconda Estate.

My mother and my father had two children, my brother and I. We all lived on the estate. My father was at first a cane-weigher. At the derrick they weigh the cane and drop it in the trucks that carry it in the factory. After that he worked at Petit Morne Estate as a clerk.

While there, he got a promotion because he was honest and always doing good for the company, so Petit Morne Estate made him farmers' overseer to look after the farmers on Golconda, Petit Morne and Tarouba. They had given him a horse to go around to these places and when he comes home he had nothing to do, only reading the papers. After that they called him at the office and say they like him to be acting overseer in the absence of the overseer.

I know all the overseer names. The first was Mallalieux, then Dixon, then Goddard, Ince, and the last one was Haynes. All were white men. I not sure but Dixon was Bajan white. My aunt husband was Dopson, a mulatto white. He was white from another country like Barbados. He was an overseer in Woodland Estate where my aunt and Dopson get together and they had their children.

White men used to get involved with Indian women when they're attractive. My aunt was like me, she had nice eyes. They have five children together. They look white, real handsome men. Women used to run after them. They didn't marry them, they used to just be with them. She was with the white man named Dopson.

None of us carried Indian names. My first cousin was Johnny Dopson, then Malligan Dopson, Dolly and Pearl Dopson and Cecil Dopson, the last one.

I used to spend holidays with them, but I had to get back home soon. My aunt had to take a bus to Cross Crossing, from there take the train to Golconda. Then we'll walk up the estate. It wasn't too long a walk from the cabin. She drop me, spend some time and go back in the afternoon. My brother would still be there because he like the company. I cry to come home but he was eight years older. He have more fun with them.

They used to go all about and catch doves. I used to be sorry for them when they bring them to roast. Malligan was going with them with the gun. He had a belt with cartridges. Last time I went he had lost the belt. When you go Golconda with Mr Brash, a next overseer, maybe his father friend, they go hunting together. When they had little hunt my brother and Cecil did that with slinging shot. That's what they used to kill the birds with and they bring home them, five or six. They clean and roast it with salt and pepper.

My mother was Dalia, an Indian name. She and my father had two children. She was a water carrier, she carry a tin of water on her head to the cane-field for the workers to drink. It didn't have no pipe. All the gangs, weeding gang, planting gang, forking gang had a water carrier.

Since I know my grandmother she never work on the estate because my uncle used to work and sometimes they give her something and sometimes she self-dependent. She make *Bara* and channa, the real *Bara*, not the flour one. Sometimes she make sugar cake to sell. That's how she make a living, and my mother give her something.

But we all live together in one barrack. Going to the back toilet, was another barrack there and she lived in the first room, so she could walk over in a few steps.

She would mind ducks and fowl. When she want to eat one, she call my uncle, he lived on the estate too, he will kill and clean it. He will say he want something to drink before we eat this. He had a little petit quart. He will buy that and bring it.

When my uncle take out his food, he could eat a big meal in a small basin and put *Dhal* over it and the duck or chicken. He will eat that and take two drink. He lived at the next end of the estate. There was a big cistern fifty feet deep that provide water for the people. We kept drinking water in the gallery.

We had a next place where my mother cook and we had two barrels there connect to the spout. We had that for drinking but to wash you go to the cistern with a pitch oil tin. My uncle will go up on it and will take a bucket on a rope and send it down and pull it up. While they holding their pan on their head he will throw it easy till it full. That's what they used for washing. Is afterwards we get pipe. There was one tap where the Sunday school is, the first barrack. But before that my *Nanee* would take me with her down by the cricket field where the river ran to the pond. She took a little pan and dip the water from the spring and take it home to drink. She gave me a small pan to carry on my head. It was fun. All the girls and boys did it.

I had goat and sheep to mind. I have to tie them out on mornings before school, and weekend I have to clean the pen. I had a whole room in the barrack for my goat and sheep.

It had five rooms. We took three of the big rooms. There was an old man named Sobratie. My father called him and tell him to come, he have place for him. We had four extra barrels and he have to full them up, toting the bucket from the standpipe. My sister in law when she get married she never go to the pipe stand. This old man was there to fill the water for us.

My mother would come from work, take a half hour rest, then she go in the garden. When she go to the garden she will plant. She have peas, mustard *Bhagi,* cucumber, cassava and bodi. She planted that because her brother used to go with her and fork up the land for her. We never buy anything like that. We get it there, plus my uncle had a whole big place where he had everything planted and he used to make a little extra money selling: *Baigan*, chennet, pumpkin, *Seim* and bodi. He would bag it and take it San Fernando market and sell. Mammy would send me there for it. We had small bhaji, no chemical, you just had to pick it, break it in two and wash and cook it. You could get some any time of the day.

I only spoke Hindi with my *Nanee*. Otherwise we talk English but dialect. Nowadays is so different. Those days everybody was the same, speak the same. I just had one uncle and everybody in that estate was *Maai, Mamoo, Mowsee,* mother sister. We lived like that. Everybody was a family. We never call big people by their names. I knew every barrack in the estate and who lived there.

Reading and fear

When I receive that cut in my foot, I really couldn't go to school. I went to school a little bit and I find that I couldn't take the education, so I had was to stop school. I had maybe eleven, twelve years, about there. I was playing and a bottle cut me in my foot. Usually I used to play cricket, football. We had a game they call 'Goes In, Goes Out.' This game goes like, one with the bat batting, and it have a set of boys fielding. And anyone get the ball, they will bowl the ball, and if they bowl out the one that batting, they getting chance to bat. So that is how it goes because everybody see anywhere the ball go now. We have to rush, so it means that a few of us nearer to the ball will run to get the ball. I could remember a bigger boy push me down, rushing for the ball, and I fall down on my knee, and I started to cry. And when I go home now, crying, and my father see me crying, he take out his big belt and start to beat me. He was warning us not to play with the boys, bigger boys and them.

So when my mother see I getting licks now, she telling him, 'Why you hit the boy for, you ent see the boy foot bleeding?' And then he started. My mother come between to block me from getting licks, and he started to beat my mother instead. And then after he started to run me, I run in quite by another neighbour house, and they save me. That was one incident I could remember.

I had one reading book, and that was I think the West Indian Reader at the time. That was what I used to read. And one copy book. I did a little, but I really can't explain so much, cause to the end of the day, when I recognise that I couldn't read or anything I didn't learn much. The onliest time I learn to read really, when I grow up a little more, is when I get baptised, and I started to read the bible. When I was to read the bible, I couldn't understand. My sister give me a bible which have concordance in it, and under every word, every big word, have the meaning of it. So then I start. I couldn't even pronounce the word properly. I start to read, and I start to pronounce, with the concordance, I start to understand. And now I does read a little, so up to today I does still go to church.

My neighbour, which was Mohan, was a teacher in school. He really was, I would say, a good teacher, because he wanted us to learn.

And I grow up in a kind of way was a fighter boy from small, so I wanted to fight. I went to school one day and something he tell me to do I didn't do it. He started to beat me with a whip. Mr. Daney was the headmaster, and he had a son like to fight, which is Mark, and during that school time I tell you, twelve, around twelve years, I used to be fighting. Every day we fighting. The scheme boys, the village boys, one day one of my friend, Soogrim, and one of them, Briss, both of them was brothers and Mr Hugh which was the Headmaster, saw his son fighting with Briss. And is Negro and Indian, and Mr Hugh thought that his son would have beat Briss, but it didn't happen so, Briss beat his son, and he was annoyed about it. He didn't like Briss beat him.

I had some fear, plenty fear. I didn't want to go to school

[. . .]

Chicken and rice

Lystra Samaroo

I started school at the age of five years old. I attend Penal Rock Road Hindu School. The first day I went to school, I was scared because the teacher had a whip and my mother kept saying, 'If you don't do your school work, the teacher will beat you.' She also keep saying, 'You lazy and you don't like house work, so you better take education.' I was a bright student and did well and passed Common Entrance. My mother was proud because I was the eldest, and they didn't have much Secondary School, and I was one of the few students in the community who had passed.

I attend Penal Junior Secondary for three years. I remember one day we had an excursion in Form Three and I tell my mother to make fried rice and chicken for me. We went to the zoo and then we had lunch at the Botanic Gardens. When every one of my friends took out their lunch, I feeling ashamed because my mother do not know how to make fried rice, so she boil the rice separate and strain it, curry the chicken and then throw the rice in the chicken and turn it up. So all my friends' mother made fried rice and they fried rice looking different from my one, because they mother know how to make it the correct way and they all offering the teacher. So the teacher ask me, 'So how come you not offering me what you bring for lunch?"

So reluctantly, I took out my lunch and my friends ask, 'What is that you bring?' The teacher realised I was ashamed and he refused all of their lunch and share my lunch and make my day good.

Notes

1   *People and Their Pasts*, edited Paul Ashton and Hilda Kean, Palgrave Macmillan, 2009 – quote taken from launch presentation, February 25th, 2009.
2   Ibid.

Chapter 18

Michael Belgrave

SOMETHING BORROWED, SOMETHING NEW

History and the Waitangi Tribunal

A S KEITH SINCLAIR WAS REDISCOVERING the Aborigines Protection Society in London after the Second World War, a Royal Commission into Surplus Lands was undertaking its own investigation into the years immediately prior to the Treaty of Waitangi.[1] The Commission struggled with its own surfeit of primary sources. Hundreds of early land deeds and correspondence on Old Land Claims were transcribed and typed with multiple carbon copies and translations from Maori where necessary.[2] These were pored over by the three-man Commission and counsel representing the Crown and Maori. It was far from an academic exercise No historians appeared as witnesses and the only secondary material used by the Commission was Ethel Wilson's *Land Problems of the New Zealand Settlers of the 'Forties* published from an MA thesis in 1936.[3] The Commission's report, published in 1948, presented its own narrative of race relations in the 1830s, but from a parallel and very different perspective from Sinclair's.

It was not until the late 1970s that academic historians began to show an active interest in attempts by the political and legal process to reconsider the colonial past as a site for contemporary conflicts over land and other aboriginal rights. The preparation of historical submissions on behalf of Tauranga Moana in 1979 marks the first attempt to meld these legal, political and academic processes. The Waitangi Tribunal's acquisition of a historical jurisdiction in 1985 led historians to become actively involved in giving evidence or in the writing of historically based reports for courts and commissions of inquiry. Partly because of this new academic involvement and partly because of the Tribunal's novel Treaty-based jurisdiction, there was a tendency to see the Tribunal's exploration of New Zealand's past as a new departure.[4] This 'new history' has been seen as unhindered by troublesome antecedents. A Maori majority and marac-based hearings also suggested that this 'new history' would be Maori centred and Maori directed. Yet despite much that was novel, there was also much that was borrowed from a long quasi-judicial tradition of interpreting and reinterpreting activities involving Maori and the Crown. Forgetting this borrowed legal historiography makes it difficult to understand the Tribunal's emerging reinterpretation of this area of the country's history. While the Tribunal and the historians in the late 1980s stressed their new approach to the investigation of Maori rights under the Treaty of Waitangi, their attempts to free themselves from the weight of past assumptions and interpretations looks less successful a decade on.

This chapter looks at the Waitangi Tribunal and the Treaty settlement process in their historical roots, identifying the extent to which they can only be explained within a long-term quasi-judicial and political process. Older inquiries and earlier settlements cast a long shadow over Tribunal research, reports and settlements. The Treaty jurisdiction has updated old settlements, allowed new historical arguments to inform judicial opinion, and given Maori a greater voice, but the precedent of legal process and earlier values about what constitutes a claim or a settlement remain. Here I review these persistent processes and values, exploring their impact on current inquiries and moves to settle claims.

The Surplus Lands Commission illustrates the age and extent of the earlier judicial and political tradition. It was far from the first time that a commission of inquiry had investigated the nature of pre-1840 sales. The first Land Claims Commission met in 1841 to investigate private purchases and recommend awards of land to settlers, while William Spain's Land Claims Commission examined the pretentious land claims of the New Zealand Company.[5] Although these Commissions dealt with comparatively recent events, they were still involved in historical reconstructions. They heard Maori and European witnesses and they tried to impose European understandings of cultural notions such as sale and price on a host of loose and informal transactions brought by petitioners hoping to get a grant of land. What all of this meant was not finalised until 1862 when Francis Dillon Bell's land claims commission fixed these early transactions on the ground with surveys and final awards.[6] Bell heard his evidence in the late 1850s, but many of the records he interpreted were already two to three decades old. Bell's awards are often used as accurate descriptions of these pre-1840 land sales.[7] Rather than describe historical transactions, these awards served colonial needs of the late 1850s, in particular the need to survey land and secure titles for settlement. In contrast with the commissions of the 1840s, the state was, in Northland where most of the claims were located, increasingly able to assert its ascendancy over Maori. There were a host of later commissions, all dealing with a Maori complaint that the Crown had unjustly acquired title to large areas of land through this process. The Surplus Lands Commission was itself created to deal with a series of petitions referred in the 1920s to the Sim Commission into confiscated lands but ruled outside that commission's terms of reference.[8]

Commissions, petitions to the House and individual complaints were a common feature of Native and Maori affairs from the 1840s. Where the political pressure from Maori carried some weight, they were referred to commissions of inquiry or to the Native Land Court to investigate. The Sim and Surplus Lands Commissions were both created to serve political ends, Sim to undermine Ratana's growing influence and Surplus Lands in recognition of Labour's dependence on its four Maori members for its 1946/9 majority. Many major grievances, South Island Crown purchases, confiscations and Old Land Claims were the subject of a host of inquiries over many decades. The results were mixed. These last three led to successful recommendations for compensation in 1921, 1928 and 1948 respectively for some but not all of the petitioners.[9] A lesser range of inquiries resulted in areas of land being returned or small amounts of compensation being paid.

Most petitions or complaints that land was acquired illegally were responded to by an internal investigation by staff of the departments of Lands or Native Affairs. A report, often a letter, was prepared describing the block history of the land, tracing the extinguishing of customary title (through a Crown purchase, Old Land Claim or Land Court order) and a description of its alienation by sale or taking of any interests Maori retained in the land. The Crown defended its title by these formulaic block histories aimed at showing that the land belonged to a particular group of Maori (and therefore no other) and that at some point in its history these owners had either voluntarily alienated it, or had it taken by confiscation or for public works. Even where there had been evidence of mistakes or unjust processes, later attempts to alleviate these by an additional payment or a settlement of

Crown land were used to close the door on any further negotiation for settlement. The return of all of the original land was rarely if ever contemplated. And even where land was returned it was almost invariably done so in a form that extinguished any remaining customary title.

The process of dealing with complaints was kept alive but marginalised by Maori inclusion in the political and inquisitorial process. Maori were a small minority in both Houses of Parliament, but they could sometimes sneak a majority in the Native Affairs Committee where their voting strength was much stronger, and by the twentieth century were made minority members on the inquiries themselves. The progression of reports on Maori complaints published in parliamentary reports had a familiar pattern. While concerned with an ill-defined concept of justice they assumed Crown sovereignty and limited complaints to those relating to land and other property. Without any legal access to the Treaty these reports looked at whether Crown actions were legal, had Maori consent and were undertaken in 'good faith'. These issues were essentially regarded as legal and lay rather than historical issues. In the Royal Commissions, historical evidence provided the background arguments. Sometimes this was, as in the preparation of the claimants' case in the Sim Commission, informed by good reading of the available secondary sources, but it was not seen as necessary to have historians prepare the evidence or interpret it to the Commissions. Historians on their part remained aloof from such applied concerns.

It took a considerable time before the participation of historians was accepted at all. In 1975, when the Waitangi Tribunal was first established, history was seen as having little to do with recognising the Treaty. An unsuccessful attempt was made to give the Tribunal a retrospective jurisdiction to 1900, but the final legislation gave the Tribunal jurisdiction only over post-1975 Crown actions. The chief issues of Maori concern at the time were continued alienation of Maori land through the Maori Affairs Act 1953 (as amended in 1967) and, soon after 1975, the new emphasis on 'think big' style development on the top of or alongside Maori communities. Underpinning early developments was an untested belief, backed by some historians, that all but a few historical claims had been solved. Briefing papers to the incoming Minister of Maori Affairs, Ben Couch, in 1976 identified only a handful of claims needing his attention, including those involving Orakei, Tauranga confiscations and Hauraki goldfields. Claudia Orange's MA thesis on the First Labour Government's Maori policy saw the settlements of the 1940s as largely successful. She identified grumbling from some quarters about the termination of annual payments, but no groundswell of Maori demands for a new wave of Treaty-based land settlements.[10]

The Tauranga Moana confiscation settlement, the major revisionist settlement of the late 1970s, illustrates the extent to which the 1940s model of negotiated settlements was very much alive even after the Tribunal's establishment. In contrast to Taranaki and Waikato, Bay of Plenty iwi had received less sympathetic hearings from the Sim Commission in 1928. Sim considered that the Tauranga and southern Bay of Plenty confiscations were justified. It was only with strong lobbying from Tauranga and new historical submissions from Keith Sorrenson and Evelyn Stokes that new grounds were established for reaching a settlement.[11] Stokes and Sorrenson were able to show that the Sim conclusions were historically unsound. The Tauranga Moana Maori Trust Board was established with joint Ngai Te Rangi and Ngati Ranginui membership and $200,000 in compensation. In less than a decade, as the process of revising the Treaty and its history took place, this settlement was in tatters. There was intense tribal conflict as a new Ngati Ranginui leadership felt increasingly unhappy with a Ngai Te Rangi led settlement, particularly as the 50,000 acres finally confiscated had been largely their land. By the mid 1980s the size of the confiscation package appeared exceedingly small and its form as a cash payment inappropriate in a climate where claimants demanded that land be given in compensation for land taken.

With the Tribunal's jurisdiction extended back to 1840 by the Fourth Labour Government in 1985, there was a renewed interest in historical claims, but no great sense of urgency on behalf of the Government. Despite the Tribunal raking over the ashes of the lower Waikato and Taranaki confiscations, there was no sense that a new era of historical revision and resettlement of claims had begun, let alone any expectation that the door might be opening to a flood of other as yet unknown grievances. The Fourth Labour Government appointed a seven-member Tribunal under the new jurisdiction. Appointments were delayed and the first Tribunal hearings did not begin until late 1986. None of the seven members were trained historians. Professor Keith Sorrenson sat at many of the early hearings only as a deputy member. When the Ngai Tahu hearings began in August 1987, none of the members were academically practising or even trained historians.

The inclusion of academic witnesses to interpret evidence was a major innovation in itself. The growth of claims history from 1987 was a logical result of the retrospective juris- diction of the Tribunal since 1985, but the central role of historians should not just be assumed. In Australia, the United States and Canada, historians have been less successful in capturing the market for claims research. In these countries, outside of Treaty-based claims, native title claims demanded the corroboration of anthropologists and archaeologists. Aboriginal title depended on evidence of occupation and cultivation over long periods of time. In New Zealand the question of Maori title to land had been resolved in the 1840s. Maori claims to every acre, mountain and river were supported by Crown purchase deeds, land court titles and proclamations. There was no need for anthropologists to scramble around interpreting folklore or for archaeologists to trawl though midden and grave sites to prove ancestral links to the land. Judges and land purchase officers had already done this as a legal rather than academic process. It then fell to historians to reassemble the paper trail and to interpret to the Tribunal and to other courts the process of extinguishment of title.

It was the hope of Chief Judge Durie, as Chairperson of the Tribunal, that historical research would be able to go behind the narrow legalese of the deeds and court orders to show the broader context of the alienation of Maori land. Academics could break the long civil service tradition of rejecting consideration of claims because 'the land had been sold', 'was confiscated after the Maori wars', or 'taken by the Public Works Act'. Historians, he hoped, could use the Tribunal's reliance on the 'principles of the Treaty' rather than legality as the test of validity. To do this required knowledge of historical context and of culture. The Chief Judge's expectations of Tribunal research were onerous. While historians had many of the skills required for working in the field, to equate Tribunal research with academic history was as inappropriate in the 1980s as it is today. Historians did not and still do not have the skills and training to undertake all that was required to investigate a claim to the Tribunal. Historians have skills in locating and analysing archival material, in report presentation, in placing historical events within the context of their times, in analysing government policy and in reviewing events in the light of the best historical literature. But there are many other areas where academic historians are less well prepared to undertake Tribunal research. Without linguistic skills in Te Reo Maori, with both oral and written sources, much of the attempt to deconstruct English language descriptions of events with Maori participants is seriously flawed. Knowledge of culture and cultural interaction is also often missing from the repertoire of most history graduates. History departments have often viewed Tribunal history with disdain, concerned with its perceived lack of rigour and fearing bias. History programmes have rarely trained historians in the specific skills required to work either for the Tribunal, or for parties before it. Even more important, the reification of professional history threatens an acknowledgement of Maori historical processes and knowledge.

Tribunal research is also a speciality all of its own. Preparing evidence or writing legal reports is a very different process from writing academic history. Not only is the product different, but so are the rules of the game. Academic evidence is tested by peer review, either before or after publication, by dissemination in the field and by re-testing the evidence through footnotes and sources. Tribunal evidence is tested by cross-communion and by the status and reputation of its presenter. Counsel leads evidence and it is counsel not the academic who interprets and suggest its significance to the inquiry. Witnesses with differing viewpoints appear and are matched against each other, but not directly. Their evidence is always mediated through counsel. The legal processes are designed not to allow evidence to be decided upon by informed insiders but by outsiders, by judges without either a general or specific knowledge of the discipline at hand. There are significant differences between the High Court and a Court of Inquiry, such as the Waitangi Tribunal. The High Court's rules of evidence would rule out almost all whakapapa as evidence. A Commission of Inquiry has much more freedom to accept different forms of evidence. It can also refer to a general secondary literature in its reports, without having been referred to that in evidence. However, it would be unwise for a Commission of Inquiry to rely too heavily on any material that had been acquired outside the formal processes of the inquiry.

The difference between academic debate and evidence before an inquiry is best illustrated by the research of Michele Dominy prepared for submission to the Ngai Tahu claim. Dominy was commissioned as an anthropologist by high country farmers in order to show their 'spiritual' connections with the land. Here, it was the Pakeha farmers who needed to use an anthropologist to prove their relationship with the land, or to show that this relationship was based on more than simply making money and profit taking. Dominy's evidence was turned into an academic article published in *Anthropology Today*. The article promoted an intense debate over the nature of her evidence. Should an anthropologist have prepared evidence against an indigenous claim? Can non-indigenous people have a spiritual relationship with the land, or with anything for that matter? The irony was that this entire debate was completely lost on the Tribunal. Her evidence was not presented orally, she had not been called as a witness, had not been examined by counsel, and her arguments, although internationally published, did not reach the forum for which they were designed. All that had been done was that her report had been attached to the back of an affidavit of one of the high country farmers, where it had languished unnoticed among the twenty-six metres of written evidence. If the Tribunal needed evidence of the high country farmers' relationship with the land they got it – and more effectively – from the farmers themselves.

The stark differences between academic and legal forums were not really tested until the Ngai Tahu claim began in August 1987. Professor Alan Ward, then at La Trobe University, was commissioned to provide an overview report on the claim because of the lack of historical expertise on the Tribunal. The Crown, led by Shonagh Kenderdine of Crown Law, went into the hearings not expecting to have to commission researchers at all. The case for the never awarded Otakou Tenths and for the other failures of the early land purchase officers appeared, even to the Crown at first glance, open and shut. Ngai Tahu were acknowledged to have undertaken a long programme of research and were expected to outline a damning and unanswerable chronicle of Crown breaches of the Treaty. It soon became evident that not only were the claimants unprepared for the depth of historical inquiry required for the claim, but that the historical evidence was far from clear cut and that even the case for the Otakou Tenths was tenuous and a matter of interpretation.

The Crown then collected its own team of historians and was the first group to give its research team the collective label 'historians'. Crown, claimant and Tribunal historians then began the process of locating, interpreting and misinterpreting an increasing fund of evidence. Tribunal members were continually struck by the sheer bulk of the documentary evidence discovered. Research was undertaken in great haste, with often no more than a few days provided for briefing, archival searching, writing and presentation. The Crown response to the Maori Reserved Land Claim was prepared and presented in two weeks.[12] Given the time available, it was a creditable piece of research for a claim, even at that time, being seriously considered for negotiation with the cost involved set at many tens of millions of dollars.

Far from being unchallenging academically, the issues arising in the Ngai Tahu claim were extremely complex. Most historical research allows a negotiation between the matters of interest and the available evidence. Sparse evidence simply leads to modifying the scope of the research – a study broadens or shifts to cover hew evidence and the topic is allowed to evolve. With a Treaty claim, however, a decision has to be made irrespective of whether there is adequate evidence to determine what actually happened. The Ngai Tahu claim that a large strip of land including most of the Southern Alps had never been sold to the Crown is a case in point. The claimants' case rested on eyewitness evidence presented in 1879 and 1880 to the Smith-Nairn Commission, one of the perennial commissions investigating the Ngai Tahu claim. According to many of these witnesses, H. T. Kemp had purchased a much smaller block of land in 1848 than appeared on the official deed map. These witnesses maintained that Kemp did not show them the map and that they were forced into the sale by threats of military action against them. Their arguments were contradicted by a good deal of Maori evidence from the time of the sale. Claimant, Crown and Tribunal historians vigorously attempted to reconcile this later Maori evidence with that from the time of the sale. In the end the Tribunal remained unconvinced by the oral testimony of the 'hole-in-the-middle'. Nonetheless the Tribunal completed its report without having explained the differences between different forms of evidence. To this extent the Tribunal's findings fell short of the kind of explanation expected of an academic debate. All the Tribunal had to do was to choose the scenario presented in the evidence that was more probable than the others.

Tribunal history has also allowed teams of historians to be assembled to work on similar or related issues, something rare in a country with so small an academic community. The adversarial system makes cooperation between different researchers difficult, and encourages confrontation. The Tribunal has always attempted to be inquisitorial in its processes, looking for the evidence wherever it may be rather than allowing one side to make a case for the other side to knock it down. This inquisitorial line of inquiry has been steadily undermined and not just by the Crown as the issues involved have become more complex and the resources involved more valuable. Early Tribunal hearings were more informal, witnesses were barely cross-examined and there were few legal counsel involved. Those that were there were often unsure of the process. Following the State Owned Enterprise case before the Court of Appeal in 1987, and the possibility of substantial remedies being transferred to Maori claimants, the stakes just got higher. Other interested groups entered, often bringing with them expensive and experienced counsel. The Tribunal's processes came under increasing scrutiny and there was more pressure to cross-examine witnesses.

The Ngai Tahu, Te Roroa, Te Ngae and Pouakani claims were all heard as the evidence was produced, often with briefs of evidence being presented to the Tribunal without prior filing. Evidence was read by witnesses and questions asked by Tribunal members and counsel. While never actually banning formal examination of witnesses by counsel, the Tribunal tried to establish alternative processes of testing evidence. In the Ngai Tahu claim, professional evidence was presented and the other parties were given the opportunity of filing comments with a right of reply. Because of the haste involved, evidence was often raw, references unchecked and often with analysis needing more extensive consideration. Despite this there were some exceptional pieces of research undertaken, most notably by Don Loveridge, the Crown's leading historical witness.[13] Overview reports by Tribunal commissioned researchers led by Alan Ward reviewed all the historical evidence and this was extensively cross-examined by counsel.[14] Hearings were of course expensive to run and tied up Tribunal members and researchers for weeks without necessarily resolving issues in dispute. The process put an intolerable strain on National Archives as all relevant files had to be copied and placed in evidence. Researchers were faced with crushing deadlines and intense and often unresolved debates with lawyers and claimants over issues of relevance and reliability.

To reduce the need for hearings and to try to ease costs for claimants and others, the Tribunal has attempted to get as much research undertaken prior to hearing. For claims linked to confiscation the Tribunal commissioned a very substantial document bank of official published and unpublished material.[15] A casebook approach now operates with each region preparing a collection of pre-hearing research in the hope that this will inform all the issues of debate before the Tribunal once the hearings commence. Casebooks have allowed very substantial amounts of evidence to be commissioned and reviewed prior to a claim going to hearing. This has not speeded up the process, but it has allowed the Tribunal to move ahead with investigations into many more claims. Something has also been lost. Historians have been more able to work according to standard historical criteria for evaluating evidence, but at the potential cost of alienating the research from the legal process.

Historians are commissioned to do research for the Tribunal from a variety of different sources. In rare instances the historian works directly for the claimants, sometimes for payment, sometimes not. Other groups with an interest in the inquiry, farmers or the fishing industry, have also commissioned historical research. Mostly, however, the historian is commissioned by the Tribunal, by the Crown, or by the claimants. Most claimant history is funded by the Tribunal or by the Crown Forestry Rental Trust (CFRT). The CFRT has by far the largest resources in the field. It was established as part of a separate SOE settlement on Crown-owned forests to manage royalties on ground rentals where cutting rights have been privatised, until the underlying ownership of the land has been settled. The interest of a capital fund (worth more than $161 million by 1997) can be applied to claims resolution for claimants, including research.[16] Claims do have to have a relationship with Crown forests, but many large iwi-based claims meet this criterion. A considerable amount of historical research has been commissioned through this fund, although there are continued problems of relevance and focus. The Trust is at arm's length from the Tribunal or from the negotiation process and its research is often prepared blind, for hearings or negotiations sometimes many years in the future.

Research commissioned by the Tribunal is public research, but research commissioned by other bodies can be private. Claimants do their own research, often with CFRT support. This may or may not be submitted to the Tribunal. Tribunal-commissioned research, for the Tribunal and for claimants, must under the Treaty of Waitangi Act 1975 be submitted to the Tribunal, distributed to parties and be examined at a hearing if necessary. Evidence before the Tribunal is generally public, and the professional reports of historians are presented in open hearing. Once the Tribunal issues its report, it is subject to public comment. However, the Crown has never regarded findings and recommendations made by the Tribunal as binding on it, outside the SOE provisions introduced in 1988. Further reviews of the evidence then take place behind closed doors.[17] Negotiations with claimants for settlement may be on the basis of the Tribunal's reports, where these exist. Even when there is a report the final grounds for settlement may have shifted in the negotiation. If, as in the Tainui example, the parties settle without a Tribunal investigation, then none of the deciding evidence is open to professional or lay scrutiny. The Tribunal reports, not the historians' evidence, are seen as the product of the historical research. The reports receive national publicity and are read widely. Little of the evidence makes its way into the academic literature.

Working for fee-paying clients creates its own problems. University historians cherish the independence of academic study and look askance at historians for hire in the public market-place. To what extent are historians under pressure to provide evidence that supports the clients? The development of claims history has produced a wealth of historical research since 1987, a time when Pakeha historians were tending to withdraw from what was then referred to as 'race relations' history. Maori have generally accepted outsider expertise, whether from Maori or from Pakeha, because claimants feel that they are in control. Some of this is through a naive belief, one shared by the Crown in this process, that any research will support their grievance and show the Crown's failings to adhere to the Treaty. The reality is a little different. Far from clarifying government iniquities, detailed historical research often only muddies the waters. Sometimes this research demonstrates Maori collusion in processes of alienation, or illustrates embarrassing inter- and intra-whanau and hapu conflicts. At other times the oral tradition cannot be easily meshed with the written sources, even those sources written by Maori. There are as yet little in the way of ethical or professional guidelines to protect historians should conflicts arise between professional judgement and client needs.

Sides are still important. The Tribunal is an adversarial forum and however much historians act professionally, the legal imperatives of claim and response seem to have a remarkable impact on the evidence. In the Ngai Tahu claim, Harry Evison and Jim McAloon found arguments that Ngai Tahu had not sold a good proportion of the South Island convincing. Don Loveridge, for the Crown, found these arguments fanciful and untenable.[18] In the Muriwhenua claim, Philippa Wyatt and Margaret Mutu argued that early deeds were returnable gifts rather than sales, while the Crown historians Tony Walzl and Fergus Sinclair argued the reverse.[19] Crown historians have rarely tried to exonerate the Crown, but their evidence has often sought explanations for dispossession external to the Crown. Claimant historians have been much more concerned to show Crown actions in a less favourable light, and to attribute contemporary social and economic conditions to Crown failures of the past. These differences suggest a deeper problem than one of individual bias or even too much attention to the needs of the client. Evidence serves a legal process aimed at a political end. Historians need to always be aware that they are producing evidence for a Tribunal report. Neither product is history in an academic sense. They contribute to a process aimed at redistributing a politically controlled fund of resources to Maori. It is also not a question of academic pluralism Historians do not produce evidence in negotiation with other disciplines, with lawyers, anthropologists and Maori scholars.

The Ngai Tahu report raised a whole series of new problems for government in dealing with questions of comparative loss. Ngai Tahu had, according to the Tribunal's narrative, lost a good deal. Putting fisheries aside they had been deprived through Crown failures of a decent stake in over half the territory of the country. The Tribunal made a series of startling revelations about the processes of land alienation, but its overall findings and recommendations were largely consistent with the progression of pre-1975 hearings that had preceded its inquiry. Ngai Tahu, in the Tribunal's view, had negotiated to sell great parts of their lands to the Crown, being promised substantial reserves never provided.[20] The Tribunal had updated the claim, with its Treaty jurisdiction. Partnership, reconciliation and tribal development were themes that allowed Ngai Tahu to assert significant and new claims for compensation and for a say in the governance of Te Waipounamu.

As government struggled in the early 1990s to find an overall policy resolving Maori claims against the Crown, the Ngai Tahu report created new and pressing problems. Did the Crown accept the Tribunal's historical narrative and buy into a significant compensatory scheme without further testing of the argument? And if large payments were made to Ngai Tahu, then what were the implications of this for dealing with claims for settlements from the much more populous North Island? When the Tribunal retold their histories, would the precedents set in the South Island become precedents for exponentially larger payouts in the North? How was loss to be quantified? Was an invasion of the Waikato worth two poor Crown land purchases in the Crown colony period? Did larger tribes deserve more compensation than smaller ones? All of these questions, and opposition to settlements at all in Cabinet and Caucus, led the National Government to its 'fiscal envelope' policy, unveiled with vitriolic criticism in 1994.[21] According to the policy, all claims would be settled by 2000 with full and final settlements, and the total bill to the state would be no more than one billion dollars. Few actions by government since 1840 so dramatically united Maori against the Crown.[22] Relativities had to be argued between tribes, and between grievances. Government needed to be sure that in agreeing to provide $100,000 compensation for land taken under one statute for one hapu, it was not making the case for a $10m package somewhere else. One group's history was then to compete with another's, according to a scale as yet undetermined.

The Tribunal initiated its own response to these problems by developing the Rangahaua Whanui programme.[23] Led by Alan Ward, the programme was designed to provide an over-view of claims across the country to 1939. Regional studies explored existing and potential claims from a review of the history of Crown-Maori relations. National studies examined specific issues, such as Old Land Claims, the Native Land Court, Public Works Acts and the like. Ward then provided a national overview bringing together all the different themes and trying to identify key issues that would require some form of negotiated settlement. The project was very extensive and required considerable Tribunal resources for over three years, but should provide a basis for more in-depth research on a regional basis leading to hearing. From 1997 the Tribunal's priorities have returned to hearing claims, although more by regions than on the iwi basis of earlier Tribunal inquiries.

Historians have tended to seek out evidence and to provide an analysis of this evidence according to standard historical tests of significance. The question of whether the Crown actions involved breached the 'principles of the Treaty of Waitangi' was left to the parties through their counsel and for the Tribunal to decide. There is a good reason for this distinc-tion. Historians may suggest that mercy should be shown some Crown purchase officer for a failure to realise that the Treaty of Waitangi his masters had disowned should have been his guiding text in his dealings with Maori. The Tribunal need have no such scruples. The 'prin-ciples of the Treaty' are an ahistorical test of past policies and practices. Retrospectively applied, these principles are determined by the Tribunal according to a present-day interpre-tation of the Treaty. Having discovered a previously unknown principle of the Treaty in 1988, there is no problem in applying this to the actions of individual Crown agents in the 1840s. This interpretation may have been informed by the best and most recent historical research, but is not bound by this research. For this reason there is sense in historians leaving such issues aside. Historical actions are being judged according to criteria developed well after the events themselves.

Despite the absence of a method for differentiating between these histories, in government's eyes, some historic actions were officially more worthy of recognition than others. Government ministers for most of the 1990s had their eyes on what they called the 'big claims' – those that involved large compensation packages. As negotiations with Tainui and Ngai Tahu progressed, the characteristics of a 'big claim' emerged. Tainui, Taranaki and Ngai Tahu were big claims, and beneath them were the other confiscation claims, Tauranga Moana, Ngati Awa, Whakatohea and Tuhoe and the confiscations in Poverty Bay. With fisheries also to come out of the 'fiscal envelope', there was only going to be small change for those tribes whose concerns were with Old Land Claims, the Native Lands Acts or takings under the Public Works Acts. Confiscation without compensation provided the chief justificationforclaim.Individualisationoftitle,government'sassaultonthecollectivesocialorganis-ation of Maori customary society and unnecessary acquisition of Maori land with full compensation were, as a matter of policy and settlement expectations, seen by Ministers as being minor grievances of little compensatable value. In short the Crown's list of suitable final settlements for the 1990s was the same as it had been in the 1940s and then in the 1970s. If unchallenged, such a priority list would show that despite the supposed new history and the reinterpretative passion of Tribunal history since the 1980s, the old game of claim and response from government remained intact, untouched by new understandings and negotiations. Negotiating escalation clauses with Tainui and Ngai Tahu, so that 34 per cent of any expenditure over the magic billion goes to these tribes, has locked in the reasoning of the 1940s.

With overview to the *Rangabawa Whanui Report* was a response to the deadlock and also a departure from the practice of keeping the historians out of commenting on Treaty loss and remedies. In 1996 the Tribunal commissioned him to 'suggest in his report some optional strategies about how the historical claims might best be dealt with'.[24] Although this did not go so far as to include a discussion on Treaty principles, it did make suggestions about both the future processing of claims and remedies. A direct attempt to comment on comparative loss in historical terms aimed at giving government a greater understanding of the various forms of loss experienced by Maori and breaking the confiscation/unfulfilled contract barrier. The report can also be seen as providing some assistance to government in its dilemma over comparative compensation. If it were possible to find out how many tribal groups were affected by particular policies, how many were the subject of compulsory public works takings or the 1890s Liberal land grab, then government could make better risk assessments of its overall liability.

The Tribunal, too, was responding to government concerns about comparative liability and was attempting to broaden government understandings of Maori perspectives of loss. The first Taranaki Report stressed the uniqueness of the Taranaki grievance, and asserted the continuing nature of the grievance. The Tribunal wanted to make it clear that Taranaki's history was living, that the muru and raupatu continued to be part of the everyday.[25] Taranaki's use of the terms muru for the wartime confiscation and raupatu for land lost to perpetual leases underlined a Maori sense that confiscation has occurred in many forms over a long period of time. In other areas raupatu refers to direct confiscation during the wars. The Tribunal took the unusual step of warning the Minister of Maori Affairs, John Luxton, that 'you may be dealing with the country's largest claim'.[26] The wars were not isolated to the period 1860 to 1869, but were preceded by nineteen years of 'turmoil' in attempts to 'constrain settlers and fighting among Maori groups'.[27] After the invasion of Parihaka in 1881, the drawn-out process of resolving the issues was described as perpetually postponing the peace: 'If war is the absence of peace, the war has never ended in Taranaki, because that essential prerequisite for peace among peoples, that each should be able to live with dignity on their own lands, is still absent and the protest over land rights continues to be made.'[28] The use of the terms war and confiscation (clearly established and compensatable breaches of the Treaty of Waitangi) to envelop the whole relationship between Taranaki and the Crown was as much political as it was an historical interpretation. It both fudged and broadened the Crown's notions of liability.

The Tribunal's role in an essentially legal and political process has the danger of detaching its reports from mainstream historical interpretations without fully explaining its reasoning. In some reports revisionist Maori historical narratives have been preferred over more orthodox approaches. Robin Fisher's review of the Muriwhenua report commented that from an outsider's perspective the report was a 'detailed examination, almost hectare by hectare, of the history of alienation of Muriwhenua'.[29] The Muriwhenua report actually glossed over the most difficult issues in the inquiry dealing in just five pages with a question that had occupied the minds of many of those involved over many hundreds of pages of extremely contentious evidence. Given the depth and sophistication of the debate over early Maori understandings of land transactions, the Tribunal avoided the need to review this evidence in detail. The claimants' heavily challenged view that land was provided to early purchasers as a kind of limited leasehold only was accepted without any detailed discussion of the contrary evidence. In the Taranaki report comments about the severity of the claim and comparisons with the Holocaust were clearly political rather than evidence-based findings. This trend is even truer for negotiated settlements, where there is no public review of evidence. In the Tainui raupatu claim a formula for describing the basis of settlement expressed a view of the invasion of the Waikato at variance with most of the secondary literature.

Maori claimants will continue to see academic history as yet another barrier to the recognition of Maori knowledge and whakapapa-based history. Intense debates, however, over the detail and interpretation of claims before the Tribunal, disguise an essential common ground. First, claimant historians and Crown historians are not so divided over the nature of historiography. Both sides tend to interpret events from a more or less common approach determined more by the inherited framework of earlier commissions of inquiry and always with an eye to settlement. Secondly, all participants are involved in a general shift in the more popular interpretation of New Zealand's race relations. The collective contribution to this new history is more important than differences over detail. In this the process again dominates the content. Together, these histories have two prime audiences. For settlements to be achieved, government needs to be moved from its narrow assumptions on the nature of claims and pakeha-led public opinion needs to be able to accept the cost and rationale for historical narratives of claims settlements. While all of this has provided new resources for Maori-centred history, this particular new history will flower outside of the Tribunal rather than within it. In the meantime, as long as the limitations are accepted, there is no reason not to continue the detailed research that Treaty settlements require. In 2000, Margaret Wilson, like Geoffrey Palmer and Doug Graham before her, suggested that negotiation is a short track to settlement. There is no reason to assume that her search for quick solutions will be any more successful than those of her predecessors. Durable negotiated settlements, without contested research, will only be possible in updating settlements where the Crown accepted responsibility prior to the 1980s and where the grounds for settlement remain largely unchanged.

Notes

1   Michael Myers, Hanara Tangiawha Reedy and Albert Moeller Samuel, 'Report of Royal Commission to Inquire into and Report on Claims Preferred by Members of the Maori Race Touching Certain Lands Known as Surplus Lands of the Crown', *AJHR*, 1948, G-8; Keith Sinclair, 'The Aborigines Protection Society and New Zealand – A Study in Nineteenth Century Opinion', MA thesis, Auckland University College, 1946.

2   The term used to describe Europeans' claims to land made on the basis of transfers from Maori prior to the proclamations of 30 January 1840 imposing pre-emption on European purchasers.

3   Ethel Wilson, *Land Problems of the New Zealand Settlers of the 'Forties*, Dunedin, 1936.

4   Geoffrey W. Rice (ed.), *The Oxford History of New Zealand*, 2nd ed., Oxford University Press, Auckland, 1992; M. P. K. Sorrenson, 'Towards a Radical Reinterpretation of New Zealand History: The Role of the Waitangi Tribunal', *NZJH*, vol. 2, no. 1, 1987, pp173–88.

5   Michael Belgrave, 'Pre-emption, the Treaty of Waitangi and the politics of Crown purchase', *NZJH*, vol 31, no. 1, 1997, pp23–37; Patricia Burns, *Fatal Success. A History of the New Zealand Company*, Heinemann Reed, Auckland, 1989; Waitangi Tribunal, *The Muriwhenua Land Report*, Waitangi Tribunal Reports, Wellington, 1997; Alan Ward, *National Overview*, 3 vols, Waitangi Tribunal Rangahaua Whanui Series, Wellington, 1997.

6   F. Dillon Bell, 'Land Claims Commission. Report of the Land Claims Commissioner, 8th July 1862', *AJHR*, 1862, pD-10.

7   Jack Lee, *I Have Named It the Bay of Islands*, Auckland, 1983; Jack Lee, *The Old Land Claim in New Zealand*, Kerikeri, 1993.

8   William Alexander Sim, Vernon Herbert Reed and William Cooper, 'Confiscated Native? Lands and other Grievances. Royal Commission Into Confiscations of Native Lands and other Grievances Alleged by Natives (Report Of)', *AJHR*, 1928, pG-7.

9   Michael Myers, Hanara Tangiawha Reedy and Albert Moeller Samuel; Sim, Reed and Cooper; Waitangi Tribunal, *The Ngai Tahu Report 1991*, 3 vols, Waitangi Tribunal Reports, Wellington, 1991.

10   Claudia Orange, 'A Kind of Equality: Labour and the Maori People 1935–49', MA thesis, University of Auckland, 1977.

11   Keith Sorrenson appeared before the Maori Affairs select committee and prepared a written submission, 'The Tauranga Confiscation', dated 4 September 1978; Evelyn Stokes submitted a written submission to the Committee at Tauranga in September 1978; Waitangi Tribunal, *Raupatu Document Bank*, 139 vols, Wellington, 1989.

12   David A. Armstrong and Tony Walzl, Evidence of David A. Armstrong and Tony Walzl on the origin of leasing on the West Coast, N6, Wal 27, Waitangi Tribunal; Waitangi Tribunal, *The Ngai Tahu Report 1991*, chap. 14.

13   Ibid.

14   Alan Ward, 'History and Historians before the Waitangi Tribunal: Some Reflections on the Ngai Tahu Claim', *NZJH*, vol. 24, no. 2, 1990, pp150–67.

15   Waitangi Tribunal, *Raupatu Document Bank*.

16   Crown Forestry Rental Trust, 'Report to Appointers', 1997.

17   The Labour-Alliance Government announced in July 2000 that it was going to open up the negotiation process, but this can be seen as little more than echoing similar claims by Geoffrey Palmer in 1990 and Jim Bolger in 1993.

18   Waitangi Tribunal, *The Ngai Tahu Report 1991*, chap. 8,

19   Waitangi Tribunal, *The Muriwhenua Land Report*.

20   Waitangi Tribunal, *The Ngai Tahu Report 1991*.

21   Annie Mikaere, 'Settlement of Treaty claims: Full and final, or fatally flawed?', *New Zealand Universities Law Review*, vol. 17, no. 4, 1997, pp425–55.

22   Chris Trotter, 'The Struggle for Sovereignty', *New Zealand Political Review*, vol. 4, no. 2, 1995, pp16–20.

23   Ward, *National Overview*.

24   Ibid.

25   Waitangi Tribunal, *The Taranaki Report: Kaupapa Tuatahi,* Waitangi Tribunal, Wellington, 1996.

26   Ibid.

27   Ibid.

28   Ibid.

29   Robin Fisher, review of Waitangi Tribunal, 'Muriwhenua Land Report. A Waitangi Tribunal Report', *NZJH*, vol. 31, no. 2, 1997, p272.

Chapter 19

Alan Rice

CREATING MEMORIALS, BUILDING IDENTITIES

The Politics of Memory in the Black Atlantic

[Memory can] be tapped, unleashed and mobilised through oral and public history to stand as an alternative to imposed orthodoxy and officially sanctioned versions of historical reality; it is a route to a broadly distributed authority for making new sense of the past in the present.

Michael Frisch[1]

Once the history of empire becomes a source of discomfort, shame and perplexity, its complications and ambiguities were readily set aside. Rather than work through those feelings, that unsettling history was diminished, denied and then if possible actively forgotten. The resulting silence feeds an additional catastrophe: the error of imagining that post-colonial people are only unwanted alien intruders without any substantive historical, political or cultural connections to the collective life of their fellow subjects.

Paul Gilroy[2]

PAUL GILROY'S DISCUSSION of the legacy of empire, which makes of black British people little more than 'alien intruders' in a British polity that eschews such 'unsettling history', has resonances in locations throughout the UK, but nowhere more so than in the ports that were central hubs of imperial trade, some of which now apparently show remarkably few legacies of this glorious and sordid past. For instance, there is virtually no maritime commercial activity any more on the quayside at Lancaster. The once bustling port is now home to upmarket flats and strolling tourists navigating between the old Custom House building and the maritime-themed pubs. The source of Lancaster's wealth in direct trade with the West Indies and in the transatlantic slave trade have traditionally been detailed in the rather outdated exhibits in the Maritime Museum,[3] which is housed in the Custom House, designed by the furniture manufacturer Robert Gillow in 1764; however, the city had always buried this history away in the background of its tale of civic pride through mercantile endeavour. In fact, the local oral history of Lancaster slave traders is often about how Lancaster merchants coming from the fourth largest slave port were mere gentleman amateurs in comparison to the professionals down the coast in Liverpool. However, as Melinda Elder describes in her history of the Lancaster slave trade and in subsequent research, Lancaster traders were involved in frantic and murderous slave raids on the African coast,[4] and indeed were engaged in joint ventures with Liverpool merchants, so that some voyages counted in the statistics as belonging to the larger port had such significant input from Lancaster merchants that many think they should be counted as Lancaster voyages.[5]

With very few black British residents and the large majority of these being of Asian origin rather than Caribbean or African, there has historically been little impetus in Lancaster to foreground this aspect of its past. In contradistinction to Bristol and Liverpool, with their large African-Caribbean communities, Lancaster had never experienced a sustained political demand to atone for its history of slave trading. However, many Lancastrians felt there was a political imperative for white people to remember the trade and their ancestors' exploitation of Africans for profit, and that the best way to do this was for them to be reminded, as they went about their daily life in the city, of the centrality of the slave trade to its history.

As long as the story of slavery in the city was mainly confined to the museum, it was readily ignored. Black presence, as well as contributions to the wealth of the city derived from the slave trade, had historically been completely silenced. For instance, the many black slaves/servants in the city were usually ignored in the discussion of the city's fine Georgian terraces. This was compounded by the absence of civic memorials to victims of the trade. For, as James Young has asserted, the right kind of memorial shows us 'not literally what was lost, but that loss itself is part of this neighbourhood's history, an invisible, yet essential feature of its landscape'.[6] This interesting idea that memorials are not just about remembering tangible, already well chronicled history but about witnessing the invisible and intangible as well is crucial to a city like Lancaster, where civic memorialising already bears more than sufficient witness to the achievements of its merchant class. As Marianne Hirsch and Valerie Smith remind us, 'what a culture remembers and what it chooses to forget are intricately bound up with issues of power and hegemony'.[7] Hirsch and Smith describe how this affects gender issues; however, their illuminating remarks have relevance for issues of class and race also, and it is the latter that is most important in challenging the hegemony of Lancaster's lily-white public image of itself. This challenge comes about through a new form of engagement with the past, which is determined to look beyond the traditional historical and museum archive. One Francophone historian, Catherine Reinhardt, in her seminal study *Claims to Memory* (2008), articulates a post-historical analytical methodology that the study also essays. She describes how she foregrounds:

> The dialogue between fact and fiction, between past and present that sheds light
> on obscured, silenced, forgotten and even erased fragments of the slave past. It
> is at the interstices of these documents that memory can be found.[8]

The 'erased fragments of the slave past' must crucially be reconstructed by memory work in order for the full history of Lancaster to be told. This work is best undertaken through interdisciplinary case studies that move beyond the merely documentary and historical and into the performative and contemporary realm, where the full implications of Lancaster's involvement in the slave trade can be teased out, in contradistinction to the way the traditional historical record obscures the city's involvement.

For despite the amnesia around the black presence in, and contribution to, Lancaster, local people have sought ways to memorialise these important historical figures, in particular at the remarkable and, I would contend, virtually unique gravesite of an African boy, 'Sambo' (died 1736) at Sunderland Point at the head of the Lune Estuary, which leads into the port of

Lancaster. Here painted stones, flowers and funerary ephemera surround a memorial plaque first laid in 1796. This plaque was replaced in the early 1990s after an act of vandalism, and an injunction on the new brass plate exhorts visitors to 'Respect this Lonely Grave', which broadly seems to be adhered to. I have discussed this gravesite before; however, it is such a dynamic site of memory and there has been so much new activity related to it in the last decade that it provides a compelling case study in memorialisation and merits further consideration here.

According to the *Lonsdale Magazine* of 1822, Sambo arrived around 1736 from the West Indies in the capacity of a servant to the captain of a ship (to this day unnamed):

> After she had discharged her cargo, he was placed at the inn . . . with the intention of remaining there on board wages till the vessel was ready to sail; but supposing himself to be deserted by the master, without being able, probably from his ignorance of the language, to ascertain the cause, he fell into a complete state of stupefaction, even to such a degree that he secreted himself in the loft on the brewhouses and stretching himself out at full length on the bare boards refused all sustenance. He continued in this state only a few days, when death terminated the sufferings of poor Samboo. As soon as Samboo's exit was known to the sailors who happened to be there, they excavated him in a grave in a lonely dell in a rabbit warren behind the village, within twenty yards of the sea shore, whither they conveyed his remains without either coffin or bier, being covered only with the clothes in which he died.[9]

Sambo was buried in such a lonely grave because he was not baptised and had to be laid in unconsecrated ground. Like most Africans arriving in Britain as 'servants' (usually slaves), he appeared to suffer a profound sense of culture shock, being landed amongst strangers with whom he could not communicate. There has been much speculation about the cause of his death, ranging from the pragmatic (pneumonia) to the sentimental (profound homesickness). The latter provided the grist for anti-slavery panegyrics such as the Reverend James Watson's 1796 elegy, which was eventually appended to a brass plate on a freestone slab at the site itself. James Watson's interest in the slave grave is not without irony, however, as his brother William Watson was a leading light in the Lancaster slave trade. William Watson was 'one of the most committed investors in Lancaster slavers [whose] tenacity was no doubt instrumental in keeping the slave trade alive at Lancaster'.[10] The tone of the memorial is sentimental in the extreme, praising Sambo as a 'faithful Negro' who had died because of his 'service' to his master. The poem consists of seventeen verses including the epitaph of the final three verses which appears on the grave. It reads:

> Full sixty years the angry winter wave
> Has thundering dash'd this bleak and barren shore,
> Since Sambo's head, laid in this lonely grave,
> Lies still, and ne'er will hear their turmoil more.
>
> Full many a sand-bird chirps upon the sod,
> And many a moon-flight Elfin round him trips;
> Full many a Summer's sunbeam warms the clod,
> And many a teeming cloud upon him drips.
>
> But still he sleeps, till the awak'ning sounds
> Of the Archangel's Trump new life impart;

Then the great Judge his approbation founds,
Not on man's colour, but his worth of heart.[11]

Such a clarion call for the humanity of the slave reflects the late eighteenth century construction of an anti-slavery sentiment that simultaneously elided Africans as actors in their own struggles at the exact time of the Santo Domingo uprising (1791–1803), which exemplified a revolutionary African diasporan tradition. African agency is downplayed by such a discourse, and a character like Sambo is saved from obliquity by the workings of English sentiment long after it does him any practical good. This feeling that Sambo's actual biography is misinterpreted by the poem is exacerbated by the Christian sentimentality of the final lines, which allow him life after death despite his heathenism. The later addition of a wooden cross to the grave only serves to emphasise the mismatch between the slave refused a Christian burial and subsequent Christian sentimentalists trying to reinstate him and atone for his earlier dismissal.

Watson collected the money for the memorial from visitors to Sunderland Point. These visitors would follow the trail along the terrace of houses to the footpath which starts at the inn and leads across the headland to the rabbit warren where Sambo is buried. In retracing Sambo's steps they and subsequent visitors would be able to see the upstairs room where he had died and his body had been laid out, then follow the passage of Sambo's coffin down the path. Today the trail is unaltered and the inn, now renamed Upsteps Cottage, still stands. The repeated pilgrimage over two hundred years is in itself a memorial event that works to remember not only this boy's life and death but also the larger issue of slavery. Paul Ricoeur, in his discussion of the sepulchre, notes the importance of such repeated acts of remembrance of death to the development of memorialisation:

> Sepulchre, indeed, is not only a place set apart in our cities, the place we call a cemetery and in which we depose the remains of the living who return to dust. It is an act, the act of burying. This gesture is not punctual; it is not limited to the moment of burial. The sepulchre remains because the gesture of burying remains; its path is the very path of mourning that transforms the physical absence of the lost object into an inner presence. The sepulchre as the material place thus becomes the enduring mark of mourning, the memory aid of the act of the sepulchre.
>
> It is this act of sepulchre that historiography turns into writing.[12]

In 'transforming the physical absence of the lost object into an inner presence', visitors to the site take on the task of inserting the boy into a historical record that would traditionally have reduced him to mere chattel. Ricoeur's formulation privileges the historian as transformative; Sambo's grave and memorialisation show how the actions of ordinary citizens can be just as important to effective historical retrieval. A traditional way to mark a pilgrimage to a gravesite is to bring a stone, and Sambo's grave has been replete with such markers. From at least the 1970s schoolchildren have been encouraged to bring stones painted with scenes and panegyrics to Sambo's memory, to enable them to empathise with a boy of around their own age whose life was cruelly foreshortened by the operation of a transatlantic slave trade originated in Lancaster. These stones, with their scenes of seafaring and lost African landscapes, add to the colourful and poignant scene that creates in Pierre Nora's words a *lieu de mémoire*, a site of memory, that is deeply affecting.[13] The loneliness of the grave, created by the fact of his burial in unconsecrated ground set off from other plots, adds to this sense of a desolation which visitors seek to make more palatable through inhabiting the grave with objects. In keeping with the gravesite of a child, visitors have also brought small toys, and recently young girls have been tying hair bobbles to the cross at the site, showing their intimate attachment to the story and its importance to them. These mementoes bring the grave alive in ways that help to transform Sambo's status from solitary human chattel to socialised human being, if only in death.

The most recent memorial at the site, erected in 2009, is placed several feet from the grave as if in acknowledgement of that already crowded space. It is a group of around thirty small memorial stones with personal messages from the children at Alston School, Cumbria. These are attached on top of bamboo canes, forming a circle of memory like a bunch of flowers or a group of toadstools. These organic forms have poignant personal messages in white paint from the schoolchildren.

Many might see in this memorial and in the other memorialisation gestures outlined above a sentimentalisation not that far removed from James Watson's poem; however, I prefer to think of it as important memory work that makes sure that Sambo's story is continually brought back into local discourses about slavery, emphasising the human story that the cityscape can so readily elide. In Michel de Certeau's words, this memory work could be said to 'exorcise death by inserting it into discourse'.[14] Hilda Kean, in discussing the memorialisation around the grave, describes how it is 'both a site of public history and one which has been created through the personal and unofficial acts of people operating outside the constructs of academic history'.[15] Such guerrilla memorialisation by a variety of recent visitors ensures the grave is not wholly constrained by limiting ideas of public remembrance and reduced to a part of that dry historical record which we might label 'heritage'.

Sambo has also been memorialised in folk song through Alan Bell's 'Sambo's Song', written in the 1970s, which tells the story of the lonely grave, the boy abandoned and his burial by 'kindly seamen' in its chorus and first two verses. The final verse speaks of him witnessing activities around the grave that continue today:

> Now children walk the grassy shore
> To place sweet flowers upon your grave,
> You'll never want for more.
> And traveller, if you e'er pass that way,
> Pause and think of Sambo,
> And man's old dreary ways.[16]

Similarly to Watson's poem, the song makes moral capital out of Sambo's abandonment and death, though in keeping with the more secular late twentieth century, the moral is more concerned with universal human rights than with Christianity. The song itself created controversy in left-wing folk forums in the 1970s because of Sambo's name. A senior Labour politician insisted that singing about a boy named 'Sambo' was 'offensive',[17] yet offered no alternative name. The London-born, Bajan-descended poet Dorothea Smartt responds to the problematic of Sambo's historically-freighted, racist name in her marvellously elliptical '99 Names of the Samboo'. In the title, she follows the spelling of the name on the 1796 brass grave plate, before embarking on a tour through African and European naming practices at the time of the slave trade and their legacies for good and ill. She starts with Sambo's imagined original name and then contrasts this with his slave status:

> Bilal
> ibn
> beloved
> son
> brother

husband
father
grandfather
elder
ancestor

sold
livestock
cargo
chattel
property
guinea-bird
savage
enslaved
captive
servant
worker[18]

The poem illuminates the way Africans are dehumanised through the process of enslavement and reduced to ciphers for European concepts of otherness. The sparse vocabulary of the poem emphasises the reductive nature of such a stereotyping discourse:

heathen
cannibal
beast
blackamoor
darkie
nigger
uncivilised
wog
fuzzy-wuzzy
coon
negro

tamed
eunuch
pet
uncle tom
minstrel
golliwog
survivor
mirror
mask
chameleon
creole[19]

The poem is not hidebound by this limiting discourse, and shows how, by using such techniques of masking, Africans fight back to make their own space in language. The poem circles back to Bilal, Sambo's imagined African name, which emerges triumphant despite the power of the institution of slavery and the racist discourse it promulgated. This work, and

Smartt's earlier poem sequence 'Lancaster Keys', specially commissioned for the 2003 Lancaster Litfest, writes back directly to Watson's elegy and provides at the same time a commentary on the city's wilful forgetting of the trade that made it rich. Litfest's decision to print 24,950 copies of the poem, 'each representing a person shipped into slavery by Lancaster slave traders between 1750 and 1800', and deliver them to all secondary school pupils in the district attempted to make a dramatic gesture of rememory in the cultural life of the city. This public acknowledgement of the dissident memories that Sambo's history ignites outlines a politics which seeks to intervene in the traditional amnesia of the city about its slave past and reinvigorate the narrative, not as sentimentalised panegyric, but rather as radical counter-memory; it is in keeping with Richard Price's impassioned call for diasporic memorials to run beyond building materials:

> . . . memorials [should] run less to bricks and mortars than to knowledge and its diffusion. What if we tried to make sure that every schoolchild in Europe, the Americas and Africa is exposed as fully as possible to the history of slavery and its legacies?[20]

Smartt's poem is reproduced alongside information on Lancaster's involvement in the trade, with quotations about the importance of memory. Such a pamphlet has the kind of memorial function that Price demands. It focuses not only on the direct slave trade, which indicates the interweaving of Lancaster with the slave economy, but also on the city's trade in slave-produced and harvested goods such as rice, cotton, sugar and particularly mahogany, which made the fortune of the Gillows furniture company in the eighteenth century. Smartt's poem seeks to redress the city's amnesia about the slave trade, and the opening of the section 'The brewery room' reflects on how the routes that Sambo took to get to Sunderland Point were smoothed by the commercial networks established by Lancaster merchants:

> Keys to the city awarded
> to entrepreneurs in the new world trade.
> Adventurers of high finance.
> Slavery a key to England's glory days,
> civic largesse and the city's architecture,
> of streets and the high seas
> glistening with gold.[21]

As the poem indicates, many of those involved in the trade were prominent members of the elite that ran the city, including mayors such as Dodshon Foster. Moreover, the poem delineates how the raw materials exchanged for slaves in the West Indies came back to Lancaster too, helping to create distinctive, prestigious industries at home that belied the trade in human bodies that made them possible. As detailed above, the most famous such factory in Lancaster was Gillows, where mahogany from the Caribbean was fashioned into high class furniture. Smartt's poem shows the interrelatedness of this industry and the slave economy, positing Sambo and his fellow slaves as the labourers on whose backs large profits were made:

> The Plantation Estate, brewery source,
> furnished salon of mahogany. Gillows crafted
> wood, the Sambo farmed and forested.
> Torn from root system to harden and die.
> To be shaped into something new

and of use to Lancaster Town.
A primrose path of mahogany furniture.
Fallen nature, hardness of heart,
shameless dishonesty, blood courses,
evil courses, water courses.[22]

Just as the mahogany has been 'farmed and forested', so the Africans have been uprooted to furnish labour for the plantation, becoming a human commodity which hardens and dies just like the wood to which it contributes labour value. In this way Sambo's death in Lancaster is a function of his use as a commodity and the denial of his humanity by those who benefit from the trade in all its three corners. The economy of language here, so that Sambo is both the subject and object of the verbs 'farmed and forested', points to the duality of the slaves' position, crucial to harvesting the mahogany, but also harvested themselves in Africa to provide the labour power that makes possible the operation of the colonial economy. Both labourer and commodity, Sambo is tremendously over-determined in his meanings within the British slave-owning empire. This is true too when mercantilism is superseded by sentiment in the late eighteenth century, and Smartt speaks to this in reinterpreting Sambo's perceived pining for his master, which, according to such self-serving views, led to his death:

This Sambo
pines for his master, mythical, imagined,
key and the centre-piece of his room.
But the room is but many,
in one house, in one compound, in one
village, in one district, in one country, in one
empire, in one continent spanning continents.

The 'Ship's Inn',
I the Sambo pour out of this Brewery Room
into my fermenting home brew spilling
kicked from its calabash pot.[23]

The meaning of Sambo here as sentimentalised torch-bearer for his beloved master is transformed to Sambo as avenger, whose legacy has the power to leap out of the confines of white guilt-ridden sentimentality and reinvigorate debates around slave history from the village of Sunderland Point, through cities like Lancaster to the UK and across the seas to the intertwining nexus of slave-owning empires. In this reading Sambo's fertile tale cannot be confined to its historical trace but erupts like the 'fermenting home brew' of the brewing room he is confined to by illness. Sambo's revenge is in his re-imagining by later generations which, as Smartt shows, relate how Anglo-American cultures kept 'for themselves the harvest' yet in doing so 'ferment a bitter brew'.

The Manchester-based poet SuAndi's poem about Sambo's grave envisages a similar resurrection of the boy, but this time he returns to Africa, going back through the Door of No Return in contradistinction to its historical and mythical narrative of permanent exile:

Sometimes when the moon is full
He pushes the earth aside
Scattering the gifts, toys, tokens
And stands on the highest point
Tip-toed to extend his boyish frame

And he looks out to sea
For now he can see beyond water and land
Right to the coast of Elmina
Through the Door of No Return
And into his village and his mother's arms
And he smiles once again[24]

In pushing away the freight of keepsakes left for him, the boy rejects his status as senti-mental victim of white guilt and returns to an African homeland without conflict in a fantasy projection that replaces sentimentalised white projections with a return to homespace. Hortense Spillers has talked about how African persons in the middle passage are literally 'suspended in the Oceanic',[25] and Sambo is a prime example who complicates SuAndi's wished for return. His known life was conducted almost exclusively shipboard, and in Smartt and SuAndi's imaginations his after-life legacy permeates the transatlantic world where his memory, despite all attempts, cannot be repressed or neutralised. Suspension, a negative in Spillers's theorisation, is dialogised by Smartt and SuAndi's lyrical interventions. As Aldon Nielsen succinctly describes in talking of such black Atlantic texts, 'a different kind of scholarship may be called for here, a study that listens to seas and is owned by their terrible poetry.'[26] If nothing else, Smartt's brewery room lyric and SuAndi's fantasy projection need this kind of transnational, oceanic scholarship to fully interpret their black Atlantic resonances. Their guerrilla memorialisation interprets the gravesite anew, articulating an African presence that is in contrast to sentimentalised and objectified representations.

As Smartt details in her poems on the gravesite, there are occasional reactions, such as the vandalism of the grave, which are at the least problematic and sometimes deeply disturbing. For instance, in August 2008, I visited the gravesite where a visitor had placed a small golliwog amidst the flotsam and jetsam dispersed over the grave. This example of racist memorabilia was the equivalent of graffiti, undermining the joyous cacophony of objects that spoke to a more appropriate memorialisation. It shows that guerrilla memorialisation is not necessarily always positive and that our memorial sites cannot be left entirely to those whose knowledge of the appropriate gesture might be grossly out of kilter with the site's historical resonances. But despite such potential problems, enslaved Africans dispersed throughout the Atlantic triangle are, I believe, most effectively remembered at such local sites that conjure up their thoroughly routed existence. Remembering slavery from nearby is an urgent task in all parts of the circum-Atlantic and beyond, as Livio Sansone reminds us:

> Transatlantic slavery was by definition a transnational phenomenon, which has created a universe of suffering, dehumanisation and racialisation, spanning across many regions of what we now know, after Paul Gilroy, as the black Atlantic – a region that reaches to the tropical lowlands of the Pacific coast of Central and Latin America. Yet the way in which it is remembered as well as the legacy felt within today's life and race relations, show that the memory of slavery is often a surprisingly 'local', relational and contingent construction.[27]

The imaginative leaps that Smartt and SuAndi make from this lonely gravesite to reinvigorate lives lost in the black Atlantic are exemplary moves in the light of Sansone's comments, creating poems that use the local site to make links across geographies and chronologies. They are of course memorial gestures in themselves, guerrilla memorialisations. The poem contributed to a feeling in Lancaster that the city should build an effective memorial, one used by local people to remember the horrors of the past. Lubaina Himid talked about the possibilities of building such a memorial at the launch event of the Slave Trade Arts Memorial Project (STAMP) in November 2003:

> The monument could be for the people of a city and its visitors to be able to learn to accept and give forgiveness. In which case it could relate to today, to the past, to the future and could work visually on several levels. There could be texts, there could be water, there could be structure, there could be movement, colour, and even growing, living things.
>
> A monument needs to move, to move on, to help the people who engage with it to move on, it needs to be able to change with the weather, the seasons, the political climate and the visual debates of the day.[28]

Any successful memorial would need to be a *lieu de mémoire* that would adequately represent generations to come as well as the past and the present: a memorial that conserves memory without being conservative. That is, so that it truly helps 'the people who engage with it to move on', so that it becomes associated not with stasis but with dynamism. Such a task was daunting and humbling, but it was felt that our collective amnesia must be overcome by local gestures of remembrance (however small) which raise the collective consciousness of slavery's ghostly presence that still haunts our shared circum-Atlantic space. Such memorialisation is born out of the struggle with conservative forces that prefer to bury difficult histories, and played out through a guerrilla memorialisation that refuses to accept the status quo.

In the absence of such a memorial in Lancaster, STAMP worked with a number of artist, schools and community groups to increase public awareness of the slave trade and developed a series of commemorative exhibitions and performances from 2003–6, culminating in a permanent memorial to the Africans who were transported on board Lancaster ships, unveiled in October 2005. The committee had been formed in September 2002 at a training day for teachers around issues raised by the slave trade held at the Maritime Museum. Their frustration that there was not a focus in the city for remembering victims of the slave trade that they could share with their pupils galvanised the small group of curators, educators, local NGO representatives and community workers into forming a campaign. As an academic in the field, I became STAMP'S academic advisor. Throughout the project, our committee were aware of the tortured history of British imperialism and the city's own contribution to some of its excesses, made worse by a wilful historical amnesia. Barnor Hesse outlines this problematic and the way to overcome it with a welcome articulacy:

> Part of the difficulty with the dominant cultural form of Britain is the inability or reluctance of its institutions to accept that European racism was and is a constitutive feature of British nationalism. While this remains unexamined, resistant to decolonisation in the post-colonial period, it continues to generate a myriad of resistances and challenges to its historical formations. These dislocate the narration of Britain as a serialised essence, articulating the storylines of a nation that is diversely politicised and culturally unsettled. Residual multicultural disruptions are constituted as forms of disturbance and intrusiveness by those resurgences of meaning, arising from the imperial past. They continually put into question, particularly in unexposed places and at unforeseen times, matters deemed in hegemonic discourses to be settled, buried and apparently beyond dispute.[29]

I quote Hesse in full because his intervention speaks to the legacy of UK cities like Lancaster and the possibilities of overcoming the straitjacket imposed by amnesia and indifference.

For the committee there was much unfinished business: a colonial legacy that still informed relations and ideas in the city, and which was highlighted by its involvement in the transatlantic slave trade. However, because it had never been properly debated there was a vacuum which we felt needed to be filled so that the link between current racism and the historic chattel slavery which had helped form the very bricks and mortar of the city could be foregrounded and exposed. Our aim was to use the memorial and other project activities as 'residual multicultural disruptions' in the city to help undermine what we might call, following Paul Gilroy's adoption of Patrick Wright's phrase, 'the morbidity of heritage'.[30] We wanted to make a vibrant living response to the historical legacy of slavery and imperialism that would reawaken debate and not allow a complacent settling of the debate in favour of a monoglot UK nationalism that had historically marginalised a critical stance on this contested issue. As Lessie Jo Frazier, in discussing counter-memory in Chile, contends:

> The memories of state violence incommensurable with national-state memory took the form of aberrations or flaws in what was presented as an otherwise whole cloth of national memory in a functioning political system. . . . It is possible to read the rhetorically whole cloth of national histories, not only against the grain, but in its very weave.[31]

We wanted to highlight such 'aberrations or flaws' in the history of slavery (Britain's state violence) as essential to a complete national memory with a full accounting of the historical record, and to bring back to view the full story, the 'very weave' of it, through our monument. In this, we were part of a wider movement of localism that disdained a monoglot national narrative that refused to give up nostalgia for the imperial past, and were aware too of the importance of a transnational approach to a memorial that would be truly post-imperial. As Jay Winter commented, in discussing the importance of shifting focus away from the national sphere (replete with its hubristic and often chauvinistic monuments) to smaller-scale local memorials, the most effective sites of memory are often 'created not just by nations but primarily by small groups of men and women who do the work of remembrance'.[32] Paul Ricoeur had asserted that 'the nation remains the major reference of historical memory';[33] however, for a complex black Atlantic history such as this, the local and the transnational should surely trump it. As Paul Gilroy says, anyone involved in such needful political work would best situate themselves:

> . . . close to the centre of Britain's vernacular dissidence, lending energy to an ordinary, demotic multiculturalism that is not the outcome of government drift and institutional indifference but of concrete oppositional work: political, aesthetic, cultural, scholarly.[34]

With its committee of academics, local community activists and creative workers, and with support from radical local folk, STAMP mobilised exactly the kind of vernacular dissidence that enabled the action required to build the memorial. Perhaps our agenda is best discussed in the light of the unveiling ceremony in October 2005, which was attended by around 200 people, most of them local, but which also included an African ceremony: the launching of a burning wicker boat festooned with plants used on that continent for ceremonial burials. Although the mayor of Lancaster and civic dignitaries were present, their presence did not dominate the agenda of the ceremony, which reflected the roots of the project in the local community and its links to communities from the black Atlantic and its history. Nowhere was this more evident than in the local schoolchildren playing percussion after intensive workshops with African drummers.[35] And our international speaker, the distinguished African American political scientist and civil rights activist Preston King, had been a resident of Lancaster for over a decade whilst in political exile in the UK. The project was interested in embedding memorialisation about slavery in the city, and intent on leaving a legacy so that the memorial was not felt to be imposed from above by an elite, and so that the city and its residents had ownership of the process and finally of the monument itself. However, it was felt that this ownership should be in the context of a critical take on local, national and international histories that did not allow them to remain 'settled, buried and apparently beyond dispute', as Hesse had warned in his prescient commentary. Lubaina Himid, at the public meeting which launched STAMP, articulated the need we all felt to honour the African dead and abused who had been loaded onto ships fitted out on Lancaster's quayside, and the profits from whose sale had helped build the wealth of the city:

> If you are going to honour the dead who have been ignored, suppressed or denied when in peril in the past, you must do it because as a city you want to show that you would do differently now, that you would be able to defend those people now. You will first have to acknowledge that your city would not be the city it is, without the sacrifice of those who were sold by or used by the city in the past. This city can only aspire to being truly great if it can I suppose in some way seek forgiveness. Could it be that a monument is a tangible seeking of forgiveness?[36]

The very notion of 'forgiveness' in the context of a historical wrong from two centuries ago was bound to provoke uneasiness in some sections of the populace, and a number of local residents vented their fury, particularly when the proposal originally planned to site the modern monument directly in front of the eighteenth century Custom House on the quayside.[37] Probably the most splenetic response came after the memorial design was published in the local paper, the *Lancaster Guardian*, in December 2004. James Mackie's letter left no doubt about his disgust:

> . . . to find that a green light has been given to the erection of this nonsense is just upsetting. The quay is one of the few near-perfect parts of Lancaster that still remain and the old Customs House is one of the most beautiful and interesting landmarks in the county. Who in their right minds thinks that the area will be improved by a mosaic-encrusted plinth and a vessel in the grass verge containing 20 cast iron enslaved figures? The artist's impression that you printed with the article was not very large or detailed but is quite enough to show that the proposed artwork is simply repulsive.[38]

Mackie was not alone in his opposition, and the erroneous belief that the city council was funding the monument added to the venom. *Lancaster Guardian* reader Betty Norton wrote that a monument 'depicting misery and shame is no enhancement to the city, it will turn visitors away'.[39] However, at no point did the opposition to the monument gain any political leverage on the council, nor attract support from any councillors in the ruling Labour group or their opponents. In fact, the council leader Ian Barker sprang to the defence of the STAMP committee in response to Mackie's letter, crafting an informed and elegant response:

> History is more than the sanitised version sometimes served up by the heritage industry. We are privileged to live in a historic town. An understanding of its history can teach our children and us a lot. But it won't do so if we deceive ourselves by ignoring the painful and repellent aspects of that history.

I have no doubt that some of Lancaster's prosperous slavers were outstanding men in the local community, kind and considerate to their family and neighbours and yet simultaneously capable of inflicting barbarous treatment on unknown Africans. If the Slave Trade Arts Memorial Project (STAMP) helps us reflect on that contradiction and how it could happen, it will be worthwhile.[40]

Barker's articulate support makes the point that citizens like Mackie who worry about the disruption to the 'near-perfect' quay by the visual complications of a memorial to the victims of the slave trade are merely supporters of a sanitised history that the city has been complicit in for too long. Opposition voices continued, but they never gained any coherent body of support. Maybe the fact that the council fully endorsed STAMP but did not provide any of the core funding meant that opposition was neutralised. Most of the money for the project came from the North-West Arts Council and the Millennium Commission, with the council providing vital logistical and technical support. There were no specific council grants for opponents to identify and build opposition around. Another key factor in neutralising opposition was the way the STAMP project used the money from the Arts Council to engage with local schools and community groups, running workshops that enabled thousands of locals to be engaged with the project well before the final monument was unveiled, providing a legacy with ramifications for citizens from many different backgrounds.

Allied to this community work was an awareness in the committee of the need for a different kind of engagement with the past than would normally happen in the cityscape. The committee had decided early on that they should make the encounter with this past an everyday occurrence rather than a pilgrimage or part of an educational tour. This was key to moving slavery and its important lessons about human rights and injustice from the periphery to the centre of consciousness. As Lubaina Himid articulates, this is done not by the grand gesture, or by shock tactics, but by everyday encounter:

If the person pushing their buggy past the memorial isn't thinking, 'Oh dear what a pity all those people died', but is thinking or just catches a glimpse of fabric out of the corner of their eye or a sparkle of water then there's a kind of flowing imprint, visible, physical, the sound of the water or the flash of the colour that flows into their life as they go past. There's no point even in trying to place something like that in people's lives. But memory is not about that, it's about tiny moments, little flickers of recognition. I'd want people to meet at the memorial; a place where you feel there's a kind of continuum, where there's a going on, a tomorrow. It would be there to enter into the fabric of the day.[41]

The everyday nature of the encounter with the public work of art is key to its quiet effectiveness, and Himid's future-focused intervention informed Kevin Dalton-Johnson, our commissioned sculptor, as he completed the designs for his *Captured Africans* memorial. The final design of the memorial uses a variety of materials including stone, steel and acrylic to create a multi-textured take on Lancaster's slave trade history. The plinth is a circular stone with an inlaid mosaic of the Atlantic triangle, with lines showing the movement of ships between the continents of Europe, Africa and the Americas. Above it are a series of acrylic blocks named for the goods traded – cotton, sugar, mahogany and tobacco – with wealth named at the top because it is the prime motivation, and slaves named at the bottom because they are the goods upon which the whole trade depends. Inlaid in the acrylic are icons of the goods, so that for wealth there are coins and notes, whilst for the slaves there is a diagram based on the famous depiction of the slave ship *Brookes*. Just beneath this bottom block are small bronze casts of black slave figures which Dalton-Johnson developed with young people at risk in Lancaster. He felt it was very important that at least one part of the sculpture should be created by local people who do not consider themselves artists in any professional sense. The acrylic blocks are hung by poles between a steel panel and a carved piece of local Peakamoor stone, both of which image the shapes of a ship.[42] In an interview with Dalton-Johnson, I discussed how the sculpture as commissioned fits into its location so that it can become part of the everyday life of the citizens of the town. Dalton-Johnson agreed, and describes how:

> . . . as the public come down and round the bend, just at the top of Damside, you're looking straight at the side of the sculpture, so you're looking through the spaces in between the acrylic blocks to the water on the other side, and that's picked up again by the blue of the mosaic, because it's predominantly blue, so that works really well. And the stone which is going round the outside, that once again fits with the new buildings on either side. It operates on very different levels in as much as it suits the context of a ship in the triangle, going down the slipway, off it goes after it's just dropped its cargo off. It also fits very well with aesthetic context where it's positioned, the colours of the apartments and the buildings that are built either side, and it works perfectly with the slipway going straight into the river. Having seen it erected, I'm quite confident that it'll work on different levels, both in terms of subject matter and also aesthetically in terms of the environment in which it's been placed.[43]

What the memorial successfully does is arrest the attention of passers-by when they first encounter it. For instance, a woman who did not know about the town's slave past told me how she caught out of the corner of her eye the words *Captured Africans* on the metal side of the sculpture, and was compelled to move towards it to find out more. What Dalton-Johnson wanted to do was to make the slave trade and its history central to the stories the city told about itself, so that they could never be elided again. Exhibiting the slave trade in a public space[44] away from its usual relegation to an often tired museum gallery enables its full historical and contemporary implications to be teased out. Sue Ashworth, from Lancashire County Museum Service and a founder member of the STAMP committee, discussed how important it is to move beyond the walls of the museum and how Dalton-Johnson's sculpture had achieved this:

> We've always acknowledged the slave trade ever since the Maritime Museum first opened 20 years ago. But it was always dealt with in a very dry way that just focused on the facts, the tonnage and the products involved. We saw an opportunity to let people actually contemplate what had happened rather than just be bombarded with figures. There doesn't have to be a disparity between something that's informative but also appeals to your senses.[45]

Ashworth underlines the importance of the memorial doing different memory work that foregrounds the emotions as well as the intellect. The contemplative aspect of the sculpture, however, is combined with serious political goals, as Dalton-Johnson has a strong message for contemporary race relations from his engagement with the history of slavery:

> Well, it's just a fact that black people could be treated like that, and if it could happen then, it can happen again now. The reason why we need to have a memorial is so it isn't repeated – it operates on that level. There's also the other political level, in that I'm not trying to get my own back, but I'm turning the

tables, as if to say, you're getting a taste of how that feels. Putting the slave trade almost on trial, on exhibition, in the way that it's actually being presented, and the fact that it's a black artist doing that, re-emphasises the political statement.[46]

His desire to put the slave trade on trial is because of its implications for race relations in the here and now. As Dalton-Johnson himself says, the pedagogical aspect of the memorial is very important and is 'the reason why the ships' names are there, and the actual numbers of slaves that were on those ships. They're very clear, and they're not abstracted in the way that other parts have been.'[47] Additionally, the names of the ships' captains are listed in chronological order. Many of them are traditional Lancashire surnames which might well be shared by their viewers. The sculpture does not resist such uncomfortable realities; in fact it foregrounds them to make them part of the public memory so that white Lancastrians have to acknowledge these atrocities and hopefully learn from them. At the moment, slave traders are primarily remembered as citizens of note and many were prominent in the eighteenth century polity, such as Thomas Hinde, who became mayor of the city in 1769 and has a significant plaque in his honour in the city's Priory church. Through naming these slave traders, Dalton-Johnson's statue is a guerrilla memorialisation that works against traditional historiography. Such guerrilla memorialisation confronts Lancaster's citizens with their past in ways that work against a traditional memorial praxis which has tended toward unifying viewers principally around sympathy with the victims. Dalton-Johnson does this, but also acknowledges that the perpetrators of the historical atrocity should be remembered and marked lest Lancaster's citizens forget their ancestors' role in the trade. James E. Young has talked about the importance of such reminiscence in comments about Holocaust memorials which can be related to *Captured Africans*:

> . . . [the] aim is not to reassure or console, but to haunt visitors with the unpleasant – uncanny – sensation of calling into consciousness that which has been previously – even happily – repressed.[48]

The repression of uncomfortable historical facts has been key to white British responses to slavery and colonialism, and Dalton-Johnson's 'haunting' of visitors to his memorial through the uncannily familiar names is a device he uses to counteract complacency about the historic responsibility of white Lancastrians for the trade that helped to make the city's wealth. As Dalton-Johnson explains, the memorial has different resonances for black people, himself included: 'I don't feel I have to do the sculpture in order to remember, because I won't forget'. He continues:

> So myself, and many other black people, do not necessarily need something physical in order to remember, because we live it every day, and the way that we're treated brings it all back, what our ancestors went through, even though it's not the same degree. Outside of the black perspective, inside the white community, it's very easy to forget, and I think there are many people that would like to forget; there's a combination, a mixture there, and for that reason I think this is very important, just to remember the atrocity that happened to the slave because that's got to be core.[49]

Thus the memorial is designed not simply to honour the memory of the slaves carried on the ships, but to engage with the complexities of that history, to name the perpetrators and highlight the centrality of slavery to the fiscal and cultural economy of the city as a means to move forward. As Paul Ricoeur says of such kinds of memory work, 'it is justice that turns memory into a project, and it is this same project of justice that gives the form of the future and of the imperative to the duty of memory.'[50] Memorials at their most effective speak to their future contexts as much as to the past they commemorate, to a future-orientated responsibility, rather than a guilt-charged retrieval of a static past.

Ricoeur's statement is particularly pertinent in the wake of the nearby Morecambe Bay tragedy of February 2004, where 23 ethnic Chinese cockle pickers died due to Victorian working conditions and a bonded labour regime that must to them have seemed akin to slavery.[51] Hence, the memorial now has local contemporary resonances and can speak to modern forms of bonded labour too, showing how the local community in Lancaster has to respond not only to the human rights struggles of the past but also to the corrupt practices of global capitalism that continue to throw up bodies on our beaches over 200 years after the end of Lancaster's involvement in the slave trade.

Notes

1   Quoted in H. Kean, 'Personal and public histories: issues in the presentation of the past', in B. Graham and P. Howard (eds), The *Ashgate Research Companion to Heritage and Identity* (Aldershot: Ashgate, 2008), pp55–69 (62).

2   P. Gilroy, *After Empire: Melancholia or Convivial Culture?* (London: Routledge 2004), p98.

3   I discuss in detail in Chapter 3 [of the original work] the way Lancaster used the 2007 bicentenary commemorations to inaugurate new exhibits. These temporary installations have now been removed and the Maritime Museum now has a small and much improved permanent display about Lancaster's involvement in the slave trade.

4   As Melinda Elder states, 'Lancastrians over the years gained a something of a reputation for operating outside the accepted practices of the trade.' M. Elder, *Lancaster and the African Slave Trade* (Lancaster: Lancaster City Museums, 1994), p15.

5   M. Elder, *The Slave Trade and the Economic Development of 18th Century Lancaster* (Keele: Ryburn Press 1992). Elder's subsequent research has been communicated to me and my students in slave site tours of Lancaster, which I have organised with her on a regular basis, and has been confirmed by curators at the Maritime Museum in Lancaster. It awaits a fully referenced article or the commissioning of a new edition of what is the most comprehensive book on the Lancaster slave trade.

6   J. E. Young, *At Memory's Edge: After Images of the Holocaust in Contemporary Art and Architecture* (New Haven, CT: Yale University Press, 2000), p73.

7   Quoted A. Whitehead, *Memory* (Abingdon: Routledge, 2009), p13.

8   C. A. Reinhardt, *Claims to Memory: Beyond Slavery and Emancipation in the French Caribbean* (Oxford: Berghahn Books, 2008), p15.

9   J. T., 'Samboo's Grave', *Lonsdale Magazine and Kendal Repository* III, xxix, 31 May 1822, pp188–92 (190).

10   Elder, *The Slave Trade*, p144.

11   Quoted in J. T., 'Samboo's Grave', pp191–92.

12   P. Ricoeur, *Memory, History, Forgetting*, trans. K. Bramley and D. Pellauer (Chicago: University of Chicago Press, 2004), p366.

13   P. Nora, 'Between memory and history: les lieux de memoire' in *History and Memory in African American Culture*, ed. G. Fabre and R. O'Meally (Oxford: Oxford University Press, 1994), pp284–300.

14   Quoted in Ricoeur, *Memory, History and Forgetting*, p367.

15   Kean, 'Personal and public histories', p58.

16   A. A. Bell, 'Sambo's Song' (Fleetwood: Tamlyn Music, 1973).

17   Correspondence with A. A. Bell, 13 June 2008.

18   D. Smartt, *Ship-Shape* (Leeds: Peepal Tree Press, 2008), p29.

19   Smartt, *Ship-Shape*, pp29–30.

20   R. Price, 'Monuments and silent screamings: a view from Martinique', in G. Oostinde (ed.). *Facing Up: Perspectives on the Commemoration of Slavery from Africa, the Americas and Europe* (Kingston, Jamaica: Ian Randle, 2001), pp58–62 (61).

21   D. Smartt, *Lancaster Keys* (Lancaster: Slave Trade Arts Memorial Project, 2003), n.p.

22   Smartt, *Lancaster Keys*, n.p.

23   Smartt, *Lancaster Keys*, n.p.

24   SuAndi, 'Untitled Poem', 2006, unpublished ms.

25   H. Spillers, 'Mama's Baby, Papa's Maybe: an American grammar', in A. Mitchell (ed.), *Within the Circle: An Anthology of African American Literary Criticism from the Harlem Renaissance to the Present* (Durham, NC: Duke University Press, 1994), pp454–81 (466).

26   A. L. Nielsen, *Writing between the Lines: Race and Intertextuality* (Athens, GA: University of Georgia Press, 1994), p104.

27   L. Sansone, 'Remembering slavery from nearby: heritage, Brazilian style,' in G. Oostinde (ed.), *Facing Up: Perspectives on the Commemoration of Slavery from Africa, the Americas and Europe* (Kingston, Jamaica: Ian Randle, 2001), pp83–89 (89).

28   L. Himid, 'Monument Talk', Dukes Theatre, Lancaster, 15 November 2003.

29   B. Hesse, *Unsettled Multiculturalisms: Diasporas, Entanglements, Transruptions* (Zed Books: London, 2000), p18.

30   P. Gilroy, *After Empire: Melancholia or Convivial Culture* (Abingdon: Routledge, 2004), p109.

31   L. J. Frazier, 'Subverted memories: countermourning as political action in Chile', in M. Bal, J. Crewe and L. Spitzer (eds). *Acts of Memory: Cultural Recall in the Present* (Hanover: Dartmouth College Press, 1998), pp105–19 (115).

32   J. Winter, *Remembering War: The Great War between History and Memory in the Twentieth Century* (New Haven, CT: Yale University Press, 2006), p136.

33   Ricoeur, *Memory, History, Forgetting*, p397

34   Gilroy, *After Empire*, p108.

35   The involvement of schoolchildren was vital to the legacy of the project, and in the aftermath of the unveiling of the memorial, the organisation Global Link together with the Friends of the Lancaster Maritime Museum commissioned the artist Sue Flowers and the historian Melinda Elder to work with children from Dallas Road Primary School to devise a thoroughly researched Lancaster Slave Trade Town Trail, which is available for tourists and residents for walking tours of the city. It can be downloaded at http://www.globallink.org.uk/slavery/. On the site there is also a radio programme made by children at Bowerham Primary School about slavery and inequality: http://www.globallink.org.uk/r4c/bowerham_cp_school/index.htm.

36   Himid, 'Monument talk'.

37   The monument was eventually placed above Damside slipway at the opposite end of the quay from the Custom House, due to plans for new flood defences that would have complicated its erection on the original site.

38   J. Mackie, 'Why be slaves to our past?', letter to *Lancaster Guardian*, 7 January 2005, p6.

39   P. Collins, 'Lancaster faces up to its shameful past', *Lancaster Guardian*, 28 October 2005, p2.

40   Councillor I. Barker, 'Slavery is part of what we are', letter to *Lancaster Guardian*, 14 January 2005, p6.

41   A. Rice, 'Exploring inside the invisible: an interview with Lubiana Himid', *Wasafiri* 40 (Winter 2003), pp21–26.

42   Images of the sculpture and an explanation of the STAMP project can be found at http://www.uclan.ac.uk/abolition [accessed 27 July 2009].

43   A. Rice, interview with Kevin Dalton-Johnson, August 2005 and February 2006, available at http://www.uclan.ac.uk/abolition [accessed 27 July 2009].

44   The public space where the memorial has been placed is on a main thoroughfare into the town right on the quayside. The committee and the artist felt it important that the memorial be close to the water that enabled the trade, rather than in the town centre where it would have been dwarfed by buildings and, in part at least, decontextualised.

45   Quoted in Collins, 'Lancaster faces up', p2. Later in 2007, the city's museums used the impetus from the STAMP project to commission new installations.

46   Rice, interview with Kevin Dalton-Johnson.

47   Rice, interview with Kevin Dalton-Johnson.

48   J. E. Young, 'Daniel Libeskind's Jewish Museum in Berlin: the uncanny arts of memorial architecture', in B. Zelizer (ed.), *Visual Culture and the Holocaust* (Athlone: London, 2001), pp179–97 (194).

49   Rice, interview with Kevin Dalton-Johnson.

50   Ricoeur, *Memory, History, Forgetting*, p88.

51   Nick Broomfield's film *Ghost* (London: Beyond Films, 2006) brilliantly highlights these aspects of the tragedy.

Further Reading

General introduction

Frisch, M. (ed) (1990) *A Shared Authority: Essays on the Craft and Meaning of Oral and Public History*, Albany, NY: State University of New York Press.

Gardner, J. B. (2010) 'Trust, Risk and Public History: A View from the United States', *Public History Review*, vol 17, pp52–61.

Grele, R. J. (1981) 'Whose Public? Whose History? What is the Goal of a Public Historian?', *The Public Historian*, vol 3(1) pp40–48.

Groot, J. de (2009) *Consuming History*, Abingdon, UK: Routledge.

Hill, J. (ed) (2011) *The Future of Archives and Recordkeeping: A Reader*, London: Facet Publishing.

Ho, S. (2007) 'Blogging as Popular History Making, Blogs as Public History: The Singapore Case Study', *Public History Review*, vol 14, pp64–79.

Macintyre, S. and Clark, A. (2004) *The History Wars*, Melbourne: Melbourne University Press.

Miller, D. (2008/2010) *The Comfort of Things*, Cambridge: Polity Press.

Smith, L., Shackel, P. and Campbell, G. (2011) 'Introduction: Class Still Matters', *Heritage, Labour and the Working Classes*, Abingdon, UK: Routledge.

Yeo, S. (1986) 'Whose Story? An Argument from within Current Historical Practice in Britain', *Journal of Contemporary History*, vol 21(2), pp295–320.

Part I: The past in the present: Who is making history?

Black, J. (2005) *Using History*, London: Bloomsbury.

Brocken, M. (2010) *Other Voices: Hidden Histories of Liverpool's Popular Music Scenes, 1930s–1970s*, Aldershot, UK: Ashgate.

Connerton, P. (2009) *How Modernity Forgets,* Cambridge: Cambridge University Press.

Doss, E. (2008) *The Emotional Life of Contemporary Public Memorials: Towards a Theory of Temporary Memorials*, Amsterdam: Amsterdam University Press.

Funda, A. (2003) *Stasiland: Stories from behind the Berlin Wall*, London: Granta.

Harvey, K. (ed) (2009) *History and Material Culture: A Student's Guide to Approaching Alternative Sources*, Abingdon, UK: Routledge.

Hodgkin, K. and Radstone, S. (eds) (2003) *Contested Pasts: The Politics of Memory,* Abingdon, UK: Routledge.

Rhys, O. (2011) *Contemporary Collecting: Theory and Practice,* Edinburgh: Museum Etc.

Robertson, I. (2012) *Heritage from Below,* Aldershot, UK: Ashgate.

Vulpian, A. de (2008) *Towards the Third Modernity: How Ordinary People Are Transforming the World,* Axminster, UK: Triarchy Press.

Part II: Materials and approaches to making history

Bashforth, M. (2009) 'Absent Fathers, Present Histories', in P. Ashton and H. Kean (eds) *People and their Pasts. Public History Today,* Basingstoke, UK: Palgrave Macmillan, pp203–22.

Brennan, T. (2000) 'History, Family, History', in H. Kean, P. Martin and S. J. Morgan (eds) *Seeing History, Public History in Britain Now,* London: Francis Boutle, pp37–50.

Flinn, A. (2011) 'Archival Activism: Independent and Community-led Archives. Radical Public History and the Heritage Professions', *InterActions UCAL Journal of Education and Information Studies,* vol 7(2), pp1–20.

Greenway, J. (2008) 'Desire, Delight, Regret: Discovering Elizabeth Gibson', *Qualitative Research,* vol 8(3), pp317–24.

Landsberg, A. (2004) *Prosthetic Memory: The Transformation of American Remembrance in the Age of Mass Culture,* New York, NY: Columbia University Press.

Leone, M. P. (2010) *Critical Historical Archaeology,* Walnut Creek, CA: Left Coast Press.

Pearce, S. (1998) 'The Construction of Heritage: The Domestic Context and Its Implications', *International Journal of Heritage Studies,* vol 4(2), pp86–102.

Samuel, R. (1976) 'Local history and oral history', *History Workshop Journal,* vol 1(1), pp191–208.

Sassoon, J. (2003) 'Phantoms of Remembrance: Libraries and Archives as "The Collective Memory"', *Public History Review,* vol 10, pp40–60.

Part III: Intangible and tangible presentations of the past

Agacinski, S. (2003) *Time Passing: Modernity and Nostalgia,* New York, NY: Columbia University Press.

Counsell, C. and Mock, R. (2009) *Performance, Embodiment and Cultural Memory,* Newcastle upon Tyne, UK: Cambridge Scholars Publishing.

Gough, P. and Morgan, S. J. (2004) 'Manipulating the Metonymic: The Politics of Civic Identity and the Bristol Cenotaph 1919–32', *Journal of Historical Geography,* vol 30, pp665–84.

Holtorf, C. (2009) 'Commentary: Visions of the Twentieth Century', in J. Schofield (ed) *Defining Moments: Dramatic Archaeologies of the Twentieth-Century,* Oxford: Archaeopress, pp65–82.

Morgan, S. J. (1998) 'Memory and the Merchants: Commemoration and Civic Identity', *International Journal of Heritage Studies,* vol 4(2), pp103–13.

Purbrick, L. and Wylie, D. (2010) *MAZE,* London: Steidl.

O'Malley, V., Stirling, B. and Penetito, W. (eds) (2010) *The Treaty of Waitangi Companion: Maori and Pakeha from Tasman to Today,* Auckland: Auckland University Press.

Pinder, D. (2005) *Visions of the City: Utopianism, Power and Politics in Twentieth-Century Urbanism,* Edinburgh: Edinburgh University Press, Chapter 5 'Situationist Adventures', pp127–60.

Wallace, E. (2006) *The British Slave Trade and Public Memory,* New York, NY: Columbia University Press.

Index